Presented
to
Talbotville
United
Church
in
loving memory of
Elizabeth
Fife

by
the
Wilfrid Fife
Grandchildren

VOICES UNITED

VOICES UNITED

The Hymn and Worship Book
of The United Church of Canada

THE UNITED CHURCH PUBLISHING HOUSE

Voices United

The Hymn and Worship Book of The United Church of Canada

Copyright © 1996 The United Church Publishing House

Canadian Cataloguing in Publication Data

United Church of Canada.
    Voices united : the hymn and worship book of
the United Church of Canada

Includes index.
ISBN 1-55134-017-8

1. United Church of Canada – Liturgy – Texts.
2. United Church of Canada – Hymns. 3. Hymns,
English.   I. Title.

BX9881.A67 1996   264'.0792   C95–931553–5

The United Church Publishing House
3250 Bloor Street West
Etobicoke, Ontario, Canada
M8X 2Y4

01   00   99   98   6   5   4

Printed in Canada

Contents

Preface

Voices United is the product of five years' work by the Hymn and Worship Resource Committee, following the mandate of the 33rd General Council (1990) to produce a new hymn and worship resource for The United Church of Canada. It is offered to the church in the expectation that it will be a primary resource and support for worship well into the next century.

This is the third major hymn book produced by the United Church since its formation in 1925. Each book has been a product of its time. *The Hymnary* (1930) attempted a reconciliation of the music and worship traditions of the founding Methodist, Presbyterian, and Congregationalist Churches. *The Hymn Book* (1971) was produced and published in expectation of our union with the Anglican Church and reflected the need to accommodate the hymn and worship traditions of both communions. *Voices United* is the first "United Church" book, addressing the specific needs of our own church and time.

Voices United is more than a hymn book. It reflects increased interest in and concern with liturgical renewal in two ways: a greatly expanded psalter section, and the inclusion of service material in the form of prayers, creeds, and service music.

The task facing the Hymn and Worship Resource Committee was daunting. The changes in our society, culture, and church over the past twenty-five years have been enormous. Since the production of *The Hymn Book*, issues of inclusiveness (as they relate both to persons and "God-language") have become critical in our society and our church; these have demanded the close attention of our committee. In addition, the explosion of hymn-writing during this period, much of it of very fine quality, necessitated careful consideration of what kinds and how much of this material to include. We were also diligent in our efforts to include a selection of material from the world church to reflect the "global village" in which we live. As well, we recognized the necessity of culling several well-liked but increasingly obsolescent hymns, but strove to restore, retain, and occasionally, revise the hymns that have played such an important and enduring part in the worship life of our church. We trust that *Voices United* strikes a judicious balance between the old and the new.

From the beginning of our deliberations, we lived with the challenge of meeting all needs of our diverse and inclusive church. We decided that *Voices United* was to be a "people's book," and to that end, engaged in a process of wide consultation within the church, producing two samplers of material under consideration. This process, we believe, has ensured that the book contains an abundance of material to meet the needs of all.

As co-chairs of the Hymn and Worship Resource Committee, we wish to pay tribute to the extremely diligent, careful, and inspired effort of the Committee of which we have been priviliged to be members. We met three times per year over five years; between meetings, each member undertook a huge amount of work. All met in regional sub-groups, did individual research, and served as members of text, tunes, psalter, liturgical, children and youth, and service music sub-committees. In addition, many took on responsibility for monitoring such specific areas as women's interests, heritage hymns, global music, and regional concerns to ensure that their representation in the final product would be as balanced as possible. As a result, *Voices United* is very much the product of the Hymn and Worship Resource Committee.

We as a committee and the church as a whole have been immeasurably blessed in the work of our managing editor, John Ambrose. He brought a wealth of experience as pastor, musician, and administrator to this position, and demonstrated outstanding gifts of organization, diplomacy, advocacy, sensitivity, and balance in the myriad dimensions of the task. The quality of the finished product is in no small measure due to his faithfulness and thoroughness throughout the life of the project.

Co-Chairs Nancy E. Hardy and Leonard Lythgoe
Hymn and Worship Resource Committee

Hymn and Worship Resource Committee Members

Seiichi Ariga*
Mary Beth Nicks Barbour
Catherine J. Crooks*
Nancy E. Hardy
R. Gerald Hobbs
David Kai
Susan Lukey
Leonard Lythgoe
Susan E. Marrier
Todd L. McDonald
J. Allan McIntosh
David J. A. McKane
Diana McLeod
Joan K. McMurtry

Pierann E. Moon
John Murphy
Willis Noble
Don Parsons
Lydia Pedersen
Lillian Perigoe
William A. Richards
V. Martyn Sadler
Jeeva R. Edward Sam
Betty Sangster
Stuart Semple
Louise Skibsted
Joanne B. Sorrill*
Ruth Wiwchar

Coordinator of
Liturgical Resources
Fred Kimball Graham

Ecumenical Observers
Presbyterian Church
in Canada:
Donald Anderson
Andrew Donaldson
Anglican Church of Canada:
Paul Gibson
Canadian Conference
of Catholic Bishops:
Murray Kroetsch
Loretta Manzara

*former members of committee

Introduction

*"If I pray in a tongue, my spirit prays, but my mind is unproductive. What should I do then? I will pray with the spirit, but I will pray with the mind also; **I will sing praise with the spirit, but I will sing praise with the mind also.**"*

(I Cor. 14:14-15).

These words from the Apostle Paul convey an important message to the faithful of all times and places: praise in the Christian assembly, whether in the form of prayer or song, is an activity of both spirit and mind, emotion and intellect, inspiration and integrity. In the work of Christian formation, passion and knowledge should be brought together.

Hymns have always had a central place in the making of Christians. For many, next to scripture, a hymnal is the church's most important sourcebook. It is from hymns that many learn and retain scripture stories. It is from hymns that many receive their primary and most enduring theological education. Hymns stay with us long after occasions of teaching and preaching fade from memory. Thus, the content of congregational song is of utmost importance. Hymns and songs should convey the biblical and theological substance that will help form worshipers into thinking, passionate, loving and courageous disciples of Jesus Christ.

It is less important whether a hymn is old or new, folk or classic in style, joyful or sombre in mood, simple or complex in text or music. The church has always embraced and expressed diversity in its hymns. What is more important is that its hymns be grounded in the central tenets of Christian belief, and point to the living out of these beliefs.

Voices United is very much a hymn and worship book of The United Church of Canada. It is the culmination of extensive consultation across the entire church. Rarely has a project engaged so many in helping to determine the end result. All who have worked on the Hymn and Worship Resource Committee, and in the Project Office, are deeply aware of the invaluable contribution made by so many volunteers.

Our new hymn and worship book contains a rich collection of hymns carried forward from former hymnals and supplements. Slightly more than half the collection are older hymns still in active use in worship. Added to this heritage are new hymns which express fresh images of the triune God, of the Christian journey, and of the challenges of faithful discipleship today.

The language of many older hymns has been updated in the sincere hope of extending their useable life. Most texts, especially contemporary ones, have been edited for the purpose of inclusivity. Some have been left unchanged in deference to the views of particular authors, or because it was felt that the poetry was not permitting of change.

Voices United is global in content, with many texts and tunes drawn from Christian communities around the world. These hymns have, for the most part, been selected in consultation with the various language and ethnic groups that form part of the United Church family. Phonetic transliterations have been provided with some hymns to encourage congregations to sing the songs of our sisters and brothers in their language of origin.

The words of the hymns have been placed between the staves of music in response to many requests. To ease the challenge of singing longer texts, a small diamond has been placed at the third verse to guide singers to the correct line of verse as they move from one system (line) of music to the next.

To enhance the effectiveness of *Voices United* as a worship resource, prayers for congregational use have been carefully selected and placed throughout the hymnal portion of the book. Services of daily prayer have also been included to assist laypersons and clergy asked to lead worship at committee meetings, study groups, conferences, or gatherings of the courts of the church. These services can be made as simple or as elaborate as an occasion requires.

A variety of short musical responses have been placed throughout the book. These may be used as seasonal introits or choruses, or as responses to the proclamation of the word or prayers. Their inclusion is intended to model opportunities for expanding the use of music in the worship of the United Church. Settings for Holy Communion, kyries, amens, and sung versions of the Lord's Prayer will be found in the back section of *Voices United*.

In addition, a Psalter, with both free-verse and metrical psalms, has been included to encourage greater use of this rich scriptural heritage. The selection of psalms corresponds with those recommended in the Revised Common Lectionary. The sung refrains placed with free-verse psalms provide one model for congregations that wish to recover something of the musical traditions of ancient psalmody.

A comprehensive topic and category index, as well as a hymn lectionary index, have been provided to aid in the planning of worship. These indexes should perform an invaluable service to all worship planners.

The intent of those preparing this book is not to confine the church's hymns and songs to those found in *Voices United*. This is a time when congregations turn to many resources for their song. *Voices United* is offered as a core resource, to be augmented by the many hymns—old and new— available to congregations today.

As managing editor, I have been blessed and privileged to work with exceptional colleagues whose gifts and insights carried me through five years of complex and demanding work. Members of the Hymn and Worship Resource Committee have been unfailing, and remarkably patient, in carrying out the task given to them by the 33rd General Council. Not only have they done their work well, but they have generously extended their friendship and encouragement to staff in the Project Office.

Although not individually named here, appreciation also goes to those wonderful volunteers who served as text and music consultants, proofreaders, and members of the advisory panels in the selection of hymns from other languages and cultures. Their perceptive comments, eye for detail, and suggestions have given *Voices United* the breadth, diversity and integrity that the General Council mandated in the preparation of a new hymn and worship resource for the 21st century.

My deepest appreciation must go to my staff colleagues who approached the project not just as another work assignment, but as a labour of love. I cannot find the words to tell them how grateful I am for their gifts, dedication and friendship. Each individual seemed to know instinctively how important this project was to the church. Their efforts went far beyond anything that in fairness could have been asked or expected of them. The whole church is in their debt.

It is my hope and prayer that the church's praise and discipleship will be empowered by the words and music that fill these pages, and that *Voices United* will keep us singing together until that time when the church must undertake to prepare a new resource for a new generation of Christian worshipers.

John E. Ambrose
Managing Editor

Grateful Appreciation to:

Members of the Project Management Group.

Fred Graham, Consultant for Congregational Worship, who co-ordinated the work on the services of daily prayer and the selection of seasonal and thematic prayers.

Catherine Black and Barbara Mann, who served as Project Assistants from 1991–95 and 1994–96, respectively.

Beth Parker, Director of Publishing and Graphics, who served as the co-ordinator of the hymn and worship resource project.

Catherine Wilson (served 1991–1995), Director of The United Church Publishing House, who co-ordinated the development of promotional resources.

Ann Turner, who served as music designer and engraver throughout the life of the project.

Christopher Dumas, Art Director, who supervised the design and layout of the book.

Desmond Grundy, who served as technical consultant.

Elizabeth MacLean, who proofread every page, and who, with Barbara Mann, dealt with matters of copyright.

Kenneth Inkster, who prepared the indexes of Topics and Categories, Scripture and suggested hymns for the Lectionary.

Margaret Filshie Leask, who researched information on authors, composers and sources.

William Kervin, consultant, whose biblical and theological knowledge, liturgical expertise and pastoral sensitivity served as an invaluable guide for the Managing Editor and the Hymn and Worship Resource Committee throughout the 5 years of the project.

Key to musical and textual elements

Words and Music Credits
At the bottom left of each page, Words and Music credits identify the hymn's writer and composer, and the dates of the first known version of the words and the melody. When no date is known, an approximate date (e.g., *13th century*, or *ca. 1830*) may appear. Because of space limitations, the following abbreviations are used:

alt.	altered
adapt.	adapted by
arr.	arranged by
attrib.	attributed to
ca. (with date)	circa (around)
desc.	descant by
harm.	harmonized by
para.	paraphrased by
rev.	revised by
trans.	translated by
vers.	versified by

Copyright notice
Beneath the credits, a brief notice identifies lawful owners of the words, translation, music, harmony/arrangement or descant; complete notices, if required, appear in the Copyright Acknowledgements section (see page 976).

Tune name and metre
At the bottom right is the name of the hymn tune. The sequence of numbers beneath it, sometimes followed by the letter *D* (double metre) or *with Refrain*, give the number of syllables in each phrase of the verse; this information , used with the Metrical Index of Tunes (see page 1061), helps users identify a reference to other versions of the tune elsewhere in the book. The customary use of letters instead of numbers to indicate tune metres which occur frequently (e.g., CM – common metre – 8686, or LM – long metre – 8888) has been discontinued on the hymn pages, but retained in the Metrical Index of Tunes. The suggestion of an alternative hymn tune may also appear in this area to which a hymn's words may be sung.

The Diamond Symbol ♦
A small diamond has been placed at the third verse of longer hymns to guide singers to the correct line of verse when moving from one system (line) of music to the next.

The Asterisk *
The asterisk indicates an alternative word or phrase to use, if desired, in hymn texts that could not be revised.

Hymns, Musical Responses, and Prayers

1 O Come, O Come, Emmanuel

1 O come, O come, Emmanuel,
2 O come, O Wisdom from on high,
♦ 3 O come, O come, great God of might,
4 O come, O Rod of Jesse's stem,
5 O come, O Key of David, come,

and ransom captive Israel
who orders all things mightily;
♦ who to your tribes on Sinai's height
from every foe deliver them
and open wide our heavenly home;

that mourns in lowly exile here
to us the path of knowledge show,
♦ in ancient times once gave the law
that trust your mighty power to save,
make safe the way that leads on high,

Words: from the Latin antiphons for Advent, ca. 9th century; trans. John Mason Neale 1851, et al
Music: 15th century plainsong melody; arr. Healey Willan
Words copyright © The Church Pension Fund. Used by permission. Arrangement copyright © Concordia Publishing House.

VENI EMMANUEL
8 8 8 8 with refrain

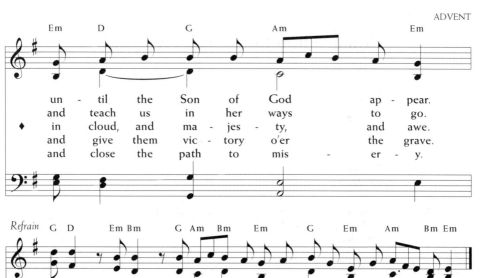

un - til the Son of God ap - pear.
and teach us in her ways to go.
in cloud, and ma - jes - ty, and awe.
and give them vic - tory o'er the grave.
and close the path to mis - er - y.

Refrain

Re-joice! Re-joice! Em-man - u-el shall come to thee, O Is - ra-el.

6 O come, O Dayspring, from on high,
and cheer us by your drawing nigh;
disperse the gloomy clouds of night,
and death's dark shadows put to flight.

Refrain

7 O come, Desire of nations, bind
all peoples in one heart and mind;
O bid our sad divisions cease,
and be for us the Prince of Peace.

Refrain

Oh, viens, Jésus, oh viens, Emmanuel

1 Oh! viens Jésus, oh! viens Emmanuel,
nous dévoiler le monde fraternel,
où ton amour, plus fort que la mort,
nous régénère au sein d'un même corps.

Refrain
Chantez! chantez! il vient à notre appel
combler nos cœurs, Emmanuel.

2 Oh! viens Berger que Dieu nous a
promis,
entends au loin ton peuple qui gémit;

dans la violence il vit son exil;
de ses souffrances, quand renaîtra-t-il?

3 Oh! viens Jésus, et dans la chair blessée,
fleuris pour nous, racine de Jessé.
Près de l'eau vive, l'arbre planté
soulève jusqu'à Dieu le monde entier.

4 Oh! viens Jésus, tracer notre chemin;
visite-nous, Étoile du matin.
Au fond de nos regards fais monter
l'éclat soudain du jour d'éternité.

Words: from the Latin ca. 9th century; English trans. John Mason Neale 1851, et al; French trans. Pierre-Yves Emery 1972
French translation copyright © AUVIDIS (Fleurus).

2 Come, Thou Long-Expected Jesus

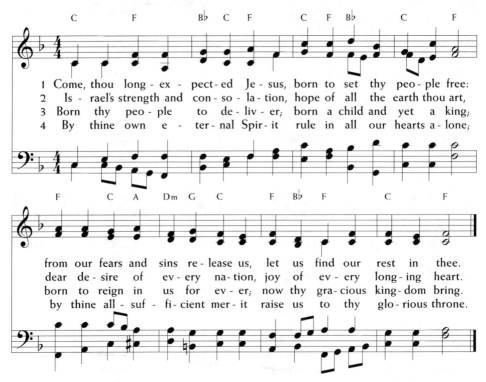

1 Come, thou long-ex-pect-ed Je-sus, born to set thy peo-ple free:
2 Is-rael's strength and con-so-la-tion, hope of all the earth thou art,
3 Born thy peo-ple to de-liv-er; born a child and yet a king;
4 By thine own e-ter-nal Spir-it rule in all our hearts a-lone;

from our fears and sins re-lease us, let us find our rest in thee.
dear de-sire of ev-ery na-tion, joy of ev-ery long-ing heart.
born to reign in us for ev-er; now thy gra-cious king-dom bring.
by thine all-suf-fi-cient mer-it raise us to thy glo-rious throne.

Words: Charles Wesley 1744
Music: Psalmodia Sacra 1715

STUTTGART
8 7 8 7
Alt. tune: Hyfrydol

3 Plus de nuit, le jour va naître

1 Plus de nuit, le jour va naître;
avancez vers le Seigneur;
dans le Christ il faut renaître;
tournez vers lui votre coeur.

2 Viens, Seigneur, sauver les hommes;
conduis-nous vers ta clarté;
tu le sais, pécheurs nous sommes;
mets en nous ta sainteté.

3 Veillez, car le jour est proche;
soyez fermes dans la foi;
amis, marchez sans reproche;
du Seigneur suivez la voie.

4 Nous préparons ta naissance;
parmi nous tu reviendras;
Fils de Dieu, par ta présence,
de joie tu nous combleras.

This French text (not a translation of the English) may be sung to the preceding tune.

Words: French para. H. Cousin 1973, rév.
STUTTGART

God of All Places

1 God of all pla - ces; pres - ent, un - seen;
2 God of all dream - ing, near and yet far;
3 God of all peo - ple, dust and the clay;

voice in our si - lence, song in our midst,
vi - sion un - heard of, wake us to rest.
breath of a new wind, fire in our hearts,

we are your peo - ple, know - ing, un - sure:
We are your pres - ence sent forth, a - fraid:
light born of heav - en, peace on the earth:

come, Lord Je - sus, come!

Words: David Haas 1988
Music: David M. Young 1988
Words copyright © 1988 G.I.A. Publications, Inc. Music copyright © David M. Young. Used by permission.

WHITTLESEY
9 9 9 5

5

All Earth Is Waiting

1 All earth is wait-ing to see the Prom-ised One,
2 Thus says the proph-et to those of Is-ra-el,
3 Moun-tains and val-leys will have to be made plain,
4 In low-ly sta-ble the Pro-mised One ap-peared.

and o-pen fur-rows a-wait the seed of God. All the
"A vir-gin moth-er will bear Em-man-u-el." One whose
o-pen new high-ways, new high-ways for our God, who is
Yet, feel that pre-sence through-out the earth to-day, for Christ

world, bound and strug-gling, seeks true lib-er-ty; it
name is "God with us," our Sav-iour shall be, through
now com-ing clos-er, so come all and see, and
lives in all Christ-ians and is with us now; a-

cries out for jus-tice and search-es for the truth.
whom hope will blos-som once more with-in our hearts.
o-pen the door-ways as wide as wide can be.
gain, on ar-riv-ing, Christ   brings us li-ber-ty.

Words: Catalonian, Alberto Taulé 1972; English trans. Gertrude C. Suppe 1987, alt.
Music: Alberto Taulé 1972, harm. Skinner Chávez-Melo 1988

TAULÉ
11 11 12 12

Words and music copyright © 1993 Centro de Pastoral Liturgica. Translation copyright ©1989 The United Methodist Publishing House
Harmony copyright © 1989 Skinner Chávez-Melo. Used by permission of Juan Francisco Chávez.

A Candle Is Burning

1 A candle is burning, a flame warm and bright,
2 A candle is burning, a candle of peace,
♦ 3 A candle is burning, a candle of joy,
4 A candle is burning, a candle of love,
5 We honour Messiah with Christ-candle's flame,

a candle of hope in December's dark night.
a candle to signal that conflict must cease:
♦ a candle to welcome brave Mary's new boy.
a candle to point us to heaven above.
our Christmas Eve candles glad tidings proclaim.

While angels sing blessings from heaven's starry sky,
for Jesus is coming to show us the way;
♦ Our hearts fill with wonder, and eyes light and glow
A baby for Christmas, a wonderful birth,
O come, all you faithful, rejoice in this night,

our hearts we prepare now for Jesus is nigh.
a message of peace humbly laid in the hay.
♦ as joy brightens winter like sunshine on snow.
for Jesus is bringing God's love to our earth.
as God comes among us, the Christian's true light.

Words: Sandra Dean 1986
Music: James R. Murray 1887
Words copyright © 1986 Sandra Dean.

AWAY IN A MANGER
6 5 6 5 D

Hope Is a Star

1 Hope is a star that shines in the night,
2 Peace is a rib-bon that cir-cles the earth,
3 Joy is a song that wel-comes the dawn,
4 Love is a flame that burns in our heart,

lead - ing us on till the morn-ing is bright.
giv - ing a prom-ise of safe-ty and worth.
tell - ing the world that the Sav-iour is born.
Je - sus has come and will nev-er de-part.

Refrain

When God is a child there's joy in our song. The last shall be first and the weak shall be strong, and none shall be a-fraid.

Words: Brian Wren 1985
Music: Joan Collier Fogg 1987
Words and music copyright © 1989 Hope Publishing Company.

MOON BEAMS
Irregular with refrain

Lo, How a Rose E'er Blooming

1 Lo, how a rose e'er bloom-ing from ten-der stem hath sprung,
2 I - sa - iah 'twas fore-told it, the Rose I have in mind,
1 D'un ar - bre sé - cu - lai - re, du vieux tronc d'I - sa - ï
2 Dieu, par la voix fer - ven - te de nom-breux ser - vi - teurs,

of Jes - se's lin - eage com - ing, as seers of old have sung.
with Ma - ry we be - hold it, the vir - gin moth - er kind.
du - rant l'hi - ver aus - tè - re, un frais ra - meau jail - lit;
à son peuple en at - ten - te, pro - met-tait un Sau - veur.

It came a blos - som bright, a - mid the
To show God's love a - right she bore for
et, sur le sol dur - ci, dans la nuit
Il vient, su - prême hon - neur, chez une hum -

cold of win - ter, when half spent was the night.
us a Sav - iour when half spent was the night.
calme et clai - re, u - ne rose a fleu - ri.
ble ser - van - te, toute à son pur bon - heur.

Words: German, 15th century; English trans. Theodore Baker 1894; French trans. L. Monastier 1926 ES IST EIN' ROS
Music: German traditional melody 1599; harm. Michael Praetorius 1609 7 6 7 6 6 7 6

9

People, Look East

1 Peo - ple, look east. The time is near
2 Fur - rows, be glad. Though earth is bare,
♦ 3 Birds, though you long have ceased to build,
4 Stars, keep the watch. When night is dim
5 Ang - els, an - nounce with shouts of mirth

of the crown - ing of the year.
one more seed is plant - ed there:
♦ guard the nest that must be filled;
one more light the bowl shall brim,
Christ who brings new life to earth.

Make your house fair as you are a - ble,
give up your strength the seed to nour - ish,
♦ ev - en the hour when wings are fro - zen
shin - ing be - yond the frost - y weath - er,
Set ev - ery peak and val - ley hum - ming

trim the hearth and set the ta - ble.
that in course the flow - er may flour - ish.
♦ God for fledg - ing time has cho - sen.
bright as sun and moon to - geth - er.
with the word, the Lord is com - ing.

Peo- ple, look east and sing to - day:

Peo- ple, look east:

Love the guest is on the way.
Love the rose is on the way.
Love the bird is on the way.
Love the star is on the way.
Love the Lord is on the way.

Peo- ple, look east:

Words: Eleanor Farjeon 1928
Music: French folk melody; harm. Martin Fallas Shaw 1928
Words copyright © David Higham Associates. Harmony copyright © Oxford University Press 1928

BESANÇON
879887

Prepare the Way of the Lord   10

Round

Pre - pare the way of the Lord! Pre - pare the way of the

Lord!   Make a straight path for him, make a straight path;

pre - pare the way of the Lord!

Words: Isaiah 40:3; adapt. Michael Burkhardt 1990
Music: Michael Burkhardt 1990

Words and music copyright © 1992 MorningStar Music Publishers.

11 An Advent Prayer

God of all wisdom,
our hearts yearn for the warmth of your love,
   and our minds search for the light of your Word.
Increase our longing for Christ our Saviour,
and strengthen us to grow in love,
   that at the dawn of his coming
   we may rejoice in his presence
   and welcome the light of his truth.
This we ask in the name of Jesus Christ. Amen.

12 She Walked in the Summer
(The Visit)

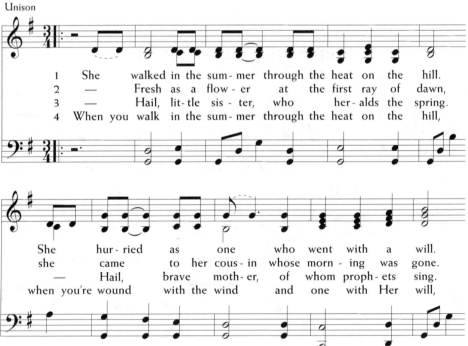

Unison

1 She walked in the sum-mer through the heat on the hill.
2 — Fresh as a flow-er at the first ray of dawn,
3 — Hail, lit-tle sis-ter, who her-alds the spring.
4 When you walk in the sum-mer through the heat on the hill,

She hur-ried as one who went with a will.
she came to her cous-in whose morn-ing was gone.
— Hail, brave moth-er, of whom proph-ets sing.
when you're wound with the wind and one with Her will,

Words: Miriam Therese Winter 1968
Music: Miriam Therese Winter 1968; accomp. Nan Thompson 1995

THE VISIT
Irregular

She danced in the sun-light when the day was done.
There leaped a lit-tle child in the an-cient womb,
— Hail to the mo-ment be - neath your breast.
be brave with the bur-den you are blessed to bear,

(v. 2)
1–3

Her heart knew no even-ing who car-ried the sun.
and there leaped a lit-tle hope— in ev-ery an - cient tomb.
May all gen - er - a - tions— call you blessed.
for it's Christ that you car-ry ev-ery—

Final

where, ev-ery-where, ev-ery-where.

An Advent Prayer

13

O God, our deliverer:
you cast down the mighty,
    and lift up those of no account;
like Elizabeth and Mary,
    who embraced one another
    with songs of liberation,
may we, pregnant with your Spirit,
affirm one another in hope for the world;
    in the name of Jesus. Amen.

Janet Morley 1988, alt.

14 To a Maid Whose Name Was Mary

1 To a maid whose name was Ma - ry, the an - gel Gab - riel came. "Fear not," the an - gel told her, "I come to bring good news, good news I come to tell you, good news, I say, good news.

2 "For you are high - ly fa - voured by God the Lord of all, who ev - en now is with you. You are on earth most blest, you are most blest, most bless - ed, God chose you, you are blest!"

3 But Mar - y was most trou - bled to hear the an - gel's word. What was the an - gel say - ing? It trou - bled her to hear, hear the an - gel's mess - age, it trou - bled her to hear.

4 "Fear not, for God is with you, and you shall bear a child. His name shall be called Je - sus, God's off - spring from on high. And he shall reign for - ev - er, for - ev - er reign on high."

Words: Gracia Grindal
Music: Rusty Edwards
Words and music copyright © 1984 Hope Publishing Company.

ANNUNCIATION
7 6 7 6 7 6

5 "How shall this be" said Mary,
   "that I should be with child?"
   The angel answered quickly,
   "The power of the Most High
   will come upon you shortly,
   your child shall be God's child."

6 As Mary heard the angel,
   she wondered at his words.
   "Behold, I am your handmaid,"
   she said unto her God.
   "So be it; I am ready
   according to your word."

Came He Not in Fire

(Advent Introit)

15

Came he not in fire, on-ward came the Lord.

Not in wind or rain, on-ward came the Lord.

Hail nor sleet or snow, on-ward came the Lord.

In a still small voice came he, on-ward came the Lord.

Words: William Farley Smith
Music: probably an African-American Spiritual, arr. William Farley Smith
Words and music copyright © 1992 Abingdon Press.

CAME HE NOT
10 10 10 12

16   Mary, Woman of the Promise

1 Mar-y, wo-man of the prom-ise, bear-er of your peo-ple's
2 Mar-y, song of ho-ly wis-dom, sung be-fore the world be-
3 Mar-y, morn-ing star of jus-tice, mir-ror of the Ra-diant
4 Mar-y, mod-el of com-pas-sion, wound-ed by your off-spring's
5 Mar-y, wom-an of the Gos-pel, pre-cious home for trea-sured

dreams, through your o - pen, will-ing spir - it wa-ters
gan, faith-ful to the Word with-in, you car-ried
Light, in the shad - ows of life's jour-ney, be a
pain, when our hearts are torn by sor - row, teach us
seed, help us to be true dis-ci-ples, bear-ing

1–4   *5*

of God's good - ness streamed.
out God's won - drous plan.
bea - con for our sight.
how to love a - gain.
fruit in word and deed.

Words: Mary Frances Fleischaker 1988
Music: Alfred V. Fedak 1988

GRATIA PLENA
8 7 8 7

O Ancient Love

Unison

1 O an - cient love, pro - cess - ing through the a - ges;
2 O home - less love, that dwells a - mong the stran - ger;
3 O gen - tle love, car - ess - ing those in sor - row;
4 O suf - fering love, that bears our hu - man weak - ness;

O hid - den love, re - vealed in hu - man form; O prom - ised
O low - ly love, that knows the might - y's scorn; O hun - gry
O ten - der love, that com - forts those for - lorn; O hope - ful
O bound - less love, that ris - es with the morn; O migh - ty

love, the dream of seers and sa - ges:
love, that lay with - in a man - ger: O liv - ing Love, with - in our
love, that prom - is - es to - mor - row:
love, con - cealed in in - fant meek - ness:

hearts be born, O liv - ing Love, with - in our hearts be borne.

Words: Michael Joncas 1994
Music: Michael Joncas 1994
Words and music copyright © 1994 G.I.A. Publications, Inc.

BEDFORD ABBEY
11 10 11 10 10

18   There's a Voice in the Wilderness

Unison

1 There's a voice in the wil-der-ness cry-ing, a
2 O Zi - on, that bring-est good tid-ings, get thee
3 But the word of our God en - dur-eth, whose
4 There's a voice in the wil-der-ness cry-ing, a

call from the ways un - trod: pre - pare in the des-ert a
up to the heights and sing! Pro - claim to a des-o-late
arm is ev - er strong; God stands in the midst of
call from the ways un - trod: pre - pare in the des-ert a

high - way, a high-way for our God! The
peo - ple the com - ing of their King. Like the
na - tions, and soon will right the wrong. God shall
high - way, a high-way for our God! The

val - leys shall be ex - alt - ed, the lof - ty hills brought
flowers of the field they per - ish, like grass our works de -
feed the flock like a shep-herd, the lambs so gen - tly
val - leys shall be ex - alt - ed, the lof - ty hills brought

Words: James Lewis Milligan 1925, alt.
Music: Henry Hugh Bancroft 1938
Music copyright © 1938 Henry Hugh Bancroft. Used by permission of Eldred Bancroft.

ASCENSION (BANCROFT)
Irregular

low; make straight all the crook - ed pla - ces
cay; the power and pomp of na - tions
hold; to pas - tures of peace will lead them,
low; make straight all the crook - ed pla - ces

where God, our God, may go!
shall pass, like a dream, a - way.
and bring them safe to fold.
where God, our God, may go!

Kindle a Flame to Lighten the Dark 19

Kin - dle a flame to light - en the dark and

take all fear a - way.

Words: The Iona Community 1987
Music: The Iona Community 1987
Music copyright © 1987 WGRG, The Iona Community (Glasgow, Scotland), G.I.A. Publications, Inc., Chicago, Illinois, exclusive agent.

20   On Jordan's Bank

Descant

5   All   praise   e - ter - nal   Son,   whose

1   On   Jor - dan's   bank,   the   Bap - tist's   cry   an -
2   Then   cleansed   be   ev - ery   life   from   sin;   make
3   In   you,   we   find   a - bun - dant   life,   our
4   Stretch   forth   your   hand,   our   health   re - store,   and
5   All   praise   to   you,   e - ter - nal   Son,   whose

ad - vent   has   our   free - dom   won;   and   praise   to   God   whom

noun - ces   that   the   Lamb   is   nigh;   a - wake   and   hear - ken,
straight   the   way   for   God   with - in;   and   let   each   heart   pre -
ref - uge   in   the   midst   of   strife;   with - out   your   grace   we
help   us   rise   to   fall   no   more.   O   let   your   face   up -
ad - vent   has   our   free - dom   won;   and   praise   to   God   whom

we   a - dore   for - ev - er - more.

for   he   brings   glad   tid - ings   of   the   King   of   Kings.
pare   a   home   where   such   a   might - y   guest   may   come.
waste   a - way,   like   flowers   that   with - er   and   de - cay.
on   us   shine,   and   fill   the   world   with   love   di - vine.
we   a - dore,   with   Ho - ly   Spir - it   ev - er - more.

Words: Latin, Charles Coffin 1763; trans. John Chandler 1837, alt.
Music: Musikalisches Handbuch, Hamburg 1690; arr. W. H. Havergal 1864; desc. Hal Hopson 1979

WINCHESTER NEW

8 8 8 8

Oh viens, Seigneur, ne tarde pas

21

1 Oh viens, Seigneur, ne tarde pas,
viens dissiper l'obscurité
où nous devons toujours marcher;
remplis nos yeux de ton éclat.

2 Brillant soleil, très pur matin,
nous aimerions te contempler,
nous réjouir de ta beauté.
Oh! lève-toi sur nos chemins.

3 Nous n'abordons jamais au port;
tous nos pas sombrent dans le soir.
Rends-nous la joie; rends-nous
l'espoir;
délivre-nous de notre mort.

4 Parais enfin et nous vivrons;
nous n'aurons plus aucune peur;
en joie tu changeras nos pleurs,
et pour toujours nous chanterons.

This French text (not a translation of the English) may be sung to the preceding tune.

Words: *Frère Pierre-Étienne 1974*
Words copyright © *Fédération Protestante de France*

WINCHESTER NEW

Wait for the Lord

22

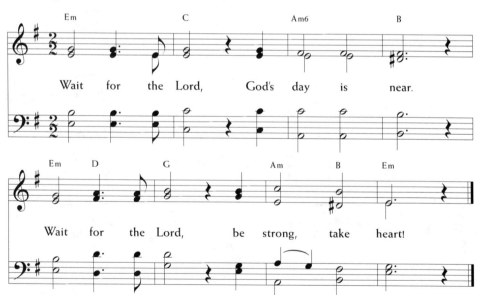

Words: *Jacques Berthier 1984*
Music: *Jacques Berthier 1984*

WAIT FOR THE LORD

Words and music copyright © *1991 Les Presses de Taizé, G.I.A. Publications, Inc., Chicago, Illinois, exclusive agent.*

23

Joy Shall Come

Words: Israeli traditional
Music: Israeli traditional, arr. Darryl Nixon 1987
Arrangement copyright © 1987 Songs for a Gospel People.

JOY SHALL COME
Irregular

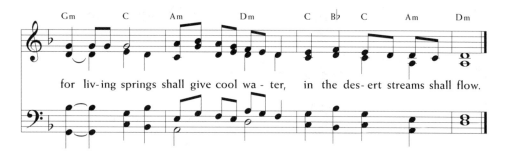

for liv-ing springs shall give cool wa - ter, in the des-ert streams shall flow.

Let the Heavens Be Glad 24

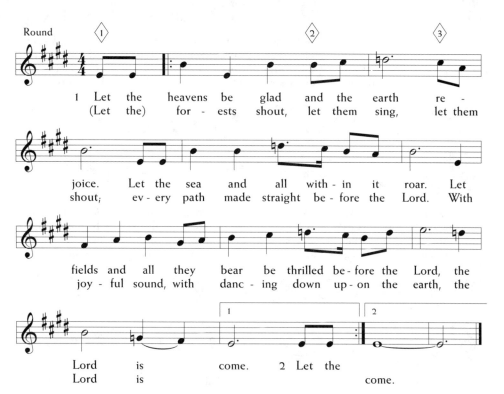

Round

1 Let the heavens be glad and the earth re-
(Let the) for - ests shout, let them sing, let them

joice. Let the sea and all with-in it roar. Let
shout; ev-ery path made straight be-fore the Lord. With

fields and all they bear be thrilled be-fore the Lord, the
joy - ful sound, with danc - ing down up-on the earth, the

Lord is come. 2 Let the
Lord is come.

Words: John B. Foley, SJ; based on Psalm 96:11–13
Music: John B. Foley, SJ
Words and music copyright © 1970, 1974 John B. Foley, SJ, and New Dawn Music.

25   Lo, He Comes with Clouds Descending

1 Lo, he comes with clouds de - scend - ing, see the Lamb for
2 Ev - ery eye shall then be - hold you, robed in awe - some
3 Now re - demp - tion, long ex - pec - ted see in sol - emn
4 Yea! A - men! Let all a - dore you, high on your e -

sin - ners slain! Thou - sand, thou - sand saints at - tend - ing
maj - es - ty; all who jeered, and mocked, and sold you,
pomp ap - pear; all the saints, by us re - ject - ed,
ter - nal throne; crowns and em - pires fall be - fore you,

join to sing the glad re - frain: hal - le - lu - jah,
pierced, and nailed you to the tree, deep - ly griev - ing,
thrill the trum - pet sound to hear: hal - le - lu - jah,
claim the king - dom for your own: O come quick - ly!

hal - le - lu - jah, hal - le - lu - jah!
deep - ly griev - ing, deep - ly griev - ing,
hal - le - lu - jah, hal - le - lu - jah!
O come quick - ly! O come quick - ly!

Words: *John Cennick 1750; rev. Charles Wesley 1758 and Martin Madan 1769; alt.*   HELMSLEY
Music: *English melody 18th century; arr. Thomas Olivers 1765*   8 7 8 7 4 7

God	ap	-	pears	on	earth		to	reign.
shall	the		true	Mes	-	si	-	ah	see.
See	the		day	of	God		ap	-	pear!
Ev	-	er	-	last	-	ing	Christ,	come	down.

An Advent Prayer — 26

Who are we, O God,
that you should come to us?
Yet you have visited your people
    and redeemed us in your Son.
As we prepare to celebrate his birth,
make our hearts leap for joy at the sound of your word,
    and move us by your spirit to bless your wonderful works.
We ask this through him whose coming is certain,
    whose day draws near, even your Son, Jesus Christ. Amen.

27   Tomorrow Christ Is Coming

1 To - mor - row Christ is com - ing, as yes - ter - day he came;
2 To - mor - row will be Christ - mas, the feast of love di - vine,
3 There will be no to - mor - rows for man - y a ba - by born;
4 Our God be - comes in - car - nate in ev - ery hu - man birth.

a child is born this mo - ment, we do not know its name.
but for the name - less mil - lions the star will nev - er shine.
Good Fri - day falls on Christ - mas when life is sown as corn.
Cre - a - ted in God's im - age, we must make peace on earth.

The world is full of dark - ness, a - gain there is no room;
Still is the cen - sus ta - ken with peo - ple on the move;
But Je - sus Christ is ris - en and comes a - gain in bread
God will ful - fil Love's pur - pose and this shall be the sign:

the sym - bols of ex - ist - ence are sta - ble, cross and tomb.
new in - fants born in sta - bles are cry - ing out for love.
to still our deep - est hun - ger and raise us from the dead.
we shall find Christ a - mong us as wo - man, child, or man.

Words: *Fred Kaan 1966*
Music: *Cecil Armstrong Gibbs 1929*

LITTLE BADDOW
7 6 7 6 D

Herald! Sound the Note of Gladness

1 Her - ald! Sound the note of glad - ness! Tell the news that
2 Her - ald! Sound the note of judge-ment, warn - ing us of
3 Her - ald! Sound the note of par - don! Those re - pent - ing
4 Her - ald! Sound the note of tri - umph! Christ has come to

Christ is here; make a path - way through the de - sert
right and wrong, turn - ing us from sin and sad - ness,
are for - given; God re - ceives these way - ward child - ren,
share our life, bring - ing God's own love and pow - er,

for the one who brings God near.
till once more we sing the song. Sound the trum - pet!
and to all new life is given.
grant - ing vic - tory in our strife.

Tell the mes - sage! Christ the Sav - ing One has come!

Words: Moir A. J. Waters 1968, alt.
Music: adapt. from Joachim Neander ca. 1680
Words copyright © 1968 Moir A. J. Waters. Used by permission of Margaret Waters.

NEANDER (UNSER HERRSCHER)
87 87 87
Alt. setting: 406

29 Hark the Glad Sound

Descant

4 Our glad ho - san - nas, Prince of Peace, your wel - come

1 Hark, the glad sound! The Sav - iour comes, the Sav - iour
2 He comes, the pris - oners to re - lease in Sa - tan's
3 He comes, the bro - ken heart to bind, the bleed - ing
4 Our glad ho - san - nas, Prince of Peace, your wel - come

shall pro - claim; and heaven's e - ter - nal arch - es

pro - mised long: let ev - ery heart pre - pare a
bond - age held; the gates of brass be - fore him
soul to cure, and with the trea - sures of his
shall pro - claim; and heaven's e - ter - nal arch - es

ring with your be - lov - ed name.

throne, and ev - ery voice a song.
burst, the i - ron fet - ters yield.
grace to bless the hum - ble poor.
ring with your be - lov - ed name.

Words: Philip Doddridge 1738, alt.
Music: Thomas Haweis 1792; adapt. Samuel Webbe 1808; desc. John Wilson
Descant copyright © Hope Publishing Company.

RICHMOND
8 6 8 6

Hail to God's Own Anointed

1 Hail to God's own a - noint - ed, great Da - vid's great - er Son!
2 Christ comes with jus - tice sure - ly to those who suf - fer wrong,
3 Christ shall come down like show - ers up - on the fruit - ful earth,
4 To him shall prayer un - ceas - ing and dai - ly vows as - cend,

Hail, in the time ap - point - ed, God's reign on earth be - gun!
to help the poor and need - y, and bid the weak be strong,
and love, joy, hope, like flow - ers, spring in his path to birth.
his king - dom still in - creas - ing, a king - dom with - out end.

Christ comes to break op - pres - sion, to set the cap - tive free,
to give them songs for sigh - ing, their dark - ness turn to light,
Be - fore him on the moun - tains shall peace the her - ald go,
The tide of time shall nev - er his cov - e - nant re - move.

to take a - way trans - gres - sion, and rule in e - qui - ty.
whose souls, con - demned and dy - ing, are pre - cious in his sight.
and righ - teous - ness in foun - tains from hill to val - ley flow.
His name shall stand for ev - er: that name to us is Love.

Words: James Montgomery 1821, alt.
Music: Johann Crüger 1640; adapt. W. H. Monk 1861

CRÜGER
7 6 7 6 D
Alt. tune: Ellacombe

31 O Lord, How Shall I Meet You

1 O Lord, how shall I meet you, how wel-come you a-right?
Your peo-ple long to greet you, my hope, my heart's de-light!
O kin-dle, then, most ho-ly, a lamp with-in my breast,
to do in spir-it low-ly all that may please you best.

2 Love caused your in-car-na-tion, love brought you here to me;
your thirst for my sal-va-tion pro-cured my lib-er-ty.
O love be-yond all tell-ing, that led you to em-brace
in love all loves ex-cel-ling our lost and fall-en race.

3 A glo-rious crown you give me, a trea-sure safe on high,
that will not fail nor leave me as earth-ly rich-es fly.
My heart shall bloom for-ev-er for you with prais-es new,
and from your name shall nev-er with-hold the hon-our due.

Words: Paul Gerhardt 1653,
trans. Catherine Winkworth 1863, et al., alt.
Music: Melchior Teschner ca. 1615; harm. William Henry Monk 1861

ST THEODULPH (VALET WILL ICH DIR GEBEN)
7 6 7 6 D
Alt. setting: 122

Seigneur, que tous s'unissent

1 Seigneur, que tous s'unissent
pour chanter ton amour.
Ton soleil de justice
se lève sur nos jours.
Le Fils de Dieu est homme
avec nous désormais.
C'est sa vie qu'il nous donne,
et nous marchons en paix.

2 Quand la terre est remplie
de bruit et de fureur,
quand nous perdons nos vies
en restant dans nos peurs,

c'est lui qui nous appelle
et vient nous délivrer.
Il est le Dieu fidèle
pour nous réconcilier.

3 Quand notre foi t'espère,
oh! viens, nous t'attendons.
Prends pitié de la terre,
ne tarde plus longtemps.
La création soupire
après la liberté.
C'est toi qu'elle désire
en ton éternité.

This French text (not a translation of the English) may be sung to the preceding tune.

Words: Louis Lévrier 1977   ST THEODULPH (VALET WILL ICH DIR GEBEN)
Words copyright © Fédération Protestante de France

Watch and Pray

Watch, watch and pray, *Je - sus, the Word, will come.

Je - sus, the Word, will come.

* Original words for Maundy Thursday, "Jesus will keep to his word"

Words: The Iona Community 1988, alt.
Music: The Iona Community 1988

34

Come Now, O God of Peace
(O-So-So)

Come now, *O God of peace, we are your peo-ple;
pour out your spir - it that we be one bod - y.

O - so - so o - so - so, pyong - hwa - ui - im - gum,
u - ri - ga han - mom i - ru - ge ha - so - so.

Additional verses (O God of love, of hope, of joy, etc.) may be sung.

Words: Korean, Geonyong Lee 1988; English trans. Marion Pope 1996, alt.
Music: Geonyong Lee 1988

O-SO-SO
6 5 5 6

Words and music copyright © 1995 Geonyong Lee. Translation copyright © 1996 Marion Pope.

And the following...

Good Christian Friends, Rejoice

35

1, 2, 3 Good Chris-tian friends, re-joice with heart and soul and

voice!
voice!
voice!

Give ye heed to what we say: News! News!
Now ye hear of end-less bliss: Joy! Joy!
Now ye need not fear the grave: Peace! Peace!

Je - sus Christ is born to - day. Ox and ass be -
Je - sus Christ was born for this! He hath o - pened
Je - sus Christ was born to save! Calls you one and

fore him bow, and he is in the man - ger now.
heav - en's door, and we are blest for - ev - er - more.
calls you all to gain his ev - er - last - ing hall.

Christ is born to - day! Christ is born to - day!
Christ was born for this! Christ was born for this!
Christ was born to save! Christ was born to save!

Words: Latin, 14th-century; trans. John Mason Neale 1853, alt.
Music: German melody; harm. Gary Alan Smith 1988

IN DULCI JUBILO
Irregular

Harmony copyright © 1989 The United Methodist Publishing House.

36   Angels, from the Realms of Glory

Descant

4 Saints be-fore the al - tar bend-ing, watch-ing long in

1 An - gels, from the realms of glo - ry, wing your flight o'er
2 Shep-herds in the field a - bid - ing, watch-ing o'er your
3 Sa - ges, leave your con - tem - pla-tions; bright - er vi - sions
4 Saints be - fore the al - tar bend - ing, watch-ing long in

hope and fear, sud - den - ly the Lord, de - scend - ing,

all the earth; ye who sang cre - a - tion's sto - ry,
flocks by night, God with us is now re - sid - ing,
beam a - far; seek the great de - sire of na - tions;
hope and fear, sud - den - ly the Lord, de - scend - ing,

in his tem - ple shall ap - pear: come and wor - ship,

now pro - claim Mes - si - ah's birth:
yon - der shines the in - fant Light:
ye have seen his na - tal star: come and wor - ship,
in his tem - ple shall ap - pear:

Words: *James Montgomery 1816*
Music: *Henry Thomas Smart 1867, alt.; desc. Ruth Girard 1994*
Descant copyright © 1996 Ruth Girard.

REGENT SQUARE
8 7 8 7 8 7

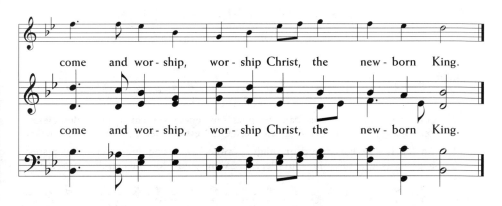

come and wor-ship, wor-ship Christ, the new-born King.

come and wor-ship, wor-ship Christ, the new-born King.

Gloria

37

(Glory to God)

Round

Glo - ri - a, glo - ri - a, in ex-cel - sis De - o!
Glo - ry to God, glo - ry to God, glo - ry in the high - est!

Glo - ri - a, glo - ri - a, al - le-lu - ia, al - le-lu - ia.
Glo - ry to God, glo - ry to God, hal - le-lu - jah, hal - le-lu - jah!

Words: trad. liturgical setting
Music: Jacques Berthier; arr. Darryl Nixon 1987

GLORIA
Irregular

38 Angels We Have Heard on High
(Les anges dans nos campagnes)

1 Les an - ges dans nos cam-pa-gnes ont en-ton-né l'hym - ne des cieux;
2 Ber - gers, pour qui cet - te fê - te? Quel est l'ob-jet de tous ces chants?

1 An - gels we have heard on high sweet-ly sing-ing o'er the plains,
2 Shep-herds, why this ju - bi - lee? Why your joy-ous strains pro-long?

et l'é - cho de nos mon - ta-gnes re - dit ce chant mé - lo - di - eux:
Quel vain-queur, quel - le con-quê - te mé - ri - te ces cris tri-om-phants?

and the moun-tains in re - ply, e - cho - ing their joy-ous strains.
What the glad - some tid - ings be which in - spire your heaven-ly song?

Refrain

Glo - - - - - - - - ri - a,

in ex - cel - sis De - o!

Words: *French trad., trans. James Chadwick 1860*
Music: *French carol melody; arr. Edward Shippen Barnes 1937*

GLORIA
7 7 7 7 with refrain

Glo - - - - - - - - ri - a, in ex - cel - sis De - - - o!

3 Ils annoncent la naissance
du libérateur d'Israël,
et pleins de reconnaissance
chantent en ce jour solennel.
Gloria in excelsis Deo!

3 Come to Bethlehem and see
Christ whose birth the angels sing;
come, adore on bended knee
Christ, the Lord, the newborn King.
Gloria in excelsis Deo!

4 See him in a manger laid,
whom the choirs of angels praise;
Mary, Joseph, lend your aid,
while our hearts in love we raise.
Gloria in excelsis Deo!

A Christmas Prayer 39

Generous God,
you gave your only-begotten Son
to take our nature upon him,
and be born of your chosen one, Mary.
Grant that we, who have been born again
and made your children by adoption and grace,
may daily be renewed by your Holy Spirit;
through our Saviour Jesus Christ,
who lives and reigns with you and the Holy Spirit,
one God now and forever. Amen.

Before the Marvel of This Night

1 Be - fore the mar - vel of this night
2 A - wake the sleep - ing world with song,
3 The love that we have al - ways known,

a - dor - ing, fold your wings and bow,
this is the day *the Lord has made;
our con-stant joy and end - less light,

then tear the sky a - part with light
as - sem - ble here, ce - les - tial throng,
now to the love - less world be shown,

and with your
in roy - al
now break up -

news the world en - dow. Pro - claim the birth of Christ and
splen-dour come ar - rayed. Give earth a glimpse of heaven - ly
on its death-ly night. In - to one song com - press the

* or "that God"

Words: Jaroslav J. Vajda 1979
Music: Carl F. Schalk 1981
Words copyright © 1981 Jaroslav J. Vajda. Music copyright © 1989 G.I.A. Publications, Inc.

MARVEL
Irregular

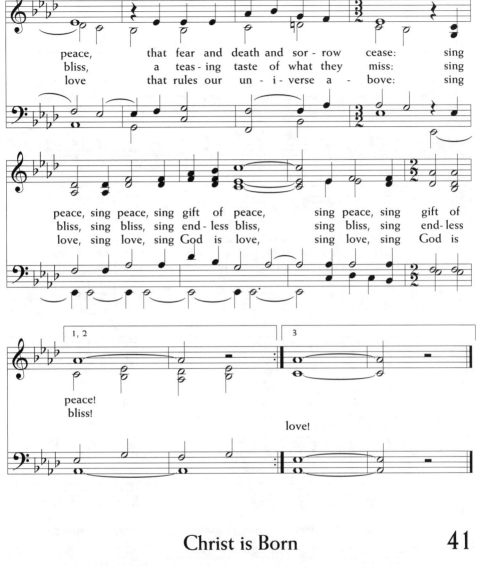

peace, that fear and death and sor-row cease: sing
bliss, a teas-ing taste of what they miss: sing
love that rules our un-i-verse a-bove: sing

peace, sing peace, sing gift of peace, sing peace, sing gift of
bliss, sing bliss, sing end-less bliss, sing bliss, sing end-less
love, sing love, sing God is love, sing love, sing God is

peace!
bliss!

love!

Christ is Born

41

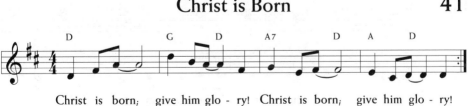

Christ is born; give him glo-ry! Christ is born; give him glo-ry!

May be sung several times; begin with solo voice, add choir, then add congregation and instruments.

Words: trad. Byzantine Christmas prayer
Music: Raquel Mora Martinez
Music copyright © 1992 Abingdon Press.

42 Down to Earth, as a Dove

1 Down to earth, as a dove, came to dwell ho - ly love:
2 This is love come to light, now is fear put to flight.
3 Christ the Lord comes to feed hun - gry souls in their need;

Je - sus Christ from a - bove bring - ing great sal - va - tion
God de - feats dark - est night, giv - ing for our sor - rows
in the house there is bread: Je - sus in a sta - ble,

Refrain

meant for ev - ery na - tion.
hope of new to - mor - rows. Let us sing,
in the church a ta - ble.

sing, sing, dance and spring, spring, spring;

Christ is here, ev - er near! Glo - ri - a in ex - cel - sis.

Words: Fred Kaan 1968
Music: melody from Piae Cantiones 1582; arr. F. R. C. Clarke 1970
Words copyright © 1968 Hope Publishing Company. Arrangement copyright © 1970 F. R. C. Clarke.

THEODORIC (PERSONENT HODIE)
6 6 6 6 6 with refrain

Go, Tell It on the Mountain

Refrain (Unison)

Go, tell it on the moun - tain, o - ver the hills and ev - ery - where.

Go, tell it on the moun - tain that Je - sus Christ is born.

Harmony

1 While shep - herds kept their watch - ing o'er si - lent flocks by night,
2 The shep - herds feared and trem - bled when lo, a - bove the earth
3 Down in a lone - ly man - ger the hum - ble Christ was born,

be - hold, through - out the heav - ens there shone a ho - ly light.
rang out the an - gel cho - rus that hailed our Sav - iour's birth!
and God sent our sal - va - tion that bless - ed Christ - mas morn.

Words: John Wesley Work II 1907
Music: African-American spiritual 19th century, arr. United Reformed Church (U.K.)
Arrangement copyright © United Reformed Church. By permission of Oxford University Press.

GO, TELL IT
Irregular

44 It Came upon the Midnight Clear

1 It came up-on the mid-night clear, that glo-rious
2 Still through the clo-ven skies they come with peace-ful
3 Yet with the woes of sin and strife the world has
4 For, lo! the days are hast-ening on, by proph-ets

song of old, from an-gels bend-ing near the earth
wings un-furled; and still their heaven-ly mu-sic floats
suf-fered long; be-neath the an-gel strain have rolled
seen of old, when with the ev-er-cir-cling years

to touch their harps of gold, "Peace on the earth, good
o'er all the wea-ry world; a-bove its sad and
two thou-sand years of wrong; and war-ring hu-man-
shall come the time fore-told, when peace shall o-ver

will to all, from heaven's all-gra-cious King!"
low-ly plains they bend on hover-ing wing,
kind hears not the love song which they bring.
all the earth its an-cient splen-dours fling,

Words: Edmund Hamilton Sears 1849, alt.
Music: Richard Storrs Willis 1850

CAROL
8 6 8 6 D

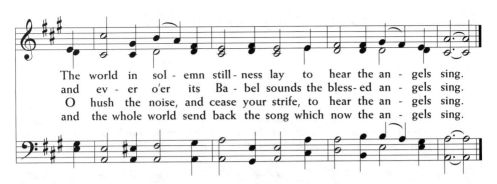

The world in sol - emn still - ness lay to hear the an - gels sing.
and ev - er o'er its Ba - bel sounds the bless- ed an - gels sing.
O hush the noise, and cease your strife, to hear the an - gels sing.
and the whole world send back the song which now the an - gels sing.

Joy Is Now in Every Place 45

1 Joy is now in ev - ery place, Christ- mas light - ens
2 May the star that shone that night, mak - ing your poor
3 Through the New Year let it stay, lead - ing us up -
4 Now and ev - er may we find your good news to

ev - ery face; now be with us, in your grace,
sta - ble bright, fill our hearts with love and light,
on your way, mak - ing Christ - mas ev - ery day,
fill our mind: peace and love to hu - man - kind,

hear us, bless us, ho - ly Je - sus.

Words: Author unknown
Music: German carol melody ca. 1500; arr. Ralph Vaughan Williams 1906
Arrangement by permission of Oxford University Press.

RESONET IN LAUDIBUS
7 7 7 6

46 Gentle Mary Laid Her Child

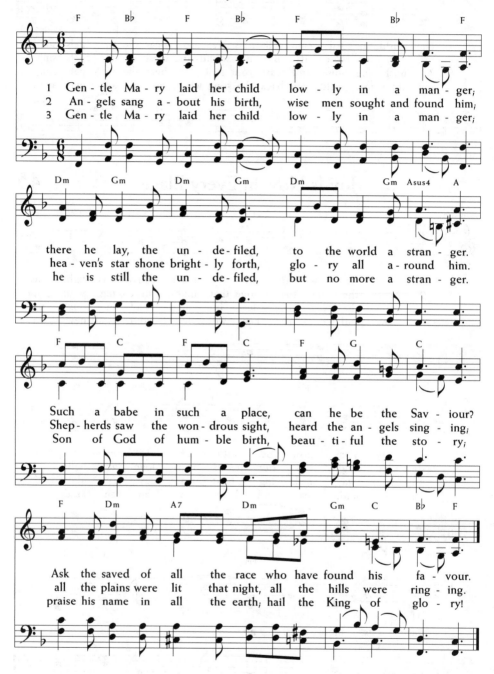

1 Gen - tle Ma - ry laid her child low - ly in a man - ger;
2 An - gels sang a - bout his birth, wise men sought and found him;
3 Gen - tle Ma - ry laid her child low - ly in a man - ger;

there he lay, the un - de - filed, to the world a stran - ger.
hea - ven's star shone bright - ly forth, glo - ry all a - round him.
he is still the un - de - filed, but no more a stran - ger.

Such a babe in such a place, can he be the Sav - iour?
Shep - herds saw the won - drous sight, heard the an - gels sing - ing;
Son of God of hum - ble birth, beau - ti - ful the sto - ry;

Ask the saved of all the race who have found his fa - vour.
all the plains were lit that night, all the hills were ring - ing.
praise his name in all the earth; hail the King of glo - ry!

Words: Joseph Simpson Cook 1919
Music: Alta Lind Cook; arr. Scott Wilkinson
Music copyright © Metropolitan United Church, Toronto.

GENTLE MARY
7 6 7 6 D

Still, Still, Still

1 Still, still, still: the night is calm and
2 Sleep, sleep, sleep: sweet Je - sus, soft - ly
3 Joy, joy, joy; glad tid - ings of great

still. The Christ - child in his crib lies sleep - ing,
sleep, while Ma - ry sings and gent - ly holds you,
joy! For through God's ho - ly in - car - na - tion

an - gels round him watch are keep - ing.
safe - ly in her arms en - folds you.
Christ is born for our sal - va - tion.

Still, still, still: the night is calm and still.
Sleep, sleep, sleep: sweet Je - sus soft - ly sleep.
Joy, joy, joy; glad tid - ings of great joy!

Words: Austrian carol; trans. John Rutter 1994
Music: Austrian melody; arr. Walter Ehret 1963

STILL, STILL, STILL
3 6 9 8 3 6

48   Hark! the Herald Angels Sing

1 Hark! the her - ald an - gels sing, "Glo - ry to the new - born King,
2 Christ, by high - est heaven a - dored, Christ, the ev - er - last - ing Lord,
3 Hail, the heaven - born Prince of Peace! Hail, the Sun of Righ - teous - ness!

peace on earth, and mer - cy mild, God and sin - ners rec - on - ciled!"
late in time be - hold him come, off - spring of a vir - gin's womb.
Light and life to all he brings, risen with heal - ing in his wings.

Joy - ful, all ye na - tions, rise, join the tri - umph of the skies;
Veiled in flesh the God - head see; hail, the in - car - nate de - i - ty,
Mild he lays his glo - ry by, born that we no more may die,

with the an - gel - ic host pro - claim, "Christ is born in Beth - le - hem!"
pleased with us in flesh to dwell, Je - sus, our Em - man - u - el!
born to raise us from the earth, born to give us sec - ond birth.

Words: Charles Wesley 1739, alt.
Music: Felix Mendelssohn 1840; adapt. William Hayman Cummings 1856

MENDELSSOHN
7 7 7 7 D *with refrain*

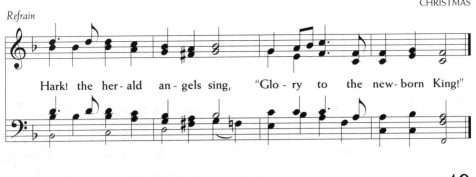

Refrain

Hark! the her-ald an-gels sing, "Glo-ry to the new-born King!"

No Crowded Eastern Street 49

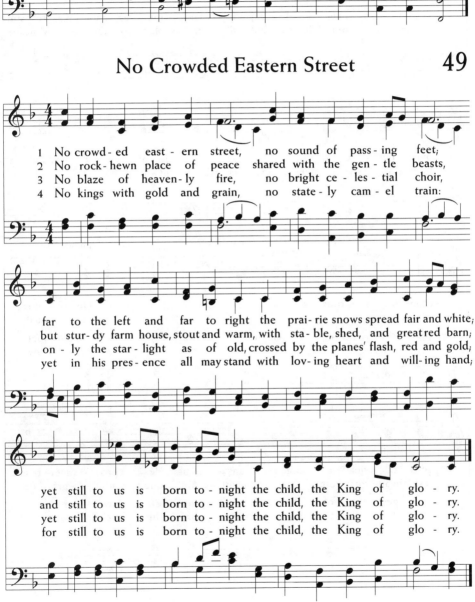

1 No crowd-ed east-ern street, no sound of pass-ing feet;
2 No rock-hewn place of peace shared with the gen-tle beasts,
3 No blaze of heaven-ly fire, no bright ce-les-tial choir,
4 No kings with gold and grain, no state-ly cam-el train:

far to the left and far to right the prai-rie snows spread fair and white;
but stur-dy farm house, stout and warm, with sta-ble, shed, and great red barn;
on-ly the star-light as of old, crossed by the planes' flash, red and gold;
yet in his pres-ence all may stand with lov-ing heart and will-ing hand;

yet still to us is born to-night the child, the King of glo-ry.
and still to us is born to-night the child, the King of glo-ry.
yet still to us is born to-night the child, the King of glo-ry.
for still to us is born to-night the child, the King of glo-ry.

Words: Frieda Major 1958
Music: Robert J. B. Fleming ca. 1970

HERITAGE
6 6 8 8 8 7

Words copyright © 1976 Frieda Major. Used by permission of St. Luke's Anglican Church, Winnipeg.
Music copyright © Robert J. B. Fleming. Used by permission of Margaret Fleming.

50

He Is Born
(Il est né)

Il est né, le di-vin En-fant, jou-ez, haut-bois, ré-son-
He is born, lit-tle Child div-ine; play on the reeds while the

nez mu-set-tes; il est né, le di-vin En-fant;
lutes are strum-ming. He is born, lit-tle Child div-ine;

chan-tons tous son a-vè-ne-ment.
join the song to an-nounce the day.

1 De-puis
2 Ah! qu'il

1 Through long
2 O how

plus de qua-tre mille ans nous le pro-met-taient
est beau, qu'il est char - mant! Ah! que ses grâ-ces
a - ges of the past, proph-ets have for -
love-ly, O how pure is this per - fect

Words: trad. 19th-century French carol; trans. George Evans 1963
Music: 18th-century French carol; harm. Carlton R. Young 1988

Translation copyright © Walton Music Corporation.
Harmony copyright © 1989 The United Methodist Publishing House.

IL EST NÉ
7 10 7 8 with refrain

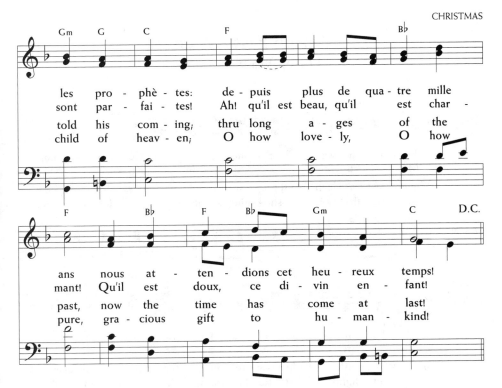

les pro - phè - tes: de - puis plus de qua - tre mille
sont par - fai - tes! Ah! qu'il est beau, qu'il est char -
told his com - ing; thru long a - ges of the
child of heav - en; O how love - ly, O how

ans nous at - ten - dions cet heu - reux temps!
mant! Qu'il est doux, ce di - vin en - fant!
past, now the time has come at last!
pure, gra - cious gift to hu - man - kind!

3 Une étable est son logement,
un peu de paille est sa couchette.
Une étable est son logement:
pour un Dieu, quel abaissement!

Refrain

4 Ô Jésus! Ô roi tout-puissant!
Tout petit enfant que vous êtes,
Ô Jésus! Ô roi tout-puissant!
Régnez sur nous entièrement.

Refrain

3 Lowly lodged in a stable poor,
laid on straw for his infant cradle.
Lowly lodged in a stable poor,
God come down to our mortal aid.

Refrain

4 Jesus, Lord of all the world,
coming as a child among us,
Jesus, Lord of all the world,
grant to us your heavenly peace.

Refrain

Prière de Noël

51

Aujourd'hui les anges chantent dans le ciel: chante avec eux!
Gloire à Dieu au plus haut des cieux!

Aujourd'hui les bergers viennent à Bethléem: viens avec eux!
Gloire à Dieu au plus haut des cieux!

Ils trouvent Joseph et Marie et l'enfant nouveau-né: cherche avec eux!
Gloire à Dieu au plus haut des cieux!

Lucien Deiss 1974

52

Sheep Fast Asleep
(Hitsuji Wa Nemure Ri)

1 Hi - tsu - ji wa ne - mu - re ri, Ku - sa - no, to - ko ni, Sa - e - yu - ku fu - yu no yo, Shi - mo mo mi - e - tsu. Ha - ru - ka ni,

2 Ma - hi - ru ni o - to - ra - nu Ku - shi - ki hi - ka - ri, Mi - so - ra no ka - na - ta ni Te - ri - ka - ga - ya - ku. Su - ku - i wo

1 Sheep fast a-sleep, there on a hill, grass for their bed; all is still. Cold win-ter night, the frost ap-pears; shep - herds keep watch by their fire. Soft there a sound,

2 Star in the sky, shi - ning so bright, si - lent and pure, won - drous light! What tid-ings brings it Is - ra - el? Can we new hope in it find? Good news it brings!

Words: Japanese, Genzo Miwa 1907, English trans. John Moss 1957, alt.
Music: Chûgoro Torii 1941; arr. David Kai 1994

KORIN
8 7 8 7 8 7 8 6

hi - bi - ku wa   Ka - ze - ka,   mi - zu ka,
mo - ta - ra - su   Ka - mi   no   mi - ko no
far, far a - way: is   it   the   stream?   Winds   at   play?
"Fear   not, I   pray!   Born   is   God's   Son,   born   to - day!

I - na - to yo   mi - tsu - ka - i   U - ta - u   mi - u - ta.
U - ma - re - shi   yo - ro - ko - bi   Tsu - gu - ru   ho - shi   ka.
Nay, friend, it is   the heaven - ly choir, sing - ing through - out the spheres.
God's gift of love to   all   the earth,   our Lord, Em - man - u - el."

3 Ame ni wa misakae
   Kami ni areya.
   Tsuchi ni wa odayaka
   Hito ni areto
   Mukashi no shirabe wo
   Ima ni kaeshi.
   Utaeya, tomora yo,
   Koemo takaku.

3 Glory to God! Glory on high!
   Sing you "Noel!" Day is nigh!
   All you who dwell on earth below,
   peace be to you, and goodwill.
   Come let us go to Bethlehem;
   follow the star, seeking him.
   Let us adore and worship still,
   in love and joy to grow.

A Christmas Prayer   53

Eternal God,
in Jesus Christ your light shines in our darkness,
      giving joy in our sorrow
      and presence in our loneliness.
Fill us with the mystery of your Word made flesh,
until our hearts overflow with praise and joy,
for he is the beginning and the end of all that exists,
      living forevermore. Amen.

54

Unto Us a Boy Is Born

Unison

1 Un - to us a boy is born! King of all cre - a - tion, came he to a world for - lorn, the Lord of ev - ery na - tion, the Lord of ev - ery na - tion.

2 Christ from heaven des - cend - ing low comes, on earth a stran - ger; ox and ass their own - er know, be - cra - dled in the man - ger, be - cra - dled in the man - ger.

♦ 3 He - rod then with fear was filled: "A prince," he said, "in Jew - ry!"; all the lit - tle boys he killed at Beth - lem in his fu - ry, at Beth - lem in his fu - ry.

4 Now may Ma - ry's son, who came so long a - go to love us, lead us all with hearts a - flame un - to the joys a - bove us, un - to the joys a - bove us.

5 O - me - ga and Al - pha he! Let the or - gan thun - der, while the choir with peals of glee doth rend the air a - sun - der, doth rend the air a - sun - der.

Words: German carol, 15th century; trans. vv. 1, 3–5, Percy Dearmer 1928;
trans. v. 2 George Ratcliff Woodward 1901
Music: German carol melody 1582; harm. Geoffrey Shaw 1928
Harmony copyright © Oxford University Press for A. R. Mowbray Ltd.

PUER NOBIS NASCITUR
76777

In the Bleak Midwinter

1 In the bleak mid-win-ter, frost-y wind made moan,
2 Our God, heaven can-not hold him, nor earth sus-tain;
3 E-nough for him, whom che-ru-bim wor-ship night and day, a
4 What can I give him, poor as I am?

earth stood hard as i-ron, wa-ter like a stone;
heaven and earth shall flee a-way when he comes to reign;
breast full of milk, and a man-ger full of hay. E-
If I were a shep-herd, I would bring a lamb;

snow had fal-len, snow on snow, snow on snow,
in the bleak mid-win-ter a sta-ble place suf-ficed the
nough for him, whom an-gels fall down be-fore, the
if I were a wise man, I would do my part; yet

in the bleak mid-win-ter, long a-go.
Lord God al-might-y, Je-sus Christ.
ox and ass and cam-el which a-dore.
what I can I give him — give my heart.

Words: Christina Georgina Rossetti ca. 1872
Music: Gustav Theodor Holst 1906

CRANHAM
Irregular

56

Jesus, Our Brother

1 Je - sus, our broth - er, kind and good, was
2 "I," said the don - key, shag - gy and brown, "I
3 "I," said the cow, all white and red, "I
4 "I," said the sheep with curl - y horn, "I

hum - bly born in a sta - ble rude, and the
car - ried the moth - er up - hill and down, I
gave him my man - ger for his bed, I
gave him my wool for his blan - ket warm, he

friend - ly beasts a - round him stood,
car - ried his moth - er to Beth - le - hem town;
gave him hay to pil - low his head;
wore my coat on Christ - mas morn;

Je - sus, our broth - er, kind and good.
I," said the don - key, shag - gy and brown.
I," said the cow, all white and red.
I," said the sheep, with cur - ly horn.

Words: French carol, 12th century; trans. Robert Davis, alt.
Music: medieval French melody; attrib. Pierre de Corbeil; harm. Carlton R. Young 1987
Translation copyright © CPP/Belwin, Inc. Harmony copyright © 1989 The United Methodist Publishing House.

ORIENTIS PARTIBUS
Irregular

5 "I," said the dove, from the rafters high,
"I cooed him to sleep that he should not
cry,
we cooed him to sleep, my mate and I;
I," said the dove, from the rafters high.

6 Thus all the beasts, by some good spell,
in the stable dark were glad to tell
of the gifts they gave Emmanuel,
the gifts they gave Emmanuel.

Oh, How Joyfully

57

1 Oh, how joy-ful-ly, oh, how hope-ful-ly, waits the world on Christ-mas Eve! Love comes heal-ing, God re-veal-ing. Friends, be joy-ful and be-lieve!

2 Oh, how joy-ful-ly, oh, how peace-ful-ly, sleeps the world on Christ-mas Night! Sins are cov-ered, grace dis-cov-ered. In our dark-ness shines the light!

3 Oh, how joy-ful-ly, oh, how thank-ful-ly, wakes the world on Christ-mas Morn! God has spo-ken, death is bro-ken. Hal-le-lu-jah! Christ is born!

Words: Brian Wren
Music: Sicilian melody, 18th century
Words copyright © 1993 Hope Publishing Company.

SICILIAN MARINERS
5 5 7 4 4 7

58 Infant Holy, Infant Lowly

1 In - fant ho - ly, in - fant low - ly, for his bed a cat - tle stall;
2 Flocks were sleep-ing; shep-herds keep-ing vig - il till the morn-ing new

ox - en low - ing, lit - tle know - ing Christ the babe is Lord of all.
saw the glo - ry, heard the sto - ry, tid - ings of a gos - pel true.

Swift are wing-ing an - gels sing-ing, no - els ring-ing, tid-ings bring-ing:
Thus re - joic-ing, free from sor - row, prais-es voic-ing greet the mor-row:

Christ the babe is born for all. Christ the babe is born for all!
Christ the babe was born for you. Christ the babe was born for you!

Words: Polish carol, trans. and para. Edith M. G. Reed 1921
Music: Polish folk melody, harm. A. E. Rusbridge
Harmony copyright © 1960 A. E. Rusbridge. Used by permission of Rosalind Rusbridge.

W ŻŁOBIE LEŻY
87 87 88 77

Joy to the World

1 Joy to the world! the Lord is come: let earth re-ceive her
2 Joy to the earth! the Sa-viour reigns: let all their songs em-
3 No more let sins and sor-rows grow, nor thorns in-fest the
4 He rules the earth with truth and grace, and makes the na-tions

King! Let ev-ery heart pre-pare him
ploy, while fields and floods, rocks, hills and
ground: he comes to make his bless-ings
prove the glo-ries of his righ-teous-

room, and heaven and na-ture sing, and heaven and na-ture
plains re-peat the sound-ing joy, re-peat the sound-ing
flow far as the curse is found, far as the curse is
ness and won-ders of his love, and won-ders of his

and heaven and na-ture sing, and

sing, and heaven, and heaven and na-ture sing.
joy, re-peat, re-peat the sound-ing joy.
found, far as, far as the curse is found.
love, and won-ders, won-ders of his love.

heaven and na-ture sing,

Words: Isaac Watts 1719, alt.
Music: attrib. George Frideric Handel 1742; arr. Lowell Mason 1836

ANTIOCH
8 6 8 6 with repeat

60 O Come, All Ye Faithful

1 O come, all ye faith-ful, joy-ful and tri-um-phant, O
2 God of God, light of light,
3 Sing, choirs of ang-els, sing in ex-ul-ta-tion,
4 See how the shep-herds sum-moned to his cra-dle,
5 Yea, Lord, we greet thee, born this hap-py morn-ing;

come ye, O come ye to Beth-le-hem:
lo, he ab-hors not the vir-gin's womb;
sing, all ye cit-i-zens of heaven a-bove;
leav-ing their flocks, draw nigh with low-ly fear;
Je-sus, to thee be glo-ry given;

come and be-hold him, born the King of an-gels;
ve-ry God, be-got-ten, not cre-a-ted:
glo-ry to God in the high-est;
we too will thi-ther bend our joy-ful foot-steps;
word of the Fa-ther, now in flesh ap-pear-ing:

Refrain

O come, let us a-dore him, O come, let us a-dore him,
ve-ni-te a-do-re-mus, ve-ni-te a-do-re-mus,

O come, let us a - dore him, Christ the Lord.
ve - ni - te a - do - re - mus Do - mi - num.

Latin:

1 Adeste, fideles, læti triumphantes,
venite, venite, in Bethlehem:
natum videte regem angelorum:
Venite, adoremus Dominum.

2 Deum de Deo, lumen de lumine,
parturit virgo mater,
Deum verum, genitum, non factum.
Venite, adoremus Dominum.

3 Cantet nunc hymnos chorus
angelorum;
cantet nunc aula cælestium:

gloria in excelsis Deo!
Venite, adoremus Dominum.

4 En grege relicto, — humiles ad
cunas
vocati pastores approperant:
et nos ovanti gradu festinemus:
venite, adoremus Dominum.

5 Ergo qui natus die hodierna,
Jesu, tibi sit gloria:
Patris aeterni verbum caro factum.
Venite, adoremus Dominum.

Words: Latin, John Francis Wade, ca. 1743

ADESTE FIDELES
Irregular

French:

1 Peuple fidèle, le Seigneur t'appelle:
c'est fête sur terre, le Christ est né.
Viens à la crèche,
voir le Roi du monde:

Refrain
En lui, viens reconnaître,
ton Dieu, ton Sauveur!

2 Verbe, Lumière, et splendeur du Pére,
il naît d'une mère, petit enfant; Dieu
véritable,
le Seigneur fait homme:

Refrain

3 Peuple, acclame, avec tous les anges,
le Maître des hommes qui vient chez
nous. Dieu qui se donne
à tous ceux qu'il aime!

Refrain

4 Peuple fidèle, en ce jour de fête,
proclame la gloire de ton Seigneur.
Dieu se fait homme; vois donc comme
il t'aime:

Refrain

Words: English trans. Frederick Oakeley 1841, et al; French trans. Claude Rozier 1950
Music: attrib. John Francis Wade ca. 1743

ADESTE FIDELES
Irregular

61   Of the Father's Love Begotten

Unison

1 *Of the Fa - ther's love be - got - ten
2 At his word the worlds were fram - ed.
3 O that birth for ev - er bless - ed!
4 This is he whom seers in old time

ere the worlds be - gan to be,
He com - mand - ed, it was done:
When the Vir - gin, full of grace,
chant - ed of with one ac - cord,

Christ is Al - pha and O - me - ga,
heaven and earth and depths of o - cean
by the Ho - ly Ghost con - ceiv - ing,
whom the voic - es of the proph - ets

Christ the source, the end - ing he,
in their three - fold or - der one;
bare the Sav - iour of our race,
pro - mised in their faith - ful word;

* or "Of God's very heart"

Words: Latin, Aurelius Clemens Prudentius ca. 405; trans. John Mason Neale 1851, alt.   DIVINUM MYSTERIUM
Music: plainsong melody, ca. 12th century; arr. Healey Willan 1933   8 7 8 7 8 7 7
Arrangement copyright © 1933. Reprinted with permission of the Estate of Healey Willan.

of the things that are and have been,
all that grows be-neath the shin - - - ing
and the babe, the world's re-deem - - - er,
now he shines, the long-ex-pect - - - ed;

and that fu - ture years shall see,
of the moon and burn - ing sun,
first re - vealed his sa - cred face,
let cre - a - tion praise its Lord,

Optional

ev - er - more and ev - er - more.
ev - er - more and ev - er - more.
ev - er - more and ev - er - more.
ev - er - more and ev - er - more. A - men.

5 O ye heights of heaven, adore him;
angel hosts, his praises sing;
powers, dominions, bow before him,
and extol our God and King;
let no tongue on earth be silent,
every voice in concert ring,
evermore and evermore.

6 Christ, to thee, with God most
blessed,
and, O Holy Ghost, to thee,
hymn and chant and high
thanksgiving
and unwearied praises be,
honour, glory, and dominion
and eternal victory,
evermore and evermore.

62 Once in Royal David's City

Descant

4 And our eyes at last shall see him, through his

1 Once in roy - al Da - vid's ci - ty stood a
2 He came down to earth from heav - en who, with
3 For he is our life - long pat - tern; dai - ly,
4 And our eyes at last shall see him, through his

own re - deem - ing love; for that child who seemed so
God, is ov - er all, and his shel - ter was a
when on earth he grew, he was temp - ted, scorned, re -
own re - deem - ing love; for that child who seemed so

help - less is our Lord in heaven a - bove; and he

ba - by in a man - ger for his bed. Ma - ry
sta - ble, and his cra - dle was a stall. There a -
jec - ted, tears and smiles like us he knew. Thus he
help - less is our Lord in heaven a - bove; and he

Words: Cecil Frances Alexander 1848, alt.
Music: Henry John Gauntlett 1849; harm. Arthur Henry Mann;
    desc. David Willcocks 1970

IRBY
878777

Harmony copyright © 1957 Novello & Co. Limited. Descant copyright © Oxford University Press 1970.

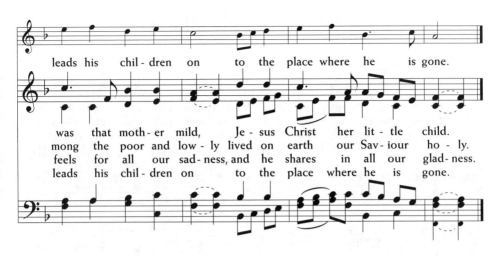

leads his chil-dren on to the place where he is gone.

was that moth-er mild, Je-sus Christ her lit-tle child.
mong the poor and low-ly lived on earth our Sav-iour ho-ly.
feels for all our sad-ness, and he shares in all our glad-ness.
leads his chil-dren on to the place where he is gone.

A Christmas Prayer of Confession   63

God of stable, stars, and surprises,
   of light and hope and new life:
open our eyes and hearts to your presence in our world;
   forgive our obsession with property and possessions;
   forgive our compromises and narrowness of vision.
Open us to your grace,
that we might hear again the song of the angels,
   and respond with a song in our hearts,
   and in our lives. Amen.

Gordon Nodwell 1980, alt.

64   O Little Town of Bethlehem

1 O lit-tle town of Beth-le-hem, how still we see thee lie!
2 For Christ is born of Ma - ry; and gath-ered all a - bove,
3 How si - lent-ly, how si - lent-ly the won-drous gift is given!
4 O ho - ly child of Beth-le-hem, de-scend to us, we pray;

A - bove thy deep and dream-less sleep the si - lent stars go by;
while mor-tals sleep, the an - gels keep their watch of won-dering love.
So God im-parts to hu - man hearts the bless-ed gift of heaven.
cast out our sin, and en - ter in; be born in us to - day.

yet in thy dark streets shin-eth the ev - er - last-ing light;
O morn-ing stars, to - ge - ther pro-claim the ho - ly birth,
No ear may hear his com-ing; but in this world of sin,
We hear the Christ-mas an - gels the great glad tid-ings tell;

the hopes and fears of all the years are met in thee to-night.
and prais-es sing to God the King, and peace to all on earth.
where meek souls will re-ceive him, still the dear Christ en-ters in.
O come to us, a-bide with us, our Lord Em-man-u-el.

Words: *Phillips Brooks* 1868
Music: *Lewis Henry Redner* 1868

ST LOUIS
8 6 8 6 7 6 8 6
Alt. tune: Forest Green

Ring a Bell for Peace

1 Ring a bell for peace, for the babe born on this night, ring a bell through the coun-try and the town; ring a bell for peace, come and see the won-drous light, ring a bell, ring it mer-ry up and down.

2 Blow a horn for joy, for the babe born in the hay, blow a horn through the coun-try and the town; blow a horn for joy, come and hear what peo-ple say, blow a horn, blow it mer-ry up and down.

3 Play a flute for hope, for the babe now fast a-sleep, play a flute through the coun-try and the town; play a flute for hope, see the shep-herds leave their sheep, play a flute, play it mer-ry up and down.

4 Beat the drum for faith, for the babe born 'neath the star, beat the drum through the coun-try and the town; beat the drum for faith, come and play where-'er you are, beat the drum, beat it mer-ry up and down.

Words: Marian Collibole
Music: Richard H. Jacquet 1975

CHESHUNT
5 7 10 D

66

A Christian Prayer

As once you came in the hush of darkness, O God,
    so still our hearts now
    by the wonder of this night.
Make us wise with the wisdom of a little one,
    that truth might be born afresh in us.
Let not our hearts be busy inns with no room,
    but doors opened wide to welcome a Holy Guest,
who is Jesus Christ, alive with you and the Holy Spirit,
    one God, now and for ever. Amen.

Robert Stark 1990, alt.

67

Silent Night, Holy Night
(Stille Nacht)

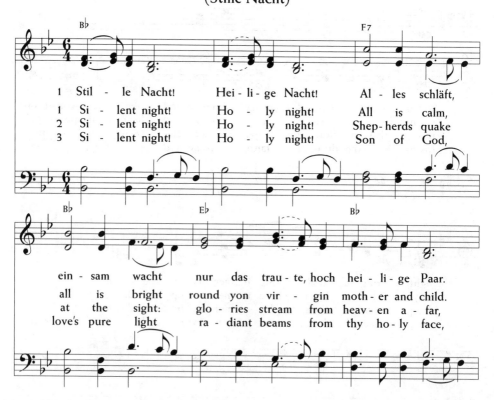

1 Stil - le Nacht! Hei - li - ge Nacht! Al - les schläft,
1 Si - lent night! Ho - ly night! All is calm,
2 Si - lent night! Ho - ly night! Shep- herds quake
3 Si - lent night! Ho - ly night! Son of God,

ein - sam wacht nur das trau - te, hoch hei - li - ge Paar.
all is bright round yon vir - gin moth - er and child.
at the sight: glo - ries stream from heav - en a - far,
love's pure light ra - diant beams from thy ho - ly face,

Words: *Joseph Mohr 1818, English trans. John Freeman Young 1863, et al.*
Music: *Franz Xavier Grüber 1818*

STILLE NACHT
Irregular

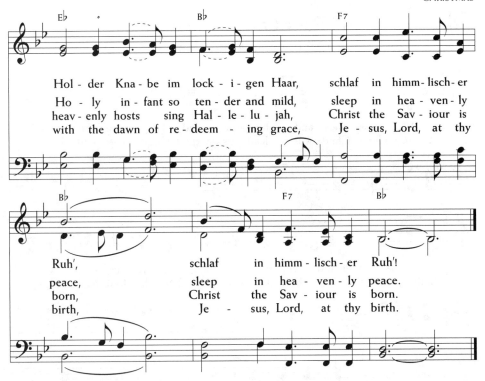

Hol - der Kna - be im lock - i - gen Haar, schlaf in himm - lisch - er
Ho - ly in - fant so ten - der and mild, sleep in hea - ven - ly
heav - enly hosts sing Hal - le - lu - jah, Christ the Sav - iour is
with the dawn of re - deem - ing grace, Je - sus, Lord, at thy

Ruh', schlaf in himm - lisch - er Ruh'!
peace, sleep in hea - ven - ly peace.
born, Christ the Sav - iour is born.
birth, Je - sus, Lord, at thy birth.

2 Stille Nacht! Heilige Nacht!
Hirten erst kundgemacht.
Durch der Engel Halleluja
tönt es laut von fern und nah:
Christ, der Retter ist da,
Christ, der Retter ist da!

3 Stille Nacht! Heilige Nacht!
Gottes Sohn, o wie lacht
Lieb' aus deinem göttlichen Mund,
da uns schlägt die rettende Stund':
Christ, in deiner Geburt.
Christ, in deiner Geburt.

Ô nuit de paix! Sainte nuit!

1 Ô nuit de paix! Sainte nuit!
Dans le ciel l'astre luit;
dans les champs tout repose en paix.
Mais soudain, dans l'air pur et frais,
le brillant choeur des anges
aux bergers apparaît.

2 Ô nuit de foi! Sainte nuit!
Les bergers sont instruits;
confiants dans la voix des cieux,
ils s'en vont adorer leur Dieu;
et Jésus en échange
leur sourit radieux.

3 Ô nuit d'amour! Sainte nuit!
Dans l'étable, aucun bruit;
sur la paille est couché l'Enfant
que la Vierge endort en chantant;
il repose en ses langes,
son Jésus ravissant.

4 Ô nuit d'espoir! Sainte nuit!
L'espérance a relui:
le Sauveur de la terre est né
c'est à nous que Dieu l'a donné.
Célébrons ses louanges:
gloire au Verbe incarné!

Words: French trans. Armand Bail

68 All Poor Ones and Humble
(All Poor Men and Humble)

1 All poor ones and hum-ble and all those who stum-ble,
2 The Christ Child will lead us, the Good Shep-herd feed us

come hast-ening, and feel not a - fraid; for Je - sus, our trea-sure,
and with us a - bide till his day. Then ha-tred he'll ban-ish;

with love past all mea-sure, in low-ly poor man-ger was laid.
then sor-row will van-ish, and death and de-spair flee a - way.

Though wise men who found him laid rich gifts a - round him,
And he shall reign ev - er, and noth - ing shall sev - er

Words: v.1 Katharine Emily Roberts 1927, alt.; v.2 William Thomas Pennar Davies 1951
Music: Welsh carol; harm. Erik Routley 1951

OLWEN
6 6 8 6 6 8 D *with refrain*

Words copyright © 1928 Oxford University Press (v. 1); © 1951 W. T. Pennar Davies (v. 2). Harmony copyright © Hope Publishing Company

yet ox-en they gave him their hay, and Je-sus in beau-ty
from us the great love of our King; his peace and his pit-y

ac-cept-ed their du-ty; con-tent-ed in man-ger he lay.
shall bless his fair cit-y; his prais-es we ev-er shall sing.

Refrain

Then haste we to show him the prais-es we owe him;

our ser-vice he ne'er can de-spise; whose love still is a-ble

to show us that sta-ble, where soft-ly in man-ger he lies.

69

Away in a Manger

1 A - way in a man - ger, no crib for a bed,
2 The cat - tle are low - ing, the ba - by a - wakes,
3 Be near me, Lord Je - sus, I ask you to stay

the lit - tle Lord Je - sus laid down his sweet head.
but lit - tle Lord Je - sus, no cry - ing he makes.
close by me for ev - er, and love me, I pray.

The stars in the bright sky looked down where he lay,
I love you, Lord Je - sus; look down from the sky,
Bless all the dear chil - dren in your ten - der care,

the lit - tle Lord Je - sus a - sleep on the hay.
and stay by my side un - til morn - ing is nigh.
and fit us for heav - en, to live with you there.

Words: Author unknown
Music: William James Kirkpatrick 1895; arr. Desmond Hassell 1992
Arrangement copyright © 1992 Desmond Hassell.

CRADLE SONG
11 11 11 11
Alt. tune: Away in a Manger

There's a Star in the East

Unison

1 There's a star in the East on Christ-mas morn,
2 If you take good heed to the an-gel's words,

rise up, shep-herd, and fol-low; it will lead to the place where the
rise up, shep-herd, and fol-low, you'll for-get your flocks, you'll for-

Harmony   Unison

Christ was born; rise up, shep-herd, and fol-low.
get your herds; rise up, shep-herd, and fol-low.

Harmony

Refrain

Fol-low, fol-low, rise up, shep-herd, and fol-low,

fol-low the Star of Beth-le-hem, rise up, shep-herd, and fol-low.

Words: African-American spiritual
Music: African-American spiritual

RISE UP, SHEPHERD
Irregular with refrain

71   'Twas in the Moon of Wintertime

Unison

1 'Twas in the moon of win-ter-time, when all the birds had fled,
2 With-in a lodge of bro-ken bark the ten-der babe was found,
3 The ear-liest moon of win-ter-time is not so round and fair
4 O chil-dren of the for-est free, the an-gel song is true;

that might-y Git-chi Man-i-tou sent an-gel choirs in-stead;
a rag-ged robe of rab-bit skin en-wrapped his beau-ty round;
as was the ring of glo-ry on the help-less in-fant there.
the ho-ly child of earth and heaven is born to-day for you.

be-fore their light the stars grew dim, and
but as the hun-ter braves drew nigh, the
The chiefs from far be-fore him knelt with
Come, kneel be-fore the ra-diant boy, who

wan-dering hun-ters heard the hymn:
an-gel song rang loud and high:
gifts of fox and bea-ver pelt.
brings you beau-ty, peace, and joy:

Words: Jean de Brébeuf ca. 1641; English trans. Jesse Edgar Middleton 1926, alt.
Music: French folksong, 16th century; arr. by H. Barrie Cabena 1970

JESOUS AHATONHIA
Irregular

Refrain

Je - sus your King is born, Je - sus is born, in ex - cel - sis glo - ri - a.

From Heaven Above to Earth I Come   72

1 From heaven a - bove to earth I come to
2 To you this night is born a child of
♦ 3 These are the signs which you will see to
4 Our hearts for ver - y joy now leap, our
5 "Glo - ry to God in high - est heaven, who

bring good news to ev - ery - one! Glad tid - ings of great
Ma - ry, cho - sen vir - gin mild; this new - born child of
♦ let you know that it is he: in man - ger bed, in
voic - es can - not si - lence keep; we too must join the
un - to us a Son has given." With an - gels sing in

joy I bring to all the world, and glad - ly sing:
low - ly birth shall be the joy of all the earth.
♦ swad - dling clothes the child who all the earth up - holds.
an - gel throng to sing with joy his cra - dle song.
pi - ous mirth: a glad new year to all the earth!

Words: Martin Luther 1535; trans. adapt. from Catherine Winkworth 1855
Music: attrib. Martin Luther; melody in Valentin Schumann's Geistliche Lieder *1539; arr. unknown*
Translation adaptation copyright © 1978 Lutheran Book of Worship. Reprinted by permission of Augsburg Fortress.

VOM HIMMEL HOCH
8 8 8 8

73 The Virgin Mary Had a Baby Boy

1 The virgin Mary had a baby boy, the virgin Mary had a baby boy, the virgin Mary had a baby boy,

2 The angels sang when the baby was born, the angels sang when the baby was born, the angels sang when the baby was born, and they

3 The shepherds came where the baby was born, the shepherds came where the baby was born, the shepherds came where the baby was born,

Words: West Indian carol, from Edric Conner Collection of West Indian Spirituals 1945
Music: West Indian carol, from Edric Conner Collection of West Indian Spirituals 1945,
    arr. John Barnard 1982

THE VIRGIN MARY
Irregular with refrain

x = clap

74

What Child Is This

1 What child is this, who laid to rest, on Mary's lap is sleeping? Whom angels greet with anthems sweet while shepherds watch are keeping?

2 Why lies he in such mean estate where ox and ass are feeding? Good Christian, fear; for sinners here the silent Word is pleading.

3 So bring him incense, gold, and myrrh; come, one and all, to own him. The King of Kings salvation brings; let loving hearts enthrone him.

Refrain

This, this is Christ the King, whom shepherds guard and angels sing;

Words: *William Chatterton Dix ca. 1865*
Music: *English melody, 16th century, harm. attrib. John Stainer 1871*

GREENSLEEVES
8 7 8 7 *with refrain*

haste, haste to bring him laud, the Babe, the Son of Ma - ry!

While Shepherds Watched Their Flocks 75

1 While shep - herds watched their flocks by night all
2 "Fear not," said he, for might - y dread had
3 "To you in Da - vid's town this day is
4 "The heaven - ly babe you there shall find to

seat - ed on the ground, the an - gel of the
seized their trou - bled mind; "glad tid - ings of great
born of Da - vid's line a Sav - iour, who is
hu - man view dis - played, all mean - ly wrapped in

Lord came down, and glo - ry shone a - round.
joy I bring to you and hu - man - kind.
Christ the Lord; and this shall be the sign:
swadd - ling bands, and in a man - ger laid."

5 Thus spake the seraph; and forthwith
appeared a shining throng
of angels praising God, who thus
addressed their joyful song:

6 "All glory be to God on high,
and to the earth be peace;
good will to all from highest heaven
begin, and never cease."

Words: Nahum Tate 1700, alt.
Music: adapt. from Este's Whole Booke of Psalmes 1592

WINCHESTER OLD
8 6 8 6

76 See amid the Winter's Snow

1 See a-mid the win-ter's snow, born for us on earth be-low,
see, the ten-der Lamb ap-pears, prom-ised from e-ter-nal years.

2 Lo, with-in a man-ger lies God who built the star-ry skies,
who en-throned in height sub-lime sits a-mid the cher-u-bim.

3 Say, ye ho-ly shep-herds, say what your joy-ful news to-day;
where-fore have ye left your sheep on the lone-ly moun-tain steep?

Refrain (Harmony)

Hail, thou ev-er-bless-ed morn; hail, re-demp-tion's hap-py dawn;
sing through all Je-ru-sa-lem, Christ is born in Beth-le-hem.

Words: Edward Caswall 1851
Music: John Goss 1871

SEE AMID THE WINTER'S SNOW
7 7 7 7 with refrain

4 "As we watched at dead of night,
lo, we saw a wondrous light;
angels singing 'Peace on earth'
told us of the Saviour's birth."

Refrain

5 Sacred infant, all divine,
what a mighty love was thine,
thus to come from highest bliss
down to such a world as this!

Refrain

In Bethlehem a Newborn Boy 77

1 In Bethlehem a newborn boy was hailed with songs of praise and joy. Then warning came of danger near: King Herod's troops would soon appear.

2 (The) soldiers sought the child in vain, not yet was he to share our pain; but down the ages rings the cry of those who saw their children die.

3 (Still) rage the fires of hate today, and innocents the price must pay, while aching hearts in every land cry out, "We cannot understand!"

4 (Lord) Jesus, through our night of loss shines out the wonder of your cross, the love that cannot cease to bear our human anguish everywhere.

5 (May) that great love our lives control and conquer hate in every soul, till, pledged to build and not destroy, we share your pain and find your joy.

Words: Rosamond E. Herklots 1969
Music: Wilbur Held 1983

IN BETHLEHEM
8 8 8 8

78 Sing till Sundown

Unison

1 Sing till sun - down, hum your joy, dress in
2 Glad - ness deep - ens in - to grace, weaves its

star - light, girl and boy. Man and wo - man climb the
light on ev - ery face. Let us wake the sleep - ing

hill, warmed be - yond De - cem - ber's chill, reel - ing,
earth, cel - e - brate the sweet - est birth, pierce the

clap - ping, touch the air: is that fra - grant mu - sic
night with fes - tive cry, bloom in col - ours of the

Words: Eileen Spinelli 1988
Music: David Bretzius 1988
Words copyright © 1988 Eileen Spinelli. Music copyright © 1988 David Bretzius.

SPRINGBROOK
7 7 7 7 7 7 7 7 7 7

there? Come the glo - ry, gone the gloom: in a
sky. Bring the flute, the tam - bour - ine, wave the

won - drous hud - dled room. Christ the Word we've longed to
branch of ev - er - green. Lost we were a grief a -

know calls us danc - ing through the snow.
go, now we're danc - ing through the snow.

And the following…

79

Arise, Your Light Is Come

Descant

4 A-rise, your light is come! The moun-tains burst in song! Rise up! Rise

A   D   (A) D   A   E   B7   E

1 A-rise, your light is come! The Spir-it's call o-bey; show
2 A-rise, your light is come! Fling wide the pris-on door; pro-
3 A-rise, your light is come! All you in sor-row born, bind
4 A-rise, your light is come! The moun-tains burst in song! Rise

up like ea-gles on the wing; God's power will make us strong.

A (E) D (A) Bm B7 E (A) D (A) Esus4 E7 A

forth the glo-ry of your God, which shines on you to-day.
claim the cap-tive's lib-er-ty, good tid-ings to the poor.
up the bro-ken-heart-ed ones and com-fort those who mourn.
up like ea-gles on the wing; God's power will make us strong.

Words: Ruth Duck 1974
Music: William H. Walker 1872; desc. Diana McLeod 1995
Words copyright © 1992 G.I.A. Publications, Inc. Descant copyright © 1995 Diana McLeod.

FESTAL SONG
6 6 8 6

80

An Epiphany Prayer

O God, our light, our beauty, our rest:
With the appearance of your Son
   you have brought us into your new creation.
Form us into your people, and order our lives in you;
   through Christ, the Living One. Amen.

Gail Ramshaw 1988

As with Gladness Men of Old

Descant

5 In the heaven-ly coun-try bright none shall need cre - a - ted light;

1 As with glad-ness men of old did the guid-ing star be-hold,
2 As with joy-ful steps they sped, to that low-ly man-ger bed,
♦ 3 As they of-fered gifts most rare at that man-ger crude and bare,
4 Ho-ly Je-sus, ev-ery day keep us in the nar-row way;
5 In the heaven-ly coun-try bright none shall need cre - a - ted light;

you its light, its joy, its crown, you its sun which goes not down;

as with joy they hailed its light, lead - ing on - ward, beam-ing bright,
there to bend the knee be-fore Christ, whom heaven and earth a - dore;
♦ so may we with ho-ly joy, pure and free from sin's al - loy,
and, when earth-ly things are past, bring our ran-somed souls at last
you its light, its joy, its crown, you its sun which goes not down;

there for ev - er may we sing hal - le - lu - jah to our King.

so, most gra-cious Lord, may we ev - er - more your splen-dour see.
so may we with ea - ger pace ev - er seek your throne of grace.
♦ all our cost-liest trea-sures bring, Christ, to you, our heaven-ly King.
where they need no star to guide, where no clouds your glo - ry hide.
there for ev - er may we sing hal - le - lu - jah to our King.

Words: William Chatterton Dix ca. 1858, alt.
Music: Conrad Kocher 1838; adapt. William H. Monk 1861; desc. Alan Gray 1920

DIX
777777

82 A Light Is Gleaming

Refrain (**Unison**)

A light is gleam - ing, spread - ing its arms through - out the night, liv - ing in the light.

Come share its glad - ness, God's ra - diant love is burn - ing bright, liv - ing in the light.

vv. 1–3   Final ending   *(to verses)*

Words: *Linnea Good 1992*
Music: *Linnea Good 1992*
Words and music copyright © *1992 Borealis Music.*

LIVING IN THE LIGHT
Irregular with refrain

1 When light comes pour - ing in - to the dark - est place,
2 When night is round us and ev - ery shad - ow grows,
3 And Je - sus showed us a bright - er path to walk.
4 So let us live in the bright - ness God has giv'n,

it hurts our eyes to see the glow.
a star is there to light our way.
He showed us things we had - n't seen.
and let us rise to see the dawn.

Some - times a word of hope re - minds us of our
It tells a sto - ry of Je - sus who came
Now we, like Je - sus, can help cre - a - tion
We trust that God is here a - spar - kle and a -

fears, our mem - or - ies and tears.
near to say: "God's light will ev - er stay."
shine, and this will be a sign:
blaze, — warm - ing all our days.

83 Break Forth, O Beauteous Heavenly Light

1 Break forth, O beau-teous heaven-ly light, and
2 All bless-ing, thanks and praise to thee, Lord

ush-er in the morn-ing; ye shep-herds, shrink not
Je-sus Christ, be giv-en: thou hast our broth-er

with af-fright, but hear the an-gel's warn-ing.
deigned to be, our foes in sun-der riv-en.

This child, now born in in-fan-cy, our
O grant us through our day of grace with

con-fi-dence and joy shall be, the power of Sa-tan
con-stant praise to seek thy face; grant us ere long in

Words: German, Johann Rist 1641; trans. Arthur Tozer Russell ca. 1851, et al.
Music: Johann Schop 1641; harm. Johann Sebastian Bach 1734

ERMUNTRE DICH
Irregular

break - ing, our peace e - ter - nal mak - ing.
glo - ry with prais - es to a - dore thee.

O Radiant Christ, Incarnate Word · 84

1 O   ra - diant Christ, in - car - nate Word, e -
2 Our   bar - tered, bus - y   lives burn dim, too
3 Your   glo - ry shone at   Jor - dan's stream, the
4 O   Light of Na - tions,   fill the earth; our

ter - nal love re - vealed in time: come, make your home with -
tired to care, too numb to feel. Come, shine up - on our
font where we were born a - new. At - tune your church to
faith and hope and love re - new. Come, lead the peo - ples

in our hearts, that we may dwell in light sub - lime.
shad - owed world: your ra - diance bathes with power to heal.
know you near; il - lu - mine all we say and do.
to your peace, as stars once led the way to you.

Words: Ruth Duck 1991
Music: Robert Schumann 1839, adapt.
Words copyright © 1992 G.I.A. Publications, Inc.

CANONBURY
8 8 8 8

85 Midnight Stars Make Bright the Sky

Unison

1 Mid - night stars make bright the skies, Beth - le - hem in slum - ber lies:
2 Mid - night slum - ber lies o'er all; one lone bright lamp lights the stall.
3 Wise men long fore - told the way, saw the strange star's shin - ing ray.

glis - tening heaven sends forth great light, shep - herds see a won - drous sight!
Choose old cloth - ing, wrap him warm - ly, man - ger shall his cra - dle be.
Knew a child was born in Jew - ry, wor - ship would be joy for aye!

An - gel ranks in cho - rus sing. Silk - en sounds from heav - en ring.
Born to save us from our sin, Word made flesh, our lives to win.
Took strong cam - els hur - ry - ing, cross - ing des - ert sought their king.

Fright - ened shep - herds hear them say: "Christ comes down to earth to - day!"
Came to earth from heav - en's throne, mor - tals' sin to bear a - lone.
Rev - erent - ly to him pre - sent gold and myrrh and frank - in - cense.

Words: Chinese, Ching-chiu Yang 1930; trans. Mildred A. Wiant 1966   HUAN-SHA-CH'I
Music: Chi-fang Liang 1934; arr. Rudolph Fellner   7 7 7 7 D with refrain
Words and music copyright © 1977 The Chinese Christian Literature Council Ltd., Hong Kong. Arrangement copyright © 1955 Houghton Mifflin Co.

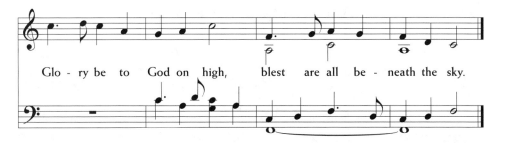

Glo - ry be to God on high, blest are all be - neath the sky.

Ming xing can lan ge

1 ming xing can lan ye wei yang,
bo li heng cheng zai shui xiang;
ye wai mu ren jian yi xiang,
tian shang jiao ran fa da quang;
tian zhi lie dui tong ge chang,
mu ren jian zhi xian jing huang;
hu wen lun yin ban jiu xiao,
xuan yan sheng zi jiang xia fang;

2 ming xing can lan ye wei yang,
gu deng ying ying zhao ke chuang;
qu lai jiu bu zuo qian bao,
ma cao quan dang yo er chuang;

wei yu jiu shi zheng xian ni,
dao cheng ren shen zhen li zhang;
cai li di zuo lin xia jie,
ren shi jian xin yi bei chang;

3 wang dao nai you san bo shi,
yang zhan yi xing fa guang wang,
cong zhi jiu zhu sheng you tai,
yi jin wei rong cheng yi chang,
jie bi ming tuo qian li zu,
ba she huang mo chao jun wang,
xie lai li wu jing xian shang,
huang jin mo yao yu ru xiang.

Refrain
zhi gao rong yao gui shang zhu!
quan di ren min fu wu jiang!

Words: Chinese, *Ching-chiu Yang 1930, translit. Christopher Cheung 1996*
Transliteration copyright © 1996 Christopher Cheung.

HUAN-SHA-CH'I

An Epiphany Prayer   86

Radiant God, light for all people and all places,
by the guidance of a star you led the Magi
    to worship the Christ Child.
By the light of faith
lead us to worship you in peace and love,
    and guide us in your way.
We pray in the name of Christ,
    light of the world. Amen.

Joan McMurtry 1990

87 I Am the Light of the World

Refrain (Unison)

"I am the light of the world! You peo-ple come and fol-low me!" If you fol-low and love you'll learn the mys-te-ry of what you were meant to do and be.

1 When the song of the an - gels is stilled, when the star in the sky is gone, when the
2 — To find the lost and lone - ly one, to heal the bro-ken soul with love, to
3 — To free the pris - oner from all chains, to make the pow-er - ful care, to
4 To bring hope to ev - ery task you do, to dance at a ba - by's new birth, to

kings and the shep - herds have found their way home, the
feed the hun - gry child - ren with warmth and good food, to
re - build the na - tions with strength of good will, to
make mu - sic in an old per - son's heart, and

work of Christ - mas is be - gun:
feel the earth be - low, the sky a - bove!
see God's chil - dren ev - ery - where!
sing to the col - ours of the earth!

Words: Jim Strathdee 1967
Music: Jim Strathdee 1967
Words and music copyright © 1969 Desert Flower Music.

LIGHT OF THE WORLD
Irregular

An Epiphany Prayer   88

God of gold, we seek your glory:
  the richness that transforms drabness into colour,
  and brightens our dullness with vibrant light;
  your wonder and joy at the heart of all life.

God of incense, we offer you our prayer:
  our spoken and unspeakable longings,
  our questioning of truth,
  our searching for your mystery deep within.

God of myrrh, we cry out to you in our suffering:
  the pain of all our rejections and bereavements,
  our baffled despair at undeserved suffering,
  our rage at continuing injustice.

In our wealth, in our yearning, in our anger and loss,
  we embrace you, God–with–us. Amen.

Jan Berry 1990

89 From a Distant Home
(De tierra lejana venimos)

peace   and   love   to   all.

y en   la   tie - rra_a - mor.

3 Frankincense I bring
  the child of God's own choosing,
  token of our prayers
  to heaven ever rising.

4 Bitter myrrh have I
  to give the infant Jesus,
  token of the pain
  that he will bear to save us.

3 Como es Dios el Niño
  le regalo incienso,
  perfume con alma
  que sube hasta el cielo.

4 Al Niño del cielo
  que bajó a la tierra,
  le regalo mirra
  que inspira tristeza.

Words: Spanish trad. Puerto Rican carol; trans. George K. Evans 1963
Music: trad. Puerto Rican carol; arr. Walter Ehret 1963
English translation and arrangement copyright © 1963, 1980 Walter Ehret and George K. Evans, by permission of Walton Music Corp.

ISLA DEL ENCANTO
12 12 with refrain

Aujourd'hui, le Roi des cieux   90
(The First Nowell)

1 Aujourd'hui, le Roi des cieux, au milieu de la nuit,
  voulut naître chez nous de la Vierge
  Marie,
  pour sauver le genre humain, l'arracher
  au péché,
  ramener au Seigneur ses enfants
  égarés.

2 En ces lieux, durant la nuit,
  demeuraient des bergers
  qui gardaient leurs troupeaux dans les
  champs de Judée.
  Tout à coup un messager apparut dans
  les cieux
  et la gloire de Dieu resplendit autour
  d'eux.

3 L'ange dit: Ne craignez pas, soyez
  tous dans la joie,
  un Sauveur vous est né: c'est le Christ
  votre Roi.
  Près d'ici vous trouverez un enfant
  nouveau né,
  dans l'étable couché, d'un lange
  emmailloté.

4 Aussitôt s'emplit le ciel de lumière et
  de chants,
  d'une armée d'anges blancs louant
  Dieu et disant:
  Gloire à Dieu dans les hauteurs et sur
  terre la paix
  pour les hommes sur qui Dieu répand
  sa bonté.

Refrain   Noël! Noël! Noël! Noël!
Jésus est né! Chantons Noël!

(The music appears on the following page.)

Words: English traditional carol, ca. 17th century; French trans. Joseph Gelineau
Translation copyright © Musique et liturgie..

THE FIRST NOWELL

91 The First Nowell

1 The first Now - ell the an - gel did say
2 They look - ed up and saw a star,
3 And by the light of that same star
4 This star drew nigh to the north - west;

was to cer - tain poor shep - herds in fields as they lay;
shin - ing in the east, be - yond them far;
three wise men came from coun - try far;
o'er Beth - le - hem it took its rest,

in fields where they lay a - keep - ing their sheep
and to the earth it gave great light,
to seek for a king was their in - tent,
and there it did both stop and stay,

on a cold win - ter's night that was so deep.
and so it con - tin - ued both day and night.
and to fol - low the star wher - ev - er it went.
right o - ver the place where Je - sus lay.

Words: English traditional carol, ca. 17th century, alt.
Music: English traditional melody, harm. John Stainer 1871, desc. and harm. Healey Willan 1926
Refrain harmony and descant copyright © 1926 Oxford University Press, Inc.

THE FIRST NOWELL
Irregular with refrain

Now - ell, Now - ell, Now - ell, Now - ell,

born is the King of Is - ra - el.

5 Then entered in those wise men
    three,
  full reverently upon their knee,
  and offered there in his presence
  their gold and myrrh and
    frankincense.

6 Then let us all with one accord
  sing praises to our heavenly Lord,
  that hath made heaven and earth of
    nought,
  and with his blood our life hath
    bought.

Refrain with descant (alt. accomp.)

Now - ell, Now - ell, Now - ell, Now - ell,

born is the King of Is - ra - el.

92   In the Darkness Shines the Splendour

1 In the dark - ness shines the splen - dour of the
2 Light of na - tions, veiled in his - tory, born of
3 Bro - ken bread, sus - tain - ing us in sor - row, wine poured
4 All God's peo - ple, sing in ju - bi - la - tion of the

Word who took our flesh, wel - com - ing, in love's sur -
wo - man's flesh and blood, call - ing to the depths of
out to toast our joy; ex - o - dus and new to -
birth that sets us free, tell - ing of the rev - e -

ren - der, death's dark shad - ow at his crèche. Bear - ing
mys - tery rest - less hearts that seek the good. Heal - ing
mor - row, life's full prom - ise to en - joy! Glad - dening
la - tion: Je - sus, God's e - piph - a - ny. Cel - e -

ev - ery hu - man sto - ry, Word made flesh re - veals his glo - ry.
ev - ery hu - man sto - ry, Word made flesh re - veals his glo - ry.
ev - ery hu - man sto - ry, Word made flesh re - veals his glo - ry.
brate the hu - man sto - ry! Word made flesh re - veals our glo - ry.

Words: Bernadette Gasslein 1992, alt.
Music: Henry John Gauntlett 1849, harm. Arthur Henry Mann 1919

IRBY
878788

Words copyright © 1992 Bernadette Gasslein. Harmony by A. H. Mann reprinted by permission of Novello and Company Limited.

When Heaven's Bright with Mystery

Unison

1 When hea - ven's bright with mys - ter - y and sci - ence search - es
2 When He - rod bar - ters power and lives and Rach - el's weep - ing
3 When fra - gile faith, like des - ert wind, blows dry and emp - ty,
4 When hea - ven's bright with mys - ter - y and stars still lead an

Harmony

na - ture's art, when all cre - a - tion yearns for peace and
fills the night, when suf - fering's mask marks ev - ery face, and
hope e - rased, when with - ered grass and fad - ing flower pro -
un - known way, when love still lights a gen - tle path where

Unison

hope sinks deep in hu - man hearts, ap - pear to us, O Ho - ly
Love's a ref - u - gee in flight, re - veal to us your word of
claim a - gain our day's brief space, breathe on the clay of our de -
courts of pow-er can hold no sway, there with the Ma - gi, let us

Harmony

Light, lift from our eyes the shades of night.
grace and make us wit - ness to your peace.
spair and work a new cre - a - tion there.
kneel, our gifts to share, God's world to heal.

Words: Rob Johns 1985
Music: English traditional melody, arr. Ralph Vaughan Williams 1919
Words copyright © 1987 Carol Johns. Used by permission of Carol Johns. Music copyright © 1931 Oxford University Press.

SUSSEX CAROL
9 9 9 9 10 9

94

Lovely Star in the Sky
(Tong bang ŭi byŏl)

Unison

1 Ha - nu - re pin - na - nun chal - lan - han byo - ra
2 A - gi - wang nu - shin - got i - su - re jot - ko
3 U - ri - nun o - tto - k'e jong - song - ul poel - kka

1 Love - ly star in the sky, ban - ish - ing the night,
2 In - fant Love ly - ing there, dew up - on his bed,
3 What can we do to show our de - vo - tion true?

u - ri - ui o - dun - gil pal - ki - o - ra
jim - sung - gwa han - ga - ji nu - u - shot - da
hyang - gi - ron je - mu - rul pa - ch'i - ol - kka

shine down and hal - low us; light our dark path.
with all the an - i - mals sleep - ing in hay;
Shall we pre - sent to him sweet - smell - ing gifts?

ji - pyong - son jo - no - mo dong - bang - ui byo - ra
chon - sa - dul kong - son - hi ju - gyong - bae - ha - ni
jo san - ui yu - hyang - gwa pa - da - ui ch'in - ju

Star shin - ing in the east, be our true guide;
an - gels sing rev - er - ent - ly, wor - ship their God,
Far moun - tain's frank - in - cense, san - dal - wood myrrh?

Words: Korean text based on "Brightest and Best Are the Suns of the Morning," Reginald Heber 1811;   *TONG BANG UI BYOL*
    English trans. Marion Kim and James Minchin   *Irregular*
Music: Un-yung La

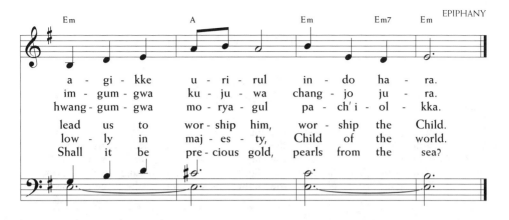

a - gi - kke u - ri - rul in - do ha - ra.
im - gum - gwa ku - ju - wa chang - jo ju - ra.
hwang - gum - gwa mo - rya - gul pa - ch'i - ol - kka.

lead us to wor - ship him, wor - ship the Child.
low - ly in maj - es - ty, Child of the world.
Shall it be pre - cious gold, pearls from the sea?

4 Kap-pi-ssan ye-mu-rul tu-rin-da-hae-do
ju-ni-mul ki-ppu-ge mo-t'a-na-ni
ju-ni-mi pa-du-shil ch'am-da-un ye-mul
jong-song-doen ye-bae-wa ki-do-ro-da.

4 None of these things of price gives
God's Child much joy;
how then, will we express thanks for
his birth?
One present, one alone, he would
desire:
love from our deepest heart, our
own best love.

Born in the Night, Mary's Child 95

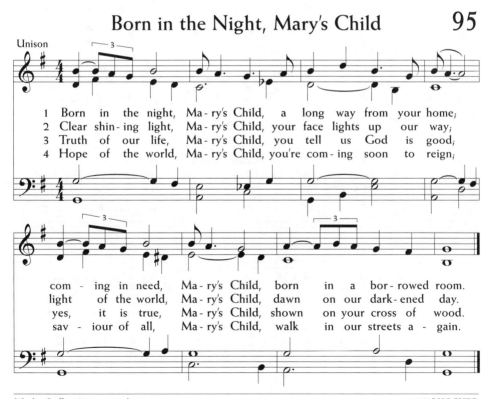

Unison

1 Born in the night, Ma - ry's Child, a long way from your home;
2 Clear shin - ing light, Ma - ry's Child, your face lights up our way;
3 Truth of our life, Ma - ry's Child, you tell us God is good;
4 Hope of the world, Ma - ry's Child, you're com - ing soon to reign;

com - ing in need, Ma - ry's Child, born in a bor - rowed room.
light of the world, Ma - ry's Child, dawn on our dark - ened day.
yes, it is true, Ma - ry's Child, shown on your cross of wood.
sav - iour of all, Ma - ry's Child, walk in our streets a - gain.

Words: Geoffrey Ainger 1964, alt.
Music: Geoffrey Ainger 1964; harm. Richard D. Wetzel 1972
Words and music copyright 1964 Stainer & Bell Ltd. Used by permission of Hope Publishing Company.

MARY'S CHILD
7 6 7 6

96   Will You Come and See the Light

1 Will you come and see the light from the sta - ble door?
It is shin - ing new - ly bright, though it shone be - fore.
It will be your guid - ing star, it will show you who you are;
will you hide, or de - cide to meet the light?

2 Will you step in - to the light that can free the slave?
It will stand for what is right, it will heal and save.
By the pyr - a - mids of greed there's a long - ing to be freed;
will you hide, or de - cide to meet the light?

♦ 3 Will you tell a - bout the light in the pri - son cell?
Though it's shack - led out of sight, it is shin - ing well.
When the truth is cut and bruised, and the in - no - cent a - bused,
will you hide, or de - cide to meet the light?

4 Will you join the hope, a - light in the young girl's eyes,
of the might - y put to flight by a ba - by's cries?
When the low - est and the least are the fore - most at the feast,
will you hide, or de - cide to meet the light?

5 Will you trav - el by the light of the babe new born?
In the can - dle lit at night there's a gleam of dawn,
and the dark - ness all a - bout is too dim to put it out:
will you hide, or de - cide to meet the light?

Words: Brian Wren 1989

Music: Traditional Scottish melody; arr. Valerie Ruddle 1993

Words and arrangement copyright © 1993 Hope Publishing Company.

KELVINGROVE
12 12 14 10
Alt setting: 567

When a Star Is Shining

Unison

1 When a Star is shin - ing o - ver east - ern hills,
2 Where the world is wait - ing for an un - known day,
3 Lead us on, O Day - star, in the qui - et night;

when the air is si - lent, and the clam - our stills,
where a voice for - got - ten cries, "Pre - pare the way!"
guide us through the shad - ow with your gen - tle light;

when the night is wait - ing, and the old hopes rise,
where an earth - ly pow - er makes the heart turn cold,
show us in a man - ger our re - demp - tion's sign;

then the time has rip - ened and the heart grows wise.
there the gifts are of - fered: in - cense, myrrh and gold.
bring us to a morn - ing where the prom - ise shines.

Words: Sylvia G. Dunstan ca. 1992
Music: Ralph Vaughan Williams 1925
Words copyright © 1995 G.I.A. Publications. Music from Enlarged Songs of Praise 1931. By permission of Oxford University Press.

KING'S WESTON
11 11 11 11

98   How Brightly Beams the Morning Star

1 How bright - ly beams the Morn - ing Star!
2 All praise to him who came to save,

What sud - den ra - diance from a - far!
who con - quered death and scorned the grave;

It cheers us with its shin - ing. Bright - ness of
each day new praise re - sound - eth to him, the

God, that breaks our night and fills the dark - ened souls with light,
life who once was slain, the friend whom none shall trust in vain,

who long for truth were pin - ing! New - ly,
whose grace for aye a - bound - eth; sing then,

Words: German, Johann Adolf Schlegel 1766; trans. Catherine Winkworth 1863
Music: adapt. from Philipp Nicolai 1597

WIE SCHÖN LEUCHTET
887D888

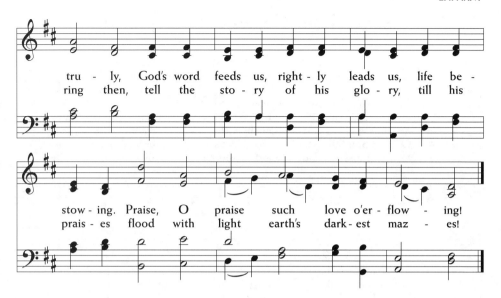

tru - ly, God's word feeds us, right - ly leads us, life be -
ring then, tell the sto - ry of his glo - ry, till his

stow - ing. Praise, O praise such love o'er - flow - ing!
prais - es flood with light earth's dark - est maz - es!

Christ, When for Us You Were Baptized 99

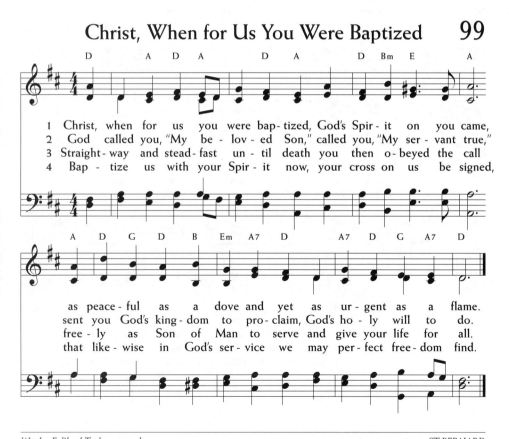

1 Christ, when for us you were bap - tized, God's Spir - it on you came,
2 God called you, "My be - lov - ed Son," called you, "My ser - vant true,"
3 Straight - way and stead - fast un - til death you then o - beyed the call
4 Bap - tize us with your Spir - it now, your cross on us be signed,

as peace - ful as a dove and yet as ur - gent as a flame.
sent you God's king - dom to pro - claim, God's ho - ly will to do.
free - ly as Son of Man to serve and give your life for all.
that like - wise in God's ser - vice we may per - fect free - dom find.

Words: F. Bland Tucker 1977, alt.

Music: melody from Tochter Sion, Cologne 1741

Words from The Hymnal 1982, copyright © Church Pension Fund. Used by permission.

ST BERNARD
8 6 8 6

100 When Jesus Comes to Be Baptized

1 When Jesus comes to be baptized,
2 The Spirit of the Lord comes down,
3 He will not quench the dying flame,
4 O Spirit help us be like Christ:
5 We praise you, God, source of all life,

he leaves the hidden years behind,
anoints the Christ to suffering,
and what is bruised he will not break,
to live in love and charity,
we praise you, Christ, eternal Word,

the years of safety and of peace,
to preach the word, to free the bound,
but heal the wound injustice dealt,
to walk in truth and justice now,
we praise you, Spirit, gracious gift;

to bear the sins of humankind.
and to the mourner, comfort bring.
and out of death his triumph make.
and grow in Christian dignity.
your triune presence fills our world.

Words: vv. 1–3 Stanbrook Abbey 1974, 1995; vv. 4, 5 Concacan Inc., 1989   *WINCHESTER NEW*
Music: Musikalisches Handbuch 1690   8 8 8 8
Words, vv. 1–3, copyright © 1974 Stanbrook Abbey; vv. 4, 5, copyright © 1989 Concacan Inc.

Songs of Thankfulness and Praise

101

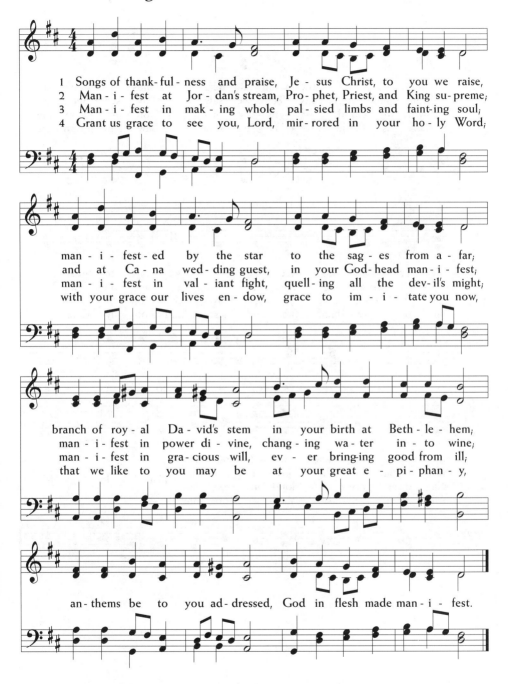

1 Songs of thank-ful-ness and praise, Je-sus Christ, to you we raise,
2 Man-i-fest at Jor-dan's stream, Pro-phet, Priest, and King su-preme;
3 Man-i-fest in mak-ing whole pal-sied limbs and faint-ing soul;
4 Grant us grace to see you, Lord, mir-rored in your ho-ly Word;

man-i-fest-ed by the star to the sag-es from a-far;
and at Ca-na wed-ding guest, in your God-head man-i-fest;
man-i-fest in val-iant fight, quell-ing all the dev-il's might;
with your grace our lives en-dow, grace to im-i-tate you now,

branch of roy-al Da-vid's stem in your birth at Beth-le-hem;
man-i-fest in power di-vine, chang-ing wa-ter in-to wine;
man-i-fest in gra-cious will, ev-er bring-ing good from ill;
that we like to you may be at your great e-pi-phan-y,

an-thems be to you ad-dressed, God in flesh made man-i-fest.

Words: Christopher Wordsworth 1862, alt.
Music: Jakob Hintze 1678; harm. adapt. from Johann Sebastian Bach ca. 1765

SALZBURG (HINTZE)
7 7 7 7 D

102   Jesus on the Mountain Peak

1 Je - sus on the moun - tain peak stands a - lone in
2 Trem - bling at his feet we saw Mo - ses and E -
3 Swift the cloud of glo - ry came, God pro - claim - ing,
4 This is God's be - lov - ed son! Law and proph - ets

glo - ry blaz - ing; let us, if we dare to speak,
li - jah speak - ing. All the proph - ets and the law
in its thun - der, Je - sus as the Son by name!
sing be - fore him, first and last and on - ly One.

join the saints and an - gels prais - ing.
shout through them their joy - ful greet - ing: Hal - le - lu - jah!
Na - tions, cry a - loud in won - der:
All cre - a - tion shall a - dore him!

Words: Brian Wren 1962, 1988
Music: Cyril Vincent Taylor 1962

MOWSLEY
7 8 7 8 4

How Good, Lord, to Be Here

Descant

5 How good, Lord, to be here! Yet we may not remain; but, since you bid us leave the mount, come with us to the plain.

1 How good, Lord, to be here! Your glory fills the night; your face and garments, like the sun, shine with unborrowed light.

2 How good, Lord, to be here, your beauty to behold, where Moses and Elijah stand, your messengers of old.

3 Fulfiller of the past and hope of things to be, we hail your body glorified, and our redemption see!

4 Before we taste of death, we see your kingdom come: we long to hold the vision bright and make this hill our home!

5 How good, Lord, to be here! Yet we may not remain; but, since you bid us leave the mount, come with us to the plain.

Words: Joseph Armitage Robinson 1888, alt.
Music: Charles Lockhart 1792; desc. Sydney H. Nicholson 1947

CARLISLE
6 6 8 6

104 We Have Come at Christ's Own Bidding

1 We have come at Christ's own bid-ding to this
2 Light breaks in up-on our dark-ness; splen-dour
3 Strength-ened by this glimpse of glo-ry, fear-ful

high and ho - ly place, where we wait with
bathes the flesh-joined Word; Mos - es and E-
lest our faith de - cline, we like Pe - ter

hope and long - ing for some to - ken of God's
li - jah mar - vel as the heaven - ly voice is
find it tempt-ing to re - main and build a

grace. Here we pray for new as - sur-ance that our
heard. Eyes and hearts be - hold with won - der how the
shrine. But true wor - ship gives us cour-age to pro -

Words: *Carl P. Daw, Jr. 1988*
Music: *Cyril Vincent Taylor 1941*
Words copyright © 1988, music copyright © 1942, (renewal) 1970 Hope Publishing Company.

ABBOT'S LEIGH
8 7 8 7 D

faith is not in vain, search - ing like those first dis -
Law and Proph - ets meet: Christ, with gar - ments drenched in
claim what we pro - fess, that our dai - ly lives may

ci - ples for a sign both clear and plain.
bright - ness, stands trans - fig - ured and com - plete.
prove us peo - ple of the God we bless.

And the following…

105 Dust and Ashes Touch Our Face

Optional   Unison

1 Dust and ash - es touch our face,
2 Dust and ash - es soil our hands—
3 Dust and ash - es choke our tongue

mark our fail - ure and our fall - ing. Ho - ly Spir - it, come,
greed of mark - et, pride of na - tion. Ho - ly Spir - it, come,
in the waste - land of de - pres - sion. Ho - ly Spir - it, come,

walk with us to - mor - row, take us as dis - ci - ples,
walk with us to - mor - row, as we pray and strug - gle
walk with us to - mor - row, through all gloom and griev - ing

washed and wak - ened by your call - ing.
through the mesh - es of op - pres - sion.
to the paths of res - ur - rec - tion.

Refrain

Take us by the hand and lead us, lead us through the
de - sert sands, bring us liv - ing wa - ter,
Ho - ly Spir - it, come.

Words: Brian Wren 1986
Music: Ron Klusmeier 1995
NEWELL
Irregular

Words copyright © 1989 Hope Publishing Company. Music copyright © 1995 Ron Klusmeier.

An Ash Wednesday Prayer   106

God our Creator,
you have formed us out of the dust of the earth.
May these ashes be to us
    a sign of our mortality and penitence,
so that we may remember
    that only by your gracious gift
    are we given everlasting life;
    through Jesus Christ our Saviour. Amen.

107 Sunday's Palms Are Wednesday's Ashes

1 *Sun-day's palms are Wednes-day's ash-es as an-oth-er Lent be-gins;

thus we kneel be-fore our Ma-ker in con-tri-tion for our sins.

We have marred bap-tis-mal pledg-es, in re-bel-lion gone a-stray;

now, re-turn-ing, seek for-give-ness; grant us par-don, God, this day!

2 We have failed to love our neighbours,
    their offences to forgive,
  have not listened to their troubles, nor
    have cared just how they live;
  we are jealous, proud, impatient, loving
    over-much our things;
  may the yielding of our failings be our
    Lenten offering.

3 We are hasty to judge others, blind to
    proof of human need;
  and our lack of understanding
    demonstrates our inner greed;
  we have wasted earth's resources; want
    and suffering we've ignored;
  come and cleanse us, then restore us;
    make new hearts within us, Lord!

* The first line of the hymn recalls the custom of burning remaining palm leaves of the previous year to form the ashes for this observance.

Words: *Rae E. Whitney 1982*
Music: *Wilbur Held 1993*
Words and music copyright © 1994 Selah Publishing Co., Inc.

SUNDAY'S PALMS
8 7 8 7 D
Alt. tune: Ebenezer

Throughout These Lenten Days and Nights 108

1 Through-out these Lent - en days and nights we
2 The pil - grim Christ, the Lamb of God, who
3 We bear the si - lence, cross and pain of
4 And though the road is hard and steep, the
5 So let us choose the path of One who
6 Re - joice, O sons and daugh - ters! Sing and

turn to walk the in - ward way, where, meet - ing Christ, our
found in weak - ness great - er power, em - brac - es us, though
Spir - it ev - er calls us on through Cal - vary's dy - ing,
wore, for us, the crown of thorn, and slept in death that
shout ho - san - nas! Raise the strain! For Christ, whose death Good

guide and light, we live in hope till Eas - ter Day.
lost and flawed, and leads us to his Ris - ing Hour.
help sus - tain our cour - age till the Feast of Life.
dark and deep, un - til we see the com - ing Dawn.
we might wake to life on Res - ur - rec - tion Morn!
Fri - day brings on Eas - ter Day will rise a - gain!

Words: James Gertmenian
Music: Musikalisches Handbuch, Hamburg 1690; arr. W. H. Havergal 1864
Words copyright © 1993 Hope Publishing Company.

WINCHESTER NEW
8 8 8 8

109

Now Quit Your Care

1 Now quit your care and anx-ious fear and wor - ry;
2 To bow the head in sack-cloth and in ash - es,
♦ 3 For is not this the fast that I have cho - sen
4 For righ-teous - ness and peace will show their fa - ces
5 Then shall your light break forth as does the morn - ing;

for schemes are vain and fret - ting brings no gain.
or rend the soul, such grief is not Lent's goal;
♦ (the pro - phet spoke) to shat - ter ev - ery yoke,
to those who feed the hun - gry in their need,
your health shall spring, the friends you make shall bring

Lent calls to prayer, to trust and ded - i - ca - tion;
but to be led to where God's glo - ry flash - es,
♦ of wick - ed - ness the griev - ous bonds to loos - en,
and wrongs re - dress, who build the old waste pla - ces,
God's glo - ry bright, your way through life a - dorn - ing;

God brings new beau - ty nigh;
God's beau - ty to come near.
♦ op - pres - sion put to flight,
and in the dark - ness shine.
and love shall be the prize.

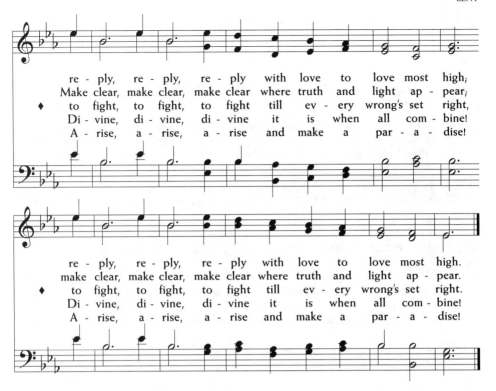

re - ply, re - ply, re - ply with love to love most high;
Make clear, make clear, make clear where truth and light ap - pear;
to fight, to fight, to fight till ev - ery wrong's set right,
Di - vine, di - vine, di - vine it is when all com - bine!
A - rise, a - rise, a - rise and make a par - a - dise!

re - ply, re - ply, re - ply with love to love most high.
make clear, make clear, make clear where truth and light ap - pear.
to fight, to fight, to fight till ev - ery wrong's set right.
Di - vine, di - vine, di - vine it is when all com - bine!
A - rise, a - rise, a - rise and make a par - a - dise!

Words: Percy Dearmer 1928, alt.
Music: French carol, harm. Martin Fallas Shaw 1928
Words and harmony copyright © 1964 Oxford University Press, Oxford.

QUITTEZ, PASTEURS
Irregular

A Lenten Prayer   110

God of love,
as in Jesus Christ you gave yourself to us,
so may we give ourselves to you,
    living according to your holy will.
Keep our feet firmly in the way
    where Christ leads us;
help our lips speak the truth
    that Christ teaches us;
fill our bodies with the life
    that is Christ within us.
In his holy name we pray. Amen.

111 As the Sun with Longer Journey

Unison

1 As the sun with long - er jour - ney melts the win - ter's
2 Through the days of wait - ing, watch - ing in the des - ert
3 Praise be giv - en to the Mak - er of the sea - sons'

snow and ice, with its slow - ly grow - ing ra - diance
of our sin, search - ing on the far ho - ri - zon
year - ly round: to the Speak - er through the Spo - ken

warms the seed be - neath the earth, may the sun of Christ's up -
for a sign of cloud or wind, we a - wait the heal - ing
in their liv - ing Breath of love as the ev - er turn - ing

ris - ing gent - ly bring our hearts to life.
wa - ters of our Sav - iour's vic - to - ry.
seas - ons roll to their e - ter - nal rest.

Words: John Patrick Earls 1981
Music: French traditional carol ca. 17th century
Words copyright © 1981, 1990 Order of St. Benedict, Inc.

PICARDY
878787

O God, How We Have Wandered

1 O God, how we have wan-dered and hid-den from your face;
2 And now at length dis-cern-ing the e-vil that we do,
3 O God of all the liv-ing, both ban-ished and re-stored,

in fool-ish-ness have squan-dered your leg-a-cy of grace.
by faith we are re-turn-ing with hope and trust in you.
com-pas-sion-ate, for-giv-ing, our peace and hope as-sured.

But how, in ex-ile dwell-ing, we turn with fear and shame,
In haste you come to meet us, and home re-joic-ing bring,
Grant now that our trans-gress-ing, our faith-less-ness may cease.

as dis-tant but com-pell-ing, you call us each by name.
in glad-ness there to greet us with calf and robe and ring.
Stretch out your hand in bless-ing, in par-don, and in peace.

Words: Kevin Nichols 1980, alt.
Music: Henry T. Smart 1836
Words copyright © 1981 International Committee on English in the Liturgy, Inc.

LANCASHIRE
7 6 7 6 D
Alt. tune: Passion Chorale

113

To the Desert Jesus Came

1 To the des-ert Je-sus came, to wres-tle and to seek God's
2 Like the He-brews long a-go who ven-tured through the des-ert
3 In the des-ert we may find the mys-ter-y of who we
4 From the ash-es to the hill, we'll trav-el on our Lent-en

way. Sun and moon rose high a-bove to watch him as he'd
sand, did he find a rock of faith, where streams of liv-ing
are, fol-low-ing a faith-ful God, so ver-y close and
road. Hand in hand we'll cross this sand, and share each oth-er's

fast and pray. To-geth-er through the val - ley, the
wat-ers ran? To-geth-er through the val - ley, so
yet so far. To-geth-er through the val - ley, we'll
heav-y load. To-geth-er through the val - ley, we'll

tempt-er led him a-round. To-geth-er through the
shall we make our way. To-geth-er through the
gath-er our dreams in prayer, to-geth-er through the
watch the chang-ing sky. To-geth-er through the

Words: *Linnea Good 1992, alt.*
Music: *Linnea Good 1992*
Words and music copyright © 1992 Borealis Music.

TOGETHER THROUGH THE VALLEY
Irregular

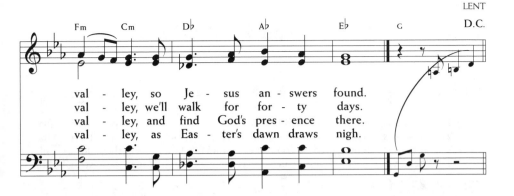

val - ley, so Je - sus an - swers found.
val - ley, we'll walk for for - ty days.
val - ley, and find God's pres - ence there.
val - ley, as Eas - ter's dawn draws nigh.

Forty Days and Forty Nights   114

1 For - ty days and for - ty nights you were fast - ing in the wild;
2 Sun - beams scorch - ing all the day, chil - ly dew-drops night- ly shed;
♦ 3 Shall not we your tri - al share, and from earth - ly joys ab- stain,
4 If temp - ta - tions, vex - ing sore, flesh or spir - it should as - sail,
5 Keep, oh keep us, Sav - iour dear, ev - er con - stant by your side;

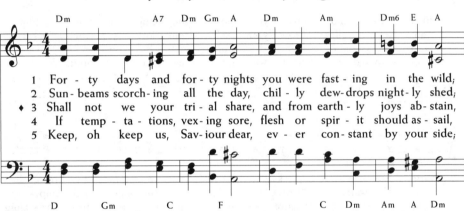

for - ty days and for - ty nights tempt - ed, and yet un - de - filed.
prowl- ing beasts a - bout your way; stones your pil - low, earth your bed.
♦ fast - ing with un - ceas - ing prayer, strong with you to suf - fer pain?
you their van-quish - er be - fore, grant we may not faint nor fail.
that with you we may ap - pear at the e - ter - nal Eas - ter - tide.

Words: *George Hunt Smyttan 1856; rev. Francis Pott 1861, alt.*
Music: *attrib. Martin Herbst 1676*

HEINLEIN
7 7 7 7

115 Jesus, Tempted in the Desert

1 Je - sus, tempt - ed in the des - ert, lone - ly, hun - gry, filled with dread: "Use your power," the tempt - er tells him; "turn these bar - ren rocks to bread!" "Not a - lone by bread," he an - swers, "can the hu - man heart be filled. On - ly by the

2 Je - sus, tempt - ed at the tem - ple, high a - bove its an - cient wall: "Throw your - self from loft - y tur - ret; an - gels wait to break your fall!" Je - sus shuns such emp - ty mar - vels, feats that fick - le crowds re - quest: "God, whose grace pro -

3 Je - sus, tempt - ed on the moun - tain by the lure of vast do - main: "Fall be - fore me! Be my ser - vant! Glo - ry, fame, you're sure to gain!" Je - sus sees the daz - zling vi - sion, turns his eyes an - oth - er way: "God a - lone de -

4 When we face temp - ta - tion's pow - er, lone - ly, strug - gling, filled with dread, Christ, who knew the tempt - er's hour, come and be our liv - ing bread. By your grace, pro - tect, pre - serve us lest we fall, your trust be - tray. Yours, a - bove all

Words: Herman Stuempfle 1990
Music: The Sacred Harp, Philadelphia 1844; harm. Ronald A. Nelson 1978, alt.

BEACH SPRING
8 7 8 7 D

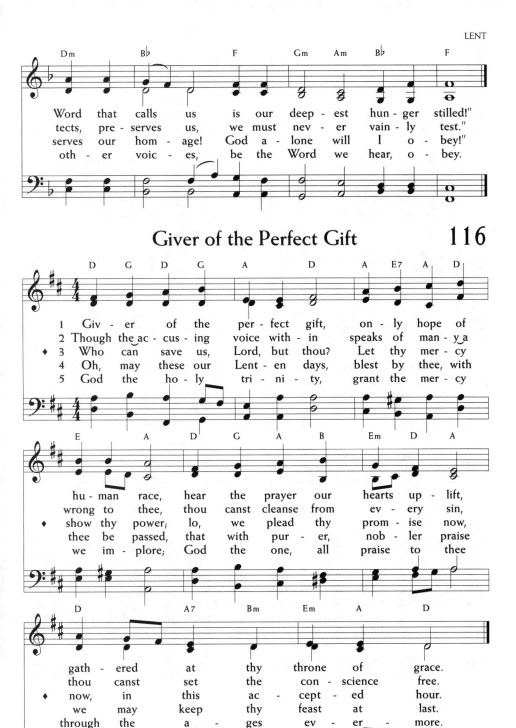

Word that calls us is our deep - est hun - ger stilled!"
tects, pre - serves us, we must nev - er vain - ly test."
serves our hom - age! God a - lone will I o - bey!"
oth - er voic - es, be the Word we hear, o - bey.

Giver of the Perfect Gift   116

1 Giv - er of the per - fect gift, on - ly hope of
2 Though the ac - cus - ing voice with - in speaks of man - y a
♦ 3 Who can save us, Lord, but thou? Let thy mer - cy
4 Oh, may these our Lent - en days, blest by thee, with
5 God the ho - ly tri - ni - ty, grant the mer - cy

hu - man race, hear the prayer our hearts up - lift,
wrong to thee, thou canst cleanse from ev - ery sin,
♦ show thy power; lo, we plead thy prom - ise now,
thee be passed, that with pur - er, nob - ler praise
we im - plore; God the one, all praise to thee

gath - ered at thy throne of grace.
thou canst set the con - science free.
♦ now, in this ac - cept - ed hour.
we may keep thy feast at last.
through the a - ges ev - er - more.

Words: from the Latin ca. 11th century; trans. John Ellerton 1891
Music: adapt. from Orlando Gibbons 1623

SONG 13
7 7 7 7

117

Jesus Christ Is Waiting

1 Je - sus Christ is wait - ing, wait - ing in the streets;
2 Je - sus Christ is rag - ing, rag - ing in the streets,
♦ 3 Je - sus Christ is heal - ing, heal - ing in the streets;
4 Je - sus Christ is danc - ing, danc - ing in the streets,
5 Je - sus Christ is call - ing, call - ing in the streets,

no one is his neigh - bour, all a - lone he eats.
where in - just - ice spi - rals and real hope re - treats.
♦ cur - ing those who suf - fer, touch - ing those he greets.
where each sign of hat - red he, with love, de - feats.
"Who will join my jour - ney? I will guide their feet."

*Lis - ten, Lord Je - sus, I am lone - ly too.
Lis - ten, Lord Je - sus, I am an - gry too.
♦ Lis - ten, Lord Je - sus, I have pit - y too.
Lis - ten, Lord Je - sus, I should tri - umph too.
Lis - ten, Lord Je - sus, let my fears be few.

* or: "Listen, my Jesus"

Words: John L. Bell 1984

Music: French carol, 15th century; harm. The Iona Community 1984

NOËL NOUVELET
11 11 10 11

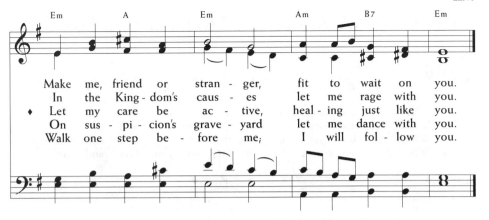

Make me, friend or stran - ger, fit to wait on you.
In the King-dom's caus - es let me rage with you.
♦ Let my care be ac - tive, heal - ing just like you.
On sus - pi - cion's grave - yard let me dance with you.
Walk one step be - fore me; I will fol - low you.

Wonder and Stare 118

Won - der and stare, fear and be - ware; hea - ven and

hell are close at hand. God's liv - ing word, Je - sus the

Lord, fol - lows where faith and love de - mand.

Words: The Iona Community 1988
Music: The Iona Community 1988
Words and harmony copyright © 1988 WGRG, The Iona Community (Glasgow, Scotland), G.I.A. Publications, Inc., Chicago, Illinois, exclusive agent.

119 When We Are Tempted to Deny Your Son

1 When we are tempt-ed to de-ny your Son, be-cause we
2 When we are tempt-ed to be-tray your Son, be-cause he
3 When we for-get the cross that held your Son, and would a-
4 When doubt ob-scures the vic-tory of your Son, and faith is

fear the an-ger of the world, and we are few who
leads us in a hard-er way, and makes de-mands we
void the bur-den of this life, the cry for jus-tice
weak and all re-solve has fled, help us to know him

bear the in-sults hurled,
do not want to pay, your will, O God, be done.
and an end to strife...
ris-en from the dead:

Words: David W. Romig 1965
Music: J. Harold Moyer 1965, The Mennonite Hymnal 1969
Words copyright © 1972 The Westminster John Knox Press. Music copyright © 1969 Faith and Life Press/Mennonite Publishing House.

FAITH
10 10 10 6

O Jesus, I Have Promised

1 O Je-sus, I have prom-ised to serve you to the end;
2 O let me feel you near me: the world is ev-er near;
3 O let me hear you speak-ing in ac-cents clear and still,
4 O Je-sus, you have prom-ised to all who fol-low you,

re-main for ev-er near me, my Sav-iour and my friend:
I see the sights that daz-zle, the tempt-ing sounds I hear;
a-bove the storms of pas-sion, the mur-murs of self-will;
that where you are in glo-ry your ser-vant shall be too.

I shall not fear the jour-ney if you are by my side,
my foes are ev-er near me, a-round me and with-in;
O speak to re-as-sure me, to hast-en or con-trol;
And Je-sus, I have prom-ised to serve you to the end;

Unison

Harmony

nor wan-der from the path-way if you will be my guide.
but, Je-sus, then draw near-er and shield my soul from sin.
now speak, and make me lis-ten, O guard-ian of my soul.
O give me grace to fol-low, my Sav-iour and my friend.

Words: John Ernest Bode ca.1866, alt.
Music: James William Elliott 1874

DAY OF REST
7 6 7 6 D

121 Tree of Life and Awesome Mystery

1 Tree of Life and awe-some mys - tery, in your death we are re - born, though you die in all of his - tory, still you rise with ev - ery morn, still you rise with ev - ery morn.

2 Seed that dies to rise in glo - ry, may we see our-selves in you, if we learn to live your sto - ry we may die to rise a - new, we may die to rise a - new.

3 We re-mem - ber truth once spo - ken, love passed on through act and word, ev - ery per - son lost and bro - ken wears the bod - y of our Lord, wears the bod - y of our Lord.

Words: Marty Haugen 1984
Music: Marty Haugen 1984
Words and music copyright © 1984 G.I.A. Publications, Inc.

THOMAS
87877

4 Gentle Jesus, mighty Spirit,
come inflame our hearts anew,
we may all your joy inherit
if we bear the cross with you,
if we bear the cross with you.

5 Christ, you lead and we shall follow,
stumbling though our steps may be,
one with you in joy and sorrow,
we the river, you the sea,
we the river, you the sea.

(Other verses to use during Lent)

General

Light of life beyond conceiving,
mighty Spirit of our Lord;
give new strength to our believing,
give us faith to live your word,
give us faith to live your word.

1st Sunday

From the dawning of creation,
you have loved us as your own;
stay with us through all temptation,
make us turn to you alone,
make us turn to you alone.

2nd Sunday

In our call to be a blessing,
may we be a blessing true;
may we live and die confessing
Christ as Lord of all we do,
Christ as Lord of all we do.

3rd Sunday

Living Water of salvation,
be the fountain of each soul;
springing up in new creation,
flow in us and make us whole,
flow in us and make us whole.

4th Sunday

Give us eyes to see you clearly,
make us children of your light;
give us hearts to live more nearly
as your gospel shining bright,
as your gospel shining bright.

5th Sunday

God of all our fear and sorrow,
God who lives beyond our death;
hold us close through each tomorrow,
love as near as every breath,
love as near as every breath.

Words: Marty Haugen 1984
Copyright © 1984 G.I.A. Publications, Inc.

And the following...

122 All Glory, Laud and Honour

Refrain

Descant

All glo-ry, laud and hon - our to you, Re-deem-er, King,

All glo-ry, laud and hon - our to you, Re-deem-er, King,

Fine

to whom the lips of chil - dren made sweet ho - san - nas ring.

to whom the lips of chil - dren made sweet ho - san - nas ring.

1 You are the King of Is - rael, and Da - vid's roy - al son,
2 The mul - ti - tude of pil - grims with palms be - fore you went;
3 To you, be - fore your pas - sion, they sang their hymns of praise;
4 Their prais - es you ac - cept - ed; ac - cept the prayers we bring,

D.C.

now in the Lord's name com - ing, our King and bless - ed one.
our praise and prayer and an - thems be - fore you we pre - sent.
to you, now high ex - alt - ed, our mel - o - dy we raise.
great auth - or of all good - ness, O good and grac - ious king.

Words: *Theodulph of Orleans ca. 820, alt.; trans. John Mason Neale 1851*   ST THEODULPH (VALET WILL ICH DIR GEBEN)
Music: *Melchior Teschner 1615; desc. Hal Hopson 1978*   7 6 7 6 D
Descant copyright © 1978 Choristers Guild.   Alt. setting: 31

Hosanna, Loud Hosanna

1 Ho - san - na, loud ho - san - na the hap - py chil - dren sang;
2 From Ol - i - vet they fol - lowed 'mid an ex - ul - tant crowd,
3 "Ho - san - na in the high - est!" That an - cient song we sing,

through pil - lared court and tem - ple the joy - ful an - them rang;
the vic - tory palm - branch wav - ing, and sing - ing clear and loud;
for Christ is our Re - deem - er; earth, let your an - thems ring.

to Je - sus, who had blessed them close fold - ed to his breast,
the Lord of earth and hea - ven rode on in low - ly state,
O may we ev - er praise him with heart and life and voice,

the chil - dren sang their prais - es, the sim - plest and the best.
con - tent that lit - tle chil - dren should on his bid - ding wait.
and in his hum - ble pres - ence e - ter - nal - ly re - joice!

Words: Jennette Threlfall 1873
Music: trad. 18th-century German tune, adapt. Xavier Ludwig Hartig 1868

ELLACOMBE
7 6 7 6 D

124 He Came Riding on a Donkey

1 He came rid - ing on a don - key, he came rid - ing
2 Then the chil - dren ga - thered, sing - ing shouts of laugh - ter,

in - to town; slow and ea - sy kind of low - ly
burst - ing cheer; in the streets their song was ring - ing,

he came rid - ing with the dawn.
"Ho - san - nas" filled the morn - ing air.

His dis - ci - ples walked be - side him, stay - ing close, a
Tim - id a - dults strained to see him, caught the Spir - it,

3 In our fasting, and our feasting,
called to follow in his way;
called to walk his road to Easter,
called to live his cross today.
    Hosanna to the Son of David,
    hosanna in the heavens above;

blessed is he who comes to save us,
blessed is he who brings his love.
Let us join to sing his praises;
open hearts and souls to God;
he is with us, Son of David;
God's Messiah, Christ the Lord.

Words: Gordon Light 1986
Music: Gordon Light 1986; arr. Nan Thompson 1995
Words and music copyright © 1986 Common Cup Company. Arrangement copyright © 1995 Nan Thompson.

DONKEY SONG
Irregular

125   Prayer for Palm Sunday

We praise you, O God,
for your redemption of the world through Jesus Christ.
Today he entered the holy city of Jerusalem in triumph
     and was proclaimed Messiah and king
        by those who spread garments and branches along his way.
Let these branches be signs of his victory,
     and grant that we who carry them
        may follow him in the way of the cross,
that, dying and rising with him, we may enter into your kingdom;
     through Jesus Christ, who lives and reigns
        with you and the Holy Spirit, now and forever. Amen.

126   Ride On, Ride On, the Time Is Right

Unison

1 Ride on, ride on, the time is right: the road - side crowds scream
2 Ride on, ride on, your crit - ics wait, in - trigue and ru - mour
♦ 3 Ride on, ride on, while well a - ware that those who shout and
4 Ride on, ride on, though blind with tears, though voice - less now and
5 Ride on, ride on, God's love de - mands. Jus - tice and peace lie

with   de - light;   palm branch - es mark the
cir -   cu - late;   new   lies a - bound   in
♦ wave   and   stare   are   mor - tals who, with
deaf   to   jeers.   Your   path is   clear, though

pil - grim   way   where   beg - gars squat and
word   and   jest,   and   truth be - comes a
♦ com - mon   breath, can   crave for life   and
few   can   tell   their   gar - ments pave the
voic - es   rhyme: you   are   the man   and

chil - dren   play.   2 Ride
sus - pect   guest.   3 Ride
♦ lust for   death.   4 Ride
road   to   hell.   5 Ride
this   the   time.   —

Fine

Words: John L. Bell 1988   RIDE ON
Music: John L. Bell 1988   8 8 8 8

127 Ride On! Ride On in Majesty!

Unison

1 Ride on! Ride on in maj - es - ty!
2 Ride on! Ride on in maj - es - ty!
3 Ride on! Ride on in maj - es - ty!
4 Ride on! Ride on in maj - es - ty!

Hark! All the tribes ho - san - na cry:
In low - ly pomp ride on to die;
The wing - ed squad - rons of the sky
In low - ly pomp ride on to die;

O Sav - iour meek, pur - sue thy road
O Christ, thy tri - umphs now be - gin
look down with sad and won - dering eyes
bow thy meek head to mor - tal pain,

with palms and scat - tered gar - ments strowed.
o'er cap - tive death and con - quered sin.
to see the ap - proach - ing sac - ri - fice.
then take, O God, thy power, and reign.

Words: Henry Hart Milman 1821
Music: Graham George 1939
Music copyright © 1941, renewed 1969 H. W. Gray Co. Inc., a division of Belwin-Mills Publishing Corp.

THE KING'S MAJESTY
8 8 8 8
Alt. tune: Winchester New

Sanna, Sannanina

* An African version of Hosanna.

Words: traditional South African

Music: traditional South African, arr. Nicholas Williams ca. 1993

Arrangement copyright © 1993 Stainer & Bell Ltd. and Methodist Church (U.K.) Division of Education and Youth. Used by permission of Hope Publishing Company.

SANNANINA

Irregular

129

Said Judas to Mary

1 Said Judas to Mary, "Now
2 "Oh Mary, oh Mary, oh
3 "To-morrow, to-morrow I'll
4 Said Jesus to Mary, "Your

what will you do with your oint-ment so rich and so rare?" "I'll
think of the poor — this oint-ment, it could have been sold,
think of the poor, to-mor-row," she said, "not to-day;
love is so deep, to-day you may do as you will. To-

pour it all o-ver the feet of the Lord and I'll
think of the blan-kets and think of the bread you could
dear-er than all of the poor in the world is my
mor-row you say I am go-ing a-way, but my

wipe it a-way with my hair," she said, —
buy with the sil-ver and gold," he said, —
love who is go-ing a-way," she said, "my
bo-dy I leave with you still," he said, "my

Words: Sydney Carter 1964
Music: Sydney Carter 1964 alt.

JUDAS AND MARY
5 8 5 6

Words copyright © 1964 and music copyright © 1964, 1969 Stainer & Bell Ltd. Used by permission of Hope Publishing Company.

"wipe it a - way with my hair."
"buy with the sil - ver and gold."
love who is go - ing a - way."
bo - dy I leave with you still."

5 "The poor of the world are my
    body," he said,
  "to the end of the world they shall
    be;
  the bread and the blankets you give
    to the poor
  you'll know, you have given to me,"
    he said,
  "you'll know you have given to me."

6 "My body will hang on the cross of
    the world
  tomorrow," he said, "not today,
  and Martha and Mary will find me
    again
  and wash all my sorrow away," he
    said,
  "wash all my sorrow away."

An Upper Room Did Our Lord Prepare 130

1 An upper room did our Lord prepare
  for those he loved until the end:
  and his disciples still gather there
  to celebrate their risen Friend.

2 A lasting gift Jesus gave his own:
  to share his bread, his loving cup.
  Whatever burdens may bow us
    down,
  he by his cross shall lift us up.

3 And after supper he washed their feet,
  for service, too, is sacrament.
  In Christ our joy shall be made
    complete:
  sent out to serve, as he was sent.

4 No end there is! We depart in peace.
  He loves beyond the uttermost:
  in every room in our Father's* house
  Christ will be there, as Lord and
    Host.

* or "Maker's"

Words: Fred Pratt Green 1973
Words copyright © 1974 by Hope Publishing Company.

O WALY WALY
9 8 9 8

131 If Our God Had Simply Saved Us

1 If our God had simply saved us, merely brought us
out of Egypt, only opened up our prison:

2 If our God had split the Red Sea: made a way through
walls of water, only opened up the waters: *Dayeinu

3 If our God had kept our feet dry, kept our heads above the
waters, kept us safely without drowning:

Refrain

Da-da-yei-nu, da-da-yei-nu, Da-da-yei-nu, da-yei-nu, Da-yei-nu, da-yei-nu! Da-da-yei-nu, da-da-yei-nu, Da-da-yei-nu, da-yei-nu, da-yei-nu!

* pronounced *Die-yea-noo*, a Hebrew word meaning 'enough'.

Words: trad. Hebrew; trans. Don Pickard 1993
Music: trad. Israeli; arr. Nicholas Williams 1993

DAYEINU
5 8 5 6

Translation and arrangement copyright © 1993 Stainer & Bell Ltd. and Methodist Church Division Of Education and Youth. Used by permission of Hope Publishing Company.

4 If our God had brought us over,
  led us safely on to dry land;
  (even though it was a desert)
  Dayeinu!

Refrain
Dadayeinu, dadayeinu.
Dadayeinu, dayeinu,
Dayeinu, dayeinu!
Dadayeinu, dadayeinu.
Dadayeinu, dayeinu,
dayeinu!

5 If our God had only led us,
  only gone ahead to guide us,
  given cloud and fire to lead us:
  Dayeinu!

Refrain

6 If our God had only brought us
  to the awful fire at Sinai:
  filled us all with dread at Sinai:
  Dayeinu!

Refrain

7 If our God had spoken to us
  only one word through the thunder
  merely whispered on the mountain:
  Dayeinu!

Refrain

8 If our God had given to us
  less than Ten Words as prescription
  simply told us: "Take the tablets!"
  Dayeinu!

Refrain

9 If our God had laid the law down:
  tabled in the words by Moses,
  only given us the Torah:
  Dayeinu!

Refrain

10 If our God had given us manna,
   daily sent down bread from heaven,
   simple manna in the desert:
   Dayeinu!

Refrain

11 If our God had only given
   seventh day for joy and gladness,
   without all the rest to help us:
   Dayeinu!

Refrain

12 If our God had from a mountain
   let us glimpse the land of promise,
   only gaze across the Jordan:
   Dayeinu!

Refrain

13 If our God had, through the river,
   led us to dry bread and water
   and not laid on milk and honey:
   Dayeinu!

Refrain

14 If our God had fed us only:
   feasted us upon the mountain —
   not inviting all the neighbours:
   Dayeinu!

Refrain

15 But, our God, who holds the
        banquet,
   calls the whole world into freedom:
   opens up the new creation:
   Dayeinu!

Refrain

A shorter version of this hymn could be used by singing the odd numbered verses only.

132 Bitter Was the Night

1 Bitter was the night, thought the cock would crow for ever.
2 Saw you passing by, told them all I did-n't know you.
3 Told them all a lie, and I told it three times o-ver.
4 What did Judas do? Sold him for a bag of sil-ver.
5 What did Judas do? Hanged himself up-on an ald-er.

Bitter was the night before the break of day.

6 Bitter was the night,
   thought there'd never be a morning.
   Bitter was the night
   before the break of day.

7 Bitter was the night,
   thought the cock would crow for ever.
   Bitter was the night
   before the break of day.

Words: Sydney Carter 1964
Music: Sydney Carter 1964
Words copyright © 1964 and music © 1964, 1969 Stainer & Bell. Used by permission of Hope Publishing Company.

BITTER WAS THE NIGHT
5 8 5 6

Go to Dark Gethsemane

1 *Go to dark Gethsemane, you that feel the tempter's power; your Redeemer's conflict see; watch with him one bitter hour; turn not from his grief away: learn from him to watch and pray.

2 See him at the judgement hall, beaten, bound, reviled, arraigned; see him meekly bearing all; love to all his soul sustained. Shun not suffering, shame, or loss: learn from Christ to bear the cross.

3 Calvary's mournful mountain view; there the Lord of glory see, made a sacrifice for you, dying on the accursed tree. "It is finished," hear his cry: trust in Christ and learn to die.

* or "Go, now, to…"

Words: James Montgomery 1820, alt.
Music: Richard Redhead 1853

REDHEAD No. 76
7 7 7 7 7 7

134 Shadows Gather, Deep and Cold

1 Shad-ows gath-er, deep and cold; lamp-light flick-ers, fades and fails.
2 In the watch-es of the night, in the hour when dark-ness reigns,

Lord, you know what day-break holds: thorns and beat-ings, cross and nails.
in the grief that has no light, in the time of fear and pain,

You will be de-nied, be-trayed when the roost-er wakes the sun.
then we hold fast to your way, to the vic-tory you have won.

Yet you kneel a-lone and pray, "Not my will, but thine be done."
Je-sus, teach us how to pray, "Not my will, but thine be done."

Words: Sylvia Dunstan ca. 1992
Music: David Kai 1994
Words copyright © 1995 G.I.A. Publications, Inc. Music copyright © 1994 David Kai.

KASLO
7 7 7 7 D

Beneath the Cross of Jesus

1 Be - neath the cross of Je - sus I fain would take my stand:
2 Up - on the cross of Je - sus my eyes at times can see
3 I take, O cross, your shad - ow for my a - bid - ing - place;

the shad - ow of a might - y rock with - in a wea - ry land,
the ver - y dy - ing form of one who suf - fered there for me;
I ask no oth - er sun - shine than the sun - shine of his face,

a home with - in the wil - der - ness, a rest up - on the way,
and from my smit - ten heart, with tears, two won - ders I con - fess,
con - tent to let the world go by, to know no gain nor loss,

from the burn - ing of the noon - tide heat and the bur - den of the day.
the won - der of his glo - rious love, and my un - wor - thi - ness.
my sin - ful self my on - ly shame, my glo - ry all, the cross.

Words: Elizabeth Cecilia Clephane 1868, alt.
Music: Frederick Charles Maker 1881

ST CHRISTOPHER
7 6 8 6 8 6 8 6

136   O Come and Mourn with Me Awhile

1 O come and mourn with me awhile;
2 Have we no tears to shed for him,
3 Seven times he spake, seven words of love;
4 O love of God! O sin - filled world!

O come now to the Sav - iour's side;
while sol - diers scoff and foes de - ride?
and all three hours his si - lence cried
In this dread act your strength is tried,

O come, to - geth - er let us mourn:
Ah! Look how pa - tient - ly he hangs:
for mer - cy on the souls of all:
and vic - to - ry re - mains with love:

Je - sus, our Love, is cru - ci - fied.

Words: Frederick William Faber 1849, alt.
Music: John Bacchus Dykes 1861

ST CROSS
8 8 8 8
Alt. tune: Apanás

The Love That Clothes Itself in Light   137

1 The Love that clothes it-self in light, stands nak-ed now, des-pised, be-trayed, re-ceiv-ing blows to face and head from hands that Love it-self has made.

2 The Love that lifts the stars and sun, col-laps-es, spent, be-neath the cross; the Love that fills the un-i-verse, goes on to death and to-tal loss.

♦ 3 Love, help-less, comes to Cal-va-ry, re-ject-ed, scorned and cru-ci-fied; Love hangs in shame, and dies a-lone; but Love a-based, is glo-ri-fied.

4 Ex-tin-guished with the sun at noon, Love's light tran-scends all his-to-ry; Love, wrapped in lin-en, Love en-tombed, still wraps all heaven in mys-ter-y.

5 Though Love is lost, Love finds us here; though Love is ab-sent, Love re-mains; where Love is fin-ished, Love be-gins; where Love is dead, Love lives and reigns!

Words: Alan Gaunt 1989
Music: Jim Strathdee 1983
Words copyright © 1991 Stainer & Bell Ltd. Used by permission of Hope Publishing Company.
Music copyright © 1983 Desert Flower Music.

APANÁS
8 8 8 8
Alt. tune: St Cross

138

Ah, Holy Jesus

1 Ah, ho - ly Je - sus, how have you of - fend - ed, that
2 Who was the guil - ty? Who brought this up - on you? A -
♦ 3 Lo, the good shep - herd for the sheep is of - fered; the
4 For me, kind Je - sus, was your in - car - na - tion, your
5 There - fore, kind Je - sus, since I can - not pay you, I

we to judge you have in hate pre - tend - ed? By foes de -
las, my trea - son, Je - sus, has un - done you; yes, I, Lord
♦ slave is guil - ty, yet the Son has suf - fered; for our a -
mor - tal sor - row, and your life's o - bla - tion; your death of
do a - dore you, and will ev - er pray you, think on your

rid - ed, by your own re - ject - ed, O most af - flict - ed.
Je - sus, I it was de - nied you, I cru - ci - fied you.
♦ tone-ment, while we noth - ing heed - ed, God in - ter - ced - ed.
an - guish and your bit - ter pas - sion, for my sal - va - tion.
pit - y and your love un - swerv - ing, not my de - serv - ing.

Words: Johann H. Heermann 1630, alt., trans. Robert Seymour Bridges 1899, et al
Music: Johann Crüger 1640; harm. adapt. from Johann Sebastian Bach

HERZLIEBSTER JESU
11 11 11 5

At the Cross Her Vigil Keeping 139

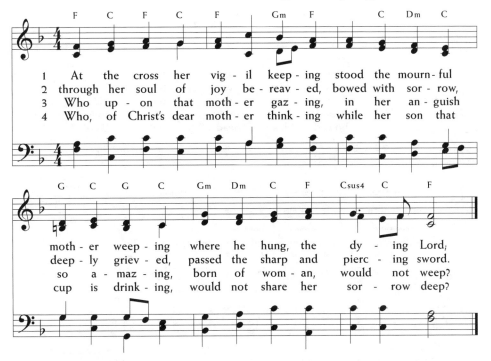

1 At the cross her vig - il keep - ing stood the mourn - ful
2 through her soul of joy be - reav - ed, bowed with sor - row,
3 Who up - on that moth - er gaz - ing, in her an - guish
4 Who, of Christ's dear moth - er think - ing while her son that

moth - er weep - ing where he hung, the dy - ing Lord;
deep - ly griev - ed, passed the sharp and pierc - ing sword.
so a - maz - ing, born of wom - an, would not weep?
cup is drink - ing, would not share her sor - row deep?

5 For his people's sins chastised
she beheld her Son despised,
scourged, and crowned with thorns
entwined,

6 saw him then from judgement taken,
and in death by all forsaken,
till his spirit he resigned.

7 Near your cross, O Christ, abiding,
grief and love my heart dividing,
I with her would take my place:

8 by your saving cross uphold me,
in your dying, Christ, enfold me,
with the deathless arms of grace.

Words: Jacopone da Todi, 13th century; trans. Edward Caswall
Music: Maintzisch Gesangbuch 1661

STABAT MATER
8 8 7

Grief and Love 140

Crucified saviour, naked God,
you hang disgraced and powerless.
Grieving, we dare to hope,
as we wait at the cross
with your mother and your friend.

141 They Crucified My Lord

Words: African-American spiritual
Music: African-American spiritual

A MUMBALIN' WORD
Irregular

Jesus, Keep Me Near the Cross

1 Je - sus, keep me near the cross; there a pre - cious foun - tain,
2 Near the cross, a trem - bling soul, love and mer - cy found me;
3 Near the cross! O Lamb of God, bring its scenes be - fore me;
4 Near the cross I'll watch and wait, hop - ing, trust - ing ev - er,

free to all, a heal - ing stream, flows from Cal - vary's moun - tain.
there the bright and morn - ing star sheds its beams a - round me.
help me walk from day to day with its shad - ow o'er me.
till I reach the gold - en strand just be - yond the riv - er.

Refrain

In the cross, in the cross, be my glo - ry ev - er,

till my rap - tured soul shall find rest be - yond the riv - er.

Words: Fanny J. Crosby 1869
Music: William Howard Doane 1869

NEAR THE CROSS
7 6 7 6 with refrain

143 My Song Is Love Unknown

1 My song is love unknown, my Saviour's love to me, love
2 He came from his blest throne salvation to bestow, but
3 Sometimes they strew his way, and his sweet praises sing, re-
4 Here might I stay and sing, no story so divine; nev-

to the loveless shown that they might lovely be.
people scorned, and none the longed-for Christ would know.
sounding all the day hosannas to their King.
er was love, dear King, never was grief like thine!

O who am I that for my sake
But O my Friend, my Friend indeed,
Then "Crucify!" is all their breath,
This is my friend, in whose sweet praise

my Lord should take frail flesh, and die?
who at my need his life did spend!
and for his death they thirst and cry.
I all my days could gladly spend.

Words: Samuel Crossman 1664
Music: John Ireland 1918
Music copyright © The John Ireland Trust.

LOVE UNKNOWN
6 6 12 4 4 8

Were You There

1 Were you there when they cru-ci-fied my Lord?
2 Were you there when they nailed him to the tree?
♦ 3 Were you there when the sun re-fused to shine? (Were you there?)
4 Were you there when they pierced him in the side?
5 Were you there when they laid him in the tomb?

Were you there when they cru-ci-fied my Lord?
Were you there when they nailed him to the tree?
♦ Were you there when the sun re-fused to shine? Oh!
Were you there when they pierced him in the side?
Were you there when they laid him in the tomb?

Some-times it caus-es me to trem-ble, trem-ble, trem-ble.

Were you there when they cru-ci-fied my Lord?
Were you there when they nailed him to the tree?
♦ Were you there when the sun re-fused to shine? (Were you there?)
Were you there when they pierced him in the side?
Were you there when they laid him in the tomb?

Words: African-American spiritual
Music: African-American spiritual; arr. Melva Wilson Costen 1987
Arrangement copyright © 1990 Melva Wilson Costen.

WERE YOU THERE
Irregular

145   O Sacred Head

1 O sa-cred head, sore wound-ed, with grief and shame weighed down;
2 Thy grief and bit-ter pas-sion were all for sin-ners' gain;
3 What lan-guage shall I bor-row to thank thee, dear-est friend,
4 Be near when I am dy-ing, O show thy cross to me;

now scorn-ful-ly sur-round-ed with thorns, thine on-ly crown:
mine, mine was the trans-gres-sion, but thine the cru-el pain.
for this thy dy-ing sor-row, thy pit-y with-out end?
and for my suc-cour fly-ing, come, Lord, to set me free.

how art thou pale with an-guish, with sore a-buse and scorn;
Lo, here I fall, my Sav-iour, turn not from me thy face;
O make me thine for-ev-er; and, should I faint-ing be,
These eyes, new faith re-ceiv-ing, from thee shall not re-move,

how does that vis-age lan-guish, which once was bright as morn!
but look on me with fa-vour, and grant to me thy grace.
Lord, let me nev-er, nev-er out-live my love to thee.
for all who die be-liev-ing, die safe-ly through thy love.

Words: Paul Gerhardt 1656, trans. James Waddell Alexander 1830, et al,
French trans. Henri Capieu 1974
Music: Hans Leo Hassler 1601, harm. Johann Sebastian Bach 1729

PASSION CHORALE
7 6 7 6 D

Ô douloureux visage

1 Ô douloureux visage
de mon humble Seigneur;
ô tête sous l'outrage,
ô front sous la douleur.
Plein des beautés divines
dans les cieux infinis,
c'est couronné d'épines
que je te vois ici.

2 C'est toi que ma main blesse,
c'est moi qui suis guéri;
c'est moi qui me redresse,
c'est toi qui est meurtri;
quel étrange partage
de ma vie et ta mort,
où ta mort est le gage
que la vie est mon sort.

3 Parmi tant de blessures
de la lance et des clous,
parmi tes meurtrissures,
la trace de mes coups;
et parmi tant d'offenses,
ton seul, ton seul pardon,
et pour seule espérance
la force de ton nom.

4 De l'humaine misère
tu t'es fait serviteur;
de chacun de tes frères,
tu portes la douleur.
Seigneur, de nos souffrances
et de nos lendemains,
garde notre espérance
en tes vivantes mains.

When Jesus Wept 146

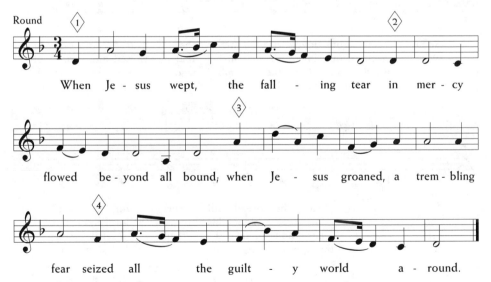

When Je-sus wept, the fall-ing tear in mer-cy
flowed be-yond all bound; when Je-sus groaned, a trem-bling
fear seized all the guilt-y world a-round.

Words: William Billings 1770
Music: William Billings, The New England Psalm Singer 1770

WHEN JESUS WEPT
Irregular

147 What Wondrous Love Is This

1 What won-drous love is this, O my soul, O my soul,
2 What won-drous love is this, O my soul, O my soul,
3 To God and to the Lamb I will sing, I will sing,
4 And when from death I'm free, I'll sing on, I'll sing on,

what won-drous love is this, O my soul!
what won-drous love is this, O my soul!
to God and to the Lamb I will sing;
and when from death I'm free, I'll sing on;

What won-drous love is this that caused the Lord of
What won-drous love is this, that caused the Lord of
to God and to the Lamb, who is the great I
and when from death I'm free, I'll sing and joy-ful

bliss to bear the dread-ful curse for my soul,
life to lay a-side his crown for my soul,
Am, while mil-lions join the theme I will sing,
be, and through e-ter-ni-ty I'll sing on,

Words: *American folk hymn ca. 1811; French trans. Claude Rozier 1972*
Music: *American folk hymn 1840; harm. Paul J. Christiansen 1955*

WONDROUS LOVE
12 9 12 9

Harmony copyright © 1978 Lutheran Book of Worship. Reprinted by permission of Augsburg Fortress.
Translation copyright © Centre Nationale de Pastorale Liturgique.

for my soul, to bear the dread-ful curse for my soul.
for my soul, to lay a-side his crown for my soul.
I will sing; while mil-lions join the theme I will sing.
I'll sing on, and through e-ter-ni-ty I'll sing on.

Ô merveilleux amour pour ma vie

1 Ô merveilleux amour pour ma vie,
   pour ma vie,
   ô merveilleux amour pour ma vie!
   Ô merveilleux amour que l'amour du
   Seigneur,
   il est venu du ciel pour ma vie, pour
   ma vie,
   il est venu du ciel pour ma vie!

2 Pour Dieu et pour l'Agneau, ma
   chanson, ma chanson,
   pour Dieu et pour l'Agneau, ma
   chanson!

Pour Dieu et pour l'Agneau je
   chanterai d'amour,
par cent millions de voix, ma chanson,
   ma chanson,
par cent millions de voix, ma chanson.

3 À ma résurrection, chanterai,
   chanterai,
   à ma résurrection, chanterai.
   À ma résurrection, je danserai de joie
   et pour l'éternité, chanterai, chanterai,
   et pour l'éternité, chanterai.

Jesus, Remember Me   148

Je-sus, re-mem-ber me when you come in-to your king-dom.

Je-sus, re-mem-ber me when you come in-to your king-dom.

Words: Luke 23:42
Music: Jacques Berthier 1978

REMEMBER ME
Irregular

149 When I Survey the Wondrous Cross
(Quand je me tourne vers la croix)

Descant

4 Were the whole realm of na - ture mine,

1 When I sur - vey the won - drous cross
2 For - bid it, Lord, that I should boast
1 Quand je me tour - ne vers la croix
2 Qui donc pour - rait cal - mer ce coeur

that were a pres - ent far too small:

on which the Prince of glo - ry died,
save in the death of Christ, my God:
où Christ ex - pi - re sur le bois
hor - mis la croix de mon Sau - veur?

love so a - maz - ing, so di - vine,

my rich - est gain I count but loss,
all the vain things that charm me most,
mon coeur bles - sé, rem - pli de deuil,
Tous mes plai - sirs, mes vains dé - sirs,

de - mands my soul, my life, my all.

G   D   Em   D   A   D

and pour con - tempt on all my pride.
I sac - ri - fice them to his blood.
prend en dé - goût mon fol or - gueil.
je veux, ô Christ, te les of - frir.

3 See from his head, his hands, his feet,
  sorrow and love flow mingled down!
  Did e'er such love and sorrow meet,
  or thorns compose so rich a crown?

3 Oh vois, des mains, de son côté,
  du front d'épines couronné,
  douleur, angoisse, amour mêlés,
  descendre pour nous racheter.

4 Were the whole realm of nature mine,
  that were a present far too small:
  love so amazing, so divine,
  demands my soul, my life, my all.

4 Si je t'offrais le monde entier
  ce don serait pris en pitié.
  Amour si grand, si pur, si doux
  veut âme, corps, mon coeur, mon tout!

Words: Isaac Watts 1707; French trans. Pauline Martin 1951, rév.
Music: second supplement to Psalmody in Miniature ca. 1780;
    adapt. Edward Miller 1790; harm. Samuel Webbe; desc. John Wilson
Descant copyright © Hope Publishing Company.

COMMUNION (ROCKINGHAM)
8 8 8 8

A Prayer for Holy Week   150

God of passionate and vulnerable love,
whose body, broken on the cross
    rebukes us still:
Save us, hold us, and forgive us,
that you as victor and victim
    might lead us from death to life;
through Jesus, the Crucified. Amen.

Paul Fayter 1990

151

Lift High the Cross

Refrain

Descant

Lift high the cross, the love of Christ pro - claim

Unison

Lift high the cross, the love of Christ pro - claim

Fine

till all the world a - dore his sac - red name.

till all the world a - dore his sac - red name.

Harmony

1 Come, Chris - tians, fol - low where our Sav - iour trod,
2 Led on their way by this tri - um - phant sign,
3 Each new - born ser - vant of the Cru - ci - fied
4 Sav - iour, once lift - ed on the glo - rious tree,
5 So shall our song of tri - umph ev - er be

Words: George William Kitchin 1887; rev. Michael Robert Newbolt 1916, alt.
Music: Sidney Hugo Nicholson 1916; desc. Richard Proulx
Words and music copyright © 1974 *Hope Publishing Company. Descant copyright* © 1985 *G.I.A. Publications, Inc.*

CRUCIFER
10 10 10 10

D.C.

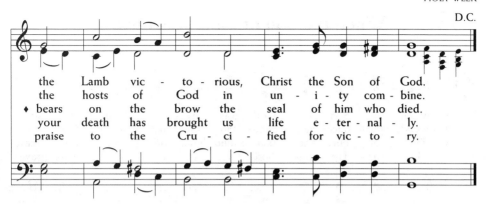

the   Lamb   vic - to - rious,   Christ   the   Son   of   God.
the   hosts   of   God   in   un - i - ty   com - bine.
♦ bears   on   the   brow   the   seal   of   him   who   died.
your   death   has   brought   us   life   e - ter - nal - ly.
praise   to   the   Cru - ci - fied   for   vic - to - ry.

There Is a Green Hill Far Away 152

1 There   is   a   green   hill   far   a - way,   out -
2 We   may   not   know,   we   can - not   tell,   what
3 There   was   no   oth - er   good   e - nough   to
4 O   dear - ly,   dear - ly   has   he   loved,   and

side   a   cit - y   wall,   where   the   dear   Lord   was
pains   he   had   to   bear;   but   we   be - lieve   it
pay   the   price   of   sin;   his   death   has   o - pened
we   must   love   him   too,   and   trust   in   his   re -

cru - ci - fied,   who   died   to   save   us   all.
was   for   us   he   hung   and   suf - fered   there.
wide   the   gate   of   heaven,   to   let   us   in.
deem - ing   blood,   and   try   his   works   to   do.

Words: Cecil Frances Alexander 1848, alt.
Music: William Horsley 1844

HORSLEY
8 6 8 6

153   When the Son of God Was Dying

1 When the Son of God was dy - ing, long a - go,
2 Crowds which once had cried, "Ho - san - na!", lost their voice:
3 Hor - ror, hurt and pain found home in Ma - ry's breast
4 Je - sus, lay your bod - y in this sad earth's grave;

some played dice and some knelt cry - ing, lost and low.
hell had grinned to hear Bar - a - bas was their choice;
watch - ing tor - ture's toll and hear - ing sol - diers jest:
on - ly one who suf - fers can pre - sume to save.

Cyn - ics sneered and wagged their tongues, mock - ers mim - icked
Ju - das hung him - self for blame; Pe - ter hung his
where was God to hear her cry? Why should her own
End hy - poc - ri - sy and lies, through our ap - a -

fu - neral songs: this, while God's own Son was dy - ing, long a - go.
head in shame, while the crowds which cried, "Ho - san - na!", lost their voice.
Je - sus die? Grief and ag - o - ny found home in Ma - ry's breast.
thy a - rise, bring us the sal - va - tion which our spir - its crave.

Words: *The Iona Community 1988*
Music: *John L. Bell 1988*

GOLGOTHA
11 11 7 7 11

Words and harmony copyright © 1988 WGRG, The Iona Community (Glasgow, Scotland), G.I.A. Publications, Inc., Chicago, Illinois, exclusive agent.

Why Has God Forsaken Me

1 "Why has God for - sak - en me?" cried out Je - sus
2 At the tomb of Laz - a - rus Je - sus wept with
3 Je - sus, as his life ex - pired, placed him - self with -
4 Mys - tery shrouds our life and death but we need not

from the cross, as he shared the lone - li - ness
o - pen grief: grant us, God, the tears which heal
in God's care: at our dy - ing, Christ, may we
be a - fraid, for the mys - tery's heart is Love,

of our deep - est grief and loss.
all our pain and un - be - lief.
trust the love which con - quers fear.
God's great love which Christ dis - played.

Words: W.L. Wallace 1979, rev. 1990
Music: Taihei Sato 1981
Words copyright © 1990 W.L. Wallace. Music copyright © 1983 Taihei Sato.

SHIMPI
7 7 7 7

And the following…

155   Jesus Christ Is Risen Today

Descant

4 Sing we to our God a-bove, hal - le - lu - jah!

1 Je - sus Christ is risen to - day,
2 Hymns of praise then let us sing
3 But the pains which he en-dured,
4 Sing we to our God a-bove,

hal - le - lu - jah!

Praise e - ter - nal as God's love; hal - le - lu - jah!

our tri - um - phant ho - ly day,
un - to Christ, our heaven - ly King,
our sal - va - tion have pro - cured;
praise e - ter - nal as God's love;

hal - le - lu - jah!

Praise our God, ye heaven - ly host, hal - le - lu - jah!

who did once, up - on the cross,
who en - dured the cross and grave,
now a - bove the sky he's King,
praise our God, ye heaven - ly host,

hal - le - lu - jah!

Words: *Lyra Davidica* 1708, *et al.*
Music: *Lyra Davidica* 1708, *desc. Derek Holman* 1971
Descant copyright © 1971 Derek Holman.

EASTER HYMN
7 7 7 7 *with hallelujahs*

Praise the Son and Ho-ly Ghost. Hal - le - lu - jah!

suf - fer to re - deem our loss.
sin - ners to re - deem and save.
where the an - gels ev - er sing. Hal - le - lu - jah!
praise the Son and Ho - ly Ghost.

Un nouveau matin se lève   156

1 Un nouveau matin se lève, Alléluia!
premier jour de la semaine; Alléluia!
regardez ma joie briller: Alléluia!
c'est Jésus qui se relève. Alléluia!

2 Tombeau vide et plus de gardes,
seul les anges me regardent;
entonnez de nouveaux chants:
c'est Jésus qui nous fait vivre.

3 Le jardin est clair et calme,
le Seigneur est là qui parle;
j'ai cru voir le jardinier:
c'est Jésus qui est lumière.

4 Il m'envoie vers vous mes frères;
lui déjà il nous précède;
écoutez mes compagnons:
c'est Jésus qui nous appelle.

This French text (not a translation of the English) may be sung to the preceding tune.

Words: Nicole Berthet
Words copyright © Centre Nationale de Pastorale Liturgique.

EASTER HYMN
7 7 7 7 with hallelujahs

Christ the Lord Is Risen Today   157

1 Christ the Lord is risen today,*
all creation join to say;
raise your joys and triumphs high;
sing, O heavens, and earth reply:

2 Love's redeeming work is done,
fought the fight, the battle won.
Lo, our sun's eclipse is o'er!
Lo, he dwells in death no more!

3 Lives again our glorious King:
where, O death, is now your sting?
Once he died, our souls to save:
where your victory, O grave?

4 Hail, the Lord of earth and heaven,
praise to you by both be given!
Every knee to you shall bow,
risen Christ, triumphant now.

* *Each line is followed by "hallelujah"*

Words: Charles Wesley 1739, alt.

EASTER HYMN
7 7 7 7 with hallelujahs

158

Christ Is Alive

Descant

5 Christ is a-live, and comes to bring good news to

1 Christ is a-live! Let Chris-tians sing. The cross stands
2 Christ is a-live! No long-er bound to dis-tant
3 In ev-ery in-sult, rift, and war, where col-our,

this and ev-ery age, till earth and sky and

emp-ty to the sky. Let streets and homes with
years in Pal-es-tine, but sav-ing, heal-ing,
scorn, or wealth div-ide, Christ suf-fers still, yet

o-cean ring with joy, with jus-tice, love and praise.

prais-es ring. Love, drowned in death, shall nev-er die.
here and now, and touch-ing ev-ery place and time.
loves the more, and lives, where e-ven hope has died.

Words: Brian Wren 1968, alt.
Music: Thomas Williams 1789; desc. John Wilson
Words and descant copyright © 1975 Hope Publishing Company.

TRURO
8 8 8 8
Alt. setting: 207

4 Women and men, in age and youth,
can feel the Spirit, hear the call,
and find the way, the life, the truth,
revealed in Jesus, freed for all.

5 Christ is alive, and comes to bring
good news to this and every age,
till earth and sky and ocean ring
with joy, with justice, love and praise.

The Strife Is O'er   159

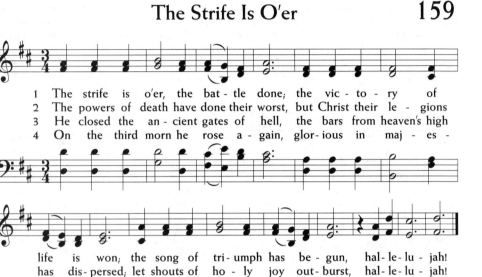

1 The strife is o'er, the bat-tle done; the vic-to-ry of
2 The powers of death have done their worst, but Christ their le - gions
3 He closed the an - cient gates of hell, the bars from heaven's high
4 On the third morn he rose a - gain, glor-ious in maj - es -

life is won; the song of tri-umph has be-gun, hal-le-lu-jah!
has dis-persed; let shouts of ho-ly joy out-burst, hal-le-lu-jah!
por-tals fell; let songs of praise his tri-umph tell, hal-le-lu-jah!
ty to reign; O let us swell the joy-ful strain, hal-le-lu-jah!

Words: from Latin 17th century; trans. Francis Pott 1861
Music: William Henry Monk 1861; from melody by Giovanni Palestrina 1591

VICTORY
8 8 8 with hallelujah
Alt. tune: Vulpius (Gelobt Sei Gott)

Louange à toi, Seigneur Jésus   160

1 Louange à toi, Seigneur Jésus!
L'humble chemin de ta venue,
guide nos pas jusqu'au salut.
Alléluia!

2 La mort n'a pu garder sa proie;
l'enfer vaincu s'ouvre à ta voix;
l'amour triomphe par la croix.
Alléluia!

3 Voici la tombe descellée,
et ses témoins, pour l'annoncer,
sont envoyés au monde entier.
Alléluia!

4 Tu es vivant, gloire à ton nom!
Hâte le temps où nous pourrons
vivre sans fin dans ta maison.
Alléluia!

This French text (not a translation of the English) may be sung to the preceding tune.

Words: Pierre-Yves Emery 1973
Words copyright © Taizé Community.

VICTORY
8 8 8 with hallelujah

161 Welcome, Happy Morning

1 Wel - come, hap - py morn - ing! age to age shall say;
2 Earth with joy - ful wel - come clothes it - self for spring;
3 Au - thor and sus - tain - er, source of life and breath;
4 Loose our souls im - pris - oned bound with Sa - tan's chain;

hell to - day is van - quished, heaven is won to - day:
greets with life re - viv - ing our re - turn - ing king:
you for our sal - va - tion trod the path of death:
all that now is fal - len, raise to life a - gain!

come then, True and Faith - ful, now ful - fil your word;
flowers in ev - ery pas - ture, leaves on ev - ery bough,
Je - sus Christ is liv - ing, God for ev - er - more!
Show your face in bright - ness, shine the whole world through;

this is your third morn - ing: rise, O bur - ied Lord!
speak of sor - rows end - ed; Je - sus tri - umphs now!
Now let all cre - a - tion hail him and a - dore.
hope re - turns with day - break, life re - turns with you.

Words: after Venantius Fortunatus ca. 582; J. Ellerton 1868; rev. Hymns for Today's Church 1982

Music: Frances Ridley Havergal 1871

Revised words copyright © 1982 Hope Publishing Company.

HERMAS

6 5 6 5 D with refrain

Refrain

Wel - come, hap - py morn - ing! age to age shall say;
hell to - day is van - quished, heaven is won to - day!

The Glory of Our King 162

1 The glo - ry of our King was seen when he came rid - ing by,
2 The glo - ry of our King was seen when, with his arms stretched wide
3 The glo - ry of our King was seen on the first Eas - ter day,

and all the chil-dren waved and sang, "Ho - san - na, King most high!"
to show his love to ev - ery - one, Je - sus was cru - ci - fied.
when Christ rose up, set free from death, to love, to guide, to stay.

Words: Margaret Beatrice Cropper 1961, alt.
Music: Wyeth's Repository of Sacred Music Part Second 1813; harm. Charles Winfred Douglas 1940

MORNING SONG
8 6 8 6

163   Hail, Glad Festival Day

Refrain (Unison)

Hail, glad fes-ti-val day! Blest day to be hal-lowed for ev - er,

day where-in Christ a - rose, break-ing the king-dom of death.

Fine

1 Lo, the fair beau-ty of earth, from the death of the win-ter a-ris - ing,
3 Mourn-ing they laid you to rest, the au-thor of life and cre-a - tion;

D.C.

ev - ery good gift of the year now with its Sav-iour re - turns.
tread-ing the path-way of death, life now be-stow-ing on all.

Words: *Venantius Fortunatus ca. 582; trans. Maurice Frederick Bell ca. 1906, et al*
Music: *Ralph Vaughan Williams 1906*
Music and translation by permission of Oxford University Press.

SALVE, FESTA DIES
Irregular

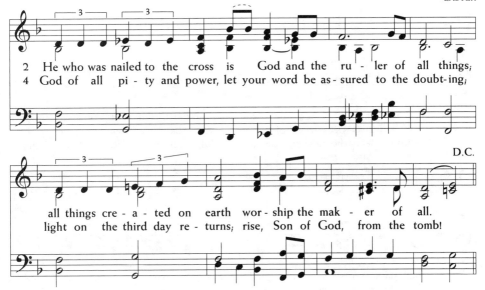

2 He who was nailed to the cross is God and the ru - ler of all things;
4 God of all pi - ty and power, let your word be as - sured to the doubt-ing;

D.C.

all things cre - a - ted on earth wor - ship the mak - er of all.
light on the third day re - turns; rise, Son of God, from the tomb!

Ascension

*1 Christ in his triumph ascends,
who has vanquished the devil's
dominion;
bright is the woodland with leaves,
brilliant the meadows with flowers.

Refrain

2 Daily the loveliness grows,
adorned with the glory of blossom,
heaven its gates now unbars,
flinging its increase of light.

Refrain

3 Jesus, the health of the world,
enlighten our minds, great Redeemer,
Son of the Father supreme,
only-begotten of God!

Refrain

4 Praise to the giver of good!
O Lover and Author of concord,
pour out your balm on our days;
order our days in your peace.

Refrain

Pentecost

*1 Lo, in the likeness of fire,
on them who await his appearing
he whom the Lord foretold
suddenly, swiftly, descends.

Refrain

2 Forth to the faithful he comes
with sevenfold mystical offering,
pouring on all human souls
infinite riches of God.

Refrain

3 Hark! for in myriad tongues
Christ's own, his chosen apostles,
preach to the ends of the earth
Christ and his wonderful works.

Refrain

4 Praise to the Spirit of life,
all praise to the fount of our being,
light that now lightens all,
life that in all now abides.

Refrain

* Note: Odd- and even-numbered verses have different tunes.

Words: Ascension verses, vv. 1-3, trans. Percy Dearmer, v. 4 George Gabriel Scott Gillett, alt.;
    Pentecost verses, trans. George Gabriel Scott Gillett, alt.
Words by permission of Oxford University Press.

164   The Day of Resurrection

1 The day of res - ur - rec - tion! Earth, tell it out a - broad;
2 Our hearts be free of e - vil, that we may see a - right
3 Now let the heavens be joy - ful, let earth its song be - gin,

the pass - o - ver of glad - ness, the pass - o - ver of God!
the Christ in rays e - ter - nal of res - ur - rec - tion light,
the round world keep high tri - umph, and all that is there - in;

From death to life e - ter - nal, from earth un - to the sky,
and, listen - ing to the ac - cents, may hear so calm and plain
let all things seen and un - seen their notes of glad - ness blend,

our Christ has brought us o - ver with hymns of vic - to - ry.
Christ's own "All hail!" and, hear - ing, may raise the vic - tor strain.
for Christ in - deed is ris - en, our Joy that has no end.

Words: John of Damascus ca. 750; trans. John Mason Neale 1862

Music: Gesangbuch der Herzogl. Wirtembergischen Katholischen Hofkapelle 1784; alt. 1868

ELLACOMBE

7 6 7 6 D

Come, You Faithful, Raise the Strain

1 Come, you faith - ful, raise the strain of tri - um - phant glad - ness:
2 'Tis the spring of souls to - day, Christ has burst his pris - on,
3 Now the queen of sea - sons, bright with the day of splen - dour,
4 Nei - ther could the gates of death, nor the tomb's dark por - tal,

God has brought forth Is - ra - el in - to joy from sad - ness,
and from three days' sleep in death as a sun has ris - en;
with the roy - al feast of feasts, comes its joy to ren - der;
nor the watch - ers, nor the seal, hold him as a mor - tal:

loosed from Phar - aoh's bit - ter yoke Ja - cob's sons and daugh - ters,
all the win - ter of our sins, long and dark, is fly - ing
comes to glad - den faith - ful hearts, who with true af - fec - tion
for to - day a - mid his own he now stands, be - stow - ing

led them with un - moist - ened foot through the Red Sea wa - ters.
from his light, to whom we give laud and praise un - dy - ing.
wel - come in un - wea - ried strains Je - sus' res - ur - rec - tion!
God's true peace which ev - er - more pass - es hu - man know - ing.

Words: John of Damascus, ca. 750; trans. John Mason Neale 1859, alt.
Music: Johann Horn 1544; adapt. J. Leisentritt 1584

AVE VIRGO VIRGINUM
7 6 7 6 D

166   Joy Comes with the Dawn

Joy comes with the dawn; joy comes with the morn- ing sun; joy springs from the tomb and scat- ters the night with her song, joy comes with the dawn.

1 Weep- ing may come; weep- ing may
2 Sor - row will turn, sor - row will
3 We will re - joice, we will re -

Words: Gordon Light 1985
Music: Gordon Light 1985, arr. Nan Thompson 1995
Words and music copyright © 1985 The Common Cup Company. Arrangement copyright © 1995 Nan Thompson.

DAWN
Irregular

come in the night, when dark shad - ows cloud our sight.
turn in - to song, and God's laugh - ter make us strong.
joice, and give praise, to the One who brings us grace.

Christ Is Risen from the Dead 167

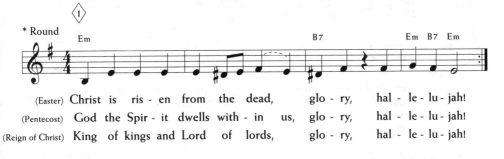

* Round

(Easter) Christ is ris - en from the dead, glo - ry, hal - le - lu - jah!
(Pentecost) God the Spir - it dwells with - in us, glo - ry, hal - le - lu - jah!
(Reign of Christ) King of kings and Lord of lords, glo - ry, hal - le - lu - jah!

Je - sus Christ is ris - en, glo - ry, hal - le - lu - jah!
God the Spir - it with us, glo - ry, hal - le - lu - jah!
Je - sus, Prince of Peace, glo - ry, hal - le - lu - jah!

* May be sung as a two-part round, the voices entering as indicated, gradually increasing tempo. The
  first half is repeated before the second voice enters.

Words: Anonymous
Music: Hasidic folk melody

KING OF KINGS

168

The Risen Christ

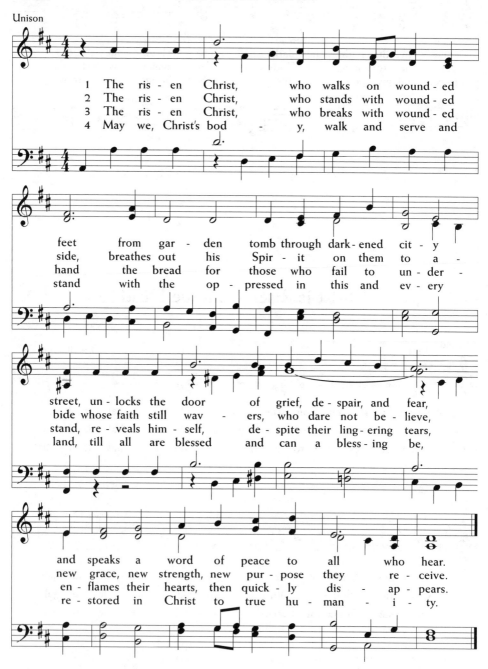

Unison

1 The ris-en Christ, who walks on wound-ed feet from gar-den tomb through dark-ened cit-y street, un-locks the door of grief, de-spair, and fear, and speaks a word of peace to all who hear.

2 The ris-en Christ, who stands with wound-ed side, breathes out his Spir-it on them to a-bide whose faith still wav-ers, who dare not be-lieve, new grace, new strength, new pur-pose they re-ceive.

3 The ris-en Christ, who breaks with wound-ed hand the bread for those who fail to un-der-stand, re-veals him-self, de-spite their ling-ering tears, en-flames their hearts, then quick-ly dis-ap-pears.

4 May we, Christ's bod-y, walk and serve and stand with the op-pressed in this and ev-ery land, till all are blessed and can a bless-ing be, re-stored in Christ to true hu-man-i-ty.

Words: Nigel Weaver 1993
Music: Walter Greatorex 1916
Words copyright © 1993 Nigel Weaver. Music by permission of Oxford University Press.

WOODLANDS
10 10 10 10

Good Christians All, Rejoice and Sing

169

1 Good Christians all, rejoice and sing!
2 The Lord of life is risen today!
3 Praise we in songs of victory
4 Your name we bless, O risen Lord,

Now is the triumph of our King!
Bring flowers of song, bedeck the way;
that love, that life which cannot die,
and sing today with one accord

To all the world glad news we bring:
let every tongue rejoice and say:
and sing with hearts uplifted high:
the life laid down, the life restored:

Hallelujah, hallelujah, hallelujah!

Words: Cyril Argentine Alington 1925, alt.
Music: melody by Melchior Vulpius 1609; arr. Ernest Campbell MacMillan ca. 1930

VULPIUS (GELOBT SEI GOTT)
8 8 8 with hallelujahs

170 O Sons and Daughters, Let Us Sing

*Hal - le - lu - jah! Hal - le - lu - jah! Hal - le - lu - jah!

1 O sons and daugh - ters, let us sing! The King of heaven, the
2 That Eas - ter morn, at break of day, the faith - ful wo - men
♦ 3 An an - gel clad in white they see, who sat and spake un -
4 That night the a - pos - tles met in fear; a - midst them came their
5 So, on this ho - ly day of days, with faith in God our

glo - rious King, o'er death and hell rose tri - umph - ing.
went their way to seek the tomb where Je - sus lay.
♦ to the three, "Your Lord doth go to Gal - i - lee."
Lord most dear, and said, "My peace be on all here."
voic - es raise in laud and ju - bi - lee and praise.

Hal - le - lu - jah! Hal - le - lu - jah!
(Tenor) Hal - le - lu - jah!

* The Hallelujahs serve as an introduction and, therefore, should be sung only at the beginning of the hymn.

Words: Jean Tisserand; trans. John Mason Neale 1851
Music: from Airs sur les hymnes sacrez, Paris 1623; arr. F. R. C. Clarke 1970
Arrangement copyright © 1971 F. R. C. Clarke.

O FILII ET FILIAE
8 8 8 with hallelujahs

(Additional verses for the Second Sunday of Easter)

1 When Thomas first the tidings heard,
how they had seen the risen Lord,
he doubted the disciples' word.
Hallelujah!

2 "My pierced side, O Thomas, see;
my hands, my feet, I show to thee;
not faithless, but believing be."
Hallelujah!

3 No longer Thomas then denied,
he saw the feet, the hands, the side;
"Thou art my Lord and God," he cried.
Hallelujah!

4 How blest are they who have not seen,
and yet whose faith has constant been,
for they eternal life shall win.
Hallelujah!

Chrétiens, chantons le Dieu vainqueur 171

1 Chrétiens, chantons le Dieu
    vainqueur;
fêtons la Pâque du Seigneur;
acclamons-le d'un même coeur.
Alléluia!

2 De son tombeau, Jésus surgit;
il nous délivre de la nuit,
et, dans nos coeurs, le jour à lui.
Alléluia!

3 Nouveau Moïse ouvrant les eaux,
il sort vainqueur de son tombeau:
il est Seigneur des temps nouveaux.
Alléluia!

4 L'agneau pascal est immolé;
il est vivant, ressuscité,
splendeur du monde racheté.
Alléluia!

5 Le coeur de Dieu est révélé;
le coeur de l'homme est délivré;
splendeur du monde racheté.
Alléluia!

6 Ô jour de joie, de vrai bonheur!
Ô Pâque sainte du Seigneur!
Par toi nous sommes tous
    vainqueurs.
Alléluia!

This French text (not a translation of the English) may be sung to the preceding tune.

Words: Jacques Servel   *Words copyright © Éditions du Chalet/Groupe MAME*

Now Christ Is Risen 172

Now Christ is ris - en from the dead! Hal - le - lu -
jah, hal - le - - - lu - jah, hal - le - lu - jah, hal - le - lu - jah!

Words: I Corinthians 15:20
Music: Adam Gumpelzhaimer
Words and music reproduced from 50 Sacred Canons and Rounds (Ed. Kenneth Simpson) by permission of Novello & Company Limited.

173

Thine Is the Glory
(À toi la gloire)

1 À toi la gloire, Ô Res - sus - ci - té!
2 Vois - le pa - raî - tre: c'est lui, c'est Jé - sus,

1 Thine is the glo - ry, ris - en, con - quering Son:
2 Lo, Je - sus meets us, ris - en from the tomb!

À toi la vic - toi - re pour l'é - ter - ni - té!
ton sau - veur, ton maî - tre! Oh! ne dou - te plus.

end - less is the vic - tory thou o'er death hast won.
Lov - ing - ly he greets us, scat - ters fear and gloom.

Bril - lant de lu - miè - re, l'ange est des - cen - du,
Sois dans l'al - lé - gres - se, peu - ple du Sei - gneur,

An - gels in bright rai - ment rolled the stone a - way,
Let the church with glad - ness hymns of tri - umph sing,

il rou - le la pier - re du tom - beau vain - cu.
et re - dis sans ces - se que Christ est vain - queur!

kept the fold - ed grave - clothes where the bod - y lay.
for the Lord now liv - eth: death hath lost its sting.

Words: Edmond Louis Budry 1884; trans. Richard Birch Hoyle 1923
Music: Harmonia Sacra ca. 1753; arr. from George Frideric Handel 1747

JUDAS MACCABAEUS
5 5 6 5 6 5 6 5 with refrain

Refrain

À toi la gloi - re, Ô Res - sus - ci - té!
Thine is the glo - ry, ris - en, con - quering Son:

À toi la vic - toi - re pour l'é - ter - ni - té!
end - less is the vic - tory thou o'er death hast won.

3 Craindrais-je encore?
   Il vit à jamais,
   celui que j'adore,
   le prince de paix;
   il est ma victoire,
   mon puissant soutien,
   ma vie et ma gloire:
   non, je ne crains rien!

   Refrain

3 No more we doubt thee,
   glorious Prince of life;
   life is nought without thee:
   aid us in our strife;
   make us more than conquerors,
   through thy deathless love;
   bring us safe through Jordan
   to thy home above.

   Refrain

Easter Prayer   174

God of resurrection,
you have rolled the stone away
    and the tomb of our world has been opened wide.
With the dawn has come a new creation.
Let our celebration today
    empty our tombs,
    renew our lives,
    and release your power;
through the risen Christ we pray. Amen.

Joan McMurtry 1991

175 This Is the Day That God Has Made

Refrain (Unison)

This is the day that God has made! Re-joice! Re-joice, and be ex-ceed-ing glad! This is the day that God has made! Re-joice! Re-joice! Hal-le-lu - jah! lu - jah!

1 Christ has con-quered death at last, left the tomb that held him fast!
2 Je - sus lives who once was dead, lives for - ev - er, as he said!

Gone the sor-row, gone the night, dawns the morn-ing clear and bright!
Ris - en now our Sav-iour, King; songs of glad-ness let us sing!

Words: Natalie Sleeth 1976, alt.
Music: Natalie Sleeth 1976
Words and music copyright © 1976 Hinshaw Music, Inc. Reprinted by permission.

EASTER JOY
Irregular

Who Is There on This Easter Morning

1 Who is there on this Eas-ter morn - ing runs not with
2 Who has not stood where Ma - ry griev - ing to that first
3 Who is there doubts that night is end - ed? Hear from on

John to find the grave? Nor sees how, death's do - min - ion scorn-ing,
Eas - ter gar - den came; for ver - y joy but half - be - liev-ing
high the trum - pets call! Christ is in tri - umph now as - cend-ed,

Je - sus is ris - en, strong to save? Who is there on this
whose is the voice that calls her name? Who has not stood where
ris - en and reign - ing, Lord of all! Who is there doubts that

Eas - ter morn - ing runs not with John to find the grave?
Ma - ry griev - ing to that first Eas - ter gar - den came?
night is end - ed? Hear from on high the trum - pets call!

Words: Timothy Dudley-Smith 1980
Music: French traditional carol; arr. Martin Fallas Shaw 1928
Words copyright © 1984 Hope Publishing Company. Arrangement by permission of Oxford University Press.

FRAGRANCE
9 8 9 8 9 8

177 This Joyful Eastertide

1 This joy - ful Eas - ter - tide, a - way with sin and
2 My flesh in hope shall rest, and for a sea - son
3 Death's flood has lost its chill, since Je - sus crossed the

sor - - - - row! My love, the cru - ci -
slum - - - - ber, till trump from east to
ri - - - - ver: lov - er of souls, from

fied, has sprung to life this mor - - - row.
west shall wake the dead in num - - - ber.
ill my pass - ing soul de - liv - - - er.

Refrain

Had Christ, who once was slain, ne'er burst his three-day pris - on,

Words: *George R. Woodward 1894, alt.*
Music: *J. Oudaen's David's Psalmen, Amsterdam 1685; harm. Charles Wood 1902*
Harmony copyright © Mowbray.

VRUECHTEN
6 7 6 7 with refrain

our faith had been in vain: but now has Christ a - ris - en,

a - ris - en, a - ris - en, a - ris - - - - en.

Because You Live, O Christ 178

1 Because you live, O Christ,
the garden of the world has come to
flower,
the darkness of the tomb
is flooded with your resurrection
power.

Refrain:
The stone has rolled away
and death cannot imprison.
O sing this Easter Day,
for Jesus Christ has risen,
has risen, has risen, has risen!

2 Because you live, O Christ,
the spirit bird of hope is freed for
flying,
our cages of despair
no longer keep us closed and life-
denying.

Refrain

3 Because you live, O Christ,
the rainbow of your peace will span
creation,
the colours of your love
will draw all humankind to adoration.

Refrain

Words: Shirley Erena Murray 1984
Words copyright © 1987 Hope Publishing Company.

VRUECHTEN
6 11 6 11 with refrain

179 Hallelujah, Hallelujah, Give Thanks

Descant

Hal - le - lu - jah, hal - le - lu - jah,

Unison (C) F Dm Gm C

Hal - le - lu - jah, hal - le - lu - jah. Give thanks to the ris - en Christ;

hal - le - lu - jah, praise to God's name.

F A Dm Gm C7 F

hal - le - lu - jah, hal - le - lu - jah! Give praise to God's name.

F Dm Bb C

1 Je - sus is Lord of all the earth,
2 Spread the good news o'er all the earth:
3 We have been cru - ci - fied with Christ,
4 Come let us praise the liv - ing God,

Words: Donald Fishel 1971, alt.
Music: Donald Fishel 1971, arr. Darryl Nixon 1987, alt.; desc. Betty Pulkingham

ALLELUIA NO. 1
Irregular

first - born   of   all   cre - a - tion.
Je - sus   has   died   and   is   ris - en.
now   we   shall   live   for   ev - er.
joy - ful - ly   sing   to   our   Sav - iour.

Christ Is Risen, Yes, Indeed   180

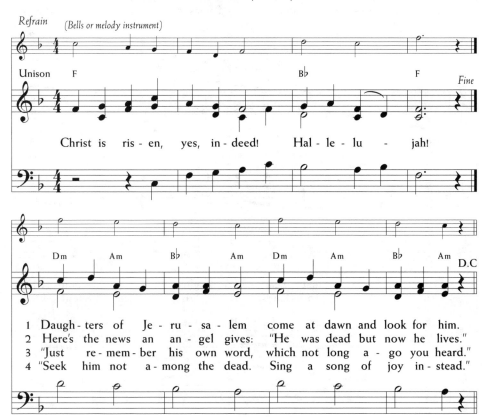

Refrain   (Bells or melody instrument)

Unison   F   Bb   F   Fine

Christ is   ris - en,   yes, in - deed!   Hal - le - lu - jah!

Dm   Am   Bb   Am   Dm   Am   Bb   Am   D.C

1 Daugh - ters of   Je - ru - sa - lem   come   at   dawn and look for   him.
2 Here's   the news   an   an - gel   gives: "He   was dead but now he lives."
3 "Just   re - mem - ber   his   own word,   which not long a - go you heard."
4 "Seek   him not   a - mong the dead.   Sing   a   song   of   joy in - stead."

Words: Dutch, *Alles wordt nieuw* 1966, 1971; *trans.* Stanley Wiersma 1982
Music: Wim ter Burg 1971
Words and music copyright © 1982 Paideia Press.

OPGESTAAN
7 7 *with refrain*

181 Midnight Sharpness, Starfields, Fading

1 Mid - night sharp - ness, star - fields, fad - ing, creep - ing
2 Cold of win - ter, dark of eve - ning, can - not

hues en - gulf the east, strips of grave - cloth cloud re -
crush the light - seed sown, flames on fro - zen, dew - wrapped

flect - ing faint - est lines in crim - son - grey: Her - ald
grass - es, spark - ling tears of Joy Un - known: Christ is

Dawn's first heart - beat glow - ing, blood - red
ris - en! Christ is ris - en! Shout O

streaks of fire flow 'cross the fields of fur - rowed
skies! Re - joice O fields! Hal - le - lu - jah! Je - sus!

la - bour, signs of liv - ing, pro - mise, hope.
Sa - viour! Let the Bells of Morn - ing peal!

Words: Neil Lemke 1990
Music: David Kai 1995

TASHME
8 7 8 7 D

Words copyright © 1990 Neil Lemke. Music copyright © 1995 David Kai.

Stay with Us through the Night   182

1 Stay with us through the night. Stay with us
2 Stay with us through the night. Stay with us
3 Stay with us through the night. Stay with us

through the pain. Stay with us, bless - ed
through the grief. Stay with us, bless - ed
through the dread. Stay with us, bless - ed

stran - ger till the morn - ing breaks a - gain.
stran - ger till the morn - ing brings re - lief.
stran - ger till the morn - ing breaks new bread.

Words: Walter Farquharson 1988
Music: Ron Klusmeier 1989

CASSWELL
6 6 7 7

Words copyright © 1986 Walter Farquharson. Music copyright © 1986 Ron Klusmeier.

183 We Meet You, O Christ

or "Christ"

Words: Fred Kaan 1966
Music: Peter D. Smith 1969, arr. Peter R. Walker 1993

LIFE

10 10 11 11

Alt. tune: Laudate Dominum

As We Walked Home at Close of Day 184

1 As we walked home at close of day, a strang-er
2 "Why wan-der furth-er with-out light? Please stay with
♦ 3 We sat to eat our sim-ple spread, then watched the
4 No strang-er he; it was our eyes which failed to
5 Hal-le-lu-jah! Hal-le-lu-jah! Hal-le-lu-

joined us on our way. He heard us speak of
us this trou-bled night. We've shared the truth of
♦ strang-er take the bread; and, as he said the
see, in strang-er's guise, the Lord who, ris-en
jah! Hal-le-lu-jah! As Mar-y and our

one who'd gone, and when we stopped, he car-ried on.
how we feel and now would like to share a meal."
♦ bless-ing prayer, we knew that some-one else was there.
from the dead, met us when read-y to be fed.
sis-ters said, the Lord is ris-en from the dead!

Words: The Iona Community 1988
Music: Georg Joseph 1657
Words and harmony copyright © 1988 WGRG, The Iona Community (Glasgow, Scotland), G.I.A. Publications, Inc., Chicago, Illinois, exclusive agent.

ANGELUS
8 8 8 8

185   You Tell Me That the Lord Is Risen

1 You tell me that the Lord is risen, that you have seen his face.
2 You claim a res - ur - rec - tion here, that God has bro - ken death.
3 "Now peace be with you. Come, my friend, my wound- ed bod - y see.
4 "How blest are they, how for - tu - nate who know with - out the sight.

Then tell me why you crouch in fear and hide with - in this place.
No eas - y words like these will soothe the pain that tears my breath.
Let the rich cour - age of your doubt bring you to fresh be - lief.
But Thom- as, you are fa - voured too, for search- ing yields its light."

You say that he spoke words of peace and stood just as be - fore.
How well do I re - call his face, com - pas - sion, strength in fear.
Fear not to won- der at the Word, to search the depths of grace.
So may each pil - grim in the Way, each road to Christ be blest,

But 'til I touch his ve - ry flesh I will not trust your joy.
How deep my grief that he should die. Spare me your words of cheer!
Reach out and touch, here is my hand. Re - ceive the gift of faith."
'til lips de - clare, "My Lord and God!", Christ's bod - y one at last.

Words: Rob Johns 1985
Music: English traditional melody, arr. Arthur Seymour Sullivan 1874
Words copyright © 1987 Sheila Johns. Used by permission of Sheila Johns.

NOËL
8 6 8 6 D

Now the Green Blade Rises

1 Now the green blade ris - es from the bur - ied grain,
2 In the grave they laid him, love by hat - red slain,
3 Forth he came at Eas - ter, like the ris - en grain,
4 When our hearts are win - try, griev - ing, or in pain,

wheat that in dark earth man - y days has lain;
think - ing that he would ne - ver wake a - gain,
he that for three days in the grave had lain;
your touch can call us back to life a - gain,

love lives a - gain, that with the dead has been:
laid in the earth like grain that sleeps un - seen;
raised from the dead, my liv - ing Lord is seen;
fields of our hearts that dead and bare have been;

love is come a - gain, like wheat a - ris - ing green.

Words: John M. C. Crum 1928
Music: mediæval French carol; harm. Martin Fallas Shaw 1928
Words and harmony copyright © 1928 Oxford University Press.

NOËL NOUVELET
11 11 10 11

187 The Spring Has Come

1 The spring has come, let all the church be part of it! The world has changed, and God is at the heart of it! New light, new day, new colour after winter grey.

2 The sun is warm, let all God's children play in it! The world expands, let's spread the Gospel way in it! New leaf, new thrust, new greening for the love of Christ.

3 The spring has come, new people are the flowers of it. Through wind and rain, new life is in the showers of it. New bud, new shoot, new hope will bear the Spirit's fruit.

Words: *Shirley Erena Murray 1990*
Music: *Colin Gibson 1990*
Words copyright © 1992 and music copyright © 1993 Hope Publishing Company.

VERVACITY
Irregular

New light,   new day,   the spring has
New leaf,   new thrust,   the sun is
New bud,   new shoot,   the spring has

come,   let all the church be   part of it!
warm,   let all God's chil - dren   play in it!
come,   new peo - ple are the   flowers of it!

Easter Prayer   188

God of grace and glory,
by the death and resurrection of your Beloved Child
your reign of wholeness has been unleashed
     within our bent and broken world.
Open us to your empowering grace
     that we may be bearers of your world-redeeming love;
through the resurrected Christ,
     our dignity, our power, and our peace. Amen.

Paul Fayter 1991

189 Hail the Day That Sees Him Rise

1 Hail the day that sees him rise, hal - le - lu - jah!
2 There the glo - rious tri - umph waits; hal - le - lu - jah!
♦ 3 Though re - turn - ing to his throne, hal - le - lu - jah!
4 See, he lifts his hands a - bove, hal - le - lu - jah!
5 Still for us he in - ter - cedes, hal - le - lu - jah!

ta - ken from our won - dering eyes, hal - le - lu - jah!
lift your heads, e - ter - nal gates; hal - le - lu - jah!
♦ still he calls the world his own; hal - le - lu - jah!
see, he shows the prints of love, hal - le - lu - jah!
his pre - vail - ing death he pleads, hal - le - lu - jah!

Christ, a - while to mor - tals given, hal - le - lu - jah!
Christ has con - quered death and sin; hal - le - lu - jah!
♦ him though high - est heaven re - ceives, hal - le - lu - jah!
hark, his gra - cious lips be - stow, hal - le - lu - jah!
near him - self pre - pares our place, hal - le - lu - jah!

re - as - cends his na - tive heaven. Hal - le - lu - jah!
take the King of Glo - ry in. Hal - le - lu - jah!
♦ still he loves the world he leaves. Hal - le - lu - jah!
bless - ing on his church be - low. Hal - le - lu - jah!
first - fruits of our hu - man race. Hal - le - lu - jah!

Words: *Charles Wesley 1739, alt.*
Music: *William Henry Monk 1861*

ASCENSION (MONK)
7 7 7 7 with hallelujah
Alt. tune: Llanfair

The Head That Once Was Crowned

1 The head that once was crowned with thorns is crowned with glo - ry now; a roy - al di - a - dem a - dorns the might - y vic - tor's brow.

2 The joy of all who dwell a - bove, the joy of all be - low, to whom he man - i - fests his love and grants his name to know.

3 To them the cross, with all its shame, with all its grace, is given, their name an ev - er - last - ing name, their joy the joy of heaven.

4 They suf - fer here with Christ be - low, they reign with him a - bove, their pro - fit and their joy to know the mys - tery of his love.

5 The cross he bore is life and health, though shame and death to him, his peo - ple's hope, his peo - ple's wealth, their ev - er - last - ing theme.

Words: Thomas Kelly 1820
Music: attrib. Jeremiah Clarke 1707; harm. William Henry Monk 1868

ST MAGNUS
8 6 8 6

191   Ascension Day Prayer

Mighty God,
by your power you raised Jesus Christ to rule over us.
We praise you that he puts down tyrannies
     that threaten to destroy us,
     and unmasks powers that claim our allegiance.
We thank you that he alone commands our lives,
     and gives us freedom to love the world.
Glory to you for the gift of his life!
Glory to you for his saving death!
Glory to you for Jesus Christ,
     who lives and reigns as our risen Lord. Amen.

192   Forsaking Chariots of Fire

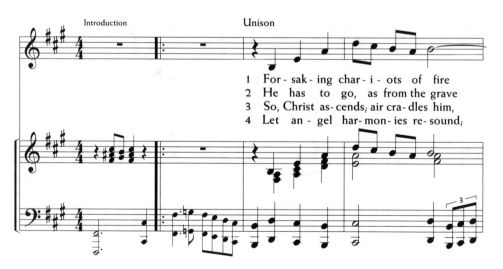

1 For - sak - ing char - i - ots of fire
2 He has to go, as from the grave
3 So, Christ as- cends; air cra- dles him,
4 Let an - gel har - mon - ies re- sound;

Words: The Iona Community 1988
Music: John L. Bell 1988

Words and harmony copyright © 1988 WGRG, The Iona Community (Glasgow, Scotland), G.I.A. Publications, Inc., Chicago, Illinois, exclusive agent.

THE SAVIOUR LEAVES
8 4 8 4 6 4

and fan- fared brass,   as strange- ly si - lent as he came,
he had to rise: in or - der to be ev - ery - where
dis - ci - ples stare.   Their Eas - ter joy, his seven weeks' stay
let trum- pets blare;   let hea- ven's ban- quet guests ap - plaud

the Sa - viour leaves   and God, with heaven's ca - ress, the Son re -
he must de - part   to live, not in one place, but in each
seem now to end.   But no! The Spir- it's send - ing they por -
the wel- comed word,   and earth an - ti - ci - pate her com- ing

1–3

ceives.
heart.
tend.

4

Lord.

And the following…

193   Gracious Spirit, Holy Ghost

1. Gracious Spirit, Holy Ghost, taught by you, we covet most of your gifts at Pentecost, holy, heavenly love.
2. Love is kind, and suffers long; love is humble, thinks no wrong; love than death itself more strong; therefore give us love.
3. Prophecy will fade away, melting in the light of day; love will ever with us stay; therefore give us love.
4. Faith will vanish into sight; hope be emptied in delight; love in heaven will shine more bright; therefore give us love.
5. Faith and hope and love we see joining hand in hand agree; but the greatest of the three, and the best, is love.

Words: Christopher Wordsworth 1862
Music: Friedrich Filitz 1847; adapt. Peter Maurice 1854

CAPETOWN
7 7 7 5

Filled with the Spirit's Power

Trumpets before each stanza (optional)

1 Filled with the Spir - it's power, with one ac -
2 Now with the mind of Christ set us on
3 Wi - den our love, good Spir - it, to em -

cord the in - fant church con - fessed its ris - en Lord.
fire, that u - ni - ty may be our great de - sire.
brace with your com - pas - sion all the hu - man race.

O Ho - ly Spir - it, in the church to - day
Give joy and peace; give faith to hear your call,
Like wind and fire with life a - mong us move,

no less your power of fel - low - ship dis - play.
and rea - di - ness in each to work for all.
till we are known as Christ's, and Christ - ian prove.

Words: J.R. Peacey 1969
Music: George William Warren 1894
Words copyright © 1978 Hope Publishing Company.

NATIONAL HYMN
10 10 10 10
Alt. tune: Ellers

195 On Pentecost They Gathered

1 On Pen-te-cost they gath-ered quite ear-ly in the day,
2 The peo-ple all a-round them were star-tled and a-mazed
3 God pours the Ho-ly Spir-it on all who would be-lieve,
4 O Spir-it, sent from heav-en on that day long a-go,

a band of Christ's dis-ci-ples, to wor-ship, sing, and pray.
to un-der-stand their lan-guage, as Je-sus Christ they praised.
on wom-en, men, and chil-dren who would God's grace re-ceive.
re-kin-dle faith a-mong us in all life's ebb and flow.

A might-y wind came blow-ing, filled all the swirl-ing air,
What u-ni-ver-sal mes-sage, what great good news was here?
That Spir-it knows no lim-it, be-stow-ing life and power.
O give us ears to lis-ten and tongues a-flame with praise,

and tongues of fire a-glow-ing in-spired each per-son there.
That Christ, once dead, is ris-en to van-quish all our fear.
The church, formed and re-form-ing, re-sponds in ev-ery hour.
so folk of ev-ery na-tion glad songs of joy shall raise.

Words: *Jane Parker Huber 1976, alt.*
Music: Neuvermehrtes Meiningisches Gesangbuch *1693, adapt. Felix Mendelssohn 1847*

MUNICH
7 6 7 6 D

Wind Who Makes All Winds That Blow 196

1 Wind who makes all winds that blow, gusts that bend the sap - lings low,
2 Fire who fuels all fires that burn, suns a - round which plan - ets turn,
3 Ho - ly Spir - it, Wind and Flame, move with - in our mor - tal frame.

gales that heave the sea in waves, stir - rings in the mind's deep caves,
bea - cons mark - ing reefs and shoals, shin - ing truth to guide our souls,
Make our hearts an al - tar pyre, kin - dle them with your own fire.

aim your breath with stead - y power on your church this day, this hour.
come to us as once you came: burst in tongues of sa - cred flame!
Breathe and blow up - on that blaze till our lives, our deeds and ways,

Raise, re - new the life we've lost, Spir - it God of Pen - te - cost.
Light and Pow - er, Might and Strength, fill your church, its breadth and length.
speak that tongue which ev - ery land by your grace shall un - der - stand.

Words: Thomas H. Troeger 1983
Music: Joseph Parry 1879
Words by permission of Oxford University Press, Inc.

ABERYSTWYTH
7 7 7 7 D

197   Prayer for Gifts of the Spirit

God, Holy Spirit, come to us, come among us;
    come as the wind, and cleanse;
    come as the fire, and burn;
    come as the dew, and refresh:
    convict, convert, and consecrate many hearts and lives
        to our great good and your greater glory. Amen.

Eric Milner-White

198   Come, O Spirit, Dwell among Us

1 Come, O Spir - it, dwell a - mong us,
2 We would raise our hal - le - lu - jahs
3 Come, O Spir - it, dwell a - mong us,

come with pen - te - cos - tal power; give the church a
for the grace of yes - ter - years; for to - mor - row's
give us words of fire and flame. Help our fee - ble

strong - er vi - sion, help us face each cru - cial hour.
un - known path - way, hear, O God, our hum - ble prayers.
lips to praise you, glo - ri - fy your ho - ly name.

Words: Janie Alford 1979
Music: Thomas John Williams 1890
Words copyright © 1979 Hope Publishing Company.

EBENEZER
8 7 8 7 D

Built up - on a firm foun - da - tion, Je - sus Christ, the
In the church's pil - grim jour - ney you have led us
God, all ho - ly, Son and Spir - it, three in one: what

cor - ner - stone, still the church is called to mis - sion
all the way, still in pres - ence move be - fore us,
mys - ter - y! We would sing our loud ho - san - nas

that God's love shall be made known.
fire by night and cloud by day.
now and through e - ter - ni - ty.

Creative Spirit, Come to Us   199

1 Creative Spirit, come to us,
  give vision to the minds you own,
  and fill the hearts which you have made
  with gifts whose grace is yours alone.

2 For you are called the Comforter,
  the glorious gift of God Most High,
  the living water, fire and love,
  outpouring of eternity.

3 Kaleidoscope of sevenfold light,
  power of the strong right hand of God,
  enriching with the promised truth
  the prophet's and the preacher's word.

4 Make our imaginations blaze,
  and fill our hearts with flowing love,
  that we, who have no strength, may know
  the strong flight of the soaring dove.

Coda: Praise to God, to Christ the Word,
  and to the Spirit: all adored. Amen

(The music appears on the following page.)

Words: Latin 9th century trans. Janet Wootton ca. 1993, alt.
Translation copyright © 1993 Stainer & Bell Ltd. and Women in Theology.
Used by permission of Hope Publishing Company.

VENI CREATOR SPIRITUS
8 7 8 7 and coda

200   O Holy Spirit, by Whose Breath

Unison

1 O Holy Spir - it, by whose breath
2 You are the seek - er's sure re - source,
♦ 3 In you God's en - er - gy is shown,
4 Flood our dull sen - ses with your light;
5 From in - ner strife grant us re - lease;

life ris - es vi - brant out of death:
of burn - ing love the liv - ing source,
to us your var - ied gifts made known.
in mu - tual love our hearts u - nite.
turn na - tions to the ways of peace.

come to cre - ate, re - new, in - spire;
pro - tec - tor in the midst of strife,
♦ Teach us to speak; teach us to hear;
Your power the whole cre - a - tion fills;
To full - er life your peo - ple bring

D.C.

come, kin - dle in our hearts your fire.
source and sus - tain - er of all life.
♦ yours is the tongue and yours the ear.
con - firm our weak, un - cer - tain wills.
that as one bod - y we may sing:

Words: 9th-century Latin, attrib. Rabanus Maurus; trans. John Webster Grant 1968, alt.
Music: plainsong melody, Mechlin; arr. Healey Willan

VENI CREATOR SPIRITUS
8 8 8 8 and coda

Translation copyright © 1971 John Webster Grant. Arrangement copyright © 1995 Waterloo Music.

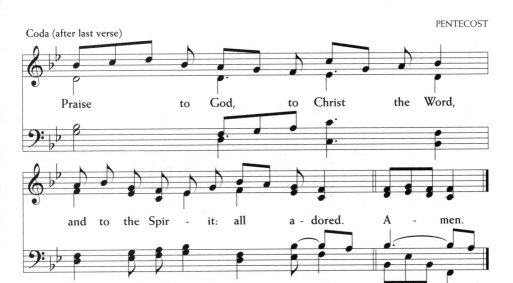

Coda (after last verse)

Praise to God, to Christ the Word,

and to the Spir - it: all a - dored. A - men.

Viens, Saint-Esprit, Dieu créateur

1 Viens, Saint-Esprit, Dieu créateur,
mettre en tout homme un nouveau
coeur;
tu veux de nous, si différents,
former un seul peuple saint.

2 Viens, Saint-Esprit consolateur,
illuminer joie et douleur;
tu sais nos élans, nos secrets,
reste avec nous à jamais.

3 Tu répands tes dons les meilleurs,
l'amour, la joie et la douceur,
toi qui viens au milieu de nous,
Esprit saint promis à tous.

4 Loué sois-tu, ô Saint-Esprit,
qui nous révèles Jésus-Christ
et nous unis au Tout-puissant;
loué soit Dieu en tout temps.

Coda: Louange à Dieu, au Christ le Verbe
et à l'Esprit: un seul Dieu trois fois saint. Amen

Words: Trans. Pierre-Étienne 1974
Translation copyright © Fédération Protestante de France.

VENI CREATOR SPIRITUS

Come, Holy Ghost   201

1 Come, Holy Ghost, our souls inspire
and lighten with celestial fire;
thou the anointing Spirit art,
who dost thy sevenfold gifts impart.

2 Thy blessed unction from above
is comfort, life, and fire of love;
enable with perpetual light
the dullness of our blinded sight;

3 anoint and cheer our soiled face
with the abundance of thy grace;
keep far our foes; give peace at home:
where thou art guide no ill can come.

4 Teach us to know the Father, Son,
and thee of both to be but one,
that through the ages all along
this still may be our endless song:

Coda: Praise to God, to Christ the Word,
and to the Spirit: all adored. Amen

Words: 9th-century Latin, attrib. Rabanus Maurus; trans. John Cosin 1627

VENI CREATOR SPIRITUS

202 O Breath of Life

1 O Breath of life, come sweep-ing through us,
2 O Wind of God, come bend us, break us
3 O Breath of love, come breathe with-in us,

re - vive your church with life and power;
till hum - bly we con - fess our need;
re - new - ing thought and will and heart;

O Breath of life, come, cleanse, re - new us
then, in your ten - der - ness re - make us,
come, love of Christ, a - fresh to win us,

and fit your church to meet this hour.
re - vive, re - store — for this we plead.
re - vive your church in ev - ery part.

Words: Elizabeth A. P. Head *ca. 1914*
Music: Mary Jane Hammond *1936*
Music copyright © Mary Jane Hammond.

SPIRITUS VITAE
9 8 9 8
Alt. tune: St. Clement

Viens, Créateur, emplis nos âmes

1 Viens, Créateur, emplis nos âmes,
Esprit-Saint, Dieu de vérité;
allume en nous la vive flamme
de ton ardente charité.

2 Présent de Dieu, don admirable,
conseiller, puissant défenseur,
tu es la source inépuisable
de la vraie vie, du vrai bonheur.

3 En nos esprits mets ta lumière;
en nos coeurs verse ton amour;
Esprit-Saint promis par le Père,
inspire-nous jour après jour.

4 Mets ta force en notre faiblesse;
loin de nous chasse l'Ennemi,
et dans la paix, par ta sagesse,
sur ton chemin garde nos vies.

This French text (not a translation of the English) may be sung to the preceding tune.

Words: Réveil

SPIRITUS VITAE

French words copyright © Réveil Publications.

Come, Holy Spirit

Come, Ho-ly Spir-it, gra-cious heaven-ly dove; come, fire of love. love.

1, 2

Last time

Words: traditional setting

Music: The Iona Community 1988

Music copyright ©1988 WGRG, The Iona Community (Glasgow, Scotland), G.I.A. Publications, Inc., Chicago, Illinois, exclusive agent.

205 Like the Murmur of the Dove's Song

1 Like the mur - mur of the dove's song, like the chal - lenge of her flight, like the vig - our of the wind's rush, like the new flame's ea - ger might: come, Ho - ly Spir - it, come.

2 To the mem - bers of Christ's bod - y, to the branch - es of the Vine, to the church in faith as - sem - bled, to our midst as gift and sign: come, Ho - ly Spir - it, come.

3 With the heal - ing of di - vi - sion, with the cease - less voice of prayer, with the power to love and wit - ness, with the peace be - yond com - pare: come, Ho - ly Spir - it, come.

Words: Carl P. Daw, Jr. 1982
Music: Peter Cutts 1969
Words copyright © 1982 and music copyright © 1969 Hope Publishing Company.

BRIDEGROOM
8 7 8 7 6

206 Pentecost Prayer

Your Spirit, God, works in our weakness
    until we are aflame with your love and power.
Fill the hearts of your faithful with living fire,
    that we may set the world ablaze;
through Jesus Christ, to whom with you and the Spirit
    be honour and praise, now and forever. Amen.

Sylvia Dunstan 1988

Spirit of God, Unleashed on Earth

Descant

3 With burn-ing words of vic - tory won in -

C · · F G7 C G

1 Spir - it of God, un - leashed on earth with
2 You came in power, the church was born; O
3 With burn - ing words of vic - tory won in -

spire our hearts grown cold with fear, re - vive in us bap -

Am G C Dm C G D G

rush of wind and roar of flame! With tongues of fire saints
Ho - ly Spir - it, come a - gain! From liv - ing wa - ters
spire our hearts grown cold with fear, re - vive in us bap -

tis - mal grace, and fan our smoul-dering lives to flame.

C D7 G G7 C Dm C G C

spread good news; earth, kin - dling, blazed its loud ac - claim.
raise new saints, let new tongues hail the ris - en Lord.
tis - mal grace, and fan our smoul-dering lives to flame.

Words: John W. Arthur 1972, alt.
Music: melody in Thomas Williams' Psalmodia Evangelica 1789; desc. John Wilson

TRURO
8 8 8 8
Alt. setting: 158

208

Come, Holy Spirit
(Veni Sancte Spiritus)

Ostinato

Ve - ni Sanc - te Spi - ri - tus.

Solo voice

1 Come, Ho - ly Spir - it, from heav - en shine forth with your glo - rious light. Ve - ni Sanc - te Spi - ri - tus.

2 Come from the four winds, O Spir - it, come, breath of God; dis - perse the shad - ows o - ver us, re - new and strength - en your peo - ple. Ve - ni Sanc - te Spi - ri - tus.

3 Guar - dian of the poor, come to our pov - er - ty. Show - er up - on us the sev - en gifts of your grace. Be the light of our lives. O come! Ve - ni Sanc - te Spi - ri - tus.

Throughout and between each verse, the soloist pauses for the indicated number of measures, while the ostinato continues uninterrupted.

Words: adapt. Jacques Berthier 1978
Music: Jacques Berthier 1978

VENI SANCTE SPIRITUS
Irregular

4 You are our on-ly com-fort-er, Peace of the soul. In the heat you shade us; in our la-bour you re-fresh us, and in trou-ble you are our strength. Ve-ni Sanc-te Spi-ri-tus.

French:

1 Viens, Saint-Es-prit, no-tre lu-miè-re é-clai-re le che-min des hom-mes. Ve-ni San-cte Spi-ri-tus.

2 Dans l'é-preu-ve, sois no-tre for-ce, dans la tris-tes-se la con-so-la-tion. Ve-ni San-cte Spi-ri-tus.

3 A-breu-ve no-tre sé-che-res-se, flé-chis no-tre du-re-té, en-flam-me no-tre tié-deur. Ve-ni San-cte Spi-ri-tus.

4 Ac-cor-de-nous d'ê-tre fi-dè-les dans la foi don-ne-nous la joie qui de-meu-re. Ve-ni San-cte Spi-ri-tus.

209 Fire of God, Undying Flame

1 Fire of God, un-dy-ing flame, Spir-it who in
2 Breath of God, that swept in power in the pen-te-
♦ 3 Strength of God, your might with-in con-quers sor-row,
4 Truth of God, your pier-cing rays pen-e-trate my
5 Love of God, your grace pro-found knows not eith-er

splen-dour came, let your heat my soul re-fine,
cos-tal hour, ho-ly breath, be now in me
♦ pain and sin: for-ti-fy from e-vil's art
se-cret ways. May the light that shames my sin
age or bound: come, my heart's own guest to be,

till it glows with love di-vine.
source of vi-tal en-er-gy.
♦ all the gate-ways of my heart.
guide me ho-lier paths to win.
dwell for ev-er-more in me.

Words: Albert Frederick Bayly 1950, alt.
Music: Johann Walther's Gesangbüchlein 1524; harm. Johann Sebastian Bach ca. 1750
Words by permission of Oxford University Press.

NUN KOMM
7 7 7 7
Alt. tune: Culbach

And the following...

You, Lord, Are Both Lamb and Shepherd 210

1 You, Lord, are both lamb and shep-herd. You, Lord, are both
2 Clothed in light up-on the moun-tain, stripped of might up-
3 You, who walk each day be-side us, sit in pow-er
4 Wor-thy is our earth-ly Je-sus! Wor-thy is our

prince and slave. You, peace-mak-er and sword-bring-er
on the cross, shin-ing in e-ter-nal glo-ry,
at God's side. You, who preach a way that's nar-row,
cos-mic Christ! Wor-thy your de-feat and vic-to-ry.

of the way you took and gave. You, the ev-er-
beg-gared by a sol-dier's toss. You, the ev-er-
have a love that reach-es wide. You, the ev-er-
Wor-thy still your peace and strife. You, the ev-er-

last-ing in-stant; you, whom we both scorn and crave.
last-ing in-stant; you who are both gift and cost.
last-ing in-stant; you, who are our pil-grim guide.
last-ing in-stant; you, who are our death and life.

(* v. 4 only)

Words: Sylvia Dunstan 1984
Music: John Van Maanen 1984
Words copyright © 1991 G.I.A. Publications Inc. Music copyright © 1984 John Van Maanen.

PARADOX
878787
Alt. tune: Westminster Abbey

211 Crown Him with Many Crowns

Descant

4 Crown him the Lord of love; be-hold his hands and side,

1 Crown him with ma-ny crowns, the Lamb up-on his throne:
2 Crown him the Lord of life, who tri-umphed o'er the grave,
3 Crown him the Lord of peace, whose power a scep-tre sways
4 Crown him the Lord of love; be-hold his hands and side,

rich wounds yet vis-i-ble a-bove, in beau-ty glo-ri-fied. All hail,

hark, how the heaven-ly an-them drowns all mu-sic but its own!
and rose vic-to-rious in the strife for those he came to save.
from pole to pole, that wars may cease, ab-sorbed in prayer and praise.
rich wounds yet vis-i-ble a-bove, in beau-ty glo-ri-fied.

Re-deem — er, hail! Thou hast died for me; thy praise

A-wake, my soul, and sing of him who died for thee,
His glo-ries now we sing who died and rose on high,
His reign shall know no end; and round his pierc-ed feet
All hail, Re-deem-er, hail! for thou hast died for me;

Words: Matthew Bridges 1851; v. 2, Godfrey Thring 1874
Music: George Job Elvey 1868; desc. Hal Hopson 1979
Descant copyright © 1979 G.I.A. Publications, Inc.

DIADEMATA
6 6 8 6 D
Alt. setting: 321

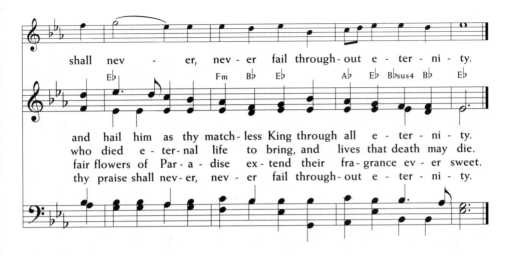

shall nev - er, nev - er fail through-out e - ter - ni - ty.

Eb   *Fm*   *Bb*   *Eb*   *Ab*   *Eb*   *Bbsus4*   *Bb*   *Eb*

and hail him as thy match-less King through all e - ter - ni - ty.
who died e - ter-nal life to bring, and lives that death may die.
fair flowers of Par - a - dise ex-tend their fra-grance ev - er sweet.
thy praise shall nev-er, nev - er fail through-out e - ter - ni - ty.

Eternal Christ, You Rule   212

Unison

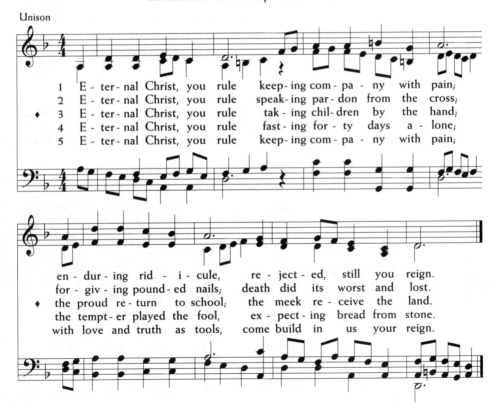

1 E - ter-nal Christ, you rule keep-ing com-pa - ny with pain;
2 E - ter-nal Christ, you rule speak-ing par-don from the cross;
3 E - ter-nal Christ, you rule tak-ing chil-dren by the hand;
4 E - ter-nal Christ, you rule fast-ing for - ty days a - lone;
5 E - ter-nal Christ, you rule keep-ing com-pa - ny with pain;

en - dur - ing rid - i - cule, re - ject - ed, still you reign.
for - giv - ing pound-ed nails; death did its worst and lost.
the proud re - turn to school; the meek re - ceive the land.
the tempt-er played the fool, ex - pect-ing bread from stone.
with love and truth as tools, come build in us your reign.

Words: Daniel Charles Damon 1990
Music: Daniel Charles Damon 1990
Words and music copyright © 1991 Hope Publishing Company.

THROCKMORTON
6 7 6 6

213

Rejoice, the Lord Is King

Descant

4 Re - joice in glo - rious hope, for Christ, the judge, shall come

1 Re - joice the Lord is King! Your ris - en Lord a - dore!
2 Je - sus the Sav - iour reigns, the God of truth and love;
3 God's king - dom can - not fail; Christ rules o'er earth and heaven;
4 Re - joice in glo - rious hope, for Christ, the judge, shall come

to glo - ri - fy the saints for their e - ter - nal home.

Re - joice, give thanks and sing and tri - umph ev - er - more.
when he had purged our sins, he took his seat a - bove.
the keys of death and hell are to our Je - sus given.
to glo - ri - fy the saints for their e - ter - nal home.

We soon shall hear the arch - an - gel's voice;

Lift up your heart, lift up your voice:
Lift up your heart, lift up your voice:
Lift up your heart, lift up your voice:
We soon shall hear the arch - an - gel's voice;

Words: Charles Wesley 1746, alt.
Music: John Darwall 1770; desc. Sidney Hugo Nicholson ca. 1947
Descant copyright © 1955 Hymns Ancient and Modern Ltd. Used by permission of Hope Publishing Company.

DARWALL'S 148TH
666688

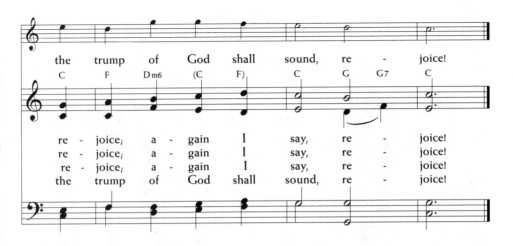

the trump of God shall sound, re - joice!

C F Dm6 (C F) C G G7 C

re - joice; a - gain I say, re - joice!
re - joice; a - gain I say, re - joice!
re - joice; a - gain I say, re - joice!
the trump of God shall sound, re - joice!

A Prayer for the Reign of Christ 214

Mighty and tender God,
    voice of the voiceless,
    power of the powerless:
we praise you for your vision
    of a community of wholeness,
    a realm of peace,
in which all who hunger and thirst are nourished,
in which the stranger is welcomed,
    the hurting are healed,
    and the captive set free.

Guide us by your truth and love,
    until we and all your people
    make manifest your reign of justice and compassion.

We pray in the name of your anointed one, our servant-king,
    to whom with you and the Spirit, one Holy God,
    be honour, glory and blessing
    this day and forever. Amen.

Paul Fayter, alt.

215
Hope of the World

1 Hope of the world, O Christ of great com - pas - sion,
2 Hope of the world, God's gift from high - est heav - en,
♦ 3 Hope of the world, a - foot on dust - y high - ways,
4 Hope of the world, who by your cross has saved us
5 Hope of the world, O Christ, o'er death vic - to - rious,

speak to our fear - ful hearts by con - flict rent;
bring - ing to hun - gry souls the bread of life,
♦ show - ing to wan - dering souls the path of light;
from death and dark de - spair, from sin and guilt;
who by this sign has con - quered grief and pain,

save us, your peo - ple, from con - sum - ing pas - sion,
still let your Spir - it un - to us be giv - en
♦ walk now be - side us lest the tempt - ing by - ways
we ren - der back the love your mer - cy gave us;
we would be faith - ful to your gos - pel glo - rious.

who by our own false hopes and aims are spent.
to heal earth's wounds and end its bit - ter strife.
♦ lure us a - way from you to end - less night.
take now our lives, with them your king - dom build.
You are our Lord! You shall for - ev - er reign.

Words: Georgia Elma Harkness 1952, alt.
Music: melody in Genevan Psalter 1551; harm. adapt. from Claude Goudimel 1565

DONNE SECOURS
11 10 11 10

Sing Praise to God, Who Reigns Above 216

1 Sing praise to God, who reigns a-bove, the God of all cre-
2 What God's al-might-y power hath made, God's gra-cious mer-cy
3 Our God is nev-er far a-way, but through all grief dis-
4 Thus all my glad-some way a-long, I sing a-loud thy

a-tion, the God of power, the God of love, the God of
keep-eth: by morn-ing glow or eve-ning shade God's watch-ful
tress-ing, an ev-er-pres-ent help and stay, our peace, and
prais-es that all may hear the grate-ful song my voice un-

our sal-va-tion; with heal-ing balm my soul is filled, and
eye ne'er sleep-eth; with-in the shel-ter of God's might, lo!
joy, and bless-ing; as with a moth-er's ten-der hand, God
wea-ried rais-es. Be joy-ful in your God, my heart! Both

ev-ery faith-less mur-mur stilled:
all is just and all is right: to God all praise and glo-ry!
gent-ly leads the cho-sen band:
soul and bod-y take your part:

Words: Johann Jacob Schütz 1675, alt.; trans. Frances Elizabeth Cox 1864, alt.
Music: Bohemian Brethren, Kirchengesang 1566; harm. Maurice F. Bell 1906

MIT FREUDEN ZART
8 7 8 7 8 8 7

217 All Creatures of Our God and King

(Vous créatures du Seigneur)

Unison

1 All crea-tures of our God and King,
2 O rush-ing winds and breez-es soft,

1 Vous cré-a-tu-res du Sei-gneur,
2 Dieu, sois lou-é pour le so-leil,

lift up your voice and with us sing:
O clouds that ride the winds a-loft,

chan-tez tou-jours en son hon-neur,
pour ce grand frè-re sans pa-reil,

Harmony

hal-le-lu-jah, hal-le-lu-jah!
sing prais-es, hal-le-lu-jah!

al-lé-lu-ia, al-lé-lu-ia!
al-lé-lu-ia, al-lé-lu-ia!

Unison

Bright burn-ing sun with gold-en beam,
O ris-ing morn, in praise re-joice;

Car c'est lui seul qu'il faut lou-er,
Et pour la lune et sa lu-eur,

Words: *St. Francis of Assisi 1225; English trans. William Henry Draper ca. 1919, alt.;*
French trans. adapt. J.-J. Bovet 1950
Music: *Geistliche Kirchengesänge, Cologne 1623; harm. Ralph Vaughan Williams 1906*
English translation copyright © G. Schirmer, Inc. Harmony by permission of Oxford University Press.

LASST UNS ERFREUEN
8 8 8 8 *with hallelujahs*

soft shin - ing moon with sil - ver gleam,
O lights of even - ing, find a voice:
il donne au so - leil sa clar - té,
pour chaque é - toi - le no - tre soeur,

Harmony

sing prais - es, sing prais - es,
sing prais - es, sing prais - es,
ren - dez gloi - re, ren - dez gloi - re,
ren - dons gloi - re, ren - dons gloi - re,

Unison

hal - le - lu - jah, hal - le - lu - jah, hal - le - lu - jah!
al - lé - lu - ia, al - lé - lu - ia, al - lé - lu - ia!

3 Earth, ever fertile, day by day
   brings forth rich blessings on our way:
   sing praises, hallelujah!
   The flowers and fruits that verdant grow,
   let them God's glory also show:
   sing praises, hallelujah!

4 And everyone of tender heart,
   forgiving others, take your part:
   sing praises, hallelujah!
   All who long pain and sorrow bear,
   praise God and yield up all your care:
   sing praises, hallelujah!

5 Let all things their Creator bless,
   and worship God in humbleness:
   sing praises, hallelujah!
   Praise God eternal, praise the Son,
   and praise the Spirit, three in one:
   sing praises, hallelujah!

3 Loué sois-tu pour sire feu,
   vivant, robuste, glorieux,
   alléluia, alléluia!
   La terre, en maternelle soeur,
   nous comble de ses mille fleurs,
   rendons gloire, alléluia!

4 Heureux les artisans de paix,
   leur nom soit béni à jamais,
   alléluia, alléluia!
   Ceux qui ont souffert et pâti,
   ils te remettent leurs soucis,
   rendons gloire, alléluia!

5 Dieu trois fois saint, nous te louons,
   nous te chantons, nous t'adorons,
   alléluia, alléluia!
   Gloire au Père et louange au Fils,
   et loué soit le Saint-Esprit,
   rendons gloire, alléluia!

218   We Praise You, O God

Descant

3 With voic - es u - nit - ed;

1 We praise you, O God, our Re - deem - er, Cre - a - tor;
2 We wor - ship you, God of our moth - ers and fa - thers,
3 With voic - es u - nit - ed our prais - es we of - fer

and glad - ly our songs of thanks - giv - ing we raise.

in grate - ful de - vo - tion our trib - ute we bring.
through tri - al and tem - pest, com - pan - ion and guide.
and glad - ly our songs of thanks - giv - ing we raise.

We pray for your bless - ing,

We lay it be - fore you; we kneel and a - dore you;
When per - ils o'er - take us, you will not for - sake us,
Our sins now con - fess - ing, we pray for your bless - ing,

Words: Julia Cory 1902, alt.

Music: Netherlands melody 1626; harm. Eduard Kremser 1877; desc. Scott Withrow 1980
Descant copyright © 1980 G.I.A. Publications, Inc.

KREMSER
12 11 12 11

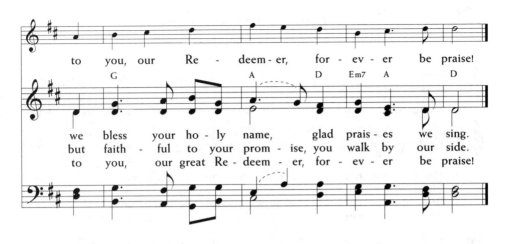

to you, our Re - deem - er, for - ev - er be praise!

G   A   D   Em7   A   D

we bless your ho - ly name, glad prais - es we sing.
but faith - ful to your prom - ise, you walk by our side.
to you, our great Re - deem - er, for - ev - er be praise!

When All Your Mercies, O My God   219

G   (D   G   Em)   C   D   A7   D   G   Em   G   D   G

1 When all your mer - cies, O my God, my ris - ing soul sur - veys,
2 Ten thou - sand thou - sand pre - cious gifts my dai - ly thanks em - ploy;
3 Through ev - ery per - iod of my life your good - ness I'll pur - sue;
4 Through all e - ter - ni - ty to you a joy - ful song I'll raise;

G   C   (D   G   Am)   G   C   D   Am   G   Em   G   D   G

trans - port - ed with the view I'm lost in won - der, love and praise.
nor is the least a cheer - ful heart that tastes those gifts with joy.
and af - ter death, in dis - tant worlds the glo - rious theme re - new.
but oh! e - ter - ni - ty's too short to ut - ter all your praise.

Words: Joseph Addison 1712, alt.
Music: William Jones 1789

ST STEPHEN
8 6 8 6

220   Praise to the Lord, the Almighty

(Peuples, criez de joie et bondissez d'allégresse)

Descant

4 Praise to the Lord! O let all that is in me a - dore him!

1 Praise to the Lord, the Al - might - y, who rules all cre - a - tion;
2 Praise to the Lord, a - bove all things so might - i - ly reign - ing,
3 Praise to the Lord who will pros - per our work and de - fend us;
4 Praise to the Lord! O let all that is in me a - dore him!

All that has life and breath come now with prais - es be - fore him!

O my soul, praise him, at all times your health and sal - va - tion.
keep - ing us safe at his side, and so gent - ly sus - tain - ing.
sure - ly his good - ness and mer - cy will dai - ly at - tend us;
All that has life and breath come now with prais - es be - fore him!

Let the A - men sound from God's peo - ple a - gain:

Come, all who hear: bro - thers and sis - ters draw near,
Have you not seen how all you need - ed has been
pon - der a - new what the Al - might - y can do,
Let the A - men sound from God's peo - ple a - gain:

Words: Joachim Neander 1680; English trans. Catherine Winkworth 1863, et al, alt.;
French trans. Didier Rimaud 1970

Music: Stralsund Gesangbuch 1665; desc. Craig Sellar Lang 1964

LOBE DEN HERREN
14 14 4 7 8

Descant copyright © Shawnee Press Inc. French translation copyright © Centre Nationale de Pastorale Liturgique.

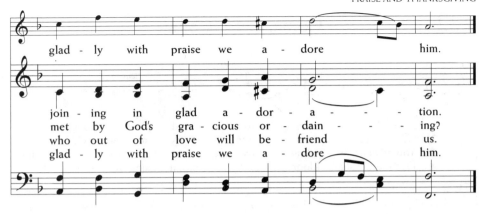

glad - ly with praise we a - dore him.

join - ing in glad a - dor - a - - - tion.
met by God's gra - cious or - dain - - - ing?
who out of love will be - friend us.
glad - ly with praise we a - dore him.

1 Peuples, criez de joie et bondissez
d'allégresse;
le Père envoie son Fils manifester sa
tendresse;
ouvrons les yeux: il est l'image de
Dieu,
pour que chacun le connaisse.

2 Loué soit notre Dieu, Source et Parole
féconde;
ses mains ont tout créé pour que nos
coeurs lui répondent;
par Jésus Christ il donne l'être et la vie
pour que sa Vie surabonde.

3 Loué soit notre Dieu, dont la splendeur
se révèle
quand nous buvons le vin pour une
terre nouvelle;
en Jésus-Christ le monde passe
aujourd'hui
vers une gloire éternelle.

4 Peuples, battez des mains et proclamez
votre fête:
le Père accueille en lui ceux que son
Verbe rachète;
par l'Esprit Saint en qui vous n'êtes plus
qu'un,
que votre joie soit parfaite!

Sing Praise to God, Who Has Shaped   221

1. Sing praise to God, who has shaped
and sustains all creation!
Sing praise, my soul, in profound and
complete adoration!
Gladsome rejoice – organ and trumpet
and voice –
joining God's great congregation.

2. Praise God, our guardian, who lovingly
offers correction,
who, as on eagle's wings, saves us from
sinful dejection.
Have you observed, how we are always
preserved
by God's parental affection?

3. Sing praise to God, with sincere thanks
for all your successes.
Merciful God ever loves to encourage
and bless us.
Only conceive what godly strength can
achieve:
strength that would touch and caress us.

4. Sing praise, my soul, the great name of
your high God commending.
All that have life and breath join you,
their notes sweetly blending.
God is your light! Soul, ever keep this in
sight:
amen, amen never ending.

Words: Joachim Neander 1680, trans. Madeleine Forell Marshall 1993
Translation copyright © 1993 Madeleine Forell Marshall.

LOBE DEN HERREN
14 14 4 7 8

222 Come, Let Us Sing

1 Come, let us sing to the Lord our song, we have stood si - lent - ly too long; sure - ly the Lord de - serves our praise, so joy - ful - ly thank God for our days.

2 O thirst - y soul, come drink at the well; God's liv - ing wa - ters will nev - er fail. Sure - ly the Lord will help you to stand, strength - ened and com - fort - ed by God's hand.

3 You dwell a - mong us and cause us to pray, and walk with each oth - er fol - lowing your way; our pre - cious broth - ers and sis - ters will grow in the ful - fill - ing love they know.

4 Des - erts shall bloom and moun - tains shall sing to the de - sire of all liv - ing things. Come, all you crea - tures, high and low, let your prais - es end - less - ly flow.

Words: Jim Strathdee 1976
Music: Jim Strathdee 1976; piano arr. Jean Strathdee 1976
Words and music copyright © 1977 Desert Flower Music. Used by permission.

FORNEY
Irregular

Eternal, Unchanging, We Sing

223

1 E - ter - nal, Un - chang - ing, we sing to your praise:
2 A - gain we re - joice in the world you have made,
3 We praise you for Je - sus, our Mas - ter and Lord,

your mer - cies are end - less, and righ - teous your ways;
your might - y cre - a - tion in beau - ty ar - rayed,
the might of his Spir - it, the truth of his word,

your ser - vants pro - claim the re - nown of your name
we thank you for life, and we praise you for joy,
his com - fort in sor - row, his pa - tience in pain,

who rules ov - er all and is ev - er the same.
for love and for hope that no power can de - stroy.
the faith sure and stead - fast that Je - sus shall reign.

Words: R.B.Y. Scott 1938
Music: Welsh folk song, arr. John Roberts (Henllan) in Caniadau y Cyssegr 1839
Words copyright © 1988 Emmanuel College, Toronto, Canada.

ST DENIO
11 11 11 11
Alt. tune: St. Basil

224

Sing a Happy Hallelujah

1 Sing a hap-py hal-le-lu-jah, sing it out with
2 We're the proof of God's good hu-mour, we're the twin-kle
3 Sar-ah laughed at God's good tim-ing, Ma-ry sang and
4 Ev-ery day sing hal-le-lu-jah! We are loved, though

Vv. 1, 4 hal-le-lu-jah,

heart and style, we're the e-cho of God's laugh-ter,
in God's eye, made to shine, re-flect the glo-ry,
Da-vid danced, Je-sus smiled and hugged the chil-dren,
so ab-surd, hu-man, fool-ish, cho-sen peo-ple,

Vv. 1, 4 hal-le-lu-jah,

Refrain (Unison)

we're the im-age of God's smile.
giv-en light and space to fly.
so is life for us en-hanced.
God still takes us at our word!

Hal-le-lu-jah,

all cre-a-tion, hal-le-lu-jah, ev-ery-one!

Words: *Shirley Erena Murray 1989*
Music: *Colin Gibson 1989*
Words and music copyright © *1992 Hope Publishing Company.*

STANSFIELD
8 7 8 7 with refrain

Hal - le - lu - jah, all cre - a - tion, hal - le - lu - jah ev - ery - one!

We Praise You for the Sun   225

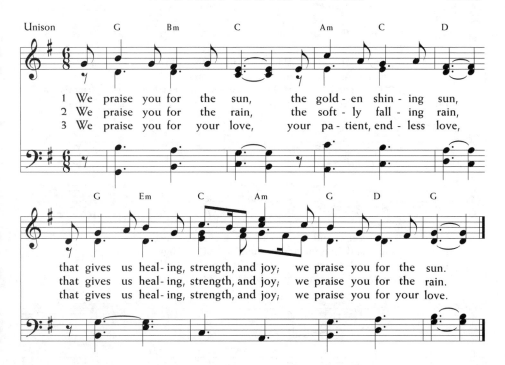

1 We praise you for the sun, the gold - en shin - ing sun,
2 We praise you for the rain, the soft - ly fall - ing rain,
3 We praise you for your love, your pa - tient, end - less love,

that gives us heal - ing, strength, and joy; we praise you for the sun.
that gives us heal - ing, strength, and joy; we praise you for the rain.
that gives us heal - ing, strength, and joy; we praise you for your love.

226

For the Beauty of the Earth

1 For the beau - ty of the earth, for the
2 For the beau - ty of each hour of the
3 For the joy of hu - man love, bro - ther,
4 For each per - fect gift sub - lime to our

glo - ry of the skies, for the love which from our
day and of the night, hill and vale, and tree and
sis - ter, par - ent, child, friends on earth, and friends a -
race so free - ly given, gra - ces hu - man and di -

birth o - ver and a - round us lies,
flower, sun and moon, and stars of light,
bove, for all gen - tle thoughts and mild,
vine, flowers of earth and buds of heaven,

God of

all, to you we raise this our hymn of grate - ful praise.

Words: Folliott Sandford Pierpoint 1864, alt.
Music: David Evans 1927
Music used by permission of Oxford University Press.

LUCERNA LAUDONIAE
7 7 7 7 7 7
Alt. tune: Dix

For the Fruit of All Creation

227

1 For the fruit of all cre - a - tion, thanks be to God.
2 In the just re - ward of la - bour, God's will is done.
3 For the har - vests of the Spir - it, thanks be to God.

For the gifts to ev - ery na - tion, thanks be to God.
In the help we give our neigh - bour, God's will is done.
For the good we all in - her - it, thanks be to God.

For the plough - ing, sow - ing, reap - ing, si - lent growth while we are
In our world - wide task of car - ing for the hun - gry and de -
For the won - ders that as - tound us, for the truths that still con -

sleep - ing, fu - ture needs in earth's safe - keep - ing, thanks be to God.
spair - ing, in the har - vests we are shar - ing, God's will is done.
found us, most of all that love has found us, thanks be to God.

Words: Fred Pratt Green 1970
Music: Welsh folk melody ca. 1784
Words copyright © 1970 Hope Publishing Company.

AR HYD Y NOS
8 4 8 4 8 8 8 4
Alt. setting: 433

228 Sing Praises to God

1 Sing prais - es to God! Sing praise in the height;
2 Sing prais - es to God! Sing praise up - on earth,
3 Sing prais - es to God, all things that give sound;
4 Sing prais - es to God! Thanks - giv - ing and song

re - joice in God's word, blest an - gels of light;
in tune - ful ac - cord, you saints of new birth;
each ju - bi - lant chord re - e - cho a - round;
be ev - er out - poured, all a - ges a - long:

high heav - ens, re - call - ing by whom you were made,
praise God, who has brought you rich grace from a - bove,
loud or - gans, your glo - ry tell out in deep tone,
for love in cre - a - tion, for hope spread a - broad,

come, of - fer your wor - ship in bright - ness ar - rayed.
and show - ered your life with a - bun - dance of love.
and trum - pets, the sto - ry of what God has done.
for grace of sal - va - tion, sing prais - es to God.

Words: Henry Williams Baker 1875, et al.
Music: C. Hubert H. Parry 1887

LAUDATE DOMINUM
10 10 11 11

God of the Sparrow

* last time

Words: Jaroslav J. Vajda 1983
Music: Carl F. Schalk 1983
Words copyright © 1983 Jaroslav Vajda. Music copyright © 1983 G.I.A. Publications, Inc.

ROEDER
5 4 6 7 7

230 Heaven Is Singing for Joy

1 Heav-en is sing-ing for joy, hal-le-lu - - jah!
2 Heav-en is sing-ing for joy, hal-le-lu - - jah!
3 Heav-en is sing-ing for joy, hal-le-lu - - jah!

for in your life and in mine is shin-ing the glo-ry of God.
for your life and mine u-nite in the love of our God.
for your life and mine will al-ways bear wit-ness to God.

Hal - le - lu - jah! Hal - le - lu - jah!

Hal - le - lu - jah! Hal - le - lu - jah!

I Sing the Mighty Power

1 I sing the might-y power of God that made the moun-tains rise,
2 I sing the good-ness of the One who filled the earth with food;
3 There's not a plant or flower be-low but makes your glo-ries known;

that spread the flow-ing seas a-broad, and built the loft-y skies.
who formed the crea-tures with a word, and then pro-nounced them good.
and clouds a-rise, and tem-pests blow, by or-der from your throne;

I sing the wis-dom that or-dained the sun to rule the day;
O God, your won-ders are dis-played where-'er I turn my eye;
while all that bor-rows life from you is ev-er in your care,

the moon shines full at God's com-mand and all the stars o-bey.
if I sur-vey the ground I tread, or gaze up-on the sky!
and ev-ery-where that I may be, you, God, are pres-ent there.

Words: Isaac Watts 1715, alt.
Music: attrib. Franz Joseph Haydn ca. 1790

HAYDN
8 6 8 6 D

232 Joyful, Joyful We Adore You

Descant

4 Mor - tals join the chor - us, hal - le - lu - jah!

Hal - le - lu - jah! Love is reign - ing o'er us,

join - ing peo - ple hand in hand. Hal - le - lu - jah!

1 Joy - ful, joy - ful we a - dore you, God of glo - ry,
2 All your works with joy sur - round you, earth and heaven re -
3 You are giv - ing and for - giv - ing, ev - er bless - ing,
4 Mor - tals join the might - y cho - rus which the morn - ing

life and love; hearts un - fold like flowers be - fore you,
flect your rays, stars and an - gels sing a - round you,
ev - er blest, well - spring of the joy of liv - ing,
stars be - gan; God's own love is reign - ing o'er us,

open - ing to the sun a - bove. Melt the clouds of
cen - tre of un - bro - ken praise. Field and for - est,
o - cean depth of hap - py rest! Source of grace and
join - ing peo - ple hand in hand. Ev - er sing - ing,

Words: Henry van Dyke 1907, alt.   *HYMN TO JOY*
Music: Ludwig van Beethoven 1824; adapt. Edward Hodges 1864; desc. Hal Hopson 1979   8 7 8 7 D
Descant copyright © 1979 G.I.A. Publications, Inc.

Hal - le - lu - jah!	Hal	-	le - lu -	jah!					

D G D B Em A7 D

sin and sad - ness, drive the gloom of doubt a - way;
vale and moun - tain, flow - ery mead - ow, flash - ing sea,
fount of bless - ing, let your light up - on us shine;
march we on - ward, vic - tors in the midst of strife;

Joy - ful mu - sic leads us sun - ward in the tri - umph song of life.

G C G D7 G

giv - er of im - mor - tal glad - ness, fill us with the light of day.
chant - ing bird and flow - ing foun - tain, sound their praise e - ter - nal - ly.
teach us how to love each oth - er, lift us to the joy di - vine.
joy - ful mu - sic leads us sun - ward in the tri - umph song of life.

À mon Dieu, je me confie   233

1 À mon Dieu, je me confie;
   sa clémence est infinie;
   ta pensée, ô Dieu d'amour,
   est fidèle pour toujours.

2 La lumière radieuse
   est ton oeuvre merveilleuse;
   ta pensée, ô Dieu d'amour,
   est fidèle pour toujours.

3 Tu consoles, tu pardonnes;
   ta bonté, sur tous, rayonne;

   ta pensée, ô Dieu d'amour,
   est fidèle pour toujours.

4 Par ta grâce prévenante,
   l'âme s'ouvre à l'espérance;
   ta pensée, ô Dieu d'amour,
   est fidèle pour toujours.

5 Tout à toi je me confie;
   ta clémence est infinie;
   ta pensée, ô Dieu d'amour,
   est fidèle pour toujours.

(The music appears on the following page.)

Words: Suzanne Bidgrain 1924, rév.

MONKLAND
8 8 7 7

234　Let Us with a Gladsome Mind

Descant

5 Let us then with glad-some mind, praise our God for-

1 Let us with a glad-some mind　praise our God, for-
2 God, with all-com-mand-ing might,　filled the new-made
♦ 3 God has with a gra-cious eye　looked up-on our
4 All things liv-ing God does feed,　with full mea-sure
5 Let us then with glad-some mind,　praise our God, for-

ev - er kind; whose great mer - cies

ev - er kind; whose great mer - cies
world with light; for God's mer - cies
♦ mis - er - y; for God's mer - cies
meets their need; for God's mer - cies
ev - er kind; whose great mer - cies

still en-dure, ev - er faith-ful, ev - er sure.

still en-dure, ev - er faith - ful, ev - er sure.

Words: *John Milton 1623, alt.*

Music: *attrib. to John Antes ca. 1800; arr. John Lees 1824; adapt. John Wilkes 1861; desc. Craig Sellar Lang*

Descant copyright © Novello and Co., Ltd.

MONKLAND
7 7 7 7

O Worship the King

1 O wor-ship the King, all glo-rious a-bove,
2 O tell of God's might, O sing of God's grace,
♦ 3 The earth with its store of won-ders un-told,
4 Your boun-ti-ful care, what tongue can re-cite?
5 Frail chil-dren of dust, and fee-ble as frail,

O grate-ful-ly sing God's power and God's love;
whose robe is the light, whose can-o-py space,
♦ Al-might-y, your power has found-ed of old;
It breathes in the air, it shines in the light;
in you do we trust, nor find you to fail;

our Shield and De-fend-er, the An-cient of Days,
whose char-iots of wrath the deep thun-der-clouds form,
♦ has stab-lished it fast by a change-less de-cree,
it streams from the hills, it de-scends to the plain,
your mer-cies how ten-der, how firm to the end,

pa-vil-ioned in splen-dour, and gird-ed with praise.
and broad is God's path on the wings of the storm.
♦ and round it has cast, like a man-tle, the sea.
and sweet-ly dis-tills in the dew and the rain.
our Mak-er, De-fend-er, Re-deem-er, and Friend.

Words: Robert Grant 1833
Music: probably by William Croft 1708

HANOVER
10 10 11 11

236 Now Thank We All Our God

1 Now thank we all our God, with heart, and hands, and voic - es,
2 O may this boun - teous God through all our life be near us,
3 All praise and thanks to God for all that has been giv - en,

who won - drous things has done, in whom this world re - joic - es;
with ev - er joy - ful hearts and bless - ed peace to cheer us,
the Son, and Spir - it blest who dwell in high - est heav - en,

who from our moth - er's arms has blessed us on our way
and keep us strong in grace, and guide us when per - plexed,
the one e - ter - nal God, whom heaven and earth a - dore;

with count - less gifts of love, and still is ours to - day.
and free us from all ill in this world and the next.
for thus it was, is now, and shall be ev - er - more.

Words: Martin Rinckart ca. 1636, English trans. Catherine Winkworth 1858, alt.,
French trans. Flossette du Pasquier 1950, rév.
Music: Johann Crüger 1647

NUN DANKET
6 7 6 7 6 6 6 6

Louons le Créateur

1 Louons le Créateur;
chantons à Dieu louanges!
Et joignons notre voix
au concert de ses anges!
Dès les bras maternels
il nous a protégés
et, jusqu'au dernier jour,
il est notre berger.

2 Loué soit notre Dieu!
Que notre vie entière
tous nous vivions joyeux
sous le regard du Père;

qu'il nous tienne en sa grâce
et nous guide toujours,
nous garde du malheur
par son unique amour.

3 De ce Dieu trois fois saint
qui règne dans la gloire,
chrétiens, empressons-nous
de chanter la victoire;
c'est lui qui nous unit
et nous fait retrouver
le chemin de l'amour
et de la liberté.

Let Us Praise the God of Truth 237

Let us praise the God of truth, let us praise the
Ren - dons grâ - ce au Dieu saint, ren - dons grâ - ce
Ba ni ngye - ti Ba Ya - we, ba ni ngye - ti

God of peace, let us praise the God of love. A - men.
au Dieu juste, ren - dons grâ - ce au Dieu bon. A - men.
Ba Ya - we, ba ni ngye - ti Ba Ya - we. A - men.

Refrain

Hal - le - lu - jah. Hal - le - lu - jah. Hal - le - lu - jah. A - men.

Words: traditional Cameroon (Mungaka); English and French adapt. R. Gerald Hobbs 1987
Music: traditional Cameroon; arr. Darryl Nixon 1987
English and French translations and arrangement copyright © 1987 Songs for a Gospel People.

BA NI NGYETI
Irregular with hallelujahs

238 O Lord My God
(How Great Thou Art)

1 O Lord my God, when I in awe-some won-der
2 When through the woods and for-est glades I wan-der,
3 But when I think that God, his Son not spar-ing,
4 When Christ shall come with shout of ac-cla-ma-tion

con-sid-er all the works thy hand hath made,
I hear the birds sing sweet-ly in the trees;
sent him to die, I scarce can take it in,
and take me home, what joy shall fill my heart!

I see the stars, I hear the might-y thun-der,
when I look down from loft-y moun-tain gran-deur
that on the cross, my bur-den glad-ly bear-ing,
Then I shall bow in hum-ble ad-o-ra-tion

thy power through-out the u-ni-verse dis-played.
and hear the brook and feel the gen-tle breeze.
he bled and died to take a-way my sin.
and there pro-claim, "My God, how great thou art!"

Words: Carl Gustav Boberg ca. 1885; English trans. Stuart K. Hine ca. 1939, rev. 1949; French tr. unknown   O STORE GUD
Music: Swedish melody; arr. Stuart K. Hine 1949   Irregular with refrain
English words and arrangement copyright © 1953 [1981] Renewal by Manna Music, Inc.

Refrain

Then sings my soul, my Sav-iour God, to thee, How great thou art!

How great thou art! Then sings my soul, my Sav-iour God, to

thee, How great thou art! How great thou art!

1 Dieu tout-puissant, quand mon coeur considère
tout l'univers créé par ton pouvoir,
le ciel d'azur, les éclairs, la tonnerre,
le matin clair et les ombres du soir,

Refrain
De tout mon être alors s'élève un chant:
Dieu tout-puissant, comme tu es grand! (bis)

2 Quand par les bois ou la forêt profonde
j'erre et m'entends tous les oiseaux chanter,
quand sur les monts la source avec son onde
livre au zéphyr son chant doux et léger,

Refrain

3 Mais quand je songe au sublime mystère,
qu'un Dieu si grand a pu penser à moi,
que son cher Fils est devenu mon frère,
et que je suis l'héritier du grand Roi,

Refrain

4 Quand mon Sauveur éclatant de lumière
se lèvera de son trône éternel,
et que, laissant les douleurs de la terre,
je pourrai voir les splendeurs de son ciel,

Refrain

Cree: (O Lord My God)

1 Kisemantoo katipeyihcikeyan
Emamaskateyitaman taapwe
Kaositayan kahkiyaw askiiya
Kisokaatsiwin misiwe nokwan.

Refrain
Ninikamon emamicimitan
Kikicaayiwin, kikicaayiwin.
Ninikamon emamicimitan
Kikicaayiwin, kikicaayiwin.

2 Ispi sakaahk mekwac epimoteyan
Nipetawaw piyesiis nikamot
Miina wacihk ohci etapiyane
Niwaapahten siipii pimiciwahk.

Refrain

3 Kikoosis nama kikiimanicihaw
Maaka nikiinipoostamakonan
Asiteyaatikohk mihko kiimekiw
Poonetamakoyahk maciihtiwin.

Refrain

4 Karayst takoteci ispimihk ohci
Nikamiyowaten kiiwetahit
Nikapatapateyimototawaw
Nikawiiten ekicaayiwiyan.

Refrain

Words: Cree trans. unknown

Ojibway: (O Lord My God)

1 N'ge zha Mun e doom, pe che me
quain duh mon suh,
Nahg duh waind mon, a zhe kwa taum
gooz yun;
Nuh wob mog nung oog, noond wog
nim keeg bah shkoom wod,
Wob je gah daig, A zhe kwa taum
gooz yun.

Refrain:
Mee suh n'guh mood, n'je chog nuh
kwa mah gad,
A zhe Q'taum gooz yun, A zhe Q'taum
gooz yun;
Mee suh n'guh mood, n'je chog nuh
kwa mah gad,
A zhe Q'taum gooz yun, A zhe Q'taum
gooz yun.

2 Pah yuh zha yon, o de ba bah yuh nah
kwog,
Noon dwog p'na sheen sug, ewh me
no maunz wod;
Oon zah be yon, o de a d'she yuh
shpaub kog,

Noon don zee beens, n'moosh toon
ewh b'guh mon muk.

Refrain

3 Pe suh ewh m'quand mon, ke be zhe
nonzh wod niwh Gwe Sun,
Che o gooj goz nid, mah suh auzh da
yah t'goong;
K'che naind moowh ning, ke zhe dah
p'non wees ge too win,
Neen je zhob we zhid, mah suh bah
toz win ing.

Refrain

4 Pe, be yod owh Christ, ka gait we
q'taum gwa waim gud,
Pe suh kee wa we zhid, ka gait n'guh
moo je gain dum;
Me suh ewh uh pe, Ge Mah ka noo
kwa twung suh,
Weend mah gah yung, A peech e
shpan dahg zid.

Refrain

Words: Ojibway trans. Stanley Williams

Mohawk: (O Lord My God)

1 Se wen niio, no nen ka non ton nion
    kwas,
  Se snon sa ke tsi niio ie ron ni,
  iah kwat ka thos tsi tes kwas wah the
    ten ni
  sa sats ten se ra te ioh re ni on.

Refrain:
  A kwa tonn hets ten sa ri wah kwa se
  Tsi ni sa ia, tah ne ra kwa.
  A kwa tonn hets ten sa ri wah kwa se
  Tsi ni sa ia, tah ne ra kwa.

2 No nen tho non I ke tsi ioh non te
    nion,
  ent kat ka tho, tsi niio ne ra kwa,
  ioh kwi ro ton tsi tha kon ti ren no
    ton
  wa ka thon te, oh neh kah tsi kon
    neh.

Refrain

3 No nen ke hia ras shon kwa wi ro ien
    ha,
  tho ten nie ton ken tho na renn he ie
  ro nek kwa on o ni son kwen he iah
    se,
  so ra ke wen, ion kwa ri wa ne ren.

Refrain

4 No nen ten tre ien ses ha tsia ten ha
    we,
  en ka na neh na tonn ha ra tse ra
  tsi nien hen we en hi sen na ien he
    ke,
  Se wen niio, sa ia tah ne ra kwa.

Refrain

Words: Mohawk trans. Josephine S. (Konwenne) Day 1905

O Great Spirit 239

Words: Doreen Clellamin 1993, adapt. 1994
Music: Doreen Clellamin 1993
Words and music adapted by Doreen Clellamin from a song by Nuxalk Young People. Copyright © 1994 Doreen Clellamin.

O GREAT SPIRIT
Irregular

240 Praise, My Soul, the God of Heaven

Unison

1 Praise, my soul, the God of heav - en, glad of heart your car-ols raise;

ran - somed, healed, re - stored, for - giv - en, who, like me, should sing God's praise.

Hal - le - lu - jah! Hal - le - lu - jah! Praise the Mak - er all your days!

*Harmony

2 Praise God for the grace and fa - vour shown our fore - bears in dis - tress;

God is still the same for - ev - er, slow to chide and swift to bless.

* Hymn can be sung throughout using harmony of verse 2.

Words: Henry Francis Lyte 1834, alt.; adapt. vv. 1–3, 5 Ecumenical Women's Center 1974   LAUDA ANIMA (PRAISE MY SOUL)
Music: John Goss 1869; desc. W. Herbert Belyea 1975   8 7 8 7 8 7
Descant copyright © 1975 Herbert Belyea.

Hal - le - lu - jah! Hal - le - lu - jah! Sing our Mak - er's faith - ful - ness!

Unison

3 Like a lov - ing par - ent car - ing, God knows well our fee - ble frame;

glad - ly all our bur - dens bear - ing, still to count - less years the same.

Hal - le - lu - jah! Hal - le - lu - jah! All with - in me, praise God's name!

4 Frail as sum - mer's flower we flour - ish; blows the wind and it is gone;

but, while mor - tals rise and per - ish, God en - dures un - chang - ing on.

Hal - le - lu - jah! Hal - le - lu - jah! Praise the high e - ter - nal one.

Descant

5 An - gels, teach us ad - or - a - tion, you be - hold God face to face;

5 An - gels, teach us ad - or - a - tion, you be - hold God face to face;

sun and moon and all cre - a - tion, dwell - ers all in time and space.

sun and moon and all cre - a - tion, dwell - ers all in time and space.

O praise God! O praise God! Praise with us the God of grace!

Hal - le - lu - jah! Hal - le - lu - jah! Praise with us the God of grace!

Oh, Sing to Our God

241

1 Oh, sing to our God, oh, sing out a new song. Oh, sing to our
2 Oh, dance for our God and blow all the trum-pets. Oh, dance for our
3 Oh, shout to our God, who gave us the Spir-it. Oh, shout to our

1 Oh, sing to our God, Oh,
2 Oh, dance for our God. Oh,
3 Oh, shout to our God. Oh,

God, oh, sing out a new song. Oh, sing to our God, oh,
God and blow all the trum-pets. Oh, dance for our God and
God, who gave us the Spir-it. Oh, shout to our God, who

sing to our God, Oh, sing, Oh
dance for our God. Oh, dance and
shout to our God. Oh, shout God

sing out a new song. Oh, sing to our God. Oh, sing to our God.
blow all the trum-pets. And sing to our God, and sing to our God.
gave us the Spir-it. Oh, sing to our God. Oh, sing to our God.

Words: Brazilian folk song; trans. Gerhard Cartford, alt.
Music: Brazilian folk song; arr. John L. Bell 1991

CANTAD AL SEÑOR
5 6 5 6 5 6 5 5

242
Let All Things Now Living

1 Let all things now living a song of thanksgiving to
2 By law God enforces, the stars in their courses and

God our Creator triumphantly raise; who fashioned and
sun in its orbit obediently shine.

made us, protected and stayed us, by guiding us on to the
mountains, the rivers and fountains, the depths of the ocean pro-

Words: Katherine K. Davis 1939, alt.
Music: Welsh folk melody; desc. Katherine K. Davis 1938
Words and descant copyright © 1939, 1966 E. C. Schirmer Music Co.

THE ASH GROVE
6 6 11 6 6 11 D
Alt. setting: 481

243

Praise to God

1 Praise to God, praise to God, for the green-ness of the trees,
2 Thanks to God, thanks to God, for the gift of friends in Christ,
3 Glo-ry to God, glo-ry to God, for the grace of Christ, the Son,

for the beau-ty of the flowers, for the blue-ness of the sky,
for the church, our house of faith, for the gift of won-drous love,
for the love of par-ent God, for the com-fort and the strength

for the great-ness of the sea. Praise to God, praise to God,
for the gift of end-less grace. Thanks to God, thanks to God,
of the Spir-it, ho-ly God. Glo-ry to God, glo-ry to God,

now and for - ev - er - more.
now and for - ev - er - more.
now and for - ev - er - more.

Words: Nobuaki Hanaoka 1980, alt.
Music: Traditional Japanese melody, arr. David Kai 1994

SAKURA
Irregular

Sing Your Praise to God Eternal

244

1 Sing your praise to God e-ter-nal, sing your praise to God the Son,
2 Join the praise of ev-ery crea-ture, sing with sing-ing birds at dawn;
3 Praise God on our days of glad-ness for the sum-mons to re-joice;

sing your praise to God the Spir-it, liv-ing and for-ev-er One.
when the stars shine forth at night-fall, hear their heav-enly an-ti-phon.
praise God in our times of sad-ness for the calm, con-sol-ing voice.

God has made us, God has blessed us, God has called us to be true.
Praise God for the light of sum-mer, au-tumn glor-ies, win-ter snows,
God our Ma-ker, strong and lov-ing, Christ our Sav-iour, Lead-er, Lord,

God rules ov-er all cre-a-tion, dai-ly mak-ing all things new.
for the com-ing of the spring-time and the life of all that grows.
liv-ing God, Cre-a-tor Spir-it, be your ho-ly name a-dored!

Words: R. B. Y. Scott 1964, alt.
Music: Welsh melody

ARFON *(major)*
8 7 8 7 D

245 Praise the Lord with the Sound of Trumpet

1 Praise the Lord with the sound of trum-pet, praise the Lord with the harp and lute, praise the Lord with the gen-tle-sound-ing flute. Praise the Lord in the field and for-est, praise the Lord in the cit-y square, praise the Lord an-y-time and an-y-where.

2 Praise the Lord with the crash-ing cym-bal, praise the Lord with the pipe and string, praise the Lord with the joy-ful songs you sing. Praise the Lord on a week-day morn-ing, praise the Lord on a Sun-day noon, praise the Lord by the light of sun or moon.

Words: Natalie Sleeth 1975
Music: Natalie Sleeth 1975
Words and music copyright © 1976 Hinshaw Music, Inc.

PRAISE THE LORD
Irregular

246

Shout for God

1 Shout for God! *(Shout for God!) Make a hap-py sound! (Make a hap-py sound!) Clap for God! (Clap for God!) God is all a-round!
2 Hush for God! (Hush for God!) Let the qui-et sing. (Let the qui-et sing.) Wait for God. (Wait for God.) Deep-est feel-ings bring.
3 Sing for God! (Sing for God!) Sing a pleas-ant song. (Sing a pleas-ant song.) Work for God. (Work for God.) Good re-pla-ces wrong.
4 Praise our God! (Praise our God!) Care for all God's friends! (Care for all God's friends!) Love our God! (Love our God!) God's love nev-er ends!

* May be sung with a leader beginning each phrase and the congregation responding.

Words: Walter Farquharson 1984
Music: Ron Klusmeier 1985
Words copyright © 1984 Walter Farquharson. Music copyright © 1985 Ron Klusmeier.

VINK
Irregular

(God   is   all   a - round!)
(Deep - est   feel - ings   bring.)
(Good   re - pla - ces   wrong.)
(God's   love   nev - er

ends!)   God's   love   nev - er   ends!

Jubilate Deo

247

Ju - bi - la - te De - o, Ju - bi - la - te De - o. Hal - le - lu - jah.

Words: trad. liturgical text
Music: Michael Praetorius

248

When Long before Time

1 When long be - fore time and the worlds were be - gun,
2 ...the si - lence was bro - ken when God sang the Song,
3 The sounds of the crea - tures were one with their Lord's,
4 Though, down through the a - ges, the Song dis - ap - peared,

when there was no earth and no sky and no sun,
and light pierced the dark - ness and rhy - thm be - gan,
their har - mon - ies sweet and be - fit - ting the Word;
its har - mon - ies bro - ken and al - most un - heard,

and all was deep si - lence and night reigned su - preme,
and with its first birth - cries cre - a - tion was born,
the Sing - er was pleased as the earth sang the Song,
the Sing - er comes to us to sing it a - gain,

and e - ven our Mak - er had on - ly a dream...
and crea - ture - ly voi - ces sang praise to the morn.
the choir of the crea - tures re - ech - oed it long.
our God - Is - with - Us in the world now as then.

Words: Peter Davison 1981
Music: Peter Davison 1981, arr. George Black 1981

THE SINGER AND THE SONG
11 11 11 11

5 The Light has returned as it came once before,
   the Song of the Lord is our own song once more;
   so let us all sing with one heart and one voice
   the Song of the Singer in whom we rejoice.

6 To you, God the Singer, our voices we raise,
   to you, Song Incarnate, we give all our praise,
   to you, Holy Spirit, our life and our breath,
   be glory for ever, through life and through death.

Rejoice in the Lord Always 249

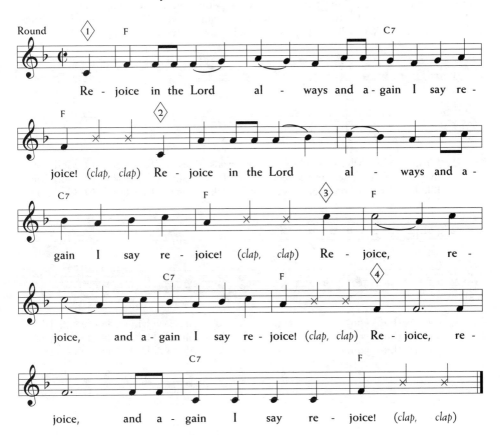

Words: traditional, anon.
Music: traditional, anon.

REJOICE IN THE LORD
Irregular

250   O God of Matchless Glory

1 O God of match-less glo - ry, of all sur-pass-ing
2 With Wis-dom as your part - ner you formed the earth and
3 Your word gives life for - ev - er; our fear of death is

worth, you fill the world with won - der; you bring the stars to
sea; and still she calls the sim - ple, "Be wise and learn from
stilled. With liv - ing bread and wa - ter our deep-est need is

birth. To whom shall we sing prais - es? To whom, O God, but
me." Who else gives rest in la - bour? Who else, O God, but
filled. To whom shall we go seek - ing? To whom, O God, but

Refrain

you? (but you?) Hal - le-lu - jah! Hal - le-lu - jah!
you? (but you?) Hal - le-lu - jah! Hal - le-lu - jah!
you? (but you?) Hal - le-lu - jah! Hal - le-lu - jah!

Words: Ruth Duck 1989
Music: Ruth Watson Henderson 1995
Words copyright © 1992 G.I.A. Publications, Inc. Music copyright © 1995 Ruth Watson Henderson.

HASTINGS
7 6 7 6 7 6 *with refrain*

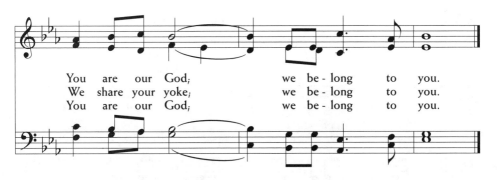

You are our God;   we be - long to you.
We share your yoke;   we be - long to you.
You are our God;   we be - long to you.

God Created Heaven and Earth   251

Unison

1 God cre - a - ted heaven and earth, all things per - fect
2 Let us praise God's mer - cy great, all our needs that
3 God is one, will ev - er be: i - dols are mere
4 But God's grace be - yond com - pare saves us all from

brought to birth;   God's great power made
love a - wait;   God, who fash - ions
van - i - ty;   hand - made gods of
death's de - spair;   so earth's crea - tures

dark and light, earth re - volv - ing day and night.
all that lives, to each one a bless - ing gives.
wood and clay can - not help us when we pray.
small and great give thanks for that bless - ed state.

Words: Taiwanese hymn; trans. Boris Anderson and Clare Anderson 1981   TOA-SIA
Music: Pi-po melody; harm. I-to Loh 1963, rev. 1982   7 7 7 7

252

Jaya Ho
(Victory Hymn)

Refrain

Ja-ya ho   a-ho

*Ja-ya ho   ja-ya ho   ja-ya ho   ja-ya ho   ja-ya ho   ja-ya ho

ja-ya ho   a-ho   ja-ya ho   a-ho   ja-ya ho   a-ho

ja-ya ho   ja-ya ho   ja-ya ho   ja-ya ho   ja-ya ho   ja-ya ho   ho

Fine

ja-ya ja-ya ja-ya ja-ya ho   ja-ya ja-ya ja-ya ja-ya ho.

Leader 1 We come be-fore thee,   O Great and Ho-ly,
2 Lord, let   us see thee, grant us   a vi-sion!
1 Te-re   sa-na mukh ham hain   a-te.

All 1   O Great and Ho-ly.
2   Grant us a vi-sion!
1   Ham hain   a-te.

* pronounced Já-hee-yah

Words: Hindi, anon., trans. Katherine R. Rohrbough 1958; phonetic transcr. I-to Loh 1988
Music: Traditional Hindi melody; arr. Victor Sherring 1955
Phonetic transcription copyright © 1989 The United Methodist Publishing House.

VICTORY HYMN
10 5 10 5 11 11 with refrain

Leader we bow our heads to thee, Great and Ho - ly,
Sins and de - ni - als, dear Lord, for - give us.
Cha ra no may hain shi - sha na - va - te.

All O Great and Ho - ly.
Dear Lord, for - give us.
Shi - sha na - va - te.

Leader low at thy feet we bow in qui - et rev - erence, then sing thy
Take us and keep us in thy strong pro - tec - tion, safe in thy
Ja - ya ja - ya te - ri ham hain ga - te. Ja - ya ja - ya

prais - es, ev - er - more re - peat - ing:
ref - uge, we will sing thy prais - es:
te - ri ham hain ga - te.

All Ja - ya ja - ya ja - ya ja - ya

D.S.

ho ja - ya ja - ya ja - ya ja - ya ho. Ja - ya

ja - ya ho Ja - ya

253

Sing Your Joy

Unison

1 Sing your joy, pro - claim God's glo - ry!
2 All the earth is filled with re - joic - ing,
3 May we learn to be - come your king - dom,
4 Light our way, O God of the liv - ing,

Rise and sing, the morn - ing has come!
light and life, the won - der of God!
may we be your kind - ness and truth!
may we learn to see with new eyes!

Bless our God and praise all cre - a - tion;
Christ has tri - umphed! Ris - en for ev - er!
Love is our call - ing, gift of your pres - ence;
Je - sus the Lord, our pow - er and prom - ise;

Words: David Haas 1987
Music: David Haas 1987
Words and music copyright © 1987 G.I.A. Publications, Inc.

SUMMIT HILL
8 8 9 9 8

* During Lent replace "Hallelujah!" with "O praise our God!".

254   Songs of Praise the Angels Sang

1 Songs of praise the an - gels sang, heaven with hal - le -
2 Songs of praise a - woke the morn when the Prince of
3 Heaven and earth must pass a - way, songs of praise shall
4 And will peo - ple si - lent be till that glo - rious

lu - jahs rang, when cre - a - tion
Peace was born; songs of praise a -
crown that day; God will make new
day they see? No, the church de -

was be - gun, when God spoke and it was done.
rose when he cap - tive led cap - tiv - i - ty.
heavens and earth, songs of praise shall hail their birth.
lights to raise psalms and hymns and songs of praise.

5 Saints below, with heart and voice,
  still in songs of praise rejoice;
  learning here, by faith and love,
  songs of praise to sing above.

6 Hymns of glory, songs of praise,
  blessed God, to you we raise.
  Jesus, Saviour, Living Word,
  with the Spirit be adored.

Words: James Montgomery 1819, alt.
Music: Scheffler's Heilige Seelenlust 1657

CULBACH
7 7 7 7

The Living God Be Praised

1 The liv-ing God be praised, who reigns en-throned a - bove,
2 Your spi - rit still flows free, high surg-ing where it will;
3 You have e - ter - nal life im - plant-ed in the soul;

an - cient of ev - er - last - ing days, and God of love.
in pro - phet's words you spoke of old and you speak still.
your love shall be our strength and stay, while a - ges roll.

Je - ho - vah, great I Am! By earth and heaven con - fessed,
Es - tab-lished is your law, and change-less it shall stand,
We praise you, liv - ing God! We praise your ho - ly name;

we bow be - fore your ho - ly name, for - ev - er blest.
in - scribed up - on the hu - man heart, on sea, or land.
the first, the last, be - yond all thought, and still the same.

Words: Daniel ben Judah 1404; trans. Max Landsberg and Newton Mann 1885, alt.
Music: Hebrew melody; adapt. Thomas Olivers and Meyer Lyon 1770

LEONI
6 6 8 4 D

256   O God beyond All Praising

Unison

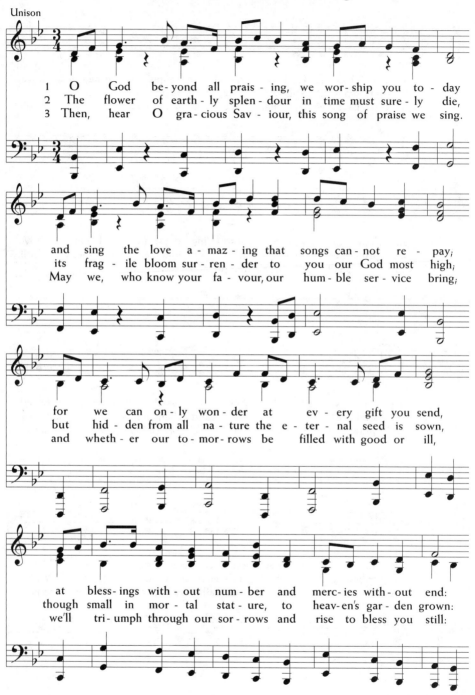

1 O God be-yond all prais - ing, we wor-ship you to - day
2 The flower of earth - ly splen - dour in time must sure - ly die,
3 Then, hear O gra - cious Sav - iour, this song of praise we sing.

and sing the love a - maz - ing that songs can-not re - pay;
its frag - ile bloom sur - ren - der to you our God most high;
May we, who know your fa - vour, our hum - ble ser - vice bring;

for we can on - ly won - der at ev - ery gift you send,
but hid - den from all na - ture the e - ter - nal seed is sown,
and wheth - er our to - mor - rows be filled with good or ill,

at bless-ings with - out num - ber and merc - ies with - out end:
though small in mor - tal stat - ure, to heav-en's gar - den grown:
we'll tri - umph through our sor - rows and rise to bless you still:

Words: Michael Perry ca. 1982, alt.
Music: Gustav Theodor Holst 1916
Words copyright © 1982 Hope Publishing Company.

THAXTED
13 13 13 13 13 13

we   lift   our hearts be - fore you and wait up- on your word,
for   Christ, your gift from heav - en, from death has set us   free,
to   mar - vel   at your beau - ty   and glo - ry in   your ways,

we   hon - our and   a - dore you, our   great and might - y   Lord.
and   we through him are giv - en   the   fi - nal vic - to - ry.
and   make   a   joy - ful du - ty   our   sac - ri - fice of   praise.

Prayer   257

Eternal God,
Light of the minds that know you,
the joy of the hearts that love you
and the strength of the wills that serve you:
grant us so to know you that we may truly love you,
    so to love you that we may fully serve you,
    whom to serve is perfect freedom. Amen.

Augustine of Hippo, 5th-century bishop and theologian, adapt.

And the following…

258

O World of God

Unison

1 O world of God, so vast and strange, pro-found and
2 O world where hu - man life is lived, so strange-ly
3 O world of time's far-stretch-ing years! There was a

won - der - ful and fair, be - yond the ut - most reach of
min - gling joy and pain, so full of e - vil and of
day when time stood still, a cen - tral mo - ment when there

thought but not be - yond our Ma - ker's care! We are not
good, so need - ful that the good shall reign! It is this
rose a cross up - on a cru - el hill;

strang - ers on this earth whirl - ing a - mid the suns of
world that God has loved, and good - ness was its Ma - ker's
death love's power was seen, the mys - ter - y of time re -

space;   we are God's chil - dren, this our home,   with those of
plan,   the prom-ise of   God's tri - umph is   a   hum - ble
vealed,   the wis-dom   of   the ways of God,   the grace through

1, 2

ev - ery clime and   race.
birth in Beth - le - hem.
which our hurt is

3

healed.

Words: R. B. Y. Scott 1965, alt.
Music: C. Hubert H. Parry 1916; harm. Gordon P. S. Jacob
Words copyright © 1988 Emmanuel College, Toronto, Canada. Music copyright © 1916, 1944, 1977 Roberton Publications.
Harmony copyright © G. Schirmer, Inc.

JERUSALEM
8 8 8 8 D
Alt. setting: 682

Prayer   259

You, O God, are mighty forever.
You cause the wind to blow and the rain to fall.
You sustain the living, give life to the dead,
    support the falling, loose those who are bound,
      and keep your faith with those that sleep in the dust.
Who is like unto you, O God of mighty acts?
Praise be to you forever. Amen.

Traditional Jewish prayer (alt.)

260 God Who Gives to Life Its Goodness

1 God who gives to life its good-ness, God cre - a - tor
2 God who fills the earth with beau - ty, God who binds each

of all joy, God who gives to us our free-dom,
friend to friend, God who names us co - cre - a - tors

God who bless - es tool and toy: teach us
God who wills that cha - os end: grant us

now to laugh and praise you, deep with - in your
now cre - a - tive spir - its, minds re - spon - sive

Words: Walter Farquharson 1970, alt.
Music: Cyril Vincent Taylor 1941

Words copyright © 1970 Walter Farquharson. Music copyright © 1942, renewal 1970 Hope Publishing Company.

ABBOT'S LEIGH
8 7 8 7 D

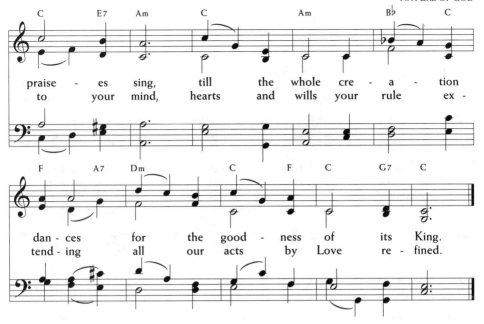

praise - es sing, till the whole cre - a - tion
to your mind, hearts and wills your rule ex -

dan - ces for the good - ness of its King.
tend - ing all our acts by Love re - fined.

C'est un rempart que notre Dieu   261

1 C'est un rempart que notre Dieu,
une invincible armure.
Notre délivrance en tout lieu,
notre défense sûre.
L'ennemi contre nous
redouble de courroux: Vaine colère!
Que pourrait l'adversaire?
L'Éternel détourne ses coups.

pour accabler l'Église,
ta Sion brave les enfers,
sur le rocher assise.
Constant dans son effort,
en vain, avec la mort,
Satan conspire;
pour briser son empire,
il suffit d'un mot du Dieu fort.

2 Seuls, nous bronchons à chaque pas;
notre force est faiblesse;
mais un héros, dans les combats,
pour nous lutte sans cesse.
Quel est ce défenseur?
C'est toi, divin Sauveur,
Dieu des armées;
tes tribus opprimées
connaissent leur libérateur.

4 Dis-le, ce mot victorieux,
dans toutes nos détresses;
répands sur nous du haut des cieux
tes divines largesses.
Qu'on nous ôte nos biens,
qu'on serre nos liens,
que nous importe!
Ta grâce est la plus forte,
et ton royaume est pour les tiens.

3 Que les démons forgent des fers

(The music appears on the following page.)

Words: Trans. Ascan Henri-Théodore Lutteroth 1845, rév.

EIN' FESTE BURG
8 7 8 7 6 6 5 7 8

262   A Mighty Fortress Is Our God

Descant

4 That word above all earth-ly powers,   no thanks to them, a-bid-eth;   the Spir - it and the gifts are ours through Christ, who with us sid-eth;   let goods and kin-dred go,

1 A might-y for-tress is our God, a bul-wark nev-er fail - ing; our help-er sure a - mid the flood of mor - tal ills pre - vail - ing: for still our an-cient foe doth

2 Did we in our own strength con - fide, our striv-ing would be los - ing, were not the right man on our side, the man of God's own choos - ing: dost ask who that may be? Christ

3 And though this world, with dev - ils filled, should threat-en to un-do us, we will not fear, for God hath willed the truth to tri - umph through us: the prince of dark - ness grim, we

4 That word a - bove all earth - ly powers, no thanks to them, a-bid - eth; the Spir - it and the gifts are ours through Christ, who with us sid - eth: let goods and kin-dred go, this

Words: Martin Luther 1529, trans. Frederick H. Hedge 1853

Music: melody Martin Luther 1529, harm. from The New Hymnal for American Youth 1930;
    desc. Scott Withrow

EIN' FESTE BURG
8 7 8 7 6 6 6 6 7

Our God's a Fortress 263

1 Our God's a fortress firm and sure,
a strong defence around us.
With him we know our cause secure,
though griefs and pains surround us.
Our old malicious foe
is set to work us woe:
both force and sly deceit
he'll use for our defeat:
no earthly power can match him.

2 Our human strength alone must fail
when evil's hosts invade us,
yet shall the one true Man prevail,
whom God has sent to aid us.
You ask who that may be:
Christ Jesus, none but he,
Lord Sabaoth alone,
of gods the mighty one—
he must maintain the battle.

3 With demons did this wide world swarm,
all eager to devour us,
we need not fear their threatened harm,
they shall not overpower us.
The leader of our foes,
though fiercely he oppose,
his kingdom shall not last;
for judgement's on him passed —
a simple word shall fell him.

4 That word all hell shall leave to stand,
nor is it by their merit:
the Lord is with us, his right hand
pours out his gifts and Spirit.
Our foes may take our life,
goods, honour, child and wife:
by faith we let them go,
they gain no victory so:
all's ours with Jesus' kingdom.

Words: Martin Luther 1529; trans. Jay Macpherson 1971
Translation copyright © 1971 Jay Macpherson.

EIN' FESTE BURG
8 7 8 7 6 6 6 6 7

264 Immortal, Invisible, God Only Wise

1 Im - mor - tal, in - vis - i - ble, God on - ly wise;
2 Un - rest - ing, un - hast - ing, and si - lent as light,
3 To all, life thou giv - est, to both great and small;
4 Thou reign - est in glo - ry, thou rul - est in light;

in light in - ac - ces - si - ble hid from our eyes;
nor want - ing, nor wast - ing, thou rul - est in might;
in all life thou liv - est, the true life of all;
thine an - gels a - dore thee, all veil - ing their sight;

most bless - ed, most glo - rious, the An - cient of Days,
thy jus - tice like moun - tains high soar - ing a - bove
we blos - som and flour - ish like leaves on the tree,
all praise we would ren - der, O help us to see

al - might - y, vic - to - rious, thy great name we praise.
thy clouds, which are foun - tains of good - ness and love.
then with - er and per - ish; but naught chang - eth thee.
'tis on - ly the splen - dour of light hid - eth thee!

Words: *Walter Chalmers Smith 1867, alt. 1987*
Music: *Welsh folk song, arr. John Roberts (Henllan)* in Caniadau y Cyssegr *1839*

ST DENIO
11 11 11 11

Creating God, Your Fingers Trace

1 Cre - at - ing God, your fin - gers trace
2 Sus - tain - ing God, your hands up - hold
3 Re - deem - ing God, your arms em - brace
4 In - dwell - ing God, your gos - pel claims

the bold de - signs of far - thest space;
earth's mys - teries known or yet un - told;
all now de - spised for creed or race;
one fam - ily with a bil - lion names;

let sun and moon and stars and light
let wa - ters frag - ile blend with air,
let peace, de - scend - ing like a dove,
let ev - ery life be touched by grace

and what lies hid - den praise your might.
en - a - bling life, pro - claim your care.
make known on earth your heal - ing love.
un - til we praise you face to face.

Words: Jeffery W. Rowthorn 1974
Music: adapt. from Franz Joseph Haydn 1798
Words copyright © 1979 The Hymn Society. Used by permission of Hope Publishing Company.

CREATION
8 8 8 8

266   Amazing Grace, How Sweet the Sound

1 A - maz - ing grace, how sweet the sound
2 'Twas grace that taught my heart to fear,
♦ 3 Through man - y dan - gers, toils, and snares,
4 The Lord has prom - ised good to me,
5 When we've been there ten thou - sand years,

that saved *a wretch like me! I once was lost,
and grace my fears re - lieved; how pre - cious did
♦ I have al - read - y come; 'tis grace that brought
this word my hope se - cures; God will my shield
bright shin - ing as the sun, we've no less days

but now am found, was blind, but now I see.
that grace ap - pear the hour I first be - lieved.
♦ me safe thus far, and grace will lead me home.
and por - tion be as long as life en - dures.
to sing God's praise than when we'd first be - gun.

* or "and strengthened"

Words: John Henry Newton *1779, alt.; v. 5 anon., from* A Collection
    of Sacred Ballads *1790*
Music: from Virginia Harmony *1831, adapt. and harm. Edwin O. Excell 1900*

AMAZING GRACE (NEW BRITAIN)
8 6 8 6

French:

1 Grâce infinie de notre Dieu
   qui un jour m'a sauvé:
   J'étais perdu, errant de lieu en lieu
   quand il m'a retrouvé.

2 La vie fut complètement changée
   au moment où j'ai cru.
   Depuis ce jour de tous les dangers,
   sa grâce m'a secouru.

3 Dans mes épreuves et mes labeurs
   suffisante est sa grâce.
   Je peux toujours compter sur sa faveur
   à chaque heure qui passe.

4 Quand nous aurons pendant mille ans
   célébré ses louanges,
   nous pourrons comme au commencement,
   lui offrir nos hommages.

Words: trans. Jacques de Réland   *Translation copyright © Jacques de Réland.*

Cree:

1 Mamaskach sakihiwewin
   Kapimachihiwet
   Pikwataw nikiwaihon
   Anoch maka niwap

2 Aspin kakitapwetaman
   Osawechikewin
   Ki otinam kostachiwin
   Kitapimachihit

3 Ata mechetwaw ayimak
   Nikipepimotan
   Kichi sawachikewinik
   Nika kewetahik

4 Mechet tato askimaka
   Kikipehayanan
   Kitaki nanskomayak
   Kisemanitowit

Translator unknown

Mohawk:

1 Ioh ne ra a kwat ra o ten raht
   ne se wa ah tsia tah kwen
   wa ka a tsia a tah ton ha tie es kwe
   ses ha tsia a tah tsen rion.

2 Ra o ten en raht ne wa kro ri
   iah te se e wak te rons.
   ne sa a ka at ka toh ra o ten en raht
   oni son tah keh tah kwe.

3 Eso te e wa ka to hets ton
   Tsi non ni i iot te ron,
   ra oh o ten en raht se wak ne ren en shon
   ra on ten raht wa ka wi.

4 No nen tho o non ien te wa we
   tsi non te e tsios we te,
   ten tsi i te e wa ri wa a kwa a se
   en tsi te wa sen na ien.

Words: trans. Josephine S. (Konwenne) Day 1978

Ojibway:

1 Kihcishawencikewin
   kaapimaaci' ikoyaan
   Ninkakippiinkwenaapan hsa
   Nookom itahsh niwaap

2 Ninkiihsekis imaa nte 'ink
   Oshawencikewin tahsh
   ninkii 'oncipisaa' nentam
   ehtepweyentamaan

Translator unknown

Inuktitut:

1 Tatamnamiik Saimaninga
  Piulilaurmanga
  Tautungnangaa Naningmanga
  Maanna Tautukpunga

2 Tusarama Saimajumik
  Tatamilauqpunga
  Ajurnirmik tataktunga
  Qaiqulirmanga

3 Iqsinaqtut tuqunaqtut
  Inuvvigijakka
  Qimakpakka pisukpunga
  Qaiqulirmanga

4 Tikinnapku Iqippanga
  Uqautivaangalu,
  "Ajurnitit piijaqpakka
  Qaigit maliklunga."

5 Tatamnamik saimaninga
  Piulilaurmanga,
  Tautungnanga naningmanga
  Maanna tautukpunga

Translator unknown

Chinese:

1 qi miao en dian he deng gan mei,
  she wo shen zhong zui qian;
  wo ceng shi sang jin bei xin hui,
  xia yan jin neng kan jian.

2 jiu shi ci en jiao wo jing wei,
  ye shi wo de an wei,
  chu xin zhi shi ji meng en hui,
  zhen shi he deng bao gui.

3 sui ran dao da guang ming di fang,
  jing li wan gu qian qiu;
  yi ran hao si zui chu jing kuang,
  yong yuan song zhu bu xiu.

Words: trans. Wing-Hee Heyward Wong 1976
Words: transliteration Christopher Cheung 1995

Words copyright © 1977 The Chinese Christian Literature Council, Ltd., Hong Kong.
Transliteration copyright © 1995 Christopher Cheung.

Japanese:

1 Wa-re o-mo   su-ku-i shi,
  ku-shi-ki me-gu-mi,
  ma-yo-i-shi   mi-mo i-ma,
  ta-chi-ka-e-ri-nu.

2 O-so-re o   shin-ko-o ni,
  ka-e-ta-ma-i-shi,
  wa-ga-shu no   mi-me-gu-mi,
  ge-ni-to-o-to-shi.

3 Ku-ru-shi-mi   na-ya-mi-mo,
  ku-shi-ki me-gu-mi,
  kyo-o-ma-de   ma-mo-ri-shi,
  shu-ni-zo ma-ka-sen.

Words: trans. Megumi Hara; transliteration Haruo Harold Aihara, Ethnic Ministries Council, The United Church of Canada 1995
Translation copyright © Sambika Committee, United Church of Christ in Japan. Transliteration copyright © Haruo Harold Aihara

Like a Mighty River Flowing

1 Like a might - y riv - er flow - ing,
2 Like the hills se - rene and e - ven,
◆ 3 Like the sum - mer breez - es play - ing,
4 Like the morn - ing sun as - cend - ed,
5 Like the a - zure o - cean swell - ing,

like a flower in beau - ty grow - ing,
like the cours - ing clouds of heav - en,
◆ like the tall trees soft - ly sway - ing,
like the scents of eve - ning blend - ed,
like the jew - el all ex - cell - ing,

far be - yond all hu - man know - ing
like the heart that's been for - giv - en
◆ like the lips of si - lent pray - ing
like a friend - ship nev - er end - ed
far be - yond our hu - man tell - ing

is the per - fect peace of God.

Words: Michael A. Perry
Music: German carol, 14th century; arr. Ralph Vaughan Williams 1906
Words copyright © 1982 Hope Publishing Company. Arrangement by permission of Oxford University Press.

QUEM PASTORES LAUDAVERE
8 8 8 7

268

Bring Many Names

1 Bring man-y names, beau-ti-ful and good,
2 Strong mo-ther God, work-ing night and day,
3 Warm fa-ther God, hug-ging ev-ery child,
4 Old, ach-ing God, grey with end-less care,

cel - e-brate, in par - a - ble and sto - ry,
plan - ning all the won - ders of cre - a - tion,
feel - ing all the strains of hu - man liv - ing,
calm - ly pierc-ing e - vil's new dis - guis - es,

ho - li - ness in glo - ry, liv-ing, lov - ing God.
set - ting each e - qua - tion, gen - i - us at play:
car - ing and for - giv - ing till we're re-con - ciled:
glad of good sur - pris - es, wis - er than de - spair:

Hail and ho - san - na! Bring man - y names!
Hail and ho - san - na, strong moth - er God!
Hail and ho - san - na, warm fa - ther God!
Hail and ho - san - na, old, ach - ing God! great, liv-ing God!

5 Young, growing God,
  eager, on the move,
  saying no to falsehood
  and unkindness,
  crying out for justice,
  giving all you have:
  Hail and hosanna,
  young, growing God!

6 Great, living God,
  never fully known,
  joyful darkness
  far beyond our seeing,
  closer yet than breathing,
  everlasting home:
  Hail and hosanna,
  great, living God!

Words: Brian Wren 1986; alt. 1993
Music: Carlton R. Young 1987
Words and music copyright ©1989 Hope Publishing Company.

WESTCHASE
9 10 11 9

The Care the Eagle Gives Her Young 269

1 The care the ea - gle gives her young,
2 As when the time to ven - ture comes,
3 And if we flut - ter help - less - ly,

safe in her loft - y nest, is like the ten - der
she stirs them out to flight, so we are pressed to
as fledg - ling ea - gles fall, be - neath us lift God's

love of God for us made man - i - fest.
bold - ly try to strive for dar - ing height.
might - y wings to bear us, one and all.

Words: R. Deane Postlethwaite 1980
Music: American camp meeting melody; harm. Robert G. McCutchan 1935
Words copyright © Marjean Postlethwaite.

CAMPMEETING
8 6 8 6

270
Dear Mother God

1 Dear Moth-er God, your wings are warm a-round us,
2 You call to us, for we are in your im-age.
3 Let not our free-dom scorn the needs of oth-ers —

we are en-fold-ed in your love and care;
We wait on you, the nest is cold and bare;
we climb the clouds un-til our strong heart sings;

safe in the dark, your heart-beat's pulse sur-rounds us,
high o-ver-head your wing-beats call us on-ward.
may we en-fold our sis-ters and our broth-ers,

you call to us, for you are al-ways there.
Filled with your power, we ride the emp-ty air.
till all are strong, till all have ea-gles' wings.

Words: Janet Wootton
Music: Richard Runciman Terry ca. 1933
Words copyright © Stainer & Bell Ltd. Used by permission of Hope Publishing Company.

HIGHWOOD
11 10 11 10

There's a Wideness in God's Mercy

1 There's a wide - ness in God's mer - cy like the wide - ness
2 There is no place where earth's sor - rows are more felt than
3 There is plen - ti - ful re - demp - tion in the blood that
4 Trou - bled souls, why will you scat - ter like a crowd of
5 For the love of God is broad - er than the mea - sures

of the sea; there's a kind - ness in God's jus - tice
up in heaven; there is no place where earth's fail - ings
Christ has shed; there is joy for all the mem - bers
fright - ened sheep? Fool - ish hearts, why will you wan - der
of the mind, and the heart of the E - ter - nal

which is more than lib - er - ty.
have such gra - cious judge - ment given.
in the sor - rows of the Head.
from a love so true and deep?
is most won - der - ful - ly kind.

Words: Frederick William Faber 1854, alt.
Music: Johann Ludwig Steiner 1723

GOTT WILL'S MACHEN
8 7 8 7
Alt. tune: Stuttgart

272 Open Your Ears, O Faithful People

1 O-pen your ears, O faith-ful peo-ple, o-pen your ears and hear God's word. O-pen your hearts, O faith-ful peo-ple, God now speaks to you.

2 They who have ears to hear the mes-sage, they who have ears, now let them hear. They who would learn the way of wis-dom, let them hear God's word.

Descant (2nd time)
God has spo-ken to the peo-ple, hal-le-lu - jah!

Refrain
God has spo-ken to the peo-ple, hal-le-lu - jah!

And those words are words of wis-dom, hal-le-lu - - - - jah!

And those words are words of wis-dom, hal-le-lu - jah! Hal-le-lu-jah! jah!

Words: from The Talmud: "Israel and the Torah are one", English, Willard F. Jabusch 1966, rev. 1985   YISRAEL V'ORAITA
Music: Hasidic melody; harm. Richard Proulx 1984   10 6 10 6 with refrain

The King of Love

1 The King of love my shep-herd is, whose good-ness
2 Where streams of liv-ing wa-ter flow my ran-somed
3 Per-verse and fool-ish oft I strayed; but yet in
4 In death's dark vale I fear no ill with thee, dear
5 Thou spread'st a ta-ble in my sight; thy unc-tion
6 And so through all the length of days thy good-ness

fail-eth nev-er; I noth-ing lack if I am
soul he lead-eth, and where the ver-dant pas-tures
love he sought me, and on his shoul-der gent-ly
Lord, be-side me; thy rod and staff my com-fort
grace be-stow-eth; and O what trans-port of de-
fail-eth nev-er: Good Shep-herd, may I sing thy

his and he is mine for-ev-er.
grow with food ce-les-tial feed-eth.
laid, and home re-joic-ing brought me.
still, thy cross be-fore to guide me.
light from thy pure chal-ice flow-eth!
praise with-in thy house for-ev-er!

Words: Henry Williams Baker 1868
Music: ancient Irish melody, arr. Charles Villiers Stanford 1906
Arrangement used by permission of Oxford University Press

ST COLUMBA
8 7 8 7

274 Your Hand, O God, Has Guided

Descant

5 Your mer-cy will not fail us, nor leave your work un-

Unison

1 Your hand, O God, has guid-ed your flock from age to
2 Your her-alds brought glad tid-ings to great-est as to
♦ 3 Through ma-ny days of dark-ness, through ma-ny scenes of
4 And we, shall we be faith-less? Shall hearts fail, hands hang
5 Your mer-cy will not fail us, nor leave your work un-

done; with your right hand to help us, the

age; the won-drous tale is writ-ten, full
least; they bade them rise, and has-ten to
♦ strife, the faith-ful few fought brave-ly to
down? Shall we e-vade the con-flict and
done; with your right hand to help us, the

vic-tory shall be won; and then, by earth and

clear, on ev-ery page. Our fore-bears owned your
share the heaven-ly feast. And this was all their
♦ guard your peo-ple's life. Their gos-pel of re-
cast a-way our crown? Not so: in God's deep
vic-tory shall be won; and then, by earth and

Words: Edward H. Plumptre 1864
Music: Basil Harwood 1898, desc. William Renwick 1991
Music published by permission of Executors of the late Dr. Basil Harwood. Descant copyright © 1991 William Renwick.

THORNBURY
7 6 7 6 D

heav - en, your name shall be a - dored, and this shall be our

good - ness, and we their deeds re - cord; and both to this bear
teach - ing, in ev - ery deed and word, to all a - like pro-
demp - tion, sin par-doned, earth re - stored, was all in this en-
coun - sels some bet - ter thing is stored; we will main-tain, un-
heav - en, your name shall be a - dored, and this shall be our

an - them: one church, one faith, one Lord.

wit - ness:
claim - ing
fold - ed: one church, one faith, one Lord.
flinch - ing,
an - them:

From God's Hands   275

It is not you who shape God;
   it is God that shapes you.
If then you are the work of God,
   await the hand of the Artist who does all things in due season.
Offer the Potter your heart,
   soft and tractable,
   and keep the form in which the Artist has fashioned you.
Let your clay be moist,
   lest you grow hard and lose
   the imprint of the Potter's fingers.

Irenaeus, 2nd Century

276 O God Who Shaped Creation

Unison

1 O God who shaped cre - a - tion at earth's cha - o - tic dawn,
2 O God, with pain and an - guish a moth - er sees her child
3 Al - though your heart is bro - ken when peo - ple scorn your ways,
4 In mer - cy and com - pas - sion your good - ness is re - vealed;

your word of power was spo - ken, and lo! the dark was gone!
em - bark on dead - end path - ways, al - lur - ing, but de - filed;
you nev - er cease your search - ing through e - vil's tan - gled maze;
with ten - der - ness you touch us, and bro - ken hearts are healed.

You framed us in your im - age, you brought us in - to birth,
so too your heart is bro - ken when hate and lust in - crease,
and when we cease our run - ning, your joys, O God, a - bound
You claim us as your chil - dren, you strip our pride - ful shame;

you blessed our in - fant foot - steps and shared your splen - doured earth.
when worlds you birthed and nur - tured spurn ways that lead to peace.
as of a search - ing wom - an when trea - sured coin is found.
with free - dom born of mer - cy we bless your ho - ly name!

Words: William Watkins Reid Jr. 1987
Music: Eric H. Thiman 1923

STOKESAY CASTLE
7 6 7 6 D

God Is Unique and One

1 God is u - nique and one: Ma - ker, Sus - tain - er, Lord!
2 Love came to earth in Christ, our com - mon life to share,
3 The Ho - ly Spir - it moves peo - ple to trace God's plan;
4 God shall for - ev - er reign, ru - ler of time and space;

Pat - terns of life were spun by that cre - a - tive word.
choos - ing to be the least, will - ing a cross to bear.
such in - spi - ra - tion proves more than the mind can span.
there, in the midst of life, seen in the hu - man face.

Of God's in - ten - tion, love and care we
He died, he rose, that we might live and
Each lis - tening heart is led to find the
We give ex - pres - sion to our creed by

are with grow - ing trust a - ware.
all our love, re - spond - ing, give.
will of God for hu - man - kind.
love in thought, in word and deed.

Words: Fred Kaan 1968
Music: Martin Shaw 1915
Words copyright © 1968 Hope Publishing Company. Music copyright © G. Schirmer, Inc.

LITTLE CORNARD
6 6 6 6 8 8

278 In the Quiet Curve of Evening

1 In the qui-et curve of eve-ning, in the sink-ing of the
2 In the rests be-tween the phras-es, in the cracks be-tween the
3 In the mys-tery of my hun-gers, in the si-lence of my

days, in the silk-y void of dark-ness, you are there.
stars, in the gaps be-tween the mean-ing, you are there.
rooms, in the cloud of my un-know-ing, you are there.

In the lap-ses of my breath-ing, in the space be-tween my ways,
In the melt-ing down of end-ings, in the cool-ing of the sun,
In the emp-ty cave of griev-ing, in the des-ert of my dreams,

in the cra-ter carved by sad-ness, you are there.
in the sol-stice of the win-ter, you are there.
in the tun-nel of my sor-row, you are there.

Words: Julie Howard 1993
Music: Julie Howard 1993, arr. Vera Lyons 1993, alt.
Words and music copyright © 1993 Order of St. Benedict, Inc.

YOU ARE THERE
Irregular with refrain

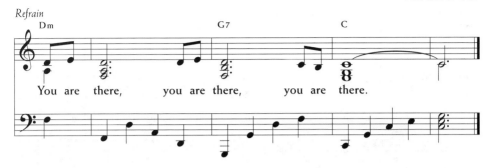

Refrain

You are there, you are there, you are there.

You, God, Are My Firmament 279

Unison

1 You, God, are my firm-a-ment, roof for my head, shel-ter from
2 You, God, are a tower of strength. I shall not fear, I shall not
3 You, God, are my guid-ing light, bea-con from birth, help-ing to

storm, nour-ish-ing bread, ten-der and warm.
fall, know-ing you're near, guard-ian of all. I will give
see, light-ing the earth, en-light-ening me.

(I will give thanks.)

thanks I will sing praise with all of my heart, all of my days.

Words: Miriam Therese Winter 1982
Music: Miriam Therese Winter 1982; accomp. Nan Thompson 1995

FIRMAMENT
7 8 8 8 9

280

Mother and God

Words: Miriam Therese Winter 1987
Music: Miriam Therese Winter 1987; arr. Nan Thompson 1995

MOTHER AND GOD
888888

Not Far beyond the Sea

1 Not far be-yond the sea nor high a-bove the heavens,
2 Root-ed and ground-ed in your love, with saints on earth
3 Help us to press to-ward that mark, and, though our vi-

but ve-ry nigh your voice, O God, is heard.
and saints a-bove we join in full ac-cord
sion now is dark, to live by what we see.

For each new step of faith we take you have more truth
to grasp the breadth, length, depth, and height, the cru-ci-fied
So, when we see you face to face, your truth and light

and light to break forth from your ho-ly word.
and ris-en might of Christ, the in-car-nate word.
our dwell-ing-place for ev-er-more shall be.

Words: George Bradford Caird 1945, alt.
Music: Samuel Sebastian Wesley 1872
Words copyright © George Bradford Caird. Used by permission of Viola M. Caird.

CORNWALL
8 8 6 D

282
Long before the Night
(This Ancient Love)

Unison

1 Long be-fore the night was born from
2 Long be-fore the grass spot-ted green the bare
♦ 3 Long be-fore a chain was forged from the
4 Long be-fore the name of God was
5 Wake - ful are our nights and slum - bers our

dark - ness Long be-fore the dawn rolled un -
hill - side Long be-fore a wing un -
♦ hill - side Long be-fore a voice ut - tered
spo - ken Long be-fore a cross was
morn - ing Stub - born is the grass sow - ing

stead - y from fire Long be-fore she wrapped her
fold - ed to wind Long be-fore she wrapped her
♦ free - dom's cry Long be-fore she wrapped her
nailed from a tree Long be-fore she laid her
green wound - ed hills As we wrap our heal - ing

scar - let arms a - round the hills there was a
long blue arm a - round the sea there was a
♦ bleed - ing arms a - round a child there was a
arm of col - ours 'cross the sky there was a
arms to hold what her arms held this an - cient

(vv. 1–4) love this an - cient love was born
(v. 5) love this ach - ing love rolls on

Words: Carolyn McDade 1988; v. 5 alt. 1995
Music: Carolyn McDade 1988; arr. David Kai 1994

THIS ANCIENT LOVE
Irregular

God Is the One Whom We Seek Together 283

Refrain (**Unison**)

God is the One whom we seek to - ge - ther, God is the Life which is
part of us all; God is the Truth and the mark of mys - te - ry,
God is the Love and the Joy that makes us whole.

Words: Colin Gibson 1978
Music: Colin Gibson 1978

GODPOINT
6 6 6 6 with refrain

284

Joyful Is the Dark

1 Joy-ful is the dark, ho - ly, hid-den God,
2 Joy-ful is the dark Spir - it of the deep,
3 Joy-ful is the dark, shad-owed sta - ble floor;
4 Joy-ful is the dark cool - ness of the tomb,
5 Joy-ful is the dark depth of love di - vine,

roll - ing cloud of night be - yond all nam - ing:
wing - ing wild - ly o'er the world's cre - a - tion,
an - gels flick - er, God on earth con - fess - ing,
wait - ing for the won - der of the morn - ing;
roar - ing, loom - ing thun - der-cloud of glo - ry,

Maj - es - ty in dark - ness, En - er - gy of love,
silk - en sheen of mid - night, plum - age black and bright,
as with ex - ul - ta - tion, Ma - ry, giv - ing birth,
nev - er was that mid - night touched by dread and gloom:
ho - ly, haunt - ing beau - ty, liv - ing, lov - ing God.

Words: Brian Wren 1986
Music: Veronica Bennetts 1986
Words and music copyright © 1989 Hope Publishing Company.

CEDARS
10 10 11 10

Word - in - Flesh, the mys - te - ry pro - claim - ing.
swoop- ing with the beau - ty of a ra - ven.
hails the in - fant cry of need and bless - ing.
dark - ness was the cra - dle of the dawn - ing.
Hal - le - lu - jah! Sing and tell the sto - ry!

Joy- ful is the dark, joy - ful is the dark, joy - ful is the dark.

Il faut qu'en Dieu l'on se confie

285

(If You Will Trust in God to Guide You)

1 Il faut qu'en Dieu l'on se confie;
la paix du coeur se trouve en lui.
On ne peut prolonger sa vie
par ses tourments, par ses soucis.
Mais en réponse à notre foi,
à toutes choses, Dieu pourvoit.

2 Au coeur humain, la joie est bonne,
et le Seigneur le sait aussi.
Pleine et parfaite, il nous la donne
dans le moment qu'il a choisi.
Il est celui qui sait le mieux
ce qu'il nous faut pour être heureux.

3 Puisqu'il me garde sur ma route,
craindre-je encor de défaillir?
Je prie et chante, et ne redoute
ni le présent, ni l'avenir.
Il est fidèle, et tous les jours
je peux compter sur son amour.

(The music appears on the following page.)

Words: Trans. Lisette Levis-Baudin
Translation copyright © Fondation d'édition des Églises Protestantes Romandes

NEUMARK
989888

286   If You Will Trust in God to Guide You

1 If you will trust in God to guide you, and hope in
2 God will em- brace your pain and weep- ing, your help- less
3 Sing, pray, and keep God's ways un- swerv- ing; so do your

God through all your ways, God will give strength, what- ever be-
an- ger and dis- tress. If you are in God's care and
own part faith- ful- ly, and trust God's word; though un- de-

tide you, and bear you through the e- vil days. Who trusts in
keep- ing, in sor- row will God love you less? For Christ, who
serv- ing, you'll find God's prom- ise true to be. God nev- er

God's un- chang- ing love builds on the rock that will not move.
took for you a cross, will bring you safe through ev- ery loss.
will for- sake in need the soul that trusts in God in- deed.

Words: *Georg Neumark 1641; vv. 1, 3 trans. Catherine Winkworth 1863, alt.; v. 2 trans. Jaroslav J. Vajda, alt.*
Music: *Georg Neumark 1657*
Translation, v. 2, copyright © 1978 Lutheran Book of Worship. Used by permission of Augsburg Fortress.

NEUMARK
9 8 9 8 8 8

Wellspring of Wisdom

1 Well - spring of wis - dom, hear our cry.
2 Dawn of a new day, put to flight
3 Gar - den of grace, your gifts a - bound,
4 Call to com - pas - sion, help us bring

The way a - head is parched and dry. We seek a source to
the ter - rors of a nu - clear night. As bear - ers of your
the sa - cred signs are all a - round, the whole of earth is
our burn - ing need for nur - tur - ing, the emp - ti - ness of

sat - is - fy our thirst for sanc - ti - fy - ing wa - ters,
lov - ing light, we hud - dle clos - er to your fire,
ho - ly ground. We learn, from all of life ex - press - ing,
ev - ery - thing to your em - brace, as we en - deav - our

wis - dom for your faith - filled sons and daugh - ters.
lift the lamp of hope a lit - tle high - er.
how to grow in sow - ing seeds of bless - ing.
to pro - claim your ho - ly name for - ev - er.

Words: Miriam Therese Winter 1987

Music: Miriam Therese Winter 1987; harm. Ruth Watson Henderson 1995

WELLSPRING
8 8 8 9 10

288 Great Is Thy Faithfulness

Descant

3 Par - don for sin and a peace that en - dur - eth,

D   G   A7   G   D

1 Great is thy faith - ful - ness, God our Cre - a - tor;
2 Sum - mer and win - ter and spring - time and har - vest,
3 Par - don for sin and a peace that en - dur - eth,

thine own dear pres - ence to cheer and to guide,

G   D   E   (B7   E7)   A

there is no shad - ow of turn - ing with thee;
sun, moon, and stars in their cours - es a - bove
thine own dear pres - ence to cheer and to guide,

strength for to - day and bright hope for to - mor - row—

A7   D   D   Em   D   G

thou chang - est not, thy com - pas - sions, they fail not;
join with all na - ture in man - i - fold wit - ness
strength for to - day and bright hope for to - mor - row—

Words: Thomas O. Chisholm 1923, alt.

Music: William M. Runyan 1923; desc. Joachim Segger 1995

FAITHFULNESS

11 10 11 10 with refrain

289 It Only Takes a Spark

(Pass It On)

1 It on - ly takes a spark to get a fire
2 What a won - drous time is spring when all the trees are
3 I wish for you, my friend, this hap - pi - ness that

go - ing, and soon all those a - round can warm up in its
bud - ding, the birds be - gin to sing, the flow - ers start their
I've found — on God you can de - pend, it mat - ters not where

glow - ing: that's how it is with God's love,
bloom - ing; that's how it is with God's love,
you're bound; I'll shout it from the moun - tain top;

once you've ex - pe - ri - enced it: you spread God's love to
once you've ex - pe - ri - enced it: you want to sing, it's
I want my world to know: the Lord of love has

Words: Kurt Kaiser 1969
Music: Kurt Kaiser 1969
Words and music used by permission of Budjohn Songs.

PASS IT ON
Irregular

ev - ery - one,   you want to pass it on.
fresh like spring, you want to pass it on.
come to me,   I want to pass it on.

Nothing Can Trouble   290
(Nada te turbe)

Noth - ing   can trou - ble,   noth - ing   can fright - en.
Na - da   te tur - be,   na - da   te es - pan - te.

Those who seek God shall nev-er go want-ing. God a-lone fills us.
Quien a Dios tie-ne na-da le fal-ta. So-lo Dios bas-ta.

Words: *Spanish St. Teresa of Jesus; trans. Taizé Community 1986*
Music: *Jacques Berthier 1991*
Words and music copyright © 1986, 1991 Taizé Community, G. I. A. Publications, Inc., Chicago, Illinois, exclusive agent.

NADA TE TURBE
Irregular

And the following...

291 All Things Bright and Beautiful

Refrain (Unison)

*All things bright and beau-ti-ful, all crea-tures great and small,
all things wise and won-der-ful: in love, God made them all.

1 Each lit-tle flower that o-pens, each lit-tle bird that sings,
2 The pur-ple-head-ed moun-tains, the riv-er run-ning by,
3 The cold wind in the win-ter, the pleas-ant sum-mer sun,
4 The rock-y moun-tain splen-dour, the lone wolf's haunt-ing call,
5 God gave us eyes to see them, and lips that we might tell

God made their glow-ing col-ours, God made their ti-ny wings.
the sun-set and the morn-ing that bright-ens up the sky;
the ripe fruits in the gar-den: God made them ev-ery one.
the great lakes and the prair-ies, the for-est in the fall;
how great is God our mak-er, who has made all things well.

* The refrain may be sung at the beginning and the end only.

Words: Cecil Frances Alexander 1848, alt.
Music: 17th-century English melody; adapt. and arr. Martin Shaw 1915

ROYAL OAK
7 6 7 6 with refrain

Creating God, We Give You Thanks

1 Cre - a - ting God, we give you thanks
2 You have not fin - ished wom - an, man,
◆ 3 Be - yond the pres - ent sin and shame,
4 What though the king - dom long de - lay,
5 Since what we choose is what we are,

that this your world is in - com - plete;
for we are in the mak - ing still,
◆ wrong's bit - ter, cru - el, scorch - ing blight,
and still with haugh - ty foes must cope?
and what we love we yet shall be,

that bat - tle calls our mar - shalled ranks,
as friends who share the Mak - er's plan,
◆ we see the beck - oning vi - sion flame,
It gives us that for which to pray,
the goal may ev - er shine a - far,

that work a - waits our hands and feet.
as those who know your lov - ing will.
◆ the bless - ed king - dom of the right.
a field for toil and faith and hope.
the will to win it makes us free.

Words: William deWitt Hyde 1903, alt.   WAREHAM
Music: William Knapp 1738   8 8 8 8

293

We Praise You, Creator
(Les cieux et la terre)

1 Les cieux et la ter - re cé - lè - brent en choeur
2 C'est lui qui nous don - ne le prin - temps joy - eux,

1 We praise you, Cre - a - tor, in earth, sea, and sky:
2 Each spring-time the blos - soms bloom frag - rant once more;

la gloi - re du Pè - re, du Dieu cré - a - teur.
les fruits de l'au - tom - ne, l'é - té ra - di - eux.

our Rul - er, our Mak - er, our Sov - ereign most high.
each sum - mer and aut - umn brings forth its rich store.

Qu'il est re - dou - ta - ble dans sa ma - jes - té!
Lar - gesse in - fi - ni - e que rien ne ta - rit!

Each new gen - er - a - tion lifts voic - es in praise;
With wit - ness com - pel - ling our praise and our prayer,

Qu'il est ad - mi - ra - ble dans sa cha - ri - té!
Sa main ras - sa - si - e tout ê - tre qui vit.

how good your cre - a - tion, how gra - cious your ways!
cre - a - tion is tell - ing of your faith - ful care.

Words: Edmund Louis Budry 1904; English trans. Andrew Donaldson 1993
Music: attrib. Johann Michael Haydn; arr. William Gardiner 1815
English words copyright © 1993 Andrew Donaldson.

LYONS
11 11 11 11

3 Mais, Ô Dieu suprême,
 plus que tous tes dons,
 c'est ton amour même
 que nous adorons.
 Ô source éternelle
 de grâce et de paix,
 ton peuple fidèle
 te loue à jamais.

3 Your wondrous works teach us,
 Creator, to trace
 the limitless reaches
 of your love and grace.
 Your grace dwells among us,
 your love goes before:
 from eldest to youngest
 we praise and adore.

Clap Your Hands

294

Clap your hands to-geth - er all ye peo - ple,

clap your hands to-geth - er all ye peo - ple,

sing un - to God with the voice of mel - o - dy,

clap your hands to - geth - er!

Words: Psalm 47:1
Music: Eleanor Daley 1988
Music copyright © 1988 Harold Flammer Music, a Division of Shawnee Press, Inc. (ASCAP).

295 The Earth and All Who Breathe

1 The earth and all who breathe ex - ist through love di - vine,
2 The good, a - bun - dant earth is ours to tend and keep;
3 Cre - a - tion now a - waits hu - man - i - ty's re - birth

who formed the sea, the flow - ering tree, the wren, the fra - grant pine.
yet land lies waste, con - sumed in haste, and hun - gry chil - dren weep.
at last to claim one com - mon aim: to nur - ture life on earth.

Each wo - man, man, and child cre - a - ted from the dust
The na - tions proud - ly build new Ba - bels to the sky.
A - wake, all hu - man - kind, the chal - lenge now em - brace;

is called to share cre - a - tion's care, a sa - cred, liv - ing trust.
Their bombs de - stroy cre - a - tion's joy; their mis - siles ter - ri - fy!
ap - ply your strength, your voice, your means, as stew - ards of God's grace.

Words: Ruth Duck 1983
Music: attrib. J. S. Bach 1736
Words copyright © 1992 G.I.A. Publications, Inc.

ICH HALTE TREULICH STILL
6 6 8 6 D

This Is God's Wondrous World

1 This is God's won-drous world, and to my listen-ing ears
2 This is God's won-drous world: the birds their car-ols raise;
3 This is God's won-drous world: O let me ne'er for-get

all na-ture sings, and round me rings the mu-sic of the spheres.
the morn-ing light, the li-ly white, de-clare their Mak-er's praise.
that though the wrong seems oft so strong, God is the rul-er yet.

This is God's won-drous world; I rest me in the thought of
This is God's won-drous world: God shines in all that's fair; in the
This is God's won-drous world: why should my heart be sad? Let

rocks and trees, of skies and seas, God's hand the won-ders wrought.
rus-tling grass or moun-tain pass, God's voice speaks ev-ery-where.
voic-es sing, let the heav-ens ring: God reigns, let earth be glad!

Words: *Maltbie Davenport Babcock 1901, alt.*
Music: *English traditional melody; adapt. Franklin L. Sheppard 1915; adapt. Stanley Oliver 1929*

TERRA BEATA
6 6 8 6 D irregular

297

All Praise to You
(Stewards of Earth)

1 All praise to you, O God of all cre - a - tion:
2 With won - drous grace you clothed the earth in splen - dour;
3 To tend the earth is our en - trust - ed du - ty,

you made the world, and it is yours a - lone.
with teem - ing life you filled the sea and land.
for earth is ours to use and not a - buse.

The plan - et earth you spun in its lo - ca - tion
In - stil in us a sense of awe and won - der
O gra - cious God, true source of all re - sour - ces,

a - mid the stars a - dorn - ing heav - en's dome.
when we be - hold the boun - ty of your hand.
for - give our greed that wields de - struc - tion's sword.

We lease the earth but for a life's dur - a - tion,
Then when we hear the voice of bird or thun - der,
Then let us serve as wise and faith - ful stew - ards

yet for this life it is our cher - ished home.
we hear the voice our faith can un - der - stand.
while earth gives glo - ry to cre - a - tion's Lord.

Words: Omer Westendorf 1984
Music: Jean Sibelius 1899; arr. The Hymnal 1933

FINLANDIA
10 10 10 10 10 10

When You Walk from Here   298

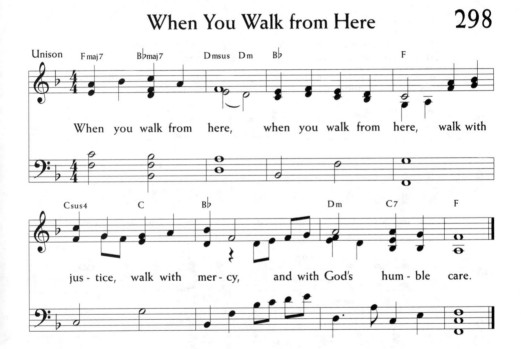

When you walk from here, when you walk from here, walk with
jus - tice, walk with mer - cy, and with God's hum - ble care.

Words: Linnea Good 1991
Music: Linnea Good 1991

WHEN YOU WALK
Irregular

299
Teach Me, God, to Wonder
(Enseigne-moi, mon Dieu)

1 Teach me, God, to won-der, teach me, God, to see;
2 Let me, God, be o-pen, let me lov-ing be;

1 En-sei-gne-moi, mon Dieu, à voir tes bien-faits,
2 Mets dans mon coeur l'a-mour né de ton Es-prit,

let your world of beau-ty cap-ture me.
let your world of peo-ple speak to me.

à ai-mer la beau-té de ton oeuvre.
pour ce monde que tu as tant ai-mé.

Refrain

Praise to you be giv-en, love for you be lived,
Gloi-re te soit ren-due pour le don de vie;

life be cel-e-brat-ed, joy you give.
nous chan-tons ton a-mour, no-tre joie.

Words: Walter Farquharson 1973; French trans. Étienne de Peyer 1983; alt. R. Gerald Hobbs 1987
Music: Ron Klusmeier 1974

MCNAUGHT
11 9 11 9

3 Let me, God, be ready,
   let me be awake,
   in your world of loving my place take.

   Refrain

4 Teach me, God, to know you,
   hear you when you speak,
   see you in my neighbour when we
   meet.

   Refrain

3 Fais de moi l'instrument
   de ta sainte paix,
   qui veut faire s'étendre ton amour.

   Refrain

4 Fais-moi te connaître,
   apprendre à t'aimer,
   fais-moi te servir, aimant mon
   prochain.

   Refrain

God, Whose Farm Is All Creation 300

1 God, whose farm is all cre-a-tion, take the gra-ti-
2 Take our plough-ing, seed-ing, reap-ing, hopes and fears of
3 All our la-bour, all our watch-ing, all our cal-en-

tude we give; take the fin-est of our har-vest,
sun and rain, all our think-ing, plan-ning, wait-ing,
dar of care, in these crops of your cre-a-tion,

crops we grow that all may live.
ripen-ing in-to fruit and grain.
take, O God: they are our prayer.

Words: John Arlott 1950, alt.
Music: English traditional melody, arr. Ralph Vaughan Williams 1906
Words copyright © The Executors of the late John Arlott. Arrangement from The English Hymnal 1906. By permission of Oxford University Press.

SHIPSTON
8 7 8 7

301 Before the Earth Had Yet Begun

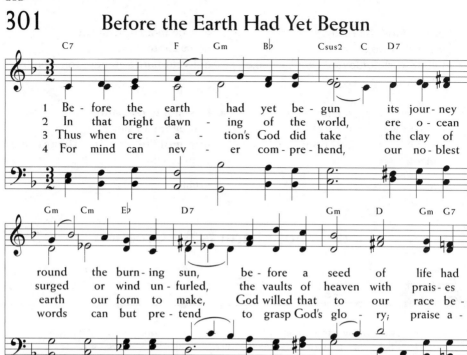

1 Be - fore the earth had yet be - gun its jour - ney
2 In that bright dawn - ing of the world, ere o - cean
3 Thus when cre - a - tion's God did take the clay of
4 For mind can nev - er com - pre - hend, our no - blest

round the burn - ing sun, be - fore a seed of life had
surged or wind un - furled, the vaults of heaven with prais - es
earth our form to make, God willed that to our race be -
words can but pre - tend to grasp God's glo - ry; praise a -

stirred, there sound - ed God's cre - a - ting Word.
rang, the morn - ing stars to - geth - er sang.
long the gifts of mu - sic, word, and song.
lone is our com - pan - ion by that throne.

Words: Herbert O'Driscoll 1986, alt.
Music: David M. Young 1986
Words copyright © 1993 Herbert O'Driscoll. Music © David M. Young. Used with permission.

CRAIGLEITH
8 8 8 8
Alt. tune: Winchester New

302 A Prayer for Forgiveness

All-merciful tender God, you have given birth to our world,
    conceiving and bearing all that lives and breathes.
We come to you as your daughters and sons,
    aware of our aggression and our drive to manipulate others.
We ask you to forgive us, and by the gentle touch of your Spirit
    help us to find a renewed sense of compassion,
      that we may truly live as your people. Amen.

Janet Berry 1989, alt.

For Beauty of Prairies

1 For beau - ty of prair - ies, for gran - deur of trees,
2 As stew - ards of beau - ty re - ceived at your hand,
3 Teach us once a - gain to be garden - ers in peace;

for flow - ers of wood - lands, for crea - tures of seas,
as crea - tures who hear your most ur - gent com - mand,
all na - ture a - round us is ours but on lease;

for all you cre - a - ted and gave us to share,
we turn from our waste - ful de - struc - tion of life,
your name we would hal - low in all that we do,

we praise you, Cre - a - tor, ex - tol - ling your care.
con - fess - ing our fail - ures, con - fess - ing our strife.
ful - fill - ing our call - ing, cre - a - ting with you.

Words: Walter Farquharson 1966, alt.
Music: Healey Willan 1927
Words copyright © 1970 Walter Farquharson. Music copyright © 1994 Waterloo Music Co. Ltd.

ST BASIL
11 11 11 11
Alt. tune: MacDowell

304 O God, beyond All Face and Form

1 O God, be-yond all face and form, you willed it that
2 The glo-ry of the gal-ax-ies, the beau-ty of
3 You gave our race both form and name, and love for us
4 Of this great love, all loves are born, of self, of neigh-

cre-a-tion's night should blaze, and cha-os still its storm,
a ba-by's hand, the thun-der-ing of rest-less seas,
was your in-tent. Then to a wom-an's womb love came,
bour, and of earth. By love shall night be turned to morn,

and birth a un-i-verse of light.
the glo-ry of the for-est's stand; All things be-low,
and on a cross was whol-ly spent.
and death shall nev-er con-quer birth.

all things a-bove are formed of your e-ter-nal love.

Words: Herbert O'Driscoll 1989
Music: Dmitri Bortnianski 1822
Words copyright © 1993 Herbert O'Driscoll.

ST PETERSBURG
8 8 8 8 8 8
Alt. setting: 804

Into the Unshaped Silence

305

*Unison

1 In - to the un - shaped si - lence sings the
2 Each day un - folds with won - ders new, first
3 The Word sings out with power once more, in -
4 A day of rest, and o'er the earth God's
5 God calls us all to join and sing the

Optional

sound of God's own voice. The dark - ness bows to
grass, first tree, first bird! Plain, peak, and vale all
to the new - made earth; and in their Mak - er's
voice a - gain is heard: a song of joy that
won - der of the earth and through our care - ful

light new - born, the moon and stars re - joice.
take their place, each shaped by God's own word.
im - age formed, wom - an and man know birth.
cel - e - brates the good - ness of the world.
stew - ard - ship to guard cre - a - tion's worth.

* May be sung as a round on selected verses.

Words: S. Curtis Tufts 1986   PRIMROSE
Music: Lucius Chapin or Amzi Chapin 1811 or 1812; A Repository of Church Music, Part Second 1813;   8 6 8 6
    arr. F. R. C. Clarke 1970, alt.

306

God of the Farmlands

1 God of the farm-lands, hear our prayer, God of the
2 God of the riv-ers in their course, God of the
3 God of the dark and som - bre mine, God of its
4 God of the cit - y's throb - bing heart, God of its
5 Source of au - thor - i - ty and right, God of all
6 God of the na - tions, wom - en, men, God of each

grow - ing seed, O bless the fields, for to your
swell - ing sea, where we must strive with na - ture's
hard - won store, your love through toil and per - il
in - dus - try, bid greed and base de - ceit de -
earth - ly power, to those who gov - ern grant your
hum - ble soul, we seek your gra - cious aid a -

care we look in all our need.
force, our guard - ian ev - er be.
shine, your strength our hope se - cure.
part, give true pros - per - i - ty.
light, your wis - dom be their dower.
gain: O come and make us whole.

Words: Thomas Charles Hunter-Clare 1949
Music: John Bacchus Dykes 1875

BEATITUDO
8 6 8 6

Touch the Earth Lightly

1 Touch the earth light - ly, use the earth gent - ly,
2 We who en - dan - ger, who cre - ate hun - ger,
3 Let there be green - ing, birth from the burn - ing,
4 God of all liv - ing, God of all lov - ing,

nour - ish the life of the world in our care:
a - gents of death for all crea - tures that live,
wa - ter that bless - es and air that is sweet,
God of the seed - ling, the snow and the sun,

gift of great won - der, ours to sur - ren - der,
we who would fos - ter clouds of di - sas - ter,
health in God's gar - den, hope in God's chil - dren,
teach us, de - flect us, Christ re - con - nect us,

trust for the child - ren to - mor - row will bear.
God of our plan - et, fore - stall and for - give!
re - gen - er - a - tion that peace will com - plete.
us - ing us gent - ly and mak - ing us one.

Words: *Shirley Erena Murray* 1991
Music: *Colin Gibson* 1991
Words and music copyright © 1992 Hope Publishing Company.

TENDERNESS
5 5 10 D

308 Many and Great, O God, Are Your Works

1 Ma - ny and great, O God, are your works, Mak - er of
2 Grant un - to us com - mu - nion with you, O star - a -

1 Ka - ti - pe - yi - ci - ket ki - si - pas - ka - mi - kaahk
2 O - pe - wii ce - wi - naan Ma - ni - to is - pi - mihk

earth and sky. Your hands have set the heav - ens with stars,
bid - ing one. Come un - to us and dwell with us,

kii - me - kiw. O - si - taw mi - na a - ca - ko - sak
oh - ci. E - ko - si wii - ci - tas - ke - mi - naan. Kih -

your fin - gers spread the moun - tains and plains. Lo, at your
with you are found the gifts of life. Bless us with

Ma - ni - to o - to - te - naw wii - ya. Ciist wii - ya
ci - me - ki - wi - na maa - ka mii - yi - naan kaa - ki -

word the wat - ers were formed; deep seas o - bey your voice.
life that has no end, e - ter - nal life with you.

ka - pi - maa - cii - ko - yahk e - pe - mi - ci - wa - ki.
ke - pi - maa - ti - si - win e - ko - te is - pi - mik.

Words: Dakota hymn, Joseph R. Renville 1842; para. Philip Frazier 1929, alt.; Cree, Stan McKay 1987
Music: Dakota melody; adapt. Joseph R. Renville 1842; harm. James R. Murray 1877
Paraphrase copyright © Dakota Conference, United Church of Christ. Cree translation and transliteration copyright © 1987 Stan McKay.

LACQUIPARLE
Irregular

Para, Para, Pitter Pat

309

1 Pa - ra,* pa - ra, pit - ter pat, see it rain, see it rain;
2 Chi - ra,* chi - ra, waft - ing down, see it snow, see it snow;
3 Ki - ra,* ki - ra, lit - tle stars, see them shine, see them shine;
4 Chu - chu,* lit - tle bird, hear it sing, hear it sing;

pa - ra, pa - ra, pit - ter pat, tell me why it rains.
chi - ra, chi - ra, waft - ing down, tell me why it snows.
ki - ra, ki - ra, lit - tle stars, tell me why you shine.
chu - chu, lit - tle bird, tell me why you sing.

So the gar - den hard and dry will be sof - tened by and by,
So the branch - es ev - ery - where will a snow - y blan - ket wear;
So that oth - ers trav - el - ling, o - ver roads a - dark - en - ing,
So that oth - ers lone - ly, lis - tening to my mel - o - dy,

and the flow - ers one by one soon will see the sun.
warm and co - sy they will stay, on a win - ter's day.
soon will find their path - ways bright, in the star - ry light.
in their hearts will hear me say, "God loves you to - day."

* Representing onomatopoeic expressions in Japanese.

Words: Ugo Nakada ca. 1920; trans. June Nakada Sumida 1981
Music: anon; harm. Masao Tomioka 1966

NAKADA
Irregular

Japanese words used by permission of JASRAC. License No. 9593114-501. Trans. copyright © 1983 June Nakada Sumida. Harmony copyright © 1966 Masao Tomioka.

310   God, Who Touches Earth with Beauty

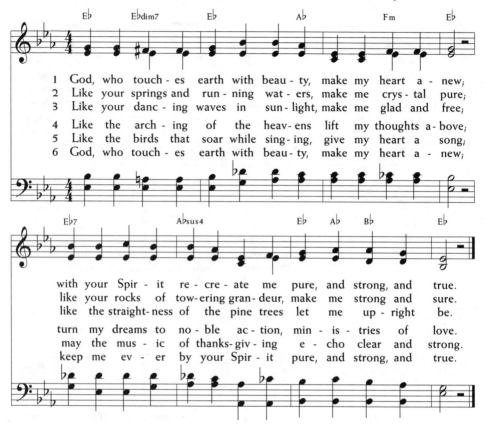

1 God, who touch-es earth with beau-ty, make my heart a-new;
2 Like your springs and run-ning wat-ers, make me crys-tal pure;
3 Like your danc-ing waves in sun-light, make me glad and free;
4 Like the arch-ing of the heav-ens lift my thoughts a-bove;
5 Like the birds that soar while sing-ing, give my heart a song;
6 God, who touch-es earth with beau-ty, make my heart a-new;

with your Spir-it re-cre-ate me pure, and strong, and true.
like your rocks of tow-ering gran-deur, make me strong and sure.
like the straight-ness of the pine trees let me up-right be.
turn my dreams to no-ble ac-tion, min-is-tries of love.
may the mus-ic of thanks-giv-ing e-cho clear and strong.
keep me ev-er by your Spir-it pure, and strong, and true.

Words: Mary S. Edgar 1925, alt.
Music: James Edmund Jones 1925
Words copyright © 1925 Mary S. Edgar.

GLEN BERNARD
8 5 8 5

311   A Prayer for the Care of Creation

O God, the only source of life and energy and wealth,
    defend our planet earth.
Teach us to conserve and not to squander the riches of nature,
    to use aright the heritage of former generations,
    and to plan for the welfare of our children's children.
Renew our wonder, awaken our concern,
    and make us better stewards and more careful tenants
    of the world you lend us as our home.
Hear us, O God, our creator and redeemer,
    in the name of Christ. Amen

Timothy Dudley-Smith 1982. Copyright © 1982 by Hope Publishing Company.

Praise with Joy the World's Creator

1 Praise with joy the world's Cre - a - tor, God of jus - tice,
2 Praise to Christ who feeds the hun - gry, frees the cap - tive,
3 Praise the Spir - it sent a - mong us, lib - er - at - ing
4 Praise the Mak - er, Christ, and Spir - it, one God in com -

love, and peace, source and end of hu - man know - ledge,
finds the lost, heals the sick, up - sets re - li - gion,
truth from pride, forg - ing bonds where race or gen - der,
mu - ni - ty, call - ing Chris - tians to em - bo - dy

God whose grace shall ne - ver cease. Cel - e - brate the
fear - less both of fate and cost. Cel - e - brate Christ's
age or na - tion dare di - vide. Cel - e - brate the
one - ness and di - ver - si - ty. This the world shall

Mak - er's glo - ry, power to res - cue and re - lease.
con - stant pres - ence: friend and strang - er, guest and host.
Spir - it's treas - ure: fool - ish - ness none dare de - ride.
see re - flect - ed: God is One and One in Three.

Words: The Iona Community 1985, alt.
Music: John Goss 1868

Words copyright © 1987 WGRG, Iona Community (Glasgow, Scotland), G.I.A. Publications, Inc., Chicago, IL, exclusive agent.

LAUDA ANIMA (PRAISE MY SOUL)
8 7 8 7 8 7
Descant: 399

313 God, Whose Almighty Word

1 God, whose al - might - y word
2 Je - sus, who came to bring
3 Spir - it of truth and love,
4 Bless - ed and ho - ly three,

cha - os and dark - ness heard, and took their flight,
on your re - deem - ing wing, heal - ing and sight,
life - giv - ing, ho - ly dove, speed forth your flight;
glo - ri - ous tri - ni - ty, wis - dom, love, might,

hear us, we hum - bly pray, and where the gos - pel day
health to the trou - bled mind, sight to the Spir - it - blind,
move on the wa - ter's face, bear - ing the lamp of grace,
bound - less as o - cean's tide roll - ing in full - est pride,

sheds not its glo - rious ray, let there be light.
O now to hu - man - kind let there be light.
and in earth's dark - est place let there be light.
through the world far and wide, let there be light.

Words: John Marriott ca. 1813, alt.
Music: adapt. from Felice de Giardini 1769

MOSCOW
6 6 4 6 6 6 4

Come Now, Almighty King

1 Come now, al - might - y King, help us your name to sing, help us to praise; one God all glo - ri - ous, ev - er vic - to - ri - ous, come and reign o - ver us, An - cient of Days.

2 Come now, in - car - nate Son, your life in us be - gun, our prayer at - tend; come, and your peo - ple bless, come, give your word suc - cess; stab - lish your righ - teous- ness, Sav - iour and friend!

3 Come ho - ly Com - for - ter, your sa - cred wit - ness bear in this glad hour; your grace to us im - part, now rule in ev - ery heart, nev - er from us de - part, Spir - it of power!

4 To the great One in Three, e - ter - nal prais - es be for ev - er - more; your sov - ereign maj - es - ty may we in glo - ry see, and to e - ter - ni - ty love and a - dore!

Words: anon. 18th century, as in George Whitfield's Collection of Hymns *1757, alt.*
Music: anon., as in Samuel Sebastian Wesley's European Psalmist *1872*

SERUG
6 6 4 6 6 6 4

315 Holy, Holy, Holy, Lord God Almighty

Descant

4 Ho - ly, ho - ly, ho - ly! Lord God al - might - y!

1 Ho - ly, ho - ly, ho - ly! Lord God al - might - y!
2 Ho - ly, ho - ly, ho - ly! All the saints a - dore thee,
3 Ho - ly, ho - ly, ho - ly! Though the dark - ness hide thee,
4 Ho - ly, ho - ly, ho - ly! Lord God al - might - y!

All thy works shall praise thy name;

Ear - ly in the morn - ing our song shall rise to thee;
cast - ing down their gold - en crowns a - round the glass - y sea;
though the eye made blind by sin thy glo - ry may not see,
All thy works shall praise thy name in earth and sky and sea;

ho - ly, ho - ly, ho - ly, mer - ci - ful and might - y,

ho - ly, ho - ly, ho - ly, mer - ci - ful and might - y,
cher - u - bim and ser - a - phim fall - ing down be - fore thee,
on - ly thou art ho - ly; there is none be - side thee,
ho - ly, ho - ly, ho - ly, mer - ci - ful and might - y,

Words: Reginald Heber ca. 1820, alt.
Music: John Bacchus Dykes 1861; desc. Godfrey Hewitt ca. 1971
Descant copyright © 1971 Godfrey Hewitt.

NICÆA
Irregular

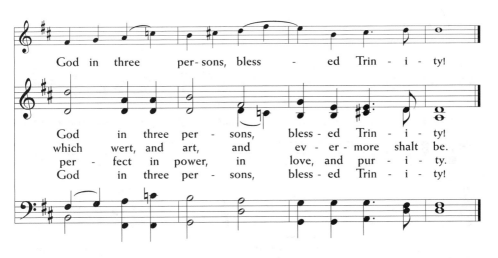

God in three per-sons, bless - ed Trin - i - ty!

God in three per - sons, bless-ed Trin - i - ty!
which wert, and art, and ev - er - more shalt be.
per - fect in power, in love, and pur - i - ty.
God in three per - sons, bless-ed Trin - i - ty!

Praise Our Maker 316

Unison

1 Praise our Mak - er, peo - ples of one fam - i - ly: God is love,
2 Love our Sav - iour, fol - low - ers of Je - sus: God is love,
3 Care for oth - ers, child - ren of the Spir - it: God is love,

God is love! Praise our Mak - er, peo - ples of one fam - i - ly:
God is love! Love our Sav - iour, fol - low - ers of Je - sus:
God is love! Care for oth - ers, child - ren of the Spir - it:

God is love, God is love!

Words: vv. 1, 2 anon. ca. 1890; adapt. and v. 3 R. Gerald Hobbs 1987
Music: Carey Bonner 1904; arr. Ruth Watson Henderson 1995

PRAISE HIM
10 6 10 6

Adaptation and verse 3 copyright © 1987 Songs for a Gospel People. Arrangement copyright © 1995 R. Watson Henderson.

317 I Bind unto Myself Today

Unison

1 I bind un - to my - self to - day the strong name
of the Trin - i - ty, by in - vo - ca - tion
of the same, the three in one and one in three.

2 I bind this day to me for - ev - er, by power of
3 I bind un - to my - self to - day the vir - tues
4 I bind un - to my - self to - day the power of
5 I bind un - to my - self the name, the strong name

faith, Christ's in - car - na - tion, his bap - tism in the
of the star - lit heav - en, the glo - rious sun's life -
God to hold and lead, his eye to watch, his
of the Trin - i - ty, by in - vo - ca - tion

Jor - dan Riv - er, his cross of death for my sal -
giv - ing ray, the white - ness of the moon at
might to stay, his ear to hear - ken to my
of the same, the three in one and one in

va - tion, his burst - ing from the spic - ed tomb, his
e - ven, the flash - ing of the light - ning free, the
need, the wis - dom of my God to teach, his
three, of whom all na - ture has cre - a - tion, e -

rid - ing up the heaven - ly way, his com - ing at the
whirl - ing wind's tem - pes - tuous shocks, the sta - ble earth, the
hand to guide, his shield to ward, the Word of God to
ter - nal Fa - ther, Spir - it, Word. Praise to the Lord of

day of doom, I bind un - to my - self to - day.
deep salt sea, a - round the old e - ter - nal rocks.
give me speech, his heaven - ly host to be my guard.
my sal - va - tion; sal - va - tion is of Christ the Lord!

Words: attrib. St. Patrick; trans. Cecil Frances Alexander 1889
Music: ancient Irish hymn melody; arr. Charles Villiers Stanford 1902

ST PATRICK
Irregular

318

Christ Be with Me

The following may be inserted between verses 4 and 5 of
"I Bind unto Myself Today" (317)

1 Christ be with me, Christ with-in me, Christ be-
2 Christ be-neath me, Christ a-bove me, Christ in

hind me, Christ be-fore me, Christ be-side me, Christ to
qui-et, Christ in dan-ger, Christ in hearts of all that

win me, Christ to com-fort and re-store me.
love me, Christ in mouth of friend and stran-ger.

Words: attrib. St. Patrick; trans. Cecil Frances Alexander 1889
Music: ancient Irish hymn melody; arr. Charles Villiers Stanford 1902

ST PATRICK
Irregular

319

A Blessing

God be in your head, and in your understanding.
God be in your eyes, and in your looking.
God be in your mouth, and in your speaking.
God be in your heart, and in your loving.
God be at your end, and at your departing.

attrib. St. Patrick 13th century

Mothering God, You Gave Me Birth

1 Moth - er - ing God, you gave me birth
2 Moth - er - ing Christ, you took my form,
3 Moth - er - ing Spir - it, nur - turing one,

in the bright morn - ing of this world.
of - fer - ing me your food of light,
in arms of pa - tience hold me close,

Cre - a - tor, source of ev - ery breath,
grain of my life, and grape of love,
so that in faith I root and grow

you are my rain, my wind, my sun.
your ver - y bod - y for my peace.
un - til I flower, un - til I know.

Words: Julian (Juliana) of Norwich ca. 1400, adapt. Jean Wiebe Janzen 1991
Music: Henry Baker 1854
Words copyright © 1991 Jean Wiebe Janzen.

HESPERUS (QUEBEC)
8 8 8 8

321

Maker, in Whom We Live

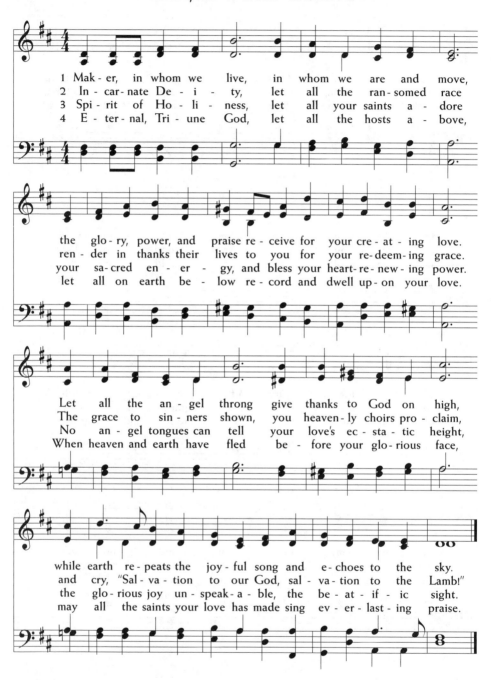

1 Mak-er, in whom we live, in whom we are and move,
2 In-car-nate De-i-ty, let all the ran-somed race
3 Spi-rit of Ho-li-ness, let all your saints a-dore
4 E-ter-nal, Tri-une God, let all the hosts a-bove,

the glo-ry, power, and praise re-ceive for your cre-at-ing love.
ren-der in thanks their lives to you for your re-deem-ing grace.
your sa-cred en-er-gy, and bless your heart-re-new-ing power.
let all on earth be-low re-cord and dwell up-on your love.

Let all the an-gel throng give thanks to God on high,
The grace to sin-ners shown, you heaven-ly choirs pro-claim,
No an-gel tongues can tell your love's ec-sta-tic height,
When heaven and earth have fled be-fore your glo-rious face,

while earth re-peats the joy-ful song and e-choes to the sky.
and cry, "Sal-va-tion to our God, sal-va-tion to the Lamb!"
the glo-rious joy un-speak-a-ble, the be-at-if-ic sight.
may all the saints your love has made sing ev-er-last-ing praise.

Words: Charles Wesley 1747, alt.
Music: George Job Elvey 1868

DIADEMATA
6 6 8 6 D
Descant: 211

O God, Whose First Creative Word 322

1 O God, whose first cre - a - tive word set un - i - ver - ses
2 O Christ who came, the liv - ing word, pro - claim - ing love's re -
3 O Spir - it, ev - er - pres - ent word, God's a - gent of trans -

in - to place, who stretched a - cross the whirl - ing void in -
deem - ing power, who drained the temp - ter's bit - ter cup and
form - ing grace, who seeks to en - ter ev - ery heart with

fin - i - ties of time and space; O speak to our cha -
tri - umphed in earth's dark - est hour; O speak to our de -
light its dark - ness to re - place; O speak with - in the

ot - ic day a word of or - dered grace, we pray.
spair and pain a word that kin - dles hope a - gain.
hearts we raise a joy - ful word of faith and praise.

Words: Judith Fetter 1985
Music: John Bacchus Dykes 1861
Words copyright © 1985 J. A. Fetter.

MELITA
8 8 8 8 8 8

323 Maker of the Sun and Moon

1 Ma-ker of the sun and moon, and moth-er of the
2 Give us grace to feel you near to sense your truth and
♦ 3 Lord of ev-ery liv-ing thing, con-ceived in wom-an's
4 Mar-y mag-ni-fies her Lord: then let us praise God's
5 Je-sus lay in Ma-ry's arms, God's fu-ture at her

earth, comes to life in hu-man form, to bless all
see; breathe in-to our lungs and limbs, that we might
♦ womb; may we find you deep in-side our lives, and
deed as God's reign be-gins this way, and we from
breast — proved his love for all the world — puts our love

Refrain

hu-man birth: to bless all hu-man birth:
ho-ly be: that we might ho-ly be:
♦ make you room: our lives, and make you room: Glo-ry to God!
sin are freed: and we from sin are freed:
to the test: puts our love to the test:

Ma-ker, Spir-it, Son! Giv-er and Gift, in love en-fold-ed in One!

Words: Peter Sharrocks 1991

Music: Peter Sharrocks 1991; arr. Simon Hester 1991

MYSTERY

7 6 7 6 6 *with refrain*

Words and music copyright © 1993 Stainer & Bell Ltd. and Methodist Church (UK) Division of Education and Youth. Used by permission of Hope Publishing Company.

Jesus, Come to Our Hearts

1 Je - sus, come to our hearts like fall - ing rain;
2 Spir - it, come to our hearts like rush - ing wind;
♦ 3 Come, God, come to our hearts like shin - ing sun;
4 Glo - ry be to the Lamb that once was slain;
5 Prais - es be to our God, the three in one;

come to re - fresh, come to re - new,
come with your fire, come with your life,
♦ come to re - veal, light - en your Word,
praise for his life, praise for his death,
praise for the sun, praise for the wind,

wash all our sins a - way.
blow all our doubts a - way.
♦ drive all our gloom a - way.
praise that he lives a - gain.
praise for the fall - ing rain.

Words: William Worley, alt. 1991
Music: William Worley 1991, arr. David Dell 1991
Words and music copyright © 1992 William Worley. Arrangement copyright © 1992 David Dell.

SOUTHLAND
10 8 6

And the following...

325   Christ Is Made the Sure Foundation

Descant

4 Laud and hon-our to the Fa-ther, laud and hon-our to the Son,

1 Christ is made the sure foun-da-tion, Christ the head and cor-ner-stone,
2 To this tem-ple where we call you, come, O Lord of hosts, to-day;
3 Here be-stow on all your ser-vants what they ask of you to gain,
4 Laud and hon-our to the Fa-ther, laud and hon-our to the Son,

laud and hon-our to the Spir-it, ev-er three and ev-er one,

cho-sen of the Lord, and pre-cious, bind-ing all the church in one,
with your faith-ful lov-ing-kind-ness hear your ser-vants as they pray,
what they gain from you for ev-er with the bless-ed to re-tain,
laud and hon-our to the Spir-it, ev-er three and ev-er one,

one in might, and one in glo-ry, while un-end-ing a - ges run.

ho-ly Zi-on's help for ev-er, and its con-fi-dence a-lone.
and your full-est be-ne-dic-tion shed with-in its walls al-way.
and here-af-ter in your glo-ry ev-er-more with you to reign.
one in might, and one in glo-ry, while un-end-ing a - ges run.

Words: Latin 7th century; trans. John Mason Neale 1851
Music: Henry Purcell ca. 1682; adapt. Ernest Hawkins 1842; desc. W. Herbert Belyea 1974
Descant copyright © 1974 W. Herbert Belyea.

WESTMINSTER ABBEY
8 7 8 7 8 7

O for a Thousand Tongues to Sing 326

Words: *Charles Wesley 1739, alt.*
Music: *Carl Gotthelf Gläser ca. 1828; adapt. and harm. Lowell Mason 1839*

AZMON
8 6 8 6
Alt. tune: Richmond

327

All Praise to Thee

Unison

1 All praise to thee, for thou, O King di - vine,
2 Thou cam'st to us in low - li - ness of thought;
♦ 3 Let this mind be in us which was in thee,
4 Where - fore, by God's e - ter - nal pur - pose, thou
5 Let ev - ery tongue con - fess with one ac - cord

didst yield the glo - ry that of right was thine,
by thee the out - cast and the poor were sought,
♦ who wast a ser - vant that we might be free,
art high ex - alt - ed o'er all crea - tures now,
in heaven and earth that Je - sus Christ is Lord;

that in our trou - bled hearts thy grace might shine:
and by thy death was God's sal - va - tion wrought:
♦ — hum - bling thy - self to death on Cal - va - ry:
and given the name to which all knees shall bow:
and God e - ter - nal be by all a - dored:

hal - le - lu - jah; hal - le - lu - jah!

Words: Francis Bland Tucker 1938, alt.
Music: Ralph Vaughan Williams 1906
Words copyright © The Church Pension Fund. Music by permission of Oxford University Press.

SINE NOMINE
10 10 10 *with hallelujahs*
Alt. setting: 705

Jesu, Joy of Our Desiring

328

1 Je - su, joy of our de - sir - ing, ho - ly wis - dom,
2 Through the way where hope is guid - ing, hark, what peace - ful

love most bright; drawn by you, our souls as - pir - ing soar to
mu - sic rings; where the flock, in you con - fid - ing, drink of

un - cre - at - ed light. Word of God, our flesh that fash - ioned,
joy from death - less springs. Theirs is beau - ty's fair - est plea - sure;

with the fire of life im - pas - sioned, striv - ing still to
theirs is wis - dom's ho - liest trea - sure. You, for - ev - er,

truth un - known, soar - ing, dy - ing round your throne.
lead your own in the love of joys un - known.

Words: Martin Janus 1661, trans. Robert Seymour Bridges, alt.
Music: Johann Schop 1642, arr. Johann Sebastian Bach 1716

JESU, JOY (WERDE MUNTER)
87 87 88 77

329

O Jesus Christ,
May Grateful Hymns Be Rising

1 O Jesus Christ, may grateful hymns be rising,
2 Grant us new courage, sacrificial, humble,
3 Show us your Spirit, brooding o'er each city,

in every city for your love and care;
strong in your strength to venture and to dare;
as you once wept above Jerusalem,

inspire our worship, grant the glad surprising
to lift the fallen, guide the feet that stumble,
seeking to gather all in love and pity,

that your blest Spirit rouses everywhere.
seek out the lonely and God's mercy share.
and healing those who touch your garment's hem.

Words: Bradford Gray Webster 1954
Music: Alfred Scott-Gatty 1900
Words copyright © 1954, renewal 1982 The Hymn Society. Used by permission of Hope Publishing Company.

WELWYN
11 10 11 10

Jesus Shall Reign

Descant

4 Let ev-ery crea-ture rise and bring pe-cu-liar

1 Je-sus shall reign wher - e'er the sun does its suc-
2 Peo-ple and realms of ev-ery tongue dwell on his
3 Bless-ings a-bound wher - e'er he reigns; and pris-oners
4 Let ev-ery crea-ture rise and bring pe-cu-liar

hon-ours to our King, an-gels de-scend with

ces-sive jour-neys run; his king-dom stretch from
love with sweet-est song, and in-fant voic-es
leap to lose their chains; the wea-ry find e -
hon-ours to our King, an-gels de-scend with

songs a-gain, and earth re-peat the loud A-men!

shore to shore, till moons shall wax and wane no more.
shall pro-claim their ear-ly bless-ings on his name.
ter-nal rest, and all who suf-fer want are blest.
songs a-gain, and earth re-peat the loud A-men!

Words: Isaac Watts 1719, alt.
Music: attrib. John Warrington Hatton 1793; desc. David McKinley Williams 1959
Descant copyright © 1959 H. W. Gray Co., Inc.

DUKE STREET
8 8 8 8

331 The Church's One Foundation

1 The church's one foun-da-tion is Je-sus Christ our Lord;
2 Called forth from ev-ery na-tion, yet one o'er all the earth;
♦ 3 Though with a scorn-ful won-der the world sees us op-pressed,
4 Mid toil and tri-bu-la-tion, and tu-mult of our war,
5 We now on earth have un-ion with God the Three in One,

we are his new cre-a-tion by wa-ter and the Word;
one char-ter of sal-va-tion: one Lord, one faith, one birth.
♦ by schi-sms rent a-sun-der, by her-e-sies dis-tressed,
we wait the con-sum-ma-tion of peace for-ev-er-more;
and share through faith com-mun-ion with those whose rest is won.

from heaven he came and sought us that we might ev-er be
One ho-ly name pro-fess-ing and at one ta-ble fed,
♦ yet saints their watch are keep-ing; their cry goes up, "How long?"
till with the vi-sion glo-rious our long-ing eyes are blest,
Oh, hap-py ones, and ho-ly! Lord, give us grace that we

his liv-ing ser-vant peo-ple, by his own death set free.
to one hope al-ways press-ing, by Christ's own Spir-it led.
♦ But soon the night of weep-ing shall be the morn of song.
and the great church vic-to-rious shall be the church at rest.
like them, the meek and low-ly, on high may dwell with thee.

Words: Samuel John Stone 1866; adapt. Laurence Hull Stookey 1983
Music: Samuel Sebastian Wesley 1864
Words (adaptation) copyright © 1983 The United Methodist Publishing House.

AURELIA
7 6 7 6 D

L'église universelle

1 L'église universelle
a pour roc Jésus Christ;
elle est l'oeuvre nouvelle
que sa parole fit.
Habitant le ciel même,
il vint se l'attacher,
et, par un don suprême,
mourut pour la sauver!

2 L'église en sa prière
unit à leur Sauveur
les peuples de la terre
soumis au seul Seigneur.
C'est son nom qu'elle acclame,
son pain qui la nourrit;
elle verse à toute âme
l'espoir qui la guérit.

3 Honnie et méconnue, menant de durs
combats,
elle attend la venue de la paix ici-bas.
Contemplant par avance la fin de son
tourment,
la grande délivrance, le repos
permanent.

4 Aujourd'hui, sur la terre,
elle est unie à Dieu,
et, par un saint mystère,
aux élus du saint lieu.
Rends-nous, comme eux, fidèles,
et reçois-nous, Seigneur,
dans la vie éternelle,
dans l'éternel bonheur!

Words: Samuel John Stone 1866; French trans. Fernand Barth 1923

The Church's One Foundation　332

1 The church's one foundation
is Jesus Christ her Lord;
she is his new creation
by water and the word;
from heaven he came and sought her
to be his holy bride;
with his own blood he bought her,
and for her life he died.

2 Elect from every nation,
yet one o'er all the earth,
her charter of salvation
one Lord, one faith, one birth;
one holy name she blesses,
partakes one holy food,
and to one hope she presses,
with every grace endued.

3 'Mid toil and tribulation
and tumult of her war,
she waits the consummation
of peace for evermore,
till with the vision glorious
her longing eyes are blest,
and the great church victorious
shall be the church at rest.

4 Yet she on earth hath union
with God the three in one,
and mystic sweet communion
with those whose rest is won.
O happy ones and holy!
Lord, give us grace that we,
like them, the meek and lowly,
on high may dwell with thee.

Words: Samuel John Stone 1866

AURELIA
7 6 7 6 D

333 Love Divine, All Loves Excelling

1 Love divine, all loves excelling, joy of heaven to earth come down, fix in us thy humble dwelling, all thy faithful mercies crown. Jesus, thou art all compassion, pure, unbounded love thou art; visit

2 Come, almighty to deliver; let us all thy grace receive; suddenly return, and never, never more thy temples leave. Thee we would be always blessing, serve thee as thy hosts above, pray, and

3 Finish, then, thy new creation; pure and spotless let us be; let us see thy great salvation perfectly restored in thee, changed from glory into glory, till in heaven we take our place, till we

Words: *Charles Wesley 1747*
Music: *Rowland Huw Prichard ca. 1831*

HYFRYDOL
8 7 8 7 D
Alt. tune: Blaenwern

us   with thy   sal - va - tion, en - ter ev - ery trem - bling heart.
praise thee, with - out ceas - ing, glo - ry in   thy per - fect love.
cast   our crowns be - fore   thee, lost in   won - der, love, and praise.

All Hail the Power of Jesus' Name   334

1 All hail   the power of Je - sus' name! Let an - gels
2 O   seed   of   Is - rael's cho - sen   race now ran - somed
♦ 3 Crown him, you mar - tyrs of your   God, who from his
4 Let ev - ery tongue and ev - ery tribe, re - spon - sive
5 O   that, with all   the sa - cred throng, we   at his

pros - trate fall;   bring forth the roy - al   di - a - dem,
from the   fall,   hail him who saves you   by his grace
♦ al - tar call;   praise him whose way of   pain you trod,
to   the   call,   to   him all maj - es - ty as - cribe
feet may   fall,   join in   the ev - er - last - ing song,

Refrain

and crown him, crown him, crown him, crown him Lord of all.

Words: Edward Perronet 1780, et al   MILES LANE
Music: William Shrubsole 1779   8 6 8 with refrain

335

At the Name of Jesus

Unison

1 At the name of Je - sus ev - ery knee shall bow,
2 Hum - bled for a sea - son to re - ceive a name
3 Name him, Chris - tians, name him, with love strong as death,
4 In your hearts en - throne him; there let him sub - due
5 Chris - tians, this Lord Je - sus shall re - turn a - gain,

ev - ery tongue con - fess him King of glo - ry now;
from the lips of sin - ners un - to whom he came,
but with awe and won - der, and with ba - ted breath;
all that is not ho - ly, all that is not true;
with his Fa - ther's glo - ry, with his an - gel train;

'tis our God's great plea - sure we should call him Lord,
faith - ful - ly he bore it, spot - less to the last,
he is God the Sav - iour, he is Christ the Lord,
crown him as your Cap - tain in temp - ta - tion's hour;
for all wreaths of em - pire meet up - on his brow,

who from the be - gin - ning was the might - y Word.
brought it back vic - to - rious when from death he passed.
ev - er to be wor - shipped, trust - ed, and a - dored.
let his will en - fold you in its light and power.
and our hearts con - fess him King of glo - ry now.

Words: *Caroline Maria Noel 1870, alt.*
Music: *Ralph Vaughan Williams 1925*
Music by permission of Oxford University Press.

KING'S WESTON
11 11 11 11

Christ Whose Glory Fills the Skies

1 Christ whose glo - ry fills the skies, Christ the true, the
2 Dark and cheer - less is the morn un - ac - com - pan -
3 Vis - it then this soul of mine, pierce the gloom of

on - ly light, sun of righ - teous - ness, a - rise,
ied by thee; joy - less is the day's re - turn,
sin and grief; fill me, ra - dian - cy di - vine,

tri - umph o'er the shades of night. Day - spring from on
till thy mer - cy's beams I see, till they in - ward
scat - ter all my un - be - lief; more and more thy -

high, be near; day - star, in my heart ap - pear.
light im - part, glad my eyes and warm my heart.
self dis - play, shin - ing to the per - fect day.

Words: Charles Wesley 1740, alt.
Music: Werner's Choralbuch 1815

RATISBON
7 7 7 7 7 7
Alt. tune: Dix

337

Blessed Assurance

1 Bless-ed as - sur - ance, Je - sus is mine! O what a fore-taste of
2 Per - fect sub - mis - sion, per-fect de-light! Vi - sions of rap-ture now
3 Per - fect sub - mis - sion, all is at rest, I in my Sav-iour am

glo - ry di - vine! Heir of sal - va - tion, pur - chase of God,
burst on my sight; an - gels de - scend - ing, bring from a - bove
hap - py and blessed; watch-ing and wait - ing, look - ing a - bove,

born of the Spir - it, washed in Christ's blood.
ech - oes of mer - cy, whis - pers of love. This is my sto - ry, this is my
filled with God's good-ness, lost in Christ's love.

song, prais-ing my Sav - iour all the day long; this is my sto - ry,

Words: Fanny J. Crosby 1873, alt.
Music: Phoebe Palmer Knapp 1873

ASSURANCE
Irregular

this is my song, prais-ing my Sav-iour all the day long.

Ask Me What Great Thing I Know 338

1 Ask me what great thing I know that de-lights and stirs me so,
2 Who de-feats my fierc-est foes? Who con-soles my sad-dest woes?
3 Who is life in life to me? Who the death of death will be?
4 This is that great thing I know; this de-lights and stirs me so:

what the high re - ward I win, whose the name I
Who re - vives my faint-ing heart, heal - ing all that
Who holds all my days se - cure, in God's heart where
faith in Christ who died to save, Christ who tri - umphed

glo - ry in: Je - sus Christ, the cru - ci - fied.
grief im - parts?
love is sure?
o'er the grave,

Words: Johann C. Schwedler ca. 1741; trans. Benjamin H. Kennedy 1863, alt.
Music: H. A. César Malan 1827

HENDON
7 7 7 7 7

339

When Morning Gilds the Skies
(Quand le soleil se lève)

Descant

4 Be this while life is mine, my can-ti-cle di-vine,

1 When morn-ing gilds the skies, my heart a-wak-ening cries:
2 To God, the Word on high, the hosts of an-gels cry:
1 Quand le so-leil se lè-ve et quand le jour s'a-chè-ve:
2 Au Cré-a-teur l'ou-vra-ge de ses mains rend hom-ma-ge:

may Je-sus Christ be praised! Be this the e-ter-nal song,

may Je-sus Christ be praised! When eve-ning shad-ows fall,
may Je-sus Christ be praised! Let mor-tals, too, up-raise
bé-ni soit Jé-sus Christ! Pour dire son al-lé-gres-se
bé-ni soit Jé-sus Christ! L'É-glise en sa pré-sen-ce

through all the a-ges long: may Je-sus Christ be praised!

this rings my cur-few call: may Je-sus Christ be praised!
their voice in hymns of praise: may Je-sus Christ be praised!
mon coeur à Dieu s'a-dres-se: bé-ni soit Jé-sus Christ!
chan-te l'a-mour im-men-se: bé-ni soit Jé-sus Christ!

Words: German hymn 1828; English trans. v. 1 and 3 Robert Seymour Bridges 1899;
v. 2 and 4 Edward Caswall 1854, alt.; French trans. Jacques Beaudon 1956; rev. R. Gerald Hobbs 1987
Music: Joseph Barnby 1868; desc. Reginald S. Thatcher 1936

LAUDES DOMINI
666666

3 Let all of humankind
　in this their concord find:
　may Jesus Christ be praised!
　Let all the earth around
　ring joyous with the sound:
　may Jesus Christ be praised!

4 Be this, while life is mine,
　my canticle divine:
　may Jesus Christ be praised!
　Be this th'eternal song,
　through all the ages long:
　may Jesus Christ be praised!

3 C'est le choeur de louanges
　qu'entonnent tous les anges:
　béni soit Jésus Christ!
　Et que la terre entière
　répète la prière:
　béni soit Jésus Christ!

4 Qu'en joie comme en détresse
　nos chants disent sans cesse:
　béni soit Jésus Christ!
　Que dans tous les langages
　ce soit le chant des âges:
　béni soit Jésus Christ!

Jesus, Friend of Little Children 340

1 Jesus, friend of little children, let me be one too;
2 Teach me how to grow in goodness, daily as I grow.
3 Never leave me, nor forsake me; ever be my friend;

take my hand, and ever keep me close to you.
You have been a child, and surely you must know.
for I need you, from life's dawning to its end.

Words: *Walter John Mathams 1882; alt.*
Music: *Gerald Wheeler 1969*
Words used by permission of Oxford University Press. Music copyright © 1969 Gerald Wheeler.

FARNHAM
8 5 8 3

341

Fairest Lord Jesus

1 *Fair - est Lord Je - sus, rul - er of all na - ture, O thou of
2 Fair are the mead - ows, fair - er still the wood - lands, robed in the
3 Fair is the sun - shine, fair - er still the moon - light, and fair the
4 All fair - est beau - ty heav - en - ly and earth - ly, won - drous - ly,

God to earth come down: thee will I cher - ish,
bloom - ing garb of spring; Je - sus is fair - er,
twink - ling, star - ry host; Je - sus shines bright - er,
Je - sus, is found in thee; none can be near - er,

thee will I hon - our, thou my soul's glo - ry, joy, and crown.
Je - sus is pur - er, who makes the trou - bled heart to sing.
Je - sus shines pur - er than all the an - gels heaven can boast.
fair - er or dear - er than thou, my Sav - iour, art to me.

* Or "Beautiful Saviour"

Words: from the German 1677; trans. Church Chorals and Choir Studies 1850, alt.
Music: Silesian folk melody in Schlesische Volkslieder 1842;
    harm. James Hopkirk 1938
Harmony copyright © Estate of James Hopkirk.

CRUSADERS' HYMN
(SCHÖNSTER HERR JESU)
5 6 8 5 5 8

You Servants of God

1 You ser - vants of God, your Sav - iour pro - claim,
2 God rules from on high, al - might - y to save,
3 Sal - va - tion to God, who sits on the throne!
4 Then let us a - dore and give as is right,

and pub - lish a - broad that won - der - ful name;
whose Word still is nigh, a pres - ence we have.
Let all cry a - loud, and hon - our the Son!
all glo - ry and power, all wis - dom and might,

the name all vic - to - rious of Je - sus ex - tol,
The great con - gre - ga - tion God's tri - umph shall sing,
The prais - es of Je - sus the an - gels pro - claim,
all hon - our and bless - ing with an - gels a - bove,

whose king - dom is glo - rious and rules o - ver all.
as - crib - ing sal - va - tion to Je - sus our King.
bow down in deep rev - erence and wor - ship the Lamb.
and thanks nev - er ceas - ing and in - fi - nite love.

Words: *Charles Wesley 1744, rev. R. Gerald Hobbs 1987*
Music: *William Gardiner 1815*
Revised words copyright © 1987 Songs for a Gospel People.

LYONS
10 10 11 11

343

I Love to Tell the Story

1. I love to tell the sto - ry of un - seen things a -
bove, of Je - sus and his glo - ry, of Je - sus and his
love. I love to tell the sto - ry, be - cause I know 'tis
true; it sat - is - fies my long-ings as noth - ing else can do.

2. I love to tell the sto - ry; more won - der - ful it
seems than all the gold - en fan - cies of all our gold - en
dreams. I love to tell the sto - ry, for some have nev - er
heard the mes - sage of sal - va - tion from God's own ho - ly Word.

3. I love to tell the sto - ry, for those who know it
best seem hun - ger - ing and thirst - ing to hear it like the
rest. And when, in scenes of glo - ry, I sing the new, new
song, 'twill be the old, old sto - ry that I have loved so long.

Words: Katherine Hankey 1866
Music: William G. Fischer 1869

HANKEY
7 6 7 6 D with refrain

Refrain

I love to tell the sto-ry, 'twill be my theme in glo-ry,

to tell the old, old sto-ry of Je-sus and his love.

How Sweet the Name of Jesus Sounds 344

1 How sweet the name of Je-sus sounds in a be-liev-er's ear!
2 It makes the wound-ed spir-it whole, and calms the trou-bled breast;
♦ 3 Dear Name! the rock on which I build, my shield and hid-ing-place,
4 Je-sus, my Shep-herd, Broth-er, Friend, my Pro-phet, Priest, and King,
5 The ef-fort of my heart is weak, and cold my warm-est thought;

It soothes the sor-rows, heals the wounds, and drives a-way all fear.
'tis man-na to the hun-gry soul, and to the wea-ry, rest.
♦ my nev-er-fail-ing trea-sury, filled with bound-less stores of grace.
my Lord, my Life, my Way, my End, ac-cept the praise I bring.
but when I see you whom I seek, I'll praise you as I ought.

Words: John Newton 1779, alt.
Music: Alexander Robert Reinagle ca. 1830

ST PETER
8 6 8 6

345   Come, Children, Join to Sing

1 Come, chil-dren, join to sing: Hal - le-lu - jah!
2 Come, lift your hearts on high: Hal - le-lu - jah!
3 Praise yet our Christ a-gain: Hal - le-lu - jah!

Praise to our Ser-vant-King: Hal - le-lu - jah!
Let prais-es fill the sky: Hal - le-lu - jah!
Raise high the joy-ous strain: Hal - le-lu - jah!

Let all with heart and voice, saved by God's gra-cious choice,
Christ calls his peo-ple friends, the help-less he de-fends,
The whole cre-a-tion o'er let all God's love a-dore,

now in this place re-joice: Hal - le-lu - jah!
a love that nev-er ends: Hal - le-lu - jah!
sing-ing for ev-er-more: Hal - le-lu - jah!

Words: Christian Henry Bateman 1843; rev. R. Gerald Hobbs 1987
Music: anon. Philadelphia 1824, alt.
Revised words copyright © 1987 Songs for a Gospel People.

MADRID
6 4 6 4 6 6 6 4

There in God's Garden

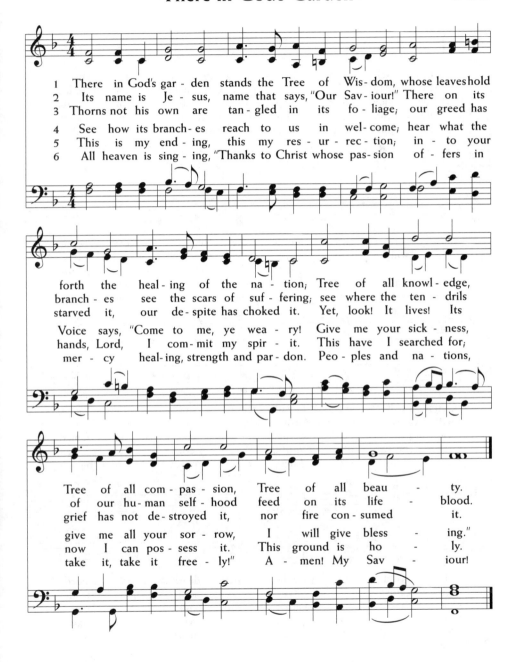

1 There in God's gar-den stands the Tree of Wis-dom, whose leaves hold
2 Its name is Je-sus, name that says, "Our Sav-iour!" There on its
3 Thorns not his own are tan-gled in its fo-liage; our greed has
4 See how its branch-es reach to us in wel-come; hear what the
5 This is my end-ing, this my res-ur-rec-tion; in-to your
6 All heaven is sing-ing, "Thanks to Christ whose pas-sion of-fers in

forth the heal-ing of the na-tion; Tree of all knowl-edge,
branch-es see the scars of suf-fering; see where the ten-drils
starved it, our de-spite has choked it. Yet, look! It lives! Its
Voice says, "Come to me, ye wea-ry! Give me your sick-ness,
hands, Lord, I com-mit my spir-it. This have I searched for;
mer-cy heal-ing, strength and par-don. Peo-ples and na-tions,

Tree of all com-pas-sion, Tree of all beau-ty.
of our hu-man self-hood feed on its life-blood.
grief has not de-stroyed it, nor fire con-sumed it.
give me all your sor-row, I will give bless-ing."
now I can pos-sess it. This ground is ho-ly.
take it, take it free-ly!" A-men! My Sav-iour!

Words: Kiràly Imre von Pécselyi ca. 1641; para. Erik Routley 1974
Music: K. Lee Scott 1976
Words (paraphrase) copyright © Hinshaw Music, Inc. Music copyright © 1987 MorningStar Music Publishers, Inc.

SHADES MOUNTAIN
11 11 11 5

347 Retell What Christ's Great Love Has Done

1 Re - tell what Christ's great love has done,
2 Re - call the cov - e - nant of grace
♦ 3 Re - view the tap - es - try of saints,
4 Re - hearse the chor - us of the heart,
5 Re - joice at what Christ yet will do,

how crib and cross the vic - tory won:
in which you free - ly find your place:
♦ that can - vas which the Spir - it paints:
let all earth's hopes and fears take part:
in - tent on mak - ing all things new:

God's call o - beyed, temp - ta - tions faced,
with wa - ter washed, at ta - ble fed,
♦ a proph - et scorned, a teach - er famed,
the shouts of youth, the cries of age,
the hun - gry filled, the peace - ful blessed,

the good news preached, then death em - braced.
in Christ a - live, to self now dead.
♦ a host un - known and un - ac - claimed,
the pris - oners' groans, the vic - tims' rage.
the wound - ed healed, each heart at rest.

Words: Jeffery Rowthorn 1986
Music: Henry James Ernest Holmes 1875
Words copyright © 1987 The Shadyside Presbyterian Church.

PATER OMNIUM
888888

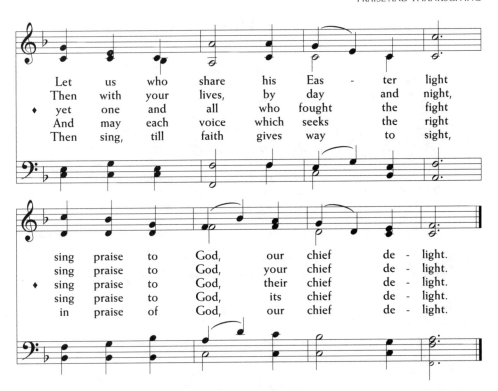

Let	us	who	share	his	Eas - ter	light
Then	with	your	lives,	by	day and	night,
◆ yet	one	and	all	who	fought the	fight
And	may	each	voice	which	seeks the	right
Then	sing,	till	faith	gives	way to	sight,

sing	praise	to	God,	our	chief de - light.
sing	praise	to	God,	your	chief de - light.
◆ sing	praise	to	God,	their	chief de - light.
sing	praise	to	God,	its	chief de - light.
in	praise	of	God,	our	chief de - light.

And the following…

348

O Love, How Deep

Descant

7 To God whose bound - less love has won
sal - va - tion for us through the Son,
to God all praise and glo - ry be

1 O love, how deep, how broad, how high!
2 God sent no an - gel to our race
◆ 3 For us he was bap - tized, and bore
4 For us he prayed, for us he taught,
5 For us to wick - ed foes be - trayed,

It fills the heart with ec - sta - sy,
of high - er or of low - er place,
◆ a ho - ly fast, and hun - gered sore;
for us great dai - ly works were wrought,
scourged, mocked, in pur - ple robe ar - rayed,

that God, in Je - sus Christ, should take
but wore the robe of hu - man frame,
◆ for us temp - ta - tions sharp - ly knew;
by words and signs, and ac - tions, thus
he bore the shame - ful cross and death;

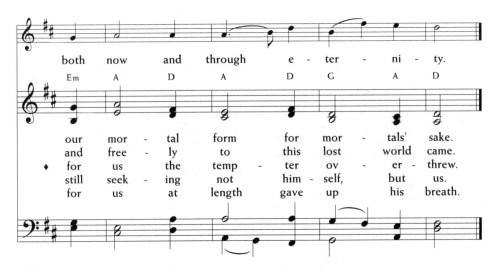

both	now	and	through	e - ter - ni - ty.
Em	A	D	A	D G A D

our	mor - tal	form	for	mor - tals'	sake.
and	free - ly	to	this	lost	world came.
for	us	the	temp - ter	ov - er - threw.
still	seek - ing	not	him - self,	but	us.
for	us	at	length	gave	up	his breath.

6 For us he rose from death again,
   for us he went on high to reign,
   for us he sent his Spirit here
   to guide, to strengthen, and
      to cheer.

7 To God whose boundless love
      has won
   salvation for us through the Son,
   to God all praise and glory be
   both now and through eternity.

Words: *from Latin, 15th century; trans. Benjamin Webb 1854, alt.*
Music: *melody from Piae Cantiones 1582, adapt Michael Praetorius 1609;*
   harm. by G. R. Woodward 1902; desc. Frances P. Macphail 1994
Harmony copyright © Mowbray. Descant copyright © 1994 Frances P. Macphail.

PUER NOBIS NASCITUR
8 8 8 8

A Prayer   349

May the Christ who walks on wounded feet
   walk with you on the road.
May the Christ who serves with wounded hands
   stretch out your hands to serve.
May the Christ who loves with a wounded heart
   open your hearts to love.
May you see the face of Christ in everyone you meet,
   and may everyone you meet
   see the face of Christ in you.

Traditional Celtic prayer

350 O Changeless Christ

Descant

6 O change-less Christ, till life is past your bless-ing still be given; then bring us home, to taste at last the time-less joys of heaven.

1 O change-less Christ, for ev-er new, who walked our earth-ly ways, still draw our hearts as once you drew the hearts of oth-er days.

2 As once you spoke by plain and hill or taught by shore and sea, so be to-day our teach-er still, O Christ of Gal-i-lee.

3 As wind and storm their mas-ter heard and his com-mand ful-filled, may trou-bled hearts re-ceive your word, the tem-pest-tossed be stilled.

4 And as of old to all who prayed your heal-ing hand was shown, so be your touch up-on us laid, un-seen but not un-known.

Words: Timothy Dudley-Smith 1981
Music: James Turle ca. 1835; desc. Norman Warren
Words copyright © 1984 and descant © 1982 Hope Publishing Company.

WESTMINSTER
8 6 8 6

5 In broken bread, in wine outpoured,
your new and living way
proclaim to us, O risen Lord,
O Christ of this our day.

6 O changeless Christ, till life is past
your blessing still be given;
then bring us home, to taste at last
the timeless joys of heaven.

With Joy We Meditate 351

1 With joy we med - i - tate the grace of our high priest a - bove; his heart is made of ten - der - ness, and o - ver - flows with love.

2 Touched with a sym - pa - thy with - in, he knows our fee - ble frame; he knows what sore temp - ta - tions mean, for he has felt the same.

3 But spot - less, in - no - cent, and pure the great Re - deem - er stood, while Sa - tan's fier - y darts he bore, and did re - sist to blood.

4 He, in the days of fee - ble flesh, poured out his cries and tears; and in his mea - sure feels a - fresh what ev - ery mem - ber bears.

5 He'll nev - er quench the smok - ing flax, but raise it to a flame; the bruis - ed reed he nev - er breaks, nor scorns the mean - est name.

6 Then let our hum - ble faith ad - dress his mer - cy and his power; we shall ob - tain de - liv - ering grace in each dis - tress - ing hour.

Words: Isaac Watts
Music: adapt. from Johann Michael Haydn 1806

SALZBURG (HAYDN)
8 6 8 6
Alt. setting: 650

352

I Danced in the Morning

1 I danced in the morn-ing when the
2 I danced for the scribe and the
3 I danced on the Sab-bath and I
4 I danced on a Fri-day when the
5 They cut me down and I

world was be-gun, and I danced in the moon and the
phar-i-see, but they would not dance and they
cured the lame; the ho-ly peo-ple
sky turned black; it's hard to dance with the
leap up high; — I am the life that will

stars and the sun, and I came from heav-en and I
would not fol-low me; I danced for the fish-er-men, for
said it was a shame; they whipped and they stripped and they
dev-il on your back; they bur-ied my bo-dy and they
nev-er, nev-er die; I'll live in you if you'll

danced on the earth; at Beth-le-hem I
James and John; they came with me and the
hung me high, and left me there on a
thought I'd gone, but I am the dance and I
live in me; — I am the Lord of the

had my birth.
dance went on.
♦ cross to die. Dance, then, wher-ev-er you may be;
still go on.
dance, said he.

I am the Lord of the dance, said he, and I'll lead you all, wher-

ev-er you may be, and I'll lead you all in the dance, said he.

Words: Sydney Carter 1963
Music: Shaker melody; adapt. and harm. Sydney Carter 1963
Words and harmony copyright © 1963 Stainer & Bell. Used by permission of Hope Publishing Company.

LORD OF THE DANCE
Irregular

'Tis the Gift to Be Simple   353
(Simple Gifts)

'Tis the gift to be simple, 'tis the gift to be free,
'tis the gift to come down where you ought to be,
and when we find ourselves in the place just right,
'twill be in the valley of love and delight.

When true simplicity is gained,
to bow and to bend we shan't be ashamed;
to turn, turn will be our delight
'til by turning, turning, we come round right.

Words: Shaker song
Music: Shaker melody

SIMPLE GIFTS
Irregular

354 In Old Galilee, When Sweet Breezes Blew

(Gariraya no kaze kaoru oka de)

1 Ga - ri - ra - ya no ka - ze ka - o - ru o - ka de
2 A - ra - shi no hi na - mi ta - ke - ru u - mi de

1 In old Gal - i - lee, when sweet breez - es blew o'er the lake,
2 On that storm - y day, when waves bil - lowed high on the lake,

hi - to bi - to ni ha - na - sa - re - ta
de - shi ta - chi o sa - to - sa - re - ta

Je - sus spoke to crowds when they came to hear,
his dis - ci - ples feared 'til he spoke to them,

me - gu - mi no mi - ko - to - ba o,
chi - ka - ra no mi - ko - to - ba o,

those words of grace that gave them prom - ise;
those words of power that gave them cour - age;

wa - ta - shi ni mo ki - ka - se - te ku - da - sa - i.
wa - ta - shi ni mo ki - ka - se - te ku - da - sa - i.

oh speak to me now, and let me hear those words of grace.
oh speak to me now, and let me hear those words of power.

Words: Nobuo Beppu 1973, para. George Gish, Jr. 1989
Music: Shoko Maita 1975

GARIRAYA NO KAZE
Irregular

Japanese words copyright © The Hymnal Committee, UCC in Japan. Words (para.) copyright © 1989 George Gish Jr. Music copyright © JASRAC License No. 9593114-501

3 Gorugota no ju-u-jika no uede
tsumi bito o mane-kareta
sukui no mikotoba o,
  watashi ni mo
kikasete kudasai.

4 Yu-u-gure no Emao e no michi de
deshi tachi ni tsuge-rareta
inochi no mikotoba o
  watashi ni mo
kikasete kudasai.

3 On that cross he hung, to die for the
  sins of the world,
from Golgotha's shame
  he called out in pain,
those saving words of hope to sinners;
oh speak to me now, and let me hear
  those saving words.

4 On that eventide two friends passing
  by Emmaus,
recognized him not 'til he spoke again
those words of life to his disciples;
oh speak to me now, and let me hear
  those words of life.

For the Crowd of Thousands — 355

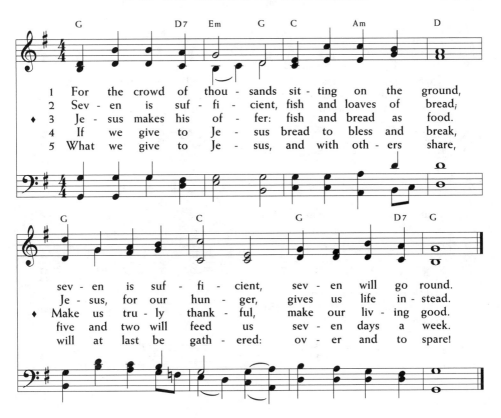

1 For the crowd of thou - sands sit - ting on the ground,
2 Sev - en is suf - fi - cient, fish and loaves of bread;
♦ 3 Je - sus makes his of - fer: fish and bread as food.
4 If we give to Je - sus bread to bless and break,
5 What we give to Je - sus, and with oth - ers share,

sev - en is suf - fi - cient, sev - en will go round.
Je - sus, for our hun - ger, gives us life in - stead.
♦ Make us tru - ly thank - ful, make our liv - ing good.
five and two will feed us sev - en days a week.
will at last be gath - ered: ov - er and to spare!

Words: Fred Kaan 1968; based on a Dutch hymn by Willem Barnard
Music: James Frederick Swift 1881
Words copyright © 1968 Hope Publishing Company.

ERNSTEIN
6 5 6 5

356 Seek Ye First the Kingdom

Descant

Hal - le - lu - jah, hal - le - lu - jah, hal - le - lu - jah, hal - le - lu - jah.

1 Seek ye first the king-dom of God and God's right-eous - ness, and all these things shall be add-ed un-to you.
2 Ask and it shall be giv-en un-to you; seek and you shall find; knock and the door shall be o-pened un-to you. Hal-le-lu, hal-le-lu - jah.
3 We do not live by bread a - lone, but by ev-ery word that pro - ceeds from the mouth of God.

Words: Karen Lafferty 1972
Music: Karen Lafferty 1972; desc. Karen Lafferty 1972
Words, music, and descant copyright © 1972 Maranatha! Music.

LAFFERTY
Irregular

Tell Me the Stories of Jesus

1 Tell me the sto-ries of Je-sus I love to hear,
2 First let me hear how the child-ren stood round his knee,
◆ 3 Tell me, in ac-cents of won-der, how rolled the sea
4 In-to the ci-ty I'd fol-low the chil-dren's band,
5 Show me that scene in the gar-den of bit-ter pain;

things I would ask him to tell me if he were here:
and I shall fan-cy his bless-ing rest-ing on me;
◆ toss-ing the boat in a tem-pest on Gal-i-lee!
wav-ing a branch of the palm tree high in my hand;
and of the cross where my Sav-iour for me was slain.

scenes by the way-side, tales of the sea,
words full of kind-ness, deeds full of grace,
◆ And how the Mas-ter, read-y and kind,
one of his her-alds, yes, I would sing
Sad ones or bright ones, so that they be

sto-ries of Je-sus, tell them to me.
all in the love-light of Je-sus' face.
◆ chid-ed the bil-lows and hushed the wind.
loud-est ho-san-nas! Je-sus is king!
sto-ries of Je-sus, tell them to me.

Words: William H. Parker 1885
Music: Frederick Arthur Challinor 1903
Words and music copyright © 1904 National Christian Education Council.

STORIES OF JESUS
8 4 8 4 5 4 5 4

358

When Jesus the Healer

1 When Jesus the healer passed through Galilee,
2 A paralyzed man was let down through a roof.
♦ 3 The death of his daughter caused Jairus to weep. Heal
4 When blind Bartimaeus cried out to the Lord,
5 The lepers were healed and the demons cast out.

the deaf came to hear and the
His sins were forgiven, his
us, heal us today! †The Lord took her hand, and he
his faith made him whole and his
A bent woman straightened to

blind came to see.
walking the proof.
♦ raised her from sleep. Heal us, *Lord Jesus!
sight was restored.
laugh and to shout.

6 The twelve were commissioned
  and sent out in twos,
Heal us, heal us today!
to make the sick whole and to spread
  the good news.
Heal us, *Lord Jesus!

7 There's still so much sickness and
  suffering today.
Heal us, heal us today!
We gather together for healing
  and pray:
Heal us, *Lord Jesus!

* or "O Jesus!"   † or "Then Christ"

Words: Peter D. Smith 1978
Music: Peter D. Smith 1978, 1979
Words © 1978 Stainer & Bell Ltd. Music © 1978, 1979 Stainer & Bell Ltd. and Methodist Church (U.K.) Division of Education and Youth.
Used by permission of Hope Publishing Company.

HEALER
11 6 11 5

He Came Singing Love

1 He came singing love and he lived singing love; he
2 He came singing faith and he lived singing faith; he
3 He came singing hope and he lived singing hope; he
4 He came singing peace and he lived singing peace; he

died singing love. He arose in silence.
died singing faith. He arose in silence.
died singing hope. He arose in silence.
died singing peace. He arose in silence.

For the love to go on we must make it our
For the faith to go on
For the hope to go on
For the peace to go on

song; you and I be the singers.

Words: Colin Gibson 1972
Music: Colin Gibson 1972
Words and music copyright © 1994 Hope Publishing Company.

SINGING LOVE
5 6 5 6 6 6 7

360 A Woman and a Coin — The Coin Is Lost

1 A wom-an and a coin — the coin is lost! How
2 A shep-herd and a sheep — the sheep is lost! Far
3 A par-ent and a child — the child is lost! The
4 Dear God, you sought us when the world was lost, you

much it means to her, what time and toil, what
from the flock, the one in hun-dred cries, then,
par-ent feeds on mem-o-ries and hope, the
gave your on-ly son at what a cost; your

part it was to play in her bright dreams! Am I that
risk-ing life, the shep-herd's voice and staff! Am I that
prod-i-gal on husks and one last chance. Am I that
spir-it wel-comes home the temp-est-tossed: now we can

trea-sured coin worth search-ing for? I'm
trea-sured sheep worth dy-ing for? I
trea-sured child worth wait-ing for? I'm
be all you were dream-ing of. We're

Words: Jaroslav J. Vajda 1990
Music: Fred Kimball Graham 1995
Words copyright © 1991 Jaroslav J. Vajda. Music © 1995 Fred Kimball Graham.

LIFE RESTORED
Irregular

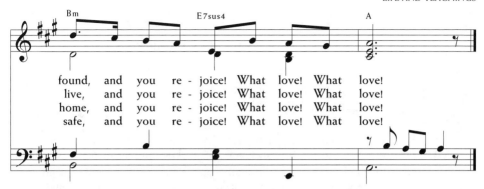

found, and you re - joice! What love! What love!
live, and you re - joice! What love! What love!
home, and you re - joice! What love! What love!
safe, and you re - joice! What love! What love!

Small Things Count — 361

1 Small things count, so Jesus said: cups of water,
2 Small things make the big things grow: grains of yeast in-
3 Every hair that's on our head, every sparrow,

crumbs of bread, small things done because we're kind
side the dough, puffs that fill a big balloon,
Jesus said, God takes care of, counts and knows,

count as big things in God's mind.
notes that make a happy tune.
God loves us from top to toes!

Words: Shirley Erena Murray 1990
Music: Jillian M. Bray 1992
Words copyright © 1992 Hope Publishing Company. Music © 1993 Jillian M. Bray.

SMALL THINGS
7 7 7 7

362 Here, O God, Your Servants Gather

(Se-ka-i no To-mo to Te o Tsu-na-gi)

Unison

1 Se - ka - i no to - mo to te o tsu - na - gi,
2 Ku - ni to ko - to - ba wa ko - to - na - re - do,

1 Here, O God, your ser-vants gath - er, hand we link with hand;
2 Man - y are the tongues we speak, scat-tered are the lands,

Jyu - ji - ka no mo - to ni ta - tsu wa - re - ra,
ko - ko - ro wa o - na - ji Shu no ta - mi zo.

look-ing to our Sav-iour's cross, joined in love we stand.
yet our hearts are one in God, one in love's de - mands.

ka - mi no mi - ku - ni o me a te to shi,
Ku - ra - ki ji - da - i no no - zo - mi na - ru,

As we seek the realm of God, we u - nite to pray:
Even in dark - ness hope ap-pears, call - ing age and youth:

Shu Ye - su no mi - chi o su - su - mi - yu - kan.
Shu Ye - su no ma - ko - to hi - ro - me - yu - kan.

Je - sus, Sav - iour, guide our steps, for you are the Way.
Je - sus, teach - er, dwell with us, for you are the Truth.

3 U-chu-u no   hi-mi-tsu
  sa-gu-ru to-mo,
  to-ki-wa no   he-i-wa
  na-o to-o-to-shi.
  Tsu-ka-re   i-ta-me-ru
  hi-to-bi-to ni,
  Shu-Yesu no   i-no-chi
  wa-ka-chi-yu-ka-n.

3 Nature's secrets open wide,
  changes never cease;
  where, O where, can weary souls
  find the source of peace?
  Unto all those sore distressed,
  torn by endless strife:
  Jesus, healer, bring your balm,
  for you are the Life.

4 Mi-chi to   ma-ko-to to
  i-no-chi na-ru,
  Shu-Yesu o   tsu-ne ni
  a-o-gi-tsu-tsu,
  a-i ni   mo-to-zu-ku
  tsu-gi no yo o,
  chi-ka-ra o   a-wa-se
  ki-zu-ki-yu-kan.

4 Grant, O God, an age renewed,
  filled with deathless love;
  help us as we work and pray,
  send us from above
  truth and courage, faith and power
  needed in our strife:
  Jesus, Saviour, be our Way,
  be our Truth, our Life.

Words: Tokuo Yamaguchi 1958; trans. and para. Everett M. Stowe 1958, alt. 1972;
phonetic transcription from Japanese I-to Loh 1988
Music: *Isao Koizumi 1958*
Words (Japanese and English) copyright © Estate of Tokuo Yamaguchi. Phonetic translation copyright © The United Methodist Publishing House.
Music used by permission of JASRAC License No. 9593114-501.

TOKYO
7 5 7 5 D

Ô Jésus, voici tes amis

1 Ô Jésus, voici tes amis,
  se tenant la main,
  regardant la croix du monde,
  signe de la vie.
  Pour connaître ton Royaume
  nous poussons le cri:
  Ô Jésus, conduis nos pas:
  toi le seul Chemin.

3 Notre monde se rénove;
  tout est merveilleux;
  mais pourquoi parmi les hommes
  tant de malheureux,
  tant de guerres, de détresses?
  Où trouver la paix?
  Ô Jésus, guéris tout homme,
  toi qui es la Vie.

2 Tant de peuples, tant de langues!
  Nous entendrons-nous?
  Mais un Père qui nous aime
  fonde notre amour.
  Tant de langues, mais la même
  pousse en nous ce cri:
  Ô Jésus, habite en nous,
  toi la Vérité.

4 Fais revivre tous les âges
  par ton seul Esprit;
  fais renaître à l'espérance
  notre humanité.
  Dieu jeunesse, Dieu courage,
  force d'unité.
  Jésus Christ, tu es Chemin,
  Vie et Vérité.

Words: Tokuo Yamaguchi 1958; trans. Claude Rozier 1972
Words (French) copyright © Centre Nationale de Pastorale Liturgique.

TOKYO
7 5 7 5 D

363
Your Coming, Lord, to Earth

1 Your com - ing, Lord, to earth in Beth - le - hem
2 That free gift of God's grace be - stowed on us
♦ 3 Come to your peo - ple as of old you came
4 Walk with us, and be known in break - ing bread:
5 Though o - ften thus you came to save and bless,

re - vealed your gra - cious will that all might live,
re - mains a foun - tain - head of joy and peace;
♦ on moun - tain - side, at ta - ble, by the sea,
those gather - ed in your name will find you here,
at last, we know, in glo - ry you will come,

by your ex - am - ple and your sac - ri - fice, in
and yet by e - vil tempt - ed and en - slaved we
♦ through doors closed on our fears and bleak dis - may: and
and shar - ing bread and wine in fel - low - ship will
in cloud and fire, with an - gels' trum - pets' sound, to

Words: Wesley Milgate 1986
Music: Lawrence F. Bartlett 1986
Words copyright © 1986 Australian Hymn Book Co. Music copyright © 1986 L. F. Bartlett. Used with permission.

GRACE
10 10 10 10

that   sal - va - tion   you   a - lone   can give.
need   to know   you   near, and find   re - lease.
in   the heart of   dark- ness light   shall be.
know   the per - fect   love that casts   out fear.
judge,   and tri - umph, and   to   claim   your own.

Forgive Our Sins as We Forgive   364

1 "For - give our sins as   we for - give," you taught us, Christ, to   pray;
2 How can your par - don reach and bless the   un - for - giv - ing   heart
3 In blaz - ing light your cross re - veals the truth we dim - ly   knew:
4 O cleanse the depths with- in   our souls and bid   re - sent - ment cease;

but   you   a - lone can grant us grace to   live the words we   say.
that broods on wrongs, and will not let old   bit - ter - ness de - part?
what triv - ial debts are owed to   us, how great our debt   to   you!
then, bound to all   in bonds of love, our   lives will spread your peace.

Words: Rosamond E. Herklots 1966
Music: William Horsley 1830
Words used by permission of Oxford University Press.

HORSLEY
8 6 8 6

365

Jesus Loves Me

1 Je-sus loves me, this I know, for the Bi-ble tells me so;
2 Je-sus loves me, this I know, as he loved so long a-go,
3 Je-sus loves me still to-day, walk-ing with me on my way,

lit-tle ones to him be-long, in his love we shall be strong.
tak-ing chil-dren on his knee, say-ing, "Let them come to me."
want-ing as a friend to give light and love to all who live.

Yes, Je-sus loves me! Yes, Je-sus loves me!

Yes, Je-sus loves me! The Bi-ble tells me so.

Words: v. 1 Anna Bartlett Warner 1859; v. 2 and 3 David Rutherford McGuire 1970
Music: William Batchelder Bradbury 1862
Words (v. 2 and 3) copyright © Cherie McGuire.

JESUS LOVES ME
7 7 7 7 with refrain

like a child

Unison

1 like a child love would send to re - veal and to mend like a
2 like a child we will meet rag - ged clothes dirt - y feet like a
3 like a child born to pray and to show us the way like a

child and a friend Je - sus comes like a child we may find claim - ing
child on the street Je - sus comes like a child we once knew com - ing
child here to stay Je - sus comes like a child we re - ceive all that

heart soul and mind like a child strong and kind Je - sus comes
back in - to view like a child born a - new Je - sus comes
love can con - ceive like a child we be - lieve Je - sus comes

Words: Daniel Charles Damon 1992
Music: Daniel Charles Damon 1992
Words and music copyright © 1993 Hope Publishing Company.

LIKE A CHILD
Irregular

And the following...

367

Come Down, O Love Divine

Descant

3 The yearn-ing strong, with which the soul will long

1 Come down, O love di-vine, seek now this soul of mine,
2 O let it free-ly burn, till earth-ly pas-sions turn
3 And so the yearn-ing strong with which the soul will long

shall far out-pass the power of hu-man tell-ing;

and vis-it it with your own ar-dour glow-ing.
to dust and ash-es in its heat con-sum-ing;
shall far out-pass the power of hu-man tell-ing;

for none can guess its grace, till love cre-ates the place

O Com-fort-er, draw near, with-in my heart ap-pear,
and let your glo-rious light shine ev-er on my sight,
for none can guess its grace, till love cre-ates the place

Words: *Bianco da Siena; trans. Richard Frederick Littledale 1867, alt.*
Music: *Ralph Vaughan Williams 1906; desc. W. Herbert Belyea 1975*
Music by permission of Oxford University Press. Descant copyright © 1975 W. Herbert Belyea.

DOWN AMPNEY
6 6 11 D

where - in the Ho - ly Spir - it makes its dwell - ing.

and kin - dle it, your ho - ly flame be - stow - ing.
and clothe me round, my on - ward path il - lum - ing.
where - in the Ho - ly Spir - it makes its dwell - ing.

Holy Spirit, Truth Divine 368

1 Ho - ly Spir - it, truth di - vine, dawn up - on this soul of mine.
2 Ho - ly Spir - it, love di - vine, glow with - in this heart of mine.
3 Ho - ly Spir - it, power di - vine, fill and nerve this will of mine.
4 Ho - ly Spir - it, law di - vine, reign with - in this soul of mine.
5 Ho - ly Spir - it, peace di - vine, still this rest - less heart of mine.
6 Ho - ly Spir - it, joy di - vine, glad - den now this heart of mine.

Voice of God and in - ward light, wake my Spir - it, clear my sight.
Kin - dle ev - ery high de - sire, pu - ri - fy me with your fire.
Bold - ly may I al - ways live, brave - ly serve, and glad - ly give.

Be my law, and I shall be firm - ly bound, for - ev - er free.
Speak to calm this toss - ing sea, grant me your tran - quil - li - ty.
In the des - ert ways I sing; spring, O liv - ing wa - ter, spring!

Words: Samuel Longfellow 1864
Music: Leighton George Hayne 1863

BUCKLAND
7 7 7 7

369 O Holy Spirit, Enter In

1 O Ho - ly Spir - it, en - ter in, and in our
2 Left to our - selves, we sure - ly stray; oh, lead us
3 O might - y Rock, O Source of life, let your good

hearts your work be - gin; now make our hearts your
on the nar - row way, with wis - est coun - sel
Word in doubt and strife be in us strong - ly

dwell - ing. Sun of the soul, O Light di -
guide us; and give us stead - fast - ness, that
burn - ing, that we be faith - ful un - to

vine, a - round and in us bright - ly shine, your
we may fol - low you for - ev - er free, no
death and live in love and ho - ly faith, from

strength in us up - well - ing. In your
mat - ter who de - rides us. Gent - ly
you true wis - dom learn - ing. God, your

ra - diance life from heav - en now is giv - en, o - ver -
heal those hearts now bro - ken; give some to - ken you are
mer - cy on us show - er; by your pow - er Christ con -

flow - ing, gift of gifts be - yond all know - ing.
near us, whom we trust to light and cheer us.
fess - ing, we will cher - ish all your bless - ing.

Words: Michael Schirmer 1640; trans. Catherine Winkworth 1863, alt.

WIE SCHÖN LEUCHTET
8 8 7 D 8 8 8

Music: Philipp Nicolai 1599

Send Your Holy Spirit

370

Send your Ho - ly Spir - it on your gath - ered peo - ple,

mer - ci - ful and lov - ing God, hear us, as we pray.

Words: Jim Strathdee 1993

JOYNER
6 6 7 5

Music: Jim Strathdee 1993

Words and music copyright © 1993 Desert Flower Music.

371 Open My Eyes, That I May See

1 O-pen my eyes, that I may see glimps-es of truth thou
2 O-pen my ears, that I may hear voic-es of truth thou
3 O-pen my mouth, and let me bear glad-ly the warm truth

hast for me; place in my hands the won-der-ful key
send-est clear; and while the wave-notes fall on my ear,
ev-ery-where; o-pen my heart and let me pre-pare

Refrain

that shall un-clasp and set me free.
ev-ery-thing false will dis-ap-pear. Si-lent-ly now I
love with thy chil-dren thus to share.

wait for thee, read-y, my God, thy will to see.

Words: Clara H. Scott 1895
Music: Clara H. Scott 1895

OPEN MY EYES
8 8 9 8 *with refrain*

O - pen my eyes,
O - pen my ears, il - lu - mine me, Spir - it di - vine!
O - pen my heart,

Though I May Speak

372

Unison

1 Though I may speak with brav - est fire, and have the
2 Though I may give all I pos - sess, and striv - ing
3 Come, Spir - it, come, our hearts con - trol, our spir - its

gift to all in - spire, and have not love, my words are
so my love pro - fess, but not be given by love with -
long to be made whole. Let in - ward love guide ev - ery

vain, as sound - ing brass, and hope - less gain.
in, the prof - it soon turns strange - ly thin.
deed; by this we wor - ship, and are freed.

Words: Hal H. Hopson 1972
Music: trad. English melody, adapt. Hal H. Hopson 1972
Words and arrangement copyright © 1972 Hope Publishing Company.

O WALY WALY (GIFT OF LOVE)
8 8 8 8

373 As Comes the Breath of Spring

1 As comes the breath of spring with light and mirth and song,
2 You come like dawn-ing day with flam-ing truth and love,
3 You come like songs at morn that fill the earth with joy,
4 You breathe and there is health; you move and there is power;

so does your Spir-it bring new days brave, free, and strong.
to chase all glooms a-way, to brace our wills to prove
till we, in Christ new-born, new strength in praise em-ploy.
you whis-per, there is wealth of love, your rich-est dower.

You come with thrill of life to chase hence win-ter's breath,
how wise, how good to choose the truth and its brave fight,
You come to rouse the heart from drift-ing to de-spair,
Your pres-ence is to us like sum-mer in the soul;

to hush to peace the strife of sin that ends in death.
to prize it, win or lose, and live on your de-light.
through high hopes to im-part life with an amp-ler air.
your joy shines forth and then life blos-soms to its goal.

Words: *David Lakie Ritchie 1929, alt.*
Music: *Charles J. Dale 1904*

DENBY
6 6 6 6 D

Come and Find the Quiet Centre

374

1 Come and find the qui - et cen - tre in the crowd-ed life we lead,
2 Si - lence is a friend who claims us, cools the heat and slows the pace,
3 In the Spir - it let us trav - el, o - pen to each oth - er's pain,

find the room for hope to en - ter, find the frame where we are freed:
God it is who speaks and names us, knows our be - ing, face to face,
let our loves and fears un - rav - el, cel - e - brate the space we gain:

clear the cha - os and the clut - ter, clear our eyes, that we can see
mak - ing space with - in our think - ing, lift - ing shades to show the sun,
there's a place for deep-est dream - ing, there's a time for heart to care,

all the things that real - ly mat - ter, be at peace, and sim - ply be.
rais-ing cour - age when we're shrink-ing, find-ing scope for faith be - gun.
in the Spir - it's live - ly schem-ing there is al - ways room to spare!

Words: Shirley Erena Murray, alt. 1989
Music: attrib. Benjamin Franklin White 1844; harm. Ronald A. Nelson 1978
Words copyright © 1992 Hope Publishing Company. Harmony copyright © 1978 Lutheran Book of Worship. Used by permission of Augsburg Fortress.

BEACH SPRING
8 7 8 7 D

375

Spirit, Spirit of Gentleness

Refrain (Unison)

Spir - it, Spir-it of gen-tle-ness, blow thro' the wil-der-ness call-ing and free, Spir - it, Spir-it of rest-less-ness, stir me from plac-id-ness, Wind, Wind on the sea.

Verses

1 You moved on the wa - ters, you called to the deep,
2 You swept thro' the des - ert, you stung with the sand,
3 You sang in a sta - ble, you cried from a hill,
4 You call from to-mor - row, you break an-cient schemes,

Words: James K. Manley 1975
Music: James K. Manley 1975
Words and music copyright © 1978 James K. Manley.

SPIRIT OF GENTLENESS
Irregular with refrain

(The French text appears on the following page.)

Souffle, vent doux du Saint-Esprit

Refrain:
Souffle, vent doux du Saint-Esprit;
ta grâce me conduit hors du désert.
Souffle, grand vent du Saint-Esprit,
secoue notre apathie,
vent, vent sur la mer.

1 Tu touchas la terre
Esprit créateur;
tu dressas les montagnes,
en gloire et splendeur;
à travers les âges,
tu crias à tous vents:
"Déployez vos ailes;
sortez du néant". *Refrain*

2 Tu choisis un peuple;
poussé par ta voix,
il quitta l'esclavage
vers une terre et une loi.
Et quand il fut trompé

par des illusions,
tu donnas aux prophètes
tes saintes visions. *Refrain*

3 Tu chantas dans l'étable,
tu gémis sur la croix;
tu rompis le silence,
par un souffle de joie;
et puis, dans les villes,
tu nous envoyas
le vent d'une tempête
qui nous ranima. *Refrain*

4 Esprit, tu écrases
l'ancien désespoir;
tu dévoiles à l'esclave
le chemin de l'espoir.
Les femmes, les hommes
reçoivent tes visions;
ton peuple se lève,
avec décision. *Refrain*

Words: James K. Manley *1975*, trans. Andrew Donaldson *1995*, alt.
Words (French translation) copyright © *1995* Andrew Donaldson.

SPIRIT OF GENTLENESS

376   Spirit of the Living God

1 Spir - it of the liv - ing God, fall a - fresh on me.
2 Spir - it of the liv - ing God, move a - mong us all;

Spir - it of the liv - ing God, fall a - fresh on me.
make us one in heart and mind, make us one in love:

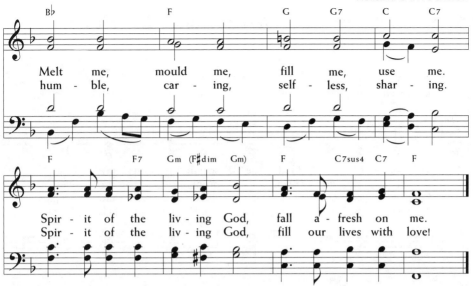

Melt me, mould me, fill me, use me.
hum - ble, car - ing, self - less, shar - ing.

Spir - it of the liv - ing God, fall a - fresh on me.
Spir - it of the liv - ing God, fill our lives with love!

Words: v. 1, Daniel Iverson 1926; v. 2, Michael Baughen 1982
Music: Daniel Iverson 1926; arr. Darryl Nixon 1987
Words (v. 1) and music copyright © 1935, 1963 Birdwing Music. Words (v. 2) copyright © 1982 Hope Publishing Company.

LIVING GOD
7 5 7 5 8 7 5

Holy Spirit, Hear Us 377

1 Ho - ly Spir - it, hear us, help us while we sing;
2 Ho - ly Spir - it, shine now on the book we read;
3 Ho - ly Spir - it, prompt us when we bow to pray;
4 Ho - ly Spir - it, help us dai - ly by your might,

breathe in - to the mu - sic of the praise we bring.
light its ho - ly pag - es with the truth we need.
speak with - in and teach us what we ought to say.
what is wrong to con - quer, and to choose the right.

Words: William H. Parker 1880, alt.
Music: James Frederick Swift 1881

ERNSTEIN
6 5 6 5

378 Spirit of God, Descend upon My Heart

1 Spi - rit of God, de - scend up - on my heart;
one ho - ly pas - sion fill - ing all my frame,
the bap - tism of the heaven - de - scend - ed dove,
stoop to my weak - ness, strength to me im - part,

2 I ask no dream, no proph - et ec - sta - cies,
no sud - den rend - ing of the veil of clay,
no an - gel vis - i - tant, no o - pening skies,

3 Have you not bid me love you, God and King;
all, all your own, soul, heart, and strength and mind?
I see your cross: there teach my heart to cling.

4 Teach me to love you as your an - gels love,
one ho - ly pas - sion fill - ing all my frame,
the bap - tism of the heaven - de - scend - ed dove,

Words: George Croly 1854, alt.
Music: Frederick C. Atkinson 1870; desc. C. David Cameron 1994
Descant copyright © 1994 C. David Cameron.

MORECAMBE
10 10 10 10

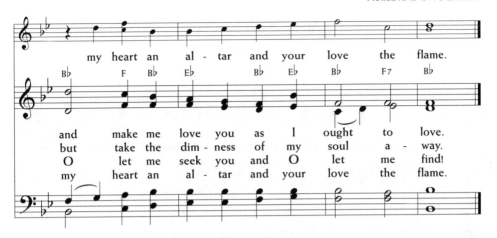

my heart an al - tar and your love the flame.

Bb | **F** | **Bb** | **Eb** | **Bb** | **Eb** | **Bb** | **F7** | **Bb**

and make me love you as I ought to love.
but take the dim - ness of my soul a - way.
O let me seek you and O let me find!
my heart an al - tar and your love the flame.

O Holy Spirit, Root of Life   379

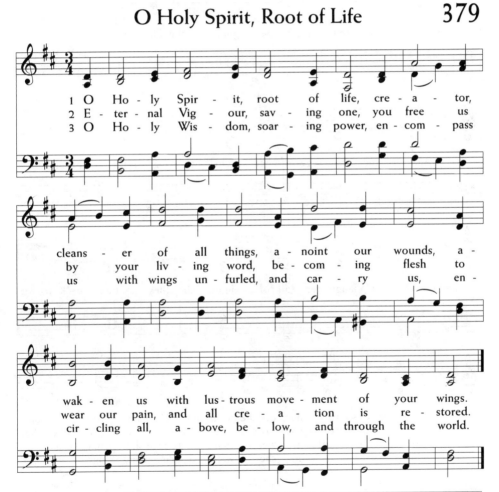

1 O Ho - ly Spir - it, root of life, cre - a - tor,
2 E - ter - nal Vig - our, sav - ing one, you free us
3 O Ho - ly Wis - dom, soar - ing power, en - com - pass

cleans - er of all things, a - noint our wounds, a -
by your liv - ing word, be - com - ing flesh to
us with wings un - furled, and car - ry us, en -

wak - en us with lus - trous move - ment of your wings.
wear our pain, and all cre - a - tion is re - stored.
cir - cling all, a - bove, be - low, and through the world.

Words: Jean Janzen 1991; based on writings by Hildegard, Abbess of Bingen 12th century   *PUER NOBIS NASCITUR*
Music: melody from 15th-century ms.; adapt. Michael Praetorius 1609; harm. George R. Woodward 1902   8 8 8 8
Words copyright © Jean Wiebe Janzen 1991. Harmony copyright © Mowbray.

380

She Comes Sailing on the Wind
(She Flies On)

Refrain (Unison)

She comes sail-ing on the wind, her wings flash-ing in the
sun; on a journ-ey just be - gun, she flies on.
And in the pas-sage of her flight, her song rings out through the
night, full of laugh-ter, full of light, she flies on. (3 To a)

1 Si - lent wa-ters rock-ing on the morn-ing of our birth, like an
2 Ma - ny were the dream-ers whose eyes were giv - en sight when the
3 gen - tle girl in Gal - i - lee, a gen - tle breeze she came, a
4 Fly - ing to the riv - er, she wait - ed cir - cling high a -

emp - ty cra - dle wait - ing to be filled. And
Spir - it filled their dreams with life and form. —
whis - per soft - ly call - ing in the dark, the
bove the child now grown so full of grace. As he

from the heart of God the Spir - it moved up - on the earth, like a
Des - erts turned to gar - dens, bro - ken hearts found new de - light, and then
prom - ise of a child of peace whose reign would nev - er end, Ma - ry
rose up from the wa - ter, she swept down from the sky, and she

1, 3

moth - er breath - ing life in - to her child. (To Verse 2)
down the a - ges still she flew
sang the Spir - it song with - in her heart. (To Verse 4)
car - ried him a - way in her em—

2, 4, 5

on. She comes
brace.

5 Long after the deep darkness that fell upon the world,
   after dawn returned in flame of rising sun,
   the Spirit touched the earth again, again her wings unfurled,
   bringing life in wind and fire as she flew on.   *Refrain*

Words: Gordon Light 1985
Music: Gordon Light 1985; arr. Andrew Donaldson 1994
Words and music copyright © 1987 Common Cup Company. Arrangement © 1994 Andrew Donaldson.

SHE FLIES ON
Irregular

381

Spirit of Life

Words: Carolyn McDade 1981
Music: Carolyn McDade 1981; harm. Grace Lewis-McLaren 1992, alt.
Words and music copyright © 1981 Carolyn McDade. Harmony © 1992 Unitarian Universalist Association.

SPIRIT OF LIFE
8 12 8 12 8 10

Breathe on Me, Breath of God

(Souffle du Dieu vivant)

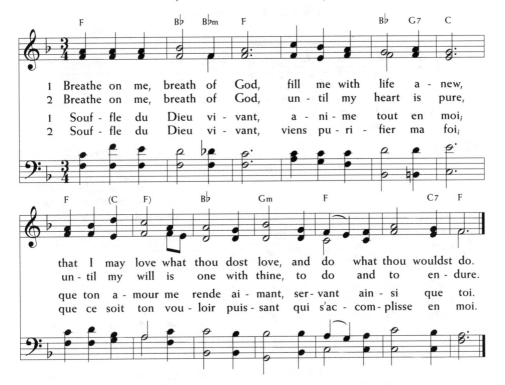

1 Breathe on me, breath of God, fill me with life a-new,
2 Breathe on me, breath of God, un-til my heart is pure,
1 Souf-fle du Dieu vi-vant, a-ni-me tout en moi;
2 Souf-fle du Dieu vi-vant, viens pu-ri-fier ma foi;

that I may love what thou dost love, and do what thou wouldst do.
un-til my will is one with thine, to do and to en-dure.
que ton a-mour me rende ai-mant, ser-vant ain-si que toi.
que ce soit ton vou-loir puis-sant qui s'ac-com-plisse en moi.

3 Breathe on me, breath of God,
till I am wholly thine,
until this earthly part of me
glows with thy fire divine.

3 Souffle du Dieu vivant,
mets ton feu dans mon coeur;
que tout en moi soit rayonnant
de ton éclat, Seigneur.

4 Breathe on me, breath of God:
so shall I never die,
but live with thee the perfect life
of thine eternity.

4 Souffle du Dieu vivant,
écarte enfin la mort;
que pour jamais, dès maintenant,
j'appartienne au Dieu fort.

Words: Edwin Hatch 1878; French trans. Suzanne Bidgrain 1937
Music: Robert Jackson 1888

TRENTHAM
6 6 8 6

383

Come, O Holy Spirit, Come
Oh viens, Esprit, viens
(Wa wa wa Emimimo)

Wa   wa   wa E - mi - mi - mo.
Come, O   Ho - ly Spir - it, come.
Oh   viens, Es - prit,   viens.

E - mi - o - lo - ye.
O wise Spir - it, come.
Es - prit de sa - gesse.

Wa   wa   wa A - lag - ba - ra.
Come, al - might - y Spir - it come.
Oh   viens, puis - sant Es - prit, viens.

A - lag - ba - ra - me - ta.
Al - might - y Tri - ni - ty.
Pui - san - te Tri - ni - té.

Wa - o   wa - o   wa - o.
Come,   come,   come.
Viens,   viens,   viens.

E - mi - mi - mo.
O Spir - it, come.
Oh viens, Es - prit.

Words: Yoruba traditional, English para. I-to Loh 1986, French, Joëlle Gouël 1990
Music: Yoruba traditional, harm. as taught by Samuel Solanke

WA WA WA EMIMIMO
Irregular

Words (Yoruban and English) copyright © 1986, (French) © 1990 and music © 1986 World Council of Churches and the Asian Institute for Liturgy and Music.

The Lone, Wild Bird

1 The lone, wild bird in loft - y flight is
2 The ends of earth are in your hand, the
3 Each se - cret thought is known to you, the
4 In se - cret depths you knit my frame, be -
5 O search me, God, my heart re - veal, re -

still with you, nor leaves your sight. And I am yours! I
sea's dark deep and far - off land. And I am yours! I
path I walk my whole life through; my days, my deeds, my
fore my birth you spoke my name; with - in my soul, as
new my life, my spir - it heal; for I am yours, I

rest in you, Great Spir - it, come, rest in me too.
rest in you, Great Spir - it, come, rest in me too.
hopes, my fears, my deep - est joys, my si - lent tears.
close as breath, so near to me, in life, in death.
rest in you, Great Spir - it, come, rest in me too.

Words: vv. 1, 2, Henry Richard McFadyen 1925, alt.; vv. 3–5 Marty Haugen 1991
Music: Walker's Southern Harmony 1835; harm. David N. Johnson 1968

PROSPECT
8 8 8 8

385 Spirit Divine, Attend Our Prayers

1 Spir-it di-vine, at-tend our prayers, and make this
2 Come as the light: to us re-veal our emp-ti-
♦ 3 Come as the wind: sweep clean a-way what dead with-
4 Come as the fire and purge our hearts like sac-ri-
5 Spir-it di-vine, at-tend our prayers: make a lost

house your home; de-scend with all your
ness and woe; and lead us in those
♦ in us lies, and search and fresh-en
fi-cial flame; let our whole life an
world your home; de-scend with all your

gra-cious powers: O come, great Spir-it, come!
paths of life where all the right-eous go.
♦ all our souls with liv-ing en-er-gies.
of-fering be to our Re-deem-er's name.
gra-cious powers: O come, great Spir-it, come!

Words: *Andrew Reed* 1829, alt.
Music: *Johann Crüger* 1647

GRÄFENBERG
8 6 8 6

386 Ô Saint-Esprit, Esprit d'amour

1 Ô Saint-Esprit, esprit d'amour,
don du Père et du Fils,
fais briller chacun de nos jours
de la splendeur du Christ.

2 Viens affermir sa vérité
dans nos coeurs inconstants;
viens offrir à sa royauté
notre vie qu'il attend.

3 Accorde-nous la soif de toi
et l'eau qui l'assouvit;
donne courage en nos combats
et lumière en la nuit.

4 Inspire-nous, quand nous prions,
pour prier comme il faut;

inspire-nous, quand nous parlons,
un amour sans défaut.

5 Baptise-nous et nous bénis
par ta force et ton feu,
et fais de nous un peuple uni
qui flambe aux mains de Dieu.

This French text (not a translation of the English) may be sung to the preceding tune.

Words: Commission d'Hymnologie de la Fédération Protestante de France 1977, d'après Romans 8,26
Words copyright © Fédération Protestante de France.

GRÄFENBERG
8 6 8 6

Loving Spirit

387

1 Lov - ing Spir - it, lov - ing Spir - it, you have
2 Like a moth - er, you en - fold me, hold my
3 Like a fa - ther, you pro - tect me, teach me
4 Friend and lov - er, in your close - ness I am
5 Lov - ing Spir - it, lov - ing Spir - it, you have

cho - sen me to be, you have drawn me to your
life with - in your own, feed me with your ver - y
the dis - cern - ing eye, hoist me up up - on your
known and held and blessed; in your prom - ise is my
cho - sen me to be, you have drawn me to your

won - der, you have set your sign on me.
bod - y, form me of your flesh and bone.
shoul - der, let me see the world from high.
com - fort, in your pres - ence I may rest.
won - der, you have set your sign on me.

Words: Shirley Erena Murray 1986
Music: Corner's Gross Catholisch Gesangbuch 1631, arr. William Smith Rockstro ca. 1895
Words copyright © 1987 The Hymn Society. Used by permission of Hope Publishing Company.

OMNI DIE (DIC MARIA)
8 7 8 7

388

Spirit Dancing

1 Spir - it danc - ing on the wa - ters, sun re - flect - ing song of grace call - ing life to all the crea - tures, giv - ing life to hu - man

2 Spir - it danc - ing on the wa - ters, nam - ing mo - ment they should part, giv - ing free - dom to the peo - ples, signed for all in dan - cer's

3 Spir - it danc - ing on the wa - ters, par - a - dox of womb and grave, wel - come now the Word child's com - ing, no one pris - oner, no one

4 Spir - it danc - ing on the wa - ters, can the dance by cross be stilled? Earth be sha - ken! Dead a - wak - en! What was emp - tied shall be

5 Spir - it danc - ing on the wa - ters, give your peo - ple their new birth, heal - ing, lov - ing one an - oth - er in com - mun - it - y with

6 Spir - it danc - ing on the wa - ters, we would come and dance with you 'til our world is filled with

Words: Walter Farquharson 1989
Music: Lori Erhardt 1988, arr. Kenneth Gray 1990

SPIRIT DANCING
8 7 8 7

race.
art.
slave.
filled.
earth.

mu - sic and in Christ all things are new.

389 God Is Here

1 God is here! As we your peo-ple meet to of-fer
2 Here are sym-bols to re-mind us of our life-long
3 Here our chil-dren find a wel-come in the Shep-herd's
4 God of all, of church and king-dom, in an age of

praise and prayer, may we find in full-er mea-sure
need of grace; here are ta-ble, font, and pul-pit;
flock and fold; here as bread and wine are tak-en,
change and doubt keep us faith-ful to the gos-pel;

what it is in Christ we share. Here, as in the world a-
here the cross has cen-tral place. Here in hon-es-ty of
Christ sus-tains us, as of old. Here the ser-vants of the
help us work your pur-pose out. Here, in this day's ded-i-

round us, all our var-ied skills and arts wait the
preach-ing, here in si-lence, as in speech, here, in
Ser-vant seek in wor-ship to ex-plore what it
ca-tion, all we have to give, re-ceive; we, who

Words: Fred Pratt Green 1978
Music: William P. Rowlands ca. 1905
Words copyright © 1979 Hope Publishing Company.

BLAENWERN
8 7 8 7 D

com - ing of the Spir - it in - to o - pen minds and hearts.
new - ness and re - new - al, God the Spir - it comes to each.
means in dai - ly liv - ing to be - lieve and to a - dore.
can - not live with - out you, we a - dore you! We be - lieve!

How Great the Mystery of Faith 390

1 How great the mys - ter - y of faith, how deep the pur - pos -
2 At - tract - ed by life's deep - est claim we wait, as - sem - bled
3 The best that we can do and say, the ut - most care of
4 Come, walk a - mong us, Ho - ly Friend, as all are gath - ered

es of God, in birth and age - ing, life and death,
in this place, with needs and hopes we can - not name,
skill and art, are sweep - ers of the Spir - it's way
and pre - pared, that scat - tered lives may meet and mend

1–3 | 4

un - veiled, yet nev - er un - der - stood!
a thirst for heal - ing, truth, and grace.
to reach the depths of ev - ery heart.
through o - pen Word and ta - ble shared.

Words: Brian Wren 1989
Music: Ron Klusmeier 1990
Words copyright © 1989 Hope Publishing Company. Music copyright © 1990 Ron Klusmeier.

OTTERSPOOR
8 8 8 8

391 God, Reveal Your Presence

1 God, re - veal your pres - ence: as we now a - dore you
2 God, re - veal your pres - ence: hear the harps re - sound - ing;
3 O great Fount of bless - ing, pur - i - fy my spir - it,

and with awe ap - pear be - fore you. Here in this your
see the crowds the throne sur - round - ing. "Ho - ly, ho - ly,
trust - ing on - ly in your mer - it; like the ho - ly

tem - ple: all with - in keep si - lence, ga - ther now with
ho - ly!" Hear the hymn as - cend - ing, an - gels, saints, their
an - gels gath - ered all be - fore you, may I cease - less -

deep - est rev - erence. You a - lone God we own,
voic - es blend - ing. Bow your ear to us here;
ly a - dore you. Let your will ev - er still

Words: *Gerhard Tersteegen 1729, trans. Frederick William Foster and John Miller 1789,*
William Mercer 1854, alt.
Music: *Joachim Neander 1680*

ARNSBERG
668D3366

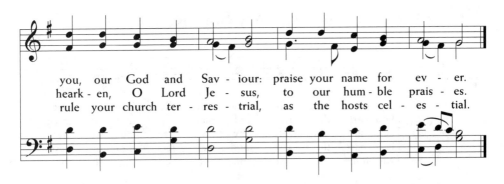

you, our God and Sav - iour: praise your name for ev - er.
heark - en, O Lord Je - sus, to our hum - ble prais - es.
rule your church ter - res - trial, as the hosts cel - es - tial.

How Sacred Is This Place 392

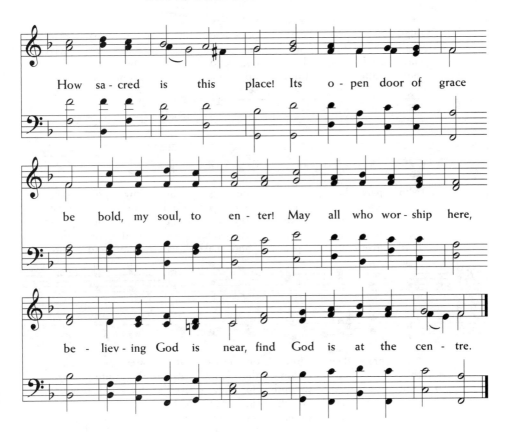

How sa - cred is this place! Its o - pen door of grace

be bold, my soul, to en - ter! May all who wor - ship here,

be - liev - ing God is near, find God is at the cen - tre.

Words: Fred Pratt Green 1982
Music: adapt. Louis Bourgeois ca. 1547; harm. Claude Goudimel ca. 1551
Words copyright © 1989 Hope Publishing Company.

LE CANTIQUE DE SIMÉON
6 6 7 6 6 7

393 I Greet Thee, Who My Sure Redeemer Art

1. I greet thee, who my sure Re-deem-er art,
   my on-ly trust and Sav-iour of my heart,
   who pain didst un-der-go for my poor sake;
   I pray thee from our hearts all cares to take.

2. Thou art the King of mer-cy and of grace,
   reign-ing om-ni-po-tent in ev-ery place:
   so come, O King, and our whole be-ing sway;
   shine on us with the light of thy pure day.

3. Thou art the life, by which a-lone we live,
   and all our sub-stance and our strength re-ceive;
   sus-tain us by thy faith and by thy power,
   and give us strength in ev-ery try-ing hour.

4. Thou hast the true and per-fect gen-tle-ness,
   no harsh-ness hast thou and no bit-ter-ness:
   O grant to us the grace we find in thee,
   that we may dwell in per-fect u-ni-ty.

5. Our hope is in no oth-er save in thee;
   our faith is built up-on thy prom-ise free;
   Lord, give us peace, and make us calm and sure,
   that in thy strength we ev-er-more en-dure.

Words: *attrib. John Calvin, French Psalter, Strassburg 1545; trans. Elizabeth Lee Smith 1868*
Music: *Orlando Gibbons 1623*

SONG 24
10 10 10 10

Moved by the Gospel, Let Us Move

394

1 Moved by the Gos - pel, let us move with ev - ery gift and art.
2 Let weav - ers form from bro - ken strands a tap - es - try of prayer.
3 O Spir - it, breathe a - mong us here; in - spire the work we do.

The im - age of cre - a - tive love in - dwells each hu - man heart.
Let art - ists paint with skil - ful hands their joy, la - ment, and care.
May hands and voic - es, eye and ear at - test to life made new.

The Mak - er calls cre - a - tion good, so let us now ex - press
Then mime the sto - ry: Christ has come. With rev - erence dance the word.
In wor - ship and in dai - ly strife cre - ate a - mong us still.

with sound and col - our, stone and wood, the shape of ho - li - ness.
With flute and or - gan, ching* and drum God's praise be ev - er heard.
Great Art - ist, form our com - mon life ac - cord - ing to your will.

* The "ching" is a Korean gong.

Words: Ruth Duck 1992
Music: Gottfried Wilhelm Fink 1842
Words copyright © 1992 G.I.A. Publications, Inc.

BETHLEHEM
8 6 8 6 D
Alt. tune: Forest Green

395

Come In, Come In and Sit Down
(Part of the Family)

Refrain (Unison)

Come in, come in and sit down, you are a part of the
fam - ily. We are lost and we are found, and we are a
part of the fam - ily.

1 — You know the rea - son
2 — God is with us
3 There's life to be shared in the
4 There's rest for the wea - ry and

why you came, — yet no rea - son
in this place, — like a moth - er's
bread and the wine; — we are the branch - es,
health for us all; there's a yoke that is eas - y, and a

Words: James K. Manley 1984, alt.
Music: James K. Manley 1984; arr. Darryl Nixon 1987
Words and music copyright © 1984 James K. Manley. Arrangement © 1987 Songs for a Gospel People.

PART OF THE FAMILY
Irregular with refrain

can ex - plain; so share in the laugh - ter and
warm em - brace. — We're all for - giv - en
Christ is the vine. — This is God's tem - ple, it's
bur - den that's small. So come in and wor - ship and

cry in the pain, for we are a part of the fam - ily.
by God's grace, for we are a part of the fam - ily.
not yours or mine, but we are a part of the fam - ily.
an - swer the call, for we are a part of the fam - ily.

Jesus, Stand among Us 396

1 Je - sus, stand a - mong us in your ris - en power;
2 Breathe the Ho - ly Spir - it in - to ev - ery heart;
3 Lead our hearts to wis - dom till our doubt - ing cease,

let this time of wor - ship be a hal - lowed hour.
bid the fears and sor - rows from each soul de - part.
and to all as - sem - bled speak your word of peace.

Words: vv. 1, 2 William Pennefather 1873; v. 3 Lydia Pedersen 1995
Music: Friedrich Filitz 1847
Words (v. 3) copyright © 1995 Lydia Pedersen.

BEMERTON (CASWALL)
6 5 6 5

397   O Praise the Gracious Power

Unison

1 O praise the gra - cious power that
2 O praise per - sis - tent truth that
3 O praise in - clu - sive love, en -
4 O praise the word of faith that
5 O praise the tide of grace that

tum - bles walls of fear and gath - ers in one
o - pens fist - ed minds and eas - es from their
cir - cling ev - ery race, ob - liv - i - ous to
claims us as God's own, a liv - ing tem - ple
laps at ev - ery shore with vi - sions of a

house of faith all stran - gers far and near:
anx - ious clutch the prej - u - dice that blinds:
gen - der, wealth, to so - cial rank or place:
built on Christ, our rock and cor - ner - stone:
world at peace, no long - er bled by war:

We praise you, Christ! Your cross has made us one!

Words: *Thomas H. Troeger* 1984
Music: *Carol Doran* 1984
Words and music copyright © 1984 Oxford University Press Inc.

CHRISTPRAISE RAY
6 6 8 6 with refrain

6 O praise the power, the truth,
  the love, the word, the tide.
  Yet more than these, O praise their
    source,
  praise Christ the crucified:
  We praise you, Christ!
  Your cross has made us one!

7 O praise the living Christ
  with faith's bright songful voice!
  Announce the gospel to the world
  and with these words rejoice:
  We praise you, Christ!
  Your cross has made us one!

Great Shepherd of Your People 398

1 Great Shepherd of your people, hear! your
2 Within these walls let holy peace and
3 May we in faith receive your word, in
4 The hearing ear, the seeing eye, the

presence now display; as you have given a
love and friendship dwell; here give the trou - bled
faith present our prayers; and in the pres - ence
con - trite heart bestow; and shine up - on us

place for prayer, so give us hearts to pray.
con - science ease, the wound - ed spir - it heal.
of our God un - bur - den all our cares.
from on high, that we in grace may grow.

Words: John Newton 1769
Music: Isaac Smith ca. 1780

ABRIDGE
8 6 8 6

399 God, Whose Love Is Reigning o'er Us

Descant
5 Lift we then our hu-man voic - es in the

1 God, whose love is *reign - ing o'er us, source of
2 Word of God from na - ture bring - ing spring- time
3 Ho - ly God of an - cient glo - ry, choos - ing
4 Cov - enant, new a - gain in Je - sus, Star - child
5 Lift we then our hu-man voic - es in the

songs that faith would bring; live we then in hu-man choic-es

all, the end - ing true; hear the u - ni - ver-sal cho-rus
green and au - tumn gold; moun-tain streams like chil-dren sing-ing,
man and wom-an, too; A - br'am's faith and Sar-ah's sto-ry
born to set us free; sent to heal us, sent to teach us
songs that faith would bring; live we then in hu-man choic-es

lives that, like our mu - sic, sing: Hal - le - lu - jah,

raised in joy - ful praise to you: Hal - le - lu - jah,
o - cean waves like thun - der bold: Hal - le - lu - jah,
formed a peo - ple bound to you. Hal - le - lu - jah,
how love's chil - dren we might be. Hal - le - lu - jah,
lives that, like our mu - sic, sing: Hal - le - lu - jah,

* or "ever with"

Words: William Boyd Grove 1980
Music: John Goss 1869, desc. Cyril Hampshire 1954

LAUDA ANIMA (PRAISE MY SOUL)
8 7 8 7

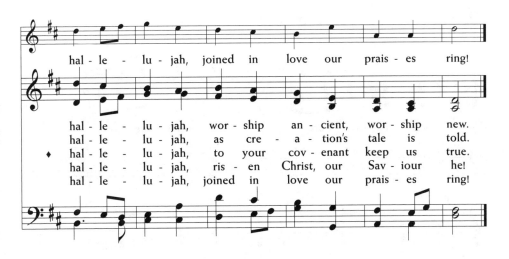

hal - le - lu - jah, joined in love our prais - es ring!

hal - le - lu - jah, wor - ship an - cient, wor - ship new.
hal - le - lu - jah, as cre - a - tion's tale is told.
hal - le - lu - jah, to your cov - enant keep us true.
hal - le - lu - jah, ris - en Christ, our Sav - iour he!
hal - le - lu - jah, joined in love our prais - es ring!

Lord, Listen to Your Children Praying 400

Lord, lis-ten to your chil-dren pray - ing, Lord, send your

Spir-it in this place; Lord, listen to your chil-dren

pray - ing, send us love, send us power, send us grace!

Words: Ken Medema 1970
Music: Ken Medema 1970
Words and music copyright © 1971 Hope Publishing Company.

CHILDREN PRAYING
9 8 9 9

401 Worship the Lord

Refrain (Unison)

Wor - ship the Lord (wor - ship the Lord)

*wor - ship the Fa - ther, the Spir - it, the Son,

rais - ing our hands (rais - ing our hands) in de -

vo - tion to God who is one! (to verses)

* or "praise the Creator, the Spirit, the Son"

Words: Fred Kaan 1972
Music: Ron Klusmeier 1977
Words copyright © 1974 Hope Publishing Company. Music © 1977 Ron Klusmeier.

LIDDLE
11 11 12 7 with refrain

1 Rais - ing our hands as a sign of re - joic - ing,
2 Pray - ing and train - ing that we be a bless - ing,
♦ 3 Called to be part - ners with God in cre - a - tion,
4 Bring - ing the bread and the wine to the ta - ble,
5 Now in re - sponse to the life you are giv - ing,

and with our lips our to - geth - er - ness voic - ing,
and by our hand - i - work dai - ly con - fess - ing:
♦ hon - our - ing Christ as the Lord of the na - tion,
ask - ing that we may be led and en - a - bled,
help us, †O Fa - ther, to of - fer our liv - ing,

giv - ing our - selves to a life of cre - a - tive - ness,
we are com - mit - ted to serv - ing hu - man - i - ty,
♦ we must be read - y for risk and for sac - ri - fice,
tru - ly u - nit - ed to build new com - mun - i - ties,
seek - ing a just and a heal - ing so - ci - e - ty,

wor - ship and work must be one!

† or "Creator"

(The French text appears on the following page..)

Louange à Dieu

Refrain

Louange à Dieu, (louange à Dieu),
louange à Dieu, au Christ et à l'Esprit.
Dieu soit loué, (Dieu soit loué)
par nos deux mains tendues vers sa vie.

1 Vers toi, ô Dieu, vois nos mains qui s'élèvent;
un chant joyeux jaillissant de nos lèvres;
reçois nos jours de travail et de fête,
règne de Dieu parmi nous!   *Refrain*

2 Vers toi, ô Dieu, nos prières s'élancent;
transforme nos mains en un chant de louange;
en servant nos prochains c'est toi qu'elles chantent,
règne de Dieu parmi nous!   *Refrain*

3 Voici un monde soumis aux souffrances,
voici nos mains pour aider sa naissance;
remplis de ta force d'amour nos gestes,
règne de Dieu parmi nous.   *Refrain*

4 Voici le pain et le vin sur la table:
fais de nous, Dieu, le ferment dans la pâte,
le sel d'une vie solidaire, amicale,
règne de Dieu parmi nous.   *Refrain*

5 Prends-nous la main quand nos forces s'épuisent;
Dieu, que ta main aujourd'hui nous conduise
là où nous verrons se lever ta justice,
règne de Dieu parmi nous.   *Refrain*

Words: Fred Kaan 1972; French trans. Nicole Berthet 1972
Words (French) copyright © 1987 Songs for a Gospel People.

LIDDLE
11 11 12 7 *with refrain*

402 We Are One

1 We are one   as we come,   as we come,   joy- ful to be
2 We are one   as we share,   as we share   bro- ken- ness and
3 We are one   as we feast,   as we feast,   peace be- comes the
4 We are one   as we hear,   as we hear,   heart and hand u-

here, / in the praise / on our lips / there's a
fear, / in the touch / of a hand / there's a
sign; / in the bread / and the wine / there's a
nite; / in the word / we re-ceive / there's a

sense / that God is near. / We are one / as we
sense / that God is here. / We are one / as we
sense / of love di-vine. / We are one / as we
sense / that God is light. / We are one / as we

sing, / as we seek, / we are found; / and we
care, / as we heal, / we are healed; / and we
come, / as we feed, / we are fed; / and we
leave, / as we love, / we are loved; / and we

come need-ful of God's grace as we meet, to-ge-ther in this place.
share warmth in God's em-brace as we pray to-ge-ther in this place.
feel God's re-fresh-ing grace as we meet at ta-ble in this place.
seek jus-tice in God's ways as we move to-ge-ther from this place.

Words: Doreen Lankshear-Smith 1988
Music: Jeeva Sam 1987; arr. David Kai 1995

WE ARE ONE
Irregular

403   Ring from Your Steeple

Unison

1 Ring from your stee - ple, bells of glad - ness!
2 Ring from your stee - ple, bells of vic - tory!
3 Ring from your stee - ple, bells of pow - er!
4 Ring from your stee - ple, bells of hea - ven!

This is the day the world was born;
This is the day death's sting was drawn;
This is the day when, at the dawn,
This is the day when none shall mourn;

God's voice rang out a - cross the dark - ness,
God's voice rang out, the tomb was emp - ty,
God's voice rang out through wind and fire,
God's voice rings out this one - in - se - ven,

Words: Michael Saward 1981
Music: Norman Warren 1982
Words and music copyright © 1982 by Hope Publishing Company.

STEEPLE BELLS
9 8 9 8

light	filled	the	sky	that	pri	-	mal
hope	sprang	a -	live	that	Eas	-	ter
fresh	came	the	Spir	- it	on		that
joy	fills	the	church	this	Sun	-	day

morn.
morn.
morn.
morn.

A Prayer at the Opening of Worship   404

As on a first day you began the work of creating us;
as on a first day you raised your Son from the dead;
so on this first day, O Lord, freshen and remake us:
and as the week is new, let our lives begin again
because of Jesus who shows us your loving power. Amen.

Thomas Caryl Micklem

405 New Every Morning

1 New ev - ery morn - ing is the love
2 New mer - cies each re - turn - ing day
3 If on our dai - ly course our mind
4 The triv - ial round, the com - mon task,
5 On - ly, O God, in your dear love

our wak - ening and up - ris - ing prove;
hov - er a - round us while we pray;
be set to hal - low all we find,
will fur - nish all we ought to ask,
fit us for per - fect rest a - bove;

through sleep and dark - ness safe - ly brought,
new per - ils past, new sins for - given,
new trea - sures still of count - less price
room to de - ny our - selves, a road
and help us, this and ev - ery day,

re - stored to life, and power, and thought.
new thoughts of God, new hopes of heaven.
God will pro - vide for sac - ri - fice.
to bring us dai - ly near - er God.
to live more near - ly as we pray.

Words: John Keble 1822
Music: Samuel Webbe 1782

MELCOMBE
8 8 8 8

See the Morning Sun Ascending 406

1 See the morn - ing sun as - cend - ing, ra - diant in the
2 So may we, in low - ly sta - tion, join the cho - ris -
3 For your lov - ing - kind - ness ev - er shed up - on our
4 "Wis - dom, hon - our, power, and bless - ing!" with the an - gel - ic

east - ern sky; hear the an - gel voic - es blend - ing
ters a - bove; sing - ing with the whole cre - a - tion,
earth - ly way; for your mer - cy, ceas - ing nev - er,
host we cry; round your throne, your name con - fess - ing,

in their praise to God on high! Hal - le - lu - jah!
prais - ing you for your great love. Hal - le - lu - jah!
for your bless - ing day by day: Hal - le - lu - jah!
now we would to you draw nigh. Hal - le - lu - jah!

Hal - le - lu - jah! Glo - ry be to God on high!
Hal - le - lu - jah! Glo - ry be to God a - bove!
Hal - le - lu - jah! Glo - ry be to God al - way!
Hal - le - lu - jah! Glo - ry be to God on high!

Words: Charles Parkin 1953
Music: Joachim Neander 1680

NEANDER (UNSER HERRSCHER)
878787
Alt. setting: 28

407   O Joy of God

1 O joy of God, we seek you in the morn - ing
2 O life of God, for you our spir - its hun - ger;
3 O peace of God, you pass our un - der - stand - ing;

and long to see the glo - ry of your face:
un - less we feed on you we sure - ly die:
safe through each mo - ment keep us ev - ery day:

rise on our dark - ness with your sun's new dawn - ing.
with love and faith re - newed and hope grown youn - ger,
with joy di - vine and mer - cy nev - er end - ing,

Flood all our be - ing in this feast of grace.
send us from here to serve you, God most high.
di - rect our path and pros - per all our way.

Words: *Cecil Henry Boutflower, rev.* Hymns for Today's Church *1982*
Music: *Richard Runciman Terry ca. 1933*
Words copyright © *1982 Hope Publishing Company. Music by permission of Oxford University Press.*

HIGHWOOD
11 10 11 10
Alt. tune: O Perfect Love

Welcome to Another Day

1 Wel - come to an - oth - er day! Night is blind - ed.
2 Wel - come to the day of prayer with God's peo - ple;
3 Wel - come is the peace that's given, sure for ev - er;

"Wel - come," let cre - a - tion say; dark - ness end - ed.
wel - come is the joy we share at this ta - ble.
wel - come is the hope of heaven when life's ov - er.

Comes the sun - shine af - ter dew, time for la - bour;
Bread and wine from heav - en fall; come, re - ceive it
As we work and as we pray, trust God's sto - ry:

time to love my God a - new and my neigh - bour.
that the Christ may reign in all who be - lieve it.
come then, as the dawn - ing day her - alds glo - ry!

Words: Michael Saward 1980
Music: Joseph David Jones ca. 1852
Words copyright © 1982 Hope Publishing Company.

GWALCHMAI
7 4 7 4 D

409

Morning Has Broken

1 Morn-ing has bro - ken like the first morn - ing,
2 Sweet the rain's new fall sun - lit from heav - en,
3 Ours is the sun - light! Ours is the morn - ing

black - bird has spo - ken like the first bird.
like the first dew - fall on the first grass.
born of the one light E - den saw play!

Praise for the sing - ing! Praise for the morn - ing!
Praise for the sweet - ness of the wet gar - den,
Praise with e - la - tion, praise ev - ery morn - ing,

Praise for them, spring - ing fresh from the Word!
sprung in com - plete - ness where God's feet pass.
God's re - cre - a - tion of the new day!

Words: Eleanor Farjeon 1931
Music: Gaelic melody; harm. Alec Wyton
Words used by permission of David Higham Associates. Harmony from The Hymnal 1982 © The Church Pension Fund.

BUNESSAN
5 5 5 4 D
Alt. setting: 484

This Day God Gives Me 410

1 This day God gives me
strength of high heaven,
sun and moon shining,
flame in my hearth,
flashing of lightning,
wind in its swiftness,
deeps of the ocean,
firmness of earth.

2 This day God sends me
strength to sustain me,
might to uphold me,
wisdom as guide.
Your eyes are watchful,
your ears are listening,
your lips are speaking,
Friend at my side.

3 God's way is my way,
God's shield is round me,
God's host defends me,
saving from ill.
Angels of heaven,
drive from me always
all that would harm me,
stand by me still.

4 Rising, I thank you,
mighty and strong One,
King of creation,
giver of rest,
firmly confessing
Threeness of Persons,
Oneness of Godhead,
Trinity blest.

Words: attrib. St. Patrick; adapt. James Quinn, SJ 1969
Words copyright © 1969, James Quinn, SJ. Used by permission of Selah Publishing Co., Inc.

BUNESSAN
5 5 5 4 D

O God We Call 411

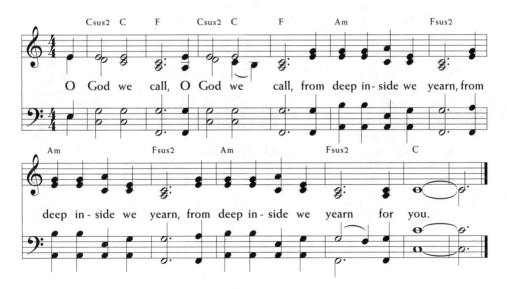

Words: Linnea Good 1994
Music: Linnea Good 1994
Words and music copyright © 1994 Borealis Music.

O GOD WE CALL
Irregular

412

This Is the Day

Unison

1,4 This is the day, this is the day that our God has made, that our
2 O - pen to us, o - pen to us your gates, O God, your
3 You are our God, your are our God, we will praise your name, we will

God has made; we will re - joice, we will re - joice, and be
gates, O God; we will go in, we will go in, to your
praise your name; we will give thanks, we will give thanks, for your

glad in it, and be glad in it. This is the day that our
ho - ly place, to your ho - ly place. O - pen to us your
faith - ful - ness, for your faith - ful - ness. You are our God, we will

God has made, we will re - joice and be glad in it.
gates, O God, we will go in to your ho - ly place.
praise your name, we will give thanks for your faith - ful - ness.

Words: v. 1 unknown; vv. 2, 3 R. Gerald Hobbs 1987, 1995
Music: Fijian folk melody; arr. Darryl Nixon 1987
Words v. 2, 3 copyright © 1987, 1995 and arrangement copyright © 1987 Songs for a Gospel People.

THIS IS THE DAY
Irregular

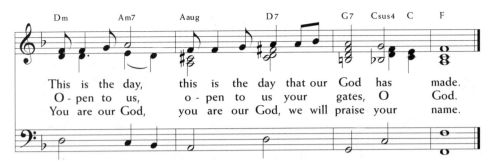

| Dm | Am7 | Aaug | D7 | G7 | Csus4 | C | F |

This is the day, this is the day that our God has made.
O - pen to us, o - pen to us your gates, O God.
You are our God, you are our God, we will praise your name.

O Splendour of God's Glory Bright 413

| D | Bm | A | D | G | D | A | D | G | D |

1 O splen - dour of God's glo - ry bright, from light e -
2 come, Ho - ly Sun of heaven - ly love, pour down your
3 O joy - ful be the pass - ing day with thoughts as
4 O Christ, with each re - turn - ing morn your im - age

| A | D | G | D | A | Bm | E7 | A | D |

ter - nal bring - ing light; O light of life, light's
ra - diance from a - bove, and to our in - ward
clear as morn - ing's ray, with faith like noon - tide
to our hearts is born; O may we ev - er

| G | D | Em | A | D | A | D | G | A | D |

liv - ing spring, true day, all days il - lu - min - ing:
hearts con - vey the Ho - ly Spir - it's cloud - less ray.
shin - ing bright, our souls un - shad - owed by the night.
see a - new our Sav - iour and our God in you!

Words: Ambrose of Milan ca. 374; trans. composite, Rejoice in the Lord 1985   *PUER NOBIS NASCITUR*
Music: Trier ms., 15th century; adapt. Michael Praetorius 1609; harm. George Ratcliff Woodward 1902   8 8 8 8
Harmony copyright © Mowbray.

414 God, Be Praised at Early Morn
(Qing-chen zao qi zan-mei Shen)

1 Qing - chen zao qi zan - mei Shen,
2 Shen di rong - guang zhao si fang,

1 God, be praised at ear - ly morn,
2 Ev - ery - where your glo - rious light,

yi - ya ping - an meng Shen en,
chong - man yu - zhou he hui - huang,

for pro - tec - tion through the night;
splen - dour fills the u - ni - verse;

Jin - ri hai qiu Zhu bao - you,
Zhen guang zhao zai wo xin shang,

bless - ing still I need this day,
true light, shine up - on my heart

Wei Zhu zuo - gong xin an - wen.
Shen en hou ai chang song - yang.

in my work, a stead - fast heart.
al - ways prais - ing your deep love.

Words: Dawei Wang 1981; English trans. G. A. Wenh-In Ng 1992
Music: Dawei Wang 1981; arr. Pen-li Chen (I-to Loh) 1990

QING-CHEN
7 7 7 7

3 Qi-qiu Sheng-ling shi da-neng
  Qu wo zui-e huan xin-ren,
  Qian-bei wen-rou xiao-fa Zhu,
  Ha-li-lu-ya rong yao Shen.

3 Holy Spirit, in your power
  cleanse my sin and make me new,
  humble, gentle, like my Lord.
  Hallelujah! Praise to God.

God, We Praise You for the Morning 415

1 God, we praise you for the morn - ing; hope springs
2 God, we praise you for cre - a - tion, moun - tains,
3 God, we praise you for com - pas - sion, all the
4 God, we praise you for your Spir - it, Com - fort -
5 God, we praise you for the Sav - iour, come that
*6 Hal - le - lu - jah, hal - le - lu - jah, hal - le -

forth with each new day, new be - gin - ning,
seas, and prai - rie land. Wak - ing souls find
lov - ing that you show; hu - man touch - ing,
er and dai - ly friend, rest - less search - er,
we may know your ways. In his lov - ing,
lu - jah, hal - le - lu - jah! Hal - le - lu - jah,

prayer, and prom - ise, joy in work and in play.
joy and heal - ing in your boun - ti - ful hand.
tears, and laugh - ter, help your chil - dren to grow.
gen - tle teach - er, strength and cour - age you send.
dy - ing, ris - ing, Christ is Lord of our days.
hal - le - lu - jah! Christ is Lord of our days!

* May be omitted during Lent.

Words: Jim Strathdee and Jean Strathdee 1984
Music: Jim Strathdee 1984
Words and music copyright © 1985 Desert Flower Music.

DICKEY
8 7 8 6

And the following...

416   Forth in Your Name, O Christ

1 Forth in your name, O Christ, we go, our daily labour to pursue, you, only you, resolved to know in all we think, or speak, or do.

2 The task your wisdom has assigned here let us cheerfully fulfil; in all our works your presence find, and prove your good and perfect will.

3 You may we set at our right hand, whose eyes our inmost secrets view, and labour on at your command and offer all our works to you.

4 Help us to bear your easy yoke, in every moment watch and pray, and still to things eternal look, and hasten to that glorious day.

5 Then with delight may we employ all that your bounteous grace has given, and run our earthly course with joy, and closely walk with you to heaven.

Words: Charles Wesley 1749, alt.
Music: Robert Schumann 1839, adapt.

CANONBURY
8 8 8 8

God, as We Rise to Leave

Words: Fred Kaan 1968
Music: Johann Crüger 1653
Words copyright © 1968 Hope Publishing Company.

LOBET DEN HERREN
11 11 11 5

418 Go Forth for God

1 Go forth for God, go to the world in peace;
be of good courage, armed with heavenly grace,
in God's good Spirit daily to increase,
till in the kingdom we see face to face.

2 Go forth for God, go to the world in love;
strengthen the faint, give courage to the weak;
help the afflicted; richly from above
God's love supplies the grace and power we seek.

3 Go forth for God, go to the world in strength;
hold fast the good, be urgent for the right;
render to no one evil; Christ at length
shall overcome all darkness with his light.

4 Go forth for God, go to the world in joy,
to serve God's people every day and hour,
and serving Christ, our every gift employ,
rejoicing in the Holy Spirit's power.

Words: J.R. Peacey ca. 1970
Music: Genevan Psalter 1551
Words copyright © 1984 Hope Publishing Company.

OLD 124TH
10 10 10 10 10

Go forth for God, go to the world in peace.
Go forth for God, go to the world in love.
Go forth for God, go to the world in strength.
Go forth for God, go to the world in joy.

May the Grace of Christ   419

1 May the grace of Christ our Sav - iour, and our
2 Thus may we a - bide in u - nion held to -

Ma - ker's bound - less love, with the Ho - ly Spi - rit's
geth - er by the Word, and pos - sess in rich com -

fa - vour, rest up - on us from a - bove.
mun - ion joys which earth can - not af - ford.

Words: John Newton 1779

OMNI DIE (DIC MARIA)
8 7 8 7

Music: Corner's Gesangbuch 1631, arr. William Smith Rockstro ca. 1895

420   Go to the World

Unison

1 Go to the world! Go in-to all the earth.
2 Go to the world! Go in-to ev-ery place.
3 Go to the world! Go strug-gle, bless and pray;
4 Go to the world! Go as the ones I send,

Go preach the cross where Christ re-news life's worth,
Go live the Word of God's re-deem-ing grace.
the nights of tears give way to joy-ous day.
for I am with you 'til the age shall end,

bap-tis-ing as the sign of our re-birth.
Go seek God's pres-ence in each time and space.
As ser-vant Church, you fol-low Christ's own way.
when all the hosts of glo-ry cry "A-men!"

Hal-le-lu-jah! Hal-le-lu-jah!

Words: Sylvia Dunstan 1985
Music: Ralph Vaughan Williams 1906

SINE NOMINE
10 10 10 4 4

Lead On, O Cloud of Presence

1 Lead on, O cloud of Pres - ence, the ex - o - dus is come.
2 Lead on, O fier - y Pil - lar, we fol - low yet with fears,
3 Lead on, O God of free - dom, and guide us on our way,

In wil - der - ness and des - ert our tribe shall make its home.
but we shall come re - joic - ing though joy be born of tears.
and help us trust the prom - ise through strug - gle and de - lay.

Our slav - ery left be - hind us, new hopes with - in us grow.
We are not lost, though wan - der - ing, for by your light we come,
We pray our sons and daugh - ters may jour - ney to that land

We seek the land of prom - ise where milk and hon - ey flow.
and we are still God's peo - ple. The jour - ney is our home.
where jus - tice dwells with mer - cy, and love is law's de - mand.

Words: Ruth Duck 1974, alt.
Music: Henry Thomas Smart 1836
Words copyright © 1992 G.I.A. Publications Inc.

LANCASHIRE
7 6 7 6 D

422 God Be with You till We Meet Again

(First tune)

1 God be with you till we meet again;
loving counsels guide, uphold you,
with a shepherd's care enfold you;
God be with you till we meet again.

2 God be with you till we meet again;
unseen wings protecting hide you,
daily manna still provide you;

3 God be with you till we meet again;
when life's perils thick confound you,
put unfailing arms around you;

4 God be with you till we meet again;
keep love's banner floating o'er you,
smite death's threatening wave before you;

Refrain

Till we meet, till we meet, till we meet at Jesus' feet; till we meet,
(till we meet, till we meet again) (till we meet) (till we meet,

till we meet, God be with you till we meet a - gain.
till we meet a - gain)

Words: Jeremiah E. Rankin 1880, alt.
Music: William G. Tomer 1880

GOD BE WITH YOU
9 8 8 9 with refrain

God Be with You till We Meet Again   423
(Second tune)

1 God be with you till we meet a - gain; lov - ing
2 God be with you till we meet a - gain; un - seen
3 God be with you till we meet a - gain; when life's
4 God be with you till we meet a - gain; keep love's

coun - sels guide, up - hold you, with a shep - herd's care
wings pro - tect - ing hide you, dai - ly man - na still
per - ils thick con - found you, put un - fail - ing arms
ban - ner float - ing o'er you, smite death's threat - ening wave

en - fold you;
pro - vide you;
a - round you;   God be with you till we meet a - gain.
be - fore you;

Words: Jeremiah Eames Rankin 1880, alt.
Music: Ralph Vaughan Williams 1906
Music by permission of Oxford University Press.

RANDOLPH
9 8 8 9

424   May the God of Hope Go with Us

1 May the God of hope go with us ev - ery day,
2 May the God of heal - ing free the earth from fear,

fill - ing all our lives with love and joy and peace.
free - ing us for peace, both trea - sured and pur - sued.

May the God of jus - tice speed us on our way,
May the God of love keep our com - mit - ment clear

bring - ing light and hope to ev - ery land and race.
to a world re - stored, to hu - man life re - newed.

*Refrain

Pray - ing, let us work for peace, sing - ing,

* If desired, the refrain may be repeated several times.

Words: v. 1 Alvin Schutmaat 1984; v. 2 Fred Kaan 1993
Music: Argentine folk melody
Words (v. 2) copyright © 1993 Hope Publishing Company.

ARGENTINA
11 11 11 11 with refrain

share our joy with all, work - ing for a

world that's new, faith - ful when we hear Christ's call.

God, Dismiss Us with Your Blessing 425

1 God, dis - miss us with your bless - ing; fill our hearts with joy and peace;
2 Thanks we give and a - do - ra - tion for your gos - pel's joy - ful sound;

let us each, your love pos - sess - ing, tri - umph in re - deem - ing grace;
may the fruits of your sal - va - tion in our hearts and lives a - bound;

O re - fresh us, O re - fresh us, trav - elling through the wil - der - ness.
may your pres - ence, may your pres - ence, with us ev - er - more be found.

Words: John Fawcett 1773, alt.
Music: from An Essay on the Church Plain Chant 1782

ALLELUIA, DULCE CARMEN
8 7 8 7 8 7

426 Saviour, Again to Your Dear Name

1 Sav - iour, a - gain to your dear name we raise
2 Grant us your peace up - on our home - ward way;
3 Grant us your peace through - out the com - ing night;
4 Grant us your peace through - out our earth - ly life,

with one ac - cord our part - ing hymn of praise;
with you be - gan, with you shall end the day;
turn all our dark - ness to your per - fect light;
com - fort in sor - row, cour - age in our strife;

we give you thanks be - fore our wor - ship cease,
guard now the lips from sin, the hearts from shame,
then, through our sleep, our hope and strength re - new,
then, when your voice shall bid our con - flict cease,

then, in the si - lence hear your word of peace.
that in this house have called up - on your name.
for dark and light are both a - like to you.
call us, at last, to your e - ter - nal peace.

Words: John Ellerton 1866, alt.
Music: Edward John Hopkins 1869

ELLERS
10 10 10 10

To Show by Touch and Word

427

1 To show by touch and word devotion
2 Renew our minds to choose the things that
3 Let love from day to day be yardstick,

to the earth, to hold in full regard all
matter most, our hearts to long for truth till
rule, and norm, and let our lives portray your

life that comes to birth, we need, O God, the
pride of self is lost. For every challenge
word in human form. Now come with us that

will to find the good you had of old in mind.
that we face we need your guidance and your grace.
we may have your wits about us where we live.

Words: Fred Kaan 1974
Music: Ron Klusmeier 1974
Words copyright © 1975 Hope Publishing Company. Music copyright © 1974 Ron Klusmeier.

LODWICK
12 12 8 8

428   A Blessing

May the blessing of the God of Sarah and Hagar,
    as of Abraham,
the blessing of the Son, born of the woman Mary,
and the blessing of the Spirit, who broods over us
    as a mother her children,
be with you all. Amen.

Lois Wilson 1982

429   May the Blessing of God Be upon You

May the bless-ing of God be up-on you. May God's love light all your way. May the grace of Christ en-fold you and peace a-round you stay. May the Spir-it of God dwell with-in you. May you live in joy each day.

Words: R. Gordon Nodwell 1989   MACRAE
Music: William H. M. Wright 1989   Irregular
Words copyright © 1995 R. Gordon Nodwell. Music copyright © 1995 William H. M. Wright.

God Be in My Head

God be in my head, and in my un-der-stand-ing;

God be in mine eyes, and in my look-ing;

God be in my mouth, and in my speak-ing;

God be in my heart, and in my think-ing;

God be at mine end, and at my de-part-ing.

Words: from The Book of Hours 1514
Music: H. Walford Davies 1910

GOD BE IN MY HEAD
Irregular

431

Sing Amen
(Asithi: Amen)

Leader:
People:
Leader:

*A - si - thi: A - men, si - ya - ku - du - mi - sa. A - si - thi:
Sing a - men: A - men, we praise your name, O God. Sing a - men:

People:
Leader: People:

A - men, si - ya - ku - du - mi - sa. A - si - thi: A - men, Ba - ba,
A - men, we praise your name, O God. Sing a - men: A - men, a - men,

a - men, Ba - ba, a - men, si - ya - ku - du - mi - sa.
a - men, a - men, a - men, we praise your name, O God.†

* Asithi: pronounced "a-see-tee"

† May be sung several times.

Words: S. C. Molefe 1977
Music: S. C. Molefe 1977, arr. Dave Dargie 1977
Words and music copyright © 1991 Lumko Institute.

ASITHI
Irregular

Now, on Land and Sea Descending 432

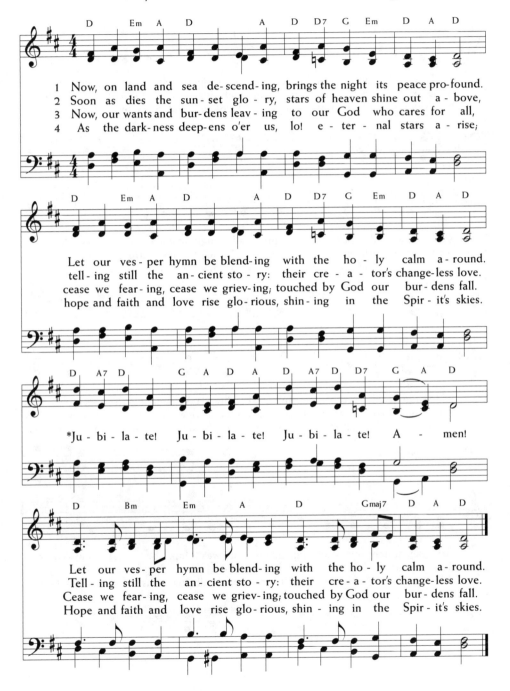

1 Now, on land and sea de-scend-ing, brings the night its peace pro-found.
2 Soon as dies the sun-set glo-ry, stars of heaven shine out a-bove,
3 Now, our wants and bur-dens leav-ing to our God who cares for all,
4 As the dark-ness deep-ens o'er us, lo! e-ter-nal stars a-rise;

Let our ves-per hymn be blend-ing with the ho-ly calm a-round.
tell-ing still the an-cient sto-ry: their cre-a-tor's change-less love.
cease we fear-ing, cease we griev-ing; touched by God our bur-dens fall.
hope and faith and love rise glo-rious, shin-ing in the Spir-it's skies.

*Ju-bi-la-te! Ju-bi-la-te! Ju-bi-la-te! A-men!

Let our ves-per hymn be blend-ing with the ho-ly calm a-round.
Tell-ing still the an-cient sto-ry: their cre-a-tor's change-less love.
Cease we fear-ing, cease we griev-ing; touched by God our bur-dens fall.
Hope and faith and love rise glo-rious, shin-ing in the Spir-it's skies.

*Pronounced: Yu-bee-lah-tay, meaning "rejoice".

Words: *Samuel Longfellow 1859*
Music: *attrib. Dimitri Bortniansky; arr. John A. Stevenson 1818*

VESPER HYMN
87878687

433 Day Is Done

1 Day is done, but love un-fail-ing dwells ev - er here;
2 Dark de-scends, but light un-end-ing shines through our night;
3 Eyes will close, but you un-sleep-ing watch by our side;

shad - ows fall, but hope, pre-vail-ing, calms ev - ery fear.
you are with us, ev - er lend-ing new strength to sight:
death may come, in love's safe-keep-ing still we a - bide.

God, our Mak - er, none for-sak - ing, take our hearts of Love's own
one in love, your truth con-fess-ing, one in hope of heav-en's
God of love, all e - vil quell-ing, sin for-giv-ing, fear dis-

mak - ing, watch our sleep-ing, guard our wak-ing, be al - ways near.
bless-ing, may we see, in love's pos-sess-ing, love's end - less light!
pell - ing, stay with us, our hearts in-dwell-ing, this e - ven - tide.

Words: James Quinn, S.J. 1969
Music: Welsh melody ca. 1784
Words copyright © 1969 James Quinn, SJ. Used by permission of Selah Publishing Co., Inc.

AR HYD Y NOS
8 4 8 4 8 8 8 4
Alt. setting: 227

O Laughing Light

Unison

1 O laugh-ing light, O first-born of cre - a - tion,
2 Day's light is frag - ile, your light is e - ter - nal;
3 Light of the world, O Je - sus, you are wor - thy!

ra - diance of glo - ry, light from light be - got - ten,
we look to you, our light with - in the shad - ow.
Giv - er of life and Child of God, we praise you.

God self - re - veal - ing, ho - ly, bright and bless - ed:
We sing to you, Cre - a - tor, Christ, and Spir - it.
Hear as the u - ni - verse now pro - claims your glo - ry!

you shine up - on us.
You shine be - fore us.
You shine a - mong us.

Words: Sylvia Dunstan 1985
Music: Poitiers Antiphoner 1746; arr. Healey Willan 1918
Words copyright © 1991 G.I.A. Publications, Inc. Music © 1918 Healey Willan. Reproduced with permission of the Estate of Healey Willan.

ISTE CONFESSOR
11 11 11 5

435 Christ, Mighty Saviour

1 Christ, might - y Sav - iour, Light of all cre - a - tion,
2 Now comes the day's end as the sun is set - ting:
3 Give heed, we pray you, to our sup - pli - ca - tion:
4 Though bod - ies slum - ber, hearts shall keep their vig - il,

you make the day - time ra - diant with the sun - light,
mir - ror of day - break, pledge of res - ur - rec - tion;
that you may grant us par - don for of - fen - ces,
for ev - er rest - ing in the peace of Je - sus,

and to the night give glit - ter - ing a - dorn - ment,
while in the heav - ens choirs of stars ap - pear - ing
strength for our weak hearts, rest for ach - ing bo - dies,
in light or dark - ness wor - ship - ping our Sav - iour

stars in the heav - ens.
hal - low the night - fall.
sooth - ing the wea - ry.
now and for ev - er.

Words: Mozarabic, 10th century; trans. Alan G. McDougall; para. Anne K. LeCroy 1982
Music: David Hurd 1983

MIGHTY SAVIOUR
11 11 11 5
Alt. tune: Flemming

Abide with Me

1 A - bide with me; fast falls the ev - en - tide;
2 Swift to its close ebbs out life's lit - tle day;
3 I need your pres - ence ev - ery pass - ing hour;
4 I have no fear with you at hand to bless;
5 Hold now your cross be - fore my clos - ing eyes;

the dark - ness deep - ens; Lord, with me a - bide;
earth's joys grow dim, its glo - ries pass a - way;
what but your grace can foil the temp - ter's power?
ills have no weight, and tears no bit - ter - ness;
shine through the gloom, and point me to the skies;

when oth - er help - ers fail, and com - forts flee,
change and de - cay in all a - round I see;
Who like your - self my guide and stay can be?
where is death's sting? Where, grave, your vic - to - ry?
heaven's morn - ing breaks, and earth's vain sha - dows flee;

help of the help - less, O a - bide with me.
O Christ, who chang - es not, a - bide with me.
Through cloud and sun - shine, O a - bide with me.
I tri - umph still, if you a - bide with me.
in life, in death, O Lord, a - bide with me.

Words: Henry Francis Lyte 1847, alt.
Music: William Henry Monk 1861

EVENTIDE
10 10 10 10

437 The Day You Gave Us, God, Is Ended

1 The day you gave us, God, is end-ed, the sun is
2 We thank you that your church un-sleep-ing, while earth rolls
3 As o'er each con-ti-nent and is-land, the dawn leads
4 The sun that bids us rest is wak-ing your church be-
5 So be it, God! Your throne shall nev-er, like earth's proud

sink-ing in the west; to you our morn-ing
on-ward in-to light, through all the world a
on an-oth-er day, the voice of prayer is
neath the west-ern sky, and hour by hour fresh
em-pires, pass a-way; your rule re-mains and

hymns as-cend-ed, your praise shall sanc-ti-fy our rest.
watch is keep-ing, and rests not now by day or night.
nev-er si-lent, nor dies the strain of praise a-way.
lips are mak-ing your won-drous do-ings heard on high.
grows for-ev-er, un-til there dawns that glo-rious day.

Words: John Ellerton 1870, alt. 1994
Music: Clement Cotterill Scholefield 1874

ST CLEMENT
9 8 9 8

The Day Thou Gavest, Lord, Is Ended 438

1 The day thou gavest, Lord, is ended;
the darkness falls at thy behest;
to thee our morning hymns ascended,
thy praise shall sanctify our rest.

2 We thank thee that thy church
unsleeping,
while earth rolls onward into light,
through all the world her watch is
keeping,
and rests not now by day or night.

3 As o'er each continent and island
the dawn leads on another day,
the voice of prayer is never silent,
nor dies the strain of praise away.

4 The sun that bids us rest is waking
our brethren 'neath the western sky,
and hour by hour fresh lips are making
thy wondrous doings heard on high.

5 So be it, Lord! Thy throne shall never,
like earth's proud empires, pass away;
thy kingdom stands and grows for ever,
till all thy creatures own thy sway.

Words: John Ellerton 1870

ST CLEMENT
9 8 9 8

Now the Day Is Over 439

1 Now the day is o - ver, night is draw-ing nigh,
2 Now the dark-ness gath - ers, stars be - gin to peep;
3 Je - sus, give the wea - ry calm and sweet re - pose;
4 Com - fort ev - ery suf - ferer watch-ing late in pain;
5 When the morn-ing wak - ens, then may I a - rise

shad - ows of the eve - ning steal a - cross the sky.
birds, and beasts, and flow - ers soon will be a - sleep.
with your ten - der bless - ing may my eye - lids close.
those who plan some e - vil from their sin re - strain.
pure, and fresh, and sin - less in your ho - ly eyes.

Words: Sabine Baring-Gould 1865
Music: Joseph Barnby 1868

EVENING
6 5 6 5

440

Glory to You, My God

1 Glory to you, my God, this night for all the blessings of the light; keep me, O keep me, King of kings, beneath your own almighty wings.

2 Forgive me, God, through your dear Son, the wrong that I this day have done, that peace with you and all may be, before I sleep, restored to me.

3 Teach me to live, that I may dread the grave as little as my bed; teach me to die, so that I may rise glorious at the awesome day.

4 O may my soul on you repose, and restful sleep mine eyelids close, sleep that shall me more vigorous make to serve my God when I awake.

5 Praise God, from whom all blessings flow; in heaven above and earth below; one God, three persons we adore— be praises given for evermore.

Words: Thomas Ken ca. 1674, alt.
Music: Thomas Tallis ca. 1561

TALLIS' CANON
8 8 8 8

And the following...

Praise and Thanksgiving

1 Praise and thanks-giv - ing be to our Cre - a - tor,
2 Not our own hol - i - ness, nor that we have striv - en
3 Come, Ho - ly Spir - it, come in vis - i - ta - tion:

source of this sac - ra - ment, Sav - iour, Med - i - a - tor.
brings us the peace which you, O Christ, have giv - en.
you are the truth, our hope and our sal - va - tion.

Bap - tize and make your own these who come be - fore you,
Bap - tize and set a - part; come, O ris - en Sav - iour,
Bap - tize with joy and power; give, O dove de - scend - ing,

while we a - dore you.
with grace and fav - our.
life nev - er end - ing.

Words: Frank Whiteley, Harold Francis Yardley 1969
Music: Johann Crüger 1653
Words copyright © 1969 Frank Whiteley and Estate of H. Francis Yardley.

LOBET DEN HERREN
11 11 11 5 Irregular

442 Wash, O God, Our Sons and Daughters

1 Wash, O God, our sons and daugh - ters, where your
2 We who bring them long for nur - ture; by your
3 O how deep your ho - ly wis - dom! Un - im -

cleans - ing wa - ters flow. Num - ber them a - mong your
milk may we be fed. Let us join your feast, par -
ag - ined, all your ways! To your name be glo - ry,

peo - ple; bless as Christ blessed long a - go. Weave them
tak - ing cup of bless - ing, liv - ing bread. God, re -
hon - our! With our lives we wor - ship, praise! We your

gar - ments bright and spar - kling; com - pass
new us, guide our foot - steps; free from
peo - ple stand be - fore you, wa - ter -

Words: Ruth Duck 1986
Music: attrib. Benjamin Franklin White 1844; harm. Ronald A. Nelson 1978

BEACH SPRING
8 7 8 7 D

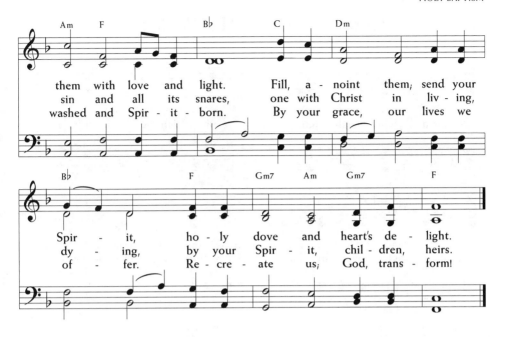

them with love and light. Fill, a - noint them; send your
sin and all its snares, one with Christ in liv - ing,
washed and Spir - it - born. By your grace, our lives we

Spir - it, ho - ly dove and heart's de - light.
dy - ing, by your Spir - it, chil - dren, heirs.
of - fer. Re - cre - ate us; God, trans - form!

Wash Us, God, Your Sons and Daughters
(For Adult Baptism)

1 Wash us, God, your sons and
daughters,
newborn creatures of your womb.
Number us among your people,
raised like Christ from death and
tomb.
Weave us garments bright and
sparkling;
compass us with love and light.
Fill, anoint us; send your Spirit,
holy dove and heart's delight.

2 Every day we need your nurture;
by your milk may we be fed.
Now we join your feast, partaking
cup of blessing, living bread.

Give us new life; guide our footsteps;
free from sin and all its snares,
one with Christ in living, dying,
by your Spirit, children, heirs.

3 O how deep your holy wisdom!
Unimagined, all your ways!
To your name be glory, honour!
With our lives we worship, praise!
We your people stand before you,
water-washed and Spirit-born.
By your grace, our lives we offer.
Recreate us; God, transform!

443 God, We Pray at This Beginning

1 God, we pray at this be-gin-ning of an
2 Help our daugh-ters face all dan-gers with the

in - fant's life - long search: bless the chil-dren of our
cour - age shown by Paul. Help our sons, like moth - er

fam - ilies, mem - bers of your chang - ing church. Make our
Ma - ry, love al - though di - sas - ter fall. Help us

sons as wise as Deb - orah, give our daugh - ters
too, with old - er vi - sion, as your chang - ing

Dan - iel's grace, for new chal - len - ges are
chil - dren grow: help us see that chang - ing

Words: *Christopher Redmond 1992*
Music: *Cyril Vincent Taylor 1941*
Words copyright © *1992 Christopher Redmond. Music © 1942, renewal 1970 Hope Publishing Company.*

ABBOT'S LEIGH
8 7 8 7 D
Alt. tune: *Hyfrydol*

Child of Blessing, Child of Promise 444

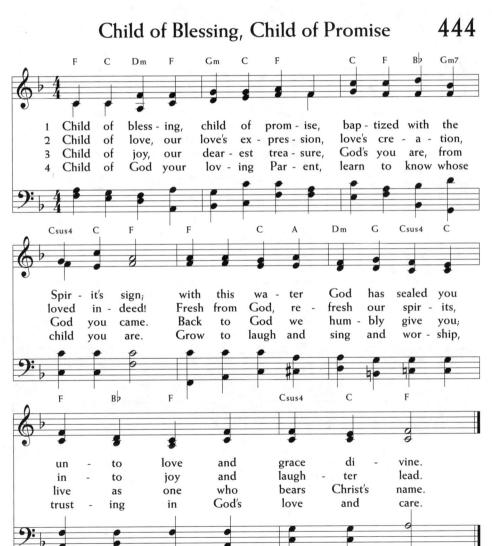

Words: Ronald S. Cole-Turner 1980
Music: attrib. Christian F. Witt, Psalmodia Sacra 1715
Words copyright © 1981 Ronald S. Cole-Turner. Used by permission.

STUTTGART
8 7 8 7

445 A Little Child the Saviour Came

1 A little child the Saviour came,
the mighty God was still his name;
and angels worshipped as he lay
the helpless infant of a day.

2 He who, a little child, began
the life divine to show God's plan
proclaims from heaven the message free,
"Let little children come to me."

3 We bring them now, and in your name
the saving love of Christ proclaim.
Through living water, grace endow;
baptize them with your Spirit now.

4 O God, who by an infant's tongue
can hear your perfect glory sung,
may these with all the heavenly throng,
praise you: Creator, Spirit, Son.

Words: William Robertson ca. 1861, alt.
Music: Trier manuscript, 15th century; adapt. Michael Praetorius 1609; harm. George R. Woodward 1902
Harmony copyright © Mowbray.

PUER NOBIS NASCITUR
8 8 8 8

O God of Life

(First tune)

1 O God of life, who wills new life to be through love cre-
2 O God of love, who gives this sign to be the out-ward
3 O God of power, whose Spir-it you have sent to be re-

at - ed: born a child, in hu-man fam-i - ly,
sym - bol of your love, the seal of u - ni - ty
ceived here, as a gift, through word and sac-ra - ment,

shaped in your im - age, this lit - tle child we bring.
which binds our chil-dren and our-selves to you:
em - power your peo - ple with stead-fast, sure in - tent;

With glad thanks-giv - ing be - fore you now we sing.
hear now the prom - ise these par - ents make a - new.
give us high pur - pose to keep this cov - e - nant.

BIRCHVIEW
Irregular

447

O God of Life
(Second tune)

Unison

1 O God of life, who wills new life to be through love cre - at - ed: born a child, in hu - man fam - i - ly, shaped

2 O God of love, who gives this sign to be the out - ward sym - bol of your love, the seal of u - ni - ty which

3 O God of power, whose Spir - it you have sent to be re - ceived here, as a gift, through word and sa - cra - ment, em -

Words: *Margaret Joyce Dickin 1967, alt.*
Music: *Ron Klusmeier 1995*

WOITTE
Irregular

in your im - age, this lit - tle child we bring.
binds our chil - dren and our - selves to you:
power your peo - ple with stead - fast, sure in - tent;

With glad thanks - giv - ing be - fore you now we
hear now the prom - ise these par - ents make a -
give us high pur - pose to keep this cov - e -

1, 2 | 3

sing.
new.
nant.

448   We Know That Christ Is Raised

Unison

1 We know that Christ is raised and dies no more.
2 We share by wa-ter in his sav-ing death.
3 The God of splend-our clothes the Son with life.
4 A new cre-a-tion comes to life and grows

Em-braced by death, he broke its fear-ful hold,
Re-born, we share with him an Eas-ter life
The Spir-it's fis-sion shakes the church of God.
as Christ's new bod-y takes on flesh and blood.

and our de-spair he turned to blaz-ing joy.
as liv-ing mem-bers of a liv-ing Christ.
Bap-tized, we live with God the Three in One.
The un-i-verse re-stored and whole will sing:

1, 2   Hal - le - lu - jah!
3   Hal - le - lu - jah!

Words: John Brownlow Geyer 1967
Music: Charles Villiers Stanford 1904
Words copyright © John B. Geyer.

ENGELBERG
10 10 10 with hallelujahs

Crashing Waters at Creation

1 Crash - ing wa - ters at cre - a - tion,
2 Part - ing wa - ter stood and trem - bled
3 Cleans - ing wa - ter once at Jor - dan
4 Liv - ing wa - ter, nev - er end - ing,

or - dered by the Spir - it's breath,
as the cap - tives passed on through,
closed a - round the one fore - told,
quench the thirst and flood the soul.

first to wit - ness day's be - gin - ning
wash - ing off the chains of bond - age—
o - pened to re - veal the glo - ry
Well - spring, Source of life e - ter - nal,

from the bright - ness of night's death.
chan - nel to a life made new.
ev - er new and ev - er old.
drench our dry - ness, make us whole.

Words: Sylvia Dunstan 1987
Music: William A. Cross 1992
Words copyright © 1994 G.I.A. Publications, Inc. Music copyright © 1994 William A. Cross.

CRASHING WATERS
8 7 8 7
Alt. tune: Stuttgart

450   Here at This Font

1 Here at this font, Source of all life, we bring a
2 Pour out this wa - ter, fresh and clear. Make it a
3 Em - brace this child with gen - tle arms, as on that
4 Guide church and par - ents in our task to teach each

child for you to bless. Met in our wor - ship,
sign of life and love. Now, as at Jor - dan
day in Gal - i - lee you called the young, and
child to walk your way. May Christ's com - mand - ments

may we know the gos - pel's way of hap - pi - ness.
long a - go, show your ap - prov - al, Ho - ly Dove.
showed to all the pow - er of hu - mil - i - ty.
be o - beyed in all we think or do or say.

Words: Alton George Demmons 1979
Music: Samuel Sebastian Wesley 1872
Words copyright © 1995 Alton George Demmons.

WINSCOTT
8 8 8 8

451   This Is the Spirit's Entry Now

1 This is the Spir - it's en - try now: the
2 This mir - a - cle of life re - born comes
3 Let wa - ter be the sa - cred sign that
4 Re - new - ing Spir - it, hear our praise for

wa - ter and the Word, the cross of Je - sus
from the Source of breath; the per - fect One from
we must die each day to rise a - gain by
your bap - tis - mal power that wash - es us through

on your brow, the seal both felt and heard.
life was torn; our life comes through Christ's death.
his de - sign as fol - lowers of his way.
all our days. Come, cleanse a - gain this hour.

Words: Thomas E. Herbranson 1965
Music: from Tochter Sion, Cologne 1741
Words copyright © Thomas E. Herbranson.

ST BERNARD
8 6 8 6

You Have Put On Christ   452

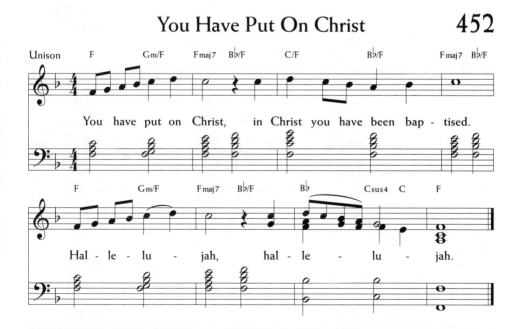

You have put on Christ, in Christ you have been bap - tised.

Hal - le - lu - jah, hal - le - lu - jah.

Words: from the Rite of Baptism, ICEL ca. 1969
Music: Howard Hughes 1977
Words copyright © 1969 and music 1977 International Committee on English in the Liturgy.

453 Out of Deep, Unordered Water

giv-er: there is wa - ter in the font.

Words: Fred Kaan 1965
Music: Ron Klusmeier 1974
Words copyright © 1968 Hope Publishing Company. Music © 1974 Ron Klusmeier.

BALGEMANN
8 7 8 7 with refrain

May God Who Creates You   454
(Baptismal Benediction)

May God who cre-ates you give you light;

may God who sus-tains you make you wise;

may God who pro-tects you give you joy,

may God who sur-rounds you give you peace.

Words: Louise Skibsted 1994
Music: Louise Skibsted 1994

Words and music copyright © 1994 Louise Skibsted.

455
This Child of Ours

1 This child of ours, this mir-a-cle. You have a dream and
2 This child of Yours, this mir-a-cle re-born of Wa-ter
3 This child of ours, this mir-a-cle whom Christ would die for,

plan for it: You wash it clean, You cra-dle it, You bless it, and You
and the Word; the Book of Life re-cords its name. You smile and an-gels
we may love, and train and raise, and teach and praise, and watch the Spir-it

call it Yours: this child of ours, this child of Yours.
cel-e-brate: this child of Yours, this child of ours.
mold a life: this child of ours, this child of Yours.

Words: Jaroslav J. Vajda 1984, rev. 1988

AIMEE
Irregular

Music: Paul D. Weber 1988, rev. 1995

Words copyright © 1984, 1988 Jaroslav J. Vajda. Music copyright © 1991 Augsburg Fortress. Used by permission of Augsburg Fortress.

And the following...

099   Christ, when for us you were baptised
644   I was there to hear your borning cry

Now to Your Table Spread

456

1 Now to your ta - ble spread we come, each one in
2 Hands of the world stretch out your mys - ter - y to
3 Here is our com - mon wealth in shar - ing what is

faith that you a - lone pro - vide the words of
touch in long - ing to be - lieve a truth be -
good, as though all hu - man - kind a - round one

life and death: in wine and bread, in
yond our reach, to sing in joy, to
ta - - - ble stood, this bread to break, this

prom - ised food we find your lov - ing heart, O God.
cry in grief, to know your mean - ing for our life.
wine to taste: one peo - ple in the name of Christ.

Words: Shirley Erena Murray 1986
Music: John Ireland 1918
Words copyright © 1987 Hope Publishing Company. Music copyright © The John Ireland Trust.

LOVE UNKNOWN
6 6 12 4 4 8

457 As We Gather at Your Table

1 As we gath-er at your ta - ble, as we list - en
2 Turn our wor-ship in-to wit - ness in the sac - ra -
3 Gra-cious Spir-it, help us sum - mon oth - er guests to

to your word, help us know, O God, your pres - ence;
ment of life; send us forth to love and serve you,
share that feast where tri - umph-ant Love will wel - come

let our hearts and minds be stirred. Nour-ish us with sa - cred
bring-ing peace where there is strife. Give us, Christ, your great com-
those who had been last and least. There no more will en - vy

sto - ry till we claim it as our own; teach us through this
pas - sion to for-give as you for-gave; may we still be -
blind us nor will pride our peace de-stroy, as we join with

Words: Carl P. Daw, Jr. 1989
Music: attrib. Benjamin Franklin White 1844; harm. Ronald A. Nelson 1978

BEACH SPRING
8 7 8 7 D

Words copyright © 1989 Hope Publishing Company. Harmony copyright © 1978 Lutheran Book of Worship. Reprinted by permission of Augsburg Fortress.

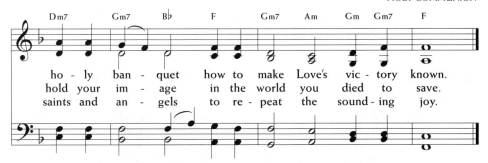

ho - ly ban - quet how to make Love's vic - tory known.
hold your im - age in the world you died to save.
saints and an - gels to re - peat the sound - ing joy.

Christ, Let Us Come with You 458

Unison

1 Christ, let us come with you to the up - per room where the
2 Teach us your serv - ing love: to be - come as friends, to be -
3 Je - sus, for - give us all that we use your name though we
4 Christ of the o - pen hands, you have brought us close to be

feast is laid, to the bread and wine where our
come as one that the world be - lieve what your
stand a - part, we re - fuse your prayer to be
loved and fed, you have touched our life, now you

peace is made: Christ, let us come with you!
life has done: teach us your serv - ing love.
one at heart: Je - sus, for - give us all.
walk a - head: Christ, let us come with you!

Words: *Shirley Erena Murray 1991, alt.*
Music: *Colin Gibson 1991, alt.*
Words and music copyright © *1992 Hope Publishing Company.*

WROSLYN ROAD
6 5 5 5 5 6

459 Here, O My Lord, I See You Face to Face

*1 Here, O my Lord, I see you face to face;
here would I touch and han-dle things un-seen,
here grasp with firm-er hand e-ter-nal grace,
and all my wear-i-ness up-on you lean.

2 Here would I feed up-on the bread of God,
here drink with you the roy-al wine of heaven;
here would I lay a-side each earth-ly load,
here taste a-fresh the calm of sin for-given.

♦ 3 This is the hour of ban-quet and of song;
this is the heaven-ly ta-ble for me spread;
here let me feast, and feast-ing, still pro-long
the fel-low-ship of liv-ing wine and bread.

4 Too soon we rise; the sym-bols dis-ap-pear.
The feast, though not the love, is past and gone;
the bread and wine re-move, but you are here,
near-er than ev-er, still my shield and sun.

5 Feast af-ter feast thus comes and pass-es by,
yet, pass-ing, points to that glad feast a-bove,
giv-ing sweet fore-taste of the fes-tal joy,
the Lamb's great brid-al feast of bliss and love.

* Verses 1 to 3 may be sung before communion, verses 4 and 5 after.

Words: Horatius Bonar 1855, alt.
Music: James Langran 1861

ST AGNES (LANGRAN)
10 10 10 10

All Who Hunger

1 All who hun-ger, gath-er glad-ly; ho-ly man-na is our bread.
2 All who hun-ger, nev-er strang-ers; seek-er, be a wel-come guest.
3 All who hun-ger, sing to-geth-er; Je-sus Christ is liv-ing bread.

Come from wil-der-ness and wan-dering. Here, in truth, we will be fed.
Come from rest-less-ness and roam-ing. Here, in joy, we keep the feast.
Come from lone-li-ness and long-ing. Here, in peace, we have been led.

You that yearn for days of full-ness, all a-round us is our food.
We that once were lost and scat-tered in com-mu-nion's love have stood.
Blest are those who from this ta-ble live their lives in grat-i-tude.

Taste and see the grace e-ter-nal. Taste and see that God is good.

Words: Sylvia G. Dunstan 1990
Music: William Moore 1825; arr. David Kai 1994, alt.
Words copyright © 1991 G.I.A. Publications, Inc. Arrangement copyright © 1994 David Kai.

HOLY MANNA
8 7 8 7 D

461

Bread of the World
(Tu es notre pain véritable)

Bread of the world, in mer-cy bro-ken, wine of the
Tu es no-tre pain vé-ri-ta-ble; tu es no-

soul in mer-cy shed, by whom the words of life were
tre sour-ce de vie; tu nous as con-viés à la

spo-ken, and in whose death our sins are dead: look on the
Ta-ble, où tu fais de nous tes a-mis. De la Table

heart by sor-row bro-ken, look on the tears by
où tu nous ras-sem-bles pour man-ger le pain

sin-ners shed; and be your feast to us the
de la vie; fais que nous par-tions tous en-

Words: Reginald Heber ca. 1820; French trans. L. Guillou
Music: melody adapt. Louis Bourgeois, Genevan Psalter 1542; arr. The English Hymnal 1933
Arrangement by permission of Oxford University Press. Translation copyright © Editions Musicales Studio S.M.

RENDEZ À DIEU
9 8 9 8 D

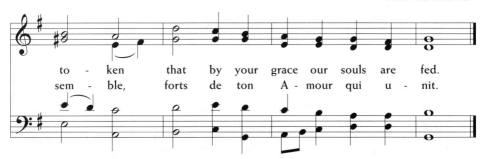

to - ken that by your grace our souls are fed.
sem - ble, forts de ton A - mour qui u - nit.

Before I Take the Body of My Lord   462

Unison

1 Be - fore I take the bod - y of my Lord, be -
2 The words of hope I of - ten failed to give, the
3 The nar - row - ness of vi - sion and of mind, the
4 Of those a - round in whom I meet my Lord, I
5 Lord Je - sus Christ, com - pan - ion at this feast, I

fore I share his life in bread and wine, I
prayers of kind - ness bur - ied by my pride, the
need for oth - er folk to serve my will, and
ask their par - don and I grant them mine that
emp - ty now my heart and stretch my hands, and

rec - og - nize the sor - ry things with - in: these I lay down.
signs of care I ar - gued out of sight: these I lay down.
ev - ery word and si - lence meant to hurt: these I lay down.
ev - ery con - tra - dic - tion to Christ's peace might be laid down.
ask to meet you here in bread and wine which you lay down.

Words: John L. Bell 1989   LAYING DOWN
Music: John L. Bell 1989   10 10 10 4

Words and music copyright © 1989 WGRG, The Iona Community, (Glasgow, Scotland), G.I.A. Publications, Inc., Chicago, Illinois, exclusive agent.

463   Deck Yourself, My Soul, with Gladness

1 Deck your - self, my soul, with glad - ness, leave the
2 Now I come be - fore you low - ly, filled with
3 Sun, which all my liv - ing bright - ens; Light, which
4 Je - sus, bread of life, I pray you let me

gloom - y haunts of sad - ness, come in - to the day - light's
joy most deep and ho - ly, as with trem - bling awe and
heart and soul en - light - ens; Joy, most sweet and spir - it
glad - ly here o - bey you; nev - er to my hurt in -

splen - dour, there with joy your prais - es ren - der
won - der on your might - y works I pon - der;
free - ing; Fount, the source of all my be - ing;
vit - ed, be your love with love re - quit - ed;

un - to Christ, whose grace un - bound - ed has this won - drous
how, by mys - ter - y sur - round - ed, depths no one has
at your feet I cry, my Mak - er, let me be a
from this ban - quet let me mea - sure, God, how vast and

Words: Johann Franck 1649, trans. Catherine Winkworth 1858, rev. 1863, alt.
Music: Johann Crüger 1649

SCHMÜCKE DICH
8 8 8 8 D

ban - quet found - ed; high o'er all the heav - ens
ev - er sound - ed, none may dare to pierce un -
fit par - tak - er of this bless - ed food from
deep its trea - sure; through the gifts you here now

reign - ing, yet to dwell with you is deign - ing.
bid - den, sec - rets that with you are hid - den.
heav - en, for our good your glo - ry giv - en.
give me, as your guest in heaven re - ceive me.

Pare-nous pour cette fête 464

1 Pare-nous pour cette fête
qu'aujourd'hui tu nous apprêtes;
Seigneur, fais briller la terre
du secret de ta lumière.
Viens nourrir notre confiance;
affermir notre espérance,
que ton pain et ta promesse
soient pour nous joie et richesse.

2 Tu prépares notre place
à ce festin de ta grâce;
tu nous donnes en silence
la douceur de ta présence.
Reçois-nous à cette table
au repas inépuisable,
avant que tu nous appelles
à tes tables éternelles.

This French text (not a translation of the English) may be sung to the preceding tune.

Words: Louis Monastier 1926, rév. 1977
Words copyright © Fédération Protestante de France.

SCHMÜCKE DICH
8 8 8 8 D

465 Christ, Be Our Host

1 Christ, be our Host, wel- com- ing, greet - ing:
2 Christ, be our Bread, bro- ken and giv - en:
3 Christ, be our Wine, gift of cre- a - tion:

After Communion:
4 Christ, be our Guest in our de- part - ing:

this is the ban- quet your love has pre - pared!
this is the ban- quet your love has pre - pared!
this is the ban- quet your love has pre - pared!

now we are fed by the food you pre - pared!

Hear us, we pray, en- trance en- treat - ing:
Here you pro- vide man- na from hea - ven:
Made by your death Cup of Sal- va - tion:

Christ, be our Strength, cour- age im- part - ing:

this is the ban- quet your love has pre - pared!
this is the ban- quet your love has pre - pared!
this is the ban- quet your love has pre - pared!

now we are fed by the food you pre - pared!

Words: Herman G. Stuempfle, Jr. 1994
Music: David N. Johnson 1968

EARTH AND ALL STARS
4 5 7 D with refrain

Words copyright © 1994 Herman G. Stuempfle, Jr. Music copyright © 1968 Augsburg Publishing House. Reprinted by permission of Augsburg Fortress.

1–3 Come to the ta - ble where mer - cies are spread!

4 Go from the feast where my mer - cies are spread!

Come to the feast, all who hun - ger!

Go, I am with you for - ev - er!

Eat This Bread

466

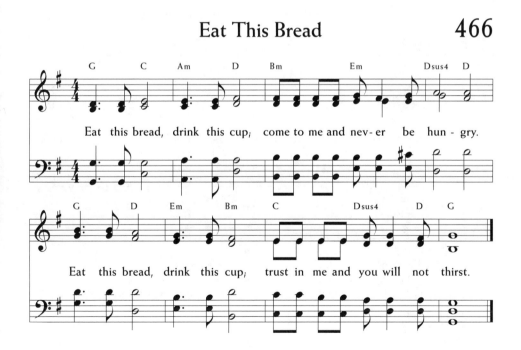

Eat this bread, drink this cup; come to me and nev-er be hun - gry.

Eat this bread, drink this cup; trust in me and you will not thirst.

Words: Robert J. Batastini and the Taizé Community 1982

Music: Jacques Berthier 1982

EAT THIS BREAD

Irregular

467 One Bread, One Body

*   Verses might be sung by soloist or choir.

Words: John B. Foley, S.J. 1978
Music: John B. Foley, S.J. 1978, harm. Gary Alan Smith 1988
Words and music copyright © 1978 John B. Foley, New Dawn Music, administered by Oregon Catholic Press.

ONE BREAD, ONE BODY
4 4 6 with refrain

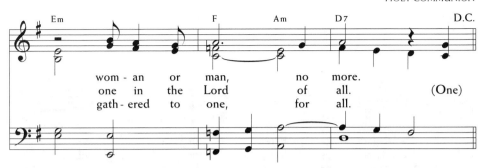

wom - an   or   man,   no   more.
one   in   the   Lord   of   all.   (One)
gath - ered to   one,   for   all.

Let Us Talents and Tongues Employ 468

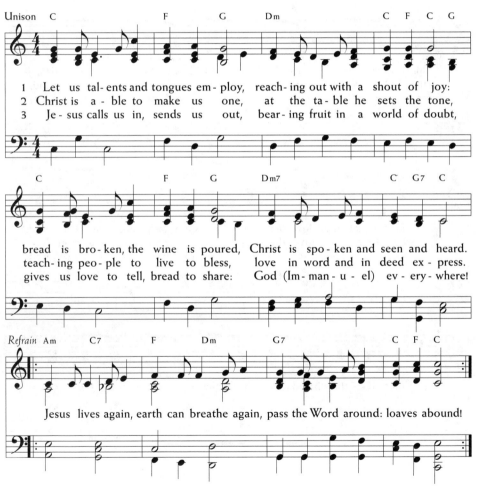

1 Let us tal - ents and tongues em - ploy, reach - ing out with a shout of joy:
2 Christ is a - ble to make us   one,   at the ta - ble he sets the tone,
3 Je - sus calls us in, sends us   out,   bear - ing fruit in a world of doubt,

bread is bro - ken, the wine is poured, Christ is spo - ken and seen and heard.
teach - ing peo - ple to live to bless, love in word and in deed ex - press.
gives us love to tell, bread to share: God (Im - man - u - el) ev - ery - where!

Refrain
Jesus lives again, earth can breathe again, pass the Word around: loaves abound!

Words: Fred Kaan 1975
Music: Jamaican folk song; adapt. Doreen Potter 1975
Words and music copyright © 1975 Hope Publishing Company.

LINSTEAD
8 8 8 8 with refrain

469

We Gather Here
(Come, Share the Lord)

1 We gath-er here in Je-sus' name,
2 He joins us here, he breaks the bread,
3 We'll gath-er soon where an-gels sing;

his love is burn-ing in our hearts like liv-ing flame;
the One who pours the cup is ris-en from the dead;
we'll see the glo-ry of our Lord and com-ing King;

for through the lov-ing son God fash-ions us as one:
the One we love the most is now our gra-cious host:
now we an-tic-i-pate the feast for which we wait:

Fine

Come take the bread, come drink the wine, come, share the Lord.

Words: *Bryan Jeffery Leech 1984, alt.*
Music: *Bryan Jeffery Leech 1984*
Words and music copyright © 1984 Fred Bock Music Company.

DIVERNON
Irregular

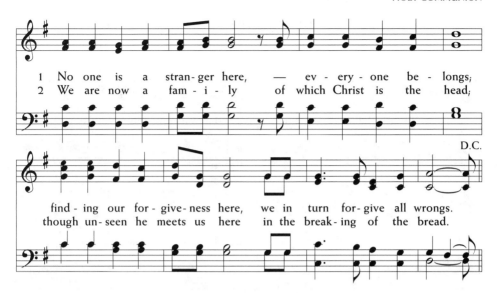

1 No one is a stran-ger here, — ev-ery-one be-longs;
2 We are now a fam-i-ly of which Christ is the head;

find-ing our for-give-ness here, we in turn for-give all wrongs.
though un-seen he meets us here in the break-ing of the bread.

For the Bread Which You Have Broken 470

1 For the bread which you have bro - ken, for the
2 By this prom - ise that you love us, by your

wine which you have poured, for the words which you have
gift of peace re - stored, by your call to heaven a-

spo - ken, now we give you thanks, O Lord.
bove us, hal - low all our lives, O Lord.

Words: Louis FitzGerald Benson 1924, alt.
Music: V. Earle Copes 1959

KINGDOM
8 7 8 7

471 Eat This Bread and Never Hunger

Refrain (Unison)

Eat this bread and nev-er hun-ger, drink this cup and nev-er thirst;

Christ in-vites us to the ta-ble where the last be-come the first. *Fine*

1 Ask - ing for a cup of wa - ter,
2 Walk - ing down a des - ert high - way,
3 Weep - ing for his friend at grave - side,

Je - sus touched for-bid-den ground; and the wom-an,
Je - sus healed a man born blind; soon the man be -
Je - sus felt the pain of death; yet he knew God's

with a ques-tion, told the world what she had found.
came a wit-ness to the truth we seek and find.
power to wak-en: liv-ing wa-ter, liv-ing breath.
D.C.

Words: Daniel Charles Damon 1992
Music: Daniel Charles Damon 1992
Words and music copyright © 1993 Hope Publishing Company.

MODESTO
8 7 8 7 with refrain

O Jesus, Joy of Loving Hearts

472

1 O Jesus, joy of loving hearts,
the fount of life, the light of all
from every bliss that earth imparts we
turn, unfilled, to hear your call.

2 Your truth unchanged has ever stood;
you plead with all to call on you,
to those who seek you, you are good, to
those who find you, life is new.

3 We taste your ever-living bread,
and long to feast upon you still;
we drink of you, the fountainhead, our
thirsting souls from you we fill.

4 O Jesus, ever with us stay;
make all our moments calm and bright;
chase the bleak night of sin away; shed
o'er the world your holy light.

Words: 12th century, trans. Ray Palmer 1858, alt.
Music: Henry Percy Smith 1874

MARYTON
8 8 8 8

473 Let All Mortal Flesh Keep Silence
(Lorsque les mortels, en silence frémiront)

Unison

1 Let all mor-tal flesh keep si - lence, and with awe and
2 King of kings, yet born of Ma - ry, as of old on

1 Lors-que les mor - tels, en si - len - ce fré - mi - ront de
2 Roi du mon - de, né de Ma - ri - e, qui fus au - tre -

rev - erence stand; pon - der noth - ing earth - ly - mind - ed,
earth he stood, Lord of lords, in hu - man ves - ture,

crain - te par - tout; lors - que fi - ni - ra l'es - pé - ran - ce,
fois un en - fant, Sei - gneur qui vé - cus no - tre vi - e,

for with bless - ing in his hand, Christ our God to
in the bod - y and the blood, he will give to

nos yeux s'ou - vri - ront tout à coup, nous ver - rons le
hom - me par le corps et le sang: tes a - mis hu -

us ap - proach - eth our full hom - age to de - mand.
all the faith - ful his own self for heaven - ly food.

Christ en gloi - re re - ce - voir l'hom - ma - ge de tous.
mains t'im - plo - rent, sau - ve - les en - cor du né - ant.

Words: *from the* Liturgy of St. James; *trans.* Gerard Moultrie *1864; French trans.* G. de Lioncourt *1972*
Music: *French traditional carol, harm.* The English Hymnal *1906*
Harmony by permission of Oxford University Press.

PICARDY
8 7 8 7 8 7

3 Rank on rank the host of heaven
  spreads its vanguard on the way,
  as the Light of light descendeth
  from the realms of endless day,
  that the powers of hell may vanish
  as the darkness clears away.

4 At his feet the six-winged seraph;
  cherubim with sleepless eye
  veil their faces to the presence,
  as with ceaseless voice they cry,
  Hallelujah, hallelujah,
  hallelujah, Lord most high!

3 Lorsque danseront les atomes
  et que surgira l'Absolu,
  fais-nous place dans ton Royaume;
  range-nous parmi tes élus.
  Le Mal à jamais s'efface,
  dans le grand soleil du salut.

4 Nous verrons la foule des anges
  soutenir les pieds du Sauveur,
  et tous les vivants crient louange
  devant l'Éternel créateur;
  les ressuscités proclament
  leur Alléluia au Seigneur.

The Son of God Proclaim 474

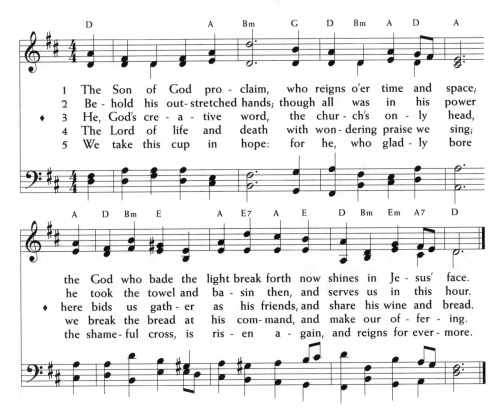

1 The Son of God proclaim, who reigns o'er time and space;
2 Behold his out-stretched hands; though all was in his power
3 He, God's creative word, the church's only head,
4 The Lord of life and death with wondering praise we sing;
5 We take this cup in hope: for he, who gladly bore

the God who bade the light break forth now shines in Jesus' face.
he took the towel and basin then, and serves us in this hour.
here bids us gather as his friends, and share his wine and bread.
we break the bread at his command, and make our offering.
the shameful cross, is risen again, and reigns for evermore.

Words: Basil E. Bridge 1962, alt.
Music: Henry Thomas Smart 1867
Words copyright © 1962 Basil E. Bridge.

SUNDERLAND
6 6 8 6

475 Now the Silence, Now the Peace

Now the si-lence Now the peace Now the emp-ty hands up-lift-ed

Now the kneel-ing Now the plea Now the Fa-ther's arms in wel-come

Now the hear-ing Now the power Now the ves-sel brimmed for pour-ing

Now the bo-dy Now the blood Now the joy-ful cel - e-bra-tion

Now the wed-ding Now the songs Now the heart for-giv - en leap-ing

Words: Jaroslav J. Vajda 1968
Music: Carl F. Schalk 1969
Words and music copyright © 1969 Hope Publishing Company.

NOW
Irregular

Now the Spir-it's vis-i-ta-tion Now the Son's e-piph-a-ny

Now the Fa-ther's bless-ing Now Now Now

C'est toi, Seigneur, le pain rompu 476

1 C'est toi, Seigneur, le pain rompu,
livré pour notre vie;
c'est toi, Seigneur, notre unité,
Jésus ressuscité!

2 Jésus, nous rappelons ta mort
et ta résurrection,
et dans la foi nous attendons
le jour de ton retour.

3 Nous partageons un même pain,
dans une même foi,
et nous formons un même corps,
l'Église de Jésus.

4 C'est maintenant le temps de Dieu:
il faut nous préparer;
c'est maintenant le temps de Dieu:
il faut changer nos coeurs.

5 Si nous souffrons en Jésus-Christ,
en lui nous règnerons;
si nous mourons en Jésus-Christ,
en lui nous revivrons.

This French text (not a translation of the English) may be sung to the tune on the following page.

Words: Jean-Paul Lecot
Words copyright © Pierre Zech.

DOVE OF PEACE
8 6 8 6 6

477 I Come with Joy

1 I come with joy, a child of God, for-giv-en,
2 I come with Chris-tians far and near to find, as
3 As Christ breaks bread, and bids us share, each proud di-
4 The Spir-it of the ris-en Christ, un-seen, but
5 To-geth-er met, to-geth-er bound by all that

loved and free, the life of Je-sus to re-call in
all are fed, the new com-mu-ni-ty of love in
vi-sion ends. The love that made us, makes us one, and
ev-er near, is in such friend-ship bet-ter known, a-
God has done, we'll go with joy, to give the world the

love laid down for me, in love laid down for me.
Christ's com-mun-ion bread, in Christ's com-mun-ion bread.
stran-gers now are friends, and stran-gers now are friends.
live a-mong us here, a-live a-mong us here.
love that makes us one, the love that makes us one.

Words: Brian Wren 1968, rev. 1993
Music: American folk tune from William Walker's Southern Harmony 1835; arr. Austin C. Lovelace 1977
Words copyright © 1971, and arrangement copyright © 1977 Hope Publishing Company.

DOVE OF PEACE
86866

You Satisfy the Hungry Heart

Unison

You sat-is-fy the hung-ry heart with gift of fin-est wheat.

Come, give to us, O sav-ing Lord, the bread of life to eat.

Fine

1 As when the shep-herd calls the sheep, they know and heed that voice,
2 With joy-ful lips we sing to you our praise and grat-i-tude,
♦ 3 Is not the cup we bless and share the blood of Christ out-poured?
4 The mys-tery of your pres-ence here no mor-tal tongue can tell;
5 In gra-cious love you give your-self; then self-less let us be,

D.C.

so when you call your fam-i-ly, we fol-low and re-joice.
that you should count us wor-thy friends, to share this heaven-ly food.
♦ Do not one cup, one loaf, de-clare our one-ness in the Lord?
whom all the world can-not con-tain comes in our hearts to dwell.
to serve each oth-er in your name in truth and char-i-ty.

Words: *Omer Westendorf 1976, alt.*
Music: *Robert E. Kreutz 1976*
Words and music copyright © 1976 Archdiocese of Philadelphia.

FINEST WHEAT (BICENTENNIAL)
8 6 8 6 with refrain

479 Draw Us in the Spirit's Tether

1 Draw us in the Spir-it's teth-er, for when hum-bly
2 As dis-ci-ples used to gath-er in the name of
3 All our meals and all our liv-ing make as sac-ra-

in your name two or three are met to-
Christ to sup, then with thanks to God the
ments of you, that by car-ing, help-ing,

geth-er, you are in the midst of them. Hal-le-
Giv-er break the bread and bless the cup. Hal-le-
giv-ing, we may be dis-ci-ples true. Hal-le-

lu-jah! Hal-le-lu-jah! Touch we now your gar-ment's hem.
lu-jah! Hal-le-lu-jah! So now bind our friend-ship up.
lu-jah! Hal-le-lu-jah! In our ser-vice faith re-new.

Words: *Percy Dearmer 1931, alt.*
Music: *Harold Friedell 1957*
Words by permission of Oxford University Press. Music copyright © 1960 The H. W. Gray Co. (renewed).

UNION SEMINARY
8 7 8 7 4 4 7

Let Us Break Bread Together

Words: African-American spiritual 19th cent.
Music: African-American spiritual 19th cent. traditional; harm. F. R. C. Clarke 1971
Harmony copyright © 1971 F. R. C. Clarke.

LET US BREAK BREAD
Irregular

481   Sent Forth by God's Blessing

1 Sent forth by God's bless-ing, our true faith con-fess-ing, the peo-ple of God from this dwell-ing take leave. The sup-per is end-ed, O now be ex-tend-ed the fruits of this ser-vice in all who be-lieve.

2 With praise and thanks-giv-ing to God ev-er liv-ing, the tasks of our ev-ery-day life we will face. Our faith ev-er shar-ing, in love ev-er car-ing, em-brac-ing God's chil-dren of each tribe and race.

Words: Omer Westendorf 1964, alt.

Music: Welsh folk tune, harm. Leland Bernhard Sateren 1972

Words copyright © 1964 World Library Publications, a division of J. S. Paluch Co., Inc.
Harmony copyright © 1972 from Contemporary Worship 4: Hymns for Baptism and Holy Communion. Reprinted by permission of Augsburg Fortress.

THE ASH GROVE
66 11 66 11 D
Alt. setting: 242

The seed of Christ's teach-ing, re-cep-tive souls
With your feast you feed us, with your light now

reach-ing, shall blos-som in ac-tion for God and for all.
lead us; u-nite us as one in this life that we share.

God's grace did in-vite us, God's love shall u-nite us
Then may all the liv-ing with praise and thanks-giv-ing

to work for the king-dom and an-swer its call.
give hon-our to Christ and the name that we bear.

482

Shout for Joy

1 Shout for joy! The Lord has let us feast;
2 No more doubt-ing, no more sense-less dread:
3 Cel - e - brate with saints who dine on high,
4 Praise the Mak - er, praise the Mak-er's Son,

heaven's own fare has fed the last and least;
God's good self has graced our wine and bread;
wit - ness - es that love can nev - er die.
praise the Spir - it, three yet ev - er one;

Christ's own peace is shared a - gain on earth;
all the won - der heaven has kept in store
"Hal - le - lu - jah!" thus their voic - es ring.
praise the God whose food and friends a - vow

(Optional bass) is shared on earth;
has kept in store
— voic - es ring:
whose friends a - vow

God the Spir - it fills us with new worth.
now is ours to keep for ev - er - more.
Noth - ing less in grat - i - tude we bring.
heaven starts here! The king - dom beck - ons now!

Words: *The Iona Community 1989*
Music: *John L. Bell 1989, alt.*

LANSDOWNE
9 9 9 9

Words and music copyright © 1989 WGRG, The Iona Community (Glasgow, Scotland), G.I.A. Publications, Inc., Chicago, Illinois, exclusive agent.

Now Let Us from This Table Rise

1. Now let us from this table rise renewed in
2. With minds a-lert, up-held by grace, to spread the
3. To fill each hu-man house with love, it is the
4. Then give us grace, Com-pan-ion-God, to choose a-

bod-y, mind and soul; with Christ we die and live a-
word in speech and deed, we fol-low in the steps of
sac-ra-ment of care; the work that Christ be-gan to
gain the pil-grim way and help us to ac-cept with

gain, his self-less love has made us whole.
Christ, at one with all in hope and need.
do we hum-bly pledge our-selves to share.
joy the chal-lenge of to-mor-row's day.

Words: Fred Kaan 1964
Music: Robert Jackson ca. 1887
Words copyright © 1968 Hope Publishing Company.

NIAGARA
8 8 8 8

484

God, the All-Holy

1 God, the All-Ho - ly, Mak - er and Moth - er,
2 Spir - it, All - See - ing, knit - ting and blend - ing
3 Christ, All - Com - plet - ing, Na - ture en - fold - ing,

glad - ly we gath - er, bring - ing in prayer
joy in de - sir - ing, friend - ship and ease,
e - vil ex - haust - ing in love's em - brace,

old hurts for heal - ing, new hopes for hold - ing,
make our be - long - ing loy - al and last - ing,
weav - ing and mend - ing, make ev - ery end - ing

giv - ing, re - ceiv - ing lov - ing and care.
so that our pledg - ing fresh - ens and frees.
God's new be - gin - ning glow - ing with grace.

Words: Brian Wren 1988
Music: Trad. Gaelic melody, harm. Martin Shaw 1931
Words copyright © 1989 Hope Publishing Company. Harmony by permission of Oxford University Press.

BUNESSAN
5 5 5 4 D
Alt. setting: 409

O God, Who Gave Humanity Its Name   485

1 O God, who gave humanity its name,
2 May through their union oth-er lives be blessed;
♦ 3 Pre-serve their days from in-ward-ness of heart;
4 From stage to stage on life's un-fold-ing way
5 God, bless us all to whom this day brings joy,

whose cov-e-nant of grace re-mains the same,
their door be wide to strang-er and to guest.
♦ to each the gift of truth-ful speech im-part.
bring to their mind the vows they make this day,
let no e-vents our u-ni-ty des-troy,

be with these two who now be-fore you wait;
Give them the un-der-stand-ing that is kind,
♦ Their bond be strong a-gainst all strain and strife
your spir-it be their guide in ev-ery move,
and help us, till all sense of time is lost,

en-large the love they come to con-se-crate.
grant them the bless-ing of an o-pen mind.
♦ a-mid the chang-es of this earth-ly life.
their faith in Christ the touch-stone of their love.
to live in love and not to count the cost.

Words: Fred Kaan 1968
Music: Roy Hopp 1989
Words copyright © 1968 Hope Publishing Company. Music copyright © 1990 Selah Publishing Co., Inc.

SHANTY CREEK
10 10 10 10
Alt. tune: Sursum Corda

486 God Who Blesses New Beginnings

1 God who bless- es new be- gin - nings, send your Spir - it
2 Give them joy to light - en sor - row! Give them hope to
3 May the grace of Christ, our Sav - iour, and our Ma - ker's

from a - bove on this Chris - tian man and wo - man, who here
bright - en life! Go with them to face the mor - row, stay with
bound - less love, with the Ho - ly Spir - it's fa - vour, rest up -

make their vows of love! Bind their hearts in true de -
them in ev - ery strife. As your word has prom - ised
on them from a - bove. May they live in last - ing

vo - tion end - less as the sea - shore's sands, bound - less
ev - er, fill them with your strength and grace, so that
u - nion with each oth - er and the Lord; find - ing

Words: vv. 1, 2 Harry N. Huxhold 1978; v. 3 John Newton 1779, alt.
Music: Roland Huw Prichard ca. 1830
Words (vv. 1, 2) copyright © 1978 Lutheran Book of Worship. Reprinted by permission of Augsburg Fortress.

HYFRYDOL
8 7 8 7 D
Alt. setting: 333

as   the deep-est o - cean, blest and sealed by your own hands.
each may serve the oth - er till   they see you face to face.
joy   in hearts' com-mu - nion: joy   to share in lives out-poured.

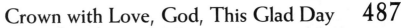

Crown with Love, God, This Glad Day   487

1 Crown with love, God, this glad day, love to hum-ble and de-light,
2 Crown with joy, God, this glad day,   joy to face life's hurt and ill,
3 Crown with peace, God, this glad day, peace the world may not in - vent,

love which un - til death will stay, test - ing all life's depth and height;
all   that tests the wed - ded way, forg - ing u - nion deep - er still;
nor mis - for - tune strip a - way from two hearts in you con - tent,

such   a love as took our part, spend-thrift in its gen-erous art.
joy   like his who, for our gain, light - ly weighed the cross and pain.
know - ing love will nev - er cease from that source who is our peace.

Words: Ian M. Fraser 1966
Music: Benjamin Milgrove 1768, alt.
Words copyright © 1969 Stainer & Bell Ltd. Used by permission of Hope Publishing Company.

HARTS
7 7 7 7 7 7

488 Friends, Let Us Love Each Other

1 Friends, let us love each oth - er, love is a gift God
2 Love is what Christ com - mand - ed, love lived out day by

gives. Friends, by the love with - in us,
day. Love bears an - oth - er's bur - den,

this world will know God lives. Love is the gift most
love walks a ten - der way. Friends, let us love each

pre - cious God gives to wo - man and man.
oth - er, love is a gift God gives.

Words: Walter Farquharson 1977
Music: Ron Klusmeier 1977

CHRISTIE
7 6 7 6 7 6 7 6

We find our life in lov - ing,
Friends, by the love with - in us,

that's our cre - a - tor's plan.
this world will know God lives.

When Love Is Found 489

1 When love is found
   and hope comes home,
sing and be glad that two are one.
When love explodes and fills the sky,
praise God, and share our
   Maker's joy.

2 When love has flowered
   in trust and care,
build both each day, that love
   may dare
to reach beyond home's
   warmth and light,
to serve and strive for truth
   and right.

3 When love is tried as loved-
   ones change,
hold still to hope, though all
   seems strange,

till ease returns and love grows wise
through listening ears and
   opened eyes.

4 When love is torn, and
   trust betrayed,
pray strength to love till
   torments fade,
till lovers keep no score of wrong,
but hear through pain love's
   Easter song.

5 Praise God for love,
   praise God for life,
in age or youth, in calm or strife.
Lift up your hearts! Let love be fed
through death and life in
   broken bread.

(The music appears on the following page.)

Words: *Brian Wren 1978, rev. 1994*
Words copyright © 1983 Hope Publishing Company.

O WALY WALY (GIFT OF LOVE)
8 8 8 8

490 Our God, Creation's Loving Source

1 Our God, Cre - a - tion's lov - ing source, in love, for
2 As God is One in Trin - i - ty, our be - ing—
♦ 3 De - sire and ten - der - ness and joy are ho - ly
4 With - in Christ's bod - y may we find our best and
5 Praise God, all liv - ing souls on earth with strings and

love has placed us here that God's own im - age, which we
bod - y, mind, and soul— is meant for u - ni - ty and
♦ gifts, and ours to share in love that's giv - ing, faith - ful,
tru - est selves re - vealed, called forth, sup - port - ed by its
trum - pets, dance, and song! God's all - sur - round - ing love will

bear, through hu - man lov - ing may shine clear.
peace, a sound and joy - ful liv - ing whole.
♦ kind, and grows in mu - tual love and care.
love to live at peace, made whole and healed.
be both home and way our whole life long!

Words: Joy F. Patterson 1993
Music: English folk melody, harm. John Weaver 1988
Words copyright © 1994 and harmony copyright © 1990 Hope Publishing Company.

O WALY WALY
8 8 8 8

O Perfect Love

1 O per - fect love, all hu - man thought tran - scend - ing,
2 O per - fect life, be al - ways their as - sur - ance
3 Grant them the joy which bright - ens earth - ly sor - row;

low - ly we kneel in prayer be - fore your throne,
of ten - der char - i - ty and stead - fast faith,
grant them the peace which calms all earth - ly strife,

that theirs may be the love that knows no end - ing,
of pa - tient hope, and qui - et brave en - dur - ance,
and to life's day the glo - rious un - known mor - row

whom, now and ev - er - more, you join in one.
with child - like trust that fears not pain nor death.
that dawns up - on e - ter - nal love and life.

Words: Dorothy Frances Gurney 1883
Music: Joseph Barnby 1889
Words by permission of Oxford University Press.

O PERFECT LOVE
11 10 11 10

And the following . . .

633 Bless now, O God, the journey

515 Holy Spirit, source of love

644 I was there to hear your borning cry

372 Though I may speak

492 God of the Living

1 God of the liv - ing, in your name as - sem - bled,
2 Help us to trea - sure all that will re - mind us
3 May we, when - ev - er tempt - ed to de - jec - tion,
4 God, you can lift us from the grave of sor - row

we join to thank you for the life re - mem - bered.
of the en - rich - ment in the days be - hind us.
strong - ly re - cap - ture thoughts of res - ur - rec - tion.
in - to the pres - ence of your own to - mor - row:

Grant us your mer - cy, to your chil - dren giv - ing
Your love has set us in the gen - er - a - tions,
You gave us Je - sus to de - feat our sad - ness
give to your peo - ple for the day's af - flic - tion

hope in be - liev - ing.
God of cre - a - tion.
with Eas - ter glad - ness.
your ben - e - dic - tion.

Words: Fred Kaan 1968
Music: Friedrich Ferdinand Flemming 1811
Words copyright © 1968 Hope Publishing Company.

FLEMMING
11 11 11 5

Today I Live

1 To-day I live, but once shall come my death;
2 How I shall die, or when, I do not know,
3 When earth-ly life shall close, as close it must,
4 Mean-while I live and move and I am glad,

one day shall still my laugh-ter and my cry-ing,
nor where, for end-less is the world's ho-ri-zon;
let Je-sus be my broth-er and my mer-it.
en-joy this life and all its in-ter-weav-ing;

bring to a halt my heart-beat and my breath:
but save me, God, from thoughts that lay me low,
Let me with-out re-gret re-call the past,
each giv-en day, as I take up the thread,

O, give me faith for liv-ing and for dy-ing.
from mor-bid fears that freeze my power of rea-son.
and then, in-to your hands com-mit my spir-it.
let love sug-gest my mode, my mood of liv-ing.

Words: Fred Kaan 1975
Music: Doreen Potter 1975
Words and music copyright © 1975 Hope Publishing Company.

BELLEGARDE
10 11 10 11

494 Those Hearts That We Have Treasured

1 Those hearts that we have trea - sured, those lives that
2 They still give hope and com - fort, they did not
3 From hearts that we have trea - sured, from lives that

we have shared, those loves that walked be - side us,
lose the fight, they showed us truth and good - ness,
we have shared, from loves that walked be - side us,

those friends for whom we've cared, their bless - ing rests up -
they shine in - to our night. Re - mem - ber days of
from friends for whom we've cared, we've learned to trea - sure

on us, their life is mem - o - ry, their suf - fer -
glad - ness; re - mem - ber times of joy; re - mem - ber
kind - ness, we've learned that grace pro - vides, we've learned to

Words: Sylvia Dunstan 1991
Music: William Walker's Southern Harmony 1835, harm. Dale Grotenhuis 1986
Words copyright © 1991 G.I.A. Publications, Inc. Harmony copyright © 1990 Dale Grotenhuis.

RESIGNATION
7 6 7 6 D
Alt. setting: 780

ing is o - ver, their spir - its are set free.
all the mo - ments that grief can not de - stroy.
be to - geth - er, we've learned that love a - bides.

Lord of All Love

495

1 Lord of all love, all life, and death, giv - er of
2 Sing us the songs we can - not sing, par - don the
3 That dark - est mys - ter - y is here, sor - row and
4 Though pre - cious dust re - turn to dust, in your good

time and place and breath, hear us as now we
praise we can - not bring, speak all the words we
pit - y, an - ger, fear; con - quer once more, dear
pur - pose will we trust, con - tent to place with -

bring our loss in - to the pres - ence of your cross.
can - not say, pray for us, Lord, we hum - bly pray.
Lord, death's sting; faith, trust, and con - so - la - tion bring.
in your care the one we love and grieve for here.

Words: Colin Gibson 1987
Music: Colin Gibson 1987
Words and music copyright © 1994 Hope Publishing Company.

HARMONY
8 8 8 8

496 Grief of Ending, Wordless Sorrow

Unison

1 Grief of end-ing, word-less sor-row, pain of part-ing,
2 Times re-mem-bered, joy dis-cov-ered, love and friend-ship,
3 Word of prom-ise, lift our sing-ing, blend-ing griev-ing
4 Christ a-mong us, Spir-it-breath-ing, safe com-pan-ion,

dry or weep-ing, on our lips and in our bod-ies,
voice and ges-ture, pre-cious, love-ly, one and on-ly,
with be-liev-ing. In your hands is all com-plet-ed,
in your keep-ing death is birth to res-ur-rec-tion,

Lov-ing God, to you we of-fer.
Giv-ing God, we tell and trea-sure.
Last-ing God, our hope and mea-sure.
Liv-ing God, our joy for-ev-er.

Words: Brian Wren 1989
Music: F. R. C. Clarke 1995
Words copyright © 1993 Hope Publishing Company. Music copyright © 1995 F. R. C. Clarke.

FIDELIS
4 4 4 4 8 8

497 Nearer, My God, to Thee
(Mon Dieu, plus près de toi)

1 Near-er, my God, to thee, near-er to thee!
2 Though, like the wan-der-er, the sun gone down,
♦ 3 There let the way ap-pear, steps un-to heaven;
4 Then, with my wak-ing thoughts bright with thy praise,
5 Or if on joy-ful wing cleav-ing the sky,

E'en though it be a cross that rais - eth me,
dark - ness be o - ver me, my rest a stone;
♦ all that thou send - est me, in mer - cy given;
out of my ston - y griefs Beth - el I'll raise;
sun, moon, and stars for - got, up - wards I fly,

still all my song shall be,
yet in my dreams I'd be
♦ an - gels to beck - on me near - er, my God, to thee;
so by my woes to be
still all my song shall be,

near - er, my God, to thee, near - er to thee!

1 Mon Dieu, plus près de toi, plus près de toi!
C'est le cri de ma foi: Plus près de toi!
Dans le jour où l'épreuve déborde comme un fleuve,
garde-moi près de toi, plus près de toi!

2 Plus près de toi, Seigneur, plus près de toi!
Tiens-moi dans ma douleur tout près de toi,
alors que la souffrance fait son oeuvre en silence,
toujours plus près de toi, plus près de toi!

3 Plus près de toi, toujours, plus près de toi!
Donne-moi ton secours, soutiens ma foi!
Que Satan se déchaîne, ton amour me ramène
toujours plus près de toi, plus près de toi!

4 Mon Dieu, plus près de toi! Dans le désert
j'ai vu, plus près de toi, ton ciel ouvert,
Pèlerin, bon courage! Ton chant brave l'orage:
Mon Dieu, plus près de toi, plus près de toi!

Words: *Sarah Flower Adams 1840; French, Charles Châtelanat 1885*
Music: *Lowell Mason 1856*

EXCELSIOR (BETHANY)
6 4 6 4 6 6 4

498 God, Who Has Caused to Be Written

1 God, who has caused to be writ-ten your word for our learn-ing,
2 Now may our God give us joy, give us peace in be-liev-ing
3 God, should the powers of the earth and the heav-ens be shak-en,

grant us that, hear-ing, our hearts may be in-ward-ly burn-ing.
all things were writ-ten in truth for our thank-ful re-ceiv-ing.
grant us to see you in all things, our vi-sion a-wak-en.

Give to us grace, that in your Son we em-brace
As Christ did preach, o'er all the world love must reach:
Help us to see, though all the earth cease to be,

life, all its glo-ry dis-cern - ing.
grant ev-ery day love's a-chiev - ing.
your truth shall ne-ver be shak - en.

Words: Herbert O'Driscoll ca. 1967
Music: F. R. C. Clarke 1967
Words copyright © 1980 Herbert O'Driscoll. Music copyright © 1971 F. R. C. Clarke.

CAUSA DIVINA
14 14 4 7 8

O Christ, the Word Incarnate

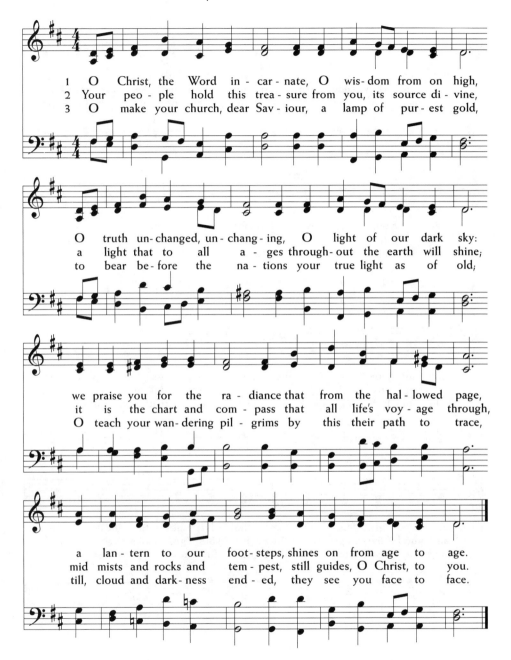

1 O Christ, the Word in-car-nate, O wis-dom from on high,
2 Your peo-ple hold this trea-sure from you, its source di-vine,
3 O make your church, dear Sav-iour, a lamp of pur-est gold,

O truth un-changed, un-chang-ing, O light of our dark sky:
a light that to all a-ges through-out the earth will shine;
to bear be-fore the na-tions your true light as of old;

we praise you for the ra-diance that from the hal-lowed page,
it is the chart and com-pass that all life's voy-age through,
O teach your wan-dering pil-grims by this their path to trace,

a lan-tern to our foot-steps, shines on from age to age.
mid mists and rocks and tem-pest, still guides, O Christ, to you.
till, cloud and dark-ness end-ed, they see you face to face.

Words: William Walsham How 1867, alt.; v. 2, rev. R. Gerald Hobbs 1987
Music: Meiningisches Gesangbuch 1693; arr. Felix Mendelssohn 1847
Revised verse 2 copyright © 1987 Songs for a Gospel People.

MUNICH
7 6 7 6 D

500   Blessed Jesus, at Your Word

1 Bless - ed Je - sus, at your word we have come a - gain to
2 All our knowl- edge, sense, and sight lie in deep - est dark - ness
3 Ra - diance of God's glo - ry bright, Light of light from God pro -

hear you; let our thoughts and hearts be stirred
shroud - ed till your Spir - it breaks the night,
ceed - ing, Je - sus, send your bless - ed light;

and in glow - ing faith be near you. As the prom - is -
fill - ing us with light un - cloud - ed. All good thoughts and
help our hear - ing, speak - ing, heed - ing, that our prayers and

es here giv - en draw us whol - ly up to heav - en.
all good liv - ing come but by your gra - cious giv - ing.
songs may please you, as with grate - ful hearts we praise you.

Words: Tobias Clausnitzer 1663; tr. Catherine Winkworth 1858, alt.
Music: melody Johann Rudolph Ahle 1664; alt. Das grosse Cantional oder Kirchen-Gesangbuch 1687;
harm. George Herbert Palmer

LIEBSTER JESU
787888

Break Now the Bread of Life

501

1 Break now the bread of life, Saviour, to me,
as once you broke the loaves beside the sea.
Beyond the sacred page I seek you, Lord;
my spirit waits for you, O Living Word.

2 Bless your own truth, dear Christ, to me, to me,
as when you blessed the bread by Galilee;
then shall all bondage cease, all fetters fall,
and I shall find my peace, my all in all.

Words: *Mary Artemisia Lathbury 1877, alt.*
Music: *William Fisk Sherwin 1877*

BREAD OF LIFE
10 10 10 10

A Prayer for Illumination

502

Eternal God, open our minds to hear your word,
our hearts to love your word,
    and our lives to be obedient to your word,
through the power of your Spirit
    and the name of Jesus Christ. Amen.

Flora Litt & Wayne Irwin 1986

503   When Seed Falls on Good Soil

Unison

1 When seed falls on good soil, it's born through qui-et toil; where
2 God's Word in Christ is seed; good soil its ur-gent need; for
3 Plough up the trod-den way, and clear the stone a-way; tear

soil re-ceives, the earth con-ceives the blade, the stem, the fruit, the
it must find in hu-man-kind the fer-tile soil in heart and
out the weed, and sow the seed. Pre-pare our hearts your Word to

leaves. Good soil, O moth-er earth, the womb, where seed takes birth.
mind. Good soil! A hu-man field! A hun-dred-fold to yield.
heed, that we good soil may be. Be-gin, O God, with me!

Words: Norman P. Olsen 1976   WALHOF
Music: Frederick F. Jackisch 1976   6 6 8 8 6 6

Words copyright © 1976 Norman P. Olsen. Music copyright © 1978 Lutheran Book of Worship. Reprinted by permission of Augsburg Fortress.

How Clear Is Our Vocation, Lord 504

Unison

1 How clear is our vo - ca - tion, Lord, when once we heed your
2 But if, for - get - ful, we should find your yoke is hard to
3 We mark your saints, how they be - come in hin - dran - ces more
4 In what you give us, here, to do, to - geth - er or a -

call: to live ac - cord - ing to your word, and
bear, if world - ly pres - sures fray the mind and
sure, whose joy - ful vir - tues put to shame the
lone, in old rou - tines and ven - tures new, may

dai - ly learn, re - freshed, re - stored, that you are o - ver
love it - self can - not un - wind its tan - gled skein of
cas - ual way we wear your name, and by our faults ob -
we not cease to look to you, the cross you hung up -

all and will not let us fall.
care: our in - ward life re - pair.
scure your power to cleanse and cure.
on — all you en - deav - oured done.

Words: Fred Pratt Green 1981
Music: C. Hubert H. Parry 1888
Words copyright © 1982 Hope Publishing Company.

REPTON
8 6 8 8 6 6
Alt. setting: 623

505   As a Chalice Cast of Gold

Unison

1 As a chal-ice cast of gold, bur-nished, bright, and
2 Save me from the sooth-ing sin of the emp-ty
3 When I bend up-on my knees, clasp my hands, or
4 When I dance or chant your praise, when I sing a

brimmed with wine, make me, God, as fit to hold grace and
cul-tic deed and the pi-ous, bab-bling din of the
bow my head, let my spo-ken, pub-lic pleas be di-
psalm or hymn, when I preach your lov-ing ways, let my

truth and love di-vine. Let my praise and
claimed but un-lived creed. Let my ac-tions,
rect-ly, sim-ply said, free of tan-gled
heart add its a-men. Let each cher-ished

wor-ship start with the cleans-ing of my heart.
God, ex-press what my tongue and lips pro-fess.
words that mask what my soul would plain-ly ask.
out-ward rite thus re-flect your in-ward light.

Words: *Thomas Troeger 1984, alt.*
Music: *Carol Doran 1984*
Words and music by permission of Oxford University Press, Inc.

INWARD LIGHT
7 7 7 D

Take My Life and Let It Be

506

Words: *Frances Ridley Havergal 1874, alt.*
Music: *unknown; desc. John T. Wilkinson 1980*
Descant copyright © 1980 enThusia Enterprises.

MOZART
7 7 7 7
Alt. tune: Hendon

507 Today We All Are Called to Be Disciples

1 To-day we all are called to be dis-ci-ples of the
2 God made the world and at its birth or-dained our hu-man
3 Pray jus-tice may come roll-ing down as in a might-y
4 May we in ser-vice to our God act out the liv-ing

Lord, to help to set the cap-tive free, make
race to live as stew-ards of the earth, re -
stream, with righ-teous-ness in field and town to
Word, and walk the road the saints have trod till

plough - share out of sword, to feed the hun - gry,
spond - ing to God's grace. But we are vain and
cleanse us and re - deem. For God is long - ing
all have seen and heard. As stew - ards of the

quench their thirst, make love and peace our fast, to
sad - ly proud, we sow not peace but strife, our
to re - store an earth where con - flicts cease, a
earth may we give thanks in one ac - cord to

Words: H. Kenn Carmichael 1985
Music: English traditional melody, arr. Arthur Seymour Sullivan 1874
Words copyright © 1989 H. Kenn Carmichael.

NOËL
8 6 8 6 D

serve the poor and home-less first, our ease and com-fort last.
dis-cord spreads a dead-ly cloud that threat-ens all of life.
world that was cre-at-ed for a har-mo-ny of peace.
God who calls us all to be dis-ci-ples of the Lord.

Just as I Am 508

1 Just as I am, with-out one plea, but that thy
2 Just as I am, poor, wretch-ed, blind; sight, rich-es,
3 Just as I am, though tossed a-bout with man-y a
4 Just as I am, thy love un-known has bro-ken

blood was shed for me, and that thou bidd'st me come to
heal-ing of the mind, yea, all I need, in thee to
con-flict, ma-ny a doubt, fight-ings and fears with-in, with-
ev-ery bar-rier down; now to be thine, yea, thine a-

thee,
find,
out,   O Lamb of God, I come, I come.
lone,

Words: Charlotte Elliott 1834
Music: William Batchelder Bradbury 1849

WOODWORTH
8 8 8 6

509

I, the Lord of Sea and Sky
(Here I Am, Lord)

1 I, the Lord of sea and sky, I have heard my peo-ple cry.
2 I, the Lord of snow and rain, I have borne my peo-ple's pain,
3 I, the Lord of wind and flame, I will tend the poor and lame,

All who dwell in deep-est sin my hand will save.
I have wept for love of them; they turn a-way.
I will set a feast for them; my hand will save.

I who made the stars of night, I will make their dark-ness bright.
I will break their hearts of stone, give them hearts for love a-lone.
Fin-est bread I will pro-vide till their hearts be sat-is-fied.

Who will bear my light to them? Whom shall I send?
I will speak my word to them. Whom shall I send?
I will give my life to them. Whom shall I send?

Words: Daniel L. Schutte 1981, alt.

Music: Daniel L. Schutte 1981, harm. Michael Pope, Daniel L. Schutte and John Weissrock 1983

Words copyright © 1981 Daniel L. Schutte and New Dawn Music.

HERE I AM, LORD
7 7 7 4 D with refrain

510   We Have This Ministry

Unison

1 We have this min-is-try and we are not dis-cour-aged; it
2 O Christ, the tree of life, our end and our be-gin-ning, we
3 The yoke of Christ is ours, the whole world is our par-ish; we

is by God's own power that we may live and serve.
grow to full-est flower when root-ed in your love.
dai-ly take the cross, the bur-den and the joy.

O-pen-ly we share God's word, speak-ing truth as we be-lieve,
Broth-ers, sis-ters, cler-gy, lay, called to ser-vice by your grace,
Bear-ing hurts of those we serve, wound-ed, bruised and bowed with pain,

pray-ing that the shad-owed world may heal-ing light re-ceive. We
diff-erent cul-tures, diff-erent gifts, the young and old a place. We
Ho-ly Spir-it, bread and wine, we die and rise a-gain. We

MINISTRY
Irregular

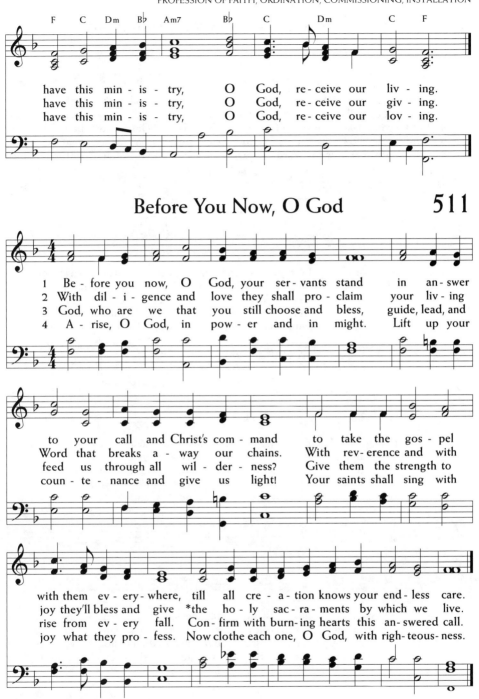

have this min - is - try, O God, re - ceive our liv - ing.
have this min - is - try, O God, re - ceive our giv - ing.
have this min - is - try, O God, re - ceive our lov - ing.

Before You Now, O God   511

1 Be - fore you now, O God, your ser - vants stand in an - swer
2 With dil - i - gence and love they shall pro - claim your liv - ing
3 God, who are we that you still choose and bless, guide, lead, and
4 A - rise, O God, in pow - er and in might. Lift up your

to your call and Christ's com - mand to take the gos - pel
Word that breaks a - way our chains. With rev - erence and with
feed us through all wil - der - ness? Give them the strength to
coun - te - nance and give us light! Your saints shall sing with

with them ev - ery - where, till all cre - a - tion knows your end - less care.
joy they'll bless and give *the ho - ly sac - ra - ments by which we live.
rise from ev - ery fall. Con - firm with burn - ing hearts this an - swered call.
joy what they pro - fess. Now clothe each one, O God, with righ - teous - ness.

* or "that ministry of hope"

Words: *Sylvia Dunstan 1985*
Music: *James Langran 1861*
Words copyright © 1992 G.I.A. Publications, Inc.

ST AGNES (LANGRAN)
10 10 10 10

512 Lord, You Give the Great Commission

1 Lord, you give the great com - mis - sion: "Heal the sick and
2 Lord, you call us to your ser - vice: "In my name bap -
3 Lord, you make the com - mon ho - ly: "This my bod - y,
4 Lord, you show us love's true mea - sure: "Fa - ther, what they
5 Lord, you bless with words as - sur - ing: "I am with you

preach the word." Lest the church ne - glect its mis - sion,
tize and teach." That the world may trust your prom - ise,
this my blood." Let us all, for earth's true glo - ry,
do, for - give." Yet we hoard as pri - vate trea - sure
to the end." Faith and hope and love re - stor - ing,

and the gos - pel go un - heard, help us wit - ness
life a - bun - dant meant for each, give us all new
dai - ly lift life heav - en - ward, ask - ing that the
all that you so free - ly give. May your care and
may we serve as you in - tend, and, a - mid the

to your pur - pose with re - newed in - teg - ri - ty;
fer - vour, draw us clos - er in com - mu - ni - ty;
world a - round us share your chil - dren's lib - er - ty;
mer - cy lead us to a just so - ci - e - ty;
cares that claim us, hold in mind e - ter - ni - ty;

Words: Jeffery W. Rowthorn 1978
Music: Cyril Vincent Taylor 1941

ABBOT'S LEIGH
8 7 8 7 D

with the Spir-it's gifts em-pow'r us for the work of min-is-try.

Give to Me, Lord, a Thankful Heart 513

Unison

1 Give to me, Lord, a thank-ful heart and a dis-cern-ing mind;
2 When, in the rush of days, my will is hab-it-bound and slow,
3 By your di-vine and ur-gent claim, and by your hu-man face,
4 Je-sus, with all your church I long to see your king-dom come;

give, as I play the Chris-tian's part, the strength to fin-ish
help me to keep in vi-sion still what love and power and
kin-dle our sink-ing hearts to flame, and as you teach the
show me your way of right-ing wrong and turn-ing sor-row

what I start and act on what I find.
peace can fill a life that trusts in you.
world your name let it be-come your place.
in-to song un-til you bring me home.

Words: Thomas Caryl Micklem 1973
Music: Thomas Caryl Micklem 1973
Words and music copyright © 1973 Thomas Caryl Micklem.

GATESCARTH
86886

514   God the Spirit, Guide and Guardian

1 God the Spir - it, guide and guard - ian, wind - sped flame and
2 Christ our Sav - iour, Sov - ereign, Shep - herd, Word made flesh, Love
3 Great Cre - a - tor, life - be - stow - er, truth be - yond all
4 Tri - une God, mys - te - rious Be - ing, un - di - vid - ed

hov - ering dove, breath of life and voice of proph - ets,
cru - ci - fied, teach - er, heal - er, suf - fering ser - vant,
thought's re - call, fount of wis - dom, womb of mer - cy,
and di - verse, deep - er than our minds can fath - om,

sign of bless - ing, power of love: give to those who
friend of sin - ners, foe of pride: in your tend - ing
giv - ing and for - giv - ing all: as you know our
great - er than our creeds re - hearse: help us in our

lead your peo - ple fresh a - noint - ing of your grace; send them
may all pas - tors learn and live a shep - herd's care; grant them
strength and weak - ness, so may those the church ex - alts ov - er -
var - ied call - ings your full im - age to pro - claim, that our

Words: Carl P. Daw, Jr. 1987
Music: William P. Rowlands ca. 1905
Words copyright © 1989 Hope Publishing Company.

BLAENWERN
8 7 8 7 D

forth as bold a-pos-tles to your Church in ev-ery place.
cour-age and com-pas-sion shown through word and deed and prayer.
see its life stead-fast-ly yet not o-ver-look its faults.
min-is-tries u-nit-ing may give glo-ry to your name.

Holy Spirit, Source of Love 515

1 Ho-ly Spir-it, source of love, who, to us, came from a-bove,
2 Give them light your truth to see, strength to serve you joy-ful-ly,
3 When the sa-cred vow is made, when the hands are on them laid,

gifts of bless-ing to be-stow on your wait-ing church be-low:
dai-ly power to con-quer sin, pa-tient faith the crown to win;
come in this most sol-emn hour, with your seven-fold gifts of power;

once a-gain in love draw near to your ser-vants gath-ered here.
shield them from temp-ta-tion's breath, keep them faith-ful un-to death.
come, O bless-ed Spir-it, come, make each ea-ger heart your home.

Words: William Dalrymple Maclagan 1875
Music: Henry Thomas Smart 1867

HEATHLANDS
7 7 7 7 7 7
Alt. tune: Dix

516 Come, You Thankful People, Come

1 Come, you thank-ful peo-ple, come, raise the song of har-vest-home!
2 All the world is God's own field, har-vests for God's praise to yield;
3 For our God, one day, shall come, and shall take this har-vest home;
4 E-ven so, God, quick-ly come to your fi-nal har-vest-home!

All is safe-ly gath-ered in, safe be-fore the storms be-gin;
wheat and weeds to-geth-er sown, here for joy or sor-row grown;
from the field shall in that day all of-fen-ces purge a-way;
Ga-ther all your peo-ple in, free from sor-row, free from sin;

God, our mak-er, does pro-vide for our needs to be sup-plied:
first the blade, and then the ear, then the full corn shall ap-pear:
giv-ing an-gels charge at last in the fire the weeds to cast;
there for ev-er pu-ri-fied, in your pres-ence to a-bide:

come to God's own tem-ple, come, raise the song of har-vest-home!
Har-vest-giv-er, grant that we whole-some grain and pure may be.
but the fruit-ful ears to store in the gar-ner ev-er-more.
come, with all your an-gels, come, raise the glo-rious har-vest-home.

Words: Henry Alford 1844, alt.
Music: George Job Elvey 1858

ST GEORGE'S, WINDSOR
7 7 7 7 D

Praise God for the Harvest

Unison

1 Praise God for the har-vest of or-chard and field,
2 Praise God for the har-vest that comes from a - far,
3 Praise God for the har-vest that's quar-ried and mined,
4 Praise God for the har-vest of sci - ence and skill,
5 Praise God for the har-vest of mer - cy and love

praise God for the peo - ple who gath - er their yield,
from mar - ket and har - bour, the sea and the shore:
then sift - ed, and smelt - ed, and shaped, and re - fined;
the urge to dis - cov - er, cre - ate, and ful - fil:
from lead - ers and peo - ples, who strug - gle and serve

the long hours of la - bour, the skills of a team,
foods packed and trans - port - ed, and gath - ered and grown
for oil and for i - ron, for cop - per and coal,
for dreams and in - ven - tions that prom - ise to gain
for fair - ness and kind - ness, that all may be led

the pa - tience of sci - ence, the power of ma - chine.
by God - giv - en neigh - bours, un - seen and un - known.
praise God, who in love has pro - vid - ed them all.
a fu - ture more hope - ful, a world more hu - mane.
in free - dom and safe - ty, and all may be fed.

Words: Brian Wren 1968, rev. 1995
Music: English traditional melody; arr. Norman L. Warren ca. 1982
Words copyright © 1978 and arrangement copyright © 1982 Hope Publishing Company.

STOWEY
11 11 11 11

518 As Those of Old Their First-fruits Brought

1 As those of old their first-fruits brought of vine-yard, flock, and field
2 A world in need now sum-mons us to la-bour, love, and give,
3 With grat-i-tude and hum-ble trust we bring our best to you,

to God, the giv-er of all good, the source of boun-teous yield;
to make our life an of-fer-ing to God, that all may live.
not just to serve your cause, but share your love with neigh-bours too.

so we to-day our first-fruits bring: the wealth of this good land,
The church of Christ is call-ing us to make the dream come true:
O God, who gave your-self to us in Je-sus Christ, your son,

of farm and mar-ket, shop and home, of mind and heart and hand.
a world re-deemed, by Christ-like love, all life in Christ made new.
help us to give our-selves each day un-til life's work is done.

Words: *Frank von Christierson 1960, alt.*
Music: *English trad. melody; harm. Ralph Vaughan Williams 1906*

Words copyright © 1961, renewal 1989 The Hymn Society. Used by permission of Hope Publishing Company.
Harmony by permission of Oxford University Press.

FOREST GREEN
8 6 8 6 D
Alt. tune: *Bethlehem*

Sing to the Lord of Harvest

519

1 Sing to the Lord of har-vest, sing songs of love and praise,
2 God makes the clouds drop fat-ness, the des-erts bloom and spring,
3 Bring to this sa-cred al-tar all things God's good-ness gave,

with joy-ful hearts and voi-ces your hal-le-lu-jahs raise;
the hills leap up in glad-ness, the val-leys laugh and sing.
the gold-en sheaves of har-vest, the souls Christ died to save:

by whom the roll-ing sea-sons in fruit-ful or-der move;
God fills them all with full-ness, all things with large in-crease,
your hearts lay down be-fore him when at his feet you fall,

sing to the Lord of har-vest a joy-ful song of love.
and crowns the year with good-ness, with plen-ty and with peace.
and with your lives a-dore him who gave his life for all.

Words: John Samuel Bewley Monsell 1866, alt.
Music: Johann Steurlein 1575; harm. Healey Willan 1958
Harmony copyright © 1969 Concordia Publishing House.

WIE LIEBLICH IST DER MAIEN
7 6 7 6 D
Alt. tune: Morning Light

520   We Plough the Fields

1 We plough the fields and scat-ter the good seed on the land,
2 You on-ly are the mak-er of all things near and far;
3 We thank you then, O Mak-er, for all things bright and good,

but it is fed and wa-tered by your al-migh-ty hand;
you paint the way-side flow-er, you light the even-ing star;
the seed-time and the har-vest, our life, our health, our food;

you send the snow in win-ter, the warmth to swell the grain,
the winds and waves o-bey you, by you the birds are fed;
ac-cept the gifts we of-fer for all your love im-parts,

the breez-es and the sun-shine, and soft re-fresh-ing rain.
much more to us, your chil-dren, you give us dai-ly bread.
and, what from us you long for, our hum-ble, thank-ful hearts.

Words: *Matthias Claudius 1782, trans. Jane Montgomery Campbell 1861, alt.*   WIR PFLÜGEN
Music: *Johann Abraham Peter Schulz 1800*   7 6 7 6 D *with refrain*

Refrain

All good gifts a - round us are sent from heaven a - bove;

we thank you, God, O ho - ly God, for all your love.

Praise to God, Immortal Praise 521

1 Praise to God, im - mor - tal praise, for the love that crowns our days;
2 for the bless - ings of the fields, for the stores the gar - den yields,
3 all that spring with boun - teous hand scat - ters o'er the smil - ing land,
4 These to you, O God, we owe, source from which all bless - ings flow;

boun - teous source of ev - ery joy, let your praise our tongues em - ploy:
flocks that whit - en all the plain, yel - low sheaves of ripen - ed grain:
all that lib - eral au - tumn pours from its rich o'er - flow - ing stores.
and for these our souls shall raise grate - ful vows and sol - emn praise.

Words: Anna Laetitia Barbauld 1772
Music: French melody, 13th century, attrib. Pierre de Corbeil; harm. Richard Redhead 1853

ORIENTIS PARTIBUS
7 7 7 7

522   Give Thanks, My Soul, for Harvest

1 Give thanks, my soul, for har-vest, for store of fruit and grain;
2 Give thanks, my soul, for rich-es of wood-land, mine, and hill;
3 Give thanks, my soul, for la-bours, that strength and days em-ploy;

but know the own-er gives so that we may share a-gain.
but know that gold and tim-ber are the Cre-a-tor's still.
but know the Mak-er's pur-pose brings toil as well as joy.

Where peo-ple suf-fer hun-ger, or lit-tle chil-dren cry,
God lends to us, as stew-ards, a-bun-dance we might share,
Show forth, O God, your pur-pose; di-rect our will and hand

with gifts from God's rich boun-ty may thank-ful-ness re-ply.
and thus pro-vide earth's chil-dren the bless-ing of God's care.
to share your love and boun-ty with all in ev-ery land.

Words: *William Watkins Reid, Sr. 1960, alt.*
Music: *Meiningisches Gesangbuch 1693; harm. Felix Mendelssohn 1847*
Words copyright © *1961, renewal 1989 The Hymn Society. Used by permission of Hope Publishing Company.*

MUNICH
7 6 7 6 D

O God of All the Many Lands

523

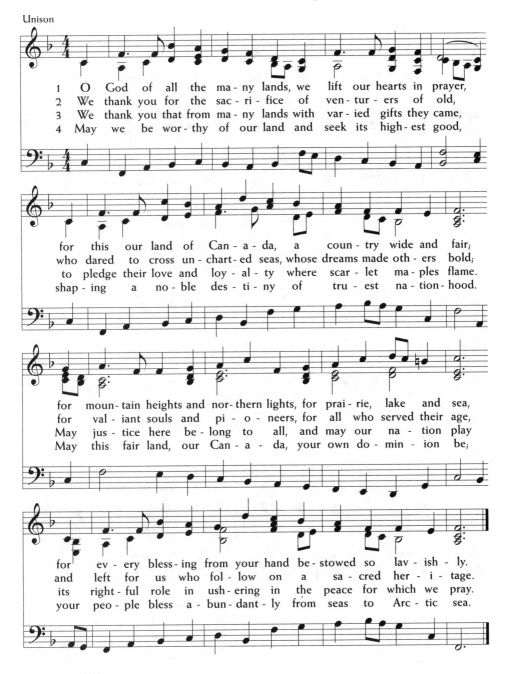

Unison

1 O God of all the many lands, we lift our hearts in prayer,
2 We thank you for the sac-ri-fice of ven-tur-ers of old,
3 We thank you that from ma-ny lands with var-ied gifts they came,
4 May we be wor-thy of our land and seek its high-est good,

for this our land of Can-a-da, a coun-try wide and fair;
who dared to cross un-chart-ed seas, whose dreams made oth-ers bold;
to pledge their love and loy-al-ty where scar-let ma-ples flame.
shap-ing a no-ble des-ti-ny of tru-est na-tion-hood.

for moun-tain heights and nor-thern lights, for prai-rie, lake and sea,
for val-iant souls and pi-o-neers, for all who served their age,
May jus-tice here be-long to all, and may our na-tion play
May this fair land, our Can-a-da, your own do-min-ion be;

for ev-ery bless-ing from your hand be-stowed so lav-ish-ly.
and left for us who fol-low on a sa-cred her-i-tage.
its right-ful role in ush-ering in the peace for which we pray.
your peo-ple bless a-bun-dant-ly from seas to Arc-tic sea.

Words: Mary Susannah Edgar 1927, alt.
Music: Keith Warren Bissell 1969
Words copyright © 1927 Mary S. Edgar. Music copyright © 1992 Keith Bissell. Used by permission of Karen Evans.

VALIANT
8 6 8 6 D

524

O Canada

O Can - a - da! Our home and na - tive land!
Ô Can - a - da! Ter - re de nos aï - eux,

True pa - triot love in all *thy sons com - mand.
ton front est ceint de fleu - rons glo - ri - eux!

With glow - ing hearts we see thee rise,
Car ton bras sait por - ter l'é - pé - e,

the True North strong and free! From far and wide,
il sait por - ter la croix! Ton his - toire est une

O Can - a - da, we stand on guard for thee.
é - po - pé - e des plus bril - lants ex - ploits.

* or "our lives"

Words: French, Adolphe B. Routhier 1880; English, Robert Stanley Weir 1908
Music: melody Calixa Lavallée ca. 1880; harm. William Smith Dingman ca. 1930

O CANADA
10 10 8 6 8 6 8 10 10

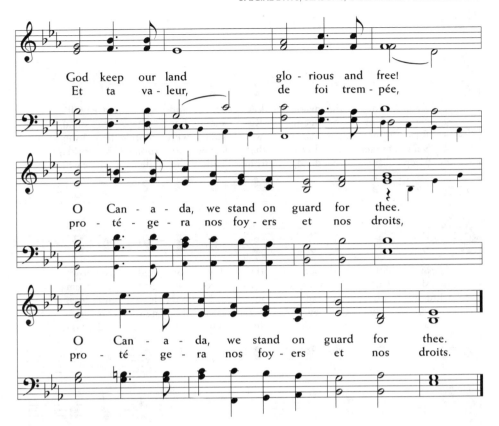

God keep our land / glo - rious and free!
Et ta va - leur, / de foi trem - pée,

O Can - a - da, we stand on guard for thee.
pro - té - ge - ra nos foy - ers et nos droits,

O Can - a - da, we stand on guard for thee.
pro - té - ge - ra nos foy - ers et nos droits.

You Embrace All Peoples 525

Eternal God,
whose image lies in the hearts of all people,
we live among peoples
    whose languages are different from our own,
    whose faiths are foreign to us,
    whose ways we fail to understand.
Help us to remember
    that you embrace all people with your love,
    that all religion is a response to you,
    that the yearnings of other hearts
    are much like our own, and are known to you.
Help us to recognize you
    in words of truth, things of beauty,
    and actions of love about us.
We pray in the name of the One who calls us
    to be neighbour and friend. Amen.

Based on a prayer by Robert H. Adams, Jr., 1965.

526

Weep for the Dead

1 Weep for the dead. Let tears and si - lence tell
2 Si - lent the dead. Re - mem - ber - ing we stand
♦ 3 Rais - ing our flag, we stand with muf - fled drum,
4 Sum - moned by love that leaves no room for pride,
5 Weep for the dead, from all the ills of earth.

of blood and bat - tle, hor - ror and re - nown.
si - lent as they, for words can - not es - teem
♦ judged by the col - ours of God's love and loss,
we pray that ev - ery con - ti - nent and isle,
Stand by the cross that bids all ha - tred cease.

The years di - min - ish, but do not dis - pel
caus - es of war, the love of na - tive land,
♦ re - call - ing as we pray, "Your king - dom come,"
wound - ed by war, war's hate may lay a - side,
March to the drums of dig - ni - ty and worth.

the pain of lives de - stroyed, and life laid down.
all that they were, and all they might have been.
♦ a pur - ple robe, and blood up - on a cross.
and find a way to heal and rec - on - cile.
Sa - lute the King of Love, the Prince of Peace.

Words: Brian Wren 1987, rev.
Music: Charles Harris
Words copyright © 1989 Hope Publishing Company.

HARRIS
10 10 10 10

God! As with Silent Hearts

1 God! As with silent hearts we bring to mind
2 Hallow our will as humbly we recall
3 Give us deep faith to comfort those who mourn,
4 So, Prince of Peace, disarm our trust in power,

how hate and war diminish humankind,
the lives of those who gave and give their all.
high hope to share with all the newly born,
teach us to coax the plant of peace to flower.

we pause, and seek in worship to increase
We thank you, God, for women, children, men
strong love in our pursuit of human worth:
May we, impassioned by your living Word,

our knowledge of the things that make for peace.
who seek to serve in love, today as then.
"lest we forget" the future of this earth.
remember forward to a world restored.

Words: Fred Kaan 1989
Music: James Langran 1861
Words copyright © 1993 Hope Publishing Company.

ST AGNES (LANGRAN)
10 10 10 10

528

God of Life

1 God of life, in Christ you lead us, guid-ing us a-
2 God of words and Word In - car - nate, words that chal - lenge
3 God of mu - sic, psalms and an - thems, help us sing your
4 God of days and years and e - ons, still you call as

long the way. In our past, through joys and sor - rows,
and em - brace, grant us bold - ness in our speak - ing,
faith a - new: mel - o - dies ex - pand - ing wor - ship,
in the past. Work un - done de - mands our la - bour;

you have been our strength and stay. Keep us faith - ful,
while we know your lov - ing grace. Give us words both
har - mo - nies en - rich - ing too. May our lives be
jus - tice yearns for peace at last. Yours the vis - ion

true dis - ci - ples, in our learn - ing and our praise,
clear and win - some, lov - ing hearts and listen - ing ears,
hymns in ac - tion, tuned to Christ in note and rhyme,
and the chal - lenge; ours the mis - sion and the praise,

Words: *Jane Parker Huber 1992*
Music: *John Zundel 1870*

Words copyright © 1992 Jane Parker Huber. Used by permission of Westminster John Knox Press.

BEECHER
8 7 8 7 D

cel - e - brat - ing past and pres - ent, con - se - crat - ing fu - ture days.
cel - e - brat - ing past and pres - ent, con - se - crat - ing fu - ture years.
cel - e - brat - ing past and pres - ent, con - se - crat - ing fu - ture time.
cel - e - brat - ing past and pres - ent, con - se - crat - ing fu - ture days.

Great God, We Sing that Mighty Hand   529

1 Great God, we sing that might - y hand by which sup -
2 With grate - ful hearts the past we own; the fu - ture,
3 In scenes ex - alt - ed or de - pressed, you are our

port - ed still we stand; the o - p'ning year your mer - cy
all to us un - known, we to your guard - ian care com -
joy, and you our rest; your good - ness all our hopes shall

shows; your mer - cy crowns it till it close.
mit, and peace - ful leave be - fore your feet.
raise, a - dored through all our chang - ing days.

Words: *Philip Doddridge ca. 1750*
Music: *William Knapp 1738*

WAREHAM
8 8 8 8

530 All Beautiful the March of Days

1 All beau-ti-ful the march of days, as sea-sons come and go;
2 O'er white ex-pans-es spark-ling pure the ra-diant morns un-fold;
3 O God, from whose un-fath-omed law the year in beau-ty flows,

the hand that shaped the rose has wrought the crys-tal of the snow,
the sol-emn splen-dours of the night burn bright-er through the cold;
your-self the vi-sion pass-ing by in crys-tal and in rose;

has sent the sil-very frost of heaven, the flow-ing wa-ters sealed,
life mounts in ev-ery throb-bing vein, love deep-ens round the hearth,
day un-to day de-clare thro' speech, and night to night pro-claim

and laid a si-lent love-li-ness on hill and wood and field.
and clear-er sounds the an-gel hymn, good will to all on earth.
in ev-er-chang-ing words of light the won-der of your name.

Words: Frances Whitmarsh Wile 1911, alt.
Music: English traditional melody; harm. Ralph Vaughan Williams 1905
Harmony by permission of Oxford University Press.

FOREST GREEN
8 6 8 6 D

Creator, Spirit, Living Word

531

1 Cre - a - tor, Spir - it, liv - ing Word, one God who calls us here: be with your peo - ple on this day; your pres - ence bring us cheer.

2 This house of God, built to your praise, we ded - i - cate to you. Ac - cept the work of ma - ny hands, the plan and pur - pose true.

3 Here at this font may par - ents see the wa - ter from a - bove, and at your ta - ble may we share the bread and wine of love.

4 When in this place your peo - ple stand as hus - band joined to wife; and when, be - reaved, they bow in prayer: give them your peace and life.

5 Here may your love be clear - ly preached by pul - pit and by pew. May we u - nite in hymn and song to cov - e - nant with you.

6 May young and old be taught your word; our church dis - cern your way; each per - son here your tem - ple be and see your glo - rious day.

Words: Alton George Demmons 1978
Music: Jeremiah Clarke 1707
Words copyright © 1995 Alton George Demmons.

ST MAGNUS
8 6 8 6

532 Creator, We Gather

1 Cre - a - tor, we gath - er to of - fer you praise, the
2 For beau - ty of build - ing in wood and in stone, where
♦ 3 For art - is - try fash - ioned in lead and in glass, for
4 For scrip - tures di - rec - ting our lives for to - day, for
5 For mu - sic of spir - it that lifts us in song, for

source of our lives and the strength of our days, re - call - ing our
Chris - tians may ga - ther, ap - proach - ing your throne, for faith, hope and
♦ love and the tal - ent that brought it to pass, for col - our in
teach - ing that o - pens our minds to your way, for words of sal -
great hymns that urge us in faith to be strong, for sounds of cre -

past, yet as - pir - ing in faith,
love which this ed - i - fice raised,
♦ na - ture our eyes can be - hold, Lord, ac - cept our thanks.
va - tion re - ceived from your Son,
a - tion, now heard in our ears,

5b* For bread and the wine we receive
once again,
For Christ who redeems us, our
lives to reclaim,
for love which he gives us, so
limitless, free,
Lord, accept our thanks.

6 To you, God Creator, the source of
all joy,
who gave varied talents, our minds
to employ,
our lives in your service we offer
anew,
Lord, accept our thanks.

*   (Optional if Holy Communion is celebrated)

Words: *Gordon M. Fleming* 1985
Music: *Gordon M. Fleming* 1995
Words and music copyright ©1995 Gordon M. Fleming.

RICHMOND HILL
11 11 11 5

When in Our Music God Is Glorified 533

1 When in our music God is glorified,
2 How often, making music, we have found
3 So has the church in liturgy and song,
4 And did not Jesus sing a psalm that night
5 Let every instrument be tuned for praise!

and adoration leaves no room for pride,
a new dimension in the world of sound,
in faith and love, through centuries of wrong,
when utmost evil strove against the light?
Let all rejoice who have a voice to raise!

it is as though the whole creation cried
as worship moved us to a more profound
borne witness to the truth in every tongue,
Then let us sing, for whom he won the fight:
And may God give us faith to sing always

Hallelujah! Hallelujah!

Words: Fred Pratt Green 1971
Music: Charles Villiers Stanford 1904
Words copyright © 1972 Hope Publishing Company.

ENGELBERG
10 10 10 with Hallelujahs
Alt. tune: Sine Nomine

534　I Cannot Dance, O Love

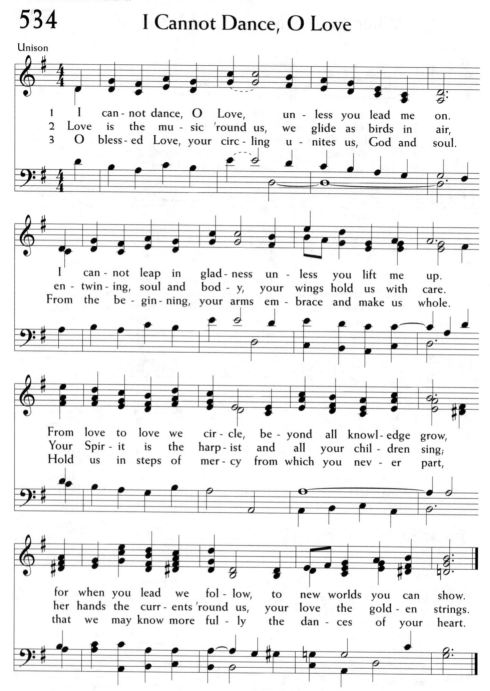

Unison

1 I can-not dance, O Love, un-less you lead me on.
2 Love is the mu-sic 'round us, we glide as birds in air,
3 O bless-ed Love, your circ-ling u-nites us, God and soul.

I can-not leap in glad-ness un-less you lift me up.
en-twin-ing, soul and bod-y, your wings hold us with care.
From the be-gin-ning, your arms em-brace and make us whole.

From love to love we cir-cle, be-yond all knowl-edge grow,
Your Spir-it is the harp-ist and all your chil-dren sing;
Hold us in steps of mer-cy from which you nev-er part,

for when you lead we fol-low, to new worlds you can show.
her hands the curr-ents 'round us, your love the gold-en strings.
that we may know more ful-ly the dan-ces of your heart.

Words: Jean Wiebe Janzen 1991, based on the writings of Mechtild of Magdeburg
Music: Ruth Wiwchar 1995

EVTON
7 6 7 6 D

For the Music of Creation

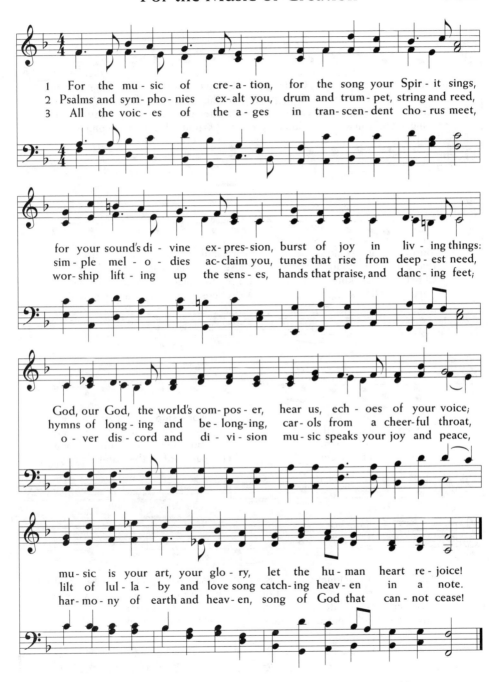

1 For the mu-sic of cre-a-tion, for the song your Spir-it sings,
2 Psalms and sym-pho-nies ex-alt you, drum and trum-pet, string and reed,
3 All the voic-es of the a-ges in tran-scen-dent cho-rus meet,

for your sound's di-vine ex-pres-sion, burst of joy in liv-ing things:
sim-ple mel-o-dies ac-claim you, tunes that rise from deep-est need,
wor-ship lift-ing up the sens-es, hands that praise, and danc-ing feet;

God, our God, the world's com-pos-er, hear us, ech-oes of your voice;
hymns of long-ing and be-long-ing, car-ols from a cheer-ful throat,
o-ver dis-cord and di-vi-sion mu-sic speaks your joy and peace,

mu-sic is your art, your glo-ry, let the hu-man heart re-joice!
lilt of lul-la-by and love song catch-ing heav-en in a note.
har-mo-ny of earth and heav-en, song of God that can-not cease!

Words: *Shirley Erena Murray* 1988
Music: *C. Hubert H. Parry* 1897
Words copyright © 1992 Hope Publishing Company.

RUSTINGTON
8 7 8 7 D

536

Born in Song

1 Born in song! God's peo-ple have al-ways been sing - ing.
2 Praise to God! Sing praise to the one who has made us.
3 Christ is king! He left all the glo-ry of heav - en.
4 Sing the song! God's Spir-it is poured out a-mong us.

Born in song! Hearts and voic - es raised.
Praise to God whose im-age we bear.
Christ is king! Born to share in our pain;
Sing the song! We're cre-at-ed a - new.

So to-day we wor-ship to-geth - er;
Heaven and earth are full of God's glo - ry;
cru - ci - fied, for sin-ners a-ton - ing,
Ev - ery mem - ber part of the Bod - y;

God a - lone is wor-thy to be praised.
let cre-a - tion praise God ev - ery-where.
ris - en, ex-alt - ed, soon to come a - gain.
giv - en God's power, God's will to seek and do.

Words: Brian R. Hoare 1979
Music: Brian R. Hoare 1979
Words and music copyright © 1983 Hope Publishing Company.

CHATSWORTH
Irregular

5 Tell the world!
   All power to Jesus is given.
   Tell the world!
   He is with us always.
   Spread the word, that all may
      receive him;
   every tongue confess and sing
      his praise.

6 Then the end!
   Christ Jesus shall reign in his glory.
   Then the end
   of all earthly days.
   Yet above the song will continue;
   all his people still shall sing
      his praise.

Your Work, O God, Needs Many Hands 537

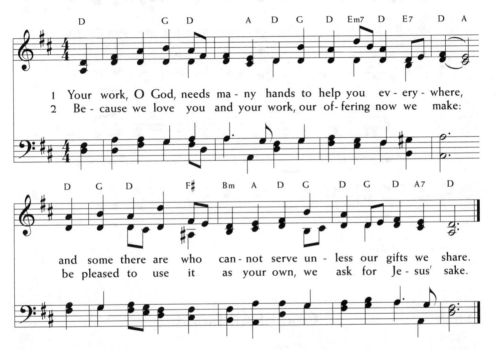

1 Your work, O God, needs ma - ny hands to help you ev - ery - where,
2 Be - cause we love you and your work, our of - fering now we make:

and some there are who can - not serve un - less our gifts we share.
be pleased to use it as your own, we ask for Je - sus' sake.

Words: *Calvin Weiss Laufer* 1927, alt.
Music: *Neil Dougall* ca. 1831

KILMARNOCK
8 6 8 6

538   For the Gift of Creation

For the gift of cre-a-tion, the gift of your love, and the gift of the
Spir-it by which we live, we thank you and give you the fruit of our
hands. May your grace be pro-claimed by the gifts that we give.

Words: Steve Garnaas-Holmes 1991
Music: Steve Garnaas-Holmes 1991
Words and music copyright © 1991 Abingdon Press.

GIFT OF CREATION
Irregular

539   God of All Good

Unison

1 God of all good, our gifts we bring to you,
2 We give our mind to un-der-stand your ways,
3 Mak - er, whose boun - ty all cre-a-tion shows,

Words: Albert F. Bayly 1962, alt.
Music: Sydney Watson 1964
Words and music by permission of Oxford University Press.

MORESTEAD
10 10 10 10

use them your ho - ly pur - pose to ful - fil;
hands, eyes and voice to serve your great de - sign;
Christ, by whose will - ing sac - ri - fice we live,

to - kens of love and pledg - es brought a - new
heart with the flame of your own love a - blaze,
Spir - it, from whom all life in full - ness flows,

that our whole life is of - fered to your will.
till for your glo - ry all our powers com - bine.
to you with grate - ful hearts our - selves we give.

Grant Us, God, the Grace   540

Grant us, God, the grace of giv - ing, with a spir - it large and free,

that our - selves and all our liv - ing we may of - fer faith - ful - ly.

Words: anonymous

Music: attrib. Christian F. Witt, Psalmodia Sacra 1715; adapt. Henry John Gauntlett 1861

STUTTGART
8 7 8 7

541 Praise God from Whom All Blessings Flow

Praise God from whom all bless-ings flow; praise God, all crea-tures
Gloire à Dieu, no-tre Cré-a-teur; gloire à Christ, no-tre

high and low; give thanks to God in love made known:
Ré-demp-teur; gloire à l'Es-prit Con-so-la-teur!

Cre-a-tor, Word and Spir-it, One.
Lou-ange et gloire à Dieu, Sau-veur.

Chinese:
pu tian zhi dia wan guo wan min,
qi sheng zan mei fu zi sheng ling,
san wei yi ti, tong rong tong zun,
wan you zhi yuan, wan fu zhi ben.

Cree:
Kain nom mau tooqk Puh tum owh woz
Kain nom moo waim uh keeng ab yaiqk
Kain nom moo wuh koung kagh tay laiqk
Kaiu nom Way gweez mint wauk W'jih joqk!

Mohawk:
Ron wa sen naiens ne Niio
ron wa sen naiens ne non kwe,
ron wa sen naiens neh ne ken
ron wa sen naiens ro ni ha.

Korean:
Man-bok-ui kun-won ha-na-nim
on paek-song ch'an-song tu-ri-go
cho ch' on-sa-yo ch'an-song-ha-se
ch'an song song-bu song-ja song-nyong

Japanese:
A-me-tsu-chi   ko-zo-ri-te
ka-shi-ko-mi   ta-ta-e-yo,
mi-me-gu-mi   a-fu-ru-ru
chi-chi-mi-ko   mi-ta-ma-o.

Spanish:
A la Divina Trinidad,
todos unido alabad,
con alegria, y gratitud,
su amor y gracia celebrad.

Words: *Thomas Ken* ca. *1674*
Music: *Genevan Psalter 1551*

OLD 100TH
8 8 8 8

We Give You But Your Own 542

We give you but your own, what-e'er the gift may be; all that we have is yours a-lone, we give it grate-ful-ly.

Words: William Walsham How 1858, alt.
Music: Johann Balthasar König 1738; adapt. William Henry Havergal 1847

FRANCONIA
6 6 8 6

We Give Thee But Thine Own 543

1 We give thee but thine own,
   what e'er the gift may be;
   all that we have is thine alone,
   a trust, O God, from thee.

2 May we thy bounties thus
   as stewards true receive,
   and gladly, as thou blessest us,
   to thee our first-fruits give.

Words: William Walsham How 1858

FRANCONIA
6 6 8 6

In Gratitude and Humble Trust 544

In gratitude and humble trust
we bring our best today
to serve your cause and share your love
with all along life's way.
O God, who gave yourself to us
in Jesus Christ, your Son,
teach us to give ourselves each day
until life's work is done.

Words: Frank von Christierson 1960, alt.
Words copyright © 1961 The Hymn Society. Used by permission of Hope Publishing Company.

FOREST GREEN
8 6 8 6 D

545

You Nourish Us

You nour - ish us with food, O God, for bod - y and for
soul; our love and ser - vice is our thanks, for
life that's free and whole, for life that's free and whole.

Words: Flora Litt and Wayne Irwin 1979
Music: Nikolaus Herman 1554; harm. Johann Sebastian Bach
Words copyright ©1979 Flora Litt and Wayne Irwin.

LOBT GOTT IHR CHRISTEN
8 6 8 6 with repeat

546

Be present at our table, Lord;
be here and everywhere adored.
This food now bless, and grant that we
may strengthened for your service be.

547

Be present at our table, Lord;
be here and everywhere adored.
thy creatures bless, and grant that we
may feast in paradise with thee.

548

We thank you, God, for this our food,
for life and health and every good.
Let manna to our souls be given —
the bread of life sent down from heaven.

Words 546, 547, 548: John Cennick 1741, alt.

The above Table Graces may be sung to the tune Old 100th, at 541.

For All Your Goodness, God 549

For all your good-ness, God, we give you thanks.

Thanks for the food we eat, and for the friends we meet;

for each new day we greet, we give you thanks.

Words: trad. American
Music: trad. German; arr. Darryl Nixon 1987, alt.
Arrangement copyright © 1987 Songs for a Gospel People.

FOR ALL YOUR GOODNESS
6 4 6 6 6 4

Bread Is Broken 550

Bread is bro-ken, friend-ship's to-ken, in our shar-ing God is known.

Words: Diane Taylor and Ken Powers 1991
Music: Diane Taylor and Ken Powers 1991
Words and music copyright © 1991 Prairie Rose Publications.

551

For Food in a World

For food in a world where ma-ny walk in hun - ger; for faith in a world where ma-ny walk in fear; for friends in a world where ma-ny walk a - lone, we give you hum - ble thanks, O Lord.

Words: German, Manfred Wester 1984; trans. unknown
Music: Robert J. Crocker 1969; arr. Mary Beth Nicks Barbour 1993

CROCKER
Irregular

552

For Food in a World

For food in a world where ma-ny walk in hun - ger, for

friends in a world where ma-ny walk a-lone, for faith in a world where

ma-ny walk in fear, we give you thanks, O God.

Words: German, Manfred Wester 1984; trans. unknown
Music: composer unknown; arr. Ruth Watson Henderson 1995
Words copyright © 1985 Gisela Wester. Used by permission. Arrangement copyright © 1995 Ruth Watson Henderson.

WORLD HUNGER
Irregular

Great God, the Giver of All Good 553

Great God, the giv-er of all good, ac-

cept our thanks and bless this food. Grace, health, and strength to

us af-ford, through Je-sus Christ, our ris-en Lord.

Words: James Skinner, Daily Service Hymnal 1863, alt.
Music: Thomas Hastings 1840

RETREAT
8 8 8 8

554 God Made from One Blood

1 God made from one blood all the fam - ilies of earth,
2 We turn to you, God, with our thanks and our tears
3 Through fam - ilies we've tast - ed the val - ue of trust
4 Help fam - ilies in all of their var - i - ous forms

the cir - cles of nur - ture that raise us from birth,
for all of the fam - ilies we've known through the years,
and felt what it means to be lov - ing and just,
to face with in - teg - ri - ty strug - gles and storms;

com - pan - ions who join us to walk through each stage
the in - ti - mate net - works on whom we de - pend
yet fam - ilies have al - so be - trayed their best goals,
grant peace in our homes that will nur - ture the bud

of child - hood and youth and a - dult - hood and age.
of par - ents and part - ners and chil - dren and friends.
mis - treat - ing their mem - bers and bruis - ing their souls.
of peace for the fam - ilies you made from one blood.

Words: Thomas H. Troeger 1988, adapt.
Music: Basque carol; arr. C. Edgar Pettman 1923; harm. music editors of The BBC Hymn Book 1951
Words copyright Oxford University Press, Inc. Harmony by permission of Oxford University Press.

NORMANDY
11 11 11 11

Our Parent, by Whose Name

1 Our Par - ent, by whose name all par - ent - hood is known,
2 O Je - sus, who, a child with - in an earth - ly home,
3 O Spir - it, who can bind our hearts in u - ni - ty,

who in your love pro - claims each fam - i - ly your own:
with heart still un - de - filed did to a - dult - hood come:
and teach us so to find the love from self set free:

di - rect all pa - rents, guard - ing well, with con - stant love as
our chil - dren bless, in ev - ery place, that they may all be -
in all our hearts such love in - crease, that ev - ery home, by

sen - ti - nel, the homes in which your peo - ple dwell.
hold your face, and know - ing you may grow in grace.
this re - lease, may be the dwell - ing place of peace.

Words: *Francis Bland Tucker 1939, alt.*
Music: *John David Edwards' Original Sacred Music ca. 1840*
Words from The Hymnal 1982 © The Church Pension Fund. Used by permission.

RHOSYMEDRE
6 6 6 6 8 8 8

556 Would You Bless Our Homes and Families

1 Would you bless our homes and fam-i-lies,
2 When our way is un-de-mand-ing,
3 From the homes in which we're nur-tured,
4 Let us reach be-yond the bound-aries

Source of life who calls us here;
let us use the time that's ours
with the love that shapes us there,
of our dai-ly thought and care

in our world of stress and ten-sion
to de-light in sim-ple plea-sures,
teach us, God, to claim as fam-i-ly
till the fam-ily you have cho-sen

teach us love that con-quers fear.
shar-ing joys in gen-tle hours.
ev-ery one whose life we share.
spills its love out ev-ery-where.

Words: Walter Farquharson 1974
Music: Ron Klusmeier 1974
Words copyright © 1977 Walter Farquharson. Music copyright © 1977 Ron Klusmeier.

AITKIN
8 7 8 7 D

Help us learn to love each oth - er with a love that
When our way is anx - ious walk - ing and a heav - y
And through all that life may of - fer, may we in your
Help us learn to love each oth - er with a love that

con - stant stays; teach us when we face our trou - bles,
path we plod, teach us trust in one an - oth - er
love re - main; may the love we share in fam - i - lies
con - stant stays; teach us when we face our trou - bles

love's ex - pressed in ma - ny ways.
and in you, our gra - cious God.
be a - live to praise your name.
love's ex - pressed in ma - ny ways.

A Prayer for Homes and Families 557

In you, O God, every family on earth receives its name.
Illumine the homes of this earth with the light of your love,
  granting courage to those who are hurt or lonely,
  endurance to those who care for sick family members,
  and wisdom to those in fearful times of change.
We thank you for gifts of love we have received
  from mother, father, spouse, child, or companion.
As we have been loved by you and by others, so may we love.
Grant us your peace, through Jesus the Christ. Amen.

Ruth Duck 1990

558 We Gather Here to Bid Farewell

1 We gath - er here to bid fare - well to
2 We bless the hand that brought you here and
3 In friend - ship's bonds our souls u - nite in
4 God guide you, keep you, lead you on from

friends who leave for oth - er parts; our prayers we pledge, our
rich - ly blessed us all in you: as now you leave for
prayer and praise and ho - ly vow: to God's great heart of
hope to hope, from strength to strength, un - til, in God's all -

love we tell, and lift to God our grate - ful hearts.
wid - er sphere God's cov - enant mer - cies we re - view.
love and light your friends in Christ com - mit you now.
glo - rious dawn, we meet be - fore the throne at length.

Words: Margaret Clarkson 1987
Music: Musikalisches Handbuch 1690; harm. William Henry Havergal 1847
Words copyright © 1987 Hope Publishing Company.

WINCHESTER NEW
8 8 8 8

Come, O Fount of Every Blessing 559

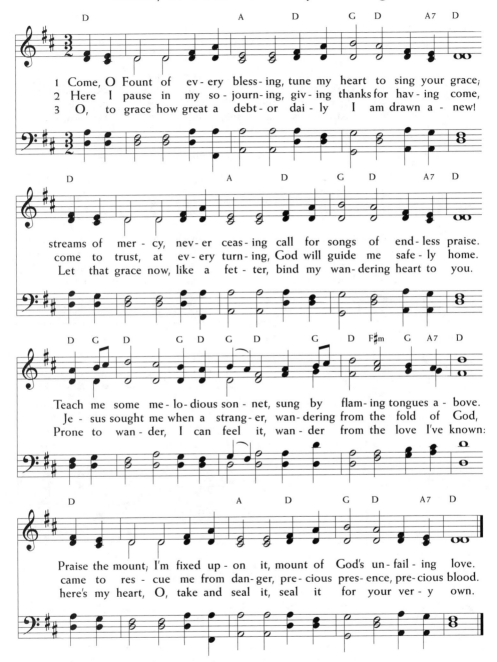

1 Come, O Fount of ev-ery bless-ing, tune my heart to sing your grace;
2 Here I pause in my so-journ-ing, giv-ing thanks for hav-ing come,
3 O, to grace how great a debt-or dai-ly I am drawn a-new!

streams of mer-cy, nev-er ceas-ing call for songs of end-less praise.
come to trust, at ev-ery turn-ing, God will guide me safe-ly home.
Let that grace now, like a fet-ter, bind my wan-dering heart to you.

Teach me some me-lo-dious son-net, sung by flam-ing tongues a-bove.
Je-sus sought me when a strang-er, wan-dering from the fold of God,
Prone to wan-der, I can feel it, wan-der from the love I've known:

Praise the mount; I'm fixed up-on it, mount of God's un-fail-ing love.
came to res-cue me from dan-ger, pre-cious pres-ence, pre-cious blood.
here's my heart, O, take and seal it, seal it for your ver-y own.

Words: Robert Robinson 1758, alt.
Music: John Wyeth, Repository of Sacred Music, Part II 1813
Word alterations copyright © 1993 The Pilgrim Press

NETTLETON
8 7 8 7 D

560 O Master, Let Me Walk with Thee

1 O Mas - ter, let me walk with thee in low - ly
2 Help me the slow of heart to move with some clear,
3 Teach me thy pa - tience; still with thee, in clos - er,
4 in hope that sends a shin - ing ray far down the

paths of ser - vice free; teach me thy se - cret,
win - ning word of love; teach me the way - ward
dear - er com - pa - ny, in work that keeps faith
fu - ture's broad - ening way, in peace that on - ly

help me bear the strain of toil, the fret of care.
feet to stay, and guide them in the home - ward way.
sure and strong, in trust that tri - umphs ov - er wrong,
thou canst give, with thee, O Mas - ter, let me live.

Words: Washington Gladden 1879, alt.
Music: Henry Percy Smith 1874

MARYTON
8 8 8 8

561 Take Up Your Cross

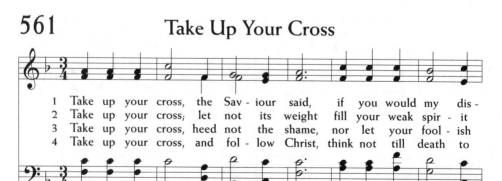

1 Take up your cross, the Sav - iour said, if you would my dis -
2 Take up your cross; let not its weight fill your weak spir - it
3 Take up your cross, heed not the shame, nor let your fool - ish
4 Take up your cross, and fol - low Christ, think not till death to

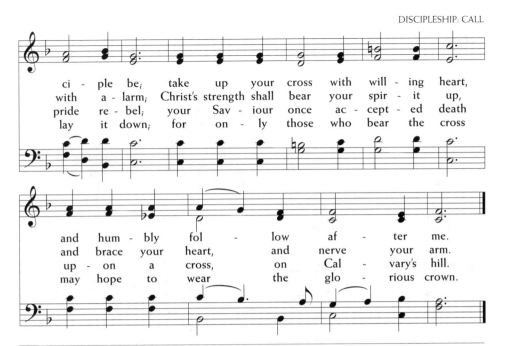

ci - ple be; take up your cross with will - ing heart,
with a - larm; Christ's strength shall bear your spir - it up,
pride re - bel; your Sav - iour once ac - cept - ed death
lay it down; for on - ly those who bear the cross

and hum - bly fol - low af - ter me.
and brace your heart, and nerve your arm.
up - on a cross, on Cal - vary's hill.
may hope to wear the glo - rious crown.

Words: Charles William Everest 1833, alt.
Music: Henry Baker 1854

HESPERUS (QUEBEC)
8 8 8 8

Jesus Calls Us 562

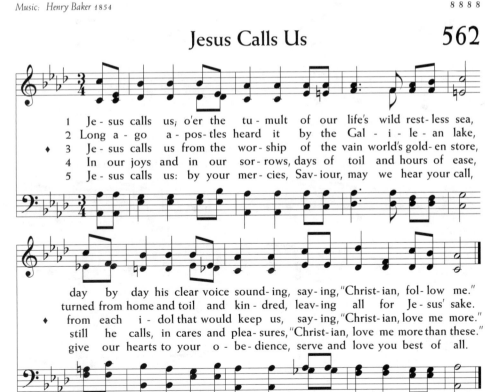

1 Je - sus calls us; o'er the tu - mult of our life's wild rest- less sea,
2 Long a - go a - pos - tles heard it by the Gal - i - le - an lake,
♦ 3 Je - sus calls us from the wor - ship of the vain world's gold- en store,
4 In our joys and in our sor - rows, days of toil and hours of ease,
5 Je - sus calls us: by your mer - cies, Sav - iour, may we hear your call,

day by day his clear voice sound- ing, say- ing,"Christ- ian, fol- low me."
turned from home and toil and kin - dred, leav- ing all for Je - sus' sake.
♦ from each i - dol that would keep us, say- ing,"Christ- ian, love me more."
still he calls, in cares and plea- sures,"Christ- ian, love me more than these."
give our hearts to your o - be - dience, serve and love you best of all.

Words: Cecil Frances Alexander 1852, alt.
Music: William Herbert Jude 1874

GALILEE
8 7 8 7

563 Jesus, You Have Come to the Lakeshore

Unison

1 Je - sus, you have come to the lake - shore
2 You know so well my pos - ses - sions;
3 You need my hands, full of car - ing
4 You, who have fished oth - er o - ceans,

look - ing nei - ther for wealth - y nor wise ones; you
my boat car - ies no gold and no weap - ons; —
through my la - bours to give oth - ers rest, and
ev - er longed for by souls who are wait - ing, my

on - ly asked me to fol - low hum - bly.
you will find there my nets and la - bour.
con - stant love that keeps on lov - ing.
lov - ing friend, as thus you call me.

Refrain

O Je - sus, with your eyes you have searched me,

Words: Cesáreo Gabaráin 1979; trans. Gertrude C. Suppe, George Lockwood,
Raquel Gutiérrez-Achón 1987
Music: Cesáreo Gabaráin 1979; harm. Skinner Chávez-Melo 1987

PESCADOR DE HOMBRES
Irregular with refrain

and while smil - ing, have spo-ken my name;

now my boat's left on the shore-line be - hind me;

by your side I will seek oth-er seas.

A Prayer for Discipleship 564

Jesus Christ, our Saviour,
    alive and at large in the world;
help us to follow and find you today
    in the places where we work and meet people,
    spend leisure time and make plans.
Teach us to see through your eyes,
    and to hear the questions you ask;
by the power of the Cross,
and in the freedom of your Spirit, we pray. Amen.

John Taylor, Bishop of Winchester 1985, alt.

565 Love, Who Made Me in Your Likeness

1 Love, who made me in your like-ness, to your im-age
2 Love, to whom my life was pre-cious, long be-fore I
3 Love, for me, you came to suf-fer and, at last, were
4 Love, my Life, my Truth, my Splen-dour, liv-ing Spir-it,
5 Love, whose yoke is laid up-on me, lib-er-at-ing

form-ing me; Love, who showed such gen - tle kind-ness
came to birth; Love, for ev - er hu - man with us,
cru-ci-fied; Love, with you, I live for ev - er,
Might-y Word; Love, by whose full self - sur-ren-der
life and mind; Love, whose grace has o - ver-come me,

when I fell, re - stor-ing me:
born to share our life on earth:
joy is end-less at your side: Love, I give my -
my heart's whole-ness is re - stored:
here is free-dom, un - con-fined:

self to be one with you, e - ter - nal - ly.

Words: German, Johann Scheffler, trans. Alan Gaunt 1991
Music: Geistreiches Gesangbuch, Darmstadt 1698
Translation copyright © 1991 Stainer & Bell, Ltd. Used by permission of Hope Publishing Company.

ALL SAINTS
878777

6 Love, your love's immense compassion
  pleads my cause at God's right hand;
  Love, redeemed from condemnation,
  in your strength, though weak, I stand:
  Love, I give myself to be
  one with you eternally.

7 Love, you are my Resurrection,
  come to call me from the dead;
  Love, I share, in your perfection,
  glory that can never fade:
  Love, I give myself to be
  one with you eternally.

Awake, O Sleeper 566

1. A-wake, O sleep-er, rise from death, and Christ shall
   give you light; so learn his love, its
   length and breadth, its full-ness, depth, and height.

2. To us on earth he came to bring from sin and
   fear re-lease, to give the Spir-it's
   u-ni-ty, the ver-y bond of peace.

3. There is one bod-y and one hope, one Spir-it
   and one call, one Lord, one faith, and
   one bap-tism, one God who made us all.

4. Then walk in love as Christ has loved, who died that
   he might save; with kind and gen-tle
   hearts for-give as God in Christ for-gave.

5. For us Christ lived, for us he died, and con-quered
   in the strife. A-wake, a-rise, go
   forth in faith, and Christ shall give you life.

Words: Francis Bland Tucker 1980
Music: Max B. Miller 1984

MARSH CHAPEL
8 6 8 6

Words copyright © 1978 Lutheran Book of Worship. Reprinted by permission of Augsburg Fortress. Music copyright © 1984 Max B. Miller.

567 Will You Come and Follow Me

Unison

1 Will you come and fol-low me if I but call your name?
2 Will you leave your-self be-hind if I but call your name?
◆ 3 Will you let the blind-ed see if I but call your name?
4 Will you love the "you" you hide if I but call your name?
5 Christ, your sum-mons e-choes true when you but call my name.

Will you go where you don't know and nev-er be the same?
Will you care for cruel and kind and nev-er be the same?
◆ Will you set the pris-oners free and nev-er be the same?
Will you quell the fear in-side and nev-er be the same?
Let me turn and fol-low you and nev-er be the same.

Will you let my love be shown, will you let my name be known,
Will you risk the hos-tile stare should your life at-tract or scare?
◆ Will you kiss the lep-er clean, and do such as this un-seen,
Will you use the faith you've found to re-shape the world a-round,
In your com-pa-ny I'll go where your love and foot-steps show.

will you let my life be grown in you and you in me?
Will you let me an-swer prayer in you and you in me?
◆ and ad-mit to what I mean in you and you in me?
through my sight and touch and sound in you and you in me?
Thus I'll move and live and grow in you and you in me.

Words: The Iona Community 1987
Music: Scottish traditional, arr. The Iona Community 1987

KELVINGROVE
7 6 7 6 7 7 7 6
Alt. setting: 96

Dear Lord, Lead Me Day by Day

568

1 Dear Lord, lead me day by day; make me stead-fast,
2 Dear Lord, lead me day by day; make me fol-low
3 Now with con-fi-dence I sing joy-ous prais-es

wise, and strong; hap-py most of all to know that my
and o-bey faith-ful-ly your words of life, that your
to our God, and with up-right heart I give ten-der

Refrain

dear Lord loves me so. Praise to God, fount of love,
love ev-er a-bide.
care and sym-pa-thy.

praise from morn till the set of sun; praise at home,

praise in church; praise to God ev-ery-where on earth.

Words: *Francisca Asuncion 1983*
Music: *Philippine folk melody, arr. by Francisca Asuncion 1983*
Words and arrangement copyright © 1983 The United Methodist Publishing House.

COTTAGE GROVE
7 7 7 7 *with refrain*

569

You Call Us Out

Unison

1 You call us out to praise you, the
2 For var - ied hues and tex - tures, new
3 The church that speaks for - give - ness, con -
4 The church that of - fers heal - ing, dis -
5 Our fee - ble voic - es strug - gle, to

God who gave us birth, to ga - ther in com - mun - ion,
pat - terns, still you search, to weave your seam - less gar - ments,
fess - es its own need; the church that feels its hun - ger,
cerns its wounds and loss; the church that fac - es dy - ing,
sing your jus - tice clear; the world has sunk in si - lence,

and trea - sure your whole earth; we are your liv - ing sto - ry,
the fab - ric of your church; our tat - tered faith you cher - ish,
finds grace to care and feed; our fam - ished world is cry - ing,
shares life be - yond the cross; to peo - ple torn and bro - ken,
each dis - cord e - choes fear; one voice a - lone is rag - ged,

to hear and to be heard; we praise your name, who writes us,
re - claim from wear and moth; we praise your name, who twines us,
its fu - ture filled with dread; we praise your name, who fills us,
your mer - cy is re - vealed; we praise your name, who loves us,
to - geth - er we are strong; we praise your name, who breathes us,

the au - thor and the word.
the weav - er and the cloth.
♦ the bak - er and the bread.
the heal - er and the healed.
the sing - er and the song.

Words: Anna Briggs 1991
Music: Basil Harwood 1898
Words copyright © 1992 The General Synod of the Anglican Church of Canada. All rights reserved. Used by permission.
Music published by permission of Executors of the late Dr. Basil Harwood.

THORNBURY
7 6 7 6 D
Descant: 274

Jesus' Hands Were Kind Hands — 570

Unison

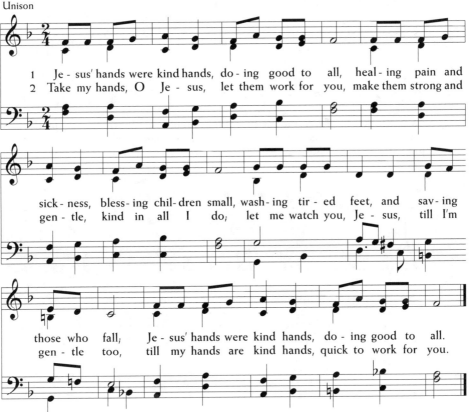

1 Je - sus' hands were kind hands, do - ing good to all, heal - ing pain and
2 Take my hands, O Je - sus, let them work for you, make them strong and

sick - ness, bless - ing chil - dren small, wash - ing tir - ed feet, and sav - ing
gen - tle, kind in all I do; let me watch you, Je - sus, till I'm

those who fall; Je - sus' hands were kind hands, do - ing good to all.
gen - tle too, till my hands are kind hands, quick to work for you.

Words: Margaret Cropper
Music: Old French melody; harm. Carlton R. Young 1988
Words copyright © 1979 Stainer & Bell Ltd. Used by permission of Hope Publishing Company. Harmony copyright © 1989 The United Methodist Publishing House.

AU CLAIR DE LA LUNE
6 5 6 5 D

571 Eternal Ruler of the Ceaseless Round

1 E - ter - nal Rul - er of the cease - less round
2 We are your own, the chil - dren of your love,
3 We would be one in ha - tred of all wrong,
4 O clothe us with your heaven - ly ar - mour, Lord,

of cir - cling plan - ets sing - ing on their way, guide of the
as dear - ly loved as your be - lov - ed Son; des - cend, O
one in our love of all things true and fair, one with the
your trust - y shield and sword of love be ours; our in - spi -

na - tions from the night pro - found in - to the glo - ry
Ho - ly Spir - it, like a dove, and rule our hearts, that
joy that finds a voice in song, one with the grief that
ra - tion be your con - stant word; we ask no vic - to -

of the per - fect day: rule in our hearts, that we may
we may be as one: as one with you, to whom we
trem - bles in - to prayer, one in the power that makes your
ries that are not yours: give or with - hold, let pain or

Words: *John White Chadwick 1864, alt.*
Music: *Orlando Gibbons 1623, alt.*

SONG 1
10 10 10 10 10 10

live a - new, guid - ed and strength-ened and up - held by you.
ev - er tend; as one with Christ, our Sav - iour and our friend.
chil - dren free to fol - low truth, and thus in you to be.
plea - sure fall; to know that we are serv - ing you is all.

Send Me, Lord 572

Leader

Send me, Lord.

All

1 Send me, Je - sus, send me, Je - sus, send me,
(2 Lead me) Je - sus, lead me, Je - sus, lead me,
(3 I will) go, Lord, I will go, Lord, in your

Leader | 1-3 | Last time

2 Lead me, Lord.
3 I will go

| 1-3 | Last time

Je - sus, send me, Lord. 2 Lead me
Je - sus, lead me, Lord. 3 I will
name, Lord, I will _____ go.

Other verses may be improvised.

Words: trad. South African text
Music: trad. South African melody
Words and music copyright © 1984 Walton Music Corporation.

THUMA MINA
Irregular

573 Eternal Spirit of the Living Christ

Unison

1 E - ter - nal Spir - it of the liv - ing Christ,
2 Come, pray in me the prayer I need this day;
3 Come with the vi - sion and the strength I need

I know not how to ask or what to say;
help me to see your pur - pose and your will,
to serve my God, and all hu - man - i - ty;

I on - ly know my need, as deep as life,
where I have failed, what I have done a - miss;
ful - fill - ment of my life in love out - poured—

and on - ly you can teach me how to pray.
held in for - giv - ing love, let me be still.
my life in you, O Christ, your love in me.

Words: Frank von Christierson 1974, 1979
Music: Alfred Morton Smith 1941

SURSUM CORDA
10 10 10 10

And the following...

504   How clear is our vocation
562   Jesus calls us; o'er the tumult
117   Jesus Christ is waiting
589   Lord, speak to me
507   Today we all are called
598   When the pain of the world

Come, Let Us Sing of a Wonderful Love 574

1 Come, let us sing of a won-der-ful love, ten-der and true,
2 Je - sus the Sav-iour this gos-pel to tell joy-ful-ly came,
3 Je - sus is seek-ing the wan-der-ers yet; why do they roam?
4 Come to my heart, O thou won-der-ful love! Come and a - bide,

ten - der and true, out of the heart of the Fa-ther a-bove,
joy - ful - ly came, came with the help-less and hope-less to dwell,
why do they roam? Love on - ly waits to for-give and for-get;
come and a - bide, lift - ing my life till it ris - es a - bove

stream - ing to me and to you: won-der-ful love,
shar - ing their sor - row and shame, seek-ing the lost,
home, wear - y wan - der - ers, home! Won-der-ful love,
en - vy and false-hood and pride: seek-ing to be,

won - der - ful love dwells in the heart of the Fa-ther a-bove.
seek - ing the lost, sav - ing, re-deem-ing at mea-sure-less cost.
won - der - ful love dwells in the heart of the Fa-ther a-bove.
seek - ing to be low - ly and hum-ble, a learn-er of thee.

Words: Robert Walmsley ca. 1900
Music: Adam Watson

WONDERFUL LOVE
10 8 10 7 8 10

575 I'm Gonna Live So God Can Use Me

1 I'm gon-na live so (live so)
2 I'm gon-na work so (work so) God can use me an-y-where, Lord,
3 I'm gon-na pray so (pray so)
4 I'm gon-na sing so (sing so)

an-y-time! I'm gon-na live so (live so)
(an-y-time!) I'm gon-na work so (work so) God can
I'm gon-na pray so (pray so)
I'm gon-na sing so (sing so)

use me an-y-where, Lord, an-y-time!
(my Lord) (an-y-time!)

Words: African-American spiritual
Music: African-American spiritual, arr. Wendell Whalum
Arrangement copyright © 1987 Estate of Wendell Whalum.

I'M GONNA LIVE
Irregular

576 A Prayer for Service to Others

Almighty God, whose son Jesus Christ has taught us
that what we do for the least of our brothers and sisters
we do also for him,
give us the will to be the servant of others
as he was the servant of all,
who gave up his life and died for us,
but is alive and reigns with you and the Holy Spirit,
one God, now and forever. Amen.

Saint Augustine of Hippo

I've Got Peace like a River

1 I've got peace like a river, I've got peace like a
2 I've got joy like a fountain, I've got joy like a
3 I've got love like an o-cean, I've got love like an

riv - er, I've got peace like a riv - er in - a my
foun - tain, I've got joy like a foun-tain in - a my
o - cean, I've got love like an o - cean in - a my

soul. I've got riv - er in - a my soul.
soul. I've got foun-tain in - a my soul.
soul. I've got o - cean in - a my soul.

Words: African-American spiritual
Music: African-American spiritual

PEACE LIKE A RIVER
7 7 11 D

578   As a Fire Is Meant for Burning

1 As a fire is meant for burn-ing with a bright and warm-ing
2 We are learn-ers; we are teach-ers; we are pil-grims on the
3 As a green bud in the spring-time is a sign of life re-

flame, so the church is meant for mis-sion, giv-ing
way. We are seek-ers; we are giv-ers; we are
newed, so may we be signs of one-ness mid earth's

glo-ry to God's name. Not to preach our creeds or
ves-sels made of clay. By our gen-tle, lov-ing
peo-ples, ma-ny-hued. As a rain-bow lights the

cus-toms, but to build a bridge of care, we join
ac-tions, we would show that Christ is light. In a
heav-ens when a storm is past and gone, may our

Words: *Ruth Duck 1983*
Music: *Marty Haugen*
Words copyright © 1992 and music copyright © 1987 G.I.A. Publications, Inc.

JOYOUS LIGHT
8 7 8 7 D
Alt. tune: Beach Spring

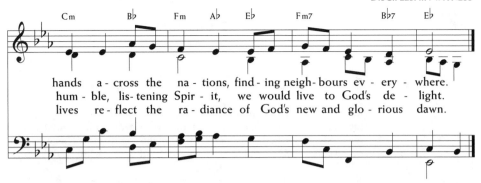

hands a-cross the na-tions, find-ing neigh-bours ev-ery-where.
hum-ble, lis-tening Spir-it, we would live to God's de-light.
lives re-flect the ra-diance of God's new and glo-rious dawn.

The Church Is Wherever God's People   579

1 The church is wher-ev-er God's peo-ple are prais-ing, sing-ing God's
2 The church is wher-ev-er God's peo-ple are help-ing, car-ing for

good-ness for joy on this day. The church is wher-ev-er dis-
neigh-bours in sick-ness and need. The church is wher-ev-er God's

ci-ples of Je-sus re-mem-ber his sto-ry and walk in his way.
peo-ple are shar-ing the words of the Bi-ble in gift and in deed.

Words: Carol Rose Ikeler 1959
Music: English carol, arr. F. R. C. Clarke 1971
Words copyright © 1963 W.L. Jenkins. Used and adapted by permission of Westminster John Knox Press. Arrangement copyright © 1971 F. R. C. Clarke.

OLD CORNISH CAROL
12 10 12 11 D

580 Faith of Our Fathers

1 Faith of our fa-thers, liv-ing still in spite of dun-geon,
2 Faith of our moth-ers, dar-ing faith, your work for Christ is
3 Faith of our sis-ters, broth-ers too, who still must bear op-
4 Faith born of God, O call us yet; bind us with all who

fire, and sword; O how our hearts beat high with joy,
love re-vealed, spread-ing God's word from pole to pole,
pres-sion's might, rais-ing on high, in pris-ons dark,
fol-low you, shar-ing the strug-gle of your cross

when-e'er we hear that glo-rious word: faith of our fa-thers,
mak-ing love known and free-dom real: faith of our moth-ers,
the cross of Christ still burn-ing bright: faith for to-day, O
un-til the world is made a-new. Faith born of God, O

ho-ly faith,
ho-ly faith,
liv-ing faith, we will be true to you till death.
liv-ing faith,

Words: v. 1 Frederick W. Faber 1849; vv. 2–4 Joseph R. Alfred 1981, alt.
Music: Henri Frederick Hemy 1864; adapt. James George Walton 1874
Words (vv. 2–4) copyright © 1981 Joseph R. Alfred.

ST CATHERINE
8 8 8 8 8 8

When We Are Living

1 When we are living, it is in Christ Je-sus,
2 Through all our liv-ing, we our fruits must give.
3 'Mid times of sor-row and in times of pain,
4 A-cross this wide world, we shall al-ways find

and when we're dy-ing, it is in the Lord.
Good works of ser-vice are for of-fer-ing.
when sens-ing beau-ty or in love's em-brace,
those who are cry-ing with no peace of mind,

Both in our liv-ing and in our dy-ing,
When we are giv-ing, or when re-ceiv-ing,
wheth-er we suf-fer, or sing re-joic-ing,
but when we help them, or when we feed them,

we be-long to God, we be-long to God.

Words: v. 1 Spanish anon.; trans. Elise S. Eslinger 1983; vv. 2–4 Roberto Escamilla 1983;
trans. George Lockwood 1987
Music: Spanish melody; harm. Carlton R. Young 1989
Translation and harmony copyright © 1989 The United Methodist Publishing House.

SOMOS DEL SEÑOR
10 10 10 10

582

There's a Spirit in the Air

Descant

Praise - the love, praise - the

1 There's a spir - it in the air, tell - ing Chris - tians
2 Lose your shy - ness, find your tongue, tell the world what
3 When be - liev - ers break the bread, when a hun - gry
4 Still the Spir - it gives us light, see - ing wrong and
5 When a stran - ger's not a - lone, where the home - less

love. Hal - le - lu - jah!

ev - ery - where: "Praise the love that Christ re - vealed,
God has done: God in Christ has come to stay.
child is fed, praise the love that Christ re - vealed,
set - ting right: God in Christ has come to stay.
find a home, praise the love that Christ re - vealed,

Hal - le - lu - jah!

liv - ing, work - ing in our world."
Live to - mor - row's life to - day!
liv - ing, work - ing in our world.
Live to - mor - row's life to - day!
liv - ing, work - ing, in our world.

Words: Brian Wren 1969
Music: John Wilson 1969, desc. John Wilson 1969
Words, music and descant copyright © 1979 Hope Publishing Company.

LAUDS
7 7 7 7
Alt. tune: Monkland

6 May the Spirit fill our praise,
  guide our thoughts and
    change our ways.
  God in Christ has come to stay,
  live tomorrow's life today.

7 There's a Spirit in the air,
  calling people everywhere:
  praise the love that Christ revealed,
  living, working, in our world.

Jesus Came, a Child like Me

583

Unison

1 Je-sus came, a child like me, so the face of God I'd see,
2 Je-sus came to show us all ways to an-swer our God's call—
3 Je-sus came God's work to do, came to live in me and you,
4 Je-sus came to show God's face, live God's love, and be God's grace.

God is not left far a-way, God is with us ev-ery day.
came to show us how to share, came to live with God's own care.
came to turn the world a-round till God's peace and love are found.
God lives now in me, in you, God's at work in what we do.

Refrain

Live, Je-sus, near us, live, Je-sus, with us,

live, Je-sus, in us, come, live in us to-day.

Words: Walter Farquharson 1987
Music: Richard D. Hall 1988
Words copyright © 1987 Walter Farquharson. Music copyright © 1988 Richard D. Hall.

JESUS CAME
7 7 7 7 with refrain

584 Through the Heart of Every City

1 Through the heart of ev-ery cit-y runs the flow of
2 Through the pass-ing gen-er-a-tions, in their spir-it,
3 Through our wor-ship and our wit-ness, Je-sus, grant that

hu-man need. 'Mid this glass and steel are puls-ing
flesh and bone, Je-sus Christ be-comes in-car-nate:
we may still hear the heart-beat of com-pas-sion

smol-der-ing wick and bruis-èd reed. Has our church a
ho-ly hearts are liv-ing stone build-ing here a
call-ing us to do your will. You, our vine, and

word to of-fer, some hope shin-ing from our creed?
house of re-fuge as a tem-ple, as a home.
we, your bran-ches, dead-ened not by an-y chill,

Words: Sylvia Dunstan 1987
Music: Charles Venn Pilcher 1935, harm. Walter MacNutt 1968
Words copyright © 1991 G.I.A. Publications, Inc. Harmony copyright © Walter MacNutt.

HERMON
8 7 8 7 D

Walk-ing through the con-crete fur-rows Je-sus sows the Word as seed.
So with-in the cit-y's shad-ow Je-sus' plant-ed Word has grown.
work-ing for that fin-al cit-y where the har-vest is ful-filled.

Jesus Bids Us Shine 585

1 Je-sus bids us shine with a pure, clear light, like a lit-tle can-dle
2 Je-sus bids us shine first of all for him; well he sees and knows it
3 Je-sus bids us shine, then, for all a-round; man-y kinds of dark-ness

burn-ing in the night. In this world is dark-ness,
if our light grows dim: Je-sus walks be-side us
in the world are found: sin, and want and sor-row;

so let us shine,
to help us shine, you in your small cor-ner, and I in mine.
so we must shine,

Words: Susan Warner 1868, alt.
Music: Edwin O. Excell

JESUS BIDS US SHINE
5 5 6 5 6 4 6 4

586 We Shall Go Out with Hope of Resurrection

1 We shall go out with hope of res - ur - rec - tion;
2 We'll give a voice to those who have not spo - ken;

we shall go out, from strength to strength go on;
we'll find the words for those whose lips are sealed;

we shall go out and tell our stor - ies bold - ly;
we'll make the tunes for those who sing no long - er,

tales of a love that will not let us go.
ex - pres - sive love a - live in ev - ery heart.

We'll sing our songs of wrongs that can be right - ed;
We'll share our joy with those who still are weep - ing,

Words: *June Boyce-Tillman 1993*
Music: *Traditional Irish melody, arr. John Barnard 1982*

LONDONDERRY AIR
11 10 11 10 D

we'll dream our dreams of hurts that can be healed;
raise hymns of strength for hearts that break in grief,

we'll weave a cloth of all the world u - ni - ted with - in the
we'll leap and dance the re - sur - rec - tion sto - ry, in - clud - ing

vi - sion of new life in Christ.
all in cir - cles of our love.

A Prayer For Hope

587

God, like a bakerwoman,
you bring the leaven
    which causes our hopes to rise.
With your strong and gentle hands,
    shape our lives.
Warm us with your love.
Take our common lives
    and touch them with your grace,
    that we may nourish hope among humanity.
We pray trusting in your name,
    through Jesus our Christ. Amen

Ruth Duck 1992

588

Many Are the Lightbeams

1 Ma - ny are the light - beams from the one light. Our one
2 Ma - ny are the branch - es of the one tree. Our one
♦ 3 Ma - ny are the gifts given, love is all one. Love's the
4 Ma - ny ways to serve God, the Spir - it is one, ser - vant
5 Ma - ny are the mem - bers, the bod - y is one, mem - bers

light is Je - sus. (Ma - ny) Ma - ny are the light - beams
tree is Je - sus. (Ma - ny) Ma - ny are the branch - es
♦ gift of Je - sus. (Ma - ny) Ma - ny are the gifts given,
spi - rit of Je - sus. (Ma - ny) Ma - ny ways to serve God, the
all of Je - sus. (Ma - ny) Ma - ny are the mem - bers, the

from the one light;
of the one tree;
♦ love is all one; we are one in Christ.
Spir - it is one;
bod - y is one;

Words: Cyprian of Carthage 252; Swedish para. Anders Frostenson 1972, rev. 1986;
English trans. David Lewis 1983
Music: Olle Widestrand 1974; arr. Len Lythgoe 1983

LAGORNA ÄR MANGA
10 6 10 5

And the following...

338   Ask me what great thing I know
714, 715   Come, we that love the Lord
289   It only takes a spark

Lord, Speak to Me

589

1 Lord, speak to me that I may speak
2 O lead me, so that I may lead
3 O teach me, so that I may teach
4 O fill me with your full - ness, Lord,

in liv - ing e - choes of your tone;
the wan - dering and the wa - vering feet;
the pre - cious truths which you im - part;
un - til my ver - y heart o'er - flows

as you have sought, so let me seek
O feed me, so that I may feed
and wing my words, that they may reach
in kin - dling thought and glow - ing word,

your stray - ing chil - dren lost and lone.
your hun - gering ones with man - na sweet.
the hid - den depths of ma - ny a heart.
your love to tell, your praise to show.

Words: Frances Ridley Havergal 1872
Music: Samuel Sebastian Wesley 1872

WINSCOTT
8 8 8 8

590 A Prophet-Woman Broke a Jar

1 A proph - et - wom - an broke a jar, by
2 A faith - ful wom - an left a tomb by
3 Though wom - an - wis - dom, wom - an - truth, for
4 The Spir - it knows, the Spir - it calls, by

Love's di - vine ap - point - ing. With rare per - fume she
Love's di - vine com - mis - sion. She saw, she heard, she
cen - tu - ries were hid - den, un - sung, un - writ - ten,
Love's di - vine or - dain - ing, the friends we need to

filled the room, pre - sid - ing and a - noint - ing.
preached the Word, a - ris - ing from sub - mis - sion.
and un - heard, de - rid - ed and for - bid - den,
serve and lead, their powers and gifts un - chain - ing.

A proph - et - wom - an broke a jar, the
A faith - ful wom - an left a tomb, with
the Spir - it's breath, the Spir - it's fire, on
The Spir - it knows, the Spir - it calls, from

Words: Brian Wren 1991
Music: Walter K. Stanton ca. 1951

MEGERRAN
8 7 8 7 D

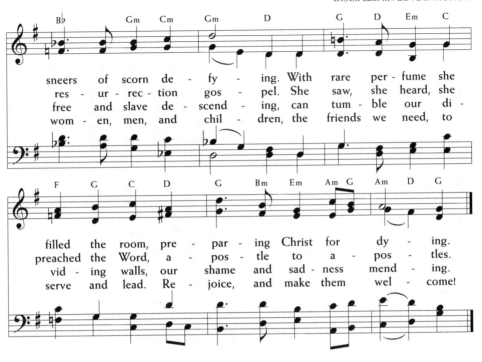

sneers of scorn de - fy - ing. With rare per - fume she
res - ur - rec - tion gos - pel. She saw, she heard, she
free and slave de - scend - ing, can tum - ble our di -
wom - en, men, and chil - dren, the friends we need, to

filled the room, pre - par - ing Christ for dy - ing.
preached the Word, a - pos - tle to a - pos - tles.
vid - ing walls, our shame and sad - ness mend - ing.
serve and lead. Re - joice, and make them wel - come!

Jesus, United by Your Grace 591

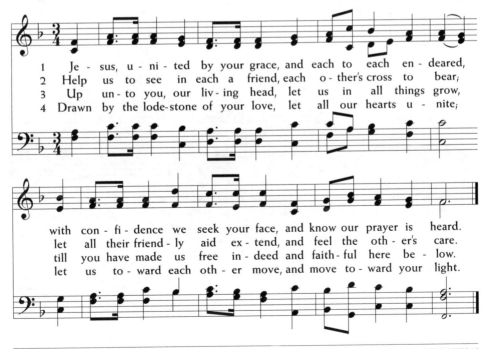

1 Je - sus, u - ni - ted by your grace, and each to each en - deared,
2 Help us to see in each a friend, each o - ther's cross to bear;
3 Up un - to you, our liv - ing head, let us in all things grow,
4 Drawn by the lode-stone of your love, let all our hearts u - nite;

with con - fi - dence we seek your face, and know our prayer is heard.
let all their friend - ly aid ex - tend, and feel the oth - er's care.
till you have made us free in - deed and faith - ful here be - low.
let us to - ward each oth - er move, and move to - ward your light.

Words: Charles Wesley 1742, alt.
Music: Thomas Augustine Arne 1762

ARLINGTON
8 6 8 6

592 Come, Now, You Blessed

Unison

1 "Come, now, you bless - ed, eat at my ta - ble,"
2 "When did we see you hun - gry or thirs - ty?
3 "When you gave bread to earth's hun - gry chil - dren,
4 Christ, when we meet you out on life's road - ways,

said the great judge to the right - eous a - bove.
When were you home - less, a strang - er a - lone?
when you gave wel - come to war's ref - u - gees,
look - ing to us in the fac - es of need,

"When I was hun - gry, thirs - ty and home - less,
When did we see you sick or in pris - on?
when you re - mem - bered those most for - got - ten,
then may we know you, wel - come, and show you

sick and in pris - on you showed me your love."
What have we done that you call us your own?"
you cared for me in the small - est of these."
love that is faith - ful in word and in deed.

(Optional interlude)

Words: Ruth Duck 1979
Music: Jeeva Sam 1995; arr. Ron Klusmeier 1995

COME, NOW, YOU BLESSED
10 10 10 10

Jesu, Jesu, Fill Us with Your Love

1 Kneels at the feet of his friends, si-lent-ly wash-es their
2 Neigh-bours are rich and poor, var-ied in col-our and
3 These are the ones we should serve, these are the ones we should
4 Kneel at the feet of our friends, si-lent-ly wash-ing their

feet, mas-ter who acts as a slave to them.
race, neigh-bours are near and far a-way.
love, all are neigh-bours to us and you.
feet, this is the way we should live with you.

* 'Jesu' may be pronounced 'Yay-soo'

Words: Tom Colvin 1969
Music: Ghanaian folk song, adapt. Tom Colvin 1969
Words and music adaptation copyright © 1969 Hope Publishing Company.

CHEREPONI
Irregular with refrain

594 O Christian, Love

1 O Chris-tian, love your sis-ter and your bro-ther!
2 Fol-low with rev-erent steps the great ex-am-ple:
3 Then shall all shack-les fall; the storm-y clan-gour

Where pit-y dwells, the peace of God is there;
Je-sus whose ho-ly work was do-ing good;
of wild war-mu-sic o'er the earth shall cease;

to wor-ship right-ly is to love each oth-er,
so shall the wide earth seem a hal-lowed tem-ple,
love shall tread out the bale-ful fire of an-ger,

each smile a hymn, each kind-ly deed a prayer.
each lov-ing life a psalm of grat-i-tude.
and in its ash-es plant the tree of peace.

Words: John Greenleaf Whittier 1848, alt.
Music: Alfred Scott-Gatty 1902

WELWYN
11 10 11 10

We Are Pilgrims
(The Servant Song)

1 We are pilgrims on a journey, fellow travellers on the road; we are here to help each other walk the mile and bear the load.

2 Sister, let me be your servant, let me be as Christ to you; pray that I may have the grace to let you be my servant too.

3 I will hold the Christ-light for you in the night-time of your fear; I will hold my hand out to you, speak the peace you long to hear.

4 I will weep when you are weeping, when you laugh I'll laugh with you; I will share your joy and sorrow, till we've seen this journey through.

5 When we sing to God in heaven, we shall find such harmony, born of all we've known together of Christ's love and agony.

6 Brother, let me be your servant, let me be as Christ to you; pray that I may have the grace to let you be my servant too.

Words: Richard Gillard, 1977
Music: Richard Gillard 1977; arr. Betty Pulkingham

SERVANT SONG
Irregular

596

Come and Bless Us, God

1 Come and bless us, God, save us from dis-sen-sion,
2 Not for us to keep do you give your bless-ing,
3 Peace you grant-ed once, peace a-gain must flour-ish;
4 Come and bless us, God, save us from dis-sen-sion,

that we may as one fur-ther your in-ten-tion.
tal-ents rich-ly given not for our pos-sess-ing.
as you prom-ised us, as the earth we nour-ish.
that we may as one fur-ther your in-ten-tion.

Nev-er on our own, yours for ev-er af-ter,
As we share our all bless-ing grows and flow-ers,
Help us stand the test! Those who sow with weep-ing,
Nev-er on our own, yours for ev-er af-ter,

both our tears and laugh-ter blessed by you a-lone.
lov-ing grace em-pow-ers, burst-ing e-vil's thrall.
when it's time for reap-ing, will find peace and rest.
both our tears and laugh-ter blessed by you a-lone.

Words: Dieter Trautwein 1979, trans. Len Lythgoe 1995
Music: Dieter Trautwein 1979, arr. Darryl Nixon 1987

FRANKFURTER SEGENSLIED
Irregular

Words and music copyright © Burckhardthaus-Laetare Verlag GmbH, Offenbach. Translation copyright © 1995 Len Lythgoe.
Arrangement copyright © 1987 Songs for a Gospel People.

Simon, Simon, a Fisherman

Words: *v. 1, 2 Robert K. N. McLean 1964, alt., v. 3–5 David McKane 1995*
Music: *Robert K. N. McLean 1964; arr. Catherine Ambrose 1996*

SIMON
99899

598

When Pain of the World

1 When pain of the world sur - rounds us with
2 We see with fear and trem - bling our
3 The church is a ho - ly ves - sel the
4 We praise you for our jour - ney and

dark - ness and de - spair, when search - ing just con -
ach - ing world in need, con - fess - ing to each
liv - ing wa - ters fill to nour - ish all its
your a - bun - dant grace, your sav - ing word that

founds us with false hopes ev - ery - where, when
oth - er our waste - ful - ness and greed. May
peo - ple, God's pur - pose to ful - fill. May
guid - ed a strug - gling hu - man race. O

lives are starved for mean - ing and des - ti - ny is
we with stead - fast car - ing the hun - gry chil - dren
we with hum - ble cour - age be o - pen to God's
God, with all cre - a - tion, your fu - ture we em -

Words: Jim Strathdee 1976
Music: Jim Strathdee 1976
Words and music copyright © 1978 Desert Flower Music.

CALLED TO FOLLOW
Irregular

bare, / feed. / will. / brace.
we are / We are / We are / We are
called to fol - low Je - sus and

let God's / let God's / let God's / let God's
heal - ing / jus - tice / spir - it / chang - es
flow through us.

Living Christ, Bring Us Love 599

Unison

1 Liv - ing Christ, bring us love, love for ev - ery strang - er;
2 Liv - ing Christ, bring us joy, joy of earth and heav - en;
♦ 3 Liv - ing Christ, bring us peace, peace with God and neigh - bour;
4 Liv - ing Christ, bring us love, love shared at your ta - ble;
5 Liv - ing Christ, lead us out, out to tell the sto - ry;

Liv - ing Christ, bring us love, love from cross and man - ger.
Liv - ing Christ, bring us joy, joy of sin for - giv - en.
♦ Liv - ing Christ, bring us peace, peace in all our la - bour.
Liv - ing Christ, bring us love, love from cross and sta - ble.
Liv - ing Christ, lead us out, out to show your glo - ry.

Words: Daniel Charles Damon 1992
Music: Daniel Charles Damon 1992
Words and music copyright © 1993 Hope Publishing Company.

LIVING CHRIST
3 3 6 D

600 When I Needed a Neighbour

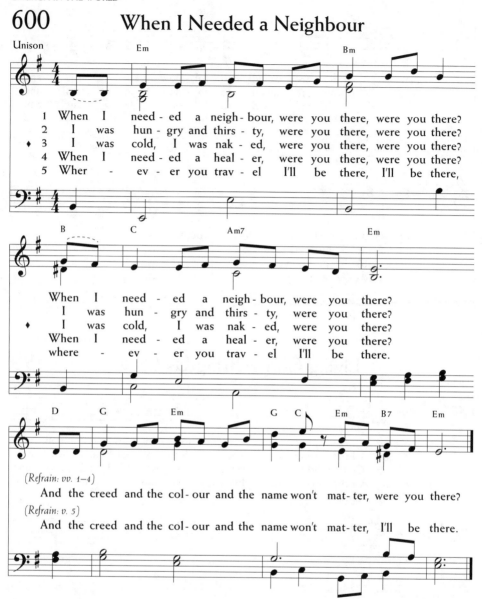

Verses for Holy Week

1 When they shouted hosanna,
were you there...?

2 When they took me to prison,
were you there...?

3 When the crosses were crooked,
were you there...?

4 When the crosses were burning,
were you there...?

Words: Sydney Carter 1962
Music: Sydney Carter, harm. Cantate Domino, full-music edition
Words and music copyright © 1965 Stainer & Bell Ltd. Used by permission of Hope Publishing Company.

NEIGHBOUR
Irregular

The Church of Christ in Every Age

601

1 The church of Christ in ev - ery age, be -
2 A - cross the world, a - cross the street the
3 Then let the ser - vant church a - rise, a
4 For Christ a - lone, whose blood was shed, can
5 We have no mis - sion but to serve in

set by change but Spi - rit led, must claim and test its
vic - tims of in - jus - tice cry for shel - ter and for
car - ing church that longs to be a part - ner in Christ's
cure the fev - er in our blood, and teach us how to
full o - bed - ience to our Lord: to care for all with -

her - i - tage and keep on ris - ing from the dead.
bread to eat, and nev - er live un - til they die.
sac - ri - fice, and clothed in Christ's hu - man - i - ty.
share our bread and feed the starv - ing mul - ti - tude.
out re - serve and spread Christ's lib - er - at - ing word.

Words: *Fred Pratt Green* 1969
Music: *James William Elliott* 1874
Words copyright © 1971 Hope Publishing Company.

CHURCH TRIUMPHANT
8 8 8 8
Alt. tune: Wareham

602   Blest Be the Tie That Binds

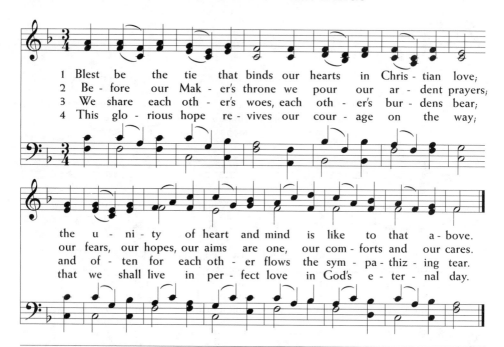

1 Blest be the tie that binds our hearts in Chris-tian love;
2 Be-fore our Mak-er's throne we pour our ar-dent prayers;
3 We share each oth-er's woes, each oth-er's bur-dens bear;
4 This glo-rious hope re-vives our cour-age on the way;

the u-ni-ty of heart and mind is like to that a-bove.
our fears, our hopes, our aims are one, our com-forts and our cares.
and of-ten for each oth-er flows the sym-pa-thiz-ing tear.
that we shall live in per-fect love in God's e-ter-nal day.

Words: John Fawcett 1782, alt.
Music: attrib. Johann G. Nägeli 1728; arr. Lowell Mason 1845

DENNIS
6 6 8 6

603   In Loving Partnership We Come

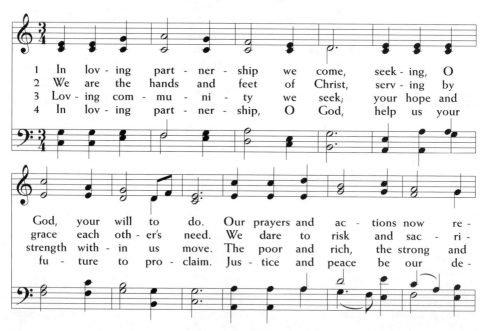

1 In lov-ing part-ner-ship we come, seek-ing, O
2 We are the hands and feet of Christ, serv-ing by
3 Lov-ing com-mu-ni-ty we seek; your hope and
4 In lov-ing part-ner-ship, O God, help us your

God, your will to do. Our prayers and ac-tions now re-
grace each oth-er's need. We dare to risk and sac-ri-
strength with-in us move. The poor and rich, the strong and
fu-ture to pro-claim. Jus-tice and peace be our de-

ceive; we free-ly of-fer them to you.
fice with truth-ful word and faith-ful deed.
weak are brought to-geth-er in your love.
sire, we hum-bly pray in Je-sus' name.

Words: Jim Strathdee 1982
Music: Jim Strathdee 1982
Words and music copyright © 1983 Desert Flower Music.

PARTNERSHIP
8 8 8 8

Not for Tongues of Heaven's Angels 604

Unison

1 Not for tongues of heav-en's an-gels, not for wis-dom to dis-
2 Love is hum-ble, love is gen-tle, love is ten-der, true, and
3 Nev-er jeal-ous, nev-er self-ish, love will not re-joice in
4 In the day this world is fad-ing faith and hope will play their

cern, not for faith that con-quers moun-tains; for this
kind; love is gra-cious, ev-er pa-tient, gen-er-
wrong; nev-er boast-ful nor re-sent-ful, love be-
part; but when Christ is seen in glo-ry love shall

bet-ter gift we yearn:
ous of heart and mind: may love be ours, O Lord.
lieves and suf-fers long:
reign in ev-ery heart:

Words: Timothy Dudley-Smith 1985
Music: Peter Cutts 1969
Words copyright © 1985 and music copyright © 1969 Hope Publishing Company.

BRIDEGROOM
8 7 8 7 6

605   Jesus, Teacher, Brave and Bold

1 Je - sus, teach - er, brave and bold,   let us serve you,
2 Je - sus, friend, so strong and true,   show us good, brave

— young and old.   Let us faith - filled work - ers be,
— work to do.   Show us those who need a friend,

all a - round, your wis - dom see.   Let us play and
all things bro - ken help us mend.   Free our minds and

dance and sing, your good - ness find in ev - ery - thing.
stretch our care, teach us to serve you ev - ery - where.

Words: Walter Farquharson 1967
Music: Ron Klusmeier 1973

OUGHTRED
7 7 7 8

In Christ There Is No East or West

606

1 In Christ there is no east or west,
2 In him shall true hearts ev — ery — where
3 Join hands, then, peo — ple of the faith,
4 In Christ now meet both east and west,

in him no south or north,
their high com — mun — ion find;
what — e'er your race may be;
in him meet south and north;

but one great fam — i — ly of love
his ser — vice is the gold — en cord
all child — ren of the liv — ing God
all Christ — like souls are one in him

through — out the whole wide earth.
close bind — ing hu — man — kind.
are sure — ly kin to me.
through — out the whole wide earth.

Words: John Oxenham 1908, alt.
Music: African-American spiritual; adapt. and harm. by Harry T. Burleigh 1939

MCKEE
8 6 8 6
Alt. tune: St. Peter

And the following...

607

O Jesus, Think on Me

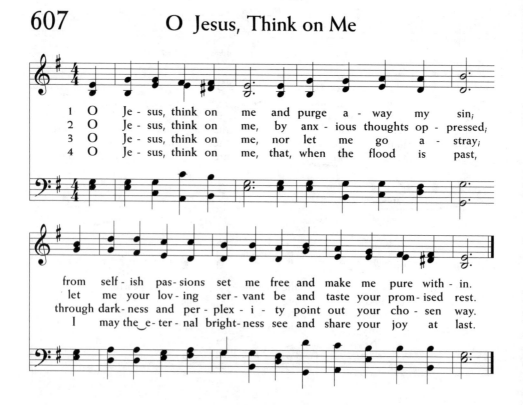

1 O Jesus, think on me and purge a-way my sin;
2 O Jesus, think on me, by anx-ious thoughts op-pressed;
3 O Jesus, think on me, nor let me go a-stray;
4 O Jesus, think on me, that, when the flood is past,

from self-ish pas-sions set me free and make me pure with-in.
let me your lov-ing ser-vant be and taste your prom-ised rest.
through dark-ness and per-plex-i-ty point out your cho-sen way.
I may the e-ter-nal bright-ness see and share your joy at last.

Words: *Synesius of Cyrene ca. 410; trans. Allen W. Chatfield, alt.*
Music: *Daman, Psalmes 1579*

SOUTHWELL
6 6 8 6

Dear God, Who Loves All Humankind   608

1 Dear God, who loves all hu-man-kind, for-
2 In sim - ple trust like theirs who heard, be-
3 O sab - bath rest by Gal - i - lee! O
4 Drop thy still dews of qui - et - ness till
5 Breathe through the heats of our de - sire thy

give our fool - ish ways; re - clothe us in our
side the Syr - ian sea, the gra - cious call - ing
calm of hills a - bove, where Je - sus knelt to
all our striv - ings cease; take from our souls the
cool - ness and thy balm; let sense be dumb, let

right - ful mind; in pur - er lives thy
of the Lord, let us, like them, with -
share with thee the si - lence of e -
strain and stress, and let our or - dered
flesh re - tire: speak through the earth - quake,

ser - vice find, in deep - er re - verence, praise.
out a word rise up, and fol - low thee.
ter - ni - ty, in - ter - pret - ed by love!
lives con - fess the beau - ty of thy peace.
wind and fire, O still small voice of calm!

Words: *John Greenleaf Whittier 1872, alt.*
Music: *Frederick Charles Maker 1887*

REST
8 6 8 8 6
Alt. tune: Repton

609 In All Our Grief and Fear

Unison

1 In all our grief and fear we turn to you. O God, you
2 Help us to put a - side the an - gry word, the clench - ing
3 You did not e - ven spare your on - ly son. He lived our
4 God, when we suf - fer all that we can bear, then let us

know all that we think or do, you know the pain we
fist, the wish and will to hurt. Teach us the way in
griefs and bore all e - vil done, but through his cross, re -
know that you in truth are near and will not leave us

put each oth - er through.
which love best is served. Lord, have mer - cy.
demp - tion was be - gun.
lost in all our fear.

Christ, have mer - cy. Lord, grant us peace.

Words: Sylvia Dunstan 1985
Music: Charles R. Anders ca. 1978

FREDERICKTOWN
10 10 10 4 4

God Remembers Pain

1 God re-mem-bers pain:
2 God re-mem-bers joy:
3 God re-mem-bers us:

nail by nail, thorn by thorn,
touch of love, taste of food,
all we were, all we are,

hun-ger, thirst and mus-cles torn.
all our sens-es know is good.
lives with-in our Lov-er's care.

Time may dull our griefs, and
Love and life flow by and
Time may dull our minds and

heal our less-er wounds, but in e-ter-nal love,
pre-cious days are gone, but in e-ter-nal love
death will take us all, but in e-ter-nal love

yes-ter-day is now, and pain is in the heart of God.
ev-ery day is now, and joy is in the heart of God.
ev-ery life is now: our life is hid with Christ in God.

Words: Brian Wren 1986
Music: Jeeva Sam 1994; arr. David Kai 1994
Words copyright © 1993 Hope Publishing Company. Music copyright © 1994 Jeeva Sam. Arrangement copyright © 1994 David Kai.

GOD REMEMBERS
Irregular

611 Out of the Depths, O God, We Call to You

1 Out of the depths, O God, we call to you.
2 Out of the depths of fear, O God, we speak.
3 God of the lov-ing heart, we praise your name.

Wounds of the past re-main, af-fect-ing all we do.
Break-ing the si-lenc-es, the sear-ing truth we seek.
Dance through our lives and loves; a-noint with Spir-it flame.

Fac-ing our lives, we need your love so much.
Safe a-mong friends, our grief and rage we share.
Your light il-lu-mines each fa-mil-iar face.

Here in this com-mu-ni-ty, heal us by your touch.
Here in this com-mu-ni-ty, hold us in your care.
Here in this com-mu-ni-ty, meet us with your grace.

Words: Ruth Duck 1988
Music: Jeeva Sam 1994; arr. David Kai 1995
Words copyright © 1992 G.I.A. Publications, Inc. Music copyright © 1994 Jeeva Sam. Arrangement copyright © 1995 David Kai.

OUT OF THE DEPTHS
10 12 10 12

There Is a Balm in Gilead

612

There is a balm in Gil-e-ad to make the wound-ed whole.

There is a balm in Gil-e-ad to heal the sin-sick soul.

1 Some-times I feel dis-cour-aged, and think my work's in vain, but
2 If you can-not preach like Pe-ter, if you can-not pray like Paul, you can

then the Ho-ly Spir-it re-vives my soul a-gain.
tell the love of Je-sus and say, "He died for all."

Words: African-American spiritual
Music: African-American spiritual; harm. David Hurd 1983
Harmony copyright © 1985 G.I.A. Publications, Inc.

BALM IN GILEAD
7 6 7 6 with refrain

613 We Cannot Measure How You Heal

1 We can - not mea - sure how you heal
2 The pain that will not go a - way,
3 But pres - ent too is love which tends
4 Your hands, though blood - ied on the cross,

or an - swer ev - ery suf - ferer's prayer,
the guilt that clings from things long past,
the hurt we nev - er hoped to find,
sur - vive to hold and heal and warn,

yet we be - lieve your grace re - sponds
the fear of what the fu - ture holds
the pri - vate ag - o - nies in - side,
to car - ry all through death to life

where faith and doubt u - nite to care.
are pres - ent as if meant to last.
the mem - o - ries that haunt the mind.
and cra - dle chil - dren yet un - born.

Words: *John Bell and Graham Maule*
Music: *Georg Joseph 1657*

ANGELUS
8 8 8 8

Words copyright © WGRG, The Iona Community (Glasgow, Scotland), G.I.A. Publications, Inc., Chicago, Illinois, exclusive agents.

5 So some have come who need your
    help,
  and some have come to make amends;
  your hands which shaped and saved
    the world
  are present in the touch of friends.

6 Lord, let your Spirit meet us here
  to mend the body, mind and soul,
  to disentangle peace from pain
  and make your broken people whole.

In Suffering Love

614

1 In suf - fering love the thread of life is
2 There is a rock, a place se - cure with -
3 In love's deep womb our fears are held; there
4 Now to our hearts your joy com - mit, in -
5 In suf - fering love our God comes now, hope's

wo - ven through our care, for God is with us,
in the storm's cold blast; con - cealed with - in the
God's rich tears are sown and bring to birth, in
to our hands your pain; so send us out to
vi - sion born in gloom; with tears and laugh - ter

not a - lone our pain and toil we bear.
suf - fering night God's cov - e - nant stands fast.
hope new - born, the strength to jour - ney on.
touch the world with bless - ings in your name.
shared and blessed the des - ert yet will bloom.

Words: Rob Johns 1983
Music: Gardiner's Sacred Melodies 1812
Words copyright © 1987 Elinor Johns. Used by permission of Elinor Johns.

BELMONT
8 6 8 6

615 When Quiet Peace Is Shattered

Unison

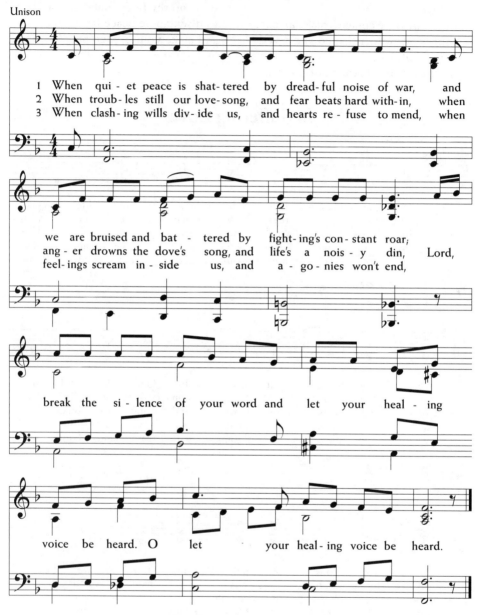

1 When qui-et peace is shat-tered by dread-ful noise of war, and
2 When troub-les still our love-song, and fear beats hard with-in, when
3 When clash-ing wills div-ide us, and hearts re-fuse to mend, when

we are bruised and bat-tered by fight-ing's con-stant roar;
ang-er drowns the dove's song, and life's a nois-y din, Lord,
feel-ings scream in-side us, and a-go-nies won't end,

break the si-lence of your word and let your heal-ing

voice be heard. O let your heal-ing voice be heard.

Words: Mary Nelson Keithahn 1991
Music: John D. Horman 1991

HEALING VOICE
Irregular

Words and music copyright © 1993 Hinshaw Music, Inc. Reprinted by permission.

A Prayer for Healing

God of our exile,
we pray for peace in a world of war,
for health in a world of hunger,
for harmony in a world of discord.
Bring us home to the world as you would have it be,
subject to the reign of your love
and grounded in the mutual care of your children.
We pray through Jesus Christ. Amen.

I Love You, God, Who Heard My Cry 617

1 I love you, God, who heard my cry
2 I love you, God, who heard my cry

and pit-ied ev - ery groan. Long as I live
and chased my grief a - way. O let my heart

and trou-bles rise, I'll has-ten to your throne.
no more de-spair while I have breath to pray.

Words: Isaac Watts 1719
Music: African-American spiritual, arr. Richard Smallwood 1975
Arrangement copyright © 1975 Richwood / Century Oak Publishing.

I LOVE THE LORD
8 7 8 7

618

God, When I Stand

1 God, when I stand, no path before me
2 When all my prayers no answer seem to
3 When the dark lord of lone-li-ness pre-
4 When, as did Thom-as, I pre-sume thee

clear, when ev-ery prayer seems pris-oner of my pain;
bring, and there is si-lence in my deep-est soul;
vails, and, all de-feat-ed, joy and friend-ship die;
dead, feel-ing and faith it-self with-in me cold,

come with a gen - tle-ness which calms my fear, Lord
when in the wil - der-ness I find no spring, Lord
come, be my joy, such love that nev-er fails, pierce
fresh-en my lips with wine, my soul with bread, ban-

of my help-less-ness, my vic-tory gain.
of the des-ert plac-es, keep me whole.
the self-pit-y of my shad-owed sky.
ish my pov-er-ty with heav-en's gold.

Words: Herbert O'Driscoll 1980
Music: Norwegian folk melody 19th century, arr. Darryl Nixon 1987

PRINCESS EUGENIE
10 10 10 10

Healer of Our Every Ill

Refrain (Unison)

Heal - er of our ev - ery ill, light of each to - mor - row,
give us peace be - yond our fear, and hope be - yond our sor - row.

1 You who know our fears and sad - ness, grace us with your
2 In the pain and joy be - hold - ing, how your grace is
3 Give us strength to love each oth - er, ev - ery sis - ter,
4 You who know each thought and feel - ing, teach us all your

peace and glad - ness. Spir - it of all com - fort, fill our hearts.
still un - fold - ing. Give us all your vi - sion, God of love.
ev - ery broth - er. Spir - it of all kind - ness, be our guide.
way of heal - ing. Spir - it of com - pas - sion, fill each heart.

Words: Marty Haugen 1987
Music: Marty Haugen 1987
Words and music copyright © 1991 G.I.A. Publications, Inc.

HEALER (HAUGEN)
Irregular

620   Silence, Frenzied, Unclean Spirit

Unison

1 "Si - lence, fren - zied, un - clean spir - it!" cried God's heal - ing
2 Lord, the de - mons still are thriv - ing in the gray cells
3 Si - lence, Lord, the un - clean spir - it in our mind and

Ho - ly One. "Cease your rant - ing! Flesh can't bear it;
of the mind: ty - rant voic - es, shrill and driv - ing,
in our heart; speak your word that when we hear it,

flee as night be - fore the sun." At Christ's words the
twist - ed thoughts that grip and bind, doubts that stir the
all our de - mons shall de - part. Clear our thought and

de - mon trem - bled, from its vic - tim
heart to pan - ic, fears dis - tort - ing
calm our feel - ing; still the frac - tured,

Words: Thomas H. Troeger 1984
Music: Carol Doran 1984
Words and music by permission of Oxford University Press, Inc.

AUTHORITY
8 7 8 7 D
Alt. tune: Ebenezer

mad - ly rushed,   while the crowd that   was as - sem - bled
rea - son's sight,   guilt that makes our   lov - ing fran - tic,
war - ring soul.   By the pow - er   of your heal - ing

stood in won - der,   stunned and hushed.
dreams that cloud the   soul with fright.
make us faith - ful,   true and whole.

Heal Me, Hands of Jesus   621

Heal me, hands of Jesus,
and search out all my pain;
restore my hope, remove my fear,
and bring me peace again.

Cleanse me, blood of Jesus,
take bitterness away;
let me forgive as one forgiven
and bring me peace today.

Know me, mind of Jesus,
and show me all my sin;
dispel the memories of guilt
and bring me peace within.

Fill me, joy of Jesus;
anxiety shall cease,
and heaven's serenity be mine,
for Jesus brings me peace.

622   Your Hands, O Christ

1 Your hands, O Christ, in days of old were
strong to heal and save; they tri - umphed o'er dis -
ease and death, fought dark - ness and the grave.
To you they went, the blind, the mute, the

2 And lo! your touch brought life and health, gave
speech and strength and sight; and youth re - newed and
health re - stored owned you, the Lord of light.
So, liv - ing Christ, draw near to bless, com -

3 O be our gra - cious heal - er still, our
God in life and death; re - store and strength - en,
soothe and bless with your life - giv - ing breath.
To hands that work and eyes that see teach

Words: Edward Hayes Plumptre 1864; rev. R. Gerald Hobbs 1987
Music: Attrib. Franz Joseph Haydn
Revised words copyright © 1987 Songs for a Gospel People.

HAYDN
8 6 8 6 D

pal - sied and the lame, the lep - er set a -
pas - sionate as be - fore; that we may touch your
wis - dom's heal - ing lore, that whole and sick, and

part and shunned, the sick with fe - vered frame.
gar - ment's fringe, walk in our streets once more.
weak and strong, we praise you ev - er - more.

And the following…

623 Dear Weaver of Our Lives' Design

Unison

1 Dear weav-er of our lives' de-sign whose
2 Take up the fab-ric of our lives with
3 Let eyes that in the plain-est cloth a

pat-terns all o-bey, with skill-ful fin-gers
hands that gen-tly hold; bind in the rag-ged
hid-den beau-ty see dis-cern in us our

gent-ly guide the stur-dy threads that will sur-vive the
edge that care would sun-der and that pain would tear, and
rich-est hues, show us the pat-terns we may use to

tan-gle of our days, the tan-gle of our days.
mend our rav-elling souls, and mend our rav-elling souls.
set our spir-its free, to set our spir-its free.

Words: Nancy C. Dorian
Music: C. Hubert H. Parry 1888, arr. Michael Fleming

REPTON
868866
Alt. setting: 504

Give To Us Laughter

624

1 Give to us laugh - ter, O Source of our life.
2 Give to us laugh - ter as sign of deep joy;
3 Why do we wor - ry that we will lose face?
4 E - ven in sor - row and hours of grief,

Laugh - ter can ban - ish so much of our strife.
let us in laugh - ing find Chris - tian em - ploy,
Why act like king for the whole hu - man race?
laugh - ter with tears brings most heal - ing re - lief.

Laugh - ter and love give us whole - ness and health.
join - ing with stars and with bright north - ern lights,
Of - ten in fam - i - ly, and of - ten with friend,
God, give us laugh - ter, and God, give us peace,

Laugh - ter and love are the coin of true wealth.
laugh - ing and prais - ing and shar - ing de - lights.
laugh - ing at pride caus - es an - guish to end.
joys of your pre - sence a - mong us in - crease.

Words: Walter Farquharson 1974
Music: Ron Klusmeier 1974, 1995

OLDHAM
10 10 10 10

625

I Feel the Winds of God

1 I feel the winds of God to-day; to-
2 It is the wind of God that dries my
3 If ev - er I for - get your love and

day my sail I lift, though heav - y oft with
vain re - gret - ful tears, un - til with brav - er
how that love was shown, lift high the blood - red

drench - ing spray and torn with man - y a rift;
thoughts shall rise the pur - er, bright - er years;
flag a - bove; it bears your name a - lone.

if hope but light the wa - ter's crest, and
if cast on shores of self - ish ease or
Great pi - lot of my on - ward way, you

Words: Jessie Adams 1907, alt.

Music: English and Irish traditional melody; arr. Ralph Vaughan Williams 1906

Words copyright © 1933 National Adult School Organisation. Arrangement by permission of Oxford University Press.

KINGSFOLD
8 6 8 6 D

Christ my bark will use, I'll seek the seas at
plea - sure I should be, O let me feel your
will not let me drift. I feel the winds of

his be - hest, and brave an - oth - er cruise.
fresh - ening breeze, and I'll put back to sea.
God to - day; to - day my sail I lift.

I Heard the Voice of Jesus 626

1 I heard the voice of Jesus say,
"Come unto me and rest;
lay down, O weary one, lay down
your head upon my breast."
I came to Jesus as I was,
weary and worn and sad;
I found in him a resting place,
and he has made me glad.

2 I heard the voice of Jesus say,
"Behold, I freely give
the living water; thirsty one,
stoop down, and drink, and live."
I came to Jesus, and I drank
of that life-giving stream;
my thirst was quenched,
    my soul revived,
and now I live in him.

3 I heard the voice of Jesus say,
"I am this dark world's light;
look unto me, your morn shall rise,
and all your day be bright."
I looked to Jesus, and I found
in him my star, my sun;
and in that light of life I'll walk
till travelling days are done.

Words: Horatius Bonar 1846

KINGSFOLD
8 6 8 6 D

627 Now There Is No Male or Female

1 Now there is no male or fe-male, now there is no
2 Cru-ci-fied with Christ the Sav-iour, bap-tised in his
3 Death has no do-min-ion o'er him, so for us death

free or slave, now there is no Jew or Gen-tile
ho-ly death, and as Christ was raised to glo-ry
holds no power; life's own wa-ters now have marked us

in the earth Christ died to save. Christ has set us
we have new life on this earth. Power of wa-ter
born to God this ve-ry hour. From this mo-ment

free for free-dom: we no more sing slav-ery's creed;
and God's nam-ing, turn-ing us from dark to light,
and for-ev-er dead to sin, a-live in Christ,

Words: Lynette Miller 1985
Music: Trier Gesangbuch 1695
Words copyright © 1985 Lynette Miller.

OMNI DIE
8 7 8 7 D

old sub - mis - sions can - not claim us, Christ has set us free in - deed.
joins us to those who, be - fore us, ran the race and fought the fight.
born of wa - ter and the Spir - it, now in Christ we find our life.

Come, My Way, My Truth 628

Unison

1 Come, my Way, my Truth, my Life: such a
2 Come, my Light, my Feast, my Strength: such a
3 Come, my Joy, my Love, my Heart: . such a

way as gives us breath, such a truth as ends all
light as shows a feast, such a feast as mends in
joy as none can move, such a love as none can

strife, such a life as kill - eth death.
length, such a strength as makes his guest.
part, such a heart as joys in love.

Words: George Herbert ca. 1633
Music: Ralph Vaughan Williams 1911; adapt. E. Harold Geer 1956
Music copyright © 1911 Stainer & Bell Ltd., London, England.

THE CALL
7 7 7 7

629 Eternal Light, Shine in My Heart

1 E - ter - nal light, shine in my heart;
2 E - ter - nal life, raise me from death;
3 un - til by your most cost - ly grace,

e - ter - nal hope, lift up my eyes;
e - ter - nal bright - ness, make me see;
in - vit - ed by your ho - ly word,

e - ter - nal power, be my sup - port;
e - ter - nal Spir - it, give me breath;
at last I come be - fore your face

e - ter - nal wis - dom, make me wise.
e - ter - nal Sav - iour, come to me.
to know you, my e - ter - nal God.

Words: from a prayer by Alcuin 8th cent., para. Christopher Idle ca. 1982
Music: John Bacchus Dykes 1866
Words (paraphrase) copyright © 1982 Hope Publishing Company.

RIVAULX
8 8 8 8

O Christ, in Thee My Soul

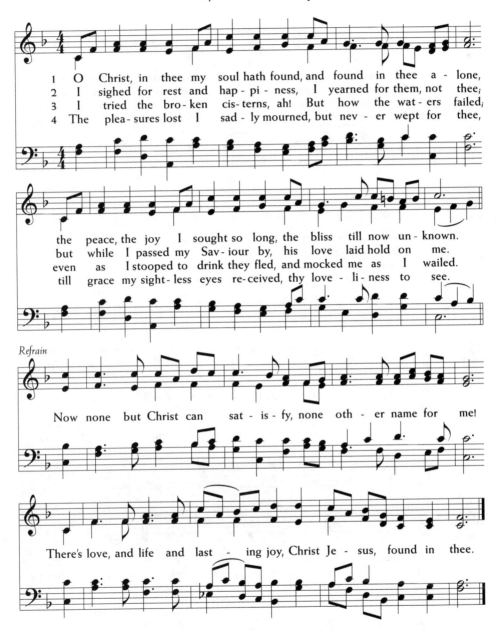

1 O Christ, in thee my soul hath found, and found in thee a - lone,
2 I sighed for rest and hap - pi - ness, I yearned for them, not thee;
3 I tried the bro - ken cis - terns, ah! But how the wat - ers failed;
4 The plea - sures lost I sad - ly mourned, but nev - er wept for thee,

the peace, the joy I sought so long, the bliss till now un - known.
but while I passed my Sav - iour by, his love laid hold on me.
even as I stooped to drink they fled, and mocked me as I wailed.
till grace my sight - less eyes re - ceived, thy love - li - ness to see.

Refrain

Now none but Christ can sat - is - fy, none oth - er name for me!

There's love, and life and last - ing joy, Christ Je - sus, found in thee.

Words: *Emma Frances Bevan ca. 1860*
Music: *James McGranahan 1881*

NONE BUT CHRIST
8 6 8 6 with refrain

631 Jesus, Your Boundless Love to Me

1 Je - sus, your bound - less love to me
2 O grant that noth - ing in my soul
3 O love, how gra - cious is your way;
4 In suf - fering, be your love my peace;

no thought can reach, no tongue de - clare.
may dwell, but your pure love a - lone;
all fear be - fore your pres - ence flies.
in weak - ness, be your love my power;

O let my heart your dwell - ing be;
O may that love pos - sess me whole,
Care, an - guish, sor - row, melt a - way
and when the storms of life shall cease,

come, reign with - out a ri - val there.
my joy, my trea - sure, and my crown.
wher - e'er your heal - ing beams a - rise.
O Je - sus, in that fin - al hour,

Words: Paul Gerhardt 1653; trans. John Wesley 1739, alt.
Music: Henry Carey 1723

SURREY
888888

Yours ful - ly, yours a - lone I am;
All cold - ness from my heart re - move;
O Je - sus, no - thing may I do,
for me be rod and staff and guide,

O let your love my heart in - flame.
my ev - ery act, my word, thought, be love.
but seek my joy in serv - ing you.
and draw me safe - ly to your side.

O Blessed Spring 632

1 O blessed spring, where Word
and sign
embrace us into Christ the Vine,
here Christ enjoins each one to be
a branch of this life giving tree.

2 Through summer heat of youthful
years,
uncertain faith, rebellious tears,
sustained by Christ's infusing rain,
the boughs will shout for joy again.

3 When autumn cools and youth is cold,
when limbs their heavy harvest hold,
then through us warm the Christ will
move
with gifts of beauty, wisdom, love.

4 As winter comes, as winters must,
we breathe our last, return to dust;
still held in Christ, our souls take wing
and trust the promise of the spring.

5 Christ, holy Vine, Christ, living Tree,
be praised for this blest mystery:
that Word and water thus revive
and join us to your Tree of Life.

Words: Susan Palo Cherwien 1993
Words copyright © 1993 Susan Palo Cherwien.

O WALY WALY (GIFT OF LOVE)
8 8 8 8

633 Bless Now, O God, the Journey

Unison

1 Bless now, O God, the jour - ney that all your peo - ple
2 Bless so - journ - ers and pil - grims who share this wind - ing
3 Di - vine E - ter - nal Lov - er, you meet us on the

make, the path through noise and si - lence, the way of give and
way, whose hope burns through the ter - rors, whose love sus - tains the
road. We wait for lands of prom - ise where milk and hon - ey

take. The trail is found in des - ert and winds the moun - tain
day. We yearn for ho - ly free - dom while of - ten we are
flow. But wait - ing not for plac - es, you meet us all a -

round, then leads be - side still wa - ters, the
bound. To - geth - er we are seek - ing the
round. Our cov - e - nant is writ - ten on

Words: Sylvia Dunstan 1989
Music: Basil Harwood 1898

THORNBURY
7 6 7 6 D

road	where	faith	is	found.
road	where	faith	is	found.
roads,	as	faith	is	found.

To Abraham and Sarah 634

1 To Abraham and Sarah
the call of God was clear:
"Go forth and I will show you
a country rich and fair.
You need not fear the journey
for I have pledged my word:
that you shall be my people
and I will be your God."

2 From Abraham and Sarah
arose a pilgrim race,
dependent for their journey
on God's abundant grace;
and in their heart was written
by God this saving word:
"that you shall be my people
and I will be your God."

3 We of this generation
on whom God's hand is laid,
can journey to the future
secure and unafraid,
rejoicing in God's goodness
and trusting in this word:
"that you shall be my people
and I will be your God."

Words: *Judith Fetter 1984*
Words copyright © 1984 Judith Fetter.

THORNBURY
7 6 7 6 D

635 All the Way My Saviour Leads Me

1 All the way my Sav-iour leads me; what have I to ask be-side?
2 All the way my Sav-iour leads me, cheers each wind-ing path I tread,
3 All the way my Sav-iour leads me; O the full-ness of his love!

Can I doubt his ten-der mer-cy who through life has been my guide?
gives me grace for ev-ery tri-al, feeds me with the liv-ing bread.
Per-fect rest to me is prom-ised in my Fa-ther's house a-bove.

Heaven-ly peace, di-vin-est com-fort, here by faith in him to dwell,
Though my wea-ry steps may falt-er, and my soul a-thirst may be,
When my spir-it, clothed, im-mor-tal, wings its flight to realms of day,

for I know, what-e'er be-fall me, Je-sus do-eth all things well.
gush-ing from the rock be-fore me, lo, a spring of joy I see!
this my song through end-less ag-es, "Je-sus led me all the way!"

Words: Fanny J. Crosby 1875
Music: Robert S. Lowry 1875

ALL THE WAY
8 7 8 7 D

Give to the Winds Your Fears

636

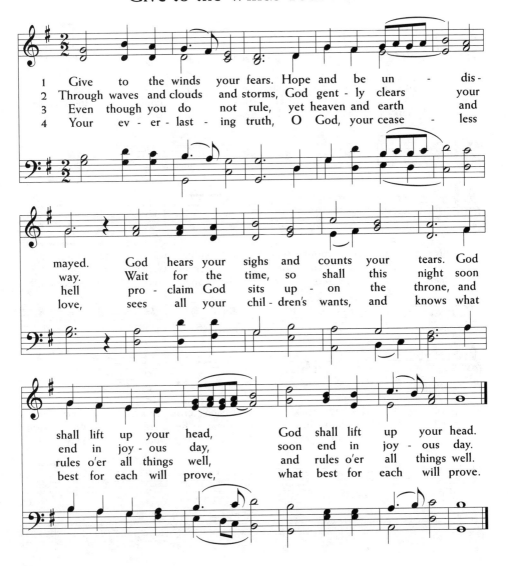

1 Give to the winds your fears. Hope and be un - dis -
2 Through waves and clouds and storms, God gent - ly clears your
3 Even though you do not rule, yet heaven and earth and
4 Your ev - er - last - ing truth, O God, your cease - less

mayed. God hears your sighs and counts your tears. God
way. Wait for the time, so shall this night soon
hell pro - claim God sits up - on the throne, and
love, sees all your chil - dren's wants, and knows what

shall lift up your head, God shall lift up your head.
end in joy - ous day, soon end in joy - ous day.
rules o'er all things well, and rules o'er all things well.
best for each will prove, what best for each will prove.

Words: Paul Gerhardt 1656; trans. John Wesley 1739, alt.
Music: Harmonia Sacra 5th ed. 1851; harm. Alice Parker 1978
Harmony copyright © 1991 Alice Parker.

HANTS
6 6 8 6 extended

637

Jesus, Saviour, Pilot Me

1 Je - sus, Sav - iour, pi - lot me over life's tem - pes - tuous sea; un - known waves be - fore me roll, hid - ing rock and treach - erous shoal; chart and com - pass come from thee, Je - sus, Sav - iour, pi - lot me.

2 As a moth - er stills her child, thou canst hush the o - cean wild; bois - terous waves o - bey thy will when thou bid - dest them "Be still." sov - ereign of the sea, Je - sus, Sav - iour, pi - lot me.

3 When at last I near the shore, and the fear - ful break - ers roar 'twixt me and the peace - ful land, still sup - port - ed by thy hand, may I hear thee say to me, "Fear not, I will pi - lot thee."

Words: Edward Hopper 1871, alt.
Music: John Edgar Gould 1871

PILOT
7 7 7 7 7 7

God, Take My Hand

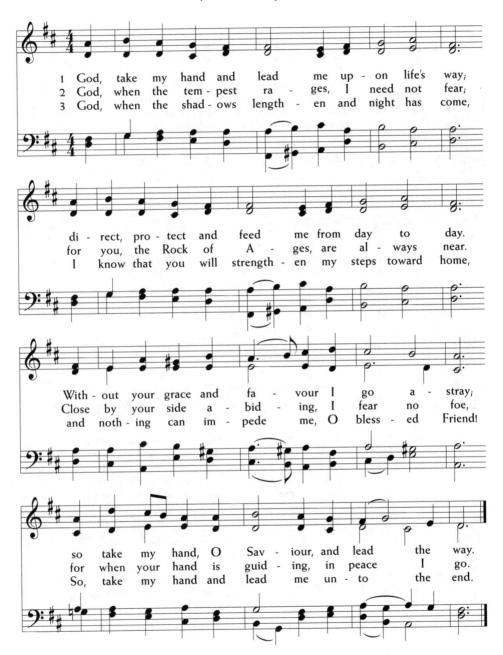

1 God, take my hand and lead me up-on life's way;
2 God, when the tem-pest ra-ges, I need not fear;
3 God, when the shad-ows length-en and night has come,

di-rect, pro-tect and feed me from day to day.
for you, the Rock of A-ges, are al-ways near.
I know that you will strength-en my steps toward home,

With-out your grace and fa-vour I go a-stray;
Close by your side a-bid-ing, I fear no foe,
and noth-ing can im-pede me, O bless-ed Friend!

so take my hand, O Sav-iour, and lead the way.
for when your hand is guid-ing, in peace I go.
So, take my hand and lead me un-to the end.

Words: Julie von Hausmann *ca.* 1862;
    trans. v. 1 Herman Brückner 1918, vv. 2,3 Rudolph A. John 1912
Music: Friedrich Silcher 1842

SO NIMM DENN MEINE HÄNDE
7 4 7 4 D

639 One More Step Along the World I Go

Words: Sydney Carter 1971
Music: Sydney Carter 1971
Words and music copyright © 1971 Stainer & Bell Ltd. Used by permission of Hope Publishing Company.

SOUTHCOTE
9 9 7 9 with refrain

Lead, Kindly Light

1 Lead, kind-ly light, a - mid the en - cir - cling gloom;
2 I was not ev - er thus, nor prayed that thou
3 So long thy power hath blest me, sure it still

lead thou me on. The night is dark, and I am far from home;
shouldst lead me on. I loved to choose and see my path, but now
will lead me on, o'er moor and fen, o'er crag and tor - rent, till

lead thou me on. Keep thou my feet; I do not ask
lead thou me on. I loved the gar - ish day, and, spite
the night is gone; and with the morn those an - gel fa -

to see the dis - tant scene, one step e - nough for me.
of fears, pride ruled my will: re - mem - ber not past years.
ces smile, which I have loved long since, and lost a - while.

Words: John Henry Newman 1833
Music: John Bacchus Dykes 1865

LUX BENIGNA
10 4 10 4 10 10
Alt. tune: Sandon

641 Lord Jesus, You Shall Be My Song
(Jésus, je voudrais te chanter)

1 Jé - sus, je vou - drais te chan - ter sur ma rou - te,
2 Jé - sus, je vou - drais te lou - er sur ma rou - te,
1 Lord Je - sus, you shall be my song as I jour - ney,
2 Lord Je - sus, I'll praise you as long as I jour - ney.

Jé - sus, je vou - drais t'an - non - cer à mes voi - sins par - tout;
Jé - sus, je vou - drais que ma voix soit l'é - cho de ta joie:
I'll tell ev - ery - bod - y a - bout you where - ev - er I go:
May all of my joy be a faith - ful re - flec - tion of you.

car toi seul es la vie et la paix et l'a - mour.
et que chan - te la terre et que chan - te le ciel;
for our life and our peace and our love is your - self.
May the earth and the sea and the sky join my song.

Words: Les Petites Soeurs de Jésus 1961; trans. Steven Somerville 1970, alt.
Music: Les Petites Soeurs de Jésus 1961; harm. T. Barrett Armstrong ca. 1973

L'ARCHE HYMN
12 14 12 12

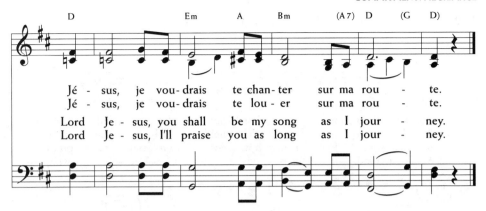

Jé - sus, je vou- drais te chan- ter sur ma rou - te.
Jé - sus, je vou- drais te lou - er sur ma rou - te.
Lord Je - sus, you shall be my song as I jour - ney.
Lord Je - sus, I'll praise you as long as I jour - ney.

3 Jésus, je voudrais te servir sur ma
    route;
  Jésus, je voudrais partager les
    souffrances de ta croix,
  car tu livres pour moi et ton corps et
    ton sang;
  Jésus, je voudrais te servir sur ma
    route.

4 Jésus, je voudrais tout au long de ma
    route,
  entendre tes pas résonner dans la
    nuit près de moi,
  jusqu'à l'aube du jour où ton peuple
    sauvé,
  Jésus, chantera ton retour sur ma
    route.

3 As long as I live, Jesus, make me
    your servant
  to carry your cross and to share all
    your burdens and tears,
  for you saved me by giving your
    body and blood.
  As long as I live, Jesus, make me
    your servant.

4 I fear in the dark and the doubt of
    my journey,
  but courage will come with the
    sound of your steps by my side;
  and with all of the family you saved
    by your love,
  we'll sing to your dawn at the end of
    our journey.

642   Be Thou My Vision

Unison

1 Be thou my vi - sion, O joy of my heart;
2 Be thou my wis - dom, my calm in all strife;
♦ 3 Be thou my bat - tle shield, sword for the fight;
4 Rich - es I heed not, nor vain emp - ty praise,
5 Great God of heav - en, af - ter vic - to - ry won,

naught be all else to me save that thou art,
I ev - er with thee, and thou in my life;
be thou my dig - ni - ty, thou my de - light,
thou mine in - her - i - tance, now and al - ways;
may I reach heav - en's joys, O bright heaven's sun!

thou my best thought, by day or by night,
thou lov - ing par - ent, thy child may I be,
thou my soul's shel - ter, thou my high tower;
thou and thou on - ly, the first in my heart,
Heart of my own heart, what - ev - er be - fall,

wak - ing or sleep - ing thy pres - ence my light.
thou in me dwell - ing, and I one with thee.
♦ raise thou me heaven - ward, O power of my power.
great God of heav - en, my trea - sure thou art.
still be my vis - ion, O rul - er of all.

Words: Irish ca. 8th century; trans. Mary Elizabeth Byrne 1905; vers. Eleanor H. Hull 1912, alt.
Music: Irish traditional melody

SLANE
10 10 10 10

Faith, While Trees Are Still in Blossom   643

1 Faith, while trees are still in blos - som, plans the
2 Long be - fore the dawn is break - ing, faith an -
3 Long be - fore the rains were com - ing, No - ah
4 Faith, up - lift - ed, tamed the wa - ter of the
5 Faith be - lieves that God is faith - ful: God will

pick - ing of the fruit; faith can feel the thrill of
ti - ci - pates the sun. Faith is ea - ger for the
went and built an ark. A - bra - ham, the lone - ly
un - di - vid - ed sea, and the peo - ple of the
be what God will be! Faith ac - cepts the call, re -

har - vest when the buds be - gin to sprout.
day - light, for the work that must be done.
mi - grant, saw the light be - yond the dark.
He - brews found the path that made them free.
spond - ing, "I am will - ing, Lord, send me."

Words: Anders Frostenson 1960; trans. Fred Kaan 1972
Music: V. Earle Copes 1960
Translation copyright © 1976 and music copyright © 1960, renewal 1988 Hope Publishing Company.

FOR THE BREAD
8 7 8 7

644 I Was There to Hear Your Borning Cry

1 I was there to hear your born-ing cry, I'll be
3 When you heard the won-der of the word, I was
5 In the mid-dle a-ges of your life, not too
7 I was there to hear your born-ing cry, I'll be

there when you are old. I re-joiced the day you
there to cheer you on; you were raised to praise the
old, no long-er young. I'll be there to guide you
there when you are old. I re-joiced the day you

were bap-tized, to see your life un-fold.
liv-ing Lord, to whom you now be-long.
through the night, com-plete what I've be-gun.
were bap-tized, to see your life un-fold.

Fine

2 I was there when you were but a child, with a
4 If you find some-one to share your time and you
6 When the eve-ning gent-ly clos-es in and you

Words: John Ylvisaker 1985
Music: John Ylvisaker 1985
Words and music copyright © 1985 John Carl Ylvisaker.

WATERLIFE
9 7 9 6 D

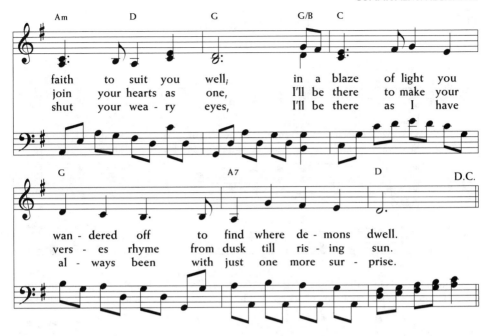

faith to suit you well; in a blaze of light you
join your hearts as one, I'll be there to make your
shut your wea - ry eyes, I'll be there as I have

wan - dered off to find where de - mons dwell.
vers - es rhyme from dusk till ris - ing sun.
al - ways been with just one more sur - prise.

Living Water, Source of Life   645

God our Mother,
Living Water,
River of Mercy,
Source of Life,
in whom we live
and move
and have our being,
who quenches our thirst,
refreshes our weariness,
bathes
and washes
and cleanses our wounds,
be for us always
a fountain of life,
and for all the world
a river of hope
springing up in the midst
of the deserts of despair.
Honour and blessing,
glory and praise
to You forever. Amen.

Miriam Therese Winter 1987

646

We Are Marching
(Siyahamba)

1 We are march - ing in the light of God, we are
2 Si - ya - hamb' e - ku - kha - nyen' kwen - khos', si - ya -

march-ing in the light of God. We are march - ing in the
hamb' e - ku - kha - nyen' kwen - khos'. Si - ya - hamb' e - ku - kha -

light of God, we are march-ing in the light of
nyen' kwen - khos', si - ya - hamb' e - ku - kha - nyen' kwen -

God. We are march-ing,_____
khos'. Si - ya - ham - ba,_____

the light of God. We are march-ing, march-ing, we are
kha - nyen' kwen - khos'. Si - ya - ham - ba, ham - ba, si - ya -

Words: South African trad. song 20th century; trans. Anders Nyberg 1984
Music: South African trad. song 20th century; arr. Anders Nyberg et al 1984
Translation and arrangement copyright © 1984 Walton Music Corporation.

SIYAHAMBA
Irregular

647

Travel On, Travel On

1 Trav-el on, trav-el on, there's a
2 Trav-el on, trav-el on, there's a
3 Trav-el on, trav-el on, there's a
4 In the king-dom of heaven is our

spir-it that is flow-ing, a spir-it that is flow-ing night and day.
spir-it that is grow-ing, the spir-it grows like flow-ers night and day.
spir-it that is play-ing, the spir-it plays like mu-sic ev-ery day.
end and our be-gin-ning, the road that we must tra-vel ev-ery day.

Trav-el on, trav-el on, with the spir-it that is
Trav-el on, trav-el on, with the spir-it that is
Trav-el on, trav-el on, with the spir-it that is
Trav-el on, trav-el on, to the king-dom that is

flow-ing, the spir-it will be with us all the way.
grow-ing, the spir-it will be with us all the way.
play-ing, the spir-it will be with us all the way.
com-ing, the king-dom will be with us all the way.

Words: Sydney Carter 1969, alt.
Music: Sydney Carter 1969

TRAVEL ON
14 10 14 10 14 10

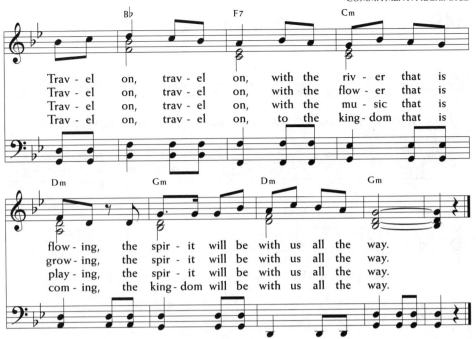

Trav - el on, trav - el on, with the riv - er that is
Trav - el on, trav - el on, with the flow - er that is
Trav - el on, trav - el on, with the mu - sic that is
Trav - el on, trav - el on, to the king - dom that is

flow - ing, the spir - it will be with us all the way.
grow - ing, the spir - it will be with us all the way.
play - ing, the spir - it will be with us all the way.
com - ing, the king - dom will be with us all the way.

A Prayer for the Journey

648

God of the Way,
    you are the road we travel,
    and the sign we follow;
    you are bread for the journey,
    and the wine of arrival.

Guide us as we follow in your way,
    holding on to each other,
    reaching out to your beloved world.

And when we stray,
    seek us out and find us,
    set our feet on the path again,
    and lead us safely home.

In the name of Jesus, our Companion, we pray. Amen.

Janet Cawley 1996

649

Walk with Me

Refrain

Walk with me, I will walk with you and build the land that
God has planned where love shines through. through.

1 When Mo-ses heard the call of God he said, "Lord, don't send me."
2 Now Pe-ter was a most un-like-ly man to lead the flock;
3 Young Ma-ry Mag-da-lene was sure her life could be much more,
4 And when you share your faith with me and work for life made new,

But God told Mo-ses, "You're the one to set my peo-ple free."
but Je-sus knew his ho-li-ness and he be-came the Rock.
and by her faith she dared to let God's love un-lock the door.
the wit-ness of your faith-ful-ness calls me to walk with you.

D.C.

Words: John S. Rice
Music: John S. Rice, arr. John Fluker
Words and music copyright © 1988 Estate of John S. Rice. Used by permission.

GLASER
9 5 9 with refrain

O God of Bethel

1 O God of Be - thel, by whose hand your
2 our vows, our prayers, we now pre - sent be -
3 Through each per - plex - ing path of life our
4 O spread your cov - ering wings a - round, till

peo - ple still are fed, who through this earth - ly
fore your throne of grace. God of past a - ges,
wan - dering foot - steps guide; give us each day our
all our wan - derings cease, and at our God's be -

pil - grim - age have all your ser - vants led:
be the God of each suc - ceed - ing race.
dai - ly bread, and shel - ter fit pro - vide.
loved a - bode our souls ar - rive in peace.

Words: Philip Doddridge 1736; John Logan 1781, alt.
Music: adapt. from Johann Michael Haydn ca. 1806

SALZBURG (HAYDN)
8 6 8 6
Alt. setting: 351

651 Guide Me, O Thou Great Jehovah
(Guide-moi, Berger fidèle)

1 Guide me, O thou great Je-ho-vah, pil-grim through this bar-ren land. I am weak, but thou art might-y, hold me with thy power-ful hand. Bread of heav-en, bread of heav-en, feed me till I want no more,

2 O-pen now the crys-tal foun-tain, whence the heal-ing stream doth flow; let the fire and cloud-y pil-lar lead me all my jour-ney through. Strong de-liv-erer, strong de-liv-er-er, be thou still my strength and shield,

1 Gui-de-moi, Ber-ger fi-dè-le, en ce mon-de pè-le-rin, prends à toi mon coeur re-bel-le, gui-de-moi, sois mon sou-tien, pain de vi-e, pain de vi-e, de ta grâ-ce nour-ris-moi,

2 Christ, tu es la sour-ce vi-ve des bi-ens les plus pré-cieux fais que pour toi seul je vi-ve, gui-de-moi du haut des cieux; viens, pro-tè-ge, viens pro-tè-ge, sois mon roc, mon bou-cli-er,

Words: Welsh, William Williams 1745, English trans. Peter Williams and William Williams 1771; French trans. Flossette du Pasquier 1951
Music: John Hughes 1905

CWM RHONDDA
8 7 8 7 8 7 *with repeat*

feed me till I want no more.
be thou still my strength and shield.
de ta grâ - ce nour - ris - moi.
sois mon roc, mon bou - cli - er.

3 When I tread the verge of Jordan,
bid my anxious fears subside;
death of death, and hell's destruction,
land me safe on Canaan's side:
songs of praises, songs of praises
I will ever give to thee
I will ever give to thee.

3 Du Jourdain je suis les rives;
quand j'ai peur, rassure-moi.
À Sion, qu'enfin j'arrive,
affermis ma faible foi;
tes louanges, tes louanges,
à jamais je chanterai,
à jamais je chanterai.

And the following...

652

Be Still, My Soul

1 Be still, my soul, for God is on your side; bear pa-tient-
2 Be still, my soul, your God will un-der-take to guide the
3 Be still, my soul, the hour is hast-ening on when we shall

ly the cross of grief or pain. Trust in your God, your
fu-ture sure-ly as the past. Your hope, your con-fi-
be for-ev-er in God's peace; when dis-ap-point-ment,

sav-iour and your guide, who through all chang-es faith-ful will re-
dence let noth-ing shake; all now mys-te-rious shall be bright at
grief and fear are gone, love's joys re-stored, our striv-ings all shall

main. Be still, my soul, your best, your heav-enly
last. Be still, my soul, life's tem-pests still o-
cease. Be still, my soul, when change and tears are

Words: Katharina von Schlegel 1752; English trans. Jane Laurie Borthwick 1855, alt.

Music: Jean Sibelius 1899, arr. The Hymnal 1933

FINLANDIA
10 10 10 10 10 10

friend through storm-y ways leads to a peace-ful end.
bey the voice that once the waves' wild fu-ry stayed.
past, all safe and bless-ed we shall meet at last.

Come, Let Us to the God of Love 653

1 Come, let us to the God of love
2 God's voice com-mands the tem - pest forth,
3 Long has the night of sor - row reigned,
4 As dew up - on the ten - der herb
5 so shall God's pres - ence bless our souls

with con - trite hearts re - turn: our God is gra - cious,
and stills the storm - y wave; and though God's arm be
the dawn shall bring us light; God shall ap - pear, and
dif - fus - ing fra - grance round, as showers that ush - er
and shed a joy - ful light; that hal - lowed morn shall

nor will leave the des - o - late to mourn.
strong to smite, 'tis al - so strong to save.
we shall rise with glad - ness at that sight.
in the spring and cheer the thirst - y ground,
chase a - way the sor - rows of the night.

Words: John Morison in Scottish Paraphrases 1781, alt.
Music: adapt. from William Gardiner's Sacred Melodies 1812

BELMONT
8 6 8 6

654 All My Hope Is Firmly Grounded

Unison

1 All my hope is firm-ly ground-ed in our great and
2 Tell me, who can trust our na - ture, hu - man, weak, and
3 But in ev-ery time and sea - son, out of love's a -
4 Thank, O thank, our great Cre-a - tor, through God's on - ly

liv - ing Lord; who, when-ev - er I most need him, nev - er
in - se - cure? Which of all the air - y cas - tles can the
bun - dant store, God sus - tains the whole cre - a - tion, fount of
Son this day; God a - lone, the heaven-ly pot - ter, made us

fails to keep his word. God I must whol - ly
hur - ri - cane en - dure? Built on sand, naught can
life for - ev - er - more. We who share earth and
out of earth and clay. Quick to heed, strong in

trust, God the ev - er good and just.
stand by our earth - ly wis - dom planned.
air count on God's un - fail - ing care.
deed, God shall all the peo - ple feed.

Words: Joachim Neander 1680, trans. Fred Pratt Green 1986
Music: Herbert Howells 1930, 1977

MICHAEL
8 7 8 7 3 3 7

All My Hope on God Is Founded 655

1 All my hope on God is founded;
who doth still my trust renew:
I through change and chance
   am guided,
only good and only true.
God unknown;
God alone
calls my heart eternally home.

2 Human pride and earthly glory,
sword and crown, betray our trust;
what with care and toil is built up,
tower and temple, fall to dust.
But God's power,
hour by hour,
is my temple and my tower.

3 Daily doth the almighty giver
bounteous gifts on us bestow.
God's desire our soul delighteth,
pleasure leads us where we go.
Love doth stand
hand in hand;
joy doth wait on God's command.

4 God's great goodness aye endureth,
deepest wisdom, passing thought:
splendour, light and life attending,
beauty springeth out of naught.
Evermore
from God's store
new-born worlds rise and adore.

Words: Joachim Neander 1680; trans. Robert Bridges 1899, alt.

MICHAEL
8 7 8 7 3 3 7

An Affirmation of Hope 656

We affirm our hope that a new day is dawning upon us.
We affirm our vision of a new heaven and a new earth.
We affirm our belief that the love of God
   which is greater than all understanding
   has the power to unite us
to participate in the creation of a new world.
We affirm the hope that turns suffering into a creative process.
We affirm the hope that enables us to act.
God we hope: help us to hope together!

Australia, Student Christian Movement

He Leadeth Me

1 He lead - eth me: O bless - ed thought! O words with
2 Some - times 'mid scenes of deep - est gloom, some - times where
3 Lord, I would clasp thy hand in mine, nor ev - er
4 And when my task on earth is done, when by thy

heaven - ly com - fort fraught! What - e'er I do, where -
E - den's bow - ers bloom, by wa - ters calm, o'er
mur - mur nor re - pine, con - tent, what - ev - er
grace the vic - tory's won, even death's cold wave I

'er I be, still 'tis God's hand that lead - eth me.
trou - bled sea, still 'tis his hand that lead - eth me.
lot I see, since 'tis my God that lead - eth me.
will not flee, since God through Jor - dan lead - eth me.

Refrain

He lead - eth me! He lead - eth me! By his own hand he lead - eth me!

Words: Joseph Henry Gilmore 1862
Music: William Batchelder Bradbury 1864

HE LEADETH ME
8 8 8 8 with refrain

His faith-ful fol-lower I would be, for by his hand he lead-eth me!

O Love That Wilt Not Let Me Go   658

1 O Love that wilt not let me go,
  I rest my wea-ry soul in thee;
  I give thee back the life I owe,
  that in thine o-cean depths its flow
  may rich-er, full-er be.

2 O Light that fol-lowest all my way,
  I yield my flick-ering torch to thee;
  my heart re-stores its bor-rowed ray,
  that in thy sun-shine's blaze its day
  may bright-er, fair-er be.

3 O Joy that seek-est me through pain,
  I can-not close my heart to thee;
  I trace the rain-bow through the rain,
  and feel the prom-ise is not vain
  that morn shall tear-less be.

4 O Cross that lift-est up my head,
  I dare not ask to fly from thee;
  I lay in dust life's glo-ry dead,
  and from the ground there blos-soms red
  life that shall end-less be.

Words: George Matheson 1881
Music: Albert Lister Peace 1884

ST MARGARET
8 8 8 8 6

659   Eternal Father, Strong to Save

1 E - ter - nal Fa - ther, strong to save, whose
2 O Christ, whose voice the wa - ters heard, and
3 O Ho - ly Spi - rit, who didst brood up -
4 O Trin - i - ty of love and power, all

arm has bound the rest - less wave, who bade the might - y
hushed their rag - ing at thy word, who walked up - on the
on the cha - os dark and rude, and bade its an - gry
trav - ellers guard in dan - ger's hour. From rock and tem - pest,

o - cean deep its own ap - point - ed lim - its keep: O
foam - ing deep, and calm a - mid the storm did sleep: O
tu - mult cease, and gave for wild con - fu - sion, peace: O
fire and foe, pro - tect them where - so - e'er they go: thus

hear us when we cry to thee for those in per - il on the sea.
hear us when we cry to thee for those in per - il on the sea.
hear us when we cry to thee for those in per - il on the sea.
ev - er - more shall rise to thee glad hymns of praise from land and sea.

Words: William Whiting 1860, alt.
Music: John Bacchus Dykes 1861

MELITA
8 8 8 8 8 8

How Firm a Foundation

1 How firm a foun - da - tion, you ser - vants of God,
2 "Fear not, I am with you; O be not dis - mayed!
3 "When through the deep wa - ters I call you to go,
4 "When through fi - ery tri - als your path - way shall lie,
5 "The soul that on Je - sus has leaned for re - pose

is laid for your faith in God's ex - cel - lent word!
For I am your God and will still give you aid;
the riv - ers of sor - row shall not o - ver - flow;
my grace, all - suf - fi - cient, shall be your sup - ply:
I will not — I will not de - sert to his foes;

What more can be said than to you has been said,
I'll strength - en and help you, and cause you to stand,
for I will be with you, your trou - bles to bless,
the flame shall not hurt you; I on - ly de - sign
that soul, though all hell should en - deav - our to shake,

to you who for re - fuge to Je - sus have fled?
up - held by my righ - teous om - ni - po - tent hand.
and sanc - ti - fy to you your deep - est dis - tress.
your dross to con - sume, and your gold to re - fine.
I'll nev - er — no, nev - er — no, nev - er for - sake!"

Words: "K" in John Rippon's *A Selection of Hymns* 1787, *alt.*
Music: *Welsh folk melody; arr. John Roberts (Henllan) in* Caniadau y Cyssegr *1839*

ST DENIO
11 11 11 11

661

Come to My Heart

1 Come, come Lord Jesus; teach me your way.
2 Fill me, Lord Jesus; teach me your way.
3 An-swer, Lord Jesus; teach me your way.

1 Come to my heart, Lord Jesus; teach me to walk in your way.
2 Fill me with love, Lord Jesus; teach me to walk in your way.
3 An-swer my prayer, Lord Jesus; teach me to walk in your way.

Come, come Lord Jesus; come to-day.
Fill me, Lord Jesus; fill me to-day.
An-swer, Lord Jesus; an-swer to-day.

Come to my heart, Lord Jesus; come to my heart to-day.
Fill me with love, Lord Jesus; fill me with love to-day.
An-swer my prayer, Lord Jesus; An-swer my prayer to-day.

Give me the peace and joy on-ly you can bring.

Give me the peace and joy that on-ly you can bring.

COME TO MY HEART
7 7 7 6 6 6 7 6

Come, come Lord Je - sus; give me a song to sing.
Fill me, Lord Je - sus; give me a song to sing.
An - swer, Lord Je - sus; give me a song to sing.

Come to my heart, Lord Je - sus; give me a song to sing.
Fill me with love, Lord Je - sus; give me a song to sing.
An - swer my prayer, Lord Je - sus; give me a song to sing.

Lead Me, God 662

Lead me, God, lead me in your righ - teous - ness;

make your way plain be - fore my face. For it is you, and

you, God on - ly, who makes me to dwell in safe - ty.

Words: based on Psalm 5:8, 4:8
Music: Samuel Sebastian Wesley 1861

LEAD ME, LORD
Irregular

663   My Faith Looks Up to Thee

1 My faith looks up to thee, thou Lamb of Cal - va - ry, Sav - iour di - vine. Now hear me while I pray; take all my guilt a - way. O let me from this day be whol - ly thine.

2 While life's dark maze I tread, and griefs a - round me spread, be thou my guide, bid dark - ness turn to day; wipe sor - row's tears a - way; nor let me ev - er stray from thee a - side.

3 May thy rich grace im - part strength to my faint - ing heart, my zeal in - spire. As thou hast died for me, O may my love to thee pure, warm, and change - less be, a liv - ing fire.

Words: Ray Palmer 1830
Music: Lowell Mason 1831

OLIVET
6 6 4 6 6 6 4

What a Friend We Have in Jesus

664

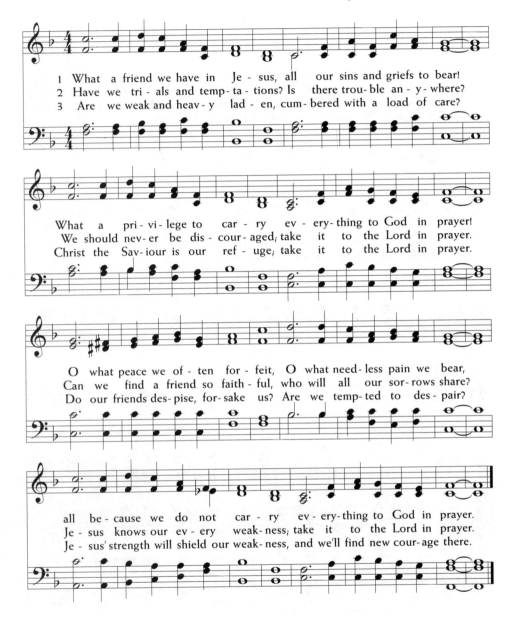

1 What a friend we have in Je - sus, all our sins and griefs to bear!
2 Have we tri - als and temp - ta - tions? Is there trou - ble an - y - where?
3 Are we weak and heav - y lad - en, cum - bered with a load of care?

What a pri - vi - lege to car - ry ev - ery - thing to God in prayer!
We should nev - er be dis - cour - aged; take it to the Lord in prayer.
Christ the Sav - iour is our ref - uge; take it to the Lord in prayer.

O what peace we of - ten for - feit, O what need - less pain we bear,
Can we find a friend so faith - ful, who will all our sor - rows share?
Do our friends des - pise, for - sake us? Are we temp - ted to des - pair?

all be - cause we do not car - ry ev - ery - thing to God in prayer.
Je - sus knows our ev - ery weak - ness; take it to the Lord in prayer.
Je - sus' strength will shield our weak - ness, and we'll find new cour - age there.

Words: Joseph Medlicott Scriven ca. 1855
Music: Charles Crozat Converse 1868

FRIENDSHIP
8 7 8 7 D
Alt. tune: Blaenwern

665 Pass Me Not, O Gentle Saviour

1 Pass me not, O gen - tle Sav - iour, hear my hum - ble cry;
2 Let me at thy throne of mer - cy find a sweet re - lief,
3 Trust - ing on - ly in thy mer - it, would I seek thy face;
4 Thou the spring of all my com - fort, more than life to me,

while on oth - ers thou art call - ing, do not pass me by.
kneel - ing there in deep con - tri - tion; help my un - be - lief.
heal my wound - ed, bro - ken spir - it, save me by thy grace.
whom have I on earth be - side thee? Whom in heaven but thee?

Refrain

Sav - iour, Sav - iour, hear my hum - ble cry;

while on oth - ers thou art call - ing, do not pass me by.

Words: Fanny J. Crosby 1868
Music: William Howard Doane 1870

PASS ME NOT
8 5 8 5 *with refrain*

In Lonely Mountain Ways

(Ya-ma-ji Ko-e-te)

1 Ya - ma - ji ko - e - te hi -
2 Mi - chi ke - wa - shi - ku yu -
3 Hi mo ku - re - na - ba i -

1 In lone - ly moun - tain ways of
2 My jour - ney may be long, the
3 And though when eve - ning falls, a

to - ri yu - ke - do shu no te ni su -
ku - te to - o - shi ko - ko - ro za - su
shi no ma - ku - ra, ka - ri - nu no yu -

this world's trial and care, my heart knows naught of
path - way rough and steep; suf - fi - cient for each
stone my pil - low shapes, the vi - sion of our

ga - re - ru mi wa ya - su - ke - shi
ka - ta ni i - tsu - ka tsu - ku - ra - n
me ni mo mi - ku - ni shi - no - ban.

fear - scarred days; the Mas - ter's hand is there.
day my song; my way the Lord does keep.
king - dom calls and here a Beth - el makes.

Words: *Sugawo Nishimura* 1903; trans. *Paul Gregory* 1981
Music: *Amzi Chapin* 1805
Translation copyright © 1983 Paul Gregory.

GOLDEN HILL
6 6 8 6

667

Jesus, Priceless Treasure

1 Je - sus, price - less trea - sure, source of pur - est plea - sure,
2 In thine arm I rest me; foes who would op - press me
3 Hence, all thoughts of sad - ness! For the Lord of glad - ness,

tru - est friend to me; long my heart hath pant - ed,
can - not reach me here. Though the earth be shak - ing,
Je - sus, en - ters in: those who love the Fa - ther,

till it well - nigh faint - ed, thirst - ing af - ter thee.
ev - ery heart be quak - ing, God dis - pels our fear;
though the storms may gath - er, still have peace with - in;

Thine I am, O spot - less Lamb, I will suf - fer
sin and hell in con - flict fell with their heav - iest
yea, what - e'er we here must bear, still in thee lies

Words: Johann Franck 1650; trans. Catherine Winkworth 1863
Music: Johann Crüger 1653; harm. Johann Sebastian Bach 1723

JESU, MEINE FREUDE
665 665 786

nought to   hide   thee, ask for nought be - side   thee.
storms as - sail   us: Je - sus will not fail   us.
pur - est plea - sure, Je - sus, price - less trea - sure!

Ô Jésus, ma joie   668

1 Ô Jésus, ma joie,
   toi que Dieu m'envoie,
   mon Sauveur, mon roi,
   viens, à ma prière,
   mettre ta lumière
   et ta vie en moi.
   De mon coeur sois le Seigneur:
   hors de toi, seul adorable,
   rien n'est désirable.

2 Quand le mal menace,
   Ô Jésus, ta grâce,
   s'offre à notre foi.
   Tu nous justifies;
   tu promets la vie
   à celui qui croit.
   Ton amour est mon recours;
   en lui seul je me confie.
   Veille sur ma vie!

3 Seul Jésus m'attire;
   seul il peut suffire
   pour remplir mon coeur.
   Il est ma richesse;
   tous les biens paraissent
   pour moi sans valeur.
   Les terreurs, ni les douleurs,
   ne méritent qu'on les craigne,
   puisque Jésus règne!

4 Sois le seul exemple
   que mes yeux contemplent,
   Ô Jésus, mon roi!
   Donne-moi de vivre
   pour t'aimer, te suivre,
   et mourir en toi.
   Chaque jour, que ton amour
   me soutienne dans ma voie,
   Ô Jésus, ma joie!

Words: Trans. Edmond Pidoux ca. 1976

French translation copyright © Fondation d'édition des Eglises protestantes romandes.

JESU, MEINE FREUDE
6 6 5 6 6 5 7 8 6

669

Jesus, Lover of My Soul

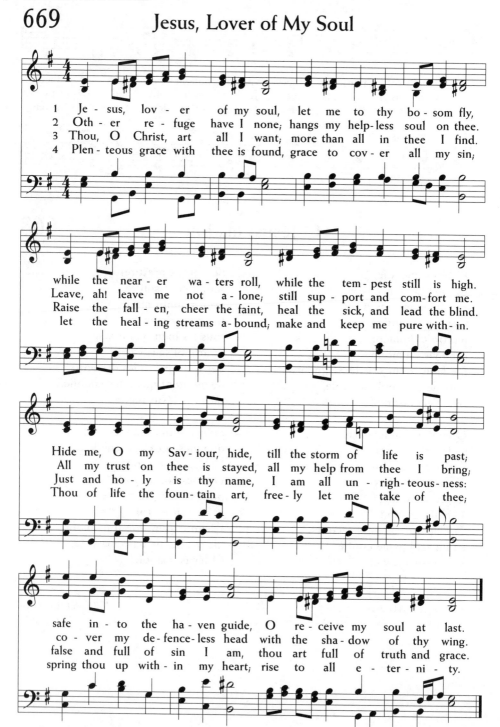

1 Je - sus, lov - er of my soul, let me to thy bo - som fly,
2 Oth - er re - fuge have I none; hangs my help - less soul on thee.
3 Thou, O Christ, art all I want; more than all in thee I find.
4 Plen - teous grace with thee is found, grace to cov - er all my sin;

while the near - er wa - ters roll, while the tem - pest still is high.
Leave, ah! leave me not a - lone; still sup - port and com - fort me.
Raise the fall - en, cheer the faint, heal the sick, and lead the blind.
let the heal - ing streams a - bound; make and keep me pure with - in.

Hide me, O my Sav - iour, hide, till the storm of life is past;
All my trust on thee is stayed, all my help from thee I bring;
Just and ho - ly is thy name, I am all un - righ - teous - ness:
Thou of life the foun - tain art, free - ly let me take of thee;

safe in - to the ha - ven guide, O re - ceive my soul at last.
co - ver my de - fence - less head with the sha - dow of thy wing.
false and full of sin I am, thou art full of truth and grace.
spring thou up with - in my heart; rise to all e - ter - ni - ty.

Words: Charles Wesley 1740
Music: Joseph Parry 1879

ABERYSTWYTH
7 7 7 7 D

Precious Lord, Take My Hand

670

1 Pre-cious Lord, take my hand, lead me on, let me stand,
2 When my way grows drear, pre-cious Lord, lin-ger near,
3 When the dark-ness ap-pears, and the night draws near,

I am tired, I am weak, I am worn;
when my life is al-most gone,
and the day is past and gone,

through the storm, through the night, lead me on to the light:
hear my cry, hear my call, hold my hand lest I fall:
at the riv-er I stand, guide my feet, hold my hand:

Refrain

take my hand, pre-cious Lord, lead me home.

Words: *Thomas A. Dorsey 1932*
Music: *George N. Allen 1844; adapt. Thomas A. Dorsey 1932*
Words and music adaptation copyright © *1938 Unichappell Music Inc.*

PRECIOUS LORD
Irregular with refrain

671 I Need Thee Every Hour

1 I need thee ev-ery hour, most gra - cious Lord;
2 I need thee ev-ery hour; stay thou near by;
3 I need thee ev-ery hour, in joy or pain;
4 I need thee ev-ery hour; teach me thy will;

no ten - der voice but thine can peace af - ford.
temp - ta - tions lose their power when thou art nigh.
come quick - ly and a - bide, or life is vain.
and thy rich prom - is - es in me ful - fil.

Refrain

I need thee, O I need thee; ev - ery hour I need thee.

O bless me now, my Sav - iour; I come to thee.

Words: *Annie Sherwood Hawks* 1872
Music: *Robert S. Lowry* 1873

DEPENDENCE (NEED)
6 4 6 4 with refrain

Take Time to Be Holy

1 Take time to be ho - ly, speak oft with your Lord;
2 Take time to be ho - ly, let him be your guide,
3 Take time to be ho - ly, be calm in your soul,

a - bide in him al - ways, and feed on his word.
and run not be - fore him, what - ev - er be - tide.
each thought and each mo - tive be - neath his con - trol.

Make friends of God's chil - dren, help those who are weak,
In joy or in sor - row, still fol - low the Lord,
Thus led by his spir - it to foun - tains of love,

for - get - ting in noth - ing his bless - ing to seek.
and, look - ing to Je - sus, still trust in his word.
you soon shall be fit - ted for ser - vice a - bove.

Words: William D. Longstaff ca. 1882
Music: George C. Stebbins 1890

HOLINESS
6 5 6 5 D

673 You Never Saw Old Galilee

Verses may be sung as a solo, with congregation joining in on the repeated last line of each verse.

Words: Herman G. Stuempfle, Jr. 1989
Music: Ben S DeVan ca. 1992

PETER'S CHANTY
8 6 8 6 6

5 We roused the Master from his sleep
  and called his name in dread:
  "Come save us from the awful deep
  or we're as good as dead,
  or we're as good as dead."

6 Then he stood up against the gale,
  and told the storm to cease.
  Tempestuous winds broke
    off their wail;
  waves calmed and lay at peace,
  waves calmed and lay at peace.

7 So, friends, although the sea be wide
  and though your boat be small,
  there's naught to fear
    from time or tide;
  the Master's Lord of all,
  the Master's Lord of all.

8 Then sing, my friends, sing merrily;
  O sing both bold and brave.
  The one who made the surging sea
  still rules the wind and wave,
  still rules the wind and wave.

Fight the Good Fight 674

1 Fight the good fight with all your might; Christ is your
2 Run the straight race through God's good grace; lift up your
3 Cast care a - side, lean on your guide; God's bound- less
4 Faint not, nor fear, God's arms are near; God chang - es

strength and Christ your right; lay hold on life, and
eyes, and seek Christ's face. Life with its path be -
mer - cy will pro - vide; trust, and the trust - ing
not and you are dear. On - ly be - lieve, and

it shall be your joy and crown e - ter - nal - ly.
fore us lies; Christ is the way, and Christ the prize.
soul shall prove Christ is its life, and Christ its love.
Christ shall be your all in all e - ter - nal - ly.

Words: *John Samuel Bewley Monsell 1863, alt.*
Music: *William Boyd 1864*

PENTECOST
8 8 8 8
Alt. tune: Duke Street

675 Will Your Anchor Hold

1 Will your an - chor hold in the storms of life?
2 It will sure - ly hold in the straits of fear,
3 It will sure - ly hold in the floods of death,
4 When our eyes be - hold, through the gath - ering night,

When the clouds un - fold their wings of strife,
when the break - ers tell that the reef is near;
when the wa - ters cold chill our lat - est breath;
the cit - y of gold, our har - bour bright,

when the strong tides lift and the ca - bles strain,
though the temp - est rave and the wild winds blow,
on the ris - ing tide it can nev - er fail
we shall an - chor fast by the heaven - ly shore,

will your an - chor drift or firm re - main?
not an an - gry wave shall our bark o'er - flow.
while our hopes a - bide with - in the veil.
with the storms all past for ev - er - more.

Words: Priscilla Jane Owens 1882
Music: William James Kirkpatrick 1882

WILL YOUR ANCHOR HOLD
10 10 10 10 with refrain

Refrain
We have an an - chor that keeps the soul stead - fast and sure while the
bil - lows roll, fast- ened to the rock which can - not move,
ground - ed firm and deep in the Sav - iour's love!

And the following…

883 Comfort, comfort, O my people
636 Give to the winds your fears
87 I heard the voice of Jesus say
286 If you will trust in God
640 Lead, kindly light
611 Out of the depths, O God
154 Why has God forsaken me

676 God, Make Us Servants of Your Peace

1 God, make us servants of your peace:
2 Where all is doubt, may we sow faith;
3 Jesus, our Lord, may we not seek
4 May we not look for love's return,
5 Dying, we live and are reborn

where there is hate, may we sow love;
where all is gloom, may we sow hope;
to be consoled, but to console,
but seek to love unselfishly.
through death's dark night to endless day;

where there is hurt, may we forgive;
where all is night, may we sow light;
nor look to understanding hearts,
For in our giving we receive,
God, make us servants of your peace

where there is strife, may we make one.
where all is tears, may we sow joy.
but look for hearts to understand.
and in forgiving are forgiven.
to wake at last in heaven's light.

Words: St. Francis of Assisi ca. 1220; para. James Quinn
Music: Samuel Sebastian Wesley 1872
Words paraphrase copyright © 1969 Selah Publishing Co., Inc.

WINSCOTT
8 8 8 8

O God of Every Nation

677

1 O God of ev-ery na-tion, of ev-ery race and land,
2 From search for wealth and pow-er and scorn of truth and right,
3 Give strength to those who la-bour that all may find re-lease
4 Keep bright in us the vi-sion of days when war shall cease,

re-deem the whole cre-a-tion with your al-might-y hand;
from trust in bombs that show-er de-struc-tion through the night,
from fear of rat-tling sa-bre, from dread of war's in-crease;
when ha-tred and di-vi-sion, give way to love and peace,

where hate and fear di-vide us and bit-ter threats are hurled,
from pride of race and sta-tion and blind-ness to your way,
when hope and cour-age fal-ter, your still small voice be heard:
till dawns the morn-ing glo-rious when peace on earth shall reign

in love and mer-cy guide us and heal our strife-torn world.
de-liv-er ev-ery na-tion, e-ter-nal God, we pray.
with faith that none can al-ter, your ser-vants un-der-gird.
and Christ shall rule vic-to-rious o'er all the world's do-main.

Words: William Watkins Reid, Jr. 1958, alt. 1972, 1995
Music: Welsh folk melody; Evans' Hymnau a Thonau 1865; arr. English Hymnal 1906

LLANGLOFFAN
7 6 7 6 D

678 For the Healing of the Nations

Descant

4 You, Cre - a - tor - God, have writ - ten your great name on

1 For the heal - ing of the na - tions, God, we pray with
2 Lead us for - ward in - to free - dom, from de - spair your
3 All that kills a - bun - dant liv - ing, let it from the
4 You, Cre - a - tor - God, have writ - ten your great name on

hu - man - kind; for our grow - ing in your like - ness

one ac - cord; for a just and e - qual shar - ing
world re - lease; that, re - deemed from war and ha - tred,
earth be banned: pride of sta - tus, race or school - ing,
hu - man - kind; for our grow - ing in your like - ness

bring the life of Christ to mind; that, by our re -

of the things that earth af - fords. To a life of
all may come and go in peace. Show us how through
dog - mas that ob - scure your plan. In our com - mon
bring the life of Christ to mind; that, by our re -

Words: Fred Kaan 1965
Music: Henry Purcell ca. 1682; desc. Darryl Nixon 1986
Words copyright © 1968 Hope Publishing Company. Descant copyright © 1987 Songs for a Gospel People.

WESTMINSTER ABBEY
878787

sponse and ser - vice, earth its des - ti - ny may find.

love in ac - tion help us rise and pledge our word.
care and good - ness fear will die and hope in - crease.
quest for jus - tice may we hal - low life's brief span.
sponse and ser - vice, earth its des - ti - ny may find.

Let There Be Light 679

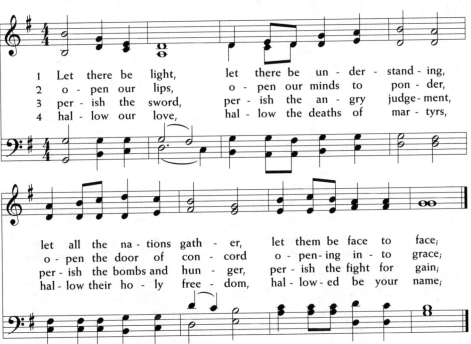

1 Let there be light, let there be un - der - stand - ing,
2 o - pen our lips, o - pen our minds to pon - der,
3 per - ish the sword, per - ish the an - gry judge - ment,
4 hal - low our love, hal - low the deaths of mar - tyrs,

let all the na - tions gath - er, let them be face to face;
o - pen the door of con - cord o - pen - ing in - to grace;
per - ish the bombs and hun - ger, per - ish the fight for gain;
hal - low their ho - ly free - dom, hal - low - ed be your name;

5 your kingdom come,
your spirit turn to language,
your people speak together,
your spirit never fade;

6 let there be light,
open our hearts to wonder,
perish the way of terror,
hallow the world God made.

Words: Frances Wheeler Davis 1968, alt.
Music: Robert J. B. Fleming 1967
Words copyright © 1970 Frances Wheeler Davis. Music copyright © 1976 Margaret Fleming.

CONCORD
4 7 7 6

680 Isaiah the Prophet Has Written of Old

1 I - sa - iah the proph - et has writ - ten of old how
2 Yet na - tions still prey on the meek of the world, and

God's new cre - a - tion shall come, in - stead of the thorn tree, the
con - flict turns par - ent from child. Your peo - ple de - spoil all the

fir tree shall grow; the wolf shall lie down with the lamb.
sweet - ness of earth; the brier and the thorn tree grow wild.

The moun - tains and hills shall break forth in - to song, the
God, bring to fru - i - tion your will for the earth, that

peo - ples be led forth in peace, for the earth shall be filled with the
no one shall hurt or de - stroy, that wis - dom and jus - tice shall

Words: Joy F. Patterson 1982

Music: American folk melody from William Walker's Southern Harmony 1835; harm. Austin C. Lovelace 1986

SAMANTHRA
11 8 11 8 D

Words copyright © 1982 The Hymn Society. Used by permission of Hope Publishing Company. Harmony copyright © 1986 G.I.A. Publications, Inc.

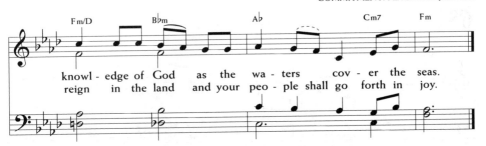

knowl - edge of God as the wa - ters cov - er the seas.
reign in the land and your peo - ple shall go forth in joy.

Where Cross the Crowded Ways of Life 681

1 Where cross the crowd - ed ways of life, where sound the
2 In haunts of wretch - ed - ness and need, on shad - owed
3 The cup of wa - ter given for you still holds the
4 O Je - sus, from the moun - tain side, make haste to
5 till all the world shall learn your love and fol - low

cries of race and clan, a - bove the noise of
thresh - olds, dark with fears, from paths where hide the
fresh - ness of your grace; yet long these mul - ti -
heal these hearts of pain; a - mong these rest - less
where your feet have trod, till glo - rious from your

self - ish strife, we hear your words of life a - gain.
lures of greed, we catch the vi - sion of your tears.
tudes to view the strong com - pas - sion of your face.
throngs a - bide, and tread the cit - y's streets a - gain,
heaven a - bove shall come the cit - y of our God.

Words: Frank Mason North 1903, alt.
Music: Gardiner's Sacred Melodies 1815

FULDA
8 8 8 8

682

O Day of Peace

Introduction

Unison

1 O day of peace that dim - ly shines through all our
2 Then shall the wolf dwell with the lamb, nor shall the

hopes and prayers and dreams, guide us to jus - tice, truth, and
fierce de - vour the small; as beasts and cat - tle calm - ly

love, de - liv - ered from our self - ish schemes. May swords of
graze, a lit - tle child shall lead them all. Then en - e -

hate fall from our hands, our hearts from en - vy find re -
mies shall learn to love, all crea - tures find their true ac -

Words: Carl P. Daw, Jr. 1982
Music: C. Hubert H. Parry 1916; arr. Janet Wyatt 1977

JERUSALEM
8 8 8 8 D
Alt. setting: 258

lease, till by God's grace our war-ring world shall see Christ's
cord; the hope of peace shall be ful-filled, for all the

Interlude

prom-ised reign of peace.
earth shall know the Lord.

Final Ending

An Affirmation of Peace 683

Peace is not the product of terror or fear.
Peace is not the silence of cemeteries.
Peace is not the silence of violent repression.
Peace is the generous, tranquil contribution of all to the good of all.
Peace is dynamism. Peace is generosity.
It is right and duty.

Oscar A. Romero; trans. James Brockman

684 Make Me a Channel of Your Peace

1 Make me a chan-nel of your peace: where there is hat-red, let me bring your love; where there is in-jur-y, your heal-ing power, — and where there's doubt, true faith in you:

2 Make me a chan-nel of your peace: there's des-pair in life, let me bring hope; where there is dark-ness, on-ly light; — and where there's sad-ness, ev-er joy. —————— O

3 Make me a chan-nel of your peace. It is in par-don-ing that we are par-doned, in giv-ing to all that we re-ceive, and in dy-ing that we're born to e-ter-nal life.

Words: attr. to St. Francis 1220
Music: Sebastian Temple 1967; arr. Betty Pulkingham 1976
Music copyright © 1968 Franciscan Communications Centre.

CHANNEL OF PEACE
Irregular

685

We Turn to You

1 We turn to you, O God of ev-ery na-tion,
2 We turn to you, that we may be for-giv-en
3 Free ev-ery heart from pride and self-re-li-ance,
4 On all who fight on earth for right re-la-tions
5 Teach us, good Lord, to serve the need of oth-ers,

giv-er of good and or-i-gin of life; your
for cru-ci-fy-ing Christ on earth a-gain. We
our ways of thought in-spire with sim-ple grace; break
we pray the light of love from hour to hour. Grant
help us to give and not to count the cost. U-

love is at the heart of all cre-a-tion,
know that we have nev-er whol-ly striv-en
down a-mong us bar-riers of de-fi-ance,
wis-dom to the lead-ers of the na-tions,
nite us all, to live as sis-ters, bro-thers,

your hurt is peo-ple's pain in war and death.
to share with all the prom-ise of your reign.
speak to the soul of all the hu-man race.
the gift of care-ful-ness to those in power.
de-feat our Bab-el with your Pen-te-cost!

Words: Fred Kaan 1965, rev. 1993
Music: Alfred Scott-Gatty 1900
Words copyright © 1968 Hope Publishing Company.

WELWYN
11 10 11 10

God of Grace and God of Glory

1 God of grace and God of glo - ry, on your peo - ple
2 Lo, the hosts of e - vil round us scorn your Christ, as -
3 Cure your child - ren's war - ring mad - ness, bend our pride to
4 Set our feet on lof - ty pla - ces, gird our lives that

pour your power; now ful - fil your chur - ch's sto - ry;
sail your ways; fears and doubts too long have bound us;
your con - trol; shame our wan - ton self - ish glad - ness,
they may be arm - oured with all Christ - like gra - ces,

bring its bud to glo - rious flower. Grant us wis - dom,
free our hearts to work and praise. Grant us wis - dom,
rich in goods and poor in soul. Grant us wis - dom,
pledged to set all cap - tives free. Grant us wis - dom,

grant us cour - age, for the fac - ing of this hour.
grant us cour - age, for the liv - ing of these days.
grant us cour - age, lest we miss your king - dom's goal.
grant us cour - age, that we fail not them nor thee.

Words: Harry Emerson Fosdick 1930, alt.
Music: Welsh traditional melody; arr. F. R. C. Clarke 1970
Arrangement copyright © 1970 F. R. C. Clarke.

RHUDDLAN
8 7 8 7 8 7
Alt. tune: Cwm Rhondda

687 When Will People Cease Their Fighting?

1 When will peo-ple cease their fight-ing? When will ar-mies
2 Floods and earth-quakes, drought and fam-ine plague the world with
3 As we strive for peace with vig-our, hop-ing to be

wage no war, na-tions con-quer not their neigh-bour,
awe-some ill, but far great-er is war's hor-ror
shown the way, we are strength-ened in the knowl-edge

weap-ons id-le, used no more? When will guns and
caused by hu-man, stub-born will. Blest are those who,
of a fu-ture, per-fect day; for we know that

bombs be si-lent? When will cap-tives be set free?
work-ing, pray-ing, pur-pose in their hearts to be
deep-er, rich-er peace is ours when Christ shall reign;

Words: Constance Cherry 1983
Music: Franz Joseph Haydn 1797
Words copyright © 1990 Constance Cherry.

AUSTRIAN HYMN
8 7 8 7 D

All cre - a - tion groans in long - ing
in - stru - ments of peace, com - mit - ted
then will all our swords be plow - shares

for the world's true lib - er - ty.
to the na - tions' har - mo - ny.
and God's chil - dren free from pain.

O Day of God, Draw Nigh 688

1 O day of God, draw nigh in beau - ty and in power,
2 Bring to our trou - bled minds, un - cer - tain and a - fraid,
♦ 3 Bring jus - tice to our land, that all may dwell se - cure,
4 Bring to our world of strife your sov - ereign word of peace,
5 O day of God, draw nigh as at cre - a - tion's birth;

come with your time - less judge - ment now to match our pres - ent hour.
the qui - et of a stead - fast faith, calm of a call o - beyed.
♦ and fine - ly build for days to come foun - da - tions that en - dure.
that war may haunt the earth no more and des - o - la - tion cease.
let there be light a - gain, and set your judge - ments in the earth.

Words: R. B. Y. Scott 1937, alt. 1972
Music: Genevan Psalter 1551
Words copyright © Emmanuel College, Toronto, Ontario.

ST MICHAEL (OLD 134TH)
6 6 8 6

689 Oh viens, jour du Seigneur

1 Oh viens, jour du Seigneur,
rayonne de clarté;
que règne dans nos faibles coeurs
l'éclat de ta beauté.

2 Et donne à nos esprits,
incertains et troublés,
le calme d'une foi qui vit,
d'un coeur qui s'est donné.

3 Apporte aux nations
l'amour et l'équité
afin que, calmes, nous vivions
dans la sécurité.

4 Accorde-nous la paix,
que tout le genre humain
connaisse enfin le don parfait
de ton salut divin.

5 Viens, jour du Dieu vivant
et, comme au premier jour,
fais resplendir sur tes enfants
ta face, ô Dieu d'amour.

(The music appears on the preceding page)

Words: R. B. Y. Scott 1937, alt. 1972; French trans. Flossette du Pasquier 1951   ST MICHAEL (OLD 134TH)

690 From the Slave Pens of the Delta

1 "From the slave pens of the del - ta, from the
2 "From the a - ging shrines and struc - tures, from the
3 When we mur - mur on the moun - tains for the
4 In the mael - strom of the na - tions, in the

ghet - toes on the Nile, let my peo - ple seek their
clois - ter and the aisle, let my peo - ple seek their
old E - gyp - tian plains, when we miss our an - cient
jour - ney in - to space, in the clash of gen - er -

Words: Herbert O'Driscoll 1971, alt.
Music: Trier Gesangbuch 1695; adapt. Luxemberg Kyriale 1768
Words copyright © 1971 The United Methodist Publishing House.

OMNI DIE
8 7 8 7 D
Alt. tune: Ebenezer

free - dom in the wil - der - ness a - while": so God
free - dom in the wil - der - ness a - while": so the
bond - age, and the hope, the prom - ise, wanes, then the
a - tions, in the hun - ger - ing for grace, in our

spoke from out of Si - nai, so God spoke and
Son of God has spo - ken, and the storm - clouds
rock shall yield its wa - ter and the man - na
ag - o - ny and glo - ry, we are called to

it was done, and a peo - ple crossed the
are un - furled, for his peo - ple must be
fall by night, and with vis - ions of a
new - er ways by the God of our to -

wa - ters toward the ris - ing of the sun.
scat - tered to be ser - vants in the world.
fu - ture shall we march to - ward the light.
mor - rows who is God of earth's to - days.

691 Though Ancient Walls

1 Though an-cient walls may still stand proud
2 When vest-ed power stands firm en-trenched
3 The truth we seek in var-ied scheme,
4 The church di-vid-ed seeks that grace,
5 This bro-ken world seeks last-ing health

and ra-cial strife be fact, though bound-aries may be
and breaks an-oth-er's back, when waste and want live
the life that we pur-sue, u-nites us in a
that new-ness we pro-claim; a u-ni-ty of
and vi-tal u-ni-ty. God's peo-ple by God's

lines of hate, pro-claim God's sav-ing act!
side by side, it's Gos-pel that we lack.
com-mon quest for self and world made new.
serv-ing love that lives praise to God's name!
Word re-newed, cast off all slav-er-y!

Refrain

Walls that di-vide are bro-ken down; Christ is our

Words: Walter Farquharson 1974
Music: Ron Klusmeier 1974, arr. 1995

KARR
8 6 8 6 with refrain

u - ni - ty! Chains that en - slave are thrown a - side;

Christ is our lib - er - ty!

(after vv. 1–4)

Prayers for Peace 692

O God, lead us from death to life,
    from falsehood to truth;
lead us from despair to hope,
    from fear to trust;
lead us from hate to love,
    from war to peace.
Let your peace fill our hearts, our world, our universe. Amen.

Satish Kumar

693

O God of many names,
Lover of all nations,
we pray for peace
    in our hearts,
    in our homes,
    in our nations,
    in our world.
For the peace you willed, we pray. Amen.

George Appleton

694 To Us All, to Every Nation

1 To us all, to ev-ery na-tion comes a mo-ment
2 Then to side with truth is no-ble when we share its
3 By the light of burn-ing mar-tyrs, Je-sus' bleed-ing
4 Though the cause of e-vil pros-per, yet 'tis truth a-

to de-cide, in the strife of truth with false-hood
wretch-ed crust, ere the cause bring fame and prof-it
feet we track, toil-ing up new Cal-varies ev-er
lone is strong, though its por-tion be the scaf-fold

for the good or ev-il side, some great cause, some
and 'tis pros-perous to be just. Then it is the
with the cross that turns not back; new oc-ca-sions
and up-on the throne be wrong. Yet that scaf-fold

mod-ern proph-et of-fering each the bloom or blight,
brave one choos-es, while the cow-ard stands a-side
teach new du-ties, time makes an-cient good un-couth:
sways the fut-ure, and, be-hind the dim un-known,

Words: James Russell Lowell 1845, adapt. W. Garrett Horder 1894, alt.
Music: Thomas John Williams 1890

EBENEZER
8 7 8 7 D

and the choice goes by for ev - er
till the mul - ti - tude make vir - tue
they must up - ward still and on - ward,
there stands God with - in the shad - ow,

'twixt that dark - ness and that light.
of the faith they had de - nied.
who would keep a - breast of truth.
keep - ing watch a - bove God's own.

God Is Passionate Life 695

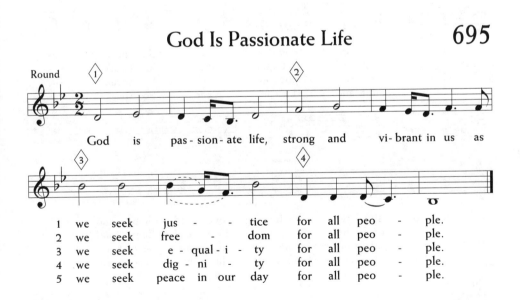

Round

God is pas - sion - ate life, strong and vi - brant in us as

1 we seek jus - tice for all peo - ple.
2 we seek free - dom for all peo - ple.
3 we seek e - qual - i - ty for all peo - ple.
4 we seek dig - ni - ty for all peo - ple.
5 we seek peace in our day for all peo - ple.

Words: Colleen Fulmer 1985
Music: Colleen Fulmer 1985
Words and music copyright © 1985 Colleen Fulmer.

PASSIONATE GOD
6 6 5 4

696 Homeless People, Will You Listen

1 "Home-less peo-ple, will you lis-ten? I, too, was a
2 "Anx-ious peo-ple, can you hear me? I was torn and
3 "Home-less peo-ple, will you lis-ten? I was al-so
4 "Anx-ious peo-ple, can you hear me? I was torn and

ref-u-gee. Poor and hun-gry of my fam-i-ly,
hurt by fear. Sick and suf-fering maimed and wound-ed,
ref-u-gee. Poor and hun-gry of my fam-i-ly,
hurt by fear. Sick and suf-fering maimed and wound-ed,

I was born in pov-er-ty." So speaks Je-sus
I knew doubt and bit-ter tear." So speaks Je-sus
I was born in pov-er-ty." So speaks Je-sus
I knew doubt and bit-ter tear." So speaks Je-sus

to our sis-ters, of-fer-ing love and hope and peace.
to our bro-thers, of-fer-ing love and hope and peace.
to his fol-lowers, friends of his must learn to give.
to his fol-lowers, friends of his must learn to give.

Words: Walter Farquharson 1977
Music: Ron Klusmeier 1977

Words copyright © 1977 Walter Farquharson. Music copyright © 1977 Ron Klusmeier.

FAIRWEATHER
8 7 8 7 D
Alt. tune: Geneva

O for a World   **697**

In this man our God has met us with a love that does not cease.
In this man our God has met us with a love that does not cease.
Life is ours to share with oth-ers. We are bound with all who live.
Life is ours to share with oth-ers. We are bound with all who live.

1 O for a world where ev - ery - one re -
2 O for a world where goods are shared and
3 We wel - come one world fam - i - ly and
4 The poor are rich, the weak are strong, the
5 O for a world pre - par - ing for God's

spects each oth - er's ways, where love is lived and
mis - er - y re - lieved, where truth is spo - ken,
strug - gle with each choice that o - pens us to
fool - ish ones are wise. Tell all who mourn: out -
glo - rious reign of peace, where time and tears will

all is done with jus - tice and with praise.
chil - dren spared, e - qual - i - ty a - chieved.
u - ni - ty and gives our vi - sion voice.
casts be - long, who per - ish - es will rise.
be no more, and all but love will cease.

Words: Miriam Therese Winter 1987
Music: Carl Gotthelf Gläser 1828; arr. Lowell Mason 1839
Words copyright © 1990 Medical Mission Sisters.

AZMON
8 6 8 6

698   With the Wings of Our Mind
(Ttŭgoŭn Maum)

1 Ttu - go - un ma - um pa - ram - e shi -
2 Ttu - go - un ma - um nun - mu - re shi -

1 With the wings of our mind on the wind fly -
2 With the wings of our tears on the wind flow -

ro sum - ma - k'in i - ttang - e po - nae - no -
ro mae - ma - run i - ttang - e po - nae - no -

ing, to the si - lent breath - less earth God's love send -
ing, to the dry and thirst - y earth God's love send -

ra chong - ui - ui kit ppa - rul hwi - nal - li -
ra sa - rang - ui saem - jul - gi t'o - ttu - ryo -

ing, let the brave jus - tice flag wave high a -
ing, let the foun - tain of love spring forth with

myo cha - yu - ui chon - ji - rul i - ru - go - chi - go.
so tta - ttu - t'an in - jong - ul p'i - u - go - chi - go.

bove, to the heavens and the earth free - dom bring - ing.
joy, 'til the flowers of our hearts ad - vent bloom - ing.

3 With the wings of our song on the
  wind flying
to the dreary desolate earth our love
  sending,
let the vision of light open wide our
  hearts
'til the songs of our hope freedom
  ringing.

3 Ttu-go-un ma-um no-rae-e shi ro
  sang-ma-kan i-ttang-e po-nae-no-ra
  o-ga-nun nun-ki-re ka-sum yŏl-go
  hi-mang-ui no-rae-rul pu-ru-go
  chi-go.

Words: Ik-Whan (Timothy) Moon; trans. A. Marion Pope 1981
Music: Don-Whan Cho 1982
Words copyright © Yongiel Park Moon. Translation copyright © A. Marion Pope. Music copyright © Don-Whan Cho.

TTUGOUN MAUM
Irregular

Live into Hope

699

1 Live in-to hope of cap-tives freed, of sight re-
2 Live in-to hope the blind shall see with in-sight
3 Live in-to hope of lib-er-ty, the right to
4 Live in-to hope of cap-tives freed from chains of

gained, the end of greed. The op-pressed shall be the
and with clar-i-ty, re-mov-ing shades of
speak, the right to be, the right to have one's
fear or want or greed. God now pro-claims our

first to see the year of God's own ju-bi-lee!
pride and fear, a vi-sion of our God brought near.
dai-ly bread, to hear God's word and thus be fed.
full re-lease to faith and hope and joy and peace.

Words: Jane Parker Huber 1976
Music: Thomas Williams' Psalmodia Evangelica, Vol. 2 1789; harm. Lowell Mason
Words copyright © 1980 Jane Parker Huber. Used by permission of Westminster John Knox Press.

TRURO
8 8 8 8

700 God of Freedom, God of Justice

Unison

1 God of free-dom, God of jus - tice, you whose love is
2 Rid the earth of tor - ture's ter - ror, you whose hands were
3 Make in us a cap - tive con - science quick to hear, to

strong as death, you who saw the dark of pris - on,
nailed to wood; hear the cries of pain and pro - test,
act, to plead; make us tru - ly sis - ters, bro - thers

you who knew the price of faith: touch our world of sad op -
you who shed the tears and blood: move in us the power of
of what - ev - er race or creed: teach us to be ful - ly

pres - sion with your Spir - it's heal - ing breath.
pit - y rest - less for the com - mon good.
hu - man, o - pen to each oth - er's need.

Words: Shirley Erena Murray 1980
Music: French traditional carol 17th century
Words copyright © 1992 Hope Publishing Company.

PICARDY
8 7 8 7 8 7

What Does the Lord Require of You   701

Words: Jim Strathdee 1986
Music: Jim Strathdee 1986
Words and music copyright © 1986 Desert Flower Music.

MOON
Irregular

702

When a Poor One

Unison

1 When a poor one who has noth-ing shares with
2 When at last all those who suf-fer find their
3 When our joy fills up our cup to o-ver-
4 When our homes are filled with good-ness in a-

strang-ers, when the thirst-y wa-ter
com-fort, when they hope though e-ven
flow-ing, when our lips can speak no
bun-dance, when we learn how to make

give un-to us all, when the wound-ed in their
hope seems hope-less-ness, when we love though hate at
words oth-er than true, when we know that love for
peace in-stead of war, when each strang-er that we

weak-ness strength-en oth-ers, then we
times seems all a-round us,
sim-ple things is bet-ter, then we
meet is called a neigh-bour,

Words: Spanish, J. A. Olivar and Miguèl Manzano 1976; trans. George Lockwood 1989, alt.
Music: J. A. Olivar and Miguèl Manzano 1976; arr. Alvin Schutmaat

EL CAMINO
12 11 12 with refrain

B♭
A7
Dm
D7
know that God still goes that road with us,
then we
Gm
A7
Dm
Gm
Dm
know that God still goes that road with us.

And the following...

5 All earth is waiting
158 Christ is alive! Let Christians sing
34 Come now, O God of peace
955 Dona nobis pacem
4 God of all places
215 Hope of the world
117 Jesus Christ is waiting
23 Joy shall come
424 May the God of hope
312 Praise with joy the world's creator
271 There's a wideness in God's mercy

703   In the Bulb There Is a Flower

Unison

1 In the bulb there is a flow-er; in the seed, an ap-ple tree;
2 There's a song in ev-ery si-lence, seek-ing word and mel-o-dy;
3 In our end is our be-gin-ning; in our time, in-fin-i-ty;

in co-coons, a hid-den prom-ise: but-ter-flies will soon be free!
there's a dawn in ev-ery dark-ness, bring-ing hope to you and me.
in our doubt there is be-liev-ing; in our life, e-ter-ni-ty.

In the cold and snow of win-ter there's a spring that waits to be,
From the past will come the fu-ture; what it holds, a mys-ter-y,
In our death, a res-ur-rec-tion; at the last, a vic-to-ry,

un-re-vealed un-til its sea-son, some-thing God a-lone can see.

PROMISE
8 7 8 7 D

God Give Us Life

1 God give us life when all a - round spells
2 God give us love in heart and hand to
3 God give us skill, in - sight and will to
4 God give us faith should all else fail and
5 Then, in the end, make death a friend, and

death and some have died; and none are clear that
hold the hurt - ing one, to free the an - ger,
find, where none are sure, new threads to mend the
death un - sheath its sting. O help us hear, through
give us strength to stand and walk to where no

hope is near or fate can be de - fied.
meet the need and wait till wait - ing's done.
web of life, new means to heal and cure.
pain and fear, the songs that an - gels sing.
eye can stare, but Christ can clasp our hand.

Words: John L. Bell 1989
Music: John L. Bell 1989
Words and music copyright © 1989 WGRG, The Iona Community (Glasgow, Scotland), G.I.A. Publications, Inc., Chicago, Illinois, exclusive agent.

CAMPBELL
8 5 8 5

705

For All the Saints

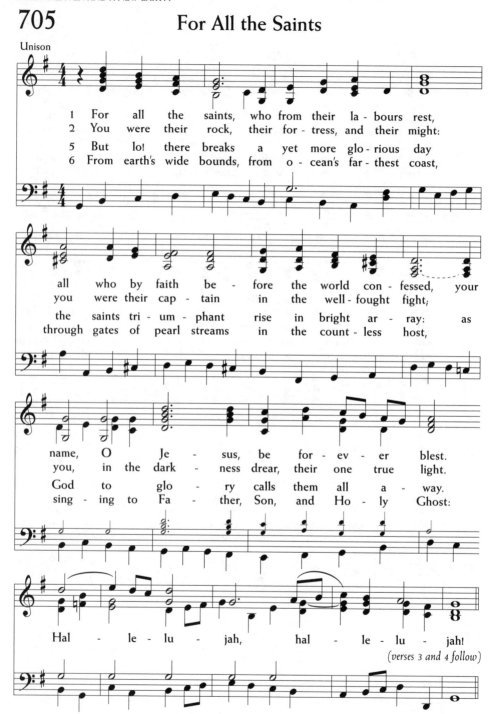

Unison

1 For all the saints, who from their la - bours rest,
2 You were their rock, their for - tress, and their might:
5 But lo! there breaks a yet more glo - rious day
6 From earth's wide bounds, from o - cean's far - thest coast,

all who by faith be - fore the world con - fessed, your
you were their cap - tain in the well - fought fight;
the saints tri - um - phant rise in bright ar - ray: as
through gates of pearl streams in the count - less host,

name, O Je - sus, be for - ev - er blest.
you, in the dark - ness drear, their one true light.
God to glo - ry calls them all a - way.
sing - ing to Fa - ther, Son, and Ho - ly Ghost:

Hal - le - lu - jah, hal - le - lu - jah!

(verses 3 and 4 follow)

Words: *William Walsham How 1864, alt.*
Music: *Ralph Vaughan Williams 1906*
Music by permission of Oxford University Press.

SINE NOMINE
10 10 10 *with hallelujahs*
Alt. setting: 327

Harmony

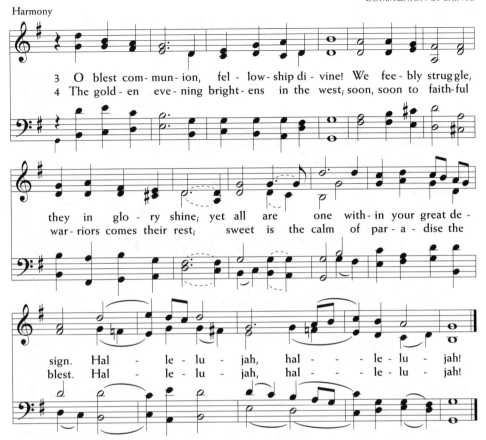

3 O blest com-mun-ion, fel-low-ship di-vine! We fee-bly struggle,
4 The gold-en eve-ning bright-ens in the west; soon, soon to faith-ful

they in glo-ry shine; yet all are one with-in your great de-
war-riors comes their rest; sweet is the calm of par-a-dise the

sign. Hal - le-lu - jah, hal - - - le-lu - jah!
blest. Hal - le-lu - jah, hal - - - le-lu - jah!

Give Thanks for Life 706

1 Give thanks for life, the measure of
   our days,
   mortal, we pass through beauty that
      decays,
   yet sing to God our hope, our love,
      our praise,
   Hallelujah, hallelujah!

2 Give thanks for those who made
      their life a light
   caught from the Christ-flame,
      bursting through the night,
   who touched the truth, who burned
      for what is right,
   Hallelujah, hallelujah!

3 And for our own, our living and our
   dead,
   thanks for the love by which our life
   is fed,
   a love not changed by time or death
      or dread,
   Hallelujah, hallelujah!

4 Give thanks for hope, that like the
      wheat, the grain
   lying in darkness does its life retain
   in resurrection to grow green again,
   Hallelujah, hallelujah!

Words: Shirley Erena Murray 1986
Words copyright © 1987 Hope Publishing Company.

SINE NOMINE
10 10 10 with hallelujahs

707 For the Faithful Who Have Answered

1 For the faith-ful who have an-swered when they heard your
2 Ma-ny eyes have glimpsed the prom-ise, ma-ny hearts have
3 For this cloud of faith-ful wit-ness, for the com-mon

call to serve, for the ma-ny ways you led them test-ing
yearned to see. Ma-ny ears have heard you call-ing us to
life we share, for the work of peace and jus-tice, for the

will and stretch-ing nerve, for their work and for their wit-ness
great-er lib-er-ty. Some have fall-en in the strug-gle,
gos-pel that we bear, for the vis-ion that our home-land

as they strove a-gainst the odds, for their cour-age and
oth-ers still are fight-ing on. You are not a-shamed
is your love — deep, high, and broad — for the dif-ferent roads

Words: Sylvia Dunstan 1986
Music: Trier Gesangbuch 1695
Words copyright © 1991 G.I.A. Publications, Inc.

OMNI DIE
8 7 8 7 D

o - be - dience we give thanks and praise, O God.
to own us. We give thanks and praise, O God.
we tra - vel we give thanks and praise, O God.

My Lord, What a Morning

708

Refrain

My Lord, what a morn - ing. My Lord, what a morn - ing.

Fine

My Lord, what a morn - ing when the stars be - gin to fall.

1 You'll hear the trum - pet sound
2 You'll hear the sin - ner cry to wake the na - tions un - der - ground,
3 You'll hear the Christ - ian shout

D.C.

Look - ing to my God's right hand when the stars be - gin to fall.

Words: African-American spiritual
Music: African-American spiritual

BURLEIGH
Irregular

709 O Holy City, Seen of John

1 O ho-ly cit-y, seen of John, where Christ, the Lamb, doth
2 Hark, now from men whose lives are held more cheap than mer-chan-
3 O shame on us who rest con-tent while lust and greed for

reign, with-in whose four-square walls shall come no
dise, from wom-en strug-gling sore for bread, from
gain in street and shop and ten-e-ment wring

night, nor need, nor pain, and where the tears are
lit-tle chil-dren's cries, there swells the sob-bing
gold from hu-man pain, and bit-ter lips in

wiped from eyes that shall not weep a-gain!
hu-man plaint that bids thy walls a-rise.
blind de-spair cry, "Christ hath died in vain!"

Words: Walter Russell Bowie 1909
Music: anon. 1811, in John Wyeth's Repository of Sacred Music, Part Second 1813;
harm. Charles Winfred Douglas 1940
Harmony from The Church Hymnal 1982 © The Church Pension Fund. Used by permission.

MORNING SONG
8 6 8 6 8 6

4 Give us, O God, the strength to build
the city that hath stood
too long a dream, whose laws are love,
whose ways are brotherhood,
and where the sun that shineth is
God's grace for human good.

5 Already in the mind of God
that city riseth fair.
Lo, how its splendour challenges
the souls that greatly dare,
yea, bids us seize the whole of life
and build its glory there!

Shall We Gather at the River 710

1 Shall we ga-ther at the riv-er, where bright an-gel feet have trod;
2 Ere we reach the shin-ing riv-er, lay we ev-ery bur-den down;
3 Soon we'll reach the shin-ing riv-er, soon our pil-grim-age will cease,

with its crys-tal tide for ev-er flow-ing by the throne of God?
grace our spir-its will de-liv-er, and pro-vide a robe and crown.
soon our hap-py hearts will quiv-er with the mel-o-dy of peace.

Refrain

Yes, we'll ga-ther at the riv-er, the beau-ti-ful, the beau-ti-ful riv-er;

ga-ther with the saints at the riv-er that flows by the throne of God.

Words: Robert S. Lowry 1864
Music: Robert S. Lowry 1864

HANSON PLACE
8 7 8 7 *with refrain*

711

Sleepers, Wake

1 "Sleep - ers, wake!" the watch are call - ing,
Mid - night comes, no long - er slum - ber,
2 Zi - on hears the sent - ries sing - ing,
For her God comes down all glo - rious,
3 Let all crea - tures sound thy prais - es,
Gates of pearl swing wide be - fore us,

1 their notes from Zi - on's watch - tower fall - ing:
nor let dull sleep your sens - es cum - ber.
2 her heart with - in for joy is spring - ing,
in grace most strong, in truth vic - to - rious,
3 now earth its voice with heav - en rais - es,
thy guests who join that bless - ed chor - us

1 "A - wake, a - wake, Je - ru - sa - lem!
Wise vir - gins, haste, or do you dream?
2 she wakes, she speeds with glad sur - prise.
her light is come, her star doth rise.
3 with harps' and cym - bals' joy - ful tone.
of an - gels that sur - round thy throne.

Words: Philip Nicolai 1598; trans. Jay Macpherson 1970
Music: Hans Sachs ca. 1513; adapt. Philip Nicolai 1599; harm. Johann Sebastian Bach 1731
Translation copyright © Jay Macpherson.

WACHET AUF
898D66488

The bride - groom draw - eth near!
Wel - come! thou wor - thy crown,
No eye hath seen, nor ear

A - rise, your lamps show clear. Hal - le - lu - jah.
Lord Je - sus, God's dear Son, ho - san - na!
was yet so blest to hear such re - joic - ing!

Your - selves ar - ray this mar - riage day
We join the throng that streams a - long
Hence - forth may we e - ter - nal - ly

to meet the bride - groom on his way."
and fills thy ban - quet hall with song.
sing hal - le - lu - jahs un - to thee.

712

Célébrons Dieu notre Père

1 Célébrons Dieu notre Père,
qui fit les astres et la terre
et le monde infini des cieux.
C'est lui qui fit les espaces
et tous les temps devant sa grâce,
et toute vie devant ses yeux.
Louange, gloire, honneur,
à toi, puissant Sauveur, alléluia!
Gloire à ton nom, Seigneur et roi,
toi qui fais naître en nous la foi.

2 Célébrons Christ notre frère,
lui qui est venu sur la terre
pour vivre et lutter avec nous.
Que nos coeurs tous glorifient
celui qui nous donna sa vie,

et ressuscita parmi nous.
Louange, gloire, honneur,
à toi, puissant Sauveur, alléluia!
Gloire à ton nom, ô Fils de Dieu,
qui règnes ici et dans les cieux.

3 Chantons l'Esprit de lumière
car sa présence reste entière
en chacun des coeurs visités.
Par lui s'ouvre l'Évangile,
et notre esprit devient paisible
et joyeux dans la vérité.
Louange, gloire, honneur,
à l'Esprit créateur, alléluia!
Gloire à l'Esprit, à l'Esprit Saint,
qui nous éclaire et nous soutient.

This French text (not a translation of the English) may be sung to the hymn on the preceding page.

Words: Commission d'Hymnologie de la Fédération Protestante de France 1972
Words copyright © Fédération Protestante de France.

713

I See a New Heaven

I see a new heaven. I see a new earth as the old

one will pass a - way, where the foun- tain of life flows

Words: Carolyn McDade 1979
Music: Carolyn McDade 1979; harm. Janet McGaughey ca. 1991, alt.
Words and music copyright © 1979 and harmony copyright © 1991 Carolyn McDade.

I SEE A NEW HEAVEN
Irregular with refrain

and with-out price goes to all peo - ple who a-bide in the land.

1 There, there on the banks of a riv - er bright and
2 There, there where death dies and our lives are born a -
3 There, there where the dark - ness brings vi - sions from a -
4 There, there where we work with the love of heal - ing

free, yield - ing her fruit, firm in her root,
gain, bod - y and soul, strug - gling but whole
bove. There where the night, bear - ing new light,
hands. La - bour we must, true to our trust

the Tree of Life will be.
like flow - ers af - ter the rain.
re - veals the prom - ise of love.
to build a prom - ised new land.

714

Come, We That Love
(First tune)

1 Come, we that love the Lord, and let our joys be known,
2 Let those re - fuse to sing who nev - er knew our God;
3 The hill of Zi - on yields a thou - sand sa - cred sweets
4 Then let our songs a - bound, and ev - ery tear be dry;

join in a song with sweet ac - cord, join
but chil - dren of the heaven - ly King, but
be - fore we reach the heaven - ly fields, be -
we're march - ing through Em - man - uel's ground, we're

in a song with sweet ac - cord and thus sur -
chil - dren of the heaven - ly King may speak their
fore we reach the heaven - ly fields or walk the
march - ing through Em - man - uel's ground to fair - er

Refrain

round the throne, and thus sur - round the throne.
joys a - broad, may speak their joys a - broad.
gold - en streets, or walk the gold - en streets.
worlds on high, to fair - er worlds on high.

We're march - ing to

Words: Isaac Watts 1707; refrain, Robert S. Lowry 1867
Music: Robert S. Lowry 1867

MARCHING TO ZION
6 6 8 8 6 6 *with refrain*

Zi - on, beau - ti - ful, beau - ti - ful Zi - on; we're march - ing

up - ward to Zi - on, the beau - ti - ful cit - y of God.

Come, We That Love

715

(Second tune)

1 Come, we that love the Lord, and let our joys be known, join
2 Let those re - fuse to sing who nev - er knew our God; but
3 The hill of Zi - on yields a thou - sand sa - cred sweets be -
4 Then let our songs a - bound, and ev - ery tear be dry; we're

in a song with sweet ac - cord, and thus sur - round the throne.
chil - dren of the heaven - ly King may speak their joys a - broad.
fore we reach the heaven - ly fields or walk the gold - en streets.
march - ing through Em - man - uel's ground, to fair - er worlds on high.

Words: Isaac Watts 1707
Music: Aaron Williams 1770

ST THOMAS
6 6 8 6

716 My Life Flows On

1 My life flows on in end-less song, a-bove earth's lam-en-
2 What though my joys and com-forts die? My Sav-iour still is
3 When ty-rants trem-ble, sick with fear, and hear their death knells
4 I lift my eyes; the cloud grows thin; I see the blue a-

ta - tion. I hear the sweet, though far off hymn that
liv - ing. What though the shad - ows gath-er 'round? A
ring - ing: when friends re-joice both far and near, how
bove it; and day by day this path-way smooths, since

hails a new cre - a - tion. Through all the tu - mult
new song Christ is giv - ing. No storm can shake my
can I keep from sing - ing? In pris - on cell and
first I learned to love it. The peace of Christ makes

and the strife, I hear the mu - sic ring - ing: It
in - most calm, while to that Rock I'm cling - ing: since
dun - geon vile our thoughts to them are wing - ing: when
fresh my heart, a foun - tain ev - er spring - ing: all

Words: *Robert S. Lowry* 1869, alt.
Music: *Robert S. Lowry* 1869, alt.

HOW CAN I KEEP FROM SINGING
8 7 8 7 D

finds an ech - o in my soul —
Love com- mands both heaven and earth, how can I keep from sing - ing?
friends by shame are un - de - filed,
things are mine since I am Christ's —

Hallelujah

717

Hal - le - lu - jah. Hal - le - lu - jah.

Hal - le - lu - jah. Hal - le - lu - jah.

Hal - le - lu - jah. Hal - le - lu - jah.

Hal - le - lu - jah. Hal - le - lu - jah.

Words: trad. liturgical text

Music: as transcribed from the singing of George Mxadana

Music copyright © WGRG The Iona Community (Glasgow, Scotland), G.I.A. Publications, Inc. Chicago, IL, exclusive agent.

HALLELUJAH (MXADANA)

Irregular

718 O God, You Gave Your Servant John

1 O God, you gave your ser - vant John a
2 Our cit - ies wear great shrouds of pain; be -
3 Come, Lord, make real John's vi - sion fair; come,

vi - sion of the world to come: a ra - diant cit - y
neath our gleam - ing towers of wealth the home - less crouch in
dwell with us, make all things new; we try in vain to

filled with light, where you with us will make your home; where
rain and snow, the poor cry out for strength and health. Youth's
save our world un - less our help shall come from you. Come,

nei - ther grief nor pain shall dwell, since for - mer things have
hope is dimmed by ig - no - rance; un - will - ing, work - ers
strength - en us to live in love; bid ha - tred, greed, in -

Words: Joy F. Patterson 1988, alt.
Music: Scottish traditional melody
Words copyright © 1989 Hope Publishing Company.

CANDLER
8 8 8 8 D

passed a - way, and where they need no sun nor
i - dled stand; in - dif - ference walks un - heed - ing
jus - tice cease. Your glo - ry all the light we

moon; your glo - ry lights e - ter - nal day.
by as hun - ger stretch - es out its hand.
need, let all our cit - ies shine forth peace.

And the following...

For the Communion of Saints 719

God of the ages,
we praise you for all your servants
who have done justice, loved mercy,
and walked humbly with their God.
We praise you for all who have sought your new creation,
and who, by their steadfast faith,
have shown their discipleship in Christ Jesus.
We praise you for those we have known and loved,
and pray that we, with them,
may follow in the way of Christ,
and, at the last, dwell in your holy city,
sharing the inheritance of the saints in light,
through your son, our Saviour, Jesus Christ. Amen.

I.   Learn these tunes before you learn any others; afterwards learn as many as you please.

II.   Sing them exactly as they are printed here, without altering or mending them at all; and if you have learned to sing them otherwise, unlearn it as soon as you can.

III.   Sing all. See that you join with the congregation as frequently as you can. Let not a slight degree of weakness or weariness hinder you. If it is a cross to you, take it up, and you will find it a blessing.

IV.   Sing lustily and with a good courage. Beware of singing as if you were half dead, or half asleep; but lift up your voice with strength. Be no more afraid of your voice now, nor more ashamed of its being heard, than when you sung the songs of Satan.

V.   Sing modestly. Do not bawl, so as to be heard above or distinct from the rest of the congregation, that you may not destroy the harmony; but strive to unite your voices together, so as to make one clear melodious sound.

VI.   Sing in time. Whatever time is sung be sure to keep with it. Do not run before nor stay behind it; but attend close to the leading voices, and move therewith as exactly as you can; and take care not to sing too slow. This drawling way naturally steals on all who are lazy; and it is high time to drive it out from us, and sing all our tunes just as quick as we did at first.

VII.   Above all sing spiritually. Have an eye to God in every word you sing. Aim at pleasing him more than yourself, or any other creature. In order to do this attend strictly to the sense of what you sing, and see that your heart is not carried away with the sound, but offered to God continually; so shall your singing be such as the Lord will approve here, and reward you when he cometh in the clouds of heaven.

From John Wesley's Select Hymns, 1761

Psalms and Scripture Songs

Psalms and Scripture Songs
An Introduction

The Psalms Heritage

The Psalms of Hebrew Scripture are the oldest worship songs of the Jewish people. According to ancient tradition, the founder of this hymnody was the shepherd-king, David, who ruled in Canaan about 1000 BCE. The work that he inspired led, over the centuries, to the emergence of the book of Psalms used for worship in the Temple at the time of Jesus. Thus it became in Hebrew, and through translation into Greek, Syriac, Latin and Coptic, the hymn book of the first Christians as well.

Christians have used psalms and songs from other parts of scripture to open their gatherings for worship ("entrance hymns" or "introits"), to respond to the lessons from other parts of scripture ("gradual hymns") and to mark different moments when celebrating communion at the Lord's table. In services of daily prayer, over the course of a week or a month, Christian communities could also say or sing their way through the whole Psalter.

With biblical translation fostered by the Reformers of the sixteenth century, the psalms, in the local language, became a part of worship in which all those gathered could share. Protestants took up the monastic practice of reading the psalms responsively, as well as singing "metrical" translations, where psalm texts were set to music with regular metre. Such versions were the only music that Anglican, Presbyterian and other Reformed congregations used in worship, until the eighteenth century, when freer paraphrases of the psalms and other scripture texts began to appear, from the pens of Isaac Watts and Charles Wesley.

The United Church of Canada inherited these traditions for reading and singing the Psalms. *The Hymnary* (1930) contained three forms: paraphrases placed throughout the hymn section, with metrical, and free-verse versions for reading or chanting appearing in the last sections of the book. Responsive readings also appeared in the closing section of *The Hymnal* (1957) of the Evangelical United Brethren churches. In *The Hymn Book* (1971) the selection of metricals and paraphrases was more limited. Free-verse psalms for choral reading had already appeared in *The Service Book* (1969).

The Language of the Psalms in *Voices United*

In *Voices United* we have brought the various traditional forms of the psalms back into one book, and included versions in more contemporary style. The approximately 150 psalms and scripture songs, including those suggested by the *Revised Common Lectionary*, appear in biblical order and, in a number of cases, with a choice of version.

The metrical psalms here include some of the most beloved in the Scots Psalter tradition. Metricals written by modern poets also appear, some to familiar melodies, some to the various forms of contemporary music.

For the free-verse psalms in *Voices United*, we have developed a version based on the *New Zealand Prayer Book* (1989), occasionally restoring more familiar expressions from the Authorised or Revised Standard versions, or using phrases from the modern Jewish version, *Tanakh* (1988). Throughout we have revised with an eye to the original Hebrew or Greek. A number of practical questions arise in all translations for public worship. In particular, we have chosen to translate the Hebrew divine name, "YHWH", as "God", following a precedent within the Psalter itself.

How the *Voices United* Psalms may be used in Worship

The metrical psalms of *Voices United* may be sung as they always have been, as hymns in their own right. As such they offer our worship their own broad expression of praise, petition, confession, lament and thanksgiving. The congregation may also sing a metrical psalm as the response to the first lesson suggested in the lectionary.

The free-verse psalms develop the spoken or chanted form used in *The Hymnary* (1930). A refrain (or a choice of refrains) introduces each psalm. The refrain echoes a key text in the psalm itself, the simple melody conveying some of the mood of the piece. Used regularly the refrains may thus help worshippers commit short passages of scripture to memory. The refrain may be sung or spoken at the beginning of the psalm, first by a leader or a choir, then by the whole congregation. The refrain is then sung or spoken again wherever the text is marked by the bold "**R**".

The text of the free-verse psalms is set out for responsive reading in two parts:

> one in ordinary type left-justified
> **and the other in bolder type indented.**

The two parts can be read responsively, between leader and congregation, or between two sections of the congregation. Occasionally a third part is set out separately, marked explicitly as for solo voice, or for the whole assembly. A few of the free-verse psalms can be sung through in their entirety. The music for such sung-through versions appear in the Music Leader's Edition.

We offer this version of Psalms and Scripture Songs in the hope that congregations in the United Church of Canada may find words here that will allow us, with those who have sung them over the last three thousand years, to "tell new generations of the wonders God has done".

Psalm 1

Refrain

T. Barrett Armstrong 1979

Bless - ed are those who fol - low the law of God.

Blessed are those who do not follow the counsel of the wicked,
or linger in the way of sinners,
or sit down among those who mock.
> **But their delight is in the law of God,**
> **and on that law they meditate day and night.**
They are like trees planted beside streams of water,
yielding their fruit in due season.
> **Their leaves do not wither,**
> **and whatever they produce shall prosper.   R**

As for the wicked, it is not so with them,
> **but they are like the chaff,**
> **driven away by the wind.**
Therefore the wicked shall not be able to stand
when judgement comes,
nor sinners in the assembly of the righteous.
> **For God watches over the way of the righteous,**
> **but the way of the wicked will perish.   R**

Psalm 2

Refrain *Hal H. Hopson 1985*

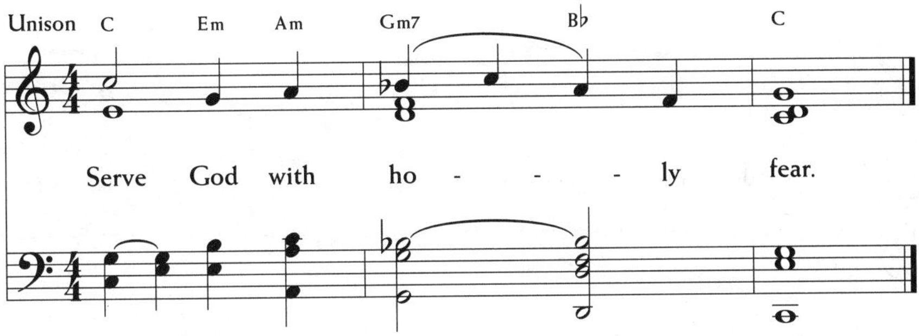

Why are the nations in turmoil,
and why are the peoples engaged in futile plotting?
The monarchs of the earth arise,
and the rulers take counsel together
against God and against God's anointed.
"Let us break their fetters," they say,
"and let us cast off their chains."
The One whose throne is in heaven laughs them to scorn,
God holds them in derision.
You speak to them in your wrath,
and terrify them in your fury.
"I myself have set up one to rule,
on Zion, my holy hill." R

I will recite the decree of God, who said to me,
"You are my child, today I have begotten you.
Ask, and I will give you the nations for your inheritance,
and the ends of the earth for your possession.
You will crush them with a rod of iron,
and break them in pieces like a potter's vessel." R

Now therefore, you monarchs, be wise;
be prudent, you rulers of the earth.
Serve God with fear,
with trembling bow down,
lest God be angry and you perish,
for God's anger is quickly kindled.
Blessed are all who put their trust in God. R

Psalm 3

Michel Guimont 1994

Refrain

God, let your mer-cy be on us as we place our trust in you.

O God, how my enemies have multiplied!
How many there are who rise up against me!
    How many there are who say of me:
    "There is no help for you in God!" R

But you, O God, are a shield about me,
you are my glory, the one who lifts up my head.
    I cry aloud to you,
    and you answer me from your holy hill.
I lie down and sleep.
I wake again, for you sustain me.
    I will not be afraid of the myriad forces
    arrayed against me on every side. R

Rise up, O God, and help me;
    you slap all my enemies on the face,
    you break the teeth of the wicked.
Deliverance belongs to God!
    May your blessing be on your people! R

Psalm 4

Refrain

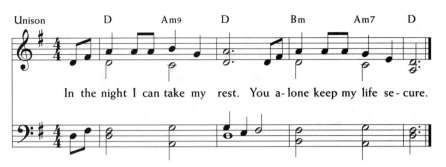

In the night I can take my rest. You a-lone keep my life se-cure.

Answer me, when I call, O God, defender of my cause,
for you set me free when I was in distress.
    Be gracious to me now
    and hear my prayer. R

How long, you people, will you defame my honour?
    How long will you love what is worthless and seek lies?
Know this, that God has chosen the faithful;
    God hears me when I call.
Stand in awe, and cease from sin;
    commune with your own heart upon your bed and be still.
Offer the sacrifices that are appointed,
    and put your trust in God. R

There are many who say,
    "O that we might see prosperity!
    Lift up the light of your face on us, O God."
But you have put gladness in my heart
more than those whose grain and wine are plentiful.
    Safe and sound, I lie down and sleep,
    for you alone, God, make me dwell in safety. R

Psalm 5

Refrain 1

Susan Marrier 1994

As morn-ing dawns, God, hear my cry.

Refrain 2

Samuel Sebastian Wesley 1861, alt.

Lead me, God, lead me in your righ-teous-ness;

make your way plain be - fore my face.

Listen to my words, O God,
give heed to the sound of my groaning.
> Hear my cry for help, my sovereign, my God,
> for to you I direct my prayer.
In the morning, God, you hear my voice;
> early in the morning I make my plea,
> and look to you for an answer.   R

For you are not a God who takes pleasure in wickedness;
no one who is evil can be your guest.
> **The boastful may not stand in your sight;**
> **you hate all those who work mischief.**
You destroy all those who speak lies;
> **the bloodthirsty and treacherous, O God, you abhor.**
But through the abundance of your steadfast love
I will come into your house,
and bow low in reverence within your holy temple.
> **Lead me, O God, in your righteousness**
> **because of my enemies.**
> **Make straight your way before my face.   R**

Let all who put their trust in you rejoice;
> **let them ever give thanks because you defend them;**
> **let those who love your name be joyful in you.**
For you give your blessing to the righteous, O God;
> **as with a shield you will surround them with your favour.   R**

Psalm 8
God, Our God, Your Glorious Name

1 God, our God, your glo - rious name all your won - drous
2 In - fant voic - es chant your praise, tell - ing of your
♦ 3 Moon and stars in shin - ing height night - ly tell their
4 Who are we that we should share in your love and
5 With do - min - ion crowned, we stand o'er the crea - tures

of your hand; all to us de - vo - tion yield,

works pro - claim; in the heavens with ra - diant signs
glo - rious ways; weak - est means work out your will,
♦ Ma - ker's might; when I view the heavens a - far,
ten - der care, raised to an ex - alt - ed height,
of your hand; all to us de - vo - tion yield,

Words: The Psalter 1912, alt.
Music: William F. Sherwin 1877; desc. Emily R. Brink 1987
Descant copyright © 1987 CRC Publications

CHAUTAUQUA (EVENING PRAISE)
77774 with refrain

in the sea and air and field. How great your name!

D7 G A7 D A7 D

ev - er - more your glo - ry shines.
might - y en - e - mies to still.
♦ then I know how small we are. How great your name!
crowned with hon - our in your sight!
in the sea and air and field.

Refrain

Ho - ly, ho - ly, how great your name! Yours the name of

G D7 G C

Ho - ly, ho - ly, ho - ly, how great your name! Yours the name of

match - less worth, ex - cel - lent in all the earth. How great your name!

G D7 G G/D D7 G

match - less worth, ex - cel - lent in all the earth. How great your name!

Psalm 8

Refrain

Michel Guimont 1990

O God, our God, how glo-rious is your name in all the earth!

O God, our God, how glorious is your name in all the earth!
From the lips of infants and children your praises reach up to the heavens.
You have set up a stronghold against your foes,
to quell the enemy and the avenger.   R

When I look to the heavens, the work of your fingers,
the moon and the stars you have set in their places,
what are we mortals that you should be mindful of us,
mere human beings that you should care for us?   R

You have made us little less than divine,
and crowned us with glory and honour.
You have made us rulers over all your creation,
and put all things under our feet,
all sheep and cattle, all creatures of the wild,
the birds of the air and the fish in the sea,
and all that make their way through the waters.   R

Psalm 9

Refrain

W. Anchors' Psalmody ca. 1721

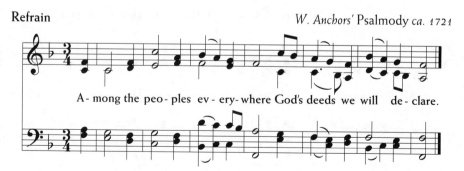

A-mong the peo-ples ev-ery-where God's deeds we will de-clare.

I will give thanks to you, God, with my whole heart;
I will tell of all your marvellous deeds.
I will be glad and rejoice in you;
I will sing praise to your name, O Most High.   R

For my enemies are driven back,
they stumble and perish before you.
> You have upheld the justice of my cause;
> seated on your throne, you have given righteous judgement.

You have rebuked the nations and destroyed the wicked;
you have blotted out their name for ever.
> Enemies have perished;
> you have made their cities a desolation;
> the very memory of them has vanished.

You have ruled from eternity;
you have established your throne for judgement.
> You will judge the world with righteousness,
> and deliver true justice to the peoples.

You are a stronghold for the oppressed,
a tower of strength in a time of trouble.
> Those who cherish your name will put their trust in you,
> for you, O God, have never failed those who seek you.

Sing praises to the One who dwells in Zion;
proclaim to the peoples the deeds God has done.
> For the One who avenges blood has remembered,
> and has not forgotten the cry of the poor.   R

Have pity on me, God;
> consider the trouble I suffer from those who hate me.

You are the One who lifts me up from the gates of death,
> so that I may recount all your praises within the gates of the city,
> and rejoice in your saving help.

The nations have fallen into a pit of their own making;
in the net they laid in secret, their own feet are entangled.
> You have made yourself known, O God, and given judgement;
> the wicked are trapped in the work of their own hands.

The wicked go down to the Dead,
all the nations that are heedless of God.
> The needy shall not always be forgotten;
> the hope of the poor shall not forever be vain.

Rise up, O God; do not let mere mortals prevail.
Call the nations to account before you.
> Put them in fear, O God;
> let the nations know that they are but human.   R

Psalm 13

Jean Sibelius 1899; arr. The Hymnal *1933*

Be still, my soul, for God is on your side.   God is on your side.

How long, O God, will you utterly forget me?
How long will you hide your face from me?
How long must I suffer anguish in my soul,
and be so grieved in my heart day and night?
How long shall my enemy triumph over me? R

Look at me, and answer me, O God my God;
give light to my eyes, lest I fall asleep in death,
lest my enemies claim to have prevailed against me,
lest my foes rejoice at my downfall.
But my trust is in your mercy.
Let my heart be joyful in your salvation.
I will sing to you, O God,
because you have dealt so lovingly with me.
I will praise your name, O God most high.   R

Psalms 14 and 53

C. *Hubert H. Parry* 1888

Refrain

The foolish have spoken in their heart,
and said " There is no God."
>They are corrupt; they do abominable things;
>there is no one who does what is good.
God looks down from heaven upon us all,
to see if any are wise and seek after God.
>But all have gone astray; all alike are corrupted;
>there is no one who does good; no, not one.   R

Have they no knowledge, all those who do evil?
>They devour my people like so much bread,
>and do not pray to God.
But see, they will tremble with fear,
for God is on the side of the righteous.
>Do not mock the hope of the poor,
>for God is their refuge.
O that deliverance for God's people would come forth from Zion!
>When God restores the fortunes of the people,
>then shall Jacob rejoice and Israel be glad.   R

Psalm 15

Thomas Tallis ca. 1567

Refrain

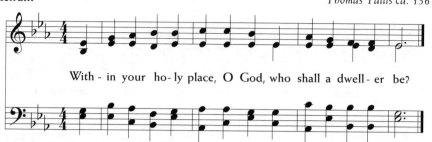

With - in your ho- ly place, O God, who shall a dwell - er be?

God, who may be a guest in your house,
    or who may dwell on your holy mountain?   R

One who leads a blameless life,
    who does what is right,
    who speaks truthfully from the heart;
one whose tongue is free from malice,
    who never wrongs a friend,
    who utters no reproach against a neighbour;
one who cannot respect the unworthy,
but honours those who fear God;
    who stands by a promise given,
    though it be to personal disadvantage;
one who will not take interest on a loan,
nor accept a bribe to testify against the innocent.
    Whoever does this shall never be overthrown.   R

Psalm 16
Protect Me, God

Unison

*1 Pro - tect me, God: I trust in you. I tell you now,
2 Your peo - ple are a cho - sen race, and I de - light
3 O God, you are my food and drink; my work for you
4 Thank you, my God, for warn- ing me; by night and day

"You are my God; on you my hap - pi - ness de - pends."
in faith - ful friends, but pa - gan ways I will not share.
is joy in - deed; glad is this her - i - tage of mine.
you guide my thoughts. With you be - fore me, I stand firm.

Refrain

Pro - tect me, God: I trust in you.

5 So now I'm glad in heart and soul,
   for I have found security;
   among the dead I shall not end.

6 Not death, but life, shall be my path;
   abundant joy your presence grants,
   an honoured place, and happiness.

Refrain

Refrain

*Verses may be spoken responsively, with refrain sung at the beginning, and after verses 2, 4, and 6.

Words: Michael Saward 1970, alt.
Music: M. Christian T. Strover 1973
Words and music copyright © 1973 Hope Publishing Company.

MEPHIBOSHETH
8 8 8 with refrain

Psalm 16

Refrain

M. Christian T. Strover 1973

Pro - tect me, God: I trust in you.

Protect me, O God, for in you I take refuge.
I have said to God, "You are my God;
from you alone comes all my prosperity."
>   All my delight is in the faithful who dwell in the land,
>   and in those who excel in virtue.
But as for those who run after other gods,
their troubles shall be multiplied.
>   Libations of blood I will not offer to those gods,
>   nor will I take their names upon my lips.   R

You, God, are my allotted portion and my cup;
>   you yourself have cast my lot.
My boundaries enclose a pleasant land;
>   indeed I have a noble heritage.
I will thank you, God, for giving me counsel;
>   at night also you teach my heart.
I keep you always before me;
>   you are on my right hand, therefore I shall not fall.   R

So my heart is glad, and my soul rejoices;
for my body shall also rest in safety.
>   For you will not surrender me to the Grave,
>   nor suffer your beloved to see the Abyss.
You will show me the path of life.
>   In your presence is fullness of joy;
>   and from your right hand flow delights for evermore.   R

Psalm 17

Hal H. Hopson 1988

Refrain

Guard me as the ap-ple of your eye;
hide me un-der the shad-ow of your wings.

Hear my just cause; attend to my cry, O God.
> **Listen to my prayer from lips that do not lie.**
Let judgement in my favour come forth from your presence;
> **and let your eyes discern what is right.**
If you examine my heart, if you visit me by night,
> **if you test me, you will find no wickedness in me.**
As for what others do, according to the command of your lips
I have kept from travelling with the violent.
> **My steps have been firm in your paths,**
> **and my feet have not stumbled.   R**

I call upon you, God, for you will answer me.
> **Incline your ear to me and hear my words.**
Show me the wonders of your steadfast love;
> **for by your right hand you save from their enemies**
> **those who take refuge in you.**
Guard me as the apple of your eye;
> **hide me under the shadow of your wings,**
from the wicked who assail me,
> **from deadly foes who surround me.**
As for me, I shall see your face because my plea is just;
> **when I awake and see your face, I shall be satisfied.   R**

Psalm 19

Refrain 1

Henry Boon 1990

The pre-cepts of our God give joy to the heart.

Refrain 2

Geoffrey Shaw

Glo - ry and praise to God whose word brings life!

The heavens declare the glory of God;
and the vault of the sky reveals God's handiwork.
> **One day speaks to another,**
> **and night shares its knowledge with night,**
and this without speech or language;
their voices are not heard.
> **But their sound goes out to all the lands,**
> **their words to the ends of the earth.   R**

In the heavens God has pitched a tent for the sun
which comes out like a bridegroom from under the canopy,
like an athlete eager to run the race.
> **Its rising is at one end of the sky,**
> **it runs its course to the other,**
> **and there is nothing that is hidden from its heat.   R**

God's law is perfect, refreshing the soul;
    God's instruction is sure,
    giving wisdom to the simple;
God's precepts are right, rejoicing the heart;
    God's commandment is pure
    giving light to the eyes;
God's fear is clean, enduring forever;
    God's judgements are true,
    every one of them righteous;
more desirable than gold, even much fine gold;
    sweeter also than honey,
    pure honey from the comb.   R

By them is your servant warned;
    for in keeping them there is great reward.
But who can discern unwitting sins?
    O cleanse me from my secret faults.
Keep your servant also from presumptuous sins,
lest they get the better of me.
    Then shall I be clean and innocent of great offence.   R

All   **Let the words of my mouth**
    and the thoughts of my heart
    be acceptable in your sight, O God,
    my strength and my redeemer.

Psalm 20

Refrain

Norman L. Warren 1972, alt.

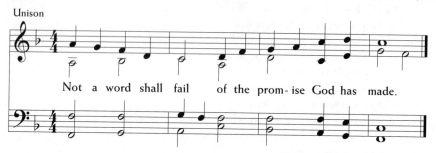

Not a word shall fail of the prom-ise God has made.

May God answer you in the day of trouble,
and the name of God defend you.
  May God send you help from the sanctuary,
  and give you support from the holy mountain.
May God remember all your offerings,
and accept your burnt sacrifices.
  May God grant you your heart's desire,
  and give success to all your plans.
May we rejoice in your victory
and triumph in the name of our God.
  May God fulfil your every wish.   R

Now I know, O God, that you help your anointed,
  and will answer from your holy heaven
  with the victorious might of your right hand.
Some put their trust in chariots,
and some in horses;
  but we will trust in the name of our God.
They will totter and fall;
  but we shall rise and stand upright.
God, save those who rule,
  and answer us when we call.   R

Psalm 22
God, Why Have You Forsaken Me

Unison

1 God, why have you for-sak-en me, and why are you so
2 Yet you are ho - ly, and the songs of praise of Is - rael
3 But I am mocked and put to scorn, all those who see me
4 A ref - uge you have been to me, my on - ly hope since

far a - way from my com-plaint and my dis - tress
are your throne; when our an - ces - tors called on you,
laugh and say, "You trust in God, so let us see
I was born; trou - ble is near me, none can help;

poured out be - fore you night and day?
you saved them, res - cued all your own.
the help of God to whom you pray."
my sav - iour, leave me not for - lorn.

Words: Christopher L. Webber 1986, alt.
Music: Sarum plainsong, 9th century; harm. Robert Hunter Bell
Words copyright © 1986 Christopher L. Webber. Arrangement copyright © 1971 Robert Hunter Bell.

CONDITOR ALME SIDERUM
8 8 8 8

Psalm 22

Refrain (for Part One)

Donatus Vervoort 1970

Music copyright © 1972 Donatus Vervoort

Part One (1–18)

My God, my God, why have you forsaken me?
> **Why are you so far from helping me,**
> **from the cry of my distress?**
O my God, I cry out in the daytime, but you do not answer;
> **at night also, but I get no relief.   R**

But you are the Holy One,
enthroned upon the praises of Israel.
> **In you our ancestors trusted;**
> **they trusted, and you delivered them.**
They called to you, and you rescued them.
> **In you they put their trust,**
> **and you did not disappoint them.**
But I am a worm, less than human,
> **an object of derision, an outcast of the people.**
All those who see me laugh me to scorn,
they curl their lips and toss their heads, saying:
> **"You trusted in God for deliverance.**
> **If God cares for you, let God rescue you!"**
But you are the One who took me out of the womb.
You kept me safe on my mother's breast.
> **On you have I depended from my birth.**
> **Even from my mother's womb, you have been my God.   R**

Do not be far from me, for trouble is close at hand,
> **and there is no one to help me.**
Many bulls encircle me, strong bulls of Bashan surround me.
> **They open wide their mouths at me,**
> **like a ravenous, roaring lion.**
My life pours out like water;
> **all my bones are out of joint;**

my heart has melted like wax within my breast;
>my mouth is parched as dry clay;
my tongue clings to my palate.
>I lie in the dust of death.
Dogs surround me;
>the wicked hem me in on every side.
They bind my hands and my feet;
>I can count all my bones,
>while they stand staring, gloating over me.
They divide my garments among themselves;
>they cast lots for my clothing.   R

Refrain (for Part Two)   *Brent Chambers 1977*

Part Two (19–22)

Do not stand far off from me, O God.
>You are my helper, come quickly to my rescue.
Deliver me from the sword,
my precious life from the mauling of dogs!
>Save me from the lion's mouth,
>my afflicted soul from the horns of the wild cattle.
Then I will declare your Name to my people.
>In the midst of the assembly I will praise you.   R

Refrain (Psalm 22)   *Brent Chambers 1977*

Part Three (23–28)

Give praise, all you who fear God!
Proclaim God's greatness, all you children of Jacob;
 stand in awe, all you children of Israel!
For God has neither despised
nor scorned the poor in their distress.
  You, O God, have not hidden your face from them.
  You heard them when they called to you.   R

You are the theme of my praise in the great assembly.
  I will keep my promise in the presence of those who fear you.
Let the poor eat to satisfaction;
let those who seek you praise you.
  May they be in good heart forever!
Let all the ends of the earth remember and turn to you, O God.
Let all the families of the nations bow down before you.
  For yours is the dominion, O God,
  you rule over the nations.   R

Part Four (29-31)

Even all who sleep in the grave shall worship you;
those who go down into the dust shall bow before you.
  I too shall live for you.
Our children shall serve you,
and tell generations yet to come about you.
  To a people yet unborn,
  they shall make known the saving deeds you have done.   R

Psalm 23
The Lord's My Shepherd

1 The Lord's my Shepherd, I'll not want;
2 My soul he doth restore again;
3 Yea, though I walk in death's dark vale,
4 My table thou hast furnished
5 Goodness and mercy all my life

he makes me down to lie in pastures green; he
and me to walk doth make within the paths of
yet will I fear no ill; for thou art with me;
in presence of my foes; my head thou dost with
shall surely follow me, and in God's house for

leadeth me, the quiet waters by.
righteousness, even for his own name's sake.
and thy rod and staff me comfort still.
oil anoint, and my cup overflows.
evermore my dwelling-place shall be.

Words: Scottish Psalter *1650*
Music: Jessie Seymour Irvine *1872*

CRIMOND
8 6 8 6

Psalm 23
God Is My Shepherd

1 God is my shep - herd, I'll not want, I
2 Re - stored to life each morn - ing new, I
3 When I must pass through shad - owed vale, where
4 No en - e - my can o - ver - come, no
5 Good - ness and mer - cy all my days will

feed in pas - tures green. God grants me rest and
rise up from the dust to fol - low God whose
loss and death a - wait, I will not fear for
power on earth de - feat the ones a - noint - ed
sure - ly fol - low me; and where God reigns in

bids me drink from wa - ters calm and clean. Through
pres - ence gives me con - fi - dence and trust. I
God is there, my shep - herd strong and great, whose
by God's grace and fed with man - na sweet. My
heaven and earth, my dwell - ing place will be. My

dai - ly tasks, I'm blessed and led by one I have not seen.
praise the name of God to - day; in God I put my trust.
rod and staff will com - fort me and all my fears a - bate.
cup is filled and o - ver - flows as I my Sav - iour greet.
shep - herd bless - es, cares, and leads through all e - ter - ni - ty.

Words: Scottish Psalter 1650; adapt. Lavon Bayler 1992
Music: James Leith Macbeth Bain 1915; harm. Gordon Jacob 1934; adapt. Walter W. Felton 1955
Words adaptations copyright © 1992 The Pilgrim Press. Harmony by permission of Oxford University Press.

BROTHER JAMES' AIR
8 6 8 6 8 6

Psalm 23

Refrain 1

Joseph Gelineau

Unison

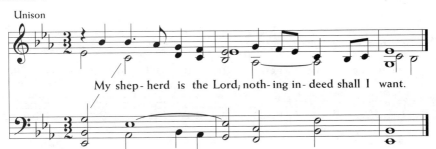

My shep-herd is the Lord; noth-ing in-deed shall I want.

Refrain 2

Charles Collignon

The God of love my shep-herd is; what can I want or need.

God is my shepherd,
>   **there is nothing I shall lack.**
You, God, make me lie down in green pastures,
>   **you lead me beside peaceful waters;**
you revive my spirit,
>   **you guide me in right pathways for your name's sake. R**

Though I walk through the valley of the shadow of death, you are with me,
>   **your rod and your staff are my comfort.**
You spread a table for me in the sight of my enemies;
>   **you anoint my head with oil; my cup is overflowing.**
Surely your goodness and mercy shall follow me all the days of my life,
>   **and I will dwell in God's house my whole life long. R**

Psalm 24
Lift Up the Gates Eternal

Refrain (Unison)

Lift up the gates e - ter - nal, lift up your voic - es:

for God in glo - ry comes, the na - tion re - joic - es.

1 See, all the earth is God's, its peo - ple and na - tions:
2 Who can go up this moun - tain, who stand in prais - ing?
◆ 3 They shall re - ceive for - give - ness, and have God's bless - ing
4 Come, lift your voic - es high, be lift - ed to glo - ry:
5 Who is this glo - rious one, for whom we are wait - ing?

God built it on the deeps and laid its foun - da - tions. (R)
Those who are pure, who come with clean hands up - rais - ing.
◆ if they will search for God, their sav - iour con - fess - ing. (R)
the sav - iour God ap - proach - es, come, shout the sto - ry.
We wait the might - y One, our God cel - e - brat - ing. (R)

Psalm 24

Andrew Mitchell Thomson
arr. F.R.C. Clarke 1971

Refrain

Lift up your heads, that God who rules in glo - ry en - ter may.

The earth is God's, and all that is in it;
the world, and those who live upon it.
> **For God founded it upon the seas,**
> **planted it firm over the waters beneath.   R**

Who may ascend the mountain of God?
Who may stand in God's holy place?
> **Those who have clean hands and a pure heart,**
> **who have not set their minds on deceit,**
> **nor made false promises;**

they shall receive God's blessing,
righteousness from the God who will save them.
> **Such are those who seek God,**
> **who seek the face of the God of Jacob.   R**

Lift up your heads, you gates!
> **Lift yourselves up, you everlasting doors,**
> **that the One who rules in glory may enter.**

Who rules in glory?
> **It is God, valiant and strong,**
> **God, who is mighty in battle.**

Lift up your heads, you gates!
> **Lift yourselves up, you everlasting doors,**
> **that the One who rules in glory may enter.**

Who rules in glory?
> **It is God of Hosts,**
> **God who rules in glory.   R**

Psalm 25

Refrain 1

Michel Guimont 1994

To you, O God, I lift my soul, to you I lift my soul.

Refrain 2

Marty Haugen

To you, O God, I lift my soul, to you I lift my soul.

To you, O God, I lift my soul; my God, in you I trust.
Let me not be put to shame, nor let my foes gloat over me.
> Let none who wait for you be shamed;
> let them be shamed who wantonly break faith.

Show me your ways; teach me your paths.
> Lead me in your truth and teach me;
> for you are God my saviour.
> For you I wait all the day long.   R

Remember your mercy, O God, and your steadfast love,
for they are as old as time.
> Do not remember the sins and offences of my youth.
> According to your steadfast love remember me,
> for your goodness' sake, O God!   R

You are upright and good, O God,
therefore you show the path to those who go astray.
> You guide the humble to do what is right,
> and teach the lowly your way.

All your ways are loving and sure
> for those who keep your covenant and commandments.   R

Psalm 27
Safe in Your Hands, O God, Who Made Me

1 Safe in your hands, O God, who made me,
what can there be that I should fear?
You are my light and my sal - va - tion, strong
is your help when foes are near.

2 This I have prayed and will seek af - ter,
that I may walk with you each day;
then will you come, shield me, give me your pro - tec - tion, no
trou - ble shall my heart dis - may.

3 God of my life, my help, my sav - iour,
fa - ther and moth - er now to me:
give me the light and my sal - va - tion, from
the threat of e - vil, lift up my soul and set me free!

4 Teach me your way and lead me on - wards,
save me from those who do me wrong;
give me the grace to wait with pa - tience, help
me to trust, hold firm, be strong.

Words: Michael Perry
Music: Christopher Norton

SAFE IN THE HANDS
9 8 9 8

Psalm 27

Refrain

Jeremiah Clarke

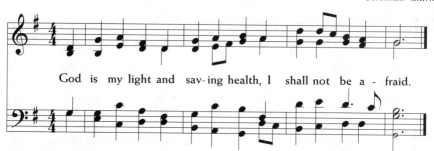

God is my light and sav-ing health, I shall not be a - fraid.

God is my light and my salvation, whom then shall I fear?
> **God is the stronghold of my life, of whom shall I be afraid?**
When the wicked close in to devour me,
> **it is they, my enemies and my foes, who stumble and fall.**
If an army should encamp against me,
my heart shall not be afraid;
> **if war should arise against me,**
> **even then I will not be dismayed. R**

One thing I have asked of God, for which I long:
that I may dwell in God's house all the days of my life,
> **to gaze on your beauty, O God,**
> **and to seek you in your temple.**
For in the time of trouble you will give me shelter;
> **you will hide me under the cover of your tent,**
> **you will set me high upon a rock.**
And now you have raised my head
above my enemies round about me.
> **Therefore I will offer in your dwelling**
> **a sacrifice with great gladness. R**

Hear my voice, O God, when I call; have mercy and answer me.
Your face, O God, I seek.
> **Do not hide your face from me;**
> **do not reject your servant in anger,**
> **you who have been my helper.**
Do not cast me off, or forsake me, O God my saviour.
> **Though my father and mother forsake me,**
> **my God will take me up. R**

Teach me your way, O God,
> **lead me on a level path, safe from those who lie in wait for me.**
Do not give me up to the will of my enemies,

(continued over)

for liars and false witnesses arise against me.
I believe that I shall see God's goodness
in the land of the living.

 Wait for God; be strong, and take courage;
 yes, wait for God!   R

Psalm 29
The God of Heaven

1 The God of heav-en thun-ders, whose voice in ca-dent
2 The des-ert writhes in tem-pest, wind whips the trees to
3 The might-y God e-ter-nal is to the throne as-

e-choes, re-sounds a-bove the wa-ters,
fu-ry, the light-ning splits the for-est,
cend-ed, and we who are God's peo-ple,

and all the world sings, "Glo-ry, glo-ry, glo-ry!"
and flame dif-fus-es Glo-ry, glo-ry, glo-ry!
with-in these walls cry, "Glo-ry, glo-ry, glo-ry!"

Words: Michael Perry 1973
Music: Norman L. Warren 1973
Words and music copyright © 1973 Hope Publishing Company.

GLORY
7 7 7 11

Psalm 29

Refrain

Winnagene Hatch 1994

Glo - ry, glo - ry, glo - ry to our God!

Ascribe to God, you powers of the heaven,
ascribe to God all glory and strength!
> **Ascribe due honour to God's holy name,**
> **and worship in the beauty of holiness.   R**

God's voice is over the waters —
God's glory thundering across the great waters.
> **God's voice is power,**
> **God's voice is full of majesty.**
God's voice shatters the cedars,
splinters the cedars of Lebanon.
> **God's voice makes Lebanon skip like a calf,**
> **Mount Hermon stampede like a wild young bull.**
God's voice forks into tongues of fire,
God's voice shakes the wilderness,
sets trembling the wilderness of Kadesh.
> **God's voice causes the oaks to whirl,**
> **stripping the forest bare;**
> **and in the temple all cry: Glory!   R**

God sits enthroned above the waters,
> **God is enthroned as sovereign forever.**
You give strength to your people, O God.
> **Now give to your people**
> **the blessing of peace.   R**

Psalm 30

Refrain

Norman L. Warren 1969

Though tears flow for a night, the morn-ing brings new joy.

I will extol you, O God, for you have lifted me up;
> you have not let my enemies triumph over me.

O God, my God, I cried to you for help,
and you restored my health.
> **You brought me back from the dead;**
> **you saved my life as I was going down to the Grave.**

Let all your servants sing praises to you,
and give thanks to your holy name.
> **Your anger is but for a moment,**
> **but your kindness is life eternal.   R**

In my prosperity I said,
> **"I shall never be shaken;**
> **your favour, O God,**
> **has made me as firm as any strong mountain."**

You turned your face away from me,
and I was greatly dismayed.
I called to you; I made my appeal:
> **"What profit is there in my death,**
> **in my going down to the Grave?**

Will the dust give you praise?
Will it proclaim your faithfulness?
> **Hear, O God, and be gracious to me;**
> **O God, be my helper."   R**

You turned my mourning into dancing;
> **you stripped off my sackcloth and clothed me with joy,**

so that my heart will sing your praise without ceasing.
> **O God, my God, I will give thanks to you forever.   R**

Psalm 31

Refrain

La Scala Santa, Ireland 1681
arr. Erik Routley 1985

I trust in you, you are my God.

Part One (1–5)

In you, O God, I have taken refuge; let me never be put to shame.
  Deliver me in your righteousness;
  incline your ear; come quickly to my rescue.   R

Be my rock of refuge, a stronghold to keep me safe.
  You are indeed my rock and fortress;
  lead me and guide me for your own name's sake.
Release me from the net that they hid for me, for you are my protector.
  Into your hands I commend my spirit,
  for you have redeemed me, O God of truth.   R

Part Two (9–14)

Have mercy on me, God, for I am in trouble;
my eyes are wasted with grief, my soul and my body also.
  My life is worn out with sorrow, and my years with sighing;
  my strength fails me in my misery, my bones are wasted away.
I am the scorn of my enemies, yes, even of my neighbours.
  My acquaintances shudder at the sight of me;
  when they see me in the street, they shrink away.
I have passed out of mind like one who is dead;
I have become like a broken vessel.
  I hear the whispering of many; fear is on every side,
  while they conspire against me, and plot to take my life.   R

Part Three (15–16)

My times are in your hands;
deliver me from the hands of my enemies, from those who pursue me.
  Let your face shine on your servant,
  and save me, for your mercy's sake.   R

Psalm 32

Refrain

Memmington ms., 17th century
Harm. George Ratcliffe Woodward 1904

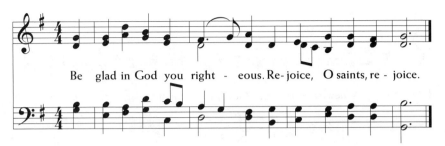

Be glad in God you right - eous. Re-joice, O saints, re - joice.

Blessed are those whose offences are forgiven,
whose sin has been put away.
> Blessed are those to whom God imputes no guilt,
> and in whose spirit there is no deceit.   R

When I kept silence, my body wasted away,
while I groaned all the day long.
> For your hand was heavy upon me day and night;
> my strength dried up as in a summer drought.
Then I acknowledged my sin to you,
my guilt I did not hide.
> I said: "I will confess my sins to God";
> and you forgave the guilt of my sin.
Therefore let all the faithful pray to you in time of trouble;
> when great floodwater rises,
> it shall not come near them.
You are a hiding place for me,
you will preserve me from trouble;
> you will surround me with shouts of deliverance.   R

I will teach you,
and guide you in the way you should go.
> I will keep you under my eye and instruct you.
Be not like a horse or mule, without understanding,
> whose course must be checked with bit and bridle.
Many pains are in store for the wicked,
> but whoever trusts in God,
> is surrounded by steadfast love.   R

Psalm 33

Refrain

Melody from A Collection of Hymns and Sacred Poems
Dublin 1749

A new song to our God pro-claim, from age to age re-joice!

Shout to God for joy, you righteous!
Praise is fitting from loyal hearts.
    Give thanks to God with the harp;
    sing praise to God with the ten-stringed lute.
Sing a new song to God;
play skillfully and with shouts of joy.
    For the word of God is true;
    God's every deed is faithful. R

You love what is right and just;
the earth is full of your constant love.
    By your word the heavens were made,
    the countless stars by the breath of your mouth.
You gathered the waters of the sea as in a goatskin;
    you stored the deep in cisterns.
Let all the earth fear you, O God,
    let all the inhabitants of the world stand in awe.
For you spoke and it came to be;
you commanded and it stood firm.
    You foil the plans of the nations,
    and frustrate the schemes of the peoples.
Your counsel, O God, shall stand forever,
the purposes of your heart through all generations.
    Happy the nation who has you as God.
    Happy the people you choose as your own.
Our heart rejoices in you, O God,
because our hope is in your holy name.
    Let your steadfast love be upon us
    as we put our trust in you. R

Psalm 34

Robert E. Kreutz

Refrain

Taste and see, taste and see the good-ness of our God.

I will bless God at all times,
God's praise will continually be in my mouth.
> **My soul will glory in God,**
> **the humble will hear and be glad.**

O magnify God with me,
let us exalt God's name together.
> **I sought God, who answered me,**
> **and freed me from all my fears.**

Look to the Most High, and let your light shine,
and your faces will not be ashamed.
> **This poor soul cried out and God heard,**
> **and saved me from all my troubles.   R**

Your angel, O God, keeps guard over those who fear you
and delivers them.
> **Taste and see that our God is good.**
> **Happy are those who take refuge in God.**

Fear God, you who are the saints,
for those who fear God lack nothing.
> **Strong lions suffer want and go hungry,**
> **but those who seek God lack no good thing.   R**

Come, my children, and listen to me,
I will teach you the fear of God.
> **Which of you delights in life,**
> **and desires many days to enjoy prosperity?**

Keep your tongue from evil, your lips from speaking lies.
Turn away from evil and do good, seek peace and pursue it.
> **God's eyes are upon the righteous,**
> **God's ears open to their cry.**

God's face is set against evil-doers,
to blot out their remembrance from the earth.
> **The righteous cry out and God hears them,**
> **and rescues them from all their troubles.   R**

(continued over)

God is near to the broken-hearted,
and saves those who are crushed in spirit.
  Many are the afflictions of the righteous,
  but God sets them free from every sorrow.
God guards every bone in their body;
not one of them will be broken.
  Evil brings death to the wicked;
  those who hate the righteous will be condemned.
But you, God, redeem the life of your servants;
  none who take refuge in you are condemned. R

Psalm 36

Refrain

Eleanor Daley 1994

Your stead-fast love, O God, ex-tends to the heavens.

Music copyright © 1994 Eleanor Daley

Your steadfast love, O God, extends to the heavens,
your faithfulness reaches to the clouds.
  Your righteousness is like the mountains, O God,
  your judgements are like the great deep;
  all living things you save. R

How precious is your steadfast love, O God!
All people may take refuge in the shadow of your wings.
  They feast on the abundance of your house,
  and you give them drink from the river of your delights. R

For with you is the fountain of life;
in your light do we see light.
  Continue your steadfast love to those who know you,
  and your salvation to the upright in heart. R

Psalm 37

New Harmony of Zion 1764

Refrain

Com- mit your way to God and trust the One who takes your part.

Do not fret because of the wicked, or envy those who do evil.
  For they soon wither like grass and fade away like the green leaf.
Trust in God and do good;
  dwell in the land and there find safe pasture.
Find your delight in God,
  who will grant the desires of your heart.   R

God will make your vindication shine like the light,
  the justice of your cause like the noonday sun.
Be still before God and wait patiently;
  do not fret because some prosper in evil schemes.
Let go of anger and abandon wrath.
  Do not fret — it can only do harm.   R

Those who do evil shall be cut off,
  but those who look to God shall inherit the earth.
In a little while the wicked will be no more;
  you will look where they were and their place will be empty.
But the meek shall inherit the earth;
  they shall enjoy fullness of peace.
Salvation for the righteous comes from God, their refuge in time of trouble.
  God helps and delivers,
  and rescues from the wicked those who seek shelter.   R

Psalm 40

Refrain

F. H. Barthélémon
adapt. Robert Simpson

You put a new song in my mouth, your name to glo - ri - fy.

I waited patiently for you, O God;
you bent down and heard my cry.
> **You lifted me out of the horrible pit,**
> **out of the miry clay,**
> **and set my feet upon a rock, making my steps secure.**
You put a new song in my mouth,
a song of praise to our God.
> **Many shall see and wonder,**
> **and will put their trust in you. R**

Blessed are those whose trust is in God,
> **who have not turned to the proud,**
> **nor to those who follow a lie.**
O God, my God, you have multiplied your wondrous deeds
> **and your thoughts toward us;**
> **none can compare with you!**
I would proclaim and tell of them,
> **but they are more than can be numbered.**
Sacrifice and offering you do not desire,
> **burnt offering and sacrifice for sin you have not required.**
But you have opened my ears to hear.
And I said: "Here I am,
ready to do what is written in the scroll of the book."
> **I delight to do your will, O my God,**
> **your law is in my heart. R**

I have told the glad news of deliverance in the great congregation;
I did not restrain my lips, as you well know.
> **I have not kept your goodness hidden in my heart,**
> **but have spoken of your faithfulness and your saving help.**
I have not concealed your steadfast love,
nor your truth from the great congregation.
> **Do not withhold from me your tender care, O God;**
> **may your love and truth ever preserve me. R**

Psalm 41

Refrain

Michel Guimont 1994

Heal me, O God, for I have sinned a - gainst you.

Blessed are those who consider the poor;
God will protect them in time of trouble.
> **God will protect them and keep them alive,**
> **so that they are counted happy in the land.**
God will never give them up to the will of their enemies.
> **God will comfort them on their sick-bed,**
> **and turn their illness into health.   R**

God, have mercy on me;
heal me, for I have sinned against you.
> **My enemies in malice say to me,**
> **"When will you die and your name perish?"**
If any come to see me, they speak insincerely;
their heart gathers mischief;
then they go out and spread it abroad.
> **All who hate me whisper together against me;**
> **they imagine about me the worst that can happen.**
They say that a deadly thing has fastened upon me;
that I will rise up no more from where I lie.
> **Even the friend I trusted, who ate bread at my table,**
> **has spun slander about me.   R**

God, have mercy upon me;
> **raise me up again, so that I may repay them.**
By this I shall know that you favour me,
in that my enemy shall not triumph over me.
> **Because of my integrity you uphold me;**
> **you have set me in your presence for ever.   R**

Psalm 42
As the Deer Pants for the Water

1 As the deer pants for the wa - ter, so my
2 I want you more than gold or sil - ver, on - ly
3 You're my friend and you are my bro - ther, e - ven

soul longs af - ter you; you a - lone are my
you can sa - tis - fy; you a - lone are the
though you are a king; I love you more than

heart's de - sire and I long to wor - ship you.
real joy - giv - er and the ap - ple of my eye.
a - ny o - ther, so much more than a - ny - thing!

You a - lone are my strength, my shield, to

Words: para. Martin Nystrom
Music: Martin Nystrom
Words and music copyright © 1983 Maranatha! Music.

AS THE DEER
8 7 8 7 with refrain

you a - lone may my spir - it yield; you a - lone are my

heart's de - sire, and I long to wor - ship you!

Psalm 42
As a Deer Seeks Flowing Waters

As a deer seeks flowing waters,
weary from the chase,
so my soul, O God, is thirsting
to behold your face.

> You command my steadfast love,
> in you my soul may quiet be;
> you, my rock, my help, my refuge,
> set my spirit free.

Day and night I cry, my heart is breaking,
tears my only food;
while my enemies jeer and taunt me saying:
"Where is now your God?"   R

Why am I so sad, so troubled; why must
suffering be so long?
I will hope in you, my God and saviour,
praise you with a song.   R

Psalm 42–43

Refrain 1

Hugh Wilson ca. 1800

Why rest- less, why cast down my soul? Hope still and you will sing!

Refrain 2

Eleanor Daley 1994

Unison

I will go to the al- tar of God, to God my ex- ceed- ing joy.

Like a deer that longs for life-giving waters,
so longs my soul for you, O God.
> **My soul thirsts for you, the source of my life.**
> **When shall I come and behold your face?**
Day and night I taste only tears,
while they steadily belittle me, saying, "Where is your God?"
> **But I remember — though my soul is distressed —**
> **how I went with the crowds to the house of God,**
our voices joyful and filled with praise,
a multitude keeping festival.   **R**

My soul is overwhelmed within me;
therefore I remember you in this land of Jordan,
in Hermon, and on Mount Mizar.
> **Like the turbulent roar of your waterfalls,**
> **all your waves and currents wash over me.**
With loving kindness you bless my days,
and by night your song is with me,
a prayer to you, Giver of life.
> **I say to God, my rock, "Why have you forgotten me?**
> **Why must I go like a mourner because my foes oppress me?"**
I am like one whose bones are broken to pieces
through the taunting of my enemies.
> **They steadily belittle me, saying, "Where is your God?"   R**

Vindicate me, O God, and plead my cause against faithless ones.
Save me from those who are deceitful and unjust.
> **You are the God in whom I take refuge. Why have you rejected me?**
> **Why must I go like a mourner because my foes oppress me?**
O send your light and your truth to lead me,
let them bring me to your holy hill and to your dwelling!
> **Then I will go to the altar of God, to God my exceeding joy.**
> **I will praise you with the harp, O God, my God.   R**

Psalm 45

Refrain   *Russian Orthodox Liturgy*

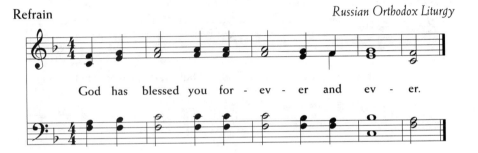

God has blessed you for - ev - er and ev - er.

My heart overflows with a noble theme;
I utter the song I have made for the king,
my tongue like the pen of a ready scribe.
> **You are the fairest, the most handsome;**
> **God endows your speech with grace;**
> **God has blessed you forever.   R**

Gird your sword on your thigh, O hero,
in splendour and majesty.
> **In your majesty ride on to conquer**
> **in the cause of truth and justice.**
Let your right hand teach by awesome deeds,
arrows sharp in the heart of royal enemies.
> **The nations shall fall at your feet.**
> **Your divine throne endures forever.**
Your royal sceptre is righteousness;
you love right and hate what is wrong.
> **Your God has anointed you**
> **with more oil of gladness than all your peers.**
All your garments are fragrant
with myrrh, aloes and cassia.
> **Out of the ivory palaces**
> **stringed music makes you glad.   R**

Psalm 46

Refrain 1 — Arthur S. Sullivan 1874

The God of Ja-cob is for us a ref-uge strong and sure.

Refrain 2 — *Martin Luther 1529; harm. The New Hymnal for American Youth, 1930*

A might-y for-tress is our God, a bul-wark nev-er fail-ing.

God is our refuge and strength,
   a very present help in trouble.
Therefore we will not fear though the earth should quake,
and the mountains fall into the depths of the sea,
   though the waters of the sea rage and foam,
   and the mountains tremble at the tumult.   R

There is a river, whose streams make glad the city of God,
sanctifying the dwelling of the Most High.
   God is in the midst of the city; it shall not be moved.
   God will help at the break of day.
Nations are in tumult, empires are shaken;
   for God speaks and the earth melts away.   R

Come and see what God has done,
the wonders wrought upon the earth.
   God makes wars to cease in all the world,
   God breaks the bow and snaps the spear,
   and burns the shields in the fire.
Be still and know that I am God,
   exalted among the nations, exalted in the earth.
The God of Hosts is with us;
   the God of Jacob is our refuge.   R

Psalm 47

Refrain 1

Eleanor Daley 1994

Hal - le - lu - jah! God has gone up with a shout!

Refrain 2

Robert Williams 1817

Praise to God who reigns a - bove! Hal - le - lu - jah!

Clap your hands, all you peoples,
cry out to God with shouts of joy!
> **For the Most High is to be feared,**
> **reigning in might, over all the earth. R**

God has subdued the peoples around us,
set nations at our feet,
> **and has chosen for us a heritage,**
> **the pride of Jacob, beloved of God.**

God has gone up with shouts of triumph,
> **has gone up with a fanfare of trumpets.**

For God reigns over all the earth!
> **Sing praises with your utmost skill. R**

God reigns over all the nations,
and sits in holiness enthroned.
> **The nobles of the nations assemble**
> **with the people of the Everlasting God.**

For earth's defenders belong to God,
> **to God the highly exalted. R**

Psalm 48

Refrain *Franz Joseph Haydn 1796*

Glo - rious things of you are spo - ken,
Zi - on, cit - y of our God.

Great is God,
and greatly to be praised
in the city of our God.
    Fair and lofty is God's holy mountain;
    it is the joy of all the earth.
On Mount Zion, in the far north,
stands the city of the Great Ruler;
    in its citadels God is known as a sure defence. R

See how the rulers assembled;
they raged together against it.
    But when they saw it, they were astounded;
    they were dismayed and ready to flee.
Trembling came upon them,
as anguish comes to a woman in childbirth;
    as when the east wind blows
    and breaks up the ships of Tarshish.
As we have heard, so have we seen,
    in the city of the God of hosts,
    the city our God upholds forever. R

We remember your steadfast love, O God,
as we gather in your temple.
> **Your name, like your praise,**
> **reaches to the ends of the earth.**

Your right hand is filled with victory.
> **Let Mount Zion rejoice,**
> **and the children of Judah be glad**
> **because of your judgements.**

Go in procession around the circuit of Zion,
count the number of its towers,
> **take note of its ramparts,**
> **examine its citadel,**

so that you may tell the next generation:
> **"Such is our God, our guide for ever." R**

Last time   *Franz Joseph Haydn 1796*

Glo - rious things of you are spo - ken,
Zi - on, cit - y of our God;

Psalm 49

Refrain

Hal H. Hopson 1986

God is our ref - uge: God is our strength.

Hear this, all you people!
Give ear, all who inhabit the world,
> you of both low and high estate,
> rich and poor together.

My mouth shall speak words of wisdom;
the thoughts of my heart are full of understanding.
> I will turn my mind to a proverb,
> and with harp and song declare its meaning. **R**

Why should I fear when the days are evil,
when the wicked stalk my steps and harass me?
> They are people who trust in their wealth,
> and boast of their abundant riches.
> We see that the wise die as well as the foolish and stupid;
> they perish, leaving their wealth to others.

But wealth cannot redeem anyone,
or pay God the value of a person's own life.
The tomb is their final home, their dwelling-place for ever,
though once they called estates by their own names.
> Like sheep, they head for the Tomb
> with Death as their shepherd.

But God will ransom my life;
> from the power of the Grave. God will save me. **R**

Psalm 50

Eleanor Daley 1994

Refrain

The might - y one, God the Sov - ereign,

speaks and sum - mons the earth.

God, the Almighty, has spoken;
    and summoned the world
    from the rising of the sun to its setting.
God shines out from Zion, a city perfect in beauty.
    Our God appears, and will not keep silence. R

Before you, God, runs a consuming fire,
and a mighty tempest rages about you.
    You call on the heavens above, and on the earth below,
    to witness the judgement of your people:
"Gather my people before me,
the people who made covenant with me by sacrifice."
    The heavens proclaim your justice, for you yourself are judge. R

Psalm 51

Refrain 1

Joseph Parry 1879

God, I call to you for help; in your mer-cy hear my prayer.

Refrain 2

Mount Angel Abbey 1976

In the a-bun-dance of your com-pas-sion, wash my sins a-way.

Music copyright © Benedictine Fathers, Mount Angel Abbey

Have mercy on me, O God, in your great kindness,
    in the fullness of your mercy blot out my offences.
Wash away all my guilt, and cleanse me from my sin.
    For I acknowledge my faults, and my sin is always before me. R

Against you, you only, have I sinned, and done evil in your sight,
    so that you are justified in your sentence,
    and blameless in your judgement.
Guilty I have been from my birth,
a sinner from the time of my conception.
    But you desire truth in our inward being,
    therefore teach me wisdom in my secret heart.
Purge me with hyssop and I shall be clean,
    wash me and I shall be whiter than snow.
Let me hear the sounds of joy and gladness,
    let the bones that you have crushed rejoice.
Turn away your face from my sins,
    and blot out all my iniquities. R

Put a new heart in me, O God,
    and give me again a constant spirit.
Do not cast me away from your presence,
    do not take your holy spirit from me.

Restore to me the joy of your salvation,
and strengthen me with a willing spirit.
>Then I will teach transgressors your ways,
>and sinners will return to you.
O God, open my lips,
>and my mouth shall proclaim your praise.   R

You desire no sacrifice, or I would give it;
>you take no delight in burnt offerings.
The sacrifice you accept, O God, is a broken spirit;
>a broken and contrite heart, O God, you will not despise.   R

Psalm 52

Refrain

Aubrey L. Butler 1971

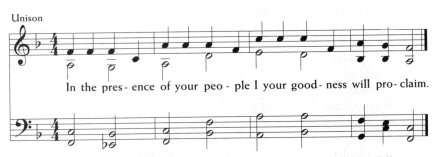

In the pres-ence of your peo-ple I your good-ness will pro-claim.

Music copyright © 1971 Broadman Press. Used by permission

Why do you boast of your evil, O brave one,
in the face of God's faithfulness?
Your tongue is like a sharpened razor, meant to cut deceitfully.
>You prefer evil to good, the lie to speaking truthfully.
>You love all words that hurt, and every deceit of the tongue!
So God will break you down forever;
>break you and tear you from your dwelling,
>root you out of the land of the living.
The righteous, looking on, will be awestruck.
Then they will laugh and say:
>here was one who did not look to God for strength,
>but trusted in great wealth and found strength in slander.   R

I am like a thriving olive tree in God's house;
>I will trust in the faithfulness of God forever.
I will praise you forever, for this was your doing;
>in the presence of the faithful I will glorify your name,
>for it is good to praise you.   R

Psalm 54

Frizzona's Canzuns Spirituaelas *1765*

Refrain

By your name, O God, now save me.

Save me, O God, by the power of your name,
and vindicate me by your might.
    Hear my prayer, O God,
    and listen to the words of my mouth.
For insolent people have risen against me,
    ruthless ones are seeking my life;
    they give no thought to God. R

But see, God is my helper;
    it is God who upholds my life.
You will repay my enemies for their evil,
    in your faithfulness, put an end to them.
The offering of a willing heart I will give you,
and praise your name, O God, in your faithfulness.
    For you have delivered me from every trouble,
    and my eye has looked in triumph on my enemies. R

Psalm 62

Refrain

Robert Batastini

Rest in God a - lone; rest in God a - lone, my soul, my soul.

How long will all of you set upon me and batter me,
as though I were a tottering wall or a leaning fence?
> **Their purpose is to thrust me down from my eminence;**
> **they delight in lies;**
> **they bless with their lips but curse me in their hearts.**
Yet be still, my soul, and wait for God,
> **from whom comes my hope of deliverance.   R**

In God is my deliverance and my honour,
the rock of my strength and my place of refuge.
> **Put your trust in God always, you people;**
> **pour out your hearts before the One who is our refuge.   R**

For we mortals are only a puff of wind;
the great among us are but illusion;
> **placed in the balance,**
> **we weigh less than a breath.**
Put no trust in extortion, set no vain hopes on plunder;
> **if riches increase, do not set your heart upon them.**
Once God has spoken, and twice have I heard it said:
"Power belongs to you, O God. Steadfast love is yours."
> **You reward us all according to our deeds.   R**

Psalm 62
My Soul Finds Rest in God Alone

1 My soul finds rest in God a-lone, on whom my help de-pends,
2 Find rest, my soul, in God a-lone, on whom my hope de-pends,
3 The great of earth are less than dust; all mor-tal strength is vain.

who is my fort-ress and my rock, who sure sal-va-tion sends.
who is my fort-ress and my rock, who sure sal-va-tion sends.
And fools a-lone re-ly on wealth or prize ill-got-ten gain.

My foes con-spire to bring me down; they scorn my trou-bled state.
My aid and hon-our come from God, my ref-uge strong and sure.
I know, O God, that you are strong, and strong your lov-ing Word.

Their lips are quick to sound my praise, but in their hearts they hate.
Now, all you peo-ple, trust in God; in whom we are se-cure.
Our ev-ery deed for good or ill, you sure-ly will re-ward.

Words: David J. Diephouse 1986, alt.
Music: Walker's Southern Harmony 1835; harm. Erik Routley 1976
Words copyright © 1987 CRC Publications. Music copyright © 1976 Hinshaw Music, Inc.

RESIGNATION
8 6 8 6 D
Alt. tune: Halifax

Psalm 63

Refrain 1

David Goodrich 1983

In the morn-ing I will sing glad songs of praise to you.

Refrain 2

Michel Guimont 1985

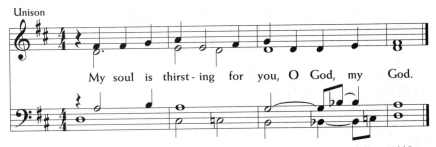

My soul is thirst-ing for you, O God, my God.

You are my God, I long for you from early morning.
My whole being desires you like a dry, worn, waterless land.
My soul thirsts for you.
> **In the sanctuary let me see how mighty are your works;**
> **your constant love is better than life itself,**
> **and so I will praise you.   R**

I will give thanks as long as I live;
I raise my hands in prayer.
> **My soul will feast and be filled,**
> **and I will sing and praise you.   R**

As I lie in bed, I remember you, O God;
I think of you all night long,
for you are my constant help.
> **In the shadow of your wings I sing for joy.**
> **I cling to you; your hand keeps me safe.   R**

Psalm 65

Refrain

Eleanor Daley 1994

Praise is due to you, O God, in Zi - on.

Praise is due to you, O God, in Zion;
to you shall vows be performed.
    You give heed to prayer; to you all mortals shall come.
The burden of our sins is too great for us,
    but you will purge them away. R

Blessed are the people you choose
and bring to dwell in your courts.
    We shall be filled with the blessings of your house, your holy temple.
With awesome deeds you answer our prayers for deliverance,
O God our saviour —
    **you that are the hope of all the ends of the earth
    and of the far-off seas.**
By your strength you make fast the mountains,
    and gird yourself round with power.
You still the raging of the seas,
    and the roaring of the waves, the tumult of the peoples.
Those who dwell at earth's farthest bounds are awed by your wonders;
    the gateways of both morning and evening shout for joy. R

You visit the earth and water it,
    you make it very fruitful.
The waters of heaven brim over their banks,
    providing us with grain, for so you have prepared the land,
drenching its furrows, settling its ridges,
    softening it with showers, and blessing its growth.
You crown the year with goodness,
    and your paths overflow with plenty.
The pastures of the wilderness abound with grass,
    and the hills are girded with joy.
The fields are clothed with sheep;
    **the valleys are decked with wheat,
    so that they shout and sing for joy. R**

Psalm 65
To Bless the Earth

1 To bless the earth God sends us from
heaven's a - bun - dant store the wa - ters of the
spring - time, en - rich - ing it once more.

2 The seed by God pro - vid - ed is
sown o'er hill and plain, and then come gen - tle
show - ers to bless the spring - ing grain.

3 God crowns the year with good - ness, the
earth God's mer - cy fills, the wil - der - ness is
fruit - ful, and joy - ful are the hills.

4 With grain the fields are cov - ered, the
flocks in pas - tures graze; all na - ture joins in
sing - ing a joy - ful song of praise.

Words: *The Psalter 1912, alt.*
Music: *Melchior Vulpius 1609*

CHRISTUS, DER IST MEIN LEBEN
7 6 7 6

Psalm 66

Refrain 1

East Indian hymn, adapt. Jeeva Sam 1992

God, our God, how glo-ri-ous is your name o'er all the earth.

Refrain 2

Konrad Kocher 1838

God of all, to you we raise this our song of joy-ful praise.

Part One (1–7)

Make a joyful noise to God, all the earth;
 sing to the honour of God's name;
 make glorious the praise of God.
How awesome are your deeds!
So great is your strength, your foes wilt before you.
 For all the world shall worship you,
 shall sing to you and praise your name. R

O come and see what God has done,
a work that is awesome to all earth's children.
 God turned the sea into dry land;
 they crossed the river on foot.
There we rejoiced in God,
who rules in power forever,
 whose eyes keep watch on the nations.
 Let not the rebellious lift up their heads. R

Part Two (8–12)

Bless our God, all peoples,
and let the sound of praise be heard.
> **God has preserved us among the living,**
> **and kept our feet from stumbling.**
For you, O God, have tested us;
you have tried us as silver is tried.
> **You led us into the desert,**
> **you laid a burden upon our back,**
you let sickness furrow our brow,
we passed through fire and water;
> **but you brought us out to a land of plenty. R**

Part Three (13–20)

I will come to your house with burnt-offerings;
I will pay you my vows,
> **the vows which I made with my lips,**
> **and swore with my mouth when I was in trouble.**
I will offer fat beasts in sacrifice,
a savoury offering of rams;
> **I will prepare you an offering of bulls and goats. R**

Come then and listen, all you that fear God,
while I tell what God has done for me.
> **I cried aloud to God;**
> **high praise was ready on my tongue.**
If I had cherished evil in my heart,
God would not have heard me.
> **But truly God has heard me,**
> **has given heed to the voice of my prayer.**
Blessed are you, O God,
for you have not rejected my prayer,
> **nor withdrawn from me your steadfast love. R**

Psalm 67

Henry Thomas Smart 1867

Refrain

Let the peo-ples praise you, God, let the na-tions shout their joy.

Be gracious unto us, O God, and bless us;
and let the light of your face shine upon us,
   that your ways may be known upon earth,
   your saving power among all nations.
Let the nations be glad, and sing for joy,
   for you judge the peoples righteously
   and guide the nations of the earth.
The earth has yielded its harvest,
and you, our God, have blessed us.
   Your blessing, O God, be upon us.
   May all the ends of the earth revere you. R

Psalm 68

Refrain

Rory Cooney 1991

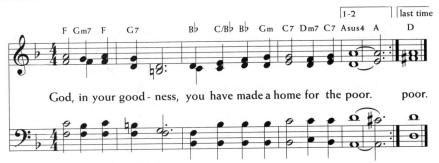

God, in your good-ness, you have made a home for the poor.   poor.

Arise, O God, and let your enemies be scattered;
let those who hate you flee before you.
> Like drifting smoke disperse them;
> like wax melting in the fire,
> let the wicked perish at your presence, **O God.**
But let the righteous be glad and exult before you;
let them rejoice with exceeding joy.
> Sing praises to God's holy name;
> make a highway for the One who rides the clouds;
> be joyful and exult in God's presence. **R**

Guardian of orphans, protector of widows,
O God, in your holy dwelling,
> you give the lonely a home in which to live;
> you lead the prisoners out to prosperity;
> but the rebels must live in a wasteland.
When you went out at the head of your people,
when you marched through the wilderness,
> the earth quaked, the heavens poured down rain
> before you, God of Sinai, God of Israel.
You sent down a generous rain;
you refreshed your heritage when it languished.
> There your people found a home,
> which in your goodness you provided for the poor. **R**

Sing to God, dominions of the earth;
praise the One who has dominion,
> the One who rides through the heavens, even the primal heavens,
> the One whose voice is the mighty thunder.
Acknowledge the power that is God's,
whose majesty is over Israel, whose strength is in the skies.
> You are awesome, **O God**, as you leave your sanctuary,
> bringing power and strength to your people.
Blessed are you, God of Israel.
> Blessed are you. **R**

Psalm 70

Refrain 1

Walker's Southern Harmony 1835
harm. Erik Routley 1982

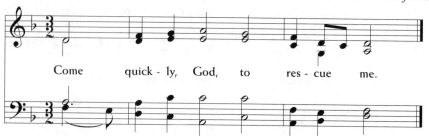

Come quick - ly, God, to res - cue me.

Refrain 2

Elaine Kirkland 1994

Has - ten to help me, O God.

O favour me, God, and save me.
Make haste, O God, and help me! R

Let those who seek my life be put to shame and confusion.
Let those who desire to hurt me collapse in dishonour.
**Let those who mock my humiliation
stumble at their own disgrace.**
But let all who seek you rejoice and be glad in you.
**Let those who long for your saving help
be ever ready to say, "God is great!" R**

As for me, I am poor and needy.
O God, come quickly to my aid!
**You are my help and my deliverer.
O God, do not delay! R**

Psalm 71

Refrain

Martin Luther 1529
harm. The New Hymnal for American Youth *1930*

A might-y for-tress is our God, a bul-wark nev-er fail - ing.

Part One (1–6)

In you, O God, I seek refuge;
may I never be disappointed.

> **In your righteousness, save and rescue me;**
> **incline your ear and deliver me.**

Be a sheltering rock for me,
a fortress where I may find safety;

> **for you are my rock and my stronghold.**

Rescue me, O God, from the hand of the wicked,
from the grasp of the unjust and cruel.

> **For you are my hope, my trust from my youth;**
> **from the time of my birth I have leaned on you. R**

Part Two (7–14)

I have become an example for many,
but you are my strength and my refuge.

> **Your praise will fill my mouth;**
> **I will sing of your glory all the day long.**

Do not cast me off in old age
or forsake me when my strength is spent;

> **for my enemies talk against me;**
> **those who lie in wait for me conspire.**

They are sure that you have forsaken me,

> **that they may pursue and lay hold of me**
> **as if there were none to deliver. R.**

O God, be not far from me;
my God, hasten to help me!

> **Let my accusers be put to shame and confusion;**
> **let those who seek my ruin**
> **be covered in scorn and disgrace.**

As for me, I will always hope;

> **I will praise your name again and again. R**

Psalm 72

Refrain   *Johann Crüger 1640*

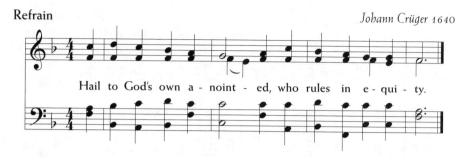

Hail to God's own a-noint-ed, who rules in e-qui-ty.

Part One (1–8)

Give the ruler your justice, O God,
and your righteousness to the royal heir,
> **for judging your people rightly,**
> **and upholding the poor with justice;**
that the mountains may bring forth peace for the people,
> **and the hills, prosperity with justice. R**

May your anointed defend the cause of the poor among the people,
save the children of the needy, and crush the oppressor.
> **May your anointed live as long as the sun endures,**
> **as long as the moon from age to age.**
May your anointed be like rain falling upon the grass,
like showers that water the earth;
> **may your anointed be one in whose days justice shall flourish**
> **and peace abound till the moon is no more. R**

Part Two (10–14)

May the rulers of Tarshish and the isles pay tribute,
the monarchs of Sheba and Seba bring gifts.
> **May all rulers do homage,**
> **and all nations render service.**
For your anointed shall deliver the needy when they cry,
the poor and those who have no helper.
> **Your anointed shall have pity on the weak and the needy,**
> **and save the lives of the poor.**
From oppression and violence your anointed shall redeem their life,
> **and count as precious their blood. R**

Part Three (18–19)

Blessed are you, O God, the God of Israel,
who alone does marvellous things.
> **Blessed is your glorious name for ever.**
> **May the whole earth be filled with your glory. R**

Psalm 77

Jeffrey Honoré ca. 1994

Refrain

Unison

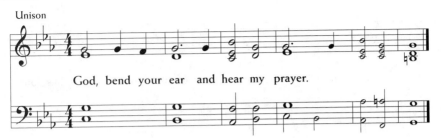

God, bend your ear and hear my prayer.

I cry aloud to God,
I cry that God may hear me.
> **In my time of distress I have turned to God;**
> **with hands uplifted I have prayed all night,**
> **but my soul refuses all comfort. R**

Then I recall your deeds, O God!
I remember your wonders of old.
I recount all your works and ponder the things you have done.
> **O God, your ways are holy.**
> **What god is as great as you!**
You are the one who works wonders;
you have shown your strength among nations.
> **By your arm you redeemed your people,**
> **the children of Jacob and Joseph. R**

The waters saw you, O God, the waters saw you and churned in fear;
> **the seas trembled to their depths.**
Clouds streamed water, the heavens rumbled;
> **your arrows bolted on every side.**
The voice of your thunder was heard in the whirlwind;
> **lightning lit up the world, the earth quaked and shuddered.**
Your way was through the sea;
> **your path, through mighty waters;**
your footprints could not be seen;
> **but by the hand of Moses and Aaron,**
> **you led your people like a flock. R**

Psalm 78

Refrain

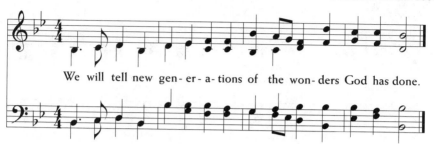

Joachim Neander 1680

We will tell new gen-er-a-tions of the won-ders God has done.

Part One (1–7)

Give heed to my teaching, O my people,
turn your ears to the words of my mouth.
> **I will open my mouth in a parable;**
> **I will reveal the hidden meaning of things in the past.**
What we have heard and known,
what our parents have told us,
we will not hide from their grandchildren,
> **but declare to the next generation**
> **the testimony that you gave to Jacob**
> **and the law you appointed in Israel,**
> **which you commanded them to teach their children,**
that the next generation might know them, children yet unborn,
and these in turn should arise, and tell their children,
> **that they should put their trust in you,**
> **and not forget your great deeds,**
> **but keep all your commandments. R**

Part Two (12–16)

Marvellous things you did in the sight of our ancestors,
in the land of Egypt, in the plain of Zoan.
> **You divided the sea and let them go through,**
> **and made the waters stand up like a wall.**
By day you led with a cloud,
and all the night long with a beacon of fire.
> **You split rocks in the wilderness,**
> **and gave drink in plenty as from the great deep.**
You brought streams out of the rock,
> **and made water run down like rivers. R**

Psalm 79

Refrain

Geistliche Volkslieder *1850*
harm. Paul Bunjes 1982

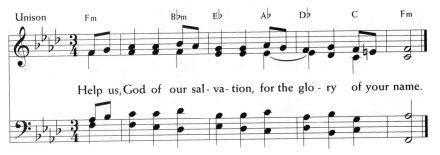

Help us, God of our sal-va-tion, for the glo-ry of your name.

O God, the nations have entered your domain,
defiled your holy temple and laid Jerusalem in ruins.
>They have left your servants' bodies for scavenging birds,
>the flesh of your faithful ones for wild beasts.
>Their blood was shed like water around Jerusalem,
>with none to bury them.
We have become the taunt of our neighbours,
mocked and scorned by those around us.
>How long, O God? Will you be angry forever?
>Will your jealous wrath burn like fire?   R

Pour out your rage on the nations that do not acknowledge you,
on the realms that will not call on your name;
>for they have devoured Jacob and desolated Israel's home.
Do not hold the sins of past generations against us;
>let your compassion come swiftly to meet us,
>for we are sunk very low.
Help us, O God our Saviour, for the glory of your name.
>Deliver us and forgive our sin, for the honour of your name.   R

Psalm 80

Refrain

John Wainright 1750, alt.

Your face, God, shine on us and give us peace.

Part One (1–7, 18–19)

Shepherd of Israel, hear us,
    you who lead Joseph like a flock,
    you who are enthroned amidst the cherubim.
Shine forth before Ephraim, Benjamin and Manasseh;
    stir up your might, come and save us. R

God of hosts, how long will you be angry with your people's prayer?
    You have fed us with the bread of weeping,
    and given us tears in plenty to drink.
You have made a mockery of us to our neighbours,
    and our enemies laugh us to scorn.
Let your hand rest on the one at your right hand,
on the one you have made strong for yourself.
    Then we will never forsake you;
    give us life, and we will call on your name. R

Part Two (1–2, 8–19)

Shepherd of Israel, hear us,
    you who lead Joseph like a flock,
    you who are enthroned amidst the cherubim.
Shine forth before Ephraim, Benjamin and Manasseh;
    stir up your might, come and save us. R

You brought a vine out of Egypt,
you drove out the nations and planted it.
    You cleared the ground for it;
    it sank deep roots, and filled the land.

The mountains were covered with its shade,
the mighty cedars with its branches.
>It stretched out its branches as far as the Sea,
>and its shoots as far as the River.
Why then have you broken down its enclosure,
so that all who go by pluck its grapes?
>The boar from the forest roots it up,
>and the beasts of the field devour it. R

Turn to us again, God of hosts,
look down from heaven and see.
>Bestow your care on this vine,
>on the stock which your right hand planted.
As for those who set it on fire, who cut it down,
may they perish at the frown of your face.
>Let your hand rest on the one by your side,
>on the one you have made strong for yourself.
Then we will never forsake you;
>give us life, and we will call on your name. R

Psalm 81

Refrain 1

Paschal Edward Jordan

Sing out with joy to God our strength.

Refrain 2

Michel Guimont 1990

Sing with joy to God!   Sing to God our help!

Part One (1–10)

Sing out with joy to God our strength,
  shout in triumph to the God of Jacob.
Raise a song, sound the tambourine,
the tuneful lyre with the harp.
  Blow the trumpet at the new moon,
  at the full moon on our festival.
For this is a statute for Israel,
a law of the God of Jacob,
  who made it a decree in Joseph,
  when they left the land of Egypt. R

I hear a voice I have not known:
  "I eased your shoulders from the burden,
  and your hands were freed from the load.
In trouble you called to me,
and I saved you;
  I answered you from the secret place of thunder,
  I put you to the test at the waters of Meribah.

Hear, O my people, while I admonish you.
O Israel, if only you would listen to me!
> **There shall be no strange god among you,**
> **nor shall you worship an alien god.**
It is I who am God,
who brought you out of the land of Egypt.
> **Open wide your mouth, and I will fill it. R**

Part Two (10 –16)

"It is I who am God,
who brought you out of the land of Egypt.
> **Open wide your mouth, and I will fill it.**
But my people would not hear my voice,
Israel would not obey me.
> **So I left them in their stubbornness of heart**
> **to follow their own devices.**
O that my people would listen to me,
that Israel would follow my paths.
> **I would soon put down their enemies,**
> **and turn a hand against their foes.**
Those who hate me would cringe before me,
their fate would be sealed forever.
> **But you I would feed with the finest of wheat,**
> **you I would satisfy with honey from the rock." R**

Psalm 81
Sing a Psalm of Joy

1 Sing a psalm of joy! Shout in cel - e - bra - tion.
2 Sound the fes - tal horn, your thanks - giv - ing voic - ing.
♦ 3 When in need you cried, I was near and saved you.
4 O my peo - ple, hear; when I call you, lis - ten.
5 I, your car - ing God, brought you out of E - gypt.

Let the tam - bou - rine and the trum - pet sound
Praise our Sav - iour God, at whose great com - mand
♦ From the cloud I spoke, an - swered your re - quest,
Choose no for - eign god, lis - ten to my plea.
I re - moved your yoke, all your needs sup - plied.

prais - es all a - round for God's great sal - va - tion.
out of E - gypt's land you came forth re - joic - ing.
♦ Mer - i - bah the test, I did not for - sake you.
Have no god but me; come and be for - giv - en.
O - pen your mouth wide: sure - ly I will fill it.

6 Oh, that Israel
would but hear my pleading!
Oh, that they would turn,
walk upon my path;
I would pour my wrath
on their foes unheeding.

7 With the finest wheat
I, your God, would feed you.
Honey from the rock
I would gladly give
that you all might live.
Hear me, O my people.

Words: Marie J. Post, 1984, alt.
Music: Genevan Psalter 1562; harm. Dale Grotenhuis 1985
Words and harmony copyright © 1987 CRC Publications.

GENEVAN 81
565556

Psalm 82

Ancient Irish hymn melody
arr. Charles Villiers Stanford 1902

Refrain

Sal - va - tion is from God, our God.

God stands in the council of heaven,
in the midst of the gods gives judgement:
**"How long will you judge unjustly,
and favour the cause of the wicked?"**
Give justice to the weak and the orphan,
maintain the right of the lowly and destitute.
**Rescue the weak and the needy,
save them from the hands of the wicked. R**

You neither know nor understand;
**you go about in darkness;
all the foundations of the earth are shaken.**
I say then to you: "Gods you all may be,
and offspring of the Most High;
**but you shall die like mortals,
and fall like any of the mighty."**
Rise up, O God, and judge the earth,
and take all the nations as your possession! R

Psalm 84

Refrain

adapt. from Johann Michael Haydn 1806

How love - ly is your dwell - ing place,
O God of hosts, to me!

How lovely is your dwelling place, God of hosts!
My soul longs, even faints for the courts of God;
my heart and my flesh cry for joy to the living God.
Even the sparrow finds a house,
and the swallow a nest where she may lay her young,
at your altars, God of hosts, my sovereign, my God. R

Happy are those who dwell in your house,
ever singing your praise.
Happy are those whose strength is in you,
who have set their heart on pilgrimage.
Going through the valley of Baca
they find a spring from which also to drink;
the early rain also covers it with pools of water.
They go from strength to strength,
to appear before God in Zion. R

O God of hosts, hear my prayer;
give ear, O God of Jacob.
Behold, O God, our shield, look on the face of your anointed.
Truly a day in your courts is better than a thousand elsewhere.
I would rather be a doorkeeper in the house of my God
than dwell in the tents of wickedness.
For you, God, are a sun and shield,
you will give grace and honour.
No good thing will you withhold
from those who live the upright life.
O God of hosts,
happy are those who put their trust in you. R

Psalm 84
How Lovely, God

Unison

1 How love - ly, God, how love - ly is your a - bid - ing place;
2 In your blest courts to wor - ship, O God, a sin - gle day
3 A sun and shield for - ev - er are you, O God Most High;

my soul is long - ing, faint - ing, to feast up - on your grace.
is bet - ter than a thou - sand if I from you should stray.
you show - er us with bless - ings; no good will you de - ny.

The spar - row finds a shel - ter, a place to build her nest;
I'd rath - er keep the en - trance and claim you as my Lord,
The saints, your grace re - ceiv - ing, from strength to strength shall go,

and so your tem - ple calls us with - in its walls to rest.
than rev - el in the rich - es the ways of sin af - ford.
and from their life shall riv - ers of bless - ing o - ver - flow.

Words: Arlo D. Duba 1984
Music: Hal H. Hopson 1983
Words copyright © 1986 and music copyright © 1983 Hope Publishing Company

MERLE'S TUNE
7 6 7 6 D

Psalm 85

Hal H. Hopson 1988

Refrain

God, show us your love, show us your love and mer - cy.

Once you were gracious to your land, O God,
you restored the fortunes of Jacob;
> **you forgave the offence of your people,**
> **and pardoned all their sin.**
You drew back all your displeasure,
and turned from your fiery wrath.
> **Restore us again, God our Saviour,**
> **and put away your just anger toward us.**
Will you be angry with us forever?
Will you prolong your wrath to all generations?
> **Will you not revive us again,**
> **that your people may rejoice in you? R**

Let me hear what you will say, O God,
for you will speak peace to your people,
to the faithful who turn their hearts to you.
> **Surely salvation is near those who fear you,**
> **and your glory will dwell in our land.**
Mercy and faithfulness will meet,
justice and peace will embrace.
> **Faithfulness will spring up from the earth,**
> **and righteousness look down from heaven.**
You, O God, will give what is good,
and our land will yield its harvest.
> **Righteousness will go before you,**
> **and the paths of your feet will be peace. R**

Psalm 86

Refrain

Jeeva Sam 1994; harm. Lydia Pedersen 1995

In the day of my trou-ble I call un-to you for you will an-swer me.

Turn your ear to me, O God, and answer me,
for I am poor and in misery.
>**Preserve my life for I am faithful;**
>**save your servant for I trust in you.**
Be merciful to me, my lord,
for I call to you all day long.
>**Gladden the heart of your servant,**
>**for to you I lift up my soul.**
For you, my lord, are good and forgiving,
and great in mercy to all who call on you.
>**Give heed, O God, to my prayer,**
>**and listen to my cry of supplication. R**

Among the gods there is none like you, my lord,
nor can the deeds of any be compared to yours.
>**All the nations you have made shall come and bow before you.**
They shall glorify your name, my lord,
>**for you are great and do marvellous things;**
>**you alone are God. R**

Turn to me then, and have mercy;
give your strength to your servant.
>**Save your handmaiden's child;**
>**give me a sign of your favour!**
Then those who hate me will see and be ashamed,
>**for you, God, have helped and comforted me. R**

Psalm 89
My Song Forever Shall Record

1 My song for-ev-er shall re-cord your ten-der mer-cies,
2 Al-might-y God, your loft-y throne has jus-tice for its
3 The swell-ing sea o-beys your will; its an-gry waves your
4 With bless-ing is the na-tion crowned whose peo-ple know the

O my God, your faith-ful-ness will I pro-claim,
cor-ner-stone; and shin-ing bright be-fore your face
voice can still. And yours, by right, the heavens and earth,
joy-ful sound; they in the light, O God, shall live,

and ev-ery age shall know your name. I sing of mer-cies
are truth and love and bound-less grace. The heavens shall join in
the world in life, in death, in birth. The whole cre-a-tion's
the light your face and fa-vour give. All glo-ry un-to

that en-dure, of faith-ful-ness for-ev-er sure.
glad ac-cord to praise your won-drous work and word.
awe-some frame pro-claims its Mak-er's glo-rious name.
God we yield, who is our con-stant help and shield.

Words: The Psalter *1912, alt.*
Music: Dmitri Stepanovitch Bortnianski *1822*

ST PETERSBURG
8 8 8 8 8
Alt. setting: 304

Psalm 90

Refrain 1

Eugene Englert

Unison

In ev-ery age, O God, you have been our ref - uge.

Music copyright © 1987 G.I.A. Publications, Inc.

Part One (1–6)

God, you have been our refuge in every generation.
Before the mountains were brought forth,
before earth and world were formed,
    from age to age everlasting, you are God.
You turn frail humans back to dust, saying: "Return, you mortals."
    For a thousand years in your sight are as yesterday,
    a day that is past, a watch in the night.
You sweep them away like a dream, like grass that is fresh in the morning,
    like grass which in the morning is green,
    but in the evening is dried up and withered. R

Part Two (7–12)

Your anger consumes us; your wrath overwhelms us.
    You set our misdeeds before you,
    our secret sins in the light of your countenance.
All our days pass away under your anger;
our years come to an end like a sigh.
    The days of our life are seventy years, even eighty, if we are strong;
but all that the years bring is toil and trouble;
    they are soon gone, and we fly away.
Yet who understands the power of your anger?
Who considers the fierceness of your wrath?
    Teach us to count our days
    that we may apply our hearts to wisdom. R

Part Three (13–17)

Turn back, O God! How long? Have compassion on your servants.
    Satisfy us in the morning with your steadfast love,
    that we may rejoice and be glad all our days.

(continued over)

Make us glad as many days as you have afflicted us,
as many years as we have suffered adversity.
>Show your servants your work, and let their children see your glory.
Let the favour of our God be upon us, and prosper the work of our hands.
>Prosper the work of our hands. R

Psalm 90

O God, Our Help in Ages Past

5 Time like an ever-rolling stream
  soon bears us all away;
  we fly forgotten, as a dream
  dies at the opening day.

6 O God, our help in ages past,
  our hope for years to come,
  be thou our guard while troubles last,
  and our eternal home.

Words: Isaac Watts 1719, alt.
Music: attrib. William Croft 1708; desc. Frances P. Macphail 1994
Descant copyright © 1994 Frances P. Macphail.

ST ANNE
8 6 8 6

Psalm 91

Refrain

Michael Joncas 1979

Words and music copyright © 1979, 1991 New Dawn Music

You who dwell in the shelter of your God,
who abide in God's shadow for life,
     say to your God: "My refuge, my rock in whom I trust!"
The snare of the fowler will never capture you,
and famine will bring you no fear:
     under God's wings your refuge, God's faithfulness your shield. R

You need not fear the terror of the night, nor the arrow that flies by day;
     though thousands fall about you, near you it shall not come.
For to the angels is given a command to guard you in all your ways;
     upon their hands they will bear you up,
     lest you dash your foot against a stone. R

"Because they have set their love upon me I will deliver them,
     I will uphold them because they know my name.
When they call to me I will answer,
     I will be with them in trouble;
I will rescue and bring them to honour.
     With long life I will satisfy them, and show them my saving power." R

Psalm 91
On Eagle's Wings

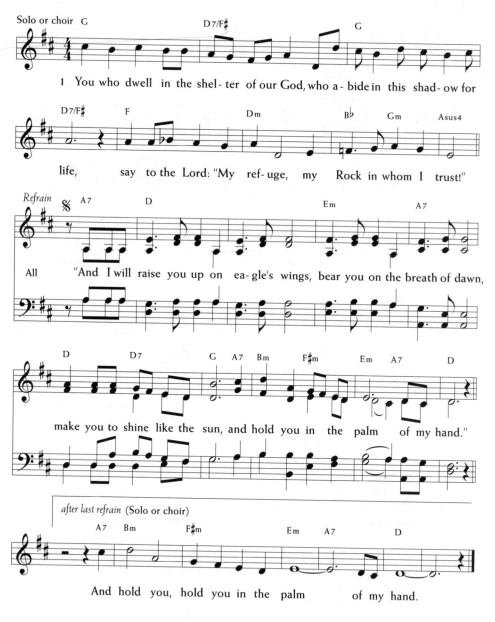

Solo or choir

1 You who dwell in the shel-ter of our God, who a-bide in this shad-ow for life, say to the Lord: "My ref-uge, my Rock in whom I trust!"

Refrain

All "And I will raise you up on ea-gle's wings, bear you on the breath of dawn,

make you to shine like the sun, and hold you in the palm of my hand."

after last refrain (Solo or choir)

And hold you, hold you in the palm of my hand.

Words: Michael Joncas 1979
Music: Michael Joncas 1979
Words and music copyright © *1979, 1991 New Dawn Music*

ON EAGLE'S WINGS
Irregular

Psalm 92

Refrain

J. Leavitt's Christian Lyre *1831*

It is good to sing your prais - es
and to thank you, O Most High.

It is good to give you thanks, O God,
to sing praises to your name, O Most High,
　　to tell of your love in the morning,
　　and your faithfulness during the night,
with a ten-stringed lute and harp,
with voice and lyre together.
　　For you, O God, have made me glad by your work;
　　I shout for joy at the works of your hands.　R

The just shall flourish like the date-palm
and increase like the cedars of Lebanon.
　　Planted in God's house,
　　they will flourish in the courts of our God.
In old age they still produce fruit,
thriving and full of vigour.
　　They will show that God is just;
　　God, our rock, in whom there is no wrong.　R

Psalm 92
To Render Thanks unto Our God

1 To render thanks unto our God
  it is a comely thing,
  and to your name, O God most high,
  due praise aloud to sing.

2 Your loving-kindness to show forth
  when shines the morning light;
  and to declare your faithfulness
  with pleasure every night,

♦ 3 upon a ten-stringed instrument,
  upon the psaltery,
  and on the harp with solemn sound,
  and grave sweet melody.

4 For you, God, by your mighty works,
  have made my heart so glad;
  and I will triumph in the works
  which by your hands were made.

5 Those that within the house of God
  are planted by your grace,
  they shall grow up, and flourish all
  within your holy place.

Words: Scottish Psalter 1650
Music: Jeremiah Clarke

BISHOPTHORPE
8 6 8 6

Psalm 93
God, You Rule with Royal Bearing

1 God, you rule with roy-al bear-ing, clothed in glo - ry,
2 In its ev - er - last-ing sta - tion earth is fixed to
3 With all tones of wa-ters blend-ing, glo-rious is the
4 God, the words your lips are tell-ing are the per - fect

love and light: you have robed your - self ma - jes - tic,
quake no more; you have laid your throne's foun - da - tion,
break-ing deep; glo-rious, beau-teous, with - out end - ing,
and the true. In your high e - ter - nal dwell-ing,

robed your - self with power and might. Hal - le - lu - jah!
you your - self are ev - er - more. Hal - le - lu - jah!
God, who reigns on heaven's high steep. Hal - le - lu - jah!
ho - li - ness shall live with you. Hal - le - lu - jah!

Hal - le - lu - jah! Hal - le - lu - jah! God who rules in depth and
Hal - le - lu - jah! Hal - le - lu - jah! God, you are for - ev - er -
Hal - le - lu - jah! Hal - le - lu - jah! Songs of o - cean nev - er
Hal - le - lu - jah! Hal - le - lu - jah! God, your word is ev - er

Words: John Keble 1839, alt. 1988
Music: William Owen 1852

BRYN CALFARIA
8 7 8 7 4 4 4 7 7

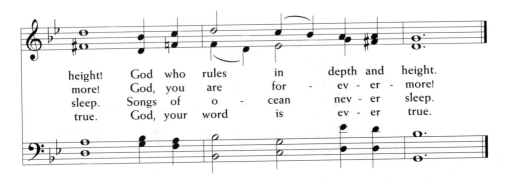

height! God who rules in depth and height.
more! God, you are for - ev - er - more!
sleep. Songs of o - cean nev - er sleep.
true. God, your word is ev - er true.

Psalm 93

William Owen 1852

Refrain

God, you rule with roy - al bear - ing,

clothed in glo - ry, love and light.

You rule, O God, clothed in majesty —
   robed, and girded with strength.
You have established the world
so that it can never be moved.
      Your throne has stood firm from of old;
      for all eternity you are God. R

The waters have lifted up, O God,
the waters have lifted up their voice;
the waters lift up their pounding waves.
      Mightier than thundering waters,
      mightier than the waves of the sea,
      mightier on high is God.
Truly your law stands firm;
      holiness adorns your house, O God, forever. R

Psalm 95

Refrain

R. Gerald Hobbs 1993

Come, let us bow down and wor - ship;

let us kneel be - fore God our mak - er.

Music copyright © 1993 R. Gerald Hobbs

Part One (1–7)

O come, let us sing to God,
> let us shout with joy to the rock of our salvation.
Let us come into God's presence with thanksgiving;
> let us joyously shout to God with songs of praise. **R**

For you are a great God,
> high sovereign above all gods.
In your hand are the depths of the earth;
> to you belong the heights of the mountains.
The sea is yours, for you made it;
> your hands also formed the dry land.
You are indeed our God;
> we are your people, the flock that you shepherd. **R**

Part Two (8–11)
(may be read by one or all)

O that today you would listen to God's voice;
"Do not harden your hearts as at Meribah,
as on that day at Massah in the wilderness;
when your forebears tried me, and put me to the test,
though they had seen my works.
Forty years I loathed that generation, and said,
'They are a people whose hearts are perverse,
for they give no heed to my ways.'
Then, I vowed in my anger:
they shall not enter my rest." **R**

Psalm 95
Come, Worship God

1 Come, wor-ship God who is wor-thy of hon-our,
2 Ruled by your might are the heights of the moun-tains,
3 We are your peo-ple, the sheep of your pas-ture,
4 Now let us lis-ten, for you speak a-mong us,

en-ter God's pres-ence with thanks and a song!
held in your hands are the depths of the earth;
you are our mak-er and to you we pray;
o-pen our hearts to re-ceive what you say:

You are the rock of your peo-ple's sal-va-tion,
yours is the sea, yours the land, for you made them,
glad-ly we kneel in o-be-dience be-fore you,
peace be to all who re-mem-ber your good-ness,

to whom our ju-bi-lant prais-es be-long.
God a-bove all gods, who gave us our birth.
great is the One whom we wor-ship this day!
trust in your word and re-joice in your way!

Words: Michael Perry 1980
Music: J. F. Thrupp
Words copyright © 1980 Hope Publishing Company.

EPIPHANY HYMN
11 10 11 10

Psalm 96

Refrain

Jane Marshall 1989

Sing a new song un-to God who has done such mar-vel-lous things.

Sing to God a new song;
    sing your praise, all the earth.
Sing and bless God's holy name,
tell the glad news of salvation from day to day.
    Declare God's glory among the nations,
    among all the peoples God's wonderful works.
For great is God and greatly to be praised,
to be revered above all the gods.
    For all the gods of the peoples are idols,
    but you, O God, made the heavens.
Honour and majesty attend you,
    strength and beauty are in your sanctuary. R

Ascribe to God, you families of peoples,
ascribe to God glory and strength.
    Ascribe glory to God's name,
    bring an offering and enter God's courts.
Worship God in the beauty of holiness,
and let the whole earth stand in awe.
    Say among the nations: It is God who reigns!
The world is made firm and cannot be shaken.
    God judges the peoples in equity. R

Let the heavens rejoice, and the earth be glad;
    let the sea roar, and all that fills it;
    let the fields exult, and all that is in them.
Then let all the trees of the forest sing for joy,
for you come, O God, to judge the earth.
    You shall judge the earth in righteousness,
    its peoples with your truth. R

Psalm 97

Refrain

Hal H. Hopson 1989

Re - joice, re - joice, let all the earth re - joice.

Music copyright © 1989 Hope Publishing Company

You reign, O God! Let the earth be glad!
Let the islands and coastlands rejoice!
> **Clouds and thick darkness are round about you;**
> **righteousness and justice the foundation of your throne.**
Fire goes before you,
consuming your enemies on every side.
> **Your lightnings light up the world;**
> **the earth trembles at the sight.**
The mountains melt like wax before you,
before the Sovereign of all the earth.
> **The heavens proclaim your righteousness,**
> **and all the peoples see your glory.   R**

Be ashamed, all you who worship images, who boast of idols;
> **bow down before God, all you gods!**
Zion hears, and is glad;
the cities of Judah rejoice, O God, at your judgements.
> **For you are the Most High, above all the earth;**
> **you are exalted far above all gods.**
You, O God, love those who hate evil.
> **You preserve the life of your saints.**
> **You deliver them from the hand of the wicked.**
Light dawns for the righteous,
and joy for the upright in heart.
> **Rejoice in God, righteous people.**
> **Give thanks to God's holy name!   R**

Psalm 98

Refrain 1

David Goodrich

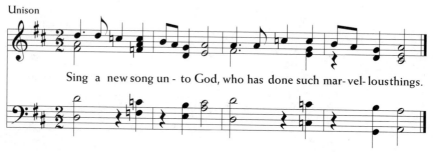

Sing a new song un-to God, who has done such mar-vel-lous things.

Refrain 2

Mary Kay Beall 1993

All the ends of the earth have seen the sav-ing pow-er of God.

Sing to God a new song,
  for God has done marvellous things.
Your right hand and your holy arm have brought victory.
    You have made known your salvation,
    and revealed before the nations your saving power.
You have remembered your steadfast love
and faithfulness to the house of Israel;
    all the ends of the earth have seen the salvation of our God. R

Make a joyful noise to God, all the earth;
  break into joyous praise, sing psalms.
Sing psalms to God with the harp,
  with the harp and melodious voice.
With trumpets, and the sound of the horn
    make a joyful noise before our sovereign God. R

Let the sea roar, and all that fills it,
  the world, and its inhabitants.
Let the rivers clap their hands,
    the hills sing together for joy before God.
You come to judge the earth, O God,
    to judge the world with righteousness,
    and the peoples with equity. R

Psalm 99

James McGranahan 1883

Refrain

You rule with jus - tice in de-light, and faith - ful - ness main-tain.

You reign, O God, and the peoples tremble,
you sit enthroned upon the cherubim, and the earth is quaking.
> **You, O God, are great in Zion,**
> **you are exalted over all the nations.**
Let them praise your great and awesome name:
holy are you and mighty, a ruler who delights in justice.
> **You have determined what is fair,**
> **you have done in Jacob what is just and right.   R**

Moses and Aaron were among your priests,
*Miriam among those who called on your name;
they called to you, God, and you answered.
> **In the pillar of cloud you spoke to them,**
> **they kept your teachings and the law that you gave them.**
O God, our God, you answered them;
> **to them you were a forgiving God,**
> **though you punished their offences.**
Proclaim the greatness of God
and worship on God's holy hill;
> **for God, our God, is the Holy One.   R**

* from Exodus 15

Psalm 100
Make a Joyful Noise

Make a joy-ful noise all the earth!

Wor - ship your God with glad - ness.

Make a joy-ful noise all the earth.

Come to this place with a song! song!

Words: Linnea Good 1991
Music: Linnea Good 1991, arr. David Kai 1994
Words and music copyright © 1991 Borealis Music. Arrangement copyright © 1994 David Kai.

PSALM 100
Irregular

Psalm 100
Vous, qui sur la terre habitez
(All People That on Earth Do Dwell)

1 Vous, qui sur la terre ha - bi - tez,
2 Sa - chez qu'il est le Sou - ve - rain,
1 All peo - ple that on earth do dwell,
2 Know that there is one God, in - deed,

chan - tez à hau - te voix, chan - tez;
qu'il nous a for - més de sa main,
sing out your faith with cheer - ful voice;
who fash - ions us with - out our aid,

ré - jou - is - sez - vous au Sei - gneur,
nous, le peu - ple qu'il veut ché - rir,
de - light in God whose praise you tell,
who claims us, gives us all we need,

par un saint hymne à son hon - neur.
et le trou - peau qu'il veut nour - rir.
whose pres - ence calls you to re - joice.
whose ten - der care will nev - er fade.

Words: French, *Théodore de Bèze* 1561, et al; English, attrib. *William Kethe* 1561; adapt. *Thomas H. Troeger* 1992, alt. OLD 100TH
Music: *Genevan Psalter* 1551 8 8 8 8

Words (adaptation) copyright © Oxford University Press, Inc.

3 Entrez dans son temple aujourd'hui;
  prosternez-vous tous devant lui,
  et, de concert avec les cieux,
  célébrez son nom glorieux.

4 C'est un Dieu rempli de bonté,
  d'une éternelle vérité,
  toujours propice à nos souhaits,
  et sa grâce dure à jamais.

3 Enter the sacred gates with praise;
  with joy approach the temple walls.
  Extol and bless our God always
  as people whom the Spirit calls.

4 Proclaim again that God is good,
  whose mercy is forever sure,
  whose truth at all times firmly stood,
  and shall from age to age endure.

(Version in *Scottish Psalter* **1650)**

1 All people that on earth do dwell,
  sing to the Lord with cheerful voice,
  him serve with mirth, his praise forth
    tell;
  come ye before him and rejoice.

2 Know that the Lord is God indeed;
  without our aid he did us make;
  we are his folk, he doth us feed,
  and for his sheep he doth us take.

3 O enter then his gates with praise,
  approach with joy his courts unto;
  praise, laud, and bless his name always,
  for it is seemly so to do.

4 For why, the Lord our God is good;
  his mercy is for ever sure;
  his truth at all times firmly stood,
  and shall from age to age endure.

Original form of melody in last line:

Psalm 100

Refrain 1

J. Jefferson Cleveland

En - ter God's gates with thanks and praise.

Refrain 2

Arthur H. Messiter 1883

Unison

Re - joice, re - joice, re - joice, give thanks, and sing.

Shout to God, all the earth:
    worship with gladness and joy.
Come before God with laughter,
    our maker to whom we belong.
To the Shepherd who tends us like sheep,
    let us raise our voices in song.

Come to God's gates with thanks;
    come to God's courts with praise.
Praise and bless God's name.
    "Truly you are good:
you are always gracious,
    and faithful age after age." R

Psalm 103

Refrain

Michael Baughen 1972;
arr. Noël Tredinnick 1990

Come, bless God, O my soul, and nev-er for-get all God's bless-ings.

Bless God, my soul,
and all my being, bless God's holy name.
> **Bless God, my soul,**
> **and forget not all God has done for you.**
Bless God, who forgives all your sin,
who heals you in all your infirmities,
> **who redeems your life from the grave**
> **and crowns you with mercy and love,**
who fills your life with good things,
so that your youth is renewed like the eagle's,
> **who works righteousness**
> **and justice for all who are wronged.   R**

O God, you showed your ways to Moses,
your deeds to the children of Israel.
> **You are compassionate and merciful,**
> **slow to anger and extravagant in love.**
You will not always accuse
nor do you keep your anger for ever.
> **You have not dealt with us according to our sins**
> **nor punished us according to our wickedness.**
For as the heavens are high above the earth,
so great is your steadfast love toward those who fear you.
> **As far as the east is from the west,**
> **so far have you put away our sins from us.**
As a father has compassion for his children,
so you have compassion for those who fear you.
> ***As a mother comforts her child,**
> **so you comfort us, O God.**
For you know how we were made.
> **You remember that we are dust.**
> **Bless God, O my soul.   R**

* from Isaiah 66:13

Psalm 104

Refrain 1

Stralsund Gesangbuch 1665

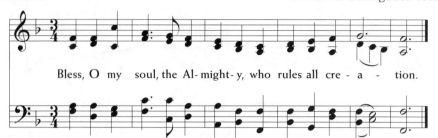

Bless, O my soul, the Al- might- y, who rules all cre - a - tion.

Refrain 2

Melchior Vulpius 1609
arr. Ernest Campbell MacMillan ca. 1930

Hal - le - lu - jah, Hal - le - lu - jah, Hal - le - lu - jah!

Part One (1–9)

Praise God, O my soul.
    Eternal God, you are great indeed.
You clothe yourself with light like a garment.
    You spread the heavens like a tent;
    you lay out the beams of your dwelling on the waters above.
You make the clouds your chariot,
and ride on the wings of the wind.
    You make the winds your messengers,
    and flames of fire your servants.
You fix the earth on its foundations,
so that it can never tremble.
    You cover the earth with the ocean as with a cloak.   R

When the waters covered the mountains,
they fled at your rebuke;
    at the sound of your thunder, they took flight.
They flowed over the mountains, ran down the valleys
to the place you had appointed for them.
    There you set limits not to be passed,
    that they might not again cover the earth.   R

Part Two (24–35)

O God, how manifold are your works!
With Wisdom at your side you made them all;
the earth is full of your creatures. R

There lies the great and mighty Sea,
teeming with living things both great and small.
Upon it sail the ships,
and there is Leviathan, the monster you made to play in it.
All these look to you,
to give them their food in due season.
What you give them they gather up.
When you open your hand,
you fill them with good things.
But when you hide your face they despair.
When you take away their breath, they die, and return to dust.
But when you send out your spirit, they live again,
and you renew the face of the earth. R

May your glory, O God, endure forever.
May you rejoice, O God, in your works.
When you look at the earth it trembles,
when you touch the mountains they smoke.
I will sing to God as long as I live.
I will praise my God while I have being. R

Psalm 105

John Medley
arr. Willis Noble 1995

Refrain

Bless God, my soul. Hal - le - lu - jah!

Part One (1–11)

Give thanks and call on God's name.
Make known to the nations what God has done.
>   **Sing, O sing the songs of praise;**
>   **tell of all God's wonderful deeds.**
Exult in God's holy name;
>   **let those who seek God be joyful in heart.   R**

Turn for help to the One who is your strength;
seek God's presence continually.
>   **Remember the marvels the Most High has done,**
>   **the wonders and judgements God has given,**
O children of Abraham and Sarah, God's servants,*
>   **O offspring of Israel, chosen of God.   R**

You are the eternal God,
>   **your justice reaches every corner of the earth.**
You are ever mindful of your covenant,
the promise you gave to a thousand generations,
>   **the covenant you made with Sarah and Abraham,**
>   **the oath you gave to Isaac.**
You confirmed it for Jacob as binding.
To Israel your everlasting covenant you declared,
>   **"To you I give the land of Canaan,**
>   **as your appointed inheritance."   R**

* from Genesis 17

Part Two (16–22)

You called down famine on the land,
and cut off the supply of bread.
> **But you sent one ahead of them,**
> **Joseph, whom they had sold as a slave.**

His feet were hurt with fetters,
his neck collared with iron;
> **until his predictions came true,**
> **your word tested him.**

Then the king sent and released him,
the ruler of nations set him free.
> **He made Joseph master of his house,**
> **ruler of all his possessions,**

to correct his officials at will,
> **to teach his counsellors wisdom.   R**

Part Three (23–26)

When Israel came to Egypt,
> **when Jacob settled in the land of Ham,**

there you made your people fruitful,
> **stronger than their foes.**

But when you turned their hearts to hate your people,
> **to deceitful dealing with your servants,**

then you sent your servant Moses,
> **and Aaron, whom you had chosen.   R**

Part Four (37–45)

You led Israel out, with spoil of silver and gold.
Among the tribes not one fell behind.
> **The Egyptians were glad when they went,**
> **for dread of Israel had fallen upon them.**

You spread cloud as a screen,
> **and fire as light by night.**

The people asked, and you sent them quail;
you filled them with bread from heaven.
> **You opened a rock and water gushed out:**
> **It flowed like a river through the arid land.   R**

For you remembered the sacred promise
you made to Abraham and Sarah, your servants.
> **You led out your people rejoicing,**
> **your chosen ones with songs of gladness.**

You gave them the lands of nations;
> **they took possession where others had toiled,**
> **that they might keep your laws and obey your teachings.   R**

Psalm 106

Refrain

John L. Bell 1988, alt.

O give thanks to God, whose love en-dures for - ev-er.

Words and music copyright © 1988 The Iona Community, G.I.A. Publications, Inc., Chicago, Illinois, exclusive agent

O give thanks, for God is good;
God's love endures forever.
> **Who can recount your mighty acts, O God,**
> **or tell of all your praise?   R**

Blessed are those who act justly,
and always do what is right.
> **Remember me, God, when you show favour to your people,**
> **and come to me with your saving help.**
May I see the prosperity of your chosen;
> **may I share the joy of your nation,**
> **and exult with the people you have made your own.   R**

We have sinned like our ancestors;
> **we have erred, and acted wickedly.**
They made a young bull at Horeb,
and worshipped that molten image.
> **They exchanged the glory of God**
> **for the image of a creature that feeds on grass.**
They forgot that you were the God who had saved them
by your mighty acts in Egypt,
> **the wonders you had done in the land of Ham,**
> **awesome deeds at the Red Sea.**
You would have destroyed them
had not Moses, your chosen one, stood in the breach.
> **He turned back your wrath from their destruction.   R**

Psalm 107

Refrain

Eleanor Daley 1994

O give thanks to God for stead - fast love.

Part One (1–9)

O give thanks, for God is gracious;
    God's steadfast love endures for ever.
Let the redeemed of God say so,
those redeemed from trouble,
    whom God gathered in from the lands,
from the east and the west,
    from the north and the south. R

Some lost their way in desert wastes,
finding no place to settle;
    hungry and thirsty, their soul fainted within them.
Then they cried to you, God, in their trouble;
you rescued them from their distress.
    You led them by a straight path,
    till they reached a place to settle.
Let them thank you, O God, for your steadfast love,
for the wonders you do for us.
    For you satisfy the thirsty,
    and fill the hungry with good things. R

Part Two (17–22)

Some suffered because of their sinful ways,
afflicted on account of their wrongdoing.
    They loathed every kind of food;
    they came close to the gates of death.
Then they cried to you, God, in their trouble.
You rescued them from their distress.
    You gave the word and healed them;
    you saved them from the grave.
Let them thank you, God, for your steadfast love,
for the wonders you do for us.
    Let them offer the sacrifice of thanksgiving,
    and tell of your deeds with shouts of joy. R

Refrain (Psalm 107)   *Eleanor Daley 1994*

O give thanks to God for stead - fast love.

Part Three (23–32)

Those who go down to the sea in ships,
those who ply their trade on great waters,
they have seen your works, O God,
and the wonders you do in the deep. R

At your command the stormy wind arose, and lifted up the waves.
Carried up to the sky, and down to the depths,
their courage melted in the face of danger;
reeling and staggering as if drunken,
their seafaring skill was to no avail.
Then they cried to you, God, in their trouble;
you rescued them from their distress.
You made the storm be still;
you hushed the roaring waves.
They rejoiced with the calm;
you brought them to the harbour for which they had longed for.
Let them thank you, God, for your steadfast love,
for the wonders that you do for us.
Let them extol you when the people gather,
and praise you when the elders take counsel. R

Part Four (33–37)

You turn rivers into desert,
springs of water into thirsty ground.
A fruitful land you make a salty waste,
because of the wickedness of its inhabitants.
But you turn desert into standing pools,
dry land into springs of water,
to give the hungry a home, a place where they can settle.
They sow fields and plant vineyards
that yield a fruitful harvest.
You bless them and their numbers increase.
You do not let their herds diminish.
Whoever is wise, ponder these things.
Consider God's unfailing love. R

Psalm 111

Hal H. Hopson 1989

Refrain

Hal - le - lu - jah. Hal - le - lu - jah. Hal - le - lu - jah.

I will thank you, God, with my whole heart,
in the company of the upright, in their assembly.
> **Great are your works, O God,**
> **studied by all who delight in them.**
Honour and majesty are your work;
your righteousness endures forever.
> **You have won renown for your wonders;**
> **you are gracious and full of compassion.   R**

You give food to those who fear you;
you keep your covenant always in mind.
> **You have shown your power in action,**
> **giving your people the heritage of nations.**
The works of your hands are faithful and just;
all your precepts trustworthy.
> **They stand fast forever and ever;**
> **grounded in justice and truth.**
You sent redemption to your people;
> **you decreed your covenant forever.**
> **Holy and awesome is your name.   R**

The fear of God is the beginning of wisdom;
> **those who practise it have good understanding.**
> **May your praise endure forever.   R**

Psalm 112

Samuel Webbe (the elder) 1782

The just shall trust in God a - lone.

Blessed are those who fear God,
    who greatly delight in God's commandments.
Their descendants will be mighty in the land,
the generation of the upright will be blessed.
    Riches and plenty shall be in their house,
    their righteousness enduring forever.
They are a light in the darkness for the upright,
being gracious, compassionate and just.
    It goes well with those who lend generously,
    who conduct their affairs with justice.   R

For the righteous will never be shaken;
they will be kept in remembrance for ever.
    They will not live in fear of bad news;
    with resolute heart they trust in God.
Their heart is steady, they do not fear;
in the end they will see their enemies' downfall.
    They distribute freely to the poor,
    their righteousness enduring forever;
    they will hold up their heads in honour.   R

Psalm 113
Praise to the Lord

1 Praise to the Lord, all of you, God's
2 There is none like our God in the heavens or on
1 Lou - ez l'É - ter - nel, ser - vi - teurs_____ de
2 Qui est comme no - tre Dieu, dans les cieux, sur la

ser - vants. Bless - ed be the name of our God
earth,_____ who lifts the poor from the dust seat - ing them
Dieu._____ Bé - ni soit son nom, main - te - nant,
ter - re, qui ex - al - te les pauvres au rang des grands

now and ev - er. From the ris - ing up of the sun_____
with the might - y,_____ who stoops to raise the weak and low:
à ja - mais._____ Du le - ver du so - leil,_____
de son peu - ple,_____ qui ma - ni - fes - te mi - sé - ri - corde?

may the Lord be praised, praise to the name of the Lord!
bé - ni soit son nom! Lou - é soit Dieu, l'É - ter - nel!

Words: Ron Klusmeier 1972; French trans. R. Gerald Hobbs 1987
Music: Ron Klusmeier 1972
Words and music copyright © 1972 Ron Klusmeier. Translation copyright © 1987 Songs for a Gospel People.

RICHARDSON-BURTON
Irregular

Psalm 116

Refrain

Stephen Dean

How can I re-pay you, God, for all the good-ness you show to me?

Music copyright © Oregon Catholic Press

I love you, God, because you heard my voice when I made supplication,
because you turned your ear to me,
when I called upon your name.
The cords of death entangled me,
and the pangs of the Grave laid hold on me;
I suffered distress and anguish.
Then I called upon the name of God:
"O God, I pray, save my life." R

How can I repay you, God,
for all the good things you have done for me?
I will take up the cup of salvation,
and call upon the name of God.
I will pay my vows in the presence of all God's people. R

Precious in the sight of God is the death of the saints.
O God, I am your servant;
I am your servant, the child of your maidservant.
You have freed me from my bonds.
I will offer a sacrifice of thanksgiving,
and will call upon the name of God.
I will pay my vows to God in the presence of all God's people,
in the courts of the house of God, in your midst, O Jerusalem. R

Psalm 118

Albert Ham ca. 1900

Hal - le - lu - jah! hal - le - lu - jah!

Part One (1–4)

Let Israel now say:
    "God's love endures for ever."
Let the house of Aaron say:
    "God's love endures for ever."
Let those who fear God say:
    "God's love endures for ever." R

Part Two (14–18)

God is my strength and my song; God has become my salvation.
    There are shouts of joy and deliverance in the tents of the righteous.
The right hand of God does mighty things; the right hand of God raises up.
    The right hand of God does mighty things.
I shall not die, but live; and I shall proclaim what God has done.
    God indeed punished me, but did not give me over to death. R

Part Three (19–24)

Open to me the gates of the temple, that I may enter and give thanks to God.
    This is the gate of God; through it the righteous shall enter.
I thank you for you have answered me; you have become my salvation.
    The stone which the builders rejected
    has become the chief cornerstone.
This is God's doing, marvellous in our eyes.
    This is the day that God has made,
    let us rejoice and be glad in it! R

Part Four (25–29)

Save us, O God, we pray;
    God, we pray, give us success.
Blessed is the one who comes in the name of God.
    We bless you from the house of God.
God, our God, has given us light;
    with palm branches in hand let us march to the altar.
You are my God, and I will thank you;
    you are my God, and I will extol you.

Psalm 119

Refrain 1

T. Barrett Armstrong 1979

Hap - py are they who fol - low your law, O God!

Part One (1–8) Aleph*

Happy are those who live a blameless life, who follow your law, O God.
> **Happy are those who keep your decrees,**
> **who seek you with their whole heart.**

They also do no wrong, but walk in your ways.
> **You have given your precepts for us to keep diligently.   R**

O that my ways might be steadfast in the keeping of your statutes.
> **Then I will not be put to shame,**
> **when I hear all your commandments.**

I will truly thank you from the heart, when I learn your righteous decrees.
> **I will keep your statutes.**
> **O do not utterly forsake me.   R**

Refrain 2

Susan Marrier 1995

Your word have I hid   in my heart that I might not sin a - gainst you.

Part Two (9–16) Beth*

How shall the young be faultless in their way?
By keeping to your words.
> **With my whole heart I seek you;**
> **let me not stray from your commandments.**

* denotes letters of the Hebrew alphabet

I treasure your word in my heart
for fear I should sin against you.
> **Blessed are you, O God; teach me your statutes.**
With my lips I proclaim all the judgements you have uttered.
> **I find more joy in the way of your commandments**
> **than in all manner of riches.**
I will meditate on your precepts; I will give heed to your ways.
> **I will delight in your statutes; I will not forget your word. R**

Refrain 3   *Thomas Attwood*

Teach me, O God, the way of your stat-utes, and I will

keep it un - to the end.

Part Three (33-40) He*

Teach me, O God, the way of your statutes,
and I will keep it unto the end.
> **Give me understanding, that I may keep your law**
> **and observe it with my whole heart.**
Lead me in the path of your commandments, for I delight in it.
> **Incline my heart to your testimonies, and not to selfish gain! R**

Turn my eyes from looking at vanities;
and give me life in your ways.
> **Confirm to your servant your promise,**
> **which is for those who fear you.**
Turn away the reproach which I dread,
for your ordinances are good.
> **Behold, I long for your precepts;**
> **in your righteousness give me life! R**

* denotes letters of the Hebrew alphabet

Psalm 119

Refrain 4

Thomas Tallis ca. 1567

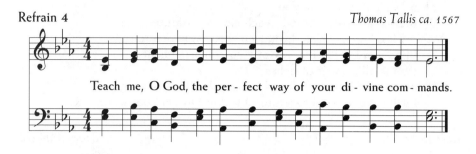

Teach me, O God, the per - fect way of your di - vine com - mands.

Part Four (97–104) Mem*

O how I love your law! It is my study all day long.
  Your commandment makes me wiser than my enemies;
  for it is always with me.
I have gained more insight than all my teachers,
for your instruction is my study.
  I have more understanding than the aged,
  for I keep your commandments.   R

I have held my feet back from every evil way,
in order to keep your word.
  I have not swerved from your judgements,
  for you, yourself, have taught me.
How sweet is your word on my tongue,
sweeter than honey in my mouth!
  Through your commandments I get understanding;
  therefore I hate every false way.   R

Refrain 5

Michael W. Smith 1984; arr. Keith Phillips, alt.

Unison

Your word is a lamp for my feet and a light for my   path.

* denotes letters of the Hebrew alphabet

Part Five (105–112) Nun*

Your word is a lamp for my feet, and a light for my path.
> I have sworn an oath and confirmed it,
> to keep your righteous judgements.
I am in deep distress;
give me life, O God, according to your word.
> Accept, O God, the willing tribute of my lips,
> and teach me your decrees.   R

I take my life into my hands continually,
yet I never forget your law;
> the wicked have laid a snare for me,
> but I have not strayed from your precepts.
Your testimonies are my heritage forever,
the very joy of my heart.
> I have set my heart to fulfil your statutes,
> forever, even to the end.   R

Refrain 6   *Eleanor Daley 1994*

Music copyright © 1994 Eleanor Daley

Part Six (137–144) Tsade*

You are righteous, O God, and your judgements are just.
> The decrees you have made are righteous and true.
I am consumed with rage because my foes neglect your words.
> Your promise is well tried, and your servant loves it.   R

Though I am belittled and despised,
I do not forget your commandments.
> Your righteousness is eternal and your teaching is true.
Though trouble and anguish come upon me,
your commandments remain my delight.
> Your righteous decrees are eternal;
> give me understanding, that I may live.   R

* denotes letters of the Hebrew alphabet

Psalm 121
Unto the Hills

1 Un-to the hills a-round do I lift up my
2 God will not suf-fer that thy foot be moved; safe
3 Je-ho-vah is in-deed thy keep-er true, thy
4 From ev-ery ev-il shall God keep thy soul, from

long-ing eyes: O whence for me shall
shalt thou be. No care-less slum-ber
change-less shade; Je-ho-vah thy de-
ev-ery sin: Je-ho-vah shall pre-

my sal-va-tion come, from whence a-rise?
shall those eye-lids close who keep-eth thee.
fence on thy right hand, thine own true aid.
serve thy go-ing out, thy com-ing in.

From God the Lord doth come my cer-tain aid, from
The One who sleep-eth not, who slum-bereth ne'er, shall
And thee no sun by day shall ev-er smite; no
A-bove thee watch-ing, God whom we a-dore shall

Words: John Campbell 1877
Music: Charles H. Purday 1860

SANDON
10 4 10 4 10 10

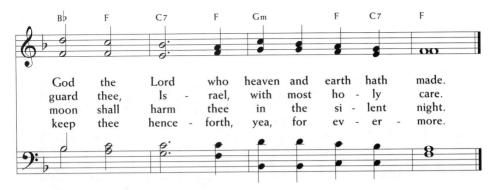

God the Lord who heaven and earth hath made.
guard thee, Is - rael, with most ho - ly care.
moon shall harm thee in the si - lent night.
keep thee hence - forth, yea, for ev - er - more.

Mohawk:

1 Se wen ni io sa wen tsi ia tion he as
   kwen ten re.
   A ia kwat ka to ne e sen ten raht ne
   tsi nen we.
   Niio tah kwa ie na wa se ha ties,
   ka ron hia ke, o ni non wen tsia ke.

2 Iah te ha we ron na ie ron hia ken te
   shon kwan hes,
   ia teh te ka ien ne na ho sen ni shon
   kwa ien a.
   Tiot kon shon kwa ni kon ra re tion
   kwe,
   ne ra o tsio kwa to o ken en ti.

3 Se wen niio i se no ri wi io ne tsi nen
   we.
   Se wen niio tas kwa as wa te ten non
   wen tsia ke.
   Ia te ka ien na ion kwa ka ron ni
   no nen i se, ie sa nia hes a on.

4 Ka ri wa ne ren e ren en weh te non
   kwa tonn hets,
   Se wen niio i se tah kwa ie na ne ia
   tion kwe.
   te tes kwa ka ne re on we ken to
   ta kwa tie na, was ne tsi nien hen we.

Words: trans. Josephine S. (Konwenne) Day 1905

Ojibway:

1 Ma gwa we je wun, ne doom be nuh
   nun Ne 'skeenzh zhe goon,
   Auh neen duh, ka oon je bah muh guk
   ewh Nooch mo go win?
   Ke sha' Muh ne do, ne guh we do kok,
   Kah we zhe tood, Ish pe ming kuh ya
   'ke.

2 Kah tah nan duh 'zee, che pung ge she
   nun; Ta ba ne gad.
   Wah weeng ga ze go ewh che ne bah
   sick, Kun wan ne mik.
   Be nuh, Je ho vah 'ke sha mun ne do
   Kah tah nee bah see kah nuh wan je
   gad.

3 Je ho vah ween kun nuh wan ne mik
   ewh, Wah ne sa yun.
   Je ho vah ween tuh nuh kuh nah wan
   don, 'Kah, we she tood.
   Kah dush ke kuh muh je do dah go
   seeg,
   'Kee soog, uh pe ne nuh ne me ze yun.

4 Che bah tah ze se wun, ke che chog
   oong, Kuh wan ne mik.
   Pa pah e zah yun suh owh, Je ho vah,
   Kun wan ne mik.
   Ish pe ming uh yah owh pa me tuh
   wind,
   Kah ke nig dush ke kah nuh wa ne
   mik.

Psalm 121

Refrain

Michel Guimont 1990

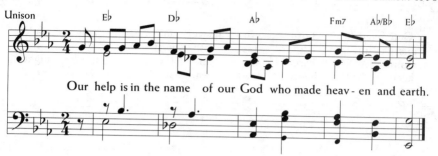

Our help is in the name of our God who made heav-en and earth.

I lift up my eyes to the hills.
From where will I look for help?
    My help comes from God, who has made heaven and earth.
God will not let your foot stumble;
the One who protects Israel will not slumber.
    The One who protects you will neither slumber nor sleep.   R

It is God who protects you,
your defence at your right hand.
    The sun shall not strike you by day,
    nor the moon by night.
God will protect you from all evil,
God will protect your life.
    God will protect your going and coming,
    now and forever.   R

Psalm 122

Thomas Hastings

Refrain

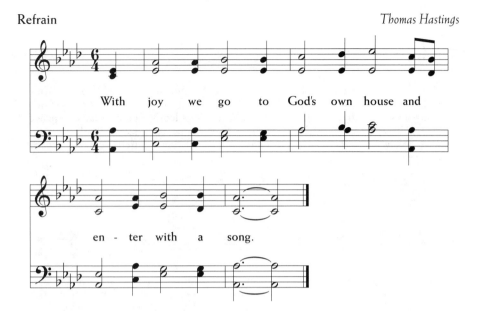

With joy we go to God's own house and en - ter with a song.

I was glad when they said to me:
Let us go to the house of God.
And now our feet are standing within your gates, O Jerusalem.
Jerusalem is built as a city bound firmly together.
There the tribes go up, the tribes of God,
to give thanks to the name of God, as was decreed for Israel.
There the thrones of justice stand,
the thrones of David's house.   R

Pray for the peace of Jerusalem.
May those who love you prosper!
May there be peace within your walls,
prosperity within your palaces!
For the sake of my kin and friends I say: Peace be with you!
For the sake of the house of our God, I will seek your good.   R

Psalm 122
I Joyed When to the House of God

1 I joyed when to the house of God "Go
2 Je - ru - sa - lem our cit - y is firm
3 Pray that Je - ru - sa - lem may have peace
4 There - fore I wish that peace may still with -
5 Now for my friends' and kin - dred's sakes "Peace

up," they said to me. Je - ru - sa - lem, with -
built and strong - ly stands; un - to that place the
and fe - lic - i - ty: let them that love thee
in thy walls re - main, and ev - er may thy
be in thee," I'll say; and for the house of

in thy gates our feet shall stand - ing be.
tribes go up, pil - grims from all its lands.
and thy peace have still pros - per - i - ty.
pal - a - ces pros - per - it - y re - tain.
God our Lord I'll seek thy good al - way.

Words: Scottish Psalter 1650, alt.
Music: Chalmers' Collection, Aberdeen 1749

ST PAUL
8 6 8 6

Psalm 123

Refrain

Hughes M. Huffman 1976

To you, O God, our eyes we raise
un - til your mer - cy we may praise.

To you I lift up my eyes,
>to you who are enthroned in the heavens.
As the eyes of servants look to their master's hands,
>as the eyes of a maid to the hand of her mistress,
so our eyes look to you, O God,
>as we wait till you show us your favour.   R

We have had more than enough of contempt.
>Too long we have suffered the scorn of the wealthy,
>and the contempt of the arrogant.   R

Psalm 124

Refrain 1

Arlo D. Duba 1980

Our help comes from God the mak-er of heav-en and earth.

Refrain 2

Michael Joncas 1978

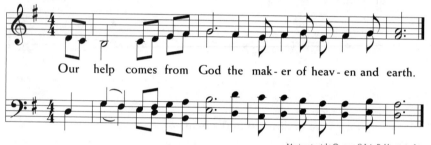

Our help comes from God the mak-er of heav-en and earth.

"If God had not been at our side,"
    now let Israel say:
"If God had not been at our side
when mortals rose up against us,
    then they would have swallowed us alive,
    when their fury was roused against us.
Then the flood would have swept us away,
and the torrent would have covered us.
    Then the raging waters
    would have gone right over our heads." R

But praised be God:
who has not given us as a prey to their teeth.
    We have escaped like a bird
    from the hunter's snare;
    the snare is broken and we are free. R

Psalm 125

Fred Kimball Graham 1995

Refrain

Those who trust in God stand fast for ev - er.

Those who trust in God are like Mount Zion,
which cannot be moved but abides forever.
> **As the mountains surround Jerusalem,**
> **so, God, you surround your people now and forever.   R**

The sceptre of the wicked shall not rest on the land assigned to the just,
lest the just should put out their hand to do evil.
> **Do good, O God, to those who are good,**
> **to those who are upright in heart.**
As for those who turn aside into crooked ways,
our God shall lead them away with evil-doers;
> **but peace shall be upon Israel.   R**

Psalm 126

Refrain 1

Norman L. Warren 1973

We'll sing the song of joy, we'll sing the song of joy!

Refrain 2

Walker's Southern Harmony 1835
harm. Erik Routley 1976

We praise the One who gave the growth, with voi - ces full and strong.

When God brought Zion's captives home,
it seemed to us like a dream.
> **But then our mouths were full of laughter,**
> **and our tongues uttered shouts of joy.**
Then they said among the nations:
"God has done great things for them."
> **Truly God has done great things for us,**
> **and therefore we rejoice.   R**

Restore our fortunes, O God, as streams refresh the Negev.
> **Those who sow in tears shall reap with shouts of joy.**
Those who go out weeping, carrying seed for sowing,
> **shall come home with songs of joy, bringing in their sheaves.   R**

Psalm 127

Refrain

David Clark Isele *1979*

The hand of God   feeds us   and   an - swers all our needs.

Unless God builds the house,
    its builders have laboured in vain.
Unless God watches over the city,
    those who keep watch stay awake in vain.
In vain you rise up early and go late to rest,
eating the bread of anxious toil;
    for those whom God loves are given sleep.   R

Truly children are a gift from God,
and offspring a reward from God's hand.
    Like arrows in a warrior's hand,
    so indeed are the children of one's youth.
Happy are those who have their quiver full of them;
    they will not be put to shame
    when they meet their adversaries at the gate.   R

Psalm 130
Up from the Depths I Cry to God

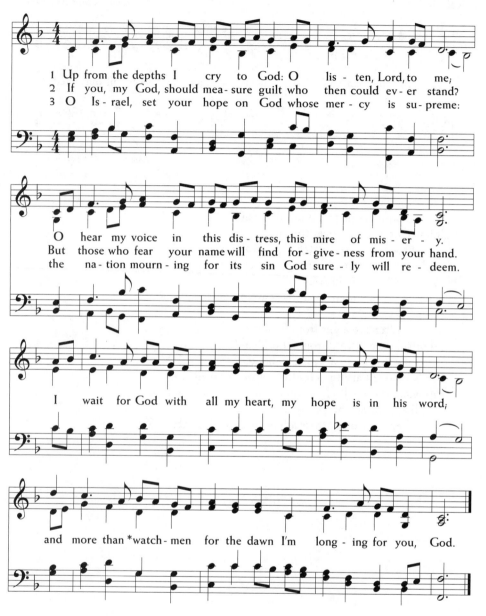

1 Up from the depths I cry to God: O lis - ten, Lord, to me;
2 If you, my God, should mea - sure guilt who then could ev - er stand?
3 O Is - rael, set your hope on God whose mer - cy is su - preme:

O hear my voice in this dis - tress, this mire of mis - er - y.
But those who fear your name will find for - give - ness from your hand.
the na - tion mourn - ing for its sin God sure - ly will re - deem.

I wait for God with all my heart, my hope is in his word;

and more than *watch - men for the dawn I'm long - ing for you, God.

* or "watchers"

Words: Christopher Idle 1975
Music: Scottish traditional melody; arr. David Iliff 1990
Words and arrangement copyright © 1990 Hope Publishing Company.

MACPHERSON'S FAREWELL
8 6 8 6 D

Psalm 130

Refrain 1

Martin Luther 1524
harm. Johann Sebastian Bach 1740, alt.

Out of the depths I cry to you; my hope is in your prom-ise true.

Refrain 2

15th-century French processional
arr. by Healey Willan, alt.

Unison

Out of the depths I cry to you; my hope is in your prom - ise true.

Out of the depths have I called to you.
O God, hear my cry!
> **Let your ears be attentive to my plea for mercy.**
If you should keep account of what is done amiss,
O God, who could stand?
> **But there is forgiveness with you,**
> **therefore we will honour you. R**

I wait for you, God;
my soul waits, and in your word is my hope.
> **My soul waits for God more than the watchers long for morning,**
> **more than the watchers long for morning.**
O Israel, wait in hope,
for with God there is love unfailing.
> **With God is great power to redeem,**
> **to redeem you, Israel, from all your sins. R**

Psalm 131

Refrain

Jean Sibelius 1899; arr. The Hymnal 1933

Be still, my soul, for God is on your side.

Arrangement copyright © 1933, renewed 1961 Presbyterian Board of Christian Education, Westminster John Knox Press

O God, my heart is not proud;
my eyes are not raised too high.
    I do not occupy myself with matters too great for me,
    with marvels that are beyond me.
But I have stilled and quieted my soul
like a weaned child nestling to its mother;
like a child is my soul within me.
    O Israel, hope in God,
    from this time forth and forevermore.   R

Psalm 132

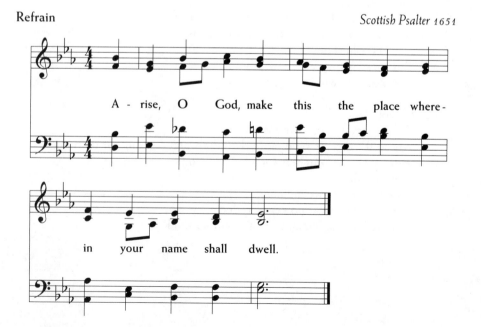

Refrain

Scottish Psalter 1651

A - rise, O God, make this the place where-

in your name shall dwell.

Part One (1–12)

O God, remember David and all the hardships he endured,
 how he swore an oath to you,
 a promise to the Mighty One of Jacob.
"I will not enter my house, nor will I climb into my bed,
I will not give sleep to my eyes, not even let my eyelids droop
 until I find a place for God,
 a dwelling for the Mighty One of Jacob." R

At Ephrathah we heard God's ark was there;
we found it in the region of Jaar.
 "Let us approach the place where the Most High rests,
 let us kneel in worship at God's footstool."
Arise, O God, and enter your resting-place,
you and your mighty ark.
 Let your priests be clothed with righteousness;
 let your faithful people shout for joy. R

For your servant David's sake, do not reject your Anointed.
 You made a sure promise to David,
 a promise that will never be revoked:
"One of your own children I will set upon your throne.
 And if they in turn keep my covenant,
 the teaching that I give them,
 their descendants too shall sit on your throne
 in succession for ever." R

Part Two (13–18)

God has chosen Zion, God desired it for a home:
 "Here I will rest for ever;
 here I will dwell, for it is my delight. R

I will bless the city with abundant food,
and satisfy its poor with bread.
 I will clothe its priests with salvation;
 its faithful people will rejoice and sing.
There I will make a branch sprout for David;
I will prepare a lamp for my Anointed.
 His enemies I will clothe with shame,
 but on his head the crown will sparkle." R

Psalm 133
Behold, How Pleasant

Words: Pablo Sosa 1974; English 1986, alt.
Music: Pablo Sosa 1974; arr. Darryl Nixon 1987
Words and music copyright ©1974 Pablo Sosa. Arrangement copyright © 1987 Songs for a Gospel People.

MIREN QUÉ BUENO
Irregular

Psalm 136
We Give Thanks unto You
(Love Is Never Ending)

Solo voice or choir   Em   Am7   B7

*1 We give thanks un - to you, O God   of   might:
2 In your wis - dom and love you shaped   the   skies:
3 You have filled all the skies with glo - ry and light:
4 From of old you have led your peo - ple in faith:
5 You de - liv - ered the ones who called   un - to you:
6 You have o - pened the sea and brought your peo - ple through:
7 You re - mem - ber your prom - ise age   to   age:
8 You give food and life to all liv - ing things:

All: Em   Am   Em   B

for your love is nev - er end - ing.

Solo voice or choir   B7   Em

We give thanks un - to you, the God of gods:
You spread out the earth up - on the sea:
The sun for the day and moon for night:
You have shown your com - pas - sion, strength and love.

From bond - age to free - dom, you brought them forth:
Brought them in - to a land that flows with life:
You show mer - cy on those of low de - gree:
We give thanks un - to you, the God of all:

All: G   Am   Em   B7   Em

for your love is nev - er end - ing.

*This psalm may be spoken in a responsive form.

Words: Marty Haugen 1987, alt.
Music: Marty Haugen 1987

Psalm 137

Refrain

Jonathan McNair 1994

By the riv-ers of Ba-by-lon, there we wept.

Music copyright © 1994 The Pilgrim Press

By the rivers of Babylon we sat down and wept
when we remembered Zion.
> There on the willows we hung up our harps
> when our captors asked us for songs.
Our tormentors called for entertainment, saying,
> "Sing us one of the songs of Zion!"   R

How could we sing the Lord's song in a strange land?
> If I forget you, O Jerusalem, let my hands wither!
Let my tongue stick to the roof of my mouth
if I do not remember you,
> if I do not set Jerusalem above my highest joy.   R

*Chorus:

Israeli melody

By the wa - ters, the wa - ters of Ba-by-lon,

We sat down and wept, and wept, for Zi - on.

We re-mem-ber, we re-mem-ber, we re-mem-ber Zi - on.

* May be sung as a round before and after the reading of the psalm.

Psalm 137
By the Babylonian Rivers

1 By the Ba - by - lo - nian riv - ers we sat
2 There our cap - tors in de - ri - sion did re -
3 How shall we sing songs of Zi - on in a

down in grief and wept, hung our harps up - on a
quire of us a song; so we sat with sta - ring
strange and bit - ter land? Can our voic - es veil the

wil - low, mourned for Zi - on while we slept.
vi - sion, and the days were hard and long.
sor - row? O God, hear your lone - ly band.

Words: Ewald Bash 1964
Music: Latvian traditional melody; arr. Darryl Nixon 1987
Words reprinted from Songs for Today, *copyright © 1964 American Lutheran Church. Used by permission of Augsburg Fortress.*

KAS DZIEDAJA
8 7 8 7

Psalm 138

Refrain

William B. Bradbury 1863

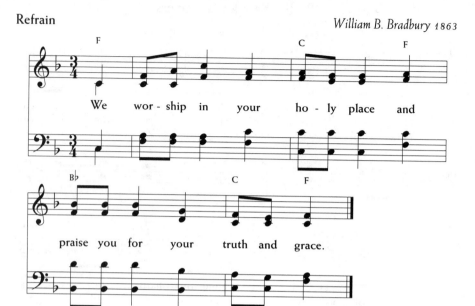

We wor-ship in your ho-ly place and praise you for your truth and grace.

I praise you, O God, with all my heart;
before the gods I will sing your praises.
> **I bow down toward your holy temple**
> **and praise your name for your love and faithfulness;**
for you have exalted your name
and your word above everything.
> **On the day that I called, you answered me,**
> **and put new strength in my soul.   R**

All earth's rulers shall praise you,
when they hear the words of your mouth.
> **They shall sing of your ways, O God,**
> **sing that your glory is great.**
For though you are high, you care for the lowly.
> **As for the proud, you humble them from afar.   R**

Though I walk in the midst of trouble, you preserve me;
> **you stretch out your hand against my enemies' rage;**
> **your powerful hand delivers me.**
You will fulfil your purpose for me.
> **Your love, O God, is eternal.**
> **Do not leave unfinished the work of your hands.   R**

Psalm 139

Refrain

Hal H. Hopson 1989

God, you have searched me, you know me through and through.

O God, you have searched me and known me.
You know when I sit down and rise up; you discern my thoughts from afar.
> **You discern my path and the places I rest;**
> **you are familiar with all my ways.**

Before a word is on my tongue, you know it, O God, completely.
You guard me from behind and before,
and lay your hand upon me.
> **It is beyond my knowledge; it is a mystery; I cannot fathom it.   R**

Where can I escape from your spirit? Where can I flee from your presence?
> **If I ascend to heaven, you are there;**
> **if I lie down in the grave, you are even there.**

If I take wing with the dawn and alight at the sea's farthest limits,
> **there also your hand will be guiding me**
> **your powerful hand holding me fast.**

If I say, "Let the darkness cover me and my day be turned to night,"
> **even darkness is not dark to you: the night is as bright as the day,**
> **for darkness is as light to you.   R**

It was you who formed my inward parts;
you fashioned me in my mother's womb.
> **I praise you, for I am fearfully, wonderfully made.**
> **Wondrous are your works; that I know very well.**

My frame was not hidden from you when I was being fashioned in secret,
intricately woven in the mystery of clay.
> **Your eyes saw my substance taking shape;**
> **in your book my every day was recorded;**
> **all my days were fashioned, even before they came to be.   R**

How deep your designs are to me, O God! How great their number!
> **I try to count them but they are more than the sand.**
> **I come to the end – I am still with you.**

Search me, O God, and know my heart;
> **test me and know my thoughts.**

Watch closely, lest I follow a path of error
> **and guide me in the everlasting way.   R**

Psalm 139
You Are before Me, God

Unison

1 You are be-fore me, God, you are be-hind,
2 Then from your spir-it where, God, shall I go;
♦ 3 If I should take my flight in-to the dawn,
4 If I should say, "Let dark-ness cov-er me,
5 Search me, O God, search me and know my heart;

and o-ver me you have spread out your hand;
and from your pres-ence where, God, shall I fly?
♦ if I should dwell on o-cean's far-thest shore,
and I shall hide with-in the veil of night,"
try me, O God, my mind and spir-it try;

such knowl-edge is too won-der-ful for me,
If I as-cend to heav-en you are there,
♦ your might-y hand will rest up-on me still,
sure-ly the dark-ness is not dark to you:
keep me from a-ny path that gives you pain,

too high to grasp, too great to un-der-stand.
and still are with me if in hell I lie.
♦ and your right hand will guard me ev-er-more.
the night is as the day, the dark-ness light.
and lead me in the ev-er-last-ing way.

Words: Ian Pitt-Watson 1973, 1989
Music: Alfred Morton Smith 1941

SURSUM CORDA
10 10 10 10

Psalm 141

Arlo D. Duba 1981
harm. Kenneth E. Williams 1982

Refrain

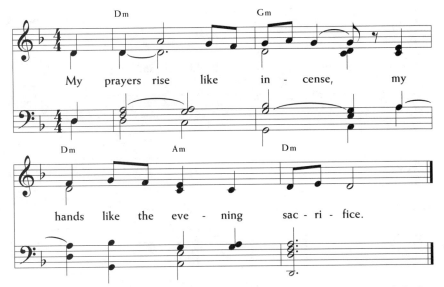

My prayers rise like in - cense, my hands like the eve - ning sac - ri - fice.

I call to you, O God; come to me quickly;
Hear my voice when I cry to you.
> Let my prayer rise before you as incense,
> the lifting up of my hands as an evening sacrifice.
Keep guard over my mouth, O God; watch the door of my lips;
keep my heart from slipping into evil.
> Let me not be busy with evil-doers;
> let me not be taken in by their sensuous delights.   R

Should the righteous rebuke me, let me accept it as grace;
but keep the oil of injustice from ever touching my head.
> I continually pray against wicked deeds;
> when we come to judgement we will know the truth of your word.
But my eyes are ever turned toward you, for you are my God;
in you I take refuge; do not deprive me of life.
> Keep me from the snare set for me by evil-doers;
> let them be ensnared, but God, grant me release.   R

Psalm 142

Refrain

Virginia Harmony 1831; adapt. Edwin. O. Excell 1900

You will my shield and por - tion be as long as life en - dures.

With my voice I cry out, O God;
>with my voice I plead for your mercy.
I pour out my trouble before you;
>I tell you of my distress.   R

When my spirit is faint within me, you know my way.
>In the path where I walk they have hidden a snare for me.
Look on my right hand and see:
there is no one who takes thought for me.
>I have no way of escape
>and no one cares for me.   R

I cry to you, God.
>I say: you are my refuge;
>you are all that I have in the land of the living.
Give heed to my cry,
for I am brought very low.
>Save me from those who pursue me,
>for they are too strong for me.
Bring me out of my prison,
so that I may give thanks to your name.
>The righteous will gather around me,
>for you will show me your loving kindness.   R

Psalm 143

George Whelpton 1897

Refrain

Hear our prayer, O God, hear our prayer, O God;
in - cline your ear to us, and grant us your peace.

Hear my prayer, O God;
in your faithfulness give heed to my pleading
and answer me in your righteousness.
> **Do not put your servant on trial,**
> **for no one living is righteous before you.**
The enemy has pursued me, crushing my life to the ground,
making me sit in darkness like those long dead.
> **Therefore my spirit faints within me,**
> **my heart is numb with grief.   R**

Yet I remember times past; I think about all you have done;
I meditate on the works of your hands.
> **I stretch out my hands to you;**
> **I thirst for you as a parched land thirsts for rain.**
Answer me quickly, O God, for my spirit is failing.
Do not hide your face from me,
or I shall be like those who go down to the dead.
> **Let me hear of your steadfast love in the morning,**
> **for in you I put my trust.**
Show me the way I should go, for on you I have set my hope.
> **Save me, O God, from my enemies; for I have fled to you for refuge.**
Teach me to do your will, for you are my God.
Let your good spirit lead me on an even path.
> **Keep me safe, O God, for your name's sake,**
> **and in your righteousness, free me from distress.   R**

Psalm 145

Refrain

Hal H. Hopson 1989

We praise you, O God: we bless your ho-ly name.

Every day we will bless you
and praise your name forever.
> **O God, you are great and highly to be praised;**
> **your greatness is beyond all measure.**
One generation shall praise your works to another,
and declare your marvellous deeds.
> **I will speak of your splendour and glory,**
> **and all your wonderful works.   R**

You, God, are righteous in all your ways,
and loving in all your deeds.
> **You are near to all who call to you,**
> **to all who call on you in truth.**
You fulfil the desire of those who revere you;
you hear their cry and you save them.
> **You watch over all who love you,**
> **but the wicked you will destroy.**
My mouth will speak your praise, O God.
> **Let every creature bless your holy name forever.   R**

Psalm 146
I'll Praise My Maker While I've Breath

1 I'll praise my Ma - ker while I've breath; and when my
2 Hap - py are those whose hopes re - ly on Is - rael's
3 For God gives eye - sight to the blind; al - so sup -
4 I'll praise you while you lend me breath; and when my

voice is lost in death, praise shall em - ploy my no - bler powers.
God, who made the sky, the earth and seas, with all their train.
ports the faint - ing mind, and sends the trou - bled con - science peace.
voice is lost in death, praise shall em - ploy my no - bler powers.

My days of praise shall ne'er be past, while life and
This truth for - ev - er stands se - cure; God saves the op -
God helps the strang - er in dis - tress, the wid - ow
My days of praise shall ne'er be past, while life and

thought and be - ing last, or im - mor - tal - i - ty en - dures.
pressed, God feeds the poor, and none shall find this prom - ise vain.
and the par - ent - less, and grants the pris - oner sweet re - lease.
thought and be - ing last, or im - mor - tal - i - ty en - dures.

Words: Isaac Watts; adapt. John Wesley 1737; alt.
Music: attrib. to Mattäeus Greiter; harm. V. Earle Copes 1964; alt.
Harmony copyright © 1964 Abingdon Press.

OLD 113TH
888888

Psalm 146

Refrain

Richard Proulx 1987

Unison

Give your praise to God, O my soul!

Praise God, O my soul. As long as I live I will praise God.
> **Yes, as long as I have life I will sing praises to God.**

Put not your trust in princes, nor in any mortal,
for in them there is no help.
> **When they breathe their last they return to dust;**
> **then their plans come to nothing.**

Happy are those whose help is the God of Jacob,
> **whose hope is the Maker of heaven and earth,**
> **the sea, and all that is in them,**

the One who keeps faith for ever,
> **who gives justice to the oppressed,**
> **who gives food to the hungry.   R**

God sets prisoners free, restores sight to the blind.
> **God straightens those who are bent;**
> **loves those who are just.**

God cares for the stranger in the land,
and sustains the widow and orphan;
> **but the way of the wicked God turns to ruin.**

God shall reign forever, O Zion,
> **your God for all generations.   R**

Psalm 147

Refrain

12th-century plainsong

Unison

Sing to God in great thanks - giv - ing.

Part One (1–11)

How good it is to sing praises to God,
>   how pleasant to laud the Most High.
You are building Jerusalem, O God,
and gathering the scattered exiles of Israel.
>   You are healing the broken-hearted,
>   and binding up their wounds.
You count the number of the stars,
and call them all by their names.
>   Great are you, O God, and mighty your power;
>   yes, and your wisdom is infinite.
You raise up the lowly,
>   and bring down the wicked to dust.   R

Sing to God in thanksgiving;
make music on the harp to our God,
>   who covers the sky with clouds,
>   who prepares rain for the earth,
>   who makes the hills green with grass.
You give the cattle their food,
and the young ravens when they cry.
>   You set no store by the power of a horse,
>   nor by the strength of a warrior's thighs.
But your delight is in those who revere you,
>   in those who rely on your mercy.   R

Part Two (12–20)

Hallelujah, O Jerusalem!
>   Zion, praise your God.
For God has strengthened the bars of your gates,
and blessed your children within you.
>   God has established peace within your borders,
>   and filled you with the finest wheat.   R

You send your word to the earth, O God;
your command runs swiftly.
>   You give snow like wool,
>   and sprinkle hoar-frost like ashes.
You scatter hailstones like bread-crumbs;
you send the cold, and the waters stand frozen.
>   You utter your word and the ice melts;
>   you blow with your wind and the waters flow.
You make known your word to Jacob,
your statutes and decrees to Israel.
>   You have not done this for any other nation,
>   nor have you taught them your laws.   R

Psalm 148
* Let All Creation Bless the Lord

1 Let all cre-a-tion bless the Lord, till heaven with praise is
2 All liv-ing things up-on the earth, green fer-tile hills and
3 O men and wom-en ev-ery-where, lift up a hymn of

ring-ing. Sun, moon, and stars peal out a chord, stir up the
moun-tains, sing to the God who gave you birth; be joy-ful,
glo-ry; all you who know God's stead-fast care, tell out sal-

an-gels' sing-ing. Sing, wind and rain! Sing, snow and sleet! make
springs and foun-tains. Lithe wa-ter-life, bright air-borne birds, wild
va-tion's sto-ry. No tongue be si-lent; sing your part, you

mu-sic, day, night, cold, and heat:
rov-ing beasts, tame flocks and herds: ex-alt the God who made you.
hum-ble souls and meek of heart:

* This hymn was originally written as paraphrase of the canticle, *Benedicite, omnia opera Domini* (A Song of Creation) from the apocryphal book, the Song of the Three Young Men.

Words: Carl P. Daw, Jr. 1988
Music: attrib. Nikolaus Decius
Words copyright © 1989 Hope Publishing Company.

ALLEIN GOTT IN DER HÖH
8 7 8 7 8 8 7
Alt. tune: Mit Freuden Zart

Psalm 148

Refrain

Jakob Hintze 1678; harm. J. S. Bach;
as in Hymns Ancient and Modern 1861

Let the whole cre - a - tion cry,

"Glo - ry be to God on high."

Praise God from the heavens; give praise in the heights!
Give praise, all you angels; praise God, all you hosts!
> **Praise God, sun and moon; give praise, stars and lights!**
> **Praise God, farthest heavens, and all waters beyond heaven! R**

Let all things praise the Holy One at whose command they were created,
who established them for all time, setting bounds, which cannot be passed.
> **Praise God from the earth, great sea creatures and ocean depths,**
> **lightning and hail, snow and frost, gales that obey God's decree,**
all mountains and hills, all fruit trees and cedars,
wild animals and cattle, creatures winged and earth-bound,
> **sovereigns who rule earth and its people,**
> **all who govern and judge this world,**
> **young men and women alike, old people and children together! R**

Let all things praise the name of God,
the name above every other, whose splendour covers heaven and earth.
> **You give strength to your people,**
> **songs of praise to your faithful,**
> **to Israel, the people dear to your heart. R**

Psalm 149
Give Praise to Our God

1 Give praise to our God and sing a new song,
amid all the saints God's praises pro - long;
a song to your mak - er and rul - er now raise,
all chil - dren of Zi - on, re - joice and give praise.

2 With timb - rel and harp and joy - ful ac - claim,
with glad - ness and mirth, we praise your great name;
for now in your peo - ple your plea - sure you seek,
with robes of sal - va - tion a - dorn - ing the meek.

3 In glo - ry ex - ult, you saints of the Word;
with songs in the night high prais - es ac - cord;
go forth in God's ser - vice, be strong in God's might
to con - quer all e - vil and stand for the right.

4 For this is God's word: the saints shall not fail,
but o - ver the earth the hum - ble pre - vail;
all rul - ers and na - tions shall yield to their sway.
To God give the glo - ry; sing prais - es for aye.

Words: The Psalter 1912, alt. 1995
Music: C. Hubert H. Parry 1887

LAUDATE DOMINUM
10 10 11 11

Psalm 149

Refrain 1

Melchior Vulpius ca. 1609
arr. Ernest Campbell MacMillan ca. 1930

Hal - le - lu - jah! Hal - le - lu - jah! Hal - le - lu - jah!

Arrangement copyright © Ernest Campbell MacMillan. Used by permission of Ross A. MacMillan

Refrain 2

C. Hubert H. Parry ca. 1887

All chil - dren of Zi - on, re - joice and give praise.

Sing to God a new song;
     give praise in the assembly of the faithful.
Let Israel rejoice in its Maker;
     let the children of Zion exult in their Sovereign!
Let them praise God's name with dancing;
     let them sing God's praise with tambourine and harp!   R

For you, O God, take delight in your people;
     you crown the humble with victory.
Let the faithful exult in their glory;
     let them sing for joy as they feast.   R

Let God's praise be on their lips,
     the two-edged sword in their hands,
to bring the nations to justice,
     and call to account the peoples,
to bind their rulers with fetters,
     their great ones with bonds of iron,
to execute on them the sentence decreed.
     This is the glory of all God's saints!   R

Psalm 150

Refrain

J. Jefferson Cleveland 1981

Praise to the Lord, hal - le - lu - jah!

Ev - ery - bod - y praise the Lord.

Words and music © 1981 J. Jefferson Cleveland

Praise God in the holy temple!
> **Praise God for mighty deeds!**
Praise God for bountiful mercies,
> **Praise God who meets all our needs!**   R

Praise God with sound of trumpet!
> **Praise God with lute and harp!**
Praise God with timbrel and dancing!
> **Praise God wherever you are!**   R

Praise God with holy cymbals!
> **Praise God with strings and with pipes!**
Praise God with clash of cymbals!
> **Praise God with all your might!**   R

Psalm 150
Praise to God, Your Praises Show

1 Praise to God, your prais - es show,
2 Earth to heaven and heaven to earth,
3 Praise to God, great mer - cies trace,
4 Strings and voi - ces, hands and hearts,

Hal - le - lu - jah!

saints with - in God's courts be - low,
tell the won - ders, sing God's worth,
praise this prov - i - dence and grace,
all in con - cert play your parts;

Hal - le - lu - jah!

an - gels round the throne a - bove,
age to age and shore to shore,
all that God for us has done;
all that breathe, your God a - dore,

Hal - le - lu - jah!

all that see and share God's love.
praise God, praise for - ev - er - more!
praise to the all - glo - rious One.
sing your praise for - ev - er - more.

Hal - le - lu - jah!

Words: *Henry Francis Lyte 1834, alt.*
Music: *Robert Williams 1817; harm. David Evans 1927*
Harmony by permission of Oxford University Press.

LLANFAIR
7777 *with hallelujahs*

Song of the Sea

Exodus 15:1–13

Refrain

TZENA (Israeli folk song)
harm. Emily R. Brink 1986

For you, my God, my strength and song, have now be - come my vic - to - ry.

Harmony copyright © 1987 CRC Publications.

I will sing to God, who has triumphed gloriously.
Horse and rider are thrown into the sea.
    God is my strength, my song, my salvation.
This is my God, whom I will praise,
our parents' God, whom I will exalt.
    God is a warrior: Eternal is God's name.   R

Pharaoh's chariots and his army are cast into the sea;
his chosen officers are sunk in the Red Sea.
    The floods covered them;
    they went down into the depths like a stone,
your right hand, O God, glorious in power,
your right hand, shattered the enemy.
    In your great majesty you overthrew your foes;
    you sent out your fury and consumed them like stubble.   R

At the blast of your nostrils the waters piled up.
    The floods stood up in a heap;
    the deeps congealed in the heart of the sea.
The enemy said,
"I will pursue, I will overtake, I will divide the spoil,
my desire shall have its fill of them.

I will draw my sword, my hand shall destroy them."
    You blew with your wind, the sea covered them;
    they sank like lead in the mighty waters.   R

Who is like you, O God, among the gods? Who is like you,
>   **majestic in holiness, awesome in splendour, wonderful in action?**
With constant love you led the people you redeemed.
>   **You guide them by your strength to your holy dwelling.**
You bring them in and plant them
on the mountain of your inheritance,
>   **the place you made your dwelling,**
>   **the sanctuary your hands have established. R**

The Ten Commandments

Exodus 20 and Deuteronomy 5

Refrain 1

Words: George Croly 1867
Music: Frederick C. Atkinson 1870

Spir - it of God, de - scend up - on my heart.

Hear the commandments which God gave Israel through Moses.
You shall have no other gods besides me.
You shall not make yourself idols,
>   nor bow down to them, nor serve them.
You shall not swear falsely, by my name.
Remember the day of rest and keep it holy.
Honour your father and your mother.   **R**

You shall not murder.
You shall not commit adultery.
You shall not steal.
You shall not bear false witness.
You shall not covet anything that is your neighbour's.   **R**

Song of Hannah
(My Soul is Filled with Joy)
I Samuel 2:1–10

1 My soul is filled with joy in my Re - deem - er,
2 All those who talk with pride now see who God is,
3 The strong have fall - en, but the weak are strength-ened;
4 O God, you set the earth on sure foun - da - tions;

for God has lift - ed me and set me high.
who weighs our deeds and knows our ev - ery move.
those who were hun - gry have e - nough to spare.
help for your saints is found in you a - lone.

There is no Ho - ly One, no Rock like our God,
Proud ones are hum - bled, but the poor are lift - ed;
She who was bar - ren sees her chil - dren's chil - dren;
Those who op - pose your truth will fall in judge - ment,

who an - swered my re - quest, who heard my cry.
all might and power are yours, O God of love.
all things are ev - er in your lov - ing care.
but you will strength - en your a - noint - ed one.

Words: Emily R. Brink 1986, alt.
Music: William Wright 1994
Words copyright © 1987 CRC Publications. Music copyright © 1994 William H. M. Wright.

DEER PARK
11 10 11 10

Isaiah 9: 2–8
(The Race That Long in Darkness Pined)

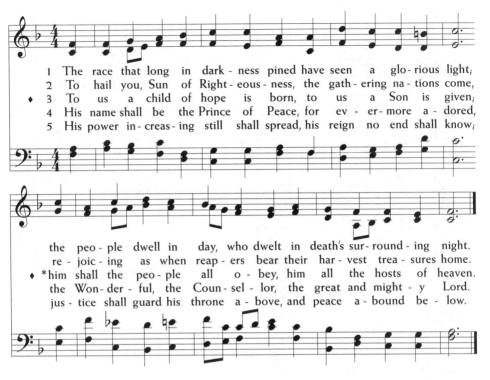

1 The race that long in dark-ness pined have seen a glo-rious light;
2 To hail you, Sun of Right-eous-ness, the gath-ering na-tions come,
3 To us a child of hope is born, to us a Son is given;
4 His name shall be the Prince of Peace, for ev-er-more a-dored,
5 His power in-creas-ing still shall spread, his reign no end shall know;

the peo-ple dwell in day, who dwelt in death's sur-round-ing night.
re-joic-ing as when reap-ers bear their har-vest trea-sures home.
*him shall the peo-ple all o-bey, him all the hosts of heaven.
the Won-der-ful, the Coun-sel-lor, the great and might-y Lord.
jus-tice shall guard his throne a-bove, and peace a-bound be-low.

* or "whom all the people shall obey, and all the hosts of heaven.

Words: John Morison, Scottish Paraphrases 1781, alt.

Music: Scottish Psalter 1615

DUNFERMLINE

8 6 8 6

Isaiah 12: 1a-6
(Give Thanks to God)

Refrain

Words and music: Joe Zsigray
arr. Catherine Ambrose 1996

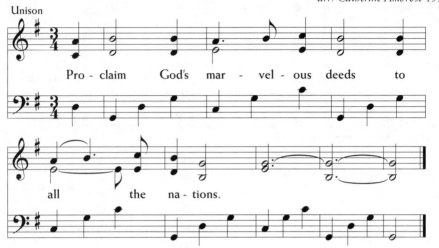

Unison

Pro-claim God's mar-vel-ous deeds to all the na-tions.

Music copyright © North American Liturgy Resources. Arrangement copyright © 1996 Catherine Ambrose.

I will praise you, O God,
> for though you were angry with me,
> your anger turned away, and you comforted me.
Surely God is my salvation.
I will trust and not be afraid,
> for you, God, are my strength and might;
> you show yourself my saviour.   R

With joy we draw water from the wells of salvation.
> Give thanks and call on God's name.
Make known God's deeds among the nations;
> proclaim that God's name is exalted.
Sing praises to God, whose work is glorious;
let it be known in all the earth.
> Shout for joy, you who dwell in Zion,
> for the Holy One of Israel is majestic among you.   R

Isaiah 35
(In the Desert)

1 When the king shall come a-gain, all his power re-veal-ing,
2 In the des-ert trees take root, fresh from God's cre-a-tion;
3 Strength-en fee-ble hands and knees; faint-ing hearts, be cheer-ful!
4 There God's high-way shall be seen where no roar-ing li-on,

splen-dour shall an-nounce his reign, life and joy and heal-ing;
plants and flowers and sweet-est fruit join the cel-e-bra-tion;
God, who comes for such as these, seeks and saves the fear-ful;
noth-ing e-vil or un-clean, walks the road to Zi-on;

earth no long-er in de-cay, hope no more frus-trat-ed;
riv-ers spring up from the earth, bar-ren lands a-dorn-ing;
deaf ears, hear the si-lent tongues sing a-way their weep-ing;
ran-somed peo-ple home-ward bound, all your prais-es voic-ing,

this is God's re-demp-tion day long-ing-ly a-wait-ed.
val-leys, this is your new birth; moun-tains, greet the morn-ing.
blind eyes, see the life-less ones walk-ing, run-ning, leap-ing.
see your Lord with glo-ry crowned, share in his re-joic-ing!

Words: Christopher Idle 1975
Music: Johann Horn 1544, Leisentritt's Gesangbuch
Words copyright © 1982 Hope Publishing Company.

AVE VIRGO VIRGINUM
7 6 7 6 D

Isaiah 40
(Prepare the Way)

1 Pre - pare the way, O Zi - on, your Christ is draw - ing near!
2 Christ brings God's rule, O Zi - on; he comes from heaven a - bove.
3 Fling wide your gates, O Zi - on; your Sav - iour's rule em - brace.

Let ev - ery hill and val - ley a lev - el way ap - pear.
His rule is peace and free - dom, and jus - tice, truth, and love.
And tid - ings of sal - va - tion pro - claim in ev - ery place.

Greet One who comes in glo - ry, fore - told in sa - cred sto - ry.
Lift high your praise re - sound - ing, for grace and joy a - bound - ing.
All lands will bow re - joic - ing, their ad - o - ra - tion voic - ing.

O blest is Christ that came in God's most ho - ly name.

Words: Frans Mikael Franzen
    adapt. Charles P. Price 1980; alt. 1989
Music: Then Swenska Psalmboken 1697; arr. American Lutheran Hymnal 1930

BEREDEN VÄG FÖR HERRAN
7 6 7 6 7 7 with refrain

Isaiah 40
(Comfort, Comfort Now My People)

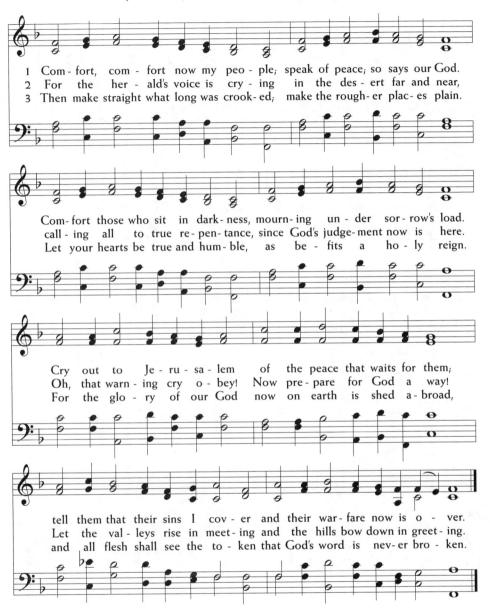

1 Com - fort, com - fort now my peo - ple; speak of peace; so says our God.
2 For the her - ald's voice is cry - ing in the des - ert far and near,
3 Then make straight what long was crook - ed; make the rough - er plac - es plain.

Com - fort those who sit in dark - ness, mourn - ing un - der sor - row's load.
call - ing all to true re - pen - tance, since God's judge - ment now is here.
Let your hearts be true and hum - ble, as be - fits a ho - ly reign.

Cry out to Je - ru - sa - lem of the peace that waits for them;
Oh, that warn - ing cry o - bey! Now pre - pare for God a way!
For the glo - ry of our God now on earth is shed a - broad,

tell them that their sins I cov - er and their war - fare now is o - ver.
Let the val - leys rise in meet - ing and the hills bow down in greet - ing.
and all flesh shall see the to - ken that God's word is nev - er bro - ken.

Words: *Johannes G. Olearius 1671; trans. Catherine Winkworth 1863, alt.*
Music: *Louis Bourgeois 1551; harm. Claude Goudimel 1564*

GENEVAN 42
8 7 8 7 7 7 8 8

Isaiah 55
(You Shall Go Out with Joy)

x=hand clapping

Words: Steffi G. Rubin 1975
Music: Stuart Dauermann 1975

TREES OF THE FIELD
Irregular

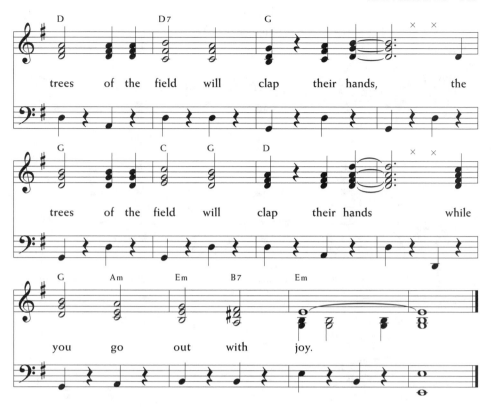

trees of the field will clap their hands, the

trees of the field will clap their hands while

you go out with joy.

Isaiah 60
(Arise, Shine)

Refrain

Lawrence M. Probes 1980

A - rise, be clothed in the light. A -

rise, be clothed in the light. Your light has come. Your

light has come. Hal - le - lu - jah.

Arise, shine, for your light has come.
God's glory has risen among you.
> Behold, darkness covers the earth,
> and thick clouds its peoples.
But upon you God shall rise.
God's glory will appear among you.
> Nations will walk by your light,
> their rulers by the brightness of your rising.   R

Raise your eyes and look around.
All gather together, all come to you.
> They will bring your sons from afar.
> They will carry your daughters like babes in arms.
Then you will see and be radiant.
Your heart will thrill and rejoice,
> because they will bring you the sea's bounty.
> The wealth of nations shall come to you.

Isaiah 40
(Comfort, Comfort Now My People)

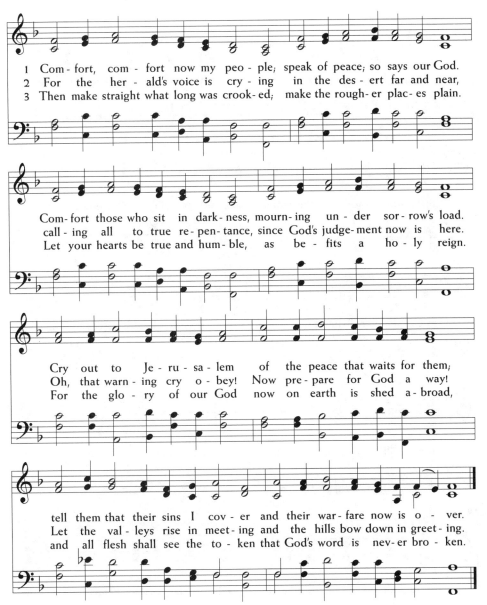

1 Com-fort, com-fort now my peo-ple; speak of peace; so says our God.
2 For the her-ald's voice is cry-ing in the des-ert far and near,
3 Then make straight what long was crook-ed; make the rough-er plac-es plain.

Com-fort those who sit in dark-ness, mourn-ing un-der sor-row's load.
call-ing all to true re-pen-tance, since God's judge-ment now is here.
Let your hearts be true and hum-ble, as be-fits a ho-ly reign.

Cry out to Je-ru-sa-lem of the peace that waits for them;
Oh, that warn-ing cry o-bey! Now pre-pare for God a way!
For the glo-ry of our God now on earth is shed a-broad,

tell them that their sins I cov-er and their war-fare now is o-ver.
Let the val-leys rise in meet-ing and the hills bow down in greet-ing.
and all flesh shall see the to-ken that God's word is nev-er bro-ken.

Words: Johannes G. Olearius 1671; trans. Catherine Winkworth 1863, alt.
Music: Louis Bourgeois 1551; harm. Claude Goudimel 1564

GENEVAN 42
87877788

Isaiah 55
(You Shall Go Out with Joy)

x=hand clapping

Words: Steffi G. Rubin 1975
Music: Stuart Dauermann 1975

TREES OF THE FIELD
Irregular

A multitude of camels will cover you,
the young camels of Midian, and Ephah, and Sheba.
> **They will bring gold and frankincense,**
> **and will herald God's glory.   R**

Your land will no longer hear the cry, "Violence!"
nor "Ruin and Destruction" your borders.
> **But you will call your walls, "Salvation,"**
> **and your gates, "Praise."**
No more will you need the sun for your light by day,
nor the moon's brightness by night,
> **but God will be your everlasting light.**
> **Your God will be your glory.   R**

Earth and All Stars

based on Daniel 3

1 Earth and all stars, loud rush-ing plan-ets
2 Steel and ma-chines, loud pound-ing ham-mers
3 Class-rooms and labs, loud boil-ing test tubes
4 Knowl-edge and truth, loud sound-ing wis-dom

sing to our God a new song!

Hail, wind, and rain, loud blow-ing snow-storm
Lime-stone and beams, loud build-ing work-ers
Ath-lete and band, loud cheer-ing peo-ple
Daugh-ter and son, loud pray-ing el-ders

sing to our God a new song!

Words: Herbert Frederick Brokering 1964
Music: David N. Johnson 1968
Words and music copyright © 1968 Augsburg Publishing House. Reprinted by permission of Augsburg Fortress.

EARTH AND ALL STARS
4 5 7 D with refrain

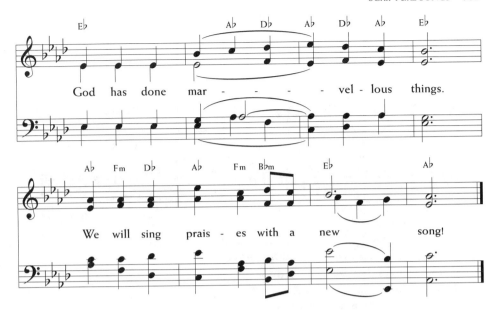

God has done mar - - - - - vel - lous things.

We will sing prais - es with a new song!

Wisdom 3
The Souls of the Righteous

Refrain

Ralph Vaughan Williams 1906

Hal - le - lu - jah! Hal - le - lu - jah!

Music by permission of Oxford University Press.

The souls of the righteous are in God's hands,
    and there no torment shall touch them.
To foolish eyes they seemed dead,
their departure reckoned as defeat,
their parting from us as disaster.
    But they are at peace. R

For though to human sight they seemed punished,
God will fulfill their hope of immortality.
    After a little chastisement they will receive great blessings,
    because God tested them and found them worthy to be God's own. R

Like gold in a crucible God put them to the test.
    God found them acceptable like an offering
    burnt whole upon the altar.
When God comes to them they will kindle into flame,
like sparks that sweep through stubble.
    They will judge nations and govern peoples,
    and God will rule forever. R

Those who put their trust in God shall know that God is true.
The faithful shall wait in love.
    They are God's chosen.
    Grace and mercy shall be theirs. R

Wisdom 7

The Nature of Wisdom

Refrain

Words: Patrick Michaels 1989
Chorale melodien zum heiligen Gesange 1808
arr. Hal H. Hopson 1991

Unison

Who comes from God, as Word and Breath? Ho - ly Wis - dom.

Wisdom is the brightness that streams from everlasting light,
 the flawless mirror of the active power of God,
 the image of God's goodness. R

Wisdom is only one, yet she can do everything;
 herself unchanging, she makes all things new.
Age after age she enters into holy souls,
and makes them God's friends and prophets.
 For none are more acceptable to God
 than those who make their home with Wisdom. R

Wisdom is more radiant than the sun.
 She surpasses every constellation.
She excels even the light of day;
for day gives way to night,
but against Wisdom no evil can prevail.
 She spans the world in power from end to end,
 and orders all things well. R

Wisdom 7
Who Comes from God

1 Who comes from God, as Word and Breath? Ho - ly Wis - dom.
2 Who lifts her voice for all to hear? Joy - ful Wis - dom.
3 Whom should we seek with all our heart? Lov - ing Wis - dom.

Who holds the keys of life and death? Might - y Wis - dom.
Who shapes a thought and makes it clear? Truth - ful Wis - dom.
Who once re - vealed, will not de - part? Faith - ful Wis - dom.

Craft - er and Cre - a - tor too, El - dest, she makes
Teach - er, draw - ing out our best, mag - ni - fies what
Part - ner, Coun - se - lor, Com - fort - er, love has found none

all things new; Wis - dom guides what God will do,
we in - vest, names our truth, di - rects our quest,
love - li - er, life is glad - ness lived with her,

Words: *Patrick Michaels 1989*
Music: Choralemelodien zum heiligen Gesange *1808; arr. Hal H. Hopson 1991*
Words copyright © *1989* arrangement copyright © *1991* Hope Publishing Company.

SALVA REGINA COELITUM
8 4 8 4 7 7 6 6

Wis- est One, Ra- diant One, wel- come, *Ho - ly Wis - dom.

* or "Great Sophia"

Wisdom 10
Wisdom and the Exodus

Refrain

Words: Patrick Michaels 1989
Choralemelodien zum heiligen Gesange 1808
arr. Hal H. Hopson 1991

Unison

Wis- est One, Ra- diant One, wel- come, Ho - ly Wis - dom.

Wisdom rescued a holy people, a blameless race,
from a nation of oppressors.
> **She inspired a servant of God,**
> **who, with signs and wonders, defied formidable rulers.**
She rewarded the labours of the holy people,
and guided them on a marvellous journey.
> **She became a shelter for them by day,**
> **a blaze of stars by night.   R**

Wisdom brought the people over the Red Sea,
guided them through its deep water.
> **But their enemies she engulfed,**
> **then cast them up again from the fathomless deep.**
So the just plundered the ungodly.
They sang the glories of your holy name, O God,
and praised with one accord your power, their champion.
> **For Wisdom taught the mute to speak,**
> **and made the tongues of infants eloquent.   R**

Song of Praise to the Holy Trinity
(Grand Dieu, Nous Te Bénissons)
Holy God, We Praise Your Name

1 Grand Dieu, nous te bé - nis - sons, nous cé - lé - brons
2 L'il - lus - tre choeur des té - moins, des dis - ci - ples,

1 Ho - ly God, we praise your name; God of all, we
2 Hark, the glad ce - les - tial hymn an - gel choirs a -

tes lou - an - ges! É - ter - nel, nous t'ex - al - tons
des pro - phè - tes; cé - lè - bre le Dieu sau - veur

bow be - fore you. All on earth your scep - tre claim;
bove are rais - ing; cher - u - bim and ser - a - phim,

de con - cert a - vec les an - ges, et pros - ter - nés
dont ils sont les in - ter - prè - tes; et ton É - glise

all in heaven a - bove a - dore you. In - fi - nite your
in un - ceas - ing cho - rus prais - ing, fill the heavens with

de - vant toi, nous t'a - do - rons: lou - ange à toi!
en tous lieux bé - nit ton nom glo - ri - eux.

vast do - main; ev - er - last - ing is your reign.
sweet ac - cord: "Ho - ly, ho - ly, ho - ly Lord."

3 Puisse ton règne de paix
s'étendre par tout le monde! Dès
  maintenant, à jamais,
que sur la terre et sur l'onde tous
  genoux soient abattus
au nom du Seigneur Jésus.

4 Gloire soit au Saint-Esprit!
Gloire soit au Dieu de vie! Gloire soit à
  Jésus Christ,
notre sauveur, notre ami! Son immense
  charité
dure à perpétuité.

3 Lo, the apostolic train
    joins your sacred name to hallow;
  prophets swell the glad refrain,
    and the white-robed martyrs follow;
  and from morn till set of sun
    through the Church the song goes on.

4 Glory through eternity:
    Spirit, Word, and blest Creator.
  God of gracious tenderness,
    at your feet we sinners gather;
  light and mercy, now, we pray,
    give your people for this day.

Words: German Ignaz Franz 1771; French trans. Henri-Louis Empeytaz 1817, rév.;
  English trans. vv 1-3 Clarence A. Walworth 1853; v. 4 R. Gerald Hobbs 1987
Music: Katholisches Gesangbuch ca. 1774
Translation (English) v. 4 copyright © 1987 Songs for a Gospel People.

GROSSER GOTT
7 8 7 8 7 7

Gloria
Luke 2: 14

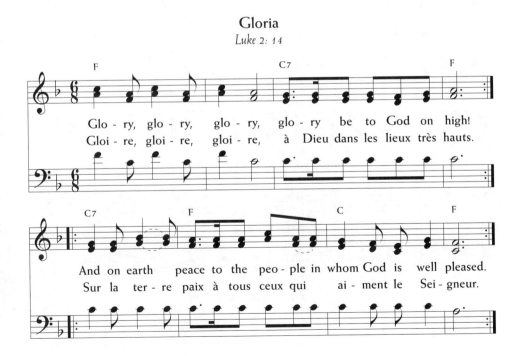

Glo - ry, glo - ry, glo - ry, glo - ry be to God on high!
Gloi - re, gloi - re, gloi - re, à Dieu dans les lieux très hauts.

And on earth peace to the peo - ple in whom God is well pleased.
Sur la ter - re paix à tous ceux qui ai - ment le Sei - gneur.

Words: traditional liturgical text
Music: Pablo Sosa
Music copyright © 1990 Pablo Sosa.

Matthew 5
(Blest Are They)

1 Blest are they, the poor in spir- it, theirs is the king- dom of God.

Blest are they, full of sor- row, they shall be con - soled.

Refrain

Re - joice _____ and be glad! _____ Bless- ed are

you, ho - ly are you! Re - joice _____ and be glad! _____

Yours is the king - dom of God.

Words: David Haas
Music: David Haas
Words and music copyright © 1985 G.I.A. Publications, Inc.

2 Blest are they, the low - ly ones, they shall in - her - it the earth.

Blest are they who hun - ger and thirst, they shall have their fill. Refrain

3 Blest are they who show mer - cy, mer - cy shall be theirs.

Blest are they, the pure of heart, they shall see God! Refrain

4 Blest are they who seek peace; they are the chil - dren of God.

Blest are they who suf - fer in faith, the glo - ry of God is theirs. Refrain

5 Blest are you who suf - fer hate, all be - cause of me. Re -

joice and be glad, yours is the king - dom; shine for all to see. Refrain

Song of Mary
(Magnificat)
Luke 1:47–55

Refrain 1

Michael Joncas 1978

To God I lift my soul in praise; in God my sav - iour I re - joice.

Refrain 2

William Richards 1995

Bless- ed are you a - mong wom- en and bless- ed the fruit of your womb.

My soul proclaims God's greatness.
> **My spirit rejoices in God my saviour.**
For you have looked with favour on your lowly servant.
> **From this day all generations will call me blessed.**
You have done great things for me, O Most Mighty.
> **Hallowed be your Name!**
You have mercy on those who fear you,
> **From one generation to another.   R**
You took action with a strong arm.
> **You scattered the proud in their conceit.**
You pulled the mighty from their thrones.
> **You raised the lowly.**
You filled the hungry with good things.
> **You sent the rich away empty.**

You come to the aid of your servant, Israel,
>for you remembered your promise of mercy,
>to our ancestors, Abraham and Sarah,
>and to their children in every age.   R

Song of Mary
(My Soul Gives Glory to My God)
Luke 1:47–55

1 My soul gives glo - ry to my God, my heart pours out its praise; God lift - ed up my low - li - ness in man - y mar - vel - lous ways.

2 My God has done great things for me: yes, ho - ly is God's name; whose peo - ple will de - clare me blessed, and bless - ings they shall claim.

3 From age to age, to all who fear, such mer - cy love im - parts, dis - pens - ing jus - tice far and near, dis - miss - ing self - ish hearts.

4 Love casts the might - y from their thrones, pro - motes the in - se - cure, leaves hun - gry spir - its sat - is - fied, the rich seem sud - den - ly poor.

5 Praise God, whose lov - ing cov - e - nant sup - ports those in dis - tress, re - mem - ber - ing past prom - is - es with pres - ent faith - ful - ness.

Words: Miriam Therese Winter 1978, 1987

Music: melody from Kentucky Harmony 1816; harm. C. Winfred Douglas 1940

MORNING SONG
8 6 8 6

Song of Zechariah
(Benedictus)
Luke 1:68–79

Refrain

Words: Michael Perry 1973;
Music: Hal H. Hopson 1983

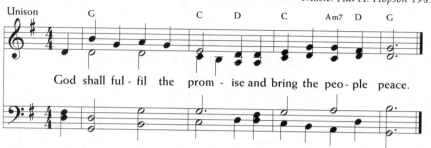

God shall ful - fil the prom - ise and bring the peo - ple peace.

Words copyright © 1973, music copyright © 1983 Hope Publishing Company.

Blessed be the God of Israel,
 who has come to the people and set them free,
who has raised up for us a mighty saviour,
 born of the house of the servant David.
Through the holy prophets of old
God promised to save us from our enemies,
 from the hands of all who hate us,
to show the mercy promised to our ancestors,
 to remember the holy covenant,
 the oath God swore to our ancestors Abraham and Sarah,
to set us free from the hands of our enemies,
 free to serve God without fear,
 holy and righteous in God's presence,
 all the days of our life.   R

And you, child,
will be called the prophet of the Most High,
for you will go before the Lord to prepare the way,
 to give the people knowledge of salvation
 by the forgiveness of their sins.
In the tender compassion of our God,
the dawn from on high shall break upon us,
 to shine on those who sit in darkness,
 in the shadow of death,
 and to guide our feet into the way of peace.   R

Song of Zechariah
(Blest Be the God of Israel)
Luke 1:68–79

1 Blest be the God of Is - rael, who comes to set us free;
2 Now from the house of Da - vid a child of grace is given;
3 On pris - on - ers of dark - ness the sun be - gins to rise,

who vis - its and re - deems us and grants us lib - er - ty.
a Sav - iour comes a - mong us to raise us up to heaven.
the dawn - ing of for - give - ness up - on the sin - ner's eyes,

The proph - ets spoke of mer - cy, of free - dom and re - lease;
Be - fore him goes the her - ald, fore - run - ner in the way,
to guide the feet of pil - grims a - long the paths of peace;

God shall ful - fil the prom - ise and bring the peo - ple peace.
the proph - et of sal - va - tion, the har - bin - ger of Day.
O bless our God and Sav - iour with songs that nev - er cease!

Words: *Michael A. Perry* 1973
Music: *Hal H. Hopson* 1983
Words copyright © 1973, music copyright © 1983 *Hope Publishing Company.*

MERLE'S TUNE
7 6 7 6 D

Song of Simeon
(Nunc Dimittis)
Luke 2: 29–35

Words: English Language Liturgical Consultation, alt.
Music: Hal H. Hopson
Music copyright © 1986 Hope Publishing Company.

SONG OF SIMEON
Irregular

Song of Simeon
(Lord, God, You Now Have Set Your Servant Free)

Luke 2: 29–35

Lord, God, you now have set your ser-vant free to go in peace as prom-ised in your word; my eyes have seen the Sav-iour, Christ the Lord, pre-pared by you for all the world to see, to shine on na-tions trapped in dark-est night, the glo-ry of your peo-ple and their light.

Words: Rae E. Whitney 1982
Music: Orlando Gibbons 1623, harm. Ralph Vaughan Williams 1906
Words copyright © 1982 The Church Pension Fund. Harmony by permission of Oxford University Press.

SONG 1
10 10 10 10 10 10

Revelation 5: 12-13
(This Is the Feast of Victory)

Refrain (Unison)

This is the feast of vic-to-ry for our God.

to verses | *last time*

Hal-le-lu-jah, hal-le-lu-jah, hal-le-lu-jah! lu-jah!

1 Wor-thy is Christ, the Lamb who was slain, whose
2 Pow-er, rich-es, wis-dom, and strength, and
3 Sing with all the peo-ple of God, and
4 For the Lamb who was slain has be-

D.C.

blood set us free to be peo-ple of God.
hon-our, bless-ing, and glo-ry are his.
join in the hymn of all cre-a-tion.
gun now to reign. Hal-le-lu-jah!

Words: adapt. John W. Arthur 1978
Music: Richard Hillert 1978

FESTIVAL CANTICLE
Irregular

Daily Prayer

Services of Daily Prayer
An Introduction

All believers share the urge to place the beginning and the ending of the day in God's hands. From earliest times, Christ's victory over death has been symbolized by the dawning of a new day and the lighting of lamps at the close of day.

When we gather in community, we express longing for fellowship with God in what is often called 'devotions'. The following services for various times of day have been prepared with this common practice in mind. They may be used by individuals or groups, in the home or the church, within meetings or informal gatherings, and adapted to suit the local context.

The **common elements** of weekday worship are **song, scripture, silence,** and **prayer**. The focus of the service is praise of God and prayer for the whole world. Symbols of our faith—a cross, a Bible, a candle—are helpful but not essential, and are always secondary to the symbol of the Christian community gathered for prayer. The sense of community is heightened when worshippers stand or sit in a circle. Leadership may be offered from within the circle or from a lectern. It is intended that the services be led by one or more lay persons.

Songs, hymns, responses, and the Lord's Prayer may all be sung, with or without accompaniment. Singing together is a powerful expression of faith.

One or more passages of **scripture** may be read. The scripture chosen should encourage praise and prayer.

Silence for the purpose of meditation and reflection is recommended following a reading from scripture. A commentary or brief meditation may be offered, but is not essential. In response to a reading, a hymn or verse of a hymn may also be sung, the people remaining seated.

Prayer may be offered in the personal words of the leader or read from among the prayers provided. Within the prayers of thanksgiving and intercession, worshippers are invited to name particular people or events. Material in square brackets may be included as appropriate. Careful explanation, perhaps prior to the service, will help worshippers enter more fully into the prayers.

When **Daily Prayer for Late Afternoon or Evening** begins with Thanksgiving for Light, the Opening Sentences, Prayer, and Evening Hymn are omitted.

As we offer praise and prayers by day or at dusk, may we find afresh the power of the resurrection in our common life in Christ.

Daily Prayer
for Morning or Mid-Day Devotions

Opening Sentences

All occasions
O God, open my lips,
   and my mouth shall proclaim your praise. (Psalm 51)

In the morning
I pray to you, O God;
   you hear my voice
   in the morning;
at sunrise I offer my prayer
   and wait for your answer.
                      (Psalm 5)

At mid-day
Those who wait for God
shall renew their strength,
   they shall mount up
   with wings like eagles;
they shall run and not be weary,
   they shall walk and not faint.
                      (Isaiah 40)

Prayer

Morning
Let us pray:

Holy God,
you call us together
   to reflect on your Word,
   and our life in your world.
Be with us now
   as we sing and pray together,
that we may hear your voice
   and understand your way.
This we pray through
   Jesus, the Christ. **Amen.**

Mid-day
Let us pray:

Sustaining God,
in the midst of our day,
   and embraced by your world,
we call upon your wisdom;
   we draw upon your strength;
   we rely upon your grace.
Help us to continue faithfully in your way,
   by the power of the Holy Spirit
   and in the name of Jesus. **Amen.**

Hymn and/or Psalm

*A hymn, if included, will be chosen to suit the time of day or occasion. A psalm for
the morning (one of psalms 51, 63, 67, or 95) or another is always appropriate.*

Scripture

At the end of the reading, the reader may say:

Hear what the Spirit
is saying to the church.
    Thanks be to God.

or   The word of God.
    Thanks be to God.

Silent reflection

Silence may be followed by a variety of responses, such as action, music, or words.

A Scripture Song (see pages 900, 901) may be sung.

Prayers of Thanksgiving and Intercession

One of the following prayers (A or B) or another may be offered. At various points during the prayers, a sung response may be used (see 948-954)

A

Thanksgiving

Generous and loving God,
we thank you for your blessings without number.
We bless you for the beauty of creation:
    for day and night, for summer and winter;
    for sun and rain, for seed-time and harvest;
    for your bounty supplying all our needs.
We bless you for protecting us in our weakness,
    and renewing our strength of spirit;
    for guiding us as we resist evil,
    and calling us to your truth, and to your service.
We praise you for sending Jesus to be among us:
    for his life on earth, his sufferings and death,
    for his resurrection to new life, and the gift of the Holy Spirit.
Grant, O God, that our hearts may grow in thankfulness
    for these and all your gifts of grace,
so that as the people of new life, we may proclaim your praise;
    [in Jesus' name. **Amen.**]

Intercessions

Each portion of the prayer may conclude:
Gracious God, hear our prayer;
and in your love, answer.

Compassionate God,
hear us as we pray:
for your church and its varied ministries . . .
for the work of justice and the healing of creation . . .
for the care of strangers, neighbours, family, friends . . .
for those isolated by sickness, sorrow, violence, fear . . .
for those broken by the world . . .
for those who face death . . .

Generous and compassionate God,
in your loving purpose, answer our prayers and fulfil our hopes;
and in all things for which we pray,
give us grace and wisdom to accept your will,
for the sake of Jesus Christ. **Amen.**

or **B**

Thanksgiving

Bountiful God, we lift our voices in prayers of praise,
for you have raised us to new life in Jesus Christ,
and your blessings to us and to your world
come in generous measure.
In our hearts and with our voices, we name before you
that for which we give thanks:

Specific events and people may be named.

Intercessions

Each portion of the prayer may conclude:
Gracious God, hear our prayer;
and in your love, answer.

Merciful God, you are close to all in need,
and by our prayers we draw close to you.
Claiming your love in Christ Jesus for the whole world,
we dare to pray for others.

Committing ourselves to care in his name for those around us,
  we bring our prayers and concerns for friend and stranger:
Prayers for people and events, both near and far, may be offered.

Gracious God, hear our prayer,
And in your love, answer.

Bountiful and merciful God,
accept the prayers of your people, and strengthen us to do your will;
through Jesus Christ. **Amen.**

Lord's Prayer

Other forms of the Prayer of Jesus may be found on page 916.

With Jesus,
we pray together, saying:

Our Father in heaven,
hallowed be your name.
Your kingdom come,
your will be done
  on earth as in heaven.
Give us today our daily bread
Forgive us our sins, as we forgive
  those who sin against us.
Save us from the time of trial,
  and deliver us from evil.
For the kingdom, the power,
  and the glory are yours,
now and forever. Amen.

As children turn to a mother
who watches over them,
let us turn to God, saying:

Our Father, who art in heaven,
  hallowed be thy name.
Thy kingdom come,
Thy will be done
  on earth as it is in heaven.
Give us this day our daily bread;
and forgive us our trespasses,
  as we forgive those
  who trespass against us;
and lead us not into temptation,
  but deliver us from evil.
For thine is the kingdom,
  and the power, and the glory,
for ever and ever. Amen.

A hymn may be sung

Blessing

May we continue to grow in the grace
and knowledge of Jesus Christ.
  Amen.
Bless God's name.
  Thanks be to God.

or The God of peace be with us.
  Amen.
Bless the name of God.
  Thanks be to God.

Daily Prayer
For Late Afternoon or Evening Devotions

The service begins with either *Thanksgiving for Light* or *Opening Sentences*

Thanksgiving for Light

After all have gathered, a candle is lit in the midst of the community.

Light and peace in Jesus Christ!
Thanks be to God.

or

Jesus Christ,
you are the light of the world,
    light shining in deepest night,
    which cannot overcome it.
Stay with us now, for it is evening;
    the day is almost over.

Let us pray:

We give you thanks and praise,
O God of endless light,
through our Saviour, Jesus Christ.
In him your light
    shines in our hearts
    and reveals the light
    that never fades.
As daylight comes to an end
    and darkness begins to fall,
we thank you for the light of day
    created for our work and pleasure,
    and bless you for the gift
    of this evening light.
All praise to you, O God,
    through Jesus Christ, in whom
all glory and honour is yours,
    with the Holy Spirit,
    in the holy church
    now and forever. **Amen.**

Opening Sentences

Our help is in the name of God,
    who made heaven and earth.

Let us give thanks
to our sovereign God
    who is worthy of all
    thanksgiving and praise.

Prayer

Let us pray:

Loving God,
in whose mercy we find our peace,
in whose presence we find our place,
in whose world we find our calling:
grant us grace to hear
    and accept your Word,
that we may be faithful followers
of your will and your way all our days.
In Jesus' name we pray. **Amen.**

or

Let us pray:

O God, our Guide and Companion,
you have brought us
    through this day
to a time of reflection and rest.
Calm our souls,
and refresh us with your peace.
In Christ, draw us closer
    to one another
in the bonds of his love.
We pray in the power of the Spirit.
Amen.

Hymn to Christ the Light

See numbers 434 and 435.

Hymn

A hymn, if included, will be chosen to suit the time of day or the occasion.

Psalm

A psalm for evening (one of Psalms 23, 51, 63, 141) or another is always appropriate.

Scripture

At the end of the reading, the reader may say:

Hear what the Spirit
is saying to the church.
Thanks be to God.

or The word of God.
Thanks be to God.

Silence may be followed by a variety of responses, such as action, music, or words.

A Scripture Song (see pages 898, 899, or 878) may be sung.

Prayers of Thanksgiving and Intercession

One of the following prayers (A or B) or another may be offered. At various points during the prayers, a sung response may be used (see 948-954)

A

Thanksgiving

Gracious and loving God,
we thank you for the blessings of life.
We bless you for the wonders of the world:
    for heights of mountains and breadth of prairie,
    for diversity of peoples and intimacy of families,
    for the goodness of all you have made.
We bless you for the gift of Jesus Christ,
    who lived and died, and lives again
    wherever justice is known, wherever love is found.
We bless you for your life among us
    forgiving sins, renewing spirits,
    and refreshing us in the fellowship of your table.

Grant, O God, that in the quietness of the evening
and in the hush of the night,
our hearts may be filled with thankfulness
for these and all your blessings;
[in the name of Jesus we pray. **Amen.**]

Intercessions

Each portion of the prayer may conclude:
Gracious God, hear our prayer;
and in your love, answer.

Mighty and tender God,
hear us as we pray,
for you bring release to the captives and rest to the weary,
and you know the way of suffering in Jesus Christ our Saviour.
We pray:
for the church throughout the world in its life and ministries . . .
for the nations as they strive for peace and justice . . .
for all who suffer: the sick, the sorrowful, the lonely, the oppressed . . .
for peaceful relationships among friends, among strangers . . .

Tender and mighty God, in your loving purpose
answer our prayers and fulfil our hopes.
In all things for which we pray,
give us the grace and wisdom to accept your will,
for the sake of Jesus Christ. **Amen.**

or **B**

Thanksgiving

We give you our praise and thanks, O Holy God,
for all the gifts of love we have received from you,
and for your light revealed in Jesus Christ.
We bless you for the wonders of creation,
the delights of human companionship
and the assurances of faith.
Especially today we thank you for . . .

Specific events and people may be named.

Intercessions

Each portion of the prayer may conclude:
     Gracious God, hear our prayer;
     and in your love, answer.

We lift up our concerns for others, O God of compassion.
In Jesus Christ, your saving love scattered the power of death
     and your eternal light shines in the darkness.
With confidence, we remember before you the suffering of humanity
     and the brokenness of the world.
Especially today we pray for . . .

Specific prayers for people and events, near and far, may be named.

Holy and compassionate God,
     accept the prayers of your people, and strengthen us to do your will;
          through Jesus Christ. **Amen.**

Lord's Prayer

Other forms of the Prayer of Jesus may be found at 916

With Jesus,
we pray together saying:

As children turn to a mother
who watches over them,
let us turn to God, saying:

Our Father in heaven,
hallowed be your name.
Your kingdom come,
your will be done
     on earth as in heaven.
Give us today our daily bread.
Forgive us our sins, as we forgive
     those who sin against us.
Save us from the time of trial,
     and deliver us from evil.
For the kingdom, the power,
     and the glory are yours,
now and forever. Amen.

Our Father, who art in heaven,
     hallowed be thy name.
Thy kingdom come,
Thy will be done
     on earth as it is in heaven.
Give us this day our daily bread;
and forgive us our trespasses,
     as we forgive those
     who trespass against us;
and lead us not into temptation,
     but deliver us from evil.
For thine is the kingdom,
     and the power, and the glory,
for ever and ever. Amen.

A hymn may be sung

Blessing

May the peace of God,
which surpasses all understanding,
guard our hearts and minds
    in Christ Jesus. **Amen.**

or May the grace of Jesus Christ,
    the love of God,
    and the communion of the Holy Spirit
      be with us all,
    this night and always. **Amen.**

At the Close of a Meeting

Eternal God,
you call us to ventures
of which we cannot see the ending,
    by paths as yet untrodden,
    through perils unknown.
Give us faith to go out with courage,
    not knowing where we go,
but only that your hand is leading us,
    and your love supporting us;
through Jesus Christ, our Lord. **Amen.**

Eric Milner-White

At Day's End

Dear Jesus,
as a hen covers her chicks
    with her wings to keep them safe,
spread out your golden wings,
    and protect us this night. **Amen.**

Traditional prayer from India

Alternate versions of the Prayer of Jesus

A Translation

Our Father-Mother, who is in the heavens,
    may your name be made holy,
    may your dominion come,
    may your will be done,
    on earth as it is in heaven.
Give us today the bread we need;
    and forgive us our debts,
    as we have forgiven our debtors;
    and do not put us to the test,
    but rescue us from evil.
For yours is the dominion, and the power,
    and the glory forever. Amen.

A Paraphrase

Eternal Spirit,
Earth-maker, Pain-bearer, Life-giver,
Source of all that is and that shall be.
Father and Mother of us all,
Loving God, in whom is heaven:

The hallowing of your name echo
    through the universe!
The way of your justice be followed
    by peoples of the world!
Your heavenly will be done
    by all created beings!
Your commonwealth of peace and freedom
    sustain our hope and come on earth.

With the bread we need for today, feed us.
In the hurts we absorb from one another, forgive us.
In times of temptation and test, strengthen us.
From trials too great to endure, spare us.
From the grip of all that is evil, free us.

For you reign in the glory of the power that is love,
now and for ever. Amen.

Affirmations of Faith, Creeds, The Lord's Prayer, Additional Prayers

THE APOSTLES' CREED

I believe in God, the Father almighty,
    creator of heaven and earth.

I believe in Jesus Christ, God's only Son, our Lord,
    who was conceived by the Holy Spirit,
    born of the Virgin Mary,
    suffered under Pontius Pilate,
    was crucified, died, and was buried;
    he descended to the dead.
    On the third day he rose again;
    he ascended into heaven,
    he is seated at the right hand of the Father,
    and he will come to judge the living and the dead.

I believe in the Holy Spirit,
    the holy catholic Church, the communion of saints,
    the forgiveness of sins, the resurrection of the body,
    and the life everlasting. Amen.

English Language Liturgical Consultation, 1988

A NEW CREED

We are not alone,
    we live in God's world.

We believe in God:
    who has created and is creating,
    who has come in Jesus,
      the Word made flesh,
      to reconcile and make new,
    who works in us and others
      by the Spirit.

We trust in God.

We are called to be the Church:
    to celebrate God's presence,
    to live with respect in Creation,
    to love and serve others,
    to seek justice and resist evil,
    to proclaim Jesus, crucified and risen,
      our judge and our hope.
In life, in death, in life beyond death,
    God is with us.
We are not alone.

    Thanks be to God.

The United Church of Canada, General Council 1968, alt.

LE SYMBOLE DES APÔTRES

Je crois en Dieu, le Père tout-puissant,
　　créateur du ciel et de la terre.

Je crois en Jésus Christ, son Fils unique, notre Seigneur,
　　qui a été conçu du Saint-Esprit,
　　est né de la vierge Marie,
　　a souffert sous Ponce Pilate,
　　a été crucifié, est mort, et a été enseveli,
　　est descendu aux enfers,
　　le troisième jour est ressuscité des morts,
　　est monté aux cieux,
　　est assis à la droite de Dieu le Père tout-puissant
　　d'où il viendra juger les vivants et les morts.

Je crois en l'Esprit Saint
　　à la sainte Église catholique,* à la communion des saints,
　　à la rémission des péchés, à la résurrection de la chair,
　　et à la vie éternelle. Amen.

* *ou* universelle

CONFESSION DE FOI DE L'ÉGLISE UNIE DU CANADA

Nous ne sommes pas seuls,
　　nous vivons dans le monde que Dieu a créé.

Nous croyons en Dieu
　　qui a créé et qui continue à créer,
　　qui est venu en Jésus, Parole faite chair,
　　pour réconcilier et renouveler,
　　qui travaille en nous et parmi nous par son Esprit.

Nous avons confiance en lui.

Nous sommes appelés à constituer l'Église:
　　pour célébrer la présence de Dieu,
　　pour vivre avec respect dans la création,
　　pour aimer et servir les autres,
　　pour rechercher la justice et résister au mal,
　　pour proclamer Jésus, crucifié et ressuscité,
　　　　notre juge et notre espérance.
Dans la vie, dans la mort,
　　et dans la vie au-delà de la mort,
　　Dieu est avec nous.
Nous ne sommes pas seuls.

　　Grâces soient rendues à Dieu.　　*French translation by Consistoire Laurentien*

THE NICENE CREED

We believe in one God,
>   the Father, the Almighty,
>   maker of heaven and earth,
>   of all that is, seen and unseen.

We believe in one Lord, Jesus Christ,
>   the only Son of God,
>   eternally begotten of the Father,
>   God from God, Light from Light,
>   true God from true God,
>   begotten, not made,
>   of one Being with the Father;
>   through him all things were made.
>   For us and for our salvation
>   he came down from heaven,
>   was incarnate of the Holy Spirit and the Virgin Mary
>   and became truly human.
>   For our sake he was crucified under Pontius Pilate;
>   he suffered death and was buried.
>   On the third day he rose again
>   in accordance with the Scriptures;
>   he ascended into heaven
>   and is seated at the right hand of the Father.
>   He will come again in glory to judge the living and the dead,
>   and his kingdom will have no end.

We believe in the Holy Spirit, the Lord, the giver of life,
>   who proceeds from the Father [and the Son],
>   who with the Father and the Son
>   is worshipped and glorified,
who has spoken through the prophets.
We believe in one holy catholic and apostolic Church.
We acknowledge one baptism for the forgiveness of sins.
We look for the resurrection of the dead,
>   and the life of the world to come. Amen.   *English Language Liturgical Consultation, 1988*

THE LORD'S PRAYER

Our Father, who art in heaven,
    hallowed be thy name,
    thy kingdom come,
    thy will be done,
    on earth, as it is in heaven.
Give us this day our daily bread,
And forgive us our trespasses,
    as we forgive those who trespass against us.
And lead us not into temptation,
    but deliver us from evil:
For thine is the kingdom, the power, and the glory
    forever and ever. Amen.

THE LORD'S PRAYER (Ecumenical Version)

Our Father in heaven,
    hallowed be your name,
    your kingdom come,
    your will be done,
    on earth as in heaven.
Give us today our daily bread.
Forgive us our sins
    as we forgive those who sin against us.
Save us from the time of trial
    and deliver us from evil.
For the kingdom, the power, and the glory are yours
    now and for ever. Amen.

English Language Liturgical Consultation, 1988

NOTRE PÈRE (Version Ecuménique)

Notre Père qui es aux cieux,
    que ton nom soit sanctifié,
    que ton règne vienne,
    que ta volonté soit faite
      sur la terre comme au ciel.
Donne-nous aujourd'hui notre pain de ce jour.
Pardonne-nous nos offenses
    comme nous pardonnons aussi à ceux qui nous ont offensés.
Et ne nous soumets pas à la tentation,
    mais délivre-nous du mal.

Car c'est à toi qu'appartiennent le règne, la puissance et la gloire,
    pour* les siècles des siècles. Amen.

* *ou* aux siècles des siècles.

French translation by Consistoire Laurentien

ᑲᑎᐯᓂᒋᑫᐨ ᐅᑕᔭᒥᐊᐧᐃᐣ The Lord's Prayer

ᓄᑕᐧᐃᓇᐣ ᑭᒋᑭᓯᑯᐠ ᑲᐃᑕᔭᐣ
ᑲᑕᐧᐃ ᑭᐢᑌᓂᒋᑲᑌᐧ ᑭᑎᓯᓂᑲᓱᐧᐃᐣ
ᑭᑐᑭᒪᐧᐃᐧᐃᐣ ᑲᑕᐧᐃ ᐅᒋᒋᐸᓂᐧ
ᑭᐟ ᐃᑌᓂᑕᒧᐧᐃᐣ ᑲᑕᐧᐃᑐᒋᑲᑌᐧ
ᐅᑕ ᐊᐢᑭᐠ ᑕᐱᐡᑯᐨ ᑭᒋᑭᓯᑯᐠ
ᒥᓂᓇᐣ ᒪᑲ ᐊᓄᐨ ᑲᑭᓯᑲᐠ ᑫᐅᒋ ᐱᒪᑎᓯᔭᐠ
ᐧᐁᐯᓂᑕᒪᐧᐃᓇᐣ ᒪᑲ ᓂᐧᐊᓂᑎᐧᐃᓂᓇᐣ
ᐁᐃᓯ ᐧᐁᐯᓂᑕᒪᐧᐃᔭᑭᒋᐠ ᑲᐧᐊᓂᑐᑕᐧᐃᔭᑭᐠ
ᒪᑲ ᒥᑕᐧᑫᓇᒪᐧᐃᓇᐣ ᒪᒋᑫᐧᑲᓇ
ᐧᐁᓴ ᑭᓇ ᑭᑎᐱᓇᐧᐁᐧᐃᓯᐣ ᐅᑭᒪᐧᐃᐧᐃᐣ ᓀᐢᑕ ᑲᐡᑭᐅᐧᐃᐣ
ᓀᐢᑕ ᑭᐢᑌᓂᑕᑯᓯᐧᐃᐣ
ᐊᓄᐨ ᓀᐢᑕ ᑲᑭᑫ. ᐁᒣᐣ.

ᔦᓇᔾᑎᐟ ᐊᔭᒥᐁᐧᐃᑲᒥᐠ ᐊᔭᒥᐊᐧᐃᐣ A New Creed

ᒧᓇ ᑭᐯᔭᑯᓇᐣ,
ᑭᑎᑕᒥᐣ ᑭᒋᒪᓂᑐ ᐅᑕᐢᑭᐠ,
ᑭᑕᐧᐯᑕᐧᐊᒥᐣ ᑭᒋᒪᓂᑐ,
ᑲᑭᐅᓯᐃᑕᐠ ᓀᐢᑕ ᑲᐱᒥᐅᓯᐃᑕᐠ,
ᒋᓴᓯᐠ ᑲᑭᐅᒋᐯᒋᑕᑯᓯᐠ,
ᐅᑎᐧᑌᐧᐃᐣ ᐧᐃᔭᓯᐠ ᑭᐃᓯᐅᓯᑕᓂᐧᐊᐣ,
ᒋᑭᐧᐁᐅᓯᑕᓂᐧᐊᐠ ᓀᐢᑕ ᒋᐅᐢᑭᐅᓯᐃᐟ,
ᐁᐊᐢᑐᐢᑫᐨ ᐱᒋ ᑭᔭᓇᐧ ᓀᐢᑕ ᑯᑕᑭᔭᐠ,
ᐊᐧᐊ ᐊᒐᐠ,
ᑭᑕᐧᐯᑕᐧᐊᓇᐧ ᑭᒋᒪᓂᑐ,
ᑭᑭᓇᑐᒥᑲᐧᐃᓇᐧ ᑭᓇᐧᐃᐟ ᑕᐱᐢᑯᐨ ᐊᔭᒥᐁᐧᐃᑲᒥᐠ ᒋᐃᑕᑯᓯᔭᐠ,
ᒋᒪᒥᒋᒪᔭᐠ ᑭᒋᒪᓂᑐ ᑲᐧᐃᒣᐧᐃᑯᔭᐠ,
ᒋᐱᒪᑎᓯᔭᐠ ᒋᑯᓯᐧᑫᑕᒪᐠ ᐅᓯᐃᑯᐧᐃᐣ,
ᒋᓴᑭᐃᐧᐁᔭᐠ ᓀᐢᑕ ᒋᐊᑐᐢᑲᐧᐊᑭᐠ ᑯᑕᑭᔭᐠ,
ᒋᓇᑐᓇᒪᐠ ᐧᑲᔭᐢᑯᑐᑕᒧᐧᐃᐣ ᓀᐢᑕ ᒋᓂᑲᑌᓇᐠ ᒪᒋᑫᐧᑲᓇ,
ᒋᑌᐧᐸᑕᑭᐠ ᒋᓴᐢ,
ᑲᑭᒋᐢᑕᐢᐧᑲᐅᐟ ᓀᐢᑕ ᑲᑭᐧᐊᓂᐡᑲᐟ,
ᑭᑎᐸᐢᑯᓂᑫᐧᐃᓂᓂᒥᓇᐧ ᓀᐢᑕ ᑭᑕᐢᐯᓂᒧᐧᐃᓂᓇᐧ,
ᐊᐣᑕ ᐱᒪᑎᓯᐧᐃᓂᐠ, ᐊᐣᑕ ᓂᐱᐧᐃᓂᐠ,
ᐱᒪᑎᓯᐧᐃᓂᐠ ᐊᐧᐊᓯᑌ ᓂᐱᐧᐃᐣ,
ᑭᒋᒪᓂᑐ ᑲᐧᐃᒣᐧᐃᑯᓇᐧ,
ᒧᓇ ᑭᐯᔭᑯᓇᐣ,
ᑭᑕᓇᓇᐢᑯᒪᑕ ᑭᒋᒪᓂᑐ.

Cree translation by Ethnic Ministry Council, The United Church of Canada

主 の 祈 り The Lord's Prayer

天に在（まし）ます我らの父よ
願わくは御名（みな）を崇（あが）めさせ給（たま）え
御国（みくに）を来（き）たらせ給え
御意（みこころ）の天に成る如（ごと）く地にも成させ給え
我らの日用の糧（かて）を今日も与え給え
我らに罪を犯す者を我らが赦（ゆる）す如く
　我らの罪をも赦し給え
我らを試みに遇（あ）わせず
　悪より救（すく）い出し給え
国と威力（ちから）と栄（さか）えとは
　限りなく汝（なんじ）の有（もの）なればなり
　　　　　　　　　　アーメン

新 信 条 A New Creed

私たちは独（ひとり）りではなく、神の世界に生きています。
私たちは天地（てんち）を創造し、今も創造されている方、
　人を和解させ、新しく創（つく）り変えるため肉となった
　御言葉、即（すなわ）ちイエスにあって来られた方、そして
　聖霊によって私たちや他人のうちに働く神を信じます。
私たちはその神に信頼します。
私たちは神の御臨在（ごりんざい）を祝うため、
　創造世界（そうぞうせかい）を尊（とうと）んで生きるため、
　他人を愛し、他人に仕（つか）えるため、
　義を求め、悪に抵抗（ていこう）するため、
　十字架にかかり、甦（よみが）えられ、私たちの裁（さば）き、
　私たちの望（のぞ）みとなられたイエスを宣（の）べ伝えるため、
　そのための教会であれ、と呼ばれています。
生きている時も死ぬ時も、また死後の命（いのち）を生きる時も、
　神が共にいて下さいます。
私たちは独りではありません。
　感謝を神に捧げます。

Japanese translation by Ethnic Ministry Council, The United Church of Canada

우리 신조   A New Creed

우리는 홀로가 아닙니다.   하나님의 세계에서 삽니다.
우리는 하나님을 믿습니다.
　만물을 창조하셨고, 지금도 창조하시며,
　화해시키고 새롭게 하기 위하여,
　말씀이 몸을 이룬 예수님 안에 오셨으며,
　우리와 남들 안에서 성령으로 역사 하십니다.
우리는 하나님을 신뢰합니다.
우리는 교회를 이루라고 부름받았습니다.
　하나님의 임재를 찬양하고, 우주 만물을 존중하며 살고,
　남들을 사랑하며 섬기고, 정의를 추구하며 악에 항거하고,
　십자가형을 당하시고 살아나셔서, 우리의 심판자와 희망이 되신
　예수님을 선포하라고 부름받았습니다.
삶에서, 죽음에서, 죽음을 넘는 삶에서 하나님이 우리와 함께 하십니다.
우리는 홀로가 아닙니다.
하나님께 감사드립니다.

주기도문   The Lord's Prayer

하늘에 계신 우리 아버지여,
　이름이 거룩히 여김을 받으시오며, 나라이 임하옵시며,
　뜻이 하늘에서 이룬 것같이 땅에서도 이루어지이다.
오늘날 우리에게 일용할 양식을 주옵시고,
　우리가 우리에게 죄 지은 자를 사하여 준 것같이
　우리 죄를 사하여 주시옵고,
　우리를 시험에 들게 하지 마옵시고, 다만 악에서 구하옵소서.
대개 나라와 권세와 영광이 아버지께 영원히 있사옵나이다. 아멘.

Korean translation by Ethnic Ministry Council, The United Church of Canada

A New Creed

信 仰 告 別

阮無孤單，阮住在屬於上帝的世界。

阮信上帝，

過去有創造現在繼續在創造，

祂對耶穌道成肉體，

使阮與上帝和好成為新的人，

通過聖神，

祂在我與別人的心內作工。

阮倚靠上帝。

阮受呼召做伙成為教會，

來讚美上帝的臨在，

來疼與服務別人，

來追求公義與拒絕罪惡，

來宣揚被釘於十字架與復活的主，

祂做阮的審判與盼望。

無論是生，是死，或是死以後，

上帝攏與阮同在。

阮無孤單。

感謝上帝！

The Lord's Prayer

主 禱 文

阮在天裡的父，

願你的名聖，

你的國臨到，

你的旨意得成，

在地裡親像在天裡。

阮的日食今仔日給阮，

赦免阮的辜負，

親像阮亦有赦免辜負阮的人。

勿得導阮入於試，

著救阮脫離彼個惡的。

因為國，權能，

榮光攏是你所有，

代代無盡。阿們。

Taiwanese translation by Ethnic Ministry Council, The United Church of Canada

主禱文　The Lord's Prayer

我們在天上的父：

　　願人都尊祢的名為聖。

　　願祢的國降臨。

　　願祢的旨意行在地上，如同行在天上。

　　我們日用的飲食，求父今日賜給我們。

　　又求饒恕我們的罪，

　　　　因為我們饒恕得罪我們的人。

　　不叫我們遇見試探，

　　拯救我們脫離兇惡；

因為國度，權柄，榮耀，全是祢的，直到永遠。

　　　　　　　　　　　　　阿們。

信仰宣言　A New Creed

我們並不孤立，我們活在上帝的世界中。

我們信上帝：

　他創造萬有，並繼續施行創造，

　道成了肉身，在耶穌裡臨世

　　　使人和好與更新，

　並藉聖靈在我們和他人當中作工。

我們信靠祂。

祂呼召我們成為教會，

　慶賀上帝的臨格，

　愛護及服務他人，持守公義，拒抗邪惡。

　宣揚耶穌為被釘十架及復活的主，

　　　是我們的審判者，也是我們的盼望。

無論生與死，今生或來世，上帝都與我們同在。

我們並不孤立。

感謝上帝。

Chinese translation by Ethnic Ministry Council, The United Church of Canada

A New Creed

KREDO NG PINAGKAISANG IGLESIA SA CANADA

Tayo ay hindi nag-iisa, nabubuhay tayo sa daigdig ng Dios.

Sumasampalataya tayo sa Dios:
 na lumalang at lumalalang,
 na naparito sa pamamagitan ni Hesus, ang Salita
  na naging laman, upang makipagkasundo
  at gawing bago,
 na gumagawa sa atin at sa lahat sa pamamagitan ng Espiritu.

Tumitiwala tayo sa Dios.

Tayo ay tinawag upang maging Iglesia:
 upang ipagdiwang ang pakikisama ng Dios,
 upang mabuhay na pinahahalagahan ang Nilalang,
 upang ibigin at paglingkuran ang kapwa,
 upang hanapin ang katarungan at bakahin ang kasamaan,
 upang ipahayag si Hesus, na napako sa krus at nabuhay na
  maguli, ating hukom at ating pag-asa.

Sa kabuhayan, sa kamatayan, sa kabuhayan sa kabila ng kamatayan,
 ang Dios ay kasama natin.

Tayo ay hindi nag-iisa.

Magpasalamat tayo sa Dios.

AMA NAMIN   The Lord's Prayer

Ama namin, sumasalangit Ka;

Sambahin ang pangalan Mo;

Dumating and kaharian Mo;

Gawin ang kalooban Mo, kung paano sa langit,
 gayon din naman sa lupa.

Ibigay Mo sa amin ang aming kakanin sa araw-araw.

Ipatawad Mo sa amin ang aming mga kasalanan, gaya
 naman namin na nagpatawad sa mga nagkasala sa amin.

At huwag Mo kaming ipahintulot sa tukso, kundi
 iligtas mo kami sa lahat ng masama;

Sapagka't Iyo ang kaharian, ang kapangyarihan;
 at ang kaluwalhatian, magpakailanman. AMEN.

Philipino translation by Ethnic Ministry Council, The United Church of Canada

Additional Prayers

Prayers of Confession

A

Holy and gracious God,
gathered as your people responding to your call,
we confess
    the self that is not aware of sinning;
    the heart that is too hardened to repent;
    the pride that dares not admit it is wrong;
    the righteousness that knows no fault;
    the callousness that has ceased to care;
    the blindness that can see nothing but its own will.
God, in your healing love, forgive us;
through our Saviour, Jesus Christ. **Amen.**

B

Gracious God,
as people called to be your presence in the world,
we search our hearts, and ask your forgiveness:
    for opportunities not taken,
    for care not given,
        forgive us, we pray.
    For sorrow not shared,
    for joy not celebrated,
        forgive us, we pray.
    For love not offered,
    forgiveness not extended,
        forgive us, we pray.
    For those failings we cannot speak aloud,
        forgive us, we pray.
Gracious God,
we seek your healing grace,
and ask forgiveness in the name of Jesus. **Amen.**

Donald Daniel 1989, alt.

A Prayer for Pardon

Merciful One,
our hearts long for your forgiveness.
Touch us with your healing,
    cleanse us of our guilt,
    renew our spirits,
that we may serve you with joy
all our days. Amen.

Elise S. Eslinger 1985, alt.

Prayers of Thanksgiving

A

Let us give thanks, always and for everything,
saying, "**We thank you, God.**"

For the beauty and wonder of creation,
    we thank you, God.
For all that is gracious in the lives of all your people,
revealing the image of Christ,
    we thank you, God.
For food and shelter, for families and friends,
    we thank you, God.
For minds to think and hearts to love,
    we thank you, God.
For the strength to work, for delight in play,
for the energy to live, and time to seek your way,
    we thank you, God.
For those who are courageous in conflict, patient in suffering,
and faithful in adversity,
    we thank you, God.
For all who pursue justice, truth, and peace,
    we thank you, God.
[Today, we give thanks especially for . . .;
for these signs of your love,
    we thank you, God.]
For all the saints who have reflected the light of Christ,
    we thank you, God.
These and all our prayers, spoken and unspoken,
we offer to you through Jesus,
your Gift and our Salvation. **Amen.**

B

Praise and thanks to you, O God,
for all you have done for us.
We thank you for the splendour of the whole creation,
for the beauty of this world, for the wonder of life,
and for the mystery of love.
We thank you for the blessing of family and friends,
and for loving care
which surrounds us on every side.
We thank you for the delight we find
in finishing well our daily tasks,
and for helping us find comfort in you,
even in failure or distress.
Above all, we thank you for your Son, Jesus Christ;
for the truth of his word and the example of his life;
for his faithfulness, his dying, his rising to life again,
by which we, too, are raised to life anew.
Grant us the gift of your Spirit,
that we may know Christ, and make him known;
and through him, at all times and in all places,
may give thanks to you in all things. **Amen.**

C

God of the heavens and the earth,
with joy we praise you,
we thank you, we honour you.

Because you have made us like yourself,
made us to be creative in your world,
we praise you.

Because you have freed us through Jesus
freed us to be people of light and love,
we thank you.

Because your Spirit is present with us,
present to guide and renew,
we honour you.

God of the heavens and the earth,
with joy we praise you,
we thank you, we honour you for ever. Amen.

Communion Settings and Additional Service Music

Communion Setting A

Lord Have Mercy (*Kyrie*)

Marty Haugen

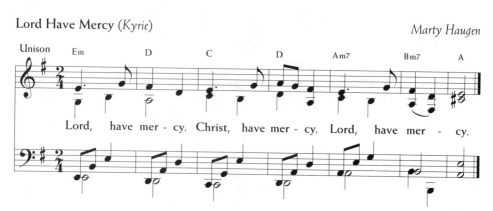

Lord, have mer - cy. Christ, have mer - cy. Lord, have mer - cy.

Holy, Holy, Holy (*Sanctus and Benedictus*)

Marty Haugen

Ho - ly, ho - ly, ho - ly are you, God of pow - er and might; heav - en and earth are filled with your glo - ry. Ho - san - na in the high - est!

Bless - ed is the one who comes in your name. Ho -

san - na in the high - est, ho - san - na in the high - est!

Memorial Acclamation

Marty Haugen

Christ has died. Christ is ris - en. Christ will come, come a - gain.

Great Amen

Marty Haugen

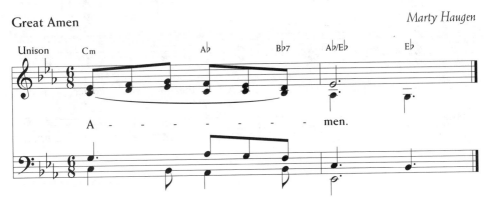

A - - - - - - men.

Communion Setting B

Lord Have Mercy (*Kyrie*)   *Stuart Semple 1989*

Lord, have mer - cy. Christ, have mer - cy. Lord, have mer - cy.

Music copyright © 1995 Stuart Semple

Holy, Holy, Holy (*Sanctus and Benedictus*)   *Stuart Semple 1989*

Ho - ly, ho - ly, ho - ly Lord, God of power and might;

heav - en and earth are full of your glo - ry. Ho - san - na

in the high - est! Bless'd is the one who comes in the

Music copyright © 1995 Stuart Semple

name of the Lord. Ho - san - na in the high - est!

Memorial Acclamation

Stuart Semple 1989

Christ has died. Christ is ris - en. Christ will come a - gain.

Great Amen

Stuart Semple 1989

A - men. A - men. A - - - men.

Communion Setting C
(The Saint Chad's Setting)

Holy, Holy, Holy (*Sanctus and Benedictus*)   *David Saint*

Ho-ly, ho-ly, ho-ly Lord, God of

power and God of might, heaven and earth are full, heaven and

earth are full, heaven and earth are full of your glo-ry. Heaven and

(unaccomp. ad lib.)

comes in the name of the Lord.

All

Bless - ed is he who comes in the name of the Lord.

Ho - san - na, ho - san - na,

(Descant) Ho - san - na.

ho - san - na in the high - est.

Memorial Acclamation

David Saint

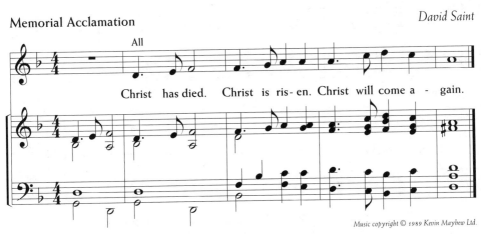

All

Christ has died. Christ is ris- en. Christ will come a - gain.

Great Amen

David Saint

All

A - men, a - men, a - - - men.

Lamb of God (*Agnus Dei*)

David Saint

First time: sopranos and altos
Second time: tenors and basses

Unison

Lamb of God, you take a-way the sins of the world;

have mer - cy on us, have mer - cy on us.

Choir (full)

Lamb of God, you take a - way the sins of the world;

All

grant us peace, grant us peace.

Communion Setting D

Holy, Holy, Holy (*Sanctus and Benedictus*)

David M. Young

Ho - ly, ho - ly, ho - ly, God of pow - er and might; heav - en and earth are full of your glo - ry. Ho - san - na in the high - est. Blessed is the one who comes in the name of God. Ho - san - na in the high - est.

Memorial Acclamation

David M. Young

Christ has died. Christ is ris - en. Christ will come a - gain.

Great Amen

David M. Young

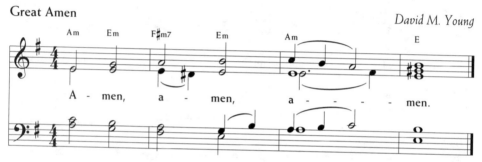

A - men, a - men, a - - - - men.

Communion Setting E

Holy, Holy, Holy (*Sanctus and Benedictus*)

from Deutsche Messe Franz Schubert 1826
adapt. Richard Proulx

Ho - ly, ho - ly, ho - ly Lord, God of power and might;

ho - ly, ho - ly, ho - ly Lord, God of power and might.

Heav'n and earth are full, full of your glo - ry.

Ho - san - na in the high - est, ho - san - na in the high - est.

Bless-ed is he who comes in the name of the Lord.

Memorial Acclamation *from Deutsche Messe Franz Schubert 1826; arr. Charles H. Webb*

Christ has died. Christ is ris - en. Christ will come a - gain.

Arrangement copyright © 1989 The United Methodist Publishing House

Great Amen *from Deutsche Messe Franz Schubert 1826; arr. Charles H. Webb*

A - men, a - men, a - men, a - - - men.

Arrangement copyright © 1989 The United Methodist Publishing House

Holy, Holy, Holy (*Santo, Santo, Santo*)

Ho - ly, ho - ly, ho - ly, ho - ly, ho - ly, ho - ly is our
San - to, san - to, san - to, san - to, san - to, san - to es nues - tro

God, God of earth and God of hea - ven. Ho - ly, ho - ly is our
Dios, Se - ñor de to - da la tie - rra. San - to, san - to es nues - tro

God. Ho - ly, ho - ly, ho - ly, ho - ly, ho - ly, ho - ly is our
Dios. San - to, san - to, san - to, san - to, san - to, san - to es nues - tro

God, God of all, and God of his - tory. Ho - ly, ho - ly is our God.
Dios, Se - ñor de to - da la his - to - ria. San - to, san - to es nues - tro Dios.

Who ac - com - pan - ies our peo - ple, who lives with - in our
Que a - com - pa - ña a nues - tro pue - blo, que vi - ve en nues - tras

strug - gles, of all the earth and heav - en the one and on - ly God.
lu - chas, del u - ni - ver - so en - te - ro el ú - ni - co Se - ñor.

Bless - ed those who in our God's name an - nounce the ho - ly Gos - pel, pro -
Ben - di - tos los que en su nom - bre el E - van - ge - lio a - nun - cian, la

claim - ing forth the good news: our li - ber - a - tion comes.
bue - na y gran no - ti - cia de la li - be - ra ción.

Words: Guillermo Joaquín Cuéllar 1980, Misa Popular Salvadoreña; *trans.* Linda McCrae
Music: Guillermo Joaquín Cuéllar 1980, Misa Popular Salvadoreña
Words and music copyright © 1980 Guillermo Joaquín Cuéllar.

SANTO
Irregular

Additional Service Music

Lord, Have Mercy (*Kyrie Eleison*)

945

Jacques Berthier

Ky - ri - e, Ky - ri - e, e - le - i - son.

Music copyright © 1978, 1980, 1981 Les Presses de Taizé (France). Used with permission of G.I.A. Publications, Inc.

946

Russian Orthodox Liturgy

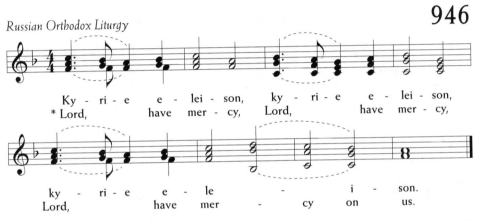

Ky - ri - e e - lei - son, ky - ri - e e - lei - son,
* Lord, have mer - cy, Lord, have mer - cy,

ky - ri - e e - le - i - son.
Lord, have mer - cy on us.

947

Paul Merritt

Unison

* Lord, have mer - cy. Christ, have

mer - cy. Lord, have mer - - - cy.

Copyright © 1995 Paul Merritt

* or: Holy One, have mercy. Blessed One, have mercy. Holy One, have mercy.

948

Prayer Responses
Jacques Berthier

O God, hear my prayer, O God, hear my prayer: when I call an-swer me. O

God, hear my prayer, O God, hear my prayer: come and lis-ten to me.

Words and music copyright © Les Presses de Taizé (France). Used with permission of G.I.A. Publications, Inc.

949

Lucien Deiss

Grant   to   us,   O   God,   a   heart   re - newed;

speak   to   us   a - fresh   your   for - giv - ing   word.

Words and music copyright © 1971 World Library Publications

950

Jacques Berthier 1982

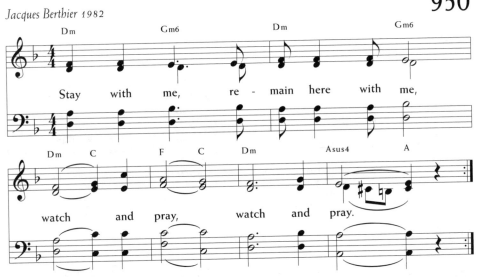

Stay with me, re-main here with me, watch and pray, watch and pray.

951

anon., Argentina

¡San - to, san - to, san - to. Mi co - ra - zón te a - do - ra! Mi
Ho - ly, ho - ly, ho - ly, my heart, my heart a - dores you! My

co - ra - zón te sa - be de - cir: San - to e - res Dios!
heart is glad to say the words: You are ho - ly, God!

952

The Iona Community

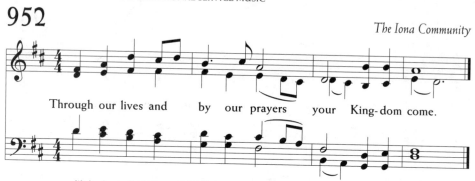

Through our lives and by our prayers your King-dom come.

953

Eleanor Daley

For God a-lone my soul a-waits in si - - - lence.

954

The Iona Community

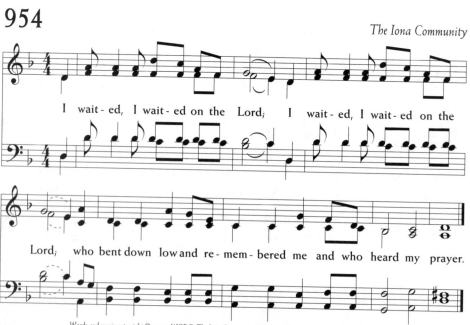

I wait-ed, I wait-ed on the Lord; I wait-ed, I wait-ed on the Lord; who bent down low and re-mem-bered me and who heard my prayer.

955

The Iona Community

Grant to us your peace on earth,
*Do - na no - bis pac - em in ter - ra,

grant to us your peace, O God.
do - na no - bis pac - em, Do - mi - ne.

* pronounced "Don-nah noh-bees pah-chem" Words and music copyright © 1987 WGRG, The Iona Community (Glasgow, Scotland),
G.I.A. Publications, Inc., Chicago, IL, exclusive agent.

Scripture Responses

956

Eleanor Daley

Your word is a lamp to my feet, and a light un - to my path.

Music copyright © 1988 Harold Flammer, Inc.

957

Ruth Watson Henderson

Before the Gospel   After the Gospel

Glo - ry to you, O Je - sus Christ.   Praise to you, O Je - sus Christ.

Music copyright © Gordon V. Thompson Music

958

Halle, Halle, Halle

Words: trad. liturgical text
Music: anon., arr. The Iona Community 1990

CARIBBEAN
Irregular

The Lord's Prayer

David Haas 1986

Our Fa - ther in heav - en, hal - low - ed be your name, your king - dom come, your will be done on earth as in heav - en. Give us to - day our dai - ly bread. For - give us our sins as

960

adapt. from a chant by R. Langdon

961

Blessings and Closing Songs

George Whelpton

Let us, O God, de-part in peace, who in your name are gath-ered here. Dis-close the bright-ness of your face, and be for-ev-er near.

962

Miriam Therese Winter

May the bless-ing of God go be-fore you. May her grace and peace a-bound. May her Spir-it live with-in you. May her love wrap you 'round. May her bless-ing re-main with you al-ways. May you walk on ho-ly ground.

Jeeva Sam 1987; Fred Kimball Graham 1995

May the grace of Christ at-tend us, and the love of God sur-round us, and the Ho-ly Spir-it keep us, now and ev-er. A - men.

964

Natalie Sleeth 1976

(may be played an octave higher)

(Keyboard or handbells)

Go now in peace, go now in peace. May the love of God sur-round you ev-ery-where, ev-ery-where you may go.

965

arr. Lowell Mason

The Lord bless thee, and keep thee: the Lord make his face shine - up-on thee, and be gra-cious un - to thee: the Lord lift up his coun - te - nance up - on thee, and give thee peace. A - men.

Amens

966   *"Dresden"*   **967**   *"Danish"*

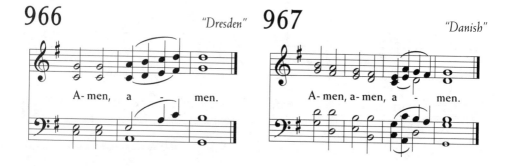

A - men, a - men.   A - men, a - men, a - men.

Norman Johnson

968

James A. Kriewald

969

A - men, a - men.

A - men, a - men, a - men.

970

Paul Merritt

A - - men, a - - men.

971

Paul Merritt

A - men, a - men, a - - - men.

972

McNeil Robinson II 1984

A - men, a - men, a - - - men.

973

John Stainer 1873

A - men, a - men, a - men, a - men.

974

Jim Strathdee 1985

A - men! A - men! Hal-le-lu - jah, a - men!

—lu - jah, a - men!

Indexes

ACKNOWLEDGEMENTS (COPYRIGHT HOLDERS)

A.R. MOWBRAY & CO. LTD., Cassell Plc., Villiers House, 41/47 Strand, London WC2N 2J3, England

ABINGDON PRESS, 201 8th Ave. S., Nashville, TN 37202, USA

AUGSBURG FORTRESS PUBLISHERS, 426 S. Fifth St., Box 1209, Minneapolis, MN 55440, USA

BOREALIS MUSIC, 311-1424 Walnut St., Vancouver, BC V6J 3R3

CHURCH PENSION FUND, Church Hymnal Corp, 445 Fifth Ave., New York, NY 10016, USA

FREDERICK R.C. CLARKE, Sydenham Street United Church, 82 Sydenham St., Kingston, ON K7L 3H4

COMMON CUP COMPANY, 7591 Gray Ave., Burnaby, BC V5J 3Z4

CONCORDIA PUBLISHING HOUSE, 3558 S. Jefferson Ave., St. Louis, MO 63118, USA

CRC PUBLICATIONS, 2850 Kalamazoo Ave. S.E., Grand Rapids, MI 49560, USA

ELEANOR DALEY, Fairlawn Heights United Church, 28 Fairlawn Ave., Toronto, ON M5M 1S7

DESERT FLOWER MUSIC, Box 1476, Carmichael, CA 95069, USA

WALTER FARQUHARSON, Box 126, Saltcoats, SK S0A 3R0

G. SCHIRMER, INC., c/o Music Sales Corporation, 257 Park Ave. S., New York, NY 10010, USA

G.I.A. PUBLICATIONS, INC., 7404 S. Mason Ave., Chicago, IL 60638, USA

RUTH WATSON HENDERSON, 23 Birchview Blvd., Etobicoke, ON M8X 1H4

HINSHAW MUSIC, INC., P.O. Box 470, Chapel Hill, NC 27514-0470, USA

HOPE PUBLISHING COMPANY, 380 S. Main Pl., Carol Stream, IL 60188, USA

INTERNATIONAL COMMITTEE ON ENGLISH IN THE LITURGY, Ste. 1000, 1522 "K" St. N.W., Washington, DC 20005-1202, USA

DAVID KAI, Orleans United Church, 1111 Orleans Blvd., Gloucester, ON K1C 7C8

RON KLUSMEIER, Suite 275, 250 Dundas St. S., Cambridge, ON N1R 8A8

MEDICAL MISSION SISTERS, Permissions Dept., 92 Sherman St., Hartford, CT 06105, USA

OREGON CATHOLIC PRESS, 5536 NE. Hassalo, Portland, OR 97213, USA

OXFORD UNIVERSITY PRESS, Arts and Reference Division, 3 Park Rd., London NW1 6XN, England

OXFORD UNIVERSITY PRESS, INC., 198 Madison Ave., New York, NY 10016-4314, USA

JEEVA SAM, Rosemont United Church, 5000 8th Ave., Regina, SK S4T 0W3

SELAH PUBLISHING CO., P.O. Box 3037, Kingston, NY 12401, USA

SHAWNEE PRESS INC., c/o Music Sales Corporation, 257 Park Ave. S., New York, NY 10010, USA

SONGS FOR A GOSPEL PEOPLE, Wood Lake Books, 10162 Newene Rd., Winfield, BC V4V 1R2

THE COPYRIGHT COMPANY, 40 Music Sq. E., Nashville, TN 37203, USA

THE PILGRIM PRESS, 700 Prospect Ave., Cleveland, OH 44115-1100, USA

THE UNITED METHODIST PUBLISHING HOUSE, Abingdon Press, 201 8th Ave. S., Nashville, TN 37202, USA

NAN THOMPSON, 1226 Longfield Ct., Cambridge, ON N3H 4W8.

JAROSLAV J. VAJDA, 3534 Brookstone S. Dr., St. Louis, MO 63129-2900, USA

WALTON MUSIC CORPORATION, 170 NE. 33rd St., Ft. Lauderdale, FL 33307, USA

WESTMINSTER JOHN KNOX PRESS, 100 Witherspoon St., Louisville, KY 40202-1396, USA

WORLD LIBRARY PUBLICATIONS, INC., a division of J.S. Paluch, 3825 N. Willow Rd., Schiller Park, IL 60176, USA

---

1 Words: © Church Pension Fund. Used by permission. Arrangement: © Concordia Publishing House, 3558 South Jefferson Ave., St. Louis, MS 63118-3968, USA. Translation: © AUVIDIS (Fleurus), BP 21, 94250 Gentilly Cedex, France.

4 Words: © 1988 G.I.A. Publications, Inc. Music: © David M. Young, 1619 Lancaster Ave., Sarnia, ON N7V 3S7. Used by permission.

5 Words, Music: © 1993 Centro de Pastoral Liturgica, administered by Oregon Catholic Press. All rights reserved. Used by permission. Translation: © 1989 The United Methodist Publishing House. Harmony: © 1989 Skinner Chávez-Melo. Used by permission of Juan Francisco Chávez, Arenal 48, Depto. 10, 01050 Mexico (San Angel), D.F. Mexico.

6 Words: © 1986 Sandra Dean, 1134 Plant Dr., Ottawa, ON K1V 9E8.

7 Words, Music: © 1989 Hope Publishing Company. All rights reserved. Used by permission.

9 Words: © David Higham Associates, 5-8 Lower John St., Golden Square, London W1R 4HA, England. Harmony: © 1928 Oxford University Press.

10 Words, Music: © 1992 MorningStar Music Publishers, 2117 59th St., St. Louis, MO 63118, USA. Used by permission.

11 Words: © 1975 International Committee on English in the Liturgy.

12 Words, Music: © 1968, 1987 Medical Mission Sisters. Accompaniment: © 1995 Nan Thompson.

13 Words: © 1988 Janet Morley, c/o Morehouse Publishing, Ste., 204, 871 Ethan Allen Highway, Ridgefield, CT 06877, USA.

14 Words, Music: © 1984 Hope Publishing Company. All rights reserved. Used by permission.

15 Words, Arrangement: © 1992 Abingdon Press.

16 Words, Music: © 1994 Selah Publishing Co., Inc. All rights reserved. Used by permission.

17 Words, Music: © 1994 G.I.A. Publications, Inc.

18 Music: © 1938 Henry Hugh Bancroft. Used by permission of Eldred Bancroft., Estate of Henry Hugh Bancroft, c/o Mr. Brian Burrows, 11331 - 75 Ave., Edmonton, AB T6G 0H6.

19 Words, Music: © WGRG, The Iona Community (Glasgow, Scotland), G.I.A. Publications, Inc., Chicago, IL, exclusive agent.

20 Descant: © 1979 G.I.A. Publications, Inc.

21 Words: © Fédération Protestante de France, 47, rue de Clichy, 75311 Paris Cedex 09, France.

22 Words, Music: © 1991 Les Presses de Taizé, G.I.A. Publications, Inc., Chicago, IL, exclusive agent.

23 Arrangement: © 1987 Songs for a Gospel People.

24 Words, Music: © 1970, 1974 John B. Foley, New Dawn Music, administered by Oregon Catholic Press.

643 Translation: © 1976, Music: © 1960, renewal 1988 Hope Publishing Company. All rights reserved. Used by permission.

644 Words, Music: © 1985 John Ylvisaker, PO Box 321, Waverly, IA 50667, USA.

645 Words: © 1987 Medical Mission Sisters.

646 Translation, Arrangement: © 1984 Walton Music Corporation.

647 Words: © 1969, 1991, Music: © 1969 Stainer & Bell Ltd. All rights reserved. Used by permission of Hope Publishing Company.

648 Words: © 1996 Janet Cawley, c/o South Hill United Church, 645 E. 47th Ave., Vancouver, BC V5W 2B5.

649 Words, Music, Arrangement: © 1988 Estate of John S. Rice, c/o Brian H. Davison, 10619 Alameda Dr., Knoxville, TN 37392-2502, USA.

652 Harmony: © 1933 renewed 1961 Presbyterian Board of Christian Education, administered by Westminster John Knox Press.

654 Translation: © 1989 Hope Publishing Company. All rights reserved. Used by permission. Music: © 1968 Novello & Company Ltd. administered by Shawnee Press Inc.

656 Words: *Your Will Be Done* 1986, reflective writings, prayers and hymns related to the discerning of God's will for our lives, alt., © 1986 Christian Conference of Asia, 96, 2nd District, Pak Tin Village, Mei Tin Rd., Shatin, N.T., Hong Kong.

661 Words, Music: © 1981 Joe Pinson, 2320 Salado, Denton, TX 76201, USA.

666 Translation: © 1983 Paul Gregory, P.O. Box 3227-145, Lancaster, PA 17604, USA.

668 Translation: © Fondation d'édition des Églises Protestantes Romandes, Cret-berard CH 1604, Puidoux, Switzerland.

670 Words, Music Adaptation: © 1938 Unichappell Music, Inc., c/o Hal Leonard Publishing Corp., P.O. Box 13819, 7777 W. Bluemound Rd., Milwaukee, WI 53213, USA. Copyright renewed. Copyright secured. International copyright secured. All rights reserved.

673 Words: © 1989 The Hymn Society. All rights reserved. Used by permission of Hope Publishing Company. Music: © 1993 Stainer & Bell Ltd. and Methodist Church (U.K.) Division of Education and Youth. Used by permission of Hope Publishing Company.

676 Words (Paraphrase): © 1969 Selah Publishing Co.

677 Words: © 1958, renewal 1986 The Hymn Society. All rights reserved. Used by permission of Hope Publishing Company.

678 Words: © 1968 Hope Publishing Company. All rights reserved. Used by permission. Descant: © 1987 Songs for a Gospel People.

679 Words: © 1970 Frances Wheeler Davis, 5205 Bellmore Ave., Montreal, PQ H4V 2C7. Music: © 1976 Margaret Fleming, 57 - 8889 212th St., Langley, BC V1M 2E8.

680 Words: © 1982 The Hymn Society. All rights reserved. Used by permission of Hope Publishing Company. Harmony: © 1986 G.I.A. Publications, Inc.

682 Words: © 1982 Hope Publishing Company. All rights reserved. Used by permission. Music, Arrangement: © 1916-44-77 Roberton Publications. Reprinted by permission of the publisher, sale representative USA and Canada, Theodore Presser Company, Presser Place, Bryn Mawr, PA 19010, USA.

683 Words: © Chicago Province of the Society of Jesus, c/o HarperCollins Publishers, 10 E. 53rd St., New York, NY 10022, USA.

684 Music, Arrangement: © 1968 Franciscan Communications Centre, 1229 S. Santee St., Los Angeles, CA 90015, USA.

685 Words: © 1968 Hope Publishing Company.

686 Arrangement: © 1970 F.R.C. Clarke.

687 Words: © 1990 Constance Cherry, 1025 Oakdale Dr., Findlay, OH 45840, USA.

688 Words: © Emmanuel College, c/o Office of the Principal, 75 Queen's Park Cr. E., Toronto, ON M5K 1K7.

690 Words: © 1971 The United Methodist Publishing House. Used by permission.

691 Words: © 1974 Walter Farquharson. Music: © 1974, Arrangement: © 1995 Ron Klusmeier.

692 Words: © Brother Tristan, SSF, Hillfield Priory, Dorchester, Dorset DT1 7BE, England.

693 Words: *Book of Common Order* (Church of Scotland) © 1940 Oxford University Press.

695 Words, Music: © 1985 Colleen Fulmer, c/o Loretto Spirituality Network, 725 Calhoun St., Albany, CA 94709 USA.

696 Words: © 1977 Walter Farquharson. Music: © 1977 Ron Klusmeier.

697 Words: © 1990 Medical Mission Sisters.

698 Words: © Yongiel Park Moon, 527-32 Suyudong, Kangbookku, Seoul 113-076, Korea. Translation: © Marion Pope, Apt. 135, 211 College St., Toronto, ON M5T 1R1. Music: © Don Whan Cho, #50-2 Dongku Song Lim 6 Dong, Song Lim Jung Anglican Methodist Church, Inchon, South Korea.

699 Words: © 1981 Jane Parker Huber. From *A Singing Faith*. Used by permission of Westminster John Knox Press.

700 Words: © 1992 Hope Publishing Company. All rights reserved. Used by permission.

701 Words, Music: © 1986 Desert Flower Music. Used by permission.

702 Words, Music, Arrangement: © 1971 J.A. Olivar, Miguel Manzano, San Pablo International-SSP, sole US agent Oregon Catholic Press. All rights reserved. Used by permission. Translation: © The United Methodist Publishing House. Used by permission.

703 Words, Music: © 1986 Hope Publishing Company. All rights reserved. Used by permission.

704 Words, Music: © 1989 WGRG, The Iona Community (Glasgow, Scotland), G.I.A. Publications, Inc., Chicago, IL, exclusive agent.

705 Music: Used by permission of Oxford University Press.

706 Words: © 1987 Hope Publishing Company. All rights reserved. Used by permission.

707 Words: © 1991 G.I.A. Publications, Inc.

709 Harmony: © 1982 Church Pension Fund. Used by permission .

711 Translation: © Jay Macpherson, 17 Berryman St., Toronto ON M5R 1M7.

712 Words: © Fédération Protestante de France, 47, rue de Clichy, 75311 Paris Cedex 09, France.

713 Words, Music: © 1979, Harmony: © 1991 Carolyn McDade, P.O. Box 510, Wellfleet, MA 02667, USA.

717 Music: © WGRG, The Iona Community (Glasgow, Scotland), G.I.A. Publications, Inc., Chicago, IL, exclusive agent.

718 Words: © 1989 Hope Publishing Company. All rights reserved. Used by permission.

719 Words: *Liturgical Year, The Worship of God, Supplemental Liturgical Resource 7*, 1992 (Presbyterian Church) © 1992 Westminster John Knox Press.

PSALMS

Ps. 1 Music: © T. Barrett Armstrong, St. Michael's Choir School, 66 Bond Street, Toronto, ON M5B 1X2.

Ps. 2 Words, Music (Refrain): © 1985 Hope Publishing Company. All rights reserved. Used by permission.

Ps. 3 Music: © 1994 G.I.A. Publications, Inc.

Ps. 4 Words, Music: © 1986 Westminster John Knox Press.

Ps. 5 Refrain 1 Words, Music: © 1994 Susan Marrier, 324 Masters St., Thunder Bay, ON P7B 6L4

Ps. 8 Descant: © 1987 CRC Publications.

Ps. 8 Refrain Music: © 1994 G.I.A. Publications, Inc.

Ps. 13 Arrangement: © 1933, renewed 1961 Presbyterian Board of Christian Education, Westminster John Knox Press.

Ps. 16 Words, Music: © 1973 Hope Publishing Company. All rights reserved. Used by permission.

Ps. 16 Refrain Words, Music: © 1973 Hope Publishing Company. All rights reserved. Used by permission.

Ps. 17 Music (Refrain): © 1988 Hope Publishing Company. All rights reserved. Used by permission.

Ps. 19 Refrain 1 Music: © Henry Boon, 985 Roseland Dr. S., Windsor, ON N9G 1T9.

Ps. 19 Refrain 2 Music: Used by permission of Oxford University Press.

Ps. 20 Music (Refrain): © 1973 Hope Publishing Company. All rights reserved. Used by permission.

Ps. 22 Words: © 1986 Christopher L. Webber, P.O. Box 1724, Sharon, CT 06069, USA. Harmony: © 1971 Robert Hunter Bell, 111 Lambertlodge Ave., Toronto, ON M6G 3X4.

Ps. 22 Refrain (for Part One) Music: © 1972 Donatus Vervoot, 15611 St. Albert Trail, Edmonton, AB T5L 4H8.

Ps. 22 Refrain (for Part Two and Repeat) Descant: © 1977 Scripture in Song, Integrity Music, administered by Maranatha! Music, c/o The Copyright Company.

Ps. 23 (God Is My Shepherd) Words: © 1992 The Pilgrim Press. Harmony: Used by permission of Oxford University Press.

Ps. 23 Refrain 1 Words, Music: © 1963, 1986 The Ladies of the Grail (England), G.I.A. Publications, Inc., Chicago, IL, exclusive agent.

Ps. 150   Refrain Words, Music: © 1981 Estate of J. Jefferson Cleveland, c/o Paul J. Cleveland, Apt. 1B, 7609 S. Coles St., Chicago, IL 60649, USA.

Ps. 150   Harmony: Used by permission of Oxford University Press.

CANTICLES

876   Harmony: © CRC Publications.

878   Words: © 1987 CRC Publications. Music: © 1994 William H.M. Wright, 165 Robert St., Toronto, ON M5S 2K6.

880   Music: Joe Zsigray © Oregon Catholic Press. Arrangement: © 1996 Catherine Ambrose, 2928 Quetta Mews, Mississauga, ON L5N 1Z7.

881   Words: © 1982 Hope Publishing Company. All rights reserved. Used by permission.

882   Words (Adaptation): © Charles P. Price, Apt. 605, 1250 S. Washington St., Alexandria, VA 22314, USA. Arrangement: © 1978 *Lutheran Book of Worship*, by permission of Augsburg Fortress.

884   Words, Music: © 1975 Lillenas Publishing Company, administered by The Copyright Company, Nashville, TN. All rights reserved. International copyright secured. Used by permission.

886   Refrain: © 1987 Lawrence M. Probes. Used by permission of Selah Publishing Co., Inc. All rights reserved.

888   Words, Music: © 1968 Augsburg Publishing House. Reprinted by permission of Augsburg Fortress.

890   Music: Used by permission of Oxford University Press.

891   Words: © 1989, Arrangement: © 1991 Hope Publishing Company. All rights reserved. Used by permission.

892   Words: © 1989, Arrangement: © 1991 Hope Publishing Company. All rights reserved. Used by permission.

893   Words: © 1989, Arrangement: © 1991 Hope Publishing Company. All rights reserved. Used by permission.

894   Words (Revised, English and French), and French Translation (Verse 3): © 1987 Songs for a Gospel People.

895   Music: © Pablo Sosa, Camacua 252, 1406 Buenos Aires, Argentina.

896   Words, Music: © 1985 G.I.A. Publications, Inc.

898   Refrain 1 Music: © 1979, 1988 G.I.A. Publications, Inc.

898   Refrain 2 Music : © 1995 William Richards, United Church Manse, Box 130, Cardiff, ON K0L 1M0.

899   Words: © 1978, 1987 Medical Mission Sisters. Harmony: ©1982 Church Pension Fund.

900   Words: © 1973, Music: © 1983 Hope Publishing Company. All rights reserved. Used by permission.

901   Words: © 1973, Music: © 1983 Hope Publishing Company. All rights reserved. Used by permission.

902   Music: © 1986 Hope Publishing Company. All rights reserved. Used by permission.

903   Words: © 1982 Church Pension Fund. Used by permission. Harmony: Used by permission of Oxford University Press.

904   Words: © 1978 *Lutheran Book of Worship*. Reprinted by permission of Augsburg Fortress. Music: © 1975, 1988 Richard Hillert, 1620 Clay Ct., Melrose Park, IL 60160, USA. Used by permission.

PRAYERS

916   Words (Translation): © 1995 The Pilgrim Press.

916   Words (Paraphrase): © 1988 James E. Cotter, c/o Cairns Publications, 47 Firth Park Ave., Sheffield S5 6HF, England.

928A   Words: *Service Book for the Use of Ministers*, 1969, p. 73, alt. Used by Permission of the United Church of Canada, 3250 Bloor St. W., Etobicoke, ON M8X 2Y4.

928B   Words: Donald A. Daniel, 1989, *Worship for All Seasons*.

929   Words: © Elise S. Eslinger, 1421 Bell St., Niles, MI 49120, USA.

929A   Words: Adapted from the *Book of Alternative Services*, 1985, alt., © 1985 The General Synod of the Anglican Church of Canada, 600 Jarvis St., Toronto, ON M4Y 2J6.

930B   Words: Adapted from the *Book of Alternative Services*, 1985, alt., © 1985 The General Synod of the Anglican Church of Canada, 600 Jarvis St., Toronto, ON M4Y 2J6.

930C   Words: *Service Book for the Use of Ministers*, 1969, p. 109, alt. Used by Permission of the United Church of Canada, 3250 Bloor S. W., Etobicoke, ON M8X 2Y4.

COMMUNION SETTINGS & ADDITIONAL SERVICE MUSIC

932   Music: © G.I.A. Publications, Inc

934   Music: © 1995 Stuart Semple, R R #2, Malagash, NS B0K 1E0.

936   Music: © 1989 Kevin Mayhew Ltd., Rattlesden, Bury St. Edmunds, Suffolk 1P30 OSZ, England. Used by permission.

941   Music: © 1988 David M. Young, 1619 Lancaster Ave., Sarnia, ON N7V 3S7.

942   Adaptation: © 1985 G.I.A. Publications, Inc. Arrangement: © 1989 The United Methodist Publishing House. Used by permission.

944   Words, Music: © 1980 Guillermo Joaquín Cuéllar Barandiarán, Residencial El Cortijo, Senda B#2, Av. Montes Urales, Colonia Montebello, San Salvador, El Salvador. Translation: © Linda McCrae, information sought.

945   Music: © 1978, 1980, 1981 Les Presses de Taizé (France), G.I.A. Publications, Inc.

947   Music: © 1995 Paul Meritt, First St. Andrews Church, 350 Queens Avenue, London, ON N6B 1X6.

948   Words, Music: © Les Presses de Taizé (France), G.I.A. Publications, Inc., Chicago, IL, exclusive agent.

949   Words, Music: © 1971 World Library Publications, Inc.

950   Words, Music: © Les Presses de Taizé (France), G.I.A. Publications, Inc., Chicago, IL, exclusive agent.

952   Words, Music: © 1987 WGRG, The Iona Community (Glasgow, Scotland), G.I.A. Publications, Inc., Chicago, IL, exclusive agent.

953   Music: © 1988 Harold Flammer Music, a division of Shawnee Press, Inc. (ASCAP). International copyright secured. All rights reserved.

954   Words, Music: © 1987 WGRG, The Iona Community (Glasgow, Scotland), G.I.A. Publications, Inc., Chicago, IL, exclusive agent.

955   Music: © 1995 WGRG, The Iona Community (Glasgow, Scotland), G.I.A. Publications, Inc. Chicago, IL, exclusive agent.

956   Music: © 1988 Harold Flammer, Inc., administered by Shawnee Press Inc., (ASCAP). International copyright secured. All rights reserved.

957   Music: © Gordon V. Thompson Music, c/o Warner Chappell, Music Div., 85 Scarsdale Rd., Don Mills, ON M3B 2R2.

958   Arrangement: © 1990 WGRG, The Iona Community (Glasgow, Scotland), G.I.A. Publications, Inc., Chicago, IL, exclusive agent.

959   Music: © 1986 G.I.A. Publications, Inc.

962   Words, Music: © 1987 Medical Mission Sisters.

963   Music: © 1987 Jeeva Sam. Harmony © 1995 Fred Kimball Graham, 17 Conrad Ave., Toronto, ON M6G 3G4.

964   Words, Music: © 1976 Hinshaw Music, Inc. Reprinted by permission.

968   Music: © 1958, 1970 Singspiration, Inc., The Benson Music Group, 365 Great Circle Rd., Nashville, TN 37228, USA.

969   Music: © 1985 The United Methodist Publishing House. Used by permission.

970   Music: © 1995 Paul Merritt, First St. Andrews Church, 350 Queens Ave., London, ON N6B 1X6.

971   Music: © 1995 Paul Merritt, First St. Andrews Church, 350 Queens Ave., London, ON N6B 1X6.

972   Music: © 1984 Theodore Presser Company, Presser Place, Bryn Mawr, PA 19010, USA. Used by permission.

974   Music: © 1985 Desert Flower Music.

HYMNS FOR THE CHURCH YEAR (LECTIONARY)

998   Revised Common Lectionary. Copyright © 1992 by The Consultation on Common Texts (CCT). All rights reserved. Used by permission.

INDEX OF AUTHORS, TRANSLATORS AND SOURCES

INDEX OF COMPOSERS, ARRANGERS AND SOURCES

Year A

Christmas Day 1
Is 62:6-12
Ps 97
Ti 3:4-7
Lk 2: (1-7), 8-20
(G) 36, 42, 46, 49, 50, 52, 57, 59,
61, 72, 77

Christmas Day 2
Is 52:7-10
Ps 98
Heb 1:1-4, (5-12)
Jn 1:1-14
(O) 72
(Ps) 59
(E) 83, 213, 413
(G) 32, 43, 53, 60, 61, 69, 81, 251,
379, 413, 435, 499

Christmas 1
Is 63:7-9
Ps 148
Heb 2:10-18
Mt 2:13-23
(O) 48, 59, 288
(Ps) 35, 217, 291
(E) 42, 83, 190, 335, 663
(G) 55, 59, 62, 74, 77, 98, 138,
190, 244, 333, 348, 473, 530,
555

Christmas 2
Jer 31:7-14 (Alt)
Sir 24:1-12 (Alt)
Ps 147:12-20 (Alt)
Wis 10:15-21 (Alt resp)
Eph 1:3-14
Jn 1:(1-9), 10-18
(O) 273, 747, 748
(G) 59, 61, 62, 83, 235, 266, 271,
335, 336, 393, 394, 521, 529,
626

Epiphany
Is 60:1-6
Ps 72:1-7, 10-14
Eph 3:1-12
Mt 2:1-12
(O) 84, 98, 679, 879
(Ps) 30
(E) 43
(G) 36, 62, 68, 71, 74, 79, 81, 84,
87, 91, 97, 330, 588, 626, 679

Baptism of Jesus
Is 42:1-9
Ps 29
Acts 10:34-43
Mt 3:13-17
(O) 330, 681
(Ps) 229
(E) 183, 678
(G) 42, 81, 84, 99, 100, 101, 335,
341, 348, 378, 384, 451, 453

Year B

Christmas Day 1
Is 62:6-12
Ps 97
Ti 3:4-7
Lk 2:(1-7), 8-20
(G) 58, 59, 60, 64, 74

Christmas Day 2
Is 52:7-10
Ps 98
Heb 1:1-4, (5-12)
Jn 1:1-14
(E) 61
(G) 48, 59, 61, 413

Christmas 1
Is 61:10-62:3
Ps 148
Gal 4:4-7
Lk 2:22-40
(G) 2, 36, 43, 48, 59, 62, 68, 236,
314, 425, 473, 529

Christmas 2
Jer 31:7-14
Sir 24:1-12 (Alt)
Ps 147:12-20 (Alt)
Wis 10:15-21 (Alt resp)
Eph 1:3-14
Jn 1:(1-9), 10-18
(O) 93, 273, 521
(G) 59, 61, 81, 83, 98, 235, 266,
271, 326, 335, 344, 352, 413,
626, 747, 748

Epiphany
Is 60:1-6
Ps 72:1-7, 10-14
Eph 3:1-12
Mt 2:1-12
(Ps) 330
(G) 30, 79, 81, 97, 98, 336, 588

Baptism of Jesus
Gn 1:1-5
Ps 29
Acts 19:1-7
Mk 1:4-11
(O) 320, 449
(G) 28, 29, 30, 84, 99, 100, 204,
208, 348, 627

Epiphany 2
1 Sm 3:1-10, (11-20)
Ps 139:1-6, 13-18
1 Cor 6:12-20
Jn 1:43-51
(O) 506
(Ps) 219
(G) 18, 81, 87, 299, 367, 385, 500,
509, 562, 879

Year C

Christmas Day 1
Is 62:6-12
Ps 97
Ti 3:4-7
Lk 2:(1-7), 8-20
(G) 8, 38, 44, 59, 64, 71, 74

Christmas Day 2
Is 52:7-10
Ps 98
Heb 1:1-4, (5-12)
Jn 1:1-14
(O) 711
(P) 59
(E) 61
(G) 36, 43, 48, 60, 69, 98, 352, 883

Christmas 1
1 Sm 2:18-20, 26
Ps 148
Col 3:12-17
Lk 2:41-52
(E) 716
(G) 62, 217, 254, 518, 530, 533

Christmas 2
Jer 31:7-14
Sir 24:1-12 (Alt)
Ps 147:12-20
Wis 10:15-21 (Alt resp)
Eph 1:3-14
Jn 1:(1-9), 10-18
(G) 35, 38, 41, 49, 54, 56, 325

Epiphany
Is 60:1-6
Ps 72:1-7, 10-14
Eph 3:1-12
Mt 2:1-12
(Ps) 30, 330
(G) 8, 74, 91, 98, 336, 413

Baptism of Jesus
Is 43:1-7
Ps 29
Acts 8:14-17
Lk 3:15-17, 21-22
(O) 660
(Ps) 220, 221
(E) 183
(G) 61, 100, 204, 218, 335, 362,
367, 375, 378, 382, 384, 409,
441, 444, 506, 651

Epiphany 2
Is 62:1-5
Ps 36:5-10
1 Cor 12:1-11
Jn 2:1-11
(O) 334
(Ps) 264, 559
(E) 208, 467, 479, 606
(G) 101, 194, 219, 226, 331, 332,
336, 367, 500, 506, 588, 667

Year A	Year B	Year C

Year A

Epiphany 2
Is 49:1-7
Ps 40:1-11
1 Cor 1:1-9
Jn 1:29-42
(O)   264, 342, 894
(G)   101, 326, 336, 348, 378, 415,
      508, 667

Epiphany 3
Is 9:1-4
Ps 27:1, 4-9
1 Cor 1:10-18
Mt 4:12-23
(O)   101, 336, 879
(Ps) 669
(E)   331, 500, 602, 654, 655
(G)   82, 83, 120, 218, 341, 413,
      562, 608, 630, 679

Epiphany 4
Mi 6:1-8
Ps 15
1 Cor 1:18-31
Mt 5:1-12
(O)   512, 701
(E)   149, 338, 642, 654, 655
(G)   68, 79, 223, 334, 499, 560,
      579, 642, 684, 686

Epiphany 5
Is 58:1-9a, (9b-12)
Ps 112:1-9, (10)
1 Cor 2:1-12, (13-16)
Mt 5:13-20
(O)   109, 326, 421, 481
(Ps) 356
(E)   215, 338, 376, 378, 416, 471,
      582
(G)   30, 62, 87, 98, 120, 236, 246,
      362, 413, 582, 583

Epiphany 6
Dt 30:15-20 (Alt)
Sir 15:15-20 (Alt)
Ps 119:1-8
1 Cor 3:1-9
Mt 5:21-37
(O)   499, 559, 560
(E)   227
(G)   220, 221, 340, 364, 368, 371,
      560, 595, 603, 639, 667

Epiphany 7
Lv 19:1-2, 9-18
Ps 119:33-40
1 Cor 3:10-11,16-23
Mt 5:38-48
(O)   255, 315
(E)   325, 331, 332, 391, 660
(G)   296, 348, 367, 595, 636, 822

Year B

Epiphany 3
Jon 3:1-5, 10
Ps 62:5-12
1 Cor 7:29-31
Mk 1:14-20
(Ps) 529
(G)   117, 342, 562, 608

Epiphany 4
Dt 18:15-20
Ps 111
1 Cor 8:1-13
Mk 1:21-28
(G)   213, 215, 313, 326, 334, 344,
      530, 620

Epiphany 5
Is 40:21-31
Ps 147:1-11, 20c
1 Cor 9:16-23
Mk 1:29-39
(Ps) 216
(G)   79, 216, 220, 221, 223, 263,
      570, 670, 709

Epiphany 6
2 Kgs 5:1-14
Ps 30
1 Cor 9:24-27
Mk 1:40-45
(E)   674
(G)   173, 266, 326, 333, 636

Epiphany 7
Is 43:18-25
Ps 41
2 Cor 1:18-22
Mk 2:1-12
(E)   326
(G)   101, 240, 385, 405, 559, 665,
      681

Epiphany 8
Hos 2:14-20
Ps 103:1-13, 22
2 Cor 3:1-6
Mk 2:13-22
(E)   376
(G)   213, 220, 221, 240, 266, 271,
      331, 332, 341

Epiphany 9
Dt 5:12-15
Ps 81:1-10
2 Cor 4:5-12
Mk 2:23-3:6
(E)   473
(G)   101, 336, 679

Epiphany Last / Transfig.
2 Kgs 2:1-12
Ps 50:1-6
2 Cor 4:3-6
Mk 9:2-9

Year C

Epiphany 3
Neh 8:1-3, 5-6, 8-10
Ps 19
1 Cor 12:12-31a
Lk 4:14-21
(Ps) 238, 330
(E)   467, 588, 606
(G)   29, 43, 87, 262, 312, 313, 315,
      325, 326, 330, 333, 626, 699

Epiphany 4
Jer 1:4-10
Ps 71:1-6
1 Cor 13:1-13
Lk 4:21-30
(O)   509
(Ps) 669
(E)   193, 262, 372, 658
(G)   193, 589, 604, 658, 660

Epiphany 5
Is 6:1-8, (9-13)
Ps 138
1 Cor 15:1-11
Lk 5:1-11
(O)   315, 509, 572, 894, 944, 951
(E)   159, 448
(G)   35, 266, 473, 506, 562, 589,
      608, 660

Epiphany 6
Jer 17:5-10
Ps 1
1 Cor 15:12-20
Lk 6:17-26
(E)   157, 180
(G)   165, 213, 215, 286, 348, 562,
      636

Epiphany 7
Gn 45:3-11, 15
Ps 37:1-11, 39-40
1 Cor 15:35-38, 42-50
Lk 6:27-38
(O)   593
(E)   159, 186, 189
(G)   190, 260, 506, 667, 677, 678,
      681

Epiphany 8
Sir 27:4-7
Is 55:10-13 (Alt)
Ps 92:1-4, 12-15
1 Cor 15:51-58
Lk 6:39-49
(O)   680
(E)   147
(G)   533, 561, 660

Year A

Epiphany 8
Is 49:8-16a
Ps 131
1 Cor 4:1-5
Mt 6:24-34
(O)   633, 650
(E)   295, 303, 643
(G)   291, 307, 356, 374, 652, 672

Epiphany 9
Dt 11:18-21, 26-28
Ps 31:1-5, 19-24
Rom 1:16-17; 3:22b-28, (29-31)
Mt 7:21-29
(O)   707
(E)   266, 559
(G)   425, 601, 654, 660

Epiphany Last / Transfig.
Ex 24:12-18
Ps 2 (Alt)
Ps 99 (Alt)
2 Pt 1:16-21
Mt 17:1-9
(O)   651
(Ps) 220, 221
(E)   98
(G)   61, 92, 101, 102, 210, 222,
      232, 264, 299, 328, 336, 415,
      894

Lent 1
Gn 2:15-17; 3:1-7
Ps 32
Rom 5:12-19
Mt 4:1-11
(O)   235
(Ps) 266
(G)   23, 114, 120, 348, 356, 559,
      611, 641

Lent 2
Gn 12:1-4a
Ps 121
Rom 4:1-5, 13-17
Jn 3:1-17 (Alt)
Mt 17:1-9 (Alt)
(0)   216, 286, 634, 657
(Ps) 636, 669
(E)   580
(G)   147, 151, 210, 308, 333, 382,
      483, 562, 663, 681

Lent 3
Ex 17:1-7
Ps 95
Rom 5:1-11
Jn 4:5-42
(O)   651
(E)   658
(G)   266, 286, 316, 328, 367, 391,
      463, 472, 478, 600, 626, 669,
      686, 811

Year B

(G)   101, 104, 327, 334, 335, 336,
      341

Lent 1
Gn 9:8-17
Ps 25:1-10
1 Pt 3:18-22
Mk 1:9-15
(E)   448
(G)   114, 119, 138, 143, 262, 263,
      266, 348, 650

Lent 2
Gn 17:1-7, 15-16
Ps 22:23-31
Rom 4:13-25
Mk 8:31-38
Mk 9:2-9 (Alt)
(G)   101, 104, 120, 149, 327, 334,
      405, 561, 634, 636, 642, 643,
      663, 681, 686

Lent 3
Ex 20:1-17
Ps 19
1 Cor 1:18-25
Jn 2:13-22
(G)   135, 149, 164, 315, 325, 335,
      499, 642, 686

Lent 4
Nm 21:4-9
Ps 107:1-3, 17-22
Eph 2:1-10
Jn 3:14-21
(E)   266, 338
(G)   147, 151, 234, 236, 266, 271,
      333, 500, 559, 669

Lent 5
Jer 31:31-34
Ps 51:1-12
Ps 119:9-16 (Alt)
Heb 5:5-10
Jn 12:20-33
(E)   143
(G)   120, 133, 135, 138, 186, 190,
      262, 330, 348, 657, 669

Palm / Passion Sunday
Mk 11:1-11
Jn 12:12-16
Ps 118:1-2, 19-29
Is 50:4-9a
Ps 31:9-16
Phil 2:5-11
Mk 14:1-15:47
Mk 15:1-39 (40-47) (Alt)
(Ps) 122
(G)   29, 123, 127, 138, 143, 145,
      149, 152, 334, 335, 348, 470,
      472

Year C

Epiphany 9
1 Kgs 8:22-23, 41-43
Ps 96:1-9
Gal 1:1-12
Lk 7:1-10
(O)   678
(G)   101, 326, 333, 619

Epiphany Last / Transfig.
Ex 34:29-35
Ps 99
2 Cor 3:12-4:2
Lk 9:28-36, (37-43)
(O)   251, 339
(E)   120, 333, 672
(G)   30, 103, 104, 264, 335, 348,
      362, 368, 371, 413, 559, 561,
      619, 678, 688

Lent 1
Dt 26:1-11
Ps 91:1-2, 9-16
Rom 10:8b-13
Lk 4:1-13
(E)   343, 444, 469, 606
(G)   114, 119, 216, 217, 262, 286,
      335, 348, 375, 380, 559, 650,
      842

Lent 2
Gn 15:1-12, 17-18
Ps 27
Phil 3:17-4:1
Lk 13:31-35
Lk 9:28-36 (Alt)
(Ps) 669
(E)   145, 421
(G)   101, 104, 269, 286, 327, 348,
      580, 636, 660, 663, 681

Lent 3
Is 55:1-9
Ps 63:1-8
1 Cor 10:1-13
Lk 13:1-9
(O)   271, 287, 612
(E)   472, 662
(G)   120, 135, 240, 266, 376, 478,
      600, 651, 658, 663, 667

Lent 4
Jos 5:9-12
Ps 32
2 Cor 5:16-21
Lk 15:1-3, 11b-32
(O)   460
(E)   112, 147, 331, 332, 333, 716
(G)   135, 271, 348, 475, 555, 636,
      660

Year A

Lent 4
1 Sm 16:1-13
Ps 23
Eph 5:8-14
Jn 9:1-41
(O) 657, 670
(Ps) 273, 747, 748
(E) 711
(G) 30, 79, 266, 326, 371, 508, 605, 626

Lent 5
Ez 37:1-14
Ps 130
Rom 8:6-11
Jn 11:1-45
(O) 186
(Ps) 611, 852
(E) 368
(G) 146, 326, 352, 378, 382, 385, 410, 474, 612

Palm / Passion Sunday
Mt 21:1-11
Ps 118:1-2, 19-29
Is 50:4-9a
Ps 31:9-16
Phil 2:5-11
Mt 26:14-27:66 (Alt)
Mt 27:11-54 (Alt)
(O) 141
(E) 334, 335
(G) 122, 123, 127, 135, 138, 143, 145, 146, 149, 151, 357, 628

Holy Thursday
Ex 12:1-4, (5-10), 11-14
Ps 116:1-2, 12-19
1 Cor 11:23-26
Jn 13:1-17, 31b-35
(O) 131
(G) 130, 132, 134, 458, 461, 593

Good Friday
Is 52:13-53:12
Ps 22
Heb 10:16-25
Heb 4:14-16; 5:7-9 (Alt)
Jn 18:1-19:42
(G) 136, 137, 139, 141, 146, 148, 149, 153, 154

Easter 1
Acts 10:34-43 (Alt)
Jer 31:1-6 (Alt)
Ps 118:1-2, 14-24
Col 3:1-4 (Alt)
Acts 10:34-43 (Alt)
Jn 20:1-18 (Alt)
Mt 28:1-10 (Alt)
(Ps) 175
(G) 155, 157, 158, 159, 160, 165, 169, 170, 173, 180, 186, 190, 211, 345, 413, 536, 651

Year B

Holy Thursday
Ex 12:1-4, (5-10), 11-14
Ps 116:1-2, 12-19
1 Cor 11:23-26
Jn 13:1-17, 31b-35
(E) 467
(G) 133, 138, 145, 333, 459, 461, 470, 480, 639, 747

Good Friday
Is 52:13-53:12
Ps 22
Heb 10:16-25
Heb 4:14-16; 5:7-9 (Alt)
Jn 18:1-19:42
(G) 119, 135, 136, 138, 139, 144, 145, 146, 147, 151, 348

Easter 1
Acts 10:34-4
Is 25:6-9 (Alt)
Ps 118:1-2, 14-24
1 Cor 15:1-11
Acts 10:34-43 (Alt)
Jn 20:1-18
Mk 16:1-8 (Alt)
(Ps) 175
(G) 155, 157, 159, 161, 163, 164, 165, 170, 352

Easter 2
Acts 4:32-35
Ps 133
1 Jn 1:1-2:2
Jn 20:19-31
(E) 479
(G) 25, 29, 169, 170, 173, 177, 260, 341, 352, 353, 396, 560, 571, 642,

Easter 3
Acts 3:12-19
Ps 4
1 Jn 3:1-7
Lk 24:36b-48
(G) 143, 159, 169, 173, 186, 190, 326, 334, 393, 627, 642, 662

Easter 4
Acts 4:5-12
Ps 23
1 Jn 3:16-24
Jn 10:11-18
(Ps) 273, 747, 748
(E) 198, 515
(G) 325, 326, 331, 332, 334, 335, 344, 542, 543

Easter 5
Acts 8:26-40
Ps 22:25-31
1 Jn 4:7-21
Jn 15:1-8

Year C

Lent 5
Is 43:16-21
Ps 126
Phil 3:4b-14
Jn 12:1-8
(O) 216
(Ps) 30
(E) 142, 149, 334, 506, 642
(G) 129, 147, 210, 215, 234, 421, 642, 667

Palm / Passion Sunday
Lk 19:28-40
Ps 118:1-2, 19-29
Is 50:4-9a
Ps 31:9-16
Phil 2:5-11
Lk 22:14-23:56
Lk 23:1-49 (Alt)
(O) 141
(Ps) 286
(G) 29, 122, 123, 126, 127, 133, 138, 143, 145, 146, 149, 335, 357, 501, 595, 618

Holy Thursday
Ex 12:1-4, (5-10,) 11-14
Ps 116:1-2, 12-19
1 Cor 11:23-26
Jn 13:1-17, 31b-35
(G) 119, 133, 138, 144, 145, 147, 348, 458, 461, 463, 480, 650

Good Friday
Is 52:13-53:12
Ps 22
Heb 10:16-25
Heb 4:14-16, 5:7-9 (Alt)
Jn 18:1-19:42
(G) 133, 138, 139, 143, 144, 145, 149, 152, 154, 614, 653

Easter 1
Acts 10:34-43
Is 65:17-25 (Alt)
Ps 118:1-2, 14-24
1 Cor 15:19-26
Acts 10:34-43 (Alt)
Jn 20:1-18
Lk 24:1-12 (Alt)
(E) 165
(G) 155, 157, 158, 159, 161, 164, 169, 170, 173, 175, 179, 186, 341, 352, 448

Easter 2
Acts 5:27-32
Ps 118:14-29
Ps 150 (Alt)
Rv 1:4-8
Jn 20:19-31

Year A

Easter 2
Acts 2:14a, 22-32
Ps 16
1 Pt 1:3-9
Jn 20:19-31
(E) 161, 164, 173
(G) 25, 159, 164, 165, 170, 171,
177, 179, 211, 335, 341, 362,
367, 382, 409, 472, 490

Easter 3
Acts 2:14a, 36-41
Ps 116:1-4, 12-19
1 Pt 1:17-23
Lk 24:13-35
(E) 337, 448, 508, 663, 667
(G) 157, 159, 169, 170, 171, 183,
190, 332, 345, 594, 667

Easter 4
Acts 2:42-47
Ps 23
1 Pt 2:19-25
Jn 10:1-10
(Ps) 273, 657, 747, 748
(E) 158, 194, 389, 479
(G) 120, 271, 342, 559, 658, 670

Easter 5
Acts 7:55-60
Ps 31:1-5, 15-16
1 Pt 2:2-10
Jn 14:1-14
(E) 285, 286, 325, 431, 459, 652,
660, 686
(G) 216, 238, 274, 331, 332, 344,
356, 362, 421, 628

Easter 6
Acts 17:22-31
Ps 66:8-20
1 Pt 3:13-22
Jn 14:15-21
(E) 217, 226, 479
(G) 143, 187, 213, 264, 333, 367,
368, 376, 396

Ascension
Acts 1:1-11
Ps 47
Ps 93 (Alt)
Eph 1:15-23
Lk 24:44-53
(E) 163, 165, 173, 189, 215, 335
(G) 211, 330, 334, 336, 367, 484

Year B

(Ps) 59, 533
(E) 229, 232
(G) 327, 333, 348, 371, 602, 603,
606

Easter 6
Acts 10:44-48
Ps 98
1 Jn 5:1-6
Jn 15:9-17
(G) 129, 190, 211, 217, 222, 308,
333, 477, 591, 628

Ascension
Acts 1:1-11
Ps 47
Ps 93 (Alt)
Eph 1:15-23
Lk 24:44-53
(G) 158, 211, 334, 336

Easter 7
Acts 1:15-17, 21-26
Ps 1
1 Jn 5:9-13
Jn 17:6-19
(G) 120, 190, 211, 215, 326, 327,
330, 334, 364, 501

Pentecost
Acts 2:1-21 (Alt)
Ez 37:1-14 (Alt)
Ps 104:24-34, 35b
Rom 8:22-27 (Alt)
Acts 2:1-21 (Alt)
Jn 15:26-27; 16:4b-15
(Ps) 235
(E) 209, 367
(G) 161, 170, 193, 201, 296, 314,
368, 376, 380, 382, 385, 515

Trinity Sunday
Is 6:1-8
Ps 29
Rom 8:12-17
Jn 3:1-17
(O) 315, 473, 572
(G) 151, 217, 313, 314, 415, 473,
509, 555, 606, 894

Year C

(Ps) 220
(E) 25
(G) 29, 170, 173, 185, 190, 213,
326, 338, 341, 367, 368, 373,
382, 396, 618, 642, 783

Easter 3
Acts 9:1-6, (7-20)
Ps 30
Rv 5:11-14
Jn 21:1-19
(E) 147, 334, 708
(G) 120, 143, 326, 345, 500, 562,
593, 653

Easter 4
Acts 9:36-43
Ps 23
Rv 7:9-17
Jn 10:22-30
(Ps) 273, 747, 748
(E) 151, 211, 342, 542, 670, 714
(G) 61, 232, 334, 337, 344, 348,
396, 461, 709, 714, 715

Easter 5
Acts 11:1-18
Ps 148
Rv 21:1-6
Jn 13:31-35
(Ps) 217, 265
(E) 362, 376, 606, 678, 709, 713
(G) 333, 372, 405, 574, 602, 658

Easter 6
Acts 16:9-15
Ps 67
Rv 21:10, 22-22:5
Jn 14:23-29
Jn 5:1-9 (Alt)
(Ps) 686, 894
(E) 559, 657, 678, 709, 710
(G) 175, 367, 368, 373, 413, 512,
559, 601, 686, 783, 808

Ascension
Acts 1:1-11
Ps 47
Ps 93 (Alt)
Eph 1:15-23
Lk 24:44-53
(E) 161, 180, 330, 334, 705
(G) 189, 211, 336

Easter 7
Acts 16:16-34
Ps 97
Rv 22:12-14, 16-17, 20-21
Jn 17:20-26
(E) 681
(G) 98, 189, 193, 194, 199, 200,
210, 213, 271, 325, 336, 348,
376, 378, 382, 415, 440, 475,
481, 571, 589, 604

Year A

Easter 7
Acts 1:6-14
Ps 68:1-10, 32-35
1 Pt 4:12-14; 5:6-11
Jn 17:1-11
(Ps) 243
(G) 187, 211, 217, 267, 296, 310, 330, 334, 336, 373, 636

Pentecost
Acts 2:1-21 (Alt)
Nm 11:24-30 (Alt)
Ps 104:24-34, 35b
1 Cor 12:3b-13 (Alt)
Acts 2:1-21 (Alt)
Jn 20:19-23 (Alt)
Jn 7:37-39 (Alt)
(Ps) 235, 296, 308
(E) 161, 163, 194, 196, 205, 367, 368, 588
(E-alt) 606
(G) 170, 198, 200, 201, 202, 209, 264, 375, 380, 382, 383, 385, 470, 472, 625

Trinity Sunday
Gn 1:1-2:4a
Ps 8
2 Cor 13:11-13
Mt 28:16-20
(O) 217, 231, 251, 291, 308, 409
(Ps) 226, 238
(G) 226, 244, 296, 315, 320, 342, 396, 420, 512, 602, 660, 894

Proper 4 [5/29–6/04] ✓
Gn 6:9-22; 7:24; 8:14-19
Ps 46
Rom 1:16-17; 3:22b-28 (29-31)
Mt 7:21-29
(G) 266, 422, 423, 606, 650, 660, 705

Proper 5 [6/05–6/11] ✓
Gn 12:1-9
Ps 33:1-12
Rom 4:13-25
Mt 9:9-13, 18-26
(O) 285, 286, 657
(Ps) 701
(E) 580
(G) 271, 304, 327, 352, 421, 477, 533, 562, 567, 594, 634, 653

Proper 6 [6/12–6/18] ✓
Gn 18:1-15, (21:1-7)
Ps 116:1-2, 12-19
Rom 5:1-8
Mt 9:35-10:8, (9-23)
(O) 264
(Ps) 342, 617, 628
(E) 149, 337, 508, 658
(G) 164, 185, 215, 262, 263, 266,

Year B

Proper 4 [5/29–6/04] ✓
1 Sm 3:1-10, (11-20)
Ps 139:1-6, 13-18
2 Cor 4:5-12
Mk 2:23-3:6
(G) 4, 101, 175, 299, 371, 510, 679

Proper 5 [6/05–6/11] ✓
1 Sm 8:4-11, (12-15), 16-20, (11:14-15)
Ps 138
2 Cor 4:13-5:1
Mk 3:20-35
(O) 533, 852
(G) 213, 238, 291, 344, 472, 556, 606, 667

Proper 6 [6/12–6/18] ✓
1 Sm 15:34-16:13
Ps 20
2 Cor 5:6-10, (11-13), 14-17
Mk 4:26-34
(G) 30, 213, 223, 288, 310, 333, 337, 362, 405, 516, 589, 605, 660, 686, 703

Proper 7 [6/19–6/25] ✓
1 Sm 17:(1a, 4-11, 19-23), 32-49
1 Sm 17:57-18:5 (10-16) (Alt)
Ps 9:9-20
Ps 133 (Alt)
2 Cor 6:1-13
Mk 4:35-41
(O) 567
(G) 120, 308, 333, 378, 562, 636, 637, 641, 652, 659, 669, 686

Proper 8 [6/26–7/02]
2 Sm 1:1, 17-27
Ps 130
2 Cor 8:7-15
Mk 5:21-43
(Ps) 852
(G) 288, 326, 352, 417, 479, 510, 542, 543, 619, 622, 636

Proper 9 [7/03–7/09]
2 Sm 5:1-5, 9-10
Ps 48
2 Cor 12:2-10
Mk 6:1-13
(E) 266
(G) 30, 40, 149, 216, 334, 362, 422, 423, 438, 481, 501, 560, 572, 639, 667

Proper 10 [7/10–7/16]
2 Sm 6:1-5, 12b-19
Ps 24
Eph 1:3-14
Mk 6:14-29
(G) 215, 240, 266, 271, 296, 315, 421, 560, 580, 691

Year C

Pentecost
Acts 2:1-21
Gn 11:1-9 (Alt)
Ps 104:24-34, 35b
Rom 8:14-17
Acts 2:1-21 (Alt)
Jn 14:8-17, (25-27)
(Ps) 321, 375
(E) 186, 195, 199, 208, 209, 367, 369, 531
(G) 161, 201, 205, 208, 325, 333, 367, 375, 380, 382, 385, 606

Trinity Sunday
Prv 8:1-4, 22-31
Ps 8
Rom 5:1-5
Jn 16:12-15
(O) 287
(Ps) 217, 232, 730
(E) 201, 266, 658
(G) 226, 235, 251, 266, 308, 313, 314, 315, 341, 345, 367, 368, 376, 377, 642, 894

Proper 4 [5/29–6/04] ✓
1 Kgs 18:20-21, (22-29), 30-39
Ps 96
Gal 1:1-12
Lk 7:1-10
(G) 326, 330, 335, 822

Proper 5 [6/05–6/11] ✓
1Kgs 17:8-16, (17-24)
Ps 146
Gal 1:11-24
Lk 7:11-17
(E) 593
(G) 213, 236, 326, 333, 339, 636

Proper 6 [6/12–6/18] ✓
1 Kgs 21:1-10, (11-14), 15-21a
Ps 5:1-8
Gal 2:15-21
Lk 7:36-8:3
(O) 677, 701
(Ps) 662
(E) 147, 581, 626, 669
(G) 218, 235, 264, 271, 330, 333, 340

Proper 7 [6/19–6/25] ✓
1 Kgs 19:1-4, (5-7), 8-15a
Ps 42 and 43
Gal 3:23-29
Lk 8:26-39
(O) 286, 612, 636, 651
(E) 456, 588, 601, 606
(G) 120, 313, 608, 620, 627

Year A	Year B	Year C

Year A

322, 367, 506, 507, 509, 512, 624,
  650, 651, 690

Proper 7 [6/19–6/25] ✓
Gn 21:8-21
Ps 86:1-10, 16-17
Rom 6:1b-11
Mt 10:24-39
(O) 560, 669
(Ps) 671
(E) 448, 451, 497
(G) 164, 169, 229, 240, 258, 271,
  288, 296, 313, 453, 509, 559,
  561, 627, 658

Proper 8 [6/26–7/02]
Gn 22:1-14
Ps 13
Rom 6:12-23
Mt 10:40-42
(O) 580
(Ps) 285, 286
(E) 120, 382, 593
(G) 164, 327, 335, 337, 561, 565,
  582, 642, 681

Proper 9 [7/03–7/09]
Gn 24:34-38, 42-49,58-67
Ps 45:10-17 or
Song 2:8-13
Rom 7:15-25a
Mt 11:16-19, 25-30
(Ps) 98
(E) 266, 292, 333, 378, 500
(G) 4, 193, 219, 285, 286, 330,
  342, 344, 352, 365, 405, 460,
  510, 603, 626, 664, 669, 681

Proper 10 [7/10–7/16]
Gn 25:19-34
Ps 119:105-112
Rom 8:1-11
Mt 13:1-9, 18-23
(E) 382, 638
(G) 31, 120, 216, 234, 300, 314,
  341, 378, 448, 481, 498, 503,
  667

Proper 11 [7/17–7/23]
Gn 28:10-19a
Ps 139:1-12, 23-24
Rom 8:12-25
Mt 13:24-30, 36-43
(O) 497, 650
(Ps) 264, 265
(E) 307, 333
(G) 314, 328, 436, 516, 606, 678,
  708

Year B

Proper 11 [7/17–7/23]
2 Sm 7:1-14a
Ps 89:20-37
Eph 2:11-22
Mk 6:30-34, 53-56
(Ps) 288
(E) 325
(G) 30, 210, 215, 273, 331, 332,
  333, 362, 605, 606, 681, 747,
  748

Proper 12 [7/24–7/30]
2 Sm 11:1-15
Ps 14
Eph 3:14-21
Jn 6:1-21
(Ps) 213
(G) 332, 348, 355, 468, 508, 555,
  608, 651, 659

Proper 13 [7/31–8/06]
2 Sm 11:26-12:13a
Ps 51:1-12
Eph 4:1-16
Jn 6:24-35
(O) 651
(G) 215, 271, 274, 332, 472, 501,
  506, 508, 571, 650, 669, 857

Proper 14 [8/07–8/13]
2 Sm 18:5-9, 15, 31-33
Ps 130
Eph 4:25-5:2
Jn 6:35, 41-51
(G) 138, 358, 461, 472, 582, 594,
  626, 636, 651, 667

Proper 15 [8/14–8/20]
1 Kgs 2:10-12; 3:3-14
Ps 111
Eph 5:15-20
Jn 6:51-58
(E) 93
(G) 190, 236, 327, 385, 461, 472,
  499, 533, 561, 582, 628, 642,
  709, 714

Proper 16 [8/21–8/27]
1 Kgs 8: (1, 6, 10-11), 22-30, 41-43
Ps 84
Eph 6:10-20
Jn 6:56-69
(E) 571, 580
(G) 119, 220, 262, 332, 333, 337,
  651

Proper 17 [8/28–9/03]
Song 2:8-13
Ps 45:1-2, 6-9
Jas 1:17-27
Mk 7:1-8, 14-15, 21-23
(E) 509
(G) 92, 226, 262, 341, 373, 505,
  508, 520, 594

Year C

Proper 8 [6/26–7/02]
2 Kgs 2:1-2, 6-14
Ps 77:1-2, 11-20
Gal 5:1, 13-15
Lk 9:51-62
(O) 207, 379
(Ps) 238, 436, 806
(E) 201, 376
(G) 219, 236, 271, 421, 560, 591,
  595, 596, 625, 627, 642

Proper 9 [7/03–7/09]
2 Kgs 5:1-14
Ps 30
Gal 6:(1-6), 7-16
Lk 10:1-11, 16-20
(O) 320, 380, 572, 575
(Ps) 611
(E) 595, 600, 602
(G) 120, 135, 227, 288, 325, 335,
  468, 509, 510, 512, 595, 619

Proper 10 [7/10–7/16]
Am 7:7-17
Ps 82
Col 1:1-14
Lk 10:25-37
(Ps) 686
(E) 581, 582, 705
(G) 326, 472, 562, 591, 593, 611,
  636, 681

Proper 11 [7/17–7/23]
Am 8:1-12
Ps 52
Col 1:15-28
Lk 10:38-42
(O) 286
(E) 364
(G) 219, 472, 506, 555, 605, 608,
  642, 667

Proper 12 [7/24–7/30]
Hos 1:2-10
Ps 85
Col 2:6-15, (16-19)
Lk 11:1-13
(Ps) 234
(E) 560, 568
(G) 236, 344, 350, 356, 364, 366,
  470, 573, 626, 650, 664

Proper 13 [7/31–8/06]
Hos 11:1-11
Ps 107:1-9, 43
Col 3:1-11
Lk 12:13-21
(O) 216, 236, 271, 276, 288
(Ps) 651
(E) 213, 448
(G) 342, 356, 472, 507, 606, 650,
  651, 658, 663

Year A

Proper 12 [7/24–7/30]
Gn 29:15-28
Ps 105:1-11, 45b or
Ps 128
Rom 8:26-39
Mt 13:31-33, 44-52
(Ps) 216
(E) 164, 205, 215, 573, 622, 658
(G) 164, 226, 264, 356, 415, 437,
438, 516, 573, 651, 660, 667,
688, 883

Proper 13 [7/31–8/06]
Gn 32:22-31
Ps 17:1-7, 15
Rom 9:1-5
Mt 14:13-21
(O) 422, 423, 642, 658,
(Ps) 665
(E) 61, 285, 286, 287, 368
(G) 165, 222, 234, 299, 326, 333,
355, 364, 417, 461, 468, 480,
501, 608, 636, 812

Proper 14 [8/07–8/13]
Gn 37:1-4, 12-28
Ps 105:1-6, 16-22, 45b
Rom 10:5-15
Mt 14:22-33
(O) 509, 657
(Ps) 220, 221
(E) 335, 343, 362
(G) 218, 264, 268, 339, 421, 562,
580, 608, 635, 636, 637, 641,
649, 659, 660, 663, 669, 675

Proper 15 [8/14–8/20]
Gn 45:1-15
Ps 133
Rom 11:1-2a, 29-32
Mt 15:(10-20), 21-28
(O) 236
(E) 271, 606
(G) 185, 238, 266, 273, 326, 358,
374, 440, 560, 602, 619, 650,
663, 686, 822

Proper 16 [8/21–8/27]
Ex 1:8-2:10
Ps 124
Rom 12:1-8
Mt 16:13-20
(O) 651
(E) 506, 518
(G) 261, 262, 335, 416, 427, 507,
508, 588, 595, 601, 603, 635

Proper 17 [8/25–9/03]
Ex 3:1-15

Year B

Proper 18 [9/04–9/10]
Prv 22:1-2, 8-9, 22-23
Ps 125
Jas 2:1-10, (11-13), 14-17
Mk 7:24-37
(E) 416, 481
(G) 29, 220, 266, 286, 326, 358,
412, 478, 570, 606, 626, 642,
681, 701

Proper 19 [9/11–9/17]
Prv 1:20-33
Ps 19
Wis 7:26-8:1 (Alt)
Jas 3:1-12
Mk 8:27-38
(Ps) 238
(E) 506, 589
(G) 149, 151, 367, 405, 497, 561,
594, 642

Proper 20 [9/18–9/24]
Prv 31:10-31
Ps 1
Jas 3:13-4:3, 7-8a
Mk 9:30-37
(E) 337, 642
(G) 236, 342, 357, 365, 368, 497,
506, 560, 662, 701

Proper 21 [9/25–10/01]
Est 7:1-6, 9-10; 9:20-22
Ps 124
Jas 5:13-20
Mk 9:38-50
(O) 216, 287
(G) 232, 261, 334, 335, 344, 378,
385, 500, 582, 642, 664, 681

Proper 22 [10/02–10/08]
Job 1:1; 2:1-10
Ps 26
Heb 1:1-4; 2:5-12
Mk 10:2-16
(Ps) 310
(E) 190, 327
(G) 211, 215, 226, 334, 340, 365,
413, 529, 555, 556, 669

Proper 23 [10/09–10/15]
Job 23:1-9, 16-17
Ps 22:1-15
Heb 4:12-16
Mk 10:17-31
(O) 670
(E) 35, 215, 499, 559, 669
(G) 96, 291, 427, 463, 506, 522,
561, 589, 630

Year C

Proper 14 [8/07–8/13]
Is 1:1, 10-20
Ps 50:1-8, 22-23
Heb 11:1-3, 8-16
Lk 12:32-40
(O) 580, 660, 701
(E) 643, 707
(G) 2, 266, 562, 635, 636, 642,
688, 704, 706, 708

Proper 15 [8/14–8/20]
Is 5:1-7
Ps 80:1-2, 8-19
Heb 11:29-12:2
Lk 12:49-56
(O) 580, 894
(Ps) 220
(G) 274, 421, 422, 562, 598, 634,
636, 642, 674, 677, 686

Proper 16 [8/21–8/27]
Jer 1:4-10
Ps 71:1-6
Heb 12:18-29
Lk 13:10-17
(0) 504
(E) 79, 262, 263, 264, 714, 715
(G) 352, 518, 642, 654, 655, 681

Proper 17 [8/28–9/03]
Jer 2:4-13
Ps 81:1, 10-16
Heb 13:1-8, 15-16
Lk 14:1, 7-14
(O) 701
(Ps) 478
(E) 120, 472, 654, 660
(G) 193, 589, 598, 600, 681

Proper 18 [9/04–9/10]
Jer 18:1-11
Ps 139:1-6, 13-18
Phlm 1-21
Lk 14:25-33
(O) 376
(Ps) 139, 265, 862
(E) 594
(G) 149, 216, 308, 310, 506, 560,
561, 593, 618, 642, 660

Proper 19 [9/11–9/17]
Jer 4:11-12, 22-28
Ps 14
1 Tm 1:12-17
Lk 15:1-10
(O) 708

Year A

Ps 105:1-6, 23-26, 45c
Rom 12:9-21
Mt 16:21-28
(G)   147, 164, 215, 235, 243, 264,
      325, 348, 405, 561, 562, 595,
      658, 806

Proper 18 [9/04–9/10]
Ex 12:1-14
Ps 149
Rom 13:8-14
Mt 18:15-20
(Ps)   234
(G)   232, 240, 241, 276, 325, 333,
      389, 396, 427, 479, 594, 674,
      690, 711

Proper 19 [9/11–9/17]
Ex 14:19-31
Ps 114
Ex 15:1b-11, 20-21 (Alt resp)
Rom 14:1-12
Mt 18:21-35
(O)   449, 651
(Ps)   216
(E)   335
(G)   164, 165, 211, 236, 240, 270,
      334, 340, 556, 581, 646, 647,
      651, 691

Proper 20 [9/18–9/24]
Ex 16:2-15
Ps 105:1-6, 37-45
Phil 1:21-30
Mt 20:1-16
(O)   216
(G)   179, 200, 216, 219, 264, 274,
      277, 321, 651

Proper 21 [9/25–10/01]
Ex 17:1-7
Ps 78:1-4, 12-16
Phil 2:1-13
Mt 21:23-32
(E)   147, 326, 335, 348
(G)   138, 213, 234, 270, 271, 338,
      347, 348, 601, 651

Proper 22 [10/02–10/08]
Ex 20:1-4, 7-9, 12-20
Ps 19
Phil 3:4b-14
Mt 21:33-46
(E)   143, 625
(G)   1, 291, 312, 467, 477, 571,
      660, 714, 715, 747, 748

Year B

Proper 24 [10/16–10/22]
Job 38:1-7 (34-41)
Ps 104:1-9, 24, 35c
Heb 5:1-10
Mk 10:35-45
(O)   229, 232, 308
(Ps)   81, 296
(G)   81, 190, 248, 264, 342, 344,
      560, 593, 603, 614, 651, 659

Proper 25 [10/23–10/29]
Job 42:1-6, 10-17
Ps 34:1-8, (19-22)
Heb 7:23-28
Mk 10:46-52
(O)   285, 296
(G)   92, 266, 286, 326, 344, 362,
      371, 642, 663, 665

Proper 26 [10/30–11/05]
Ru 1:1-18
Ps 146
Heb 9:11-14
Mk 12:28-34
(O)   262
(Ps)   326
(G)   228, 286, 299, 344, 348, 518,
      589, 593, 595, 636

All Saints [11/01]
Wis 3:1-9 (Alt))
Is 25:6-9 (Alt))
Ps 24
Rv 21:1-6a
Jn 11:32-44
(O)   682
(Ps)   705
(E)   459, 709, 718
(G)   61, 146, 154, 678

Proper 27 [11/06–11/12]
Ru 3:1-5; 4:13-17
Ps 127
Heb 9:24-28
Mk 12:38-44
(O)   356, 602
(E)   213
(G)   25, 149, 159, 236, 333, 335,
      348, 372, 516, 560, 654, 655,
      701

Proper 28 [11/13–11/19]
1 Sm 1:4-20
1 Sm 2:1-10
Heb 10:11-14 (15-18), 19-25
Mk 13:1-8
(O)   220, 221, 806, 878
(E)   711
(G)   25, 81, 147, 190, 314, 348,

Year C

(Ps)   436, 608, 852
(E)   216, 266, 559
(G)   87, 116, 149, 219, 235, 271,
      273, 276, 288, 360, 626, 641,
      646, 667, 681

Proper 20 [9/18–9/24]
Jer 8:18-9:1
Ps 79:1-9
1 Tm 2:1-7
Lk 16:1-13
(O)   608, 611, 612, 658, 669
(G)   120, 216, 236, 261, 262, 263,
      312, 335, 342, 589

Proper 21 [9/25–10/01]
Jer 32:1-3a, 6-15
Ps 91:1-6, 14-16
1 Tm 6:6-19
Lk 16:19-31
(E)   264, 473, 506, 674
(G)   207, 220, 226, 314, 580, 598,
      650, 654, 655

Proper 22 [10/02–10/08]
Lam 1:1-6
Lam 3:19-26 (resp)
Ps 137 (Alt resp)
2 Tm 1:1-14
Lk 17:5-10
(O)   378
(Ps)   611, 852
(E)   368
(G)   231, 288, 342, 405, 409, 410,
      416, 636, 663, 686

Proper 23 [10/09–10/15]
Jer 29:1, 4-7
Ps 66:1-12
2 Tm 2:8-15
Lk 17:11-19
(E)   667
(G)   119, 184, 190, 326, 338, 508,
      560, 570, 663

Proper 24 [10/16–10/22]
Jer 31:27-34
Ps 119:97-104
2 Tm 3:14-4:5
Lk 18:1-8
(O)   509, 842
(E)   499, 512, 560, 575, 578, 589
(G)   236, 261, 262, 263, 264, 271,
      498, 506, 611, 612, 664, 684,
      688, 806

Year A

Proper 23 [10/09–10/15]
Ex 32:1-14
Ps 106:1-6, 19-23
Phil 4:1-9
Mt 22:1-14
(E)   202, 375, 381
(G)   164, 175, 215, 225, 457, 465,
       471, 472, 636, 661, 664, 670,
       709, 747, 748

Proper 24 [10/16–10/22]
Ex 33:12-23
Ps 99
1 Thes 1:1-10
Mt 22:15-22
(G)   218, 220, 221, 231, 253, 256,
       288, 326, 407, 408, 478, 506,
       509, 580, 581, 663, 677

Proper 25 [10/23–10/29]
Dt 34:1-12
Ps 90:1-6, 13-17
1 Thes 2:1-8
Mt 22:34-46
(Ps)   806
(G)   228, 265, 329, 334, 347, 367,
       378, 367, 528

Proper 26 [10/30–11/05]
Jos 3:7-17
Ps 654:1-7, 33-37
1 Thes 2:9-13
Mt 23:1-12
(G)   2, 4, 260, 261, 266, 288, 338,
       352, 353, 510, 582, 688, 706,
       711

All Saints [11/01]
Rv 7:9-17
Ps 34:1-10, 22
1 Jn 3:1-3
Mt 5:1-12
(E)   211, 268, 421
(G)   342, 636, 705

Proper 27 [11/06–11/12]
Jos 24:1-3a, 14-25
Ps 78:1-7
1 Thes 4:13-18
Mt 25:1-13
(Ps)   343
(G)   25, 159, 245, 356, 375, 492,
       555, 560, 634, 705, 711, 806,
       883

Proper 28 [11/13–11/19]
Jgs 4:1-7
Ps 123
1 Thes 5:1-11
Mt 25:14-30
(Ps)   657
(E)   686
(G)   81, 169, 215, 218, 222, 223,
       244, 248, 340, 380, 571, 688

Year B

Reign of Christ [11/20–11/26]
2 Sm 23:1-7
Ps 132:1-12, (13-18)
Rv 1:4b-8
Jn 18:33-37
(Ps)   511
(O)   25
(E)   61, 330, 333,
(G)   30, 81, 211, 212, 213, 273,
       314, 335, 348, 362, 440, 473,
       475, 535, 686

Thanksgiving
Jl 2:21-27
Ps 126
1 Tm 2:1-7
Mt 6:25-33
(Ps)   326, 624, 820, 822
(O)   516
(G)   227, 232, 236, 291, 303, 356,
       519, 520, 521, 522, 650

Year C

Proper 25 [10/23–10/29]
Jl 2:23-32
Ps 65
2 Tm 4:6-8, 16-18
Lk 18:9-14
(O)   201, 208, 682
(Ps)   216, 345
(E)   658, 660, 674
(G)   217, 222, 225, 271, 288, 363,
       375, 378, 380, 382, 420, 508,
       642, 664, 665, 666, 667, 688,
       705, 706

Proper 26 [10/30–11/05]
Hb 1:1-4; 2:1-4
Ps 119:137-144
2 Thes 1:1-4, 11-12
Lk 19:1-10
(O)   642, 652, 709
(E)   685
(G)   2, 28, 232, 559, 562, 570, 598,
       660, 679, 700, 701

All Saints [11/01]
Dn 7:1-3, 15-18
Ps 149
Eph 1:11-23
Lk 6:20-31
(O)   314, 705
(Ps)   216
(E)   215, 285, 409, 580, 706
(G)   325, 334, 371, 470, 660, 677,
       691, 894

Proper 27 [11/06–11/12]
Hg 1:15b-2:9
Ps 145:1-5, 17-21
Ps 98 (Alt resp)
2 Thes 2:1-5, 13-17
Lk 20:27-38
(O)   328
(E)   390, 391, 661
(G)   1, 2, 30, 216, 217, 218, 220,
       221, 288, 325, 326, 481

Proper 28 [11/13–11/19]
Is 65:17-25
Is 12 (resp)
2 Thes 3:6-13
Lk 21:5-19
(O)   682, 714, 715
(E)   416
(G)   61, 175, 215, 314, 326, 336,
       422, 423, 566, 578, 579, 589,
       677, 681, 688, 708, 713

Reign of Christ [11/20–11/26]
Jer 23:1-6
Lk 1:68-79 (resp)
Col 1:11-20
Lk 23:33-43

Year A   Year B   Year C

Reign of Christ [11/20–11/26]
Ez 34:11-16, 20-24
Ps 100
Eph 1:15-23
Mt 25:31-46
(Ps) 220, 221, 820, 822
(G) 175, 210, 211, 212, 213, 244,
      273, 325, 339, 440, 589, 599,
      600, 681, 713

(O) 261, 262, 263, 330
(R) 901
(E) 61, 135, 142, 339
(G) 1, 30, 61, 210, 211, 212, 213,
      236, 255, 325, 326, 327, 334,
      335, 336, 342, 356, 596, 636

Thanksgiving
Dt 26:1-11
Ps 100
Phil 4:4-9
Jn 6:25-35
(O) 519
(Ps) 216, 235, 236, 242, 822
(E) 249, 213, 506
(G) 226, 227, 233, 267, 334, 463,
      464, 478, 518, 520, 582, 651,
      678

Thanksgiving
Dt 8:7-18
Ps 65
2 Cor 9:6-15
Lk 17:11-19
(O) 519
(Ps) 231
(G) 217, 219, 227, 235, 236, 266,
      303, 305, 516, 520, 523

The following Old Testament and Psalm sets (thematically related to the Gospel) may be substituted for the corresponding selections in the preceding list.

Proper 4
Dt 11:18-21, 26-28
Ps 31:1-5, 19-24
(O) 235, 343, 707
(Ps) 637

Proper 5
Hos 5:15-6:6
Ps 50:7-15
(O) 421, 653
(Ps) 296

Proper 6
Ex 19:2-8a
Ps 100
(O) 269
(Ps) 220, 221, 380, 820, 822

Proper 7
Jer 20:7-13
Ps 69:7-10, (11-15), 16-18
(O) 245, 261, 664
(Ps) 219

Proper 8
Jer 28:5-9
Ps 89:1-4, 15-18
(O) 580
(Ps) 659

Proper 9
Zec 9:9-12
Ps 145:8-14
(O) 127, 261, 262
(Ps) 232, 254, 342, 437, 438, 533

Proper 10
Is 55:10-13
Ps 65:(1-8), 9-13
(O) 59, 680
(Ps) 217, 231, 519

Proper 4
Dt 5:12-15
Ps 81:1-10
(O) 175, 305, 352, 417, 437, 438,

Proper 5
Gn 3:8-15
Ps 130
(O) 116, 292, 323
(Ps) 533

Proper 6
Ez 17:22-24
Ps 92:1-4, 12-15
(O) 227, 229, 235, 242, 296
(Ps) 533

Proper 7
Jb 38:1-11
Ps 107:1-3, 23-32
(O) 235, 242, 248, 254, 425, 659
(Ps) 218, 637, 659

Proper 8
Wis 1:13-15; 2:23-24
Lam 3:23-33 (Alt)
Ps 30
(O) 288, 405, 409
(Ps) 658

Proper 9
Ez 2:1-5
Ps 123
(O) 376, 378, 509

Proper 10
Am 7:7-15
Ps 85:8-13
(O) 5, 557
(Ps) 188, 333, 426

Proper 4
1 Kgs 8:22-23, 41-43
Ps 96:1-9
(O) 268, 317, 822, 894

Proper 5
1 Kgs 17:17-24
Ps 30
(O) 326, 448, 619

Proper 6
2 Sm 11:26-12:10, 13-15
Ps 32
(O) 295, 300, 303, 307, 508, 601

Proper 7
Is 65:1-9
Ps 22:19-28
(O) 220, 221, 264, 285, 286

Proper 8
1 Kgs 19:15-16, 19-21
Ps 16
(O) 481, 504, 560, 589

Proper 9
Is 66:10-14
Ps 66:1-9
(O) 280, 276, 280, 320, 577

Proper 10
Dt 30:9-14
Ps 25:1-10
(O) 104, 235, 337, 520

Year A	Year B	Year C

Year A

Proper 11
Wis 12:13, 16-19
Is 44:6-8 (Alt)
Ps 86:11-17
(O) 28, 173, 421, 571, 652, 688

Proper 12
1 Kgs 3:5-12
Ps 119:129-136
(O) 159, 222, 508
(Ps) 234, 288, 520

Proper 13
Is 55:1-5
Ps 145:8-9, 14-21
(O) 159, 364, 508
(Ps) 520

Proper 14
1 Kgs 19:9-18
Ps 85:8-13
(O) 608, 908
(Ps) 188, 333, 426

Proper 15
Is 56:1, 6-8
Ps 67
(O) 245, 389, 672, 701
(Ps) 185, 188, 236, 521

Proper 16
Is 51:1-6
Ps 138
(O) 235, 325, 460, 634, 643
(Ps) 105, 326, 508, 665, 669

Proper 17
Jer 15:15-21
Ps 26:1-8
(O) 105, 261, 620
(Ps) 665

Proper 18
Ez 33:7-11
Ps 119:33-40
(O) 271, 509

Proper 19
Gn 50:15-21
Ps 103: (1-7), 8-13
(O) 364, 636, 652
(Ps) 240, 266, 339

Proper 20
Jon 3:10-4:11
Ps 145:1-8
(O) 595, 653
(Ps) 217, 326, 334

Proper 21
Ez 18:1-4, 25-32
Ps 25:1-9
(O) 313, 364, 508

Year B

Proper 11
Jer 23:1-6
Ps 23
(O) 8, 360
(Ps) 273, 633, 657, 747, 748

Proper 12
2 Kgs 4:42-44
Ps 145:10-18
(O) 227, 355, 461, 480
(Ps) 232, 235, 254, 342, 363, 438,
      520, 533

Proper 13
Ex 16:2-4, 9-15
Ps 78:23-29
(O) 279, 460, 651

Proper 14
1 Kgs 19:4-8
Ps 34:1-8
(O) 114, 460, 660, 704

Proper 15
Prv 9:1-6
Ps 34:9-14
(O) 250, 287

Proper 16
Jos 24:1-2a, 14-18
Ps 34:15-22
(O) 120, 506, 508, 690

Proper 17
Dt 4:1-2, 6-9
Ps 15
(O) 235, 242, 255, 368, 523, 677,
      701

Proper 18
Is 35:4-7a
Ps 146
(O) 8, 23, 326, 881, 883
(Ps) 215

Proper 19
Is 50:4-9a
Ps 116:1-9
(O) 141, 145, 405

Proper 20
Wis 1:16-2:1, 12-22
Jer 11:18-20 (Alt)
Ps 54
(O) 5, 138, 264, 682, 708

Proper 21
Nm 11:4-6, 10-16, 24-29
Ps 19:7-14
(O) 182, 375, 460
(Ps) 499

Year C

Proper 11
Gn 18:1-10a
Ps 15
(O) 260, 643

Proper 12
Gn 18:20-32
Ps 138
(O) 223, 229, 578

Proper 13
Eccl 1:2, 12-14; 2:18-23
Ps 49:1-12
227, 287, 292, 379, 578

Proper 14
Gn 15:1-6
Ps 33:12-22
(O) 225, 269, 276, 571

Proper 15
Jer 23:23-29
Ps 82
(O) 81, 209, 573, 707

Proper 16
Is 58:9b-14
Ps 103:1-8
(O) 109, 943

Proper 17
Sir 10:12-18
Prv 25:6-7 (Alt)
Ps 112
(O) 327, 335, 367, 574, 640, 701

Proper 18
Dt 30:15-20
Ps 1
(O) 116, 292, 377

Proper 19
Ex 32:7-14
Ps 51:1-10
(O) 223, 288, 364, 690

Proper 20
Am 8:4-7
Ps 113
(O) 27, 68, 129, 394, 460, 701

Proper 21
Am 6:1a, 4-7
Ps 146
(O) 28, 688, 894

Proper 22
Hb 1:1-4; 2:1-4
Ps 37:1-9
(O) 560, 611, 672, 704

Year A

Proper 22
Is 5:1-7
Ps 80:7-15
(O) 4, 08, 205, 584
(Ps) 188, 291

Proper 23
Is 25:1-9
Ps 23
(O) 509, 614, 654, 660
(Ps) 93, 273, 360, 633, 657

Proper 24
Is 45:1-7
Ps 96:1-9, (10-13)
(O) 235, 265, 371, 426, 438, 642
(Ps) 36, 213, 249, 308, 345

Proper 25
Lv 19:1-2, 15-18
Ps 1
(O) 226, 315, 391, 441, 554, 594,
     894

Proper 26
Mi 3:5-12
Ps 43
(O) 28, 642
(Ps) 133, 173, 688

Proper 27
Wis 6:12-16
Am 5:18-24 (Alt)
Wis 6:17-20
Ps 70 (Alt resp)
(O) 5, 264, 287, 379, 678

Proper 28
Zep 1:7, 12-18
Ps 90:1-8, (9-11), 12
(O) 608, 652, 688
(Ps) 210, 264

Proper 29
Ez 34:11-16, 20-24
Ps 95:1-7a
(O) 273, 574, 747, 748
(Ps) 36, 213, 308, 345, 364

Note:

Readings and dates marked with ✓ apply *only* if after Trinity
Sunday. Month and day figures (5/29 or May 29) are inclusive.

* Year A of the lectionary cycle begins on the First Sunday of
Advent in years which can be evenly divided by three (1998,
2001, 2004, etc.)

Proper 22
Gn 2:18-24
Ps 8
(O) 217, 265, 276, 291
(Ps) 226, 238, 308

Proper 23
Am 5:6-7, 10-15
Ps 90:12-17
(O) 227, 601, 701

Proper 24
Is 53:4-12
Ps 91:9-16
(O) 138, 145, 159

Proper 25
Jer 31:7-9
Ps 126
(O) 018, 216, 342, 606
(Ps) 326, 614, 624, 821

Proper 26
Dt 6:1-9
Ps 119:1-8
(O) 255, 430, 633, 701

Proper 27
1 Kgs 17:8-16
Ps 146
(O) 633, 662, 728, 759

Proper 28
Dn 12:1-3
Ps 16
(O) 092, 277, 350, 356, 421, 635,
     636, 894
(Ps) 215

Proper 29
Dn 7:9-10, 13-14
Ps 93
(O) 227, 260, 322, 633, 822

Year C

Proper 23
2 Kgs 5:1-3, 7-15c
Ps 111
(O) 117, 326, 350, 358, 619

Proper 24
Gn 32:22-31
Ps 121
(O) 284, 875, 943

Proper 25
Sir 35:12-17
Jer 14:7-10, 19-22 (Alt)
Ps 84:1-7
(O) 5, 116, 215, 424, 654, 678

Proper 26
Is 1:10-18
Ps 32:1-7
(O) 508, 663, 669, 701

Proper 27
Jb 19:23-27a
Ps 17:1-9
(O) 149, 192, 266, 321, 661, 703

Proper 28
Mal 4:1-2a
Ps 98
(O) 48, 232, 313, 336

Proper 29
Jer 23:1-6
Ps 46
(O) 8, 185, 273, 360, 362

Holy Name
Nm 6:22-27
Ps 8
Gal 4:4-7 (Alt)
Phil 2:5-11 (Alt)
Lk 2:15-21
(E) 334, 335
(G) 36, 43, 46, 48, 60, 61, 74, 75,
     77, 218, 291, 335, 344, 375,
     394, 425, 606, 709

Year ABC

New Year
Eccl 3:1-13
Ps 8
Rv 21:1-6a
Mt 25:31-46
(O) 216, 288, 308, 529, 530, 662,
     703
(Ps) 227, 238, 806
(E) 580, 678, 709, 713
(G) 96, 218, 285, 409, 530, 582,
     662, 678, 681, 703, 750, 806,
     879

Year ABC

Ash Wednesday
Jl 2:1-2, 12-17
Is 58:1-12 (Alt)
Ps 51:1-17
2 Cor 5:20b-6:10
Mt 6:1-6, 16-21
(O)   421
(Ps) 508
(E)   105, 147, 190, 331, 333
(G)   138, 215, 266, 332, 380, 508,
      594, 611, 618, 642, 650, 651,
      662, 667, 852

Monday in Holy Week
Is 42:1-9
Ps 36:5-11
Heb 9:11-15
Jn 12:1-11
(O)   30, 251
(E)   344
(G)   120, 129, 144, 149, 271, 314,
      560, 591

Tuesday in Holy Week
Is 49:1-7
Ps 71:1-14
1 Cor 1:18-31
Jn 12:20-36
(O)   342
(G)   120, 135, 261, 262, 348, 429,
      472, 561

Wednesday in Holy Week
Is 50:4-9a
Ps 70
Heb 12:1-3
Jn 13:21-32
(O)   145
(E)   674
(G)   138, 190, 348, 364, 660, 705,
      894

Holy Thursday
Ex 12:1-4, (5-10), 11-14
Ps 116:1-2, 12-19
1 Cor 11:23-26
Jn 13:1-17, 31b-35
(O)   806
(E)   470, 480, 601
(G)   138, 147, 348, 461, 463, 464,
      479, 485, 650

Good Friday
Is 52:13-53:12
Ps 22
Heb 10:16-25 (Alt)
Heb 4:14-16; 5:7-9 (Alt)
Jn 18:1-19:42
(O)   141
(Ps) 611, 852
(G)   133, 135, 138, 143, 144, 145,
      147, 149, 152, 182, 375, 639

Year ABC

Easter Evening
Is 25:6-9
Ps 114
1 Cor 5:6b-8
Lk 24:13-49
(G)   157, 159, 164, 165, 170, 173,
      177, 213, 221, 335, 435, 436,
      636, 650, 714, 715

**THE FOLLOWING HYMNS
ARE SUITABLE FOR THE
DAYS INDICATED**

St Andrew the Apostle (Nov 30)
087, 560, 561, 562, 608

St Thomas the Apostle (Dec 21)
170, 459, 673

St Stephen (Dec 26)
345, 605, 894

St John the Evangelist (Dec 27)
138, 499, 594, 663, 669, 709, 717

Holy Innocents (Dec 28)
77, 179, 218, 244

Conversion of St Paul (Jan 25)
87, 338, 459, 506

**Presentation (Purification,
Candlemas)** (Feb 2)
138, 244, 333, 435

St Mathias the Apostle (Feb 24)
714

St Joseph of Nazareth (Mar 19)
286, 319, 463, 663, 555

Annunciation (Mar 25)
330, 362, 499, 899

St Mark the Evangelist
(April 25)
499, 705

St Philip and St James, Apostles
(May 1)
435, 628, 629, 906

Visitation of Mary to Elizabeth
(May 31)
138, 345, 676, 898, 899

St Barnabas the Apostle
(June 11)
418, 512, 542

Nativity of St John the Baptist
(June 24)
20, 235, 881

Year ABC

St Peter and St Paul (June 29)
561, 641, 674, 684

St Mary Magdalene (July 22)
326, 338, 364, 658, 684

St James the Apostle (July 25)
463, 894

Transfiguration (Aug 6)
179, 188, 352, 362, 622, 652

Mary the Mother of Jesus
(Aug 15)
8, 147, 878, 899

St Bartholomew the Apostle
(Aug 24)
345, 560

Holy Cross (Sept 14)
228, 355, 475, 542, 637, 684

St Matthew the Apostle
(Sept 21)
506, 508, 935

St Michael and All Angels
(Sept 29)
96, 138, 188, 463, 520

St Luke the Evangelist (Oct 18)
362, 382, 674

**St Simon the Zealot and St Jude
the Apostle** (Oct 28)
641, 240, 508, 598, 641, 709

**World Day of Prayer, Week of
Prayer**
129, 292, 421, 505, 602, 608, 664,
672

Earth / Environmental Day
217, 226, 227, 235, 295, 306, 307,
308

Camping Sunday
296, 310, 577, 730, 783, 823, 842

Canada Day
303, 523, 524, 580, 701

**Peace Sunday or Rememberence
Day**
421, 424, 523, 659, 677, 678, 682,
687, 688, 701

Reformation Sunday
261, 262, 263, 274, 501, 580, 660,
674

INDEX OF SCRIPTURE

INDEX OF HYMNS SUITABLE FOR USE
WITH CHILDREN AND YOUTH

INDEX OF TOPICS AND CATEGORIES

JESUS CHRIST; EPIPHANY
(see JESUS CHRIST YOUTH)

JESUS CHRIST: EXALTATION
334 All hail the power
211 Crown him
213 Rejoice, the Lord is King
173 Thine is the glory

JESUS CHRIST: EXAMPLE
133 Go to dark Gethsemane
215 Hope of the world
606 In Christ there is no east or west
591 Jesus, united by thy grace
366 like a child
001 O come, O come, Emmanuel
062 Once in royal David's city
555 Our Parent by whose Name
076 See amid the winter's snow
183 We meet you, O Christ
672 Take time to be holy

JESUS CHRIST: FAITHFULNESS
335 At the name of Jesus
133 Go to dark Gethsemane
664 What a friend

JESUS CHRIST: FRIEND
130 An upper room
652, 734, 854 Be still, my soul
180 Christ is risen
341 Fairest Lord Jesus
194 Filled with the Spirit's poer
459 Here, O my Lord, I see
098 How brightly beams
344 How sweet the name
317 I bind unto myself
626 I heard the voice
606 In Christ there is no east or west
340 Jesus, friend
669 Jesus, lover of my soul
365 Jesus loves me
056 Jesus, our brother
667 Jesus, priceless treasure
366 like a child
143 My song is love unknwon
630 O Christ, in thee my soul
120 O Jesus, I have promised
472 O Jesus, joy of loving hearts
560 O Master, let me walk
235 O worship the King
220 Praise to the Lord, the almighty
410 This day God gives

JESUS CHRIST: GRACE
445 A little child
334 All hail the power
327 All praise to thee
460 All who hunger
354 In old Galilee

JESUS CHRIST: GUIDANCE
362 Here, O God

JESUS CHRIST: GUIDE AND LEADER
635 All the way my Saviour leads me
345 Come, children, join to sing
215 Hope of the world
637 Jesus Saviour, pilot me
605 Jesus, teacher, brave and bold
421 Lead on, O cloud
151 Lift high the cross
120 O Jesus, I have promised
560 O Master, let me walk

JESUS CHRIST: HIGH PRIEST
355 For the crowd of thousands
189 Hail the day that sees him rise
344 How sweet the name
591 Jesus, united by thy grace
473 Let all mortal flesh
151 Lift high the cross
589 Lord, speak to me
565 Love who made me
560 O Master, let me walk
101 Songs of thankfulness
363 Your coming, Lord

JESUS CHRIST: IMAGES OF
068 All poor ones and humble
460 All who hunger
642 Be thou my vision
461 Bread of the world
465 Christ, be our host
325 Christ is made the sure foundation
336 Christ whose glory
628 Come, my Way, my Truth
211 Crown him with many crowns
463 Deck yourself, my soul
471, 466 Eat this bread
341 Fairest Lord Jesus
706 Give thanks for life
514 God, the Spirit, guide
399 God, whose love
048 Hark, the herald angels sing
619 Healer of our every ill
215 Hope of the world
098 How brightly beams the morning star
344 How sweet the name
352 I danced in the morning
625 I feel the winds of God
713 I see a new heaven
328 Jesu, joy
142 Jesus, keep me
056 Jesus our brother
008 Lo, how a rose
632 O blessed spring
658 O love that wilt not let me go
413 O splendour of God
213 Rejoice, the Lord is King
067 Silent night
331, 332 The church's one foundation
584 Through the heart of every city
054 Unto us a boy is born
183 We meet you, O Christ

JESUS CHRIST: INCARNATION
138 Ah, holy Jesus
038 Angels we have heard
314 Come now, almighty King
072 From heaven above
277 God is unique
048 Hark, the herald angels sing
092 In the darkness
058 Infant holy
056 Jesus, our brother
284 Joyful is the dark
473 Let all mortal flesh
008 Lo, how a rose
321 Maker, in whom
143 My song is love unknown
060 O come, all ye faithful
304 O God beyond all face and form
379 O Holy Spirit, root of lfie
064 O little town of Bethlehem
031 O Lord, how shall I meet you
348 O Love how deep
084 O radiant Christ
258 O world of God
061 Of the Father's love begotten
711 Sleepers, wake
101 Songs of thankfulness
047 Still, still, still
582 There's a Spirit in the air
584 Through the heart of every city
027 Tomorrow Christ is coming
071 'Twas in the moon of wintertime
183 We meet you, O Christ
074 What child is this
248 When long before time
153 When the Son of God was dying
075 While shepherds watched

JESUS CHRIST: KINGSHIP, CONQUEROR
334 All hail the power
122 All glory, laud and honour
327 All praise to thee
036 Angels from the realms
038 Angels we have heard
335 At the name of Jesus
536 Born in song
395 Born in the night
167 Christ is risen from
157 Christ the Lord is risen
345 Come, children, join to sing
002 Come, thou long-expected Jesus
211 Crown him
341 Fairest Lord Jesus
046 Gentle Mary
277 God is unique
030, 790 Hail to God's own anointed
050 He is born, little child
028 Herald, sound the note
215 Hope of the world, O Christ
098 How brightly beams
103 How good, Lord, to be here
344 How sweet the name
477 I come with joy
058 Infant holy
148 Jesus, remember me

METRICAL INDEX OF TUNES

INDEX OF TUNES

INDEX OF FIRST LINES OF HYMNS
AND COMMON TITLES